BARRON'S

HOW TO PREPARE FOR THE

AP®

Advanced Placement Exam

ENGLISH LITERATURE
AND COMPOSITION

George Ehrenhaft
Former Chairman of the English Department,
Mamaroneck High School, Mamaroneck, NY

BARRON'S

® AP and Advanced Placement Program are registered trademarks of the College Entrance Examination Board, which was not involved in the production of and does not endorse this book.

© Copyright 2004 by Barron's Educational Series, Inc.
© Copyright 2000, 1997, 1992, 1987, 1984, 1980, and 1974 by
Barron's Educational Series, Inc. under the title *Barron's How to
Prepare for the AP English*

All rights reserved. No part of this book may be reproduced in any
form, by photostat, microfilm, xerography, or any other means, or
incorporated into any information retrieval system, electronic or
mechanical, without the written permission of the copyright
owner.

All inquiries should be addressed to:
Barron's Educational Series, Inc.
250 Wireless Boulevard
Hauppauge, NY 11788
http://www.barronseduc.com

Library of Congress Catalog Card No. 2003062758

International Standard Book No. 0-7641-2780-2

Library of Congress Cataloging-in-Publication Data

Ehrenhaft, George.
    Barron's how to prepare for the AP English advanced placement
    examinations : literature and composition / George Ehrenhaft.—
    8th ed.
        p. cm.
    Previous ed. has subtitle: literature and composition, language
    and composition.
    Includes index.
    ISBN 0-7641-2780-2 (alk. paper)
        1. English philology—Examinations—Study guides.
    2. Advanced placement programs (Education) I. Title:
    How to prepare for the AP English advanced placement
    examinations. II. Title.

    PE66.E38   2004b
    428'.0076—dc22   2003062758

PRINTED IN THE UNITED STATES OF AMERICA
9 8 7 6 5 4 3 2

Contents

Acknowledgments

The authors gratefully acknowledge the following copyright holders for permission to reprint material used.

Page 269–270, Excerpt from Henry Fielding, *Tom Jones,* New American Library, 1963, pp. 489–490.

Page 275–276, Excerpt from Mark Twain, "Baker's Bluejay Yarn," in *The Family Mark Twain,* Harper and Bros., NY, 1935, pp. 1139–1140.

Page 286–287, Excerpt from Edith Wharton, "New Year's Day," in *Edith Wharton: Novellas and Other Writings,* The Library of America, 1990, pp. 491–492.

Page 304–305, Excerpt from George Bernard Shaw, *Man and Superman,* in *Major British Writers,* ed. G. B. Harrison, Harcourt, Brace, 1959, pp. 717–718.

Page 335, Poem: Irving Layton, "Berry Picking," *Selected Poems by Irving Layton,* 1958. Used by permission, McClelland & Stewart, Ltd. The Canadian Publishers.

Page 374–375, "Channel Firing" by Thomas Hardy from *Collected Poems,* Macmillan Co., 1925.

Page 381–382, Excerpt from Sarah Orne Jewett, "A White Heron" in *Fiction 100: An Anthology of Short Stories,* 5th ed., Macmillan, 1988, pp. 791–798.

Introducing the AP English Literature and Composition Examination

The College Board offers two different Advanced Placement examinations in English:

1. Language and Composition
2. Literature and Composition

This book will help you prepare for the exam in Literature and Composition, which focuses on close reading of literary content. The exam tests your ability to comprehend and interpret the form and substance of poems and prose passages. In addition, it asks you to write clear, concise, and persuasive analytical essays in which you must demonstrate your understanding of the broad implications of particular works of literature.

For students planning to take the AP English exam in Language and Composition, Barron's has another book available: *How to Prepare for the AP English Exam in Language and Composition.*

The Literature and Composition exam lasts three hours and consists of two sections. The first section, which takes one hour, consists of multiple-choice questions and counts for 45 percent of the total score. The second section, lasting two hours, requires you to write three essays and comprises 55 percent of your grade.

Section I	Section II
Fifty to sixty multiple-choice questions based on your reading of two or three prose fiction passages and two or three poems. (One hour)	Three essays, one on a given poem, one on a passage of prose fiction—each analyzing how form and content relate to the meaning, and a third essay on your choice of novel or play. (Two hours)

Like all other AP exams, scores are reported on a scale of 1–5. In general, scores are interpreted to mean

5 extremely well qualified
4 well qualifed
3 qualified
2 possibly qualified
1 not recommended for AP credit

A high score on this exam demonstrates a proficiency in English at least on a par with students who have successfully completed an introductory college-level course in composition or literature. Recognizing this, many colleges and universities may waive your freshman English requirement, give you academic credit for the required course, or permit you to take a more advanced course during your freshman year. Because each college and university has its own policies regarding the awarding of credit for a good score, be sure to check with the admissions office of the institution you hope to attend.

This book will familiarize you with the multiple-choice questions on the exam and give you practical help in essay writing. Sections of the book will help you develop a flair for critically evaluating poems, novels, and plays.

If you teach an AP English class, use this book as a resource. It will lighten your load because it contains a great deal of what an AP Lit course typically contains, including selected reading passages, important literary terminology, analyses of prose and poetry, sample essays with evaluations, exam questions, and several practice AP tests with answers fully explained. In addition, the literature discussed and analyzed in the text can readily be incorporated into your teaching; you might even consider it an instant syllabus. Questions and exercises throughout the book are intended to stimulate thinking and inspire students to write the kinds of in-depth analyses required on AP exams.

If you are a student, use this book to prepare for the exam. Study each chapter. Take the practice tests and check your answers. Revel in the correct ones but let the wrong answers steer you to chapters in the book that you should probably spend some time with.

To all students preparing to take the AP English exam, the author wishes the best of luck.

George Ehrenhaft

PART ONE

AP ENGLISH LITERATURE AND COMPOSITION EXAM PREPARATION

CHAPTER **1** Overview of the AP English Literature and Composition Exam

The AP English Literature and Composition exam emphasizes the analysis of poetry and prose fiction. The best preparation consists of being familiar with the format of the exam and having practiced critical reading and analysis of texts from roughly the sixteenth century to the present. Ideally, most of the works should have been written originally in English, but high-quality literature in translation, such as Greek drama and Russian novels, serve the purpose equally well.

During the exam you will be asked to analyze a number of poems and prose passages by considering, among other things, their structure, style, and dominant themes. You may also be asked to recognize and discuss such elements as figurative language, imagery, point of view, and tone. To do your best on the exam, therefore, you need to be cognizant of the ways that authors use language and literary form to convey meaning.

In addition, you should know intimately several works of literary merit by such writers as Austen, Conrad, Fitzgerald, Updike, and among the dramatists, Shakespeare (of course), Chekhov, Ibsen, and O'Neill. On the exam, you will be expected to choose a novel or play and write with precision about its meaning. You may also be asked to analyze aspects of its form and structure or to comment on the extent to which the work reflects or embodies a social or historical milieu.

Section I of the exam lasts one hour and consists of 50 to 60 multiple-choice questions. It contains two, or sometimes three, passages of prose fiction excerpted from novels and short stories, but on occasion from a play or other genre. Along with the prose passages, you'll be given two or more short poems to read and analyze. More than half the questions relate to the reading passages, the rest to the poems.

Prose Passages

Unlike the SAT I or ACT, this exam rarely asks you basic comprehension questions about the reading passages. Because AP students are assumed to have little trouble grasping the general meaning of passages, questions focus not on what the author says but on the linguistic and rhetorical choices made by the author. Emphasis is on literary technique, including, among other things, structure of the passage, effects of diction and syntax, point of view, and the relationship between parts of the passage. Instead of asking about the meaning of a particular sentence, you may be asked to determine how the structure of that sentence relates to the purpose of the whole passage. Rather than identify the meaning of an allusion, you may be asked to determine its intent. Or you might be given a particular locution and asked to interpret it. Other questions may require an analysis of an image, a figure of speech, or choice of words.

In short, you should prepare yourself to handle almost any type of analytical question. According to surveys of past AP exams, the most common questions, and therefore those you are most likely to encounter, pertain to the author's tone; shifts in the writing style within the passage; the effects of certain words and phrases, especially figures of speech; the relationship of one sentence or idea to another; the relationship of one sentence to the meaning of the passage as a whole; and the rhetorical stance of the narrator. The exam includes many other types of questions, too, all meant to test your analytical skills and perception as a reader. In addition, almost every exam contains one question on standard English grammar.

For a comprehensive review of what you are expected to know about prose fiction, please see Chapter 5.

Poetry

In addition to prose passages, you will be given two or sometimes three poems, each accompanied by eight or more questions that focus on anything from the aesthetic intent of the poet to the implications of a single word. Whatever the poet has done to create the poem is grist for the test maker's mill. You could be asked to recognize structural components, types of language, tone, diction, themes, rhetorical devices, rhythms, meter, rhymes, and more.

A survey of several recent tests reveals that the most common poetry questions asked students to define the meaning of a word or phrase in context. (Rest assured that you won't be asked about archaic words or obscure allusions; should the poem contain any, they'll probably be explained in a footnote.) Other frequently asked questions relate to the implication or meaning of figures of speech, to the tone, and to the effect of a word or phrase on the unity or meaning of the entire poem. If the poem contains a shift in the speaker's point of view or rhetorical stance, you can virtually depend on a question about that. Technical questions on poetic techniques such as meter and rhythm show up occasionally but rarely more than once per exam.

See Chapter 4 for what you need to know about poetry for the AP exam.

Once the hour-long Section I is finished, you may not return to it. Test booklets are sealed and collected, and after a five- to ten-minute break, Section II begins.

Section II consists of three essay questions to be completed in two hours. How you apportion your time is left up to you, but forty minutes is recommended for each essay.

One essay is on poetry. After reading a given poem, you must write an essay that explains how the poem conveys its meaning. You may be asked to consider its theme, structure, language, or any other literary devices you deem important.

A second essay question asks you to analyze an excerpt from a novel or story—or possibly a series of letters, a speech in a play, or some other literary passage. The question, or "prompt" will specify the purpose of your analysis, but you are free to choose the literary elements such as tone, language, structure, diction, and others to include in your discussion.

The last question asks you to write an essay on a novel or play of your choice—never on a short story, a work of nonfiction, or other genre. The "prompt" makes a general observation about life or literature. Your job is to discuss the observation as it applies to a work of "literary merit." The names of several appropriate titles are appended to the question, but you may choose any other book or play of "comparable literary merit," a phrase whose meaning is far from clear-cut, but suggests titles that have endured and deserve to be read again and again. In all likelihood, a novel or play you studied in AP English class would serve well as a subject for this essay.

Each essay will be scored holistically. That means that readers will review the essay rather quickly for an overall impression of its content and form. Readers are trained to look for clearly organized, well-developed, and forceful responses that reveal a depth of understanding and insight. Because AP students hope to earn college credit for their efforts, readers also look for prose that is worthy of mature writers. Readers will be most impressed by clarity, coherence, good reasoning, and a writing style that demonstrates—by its diction, voice, syntax, rhythm, and tone—your command of a variety of effective writing techniques. For details on how AP essays are scored, turn to page 35. Also, be sure to read the comments about the sample student essays, pages 37–58.

STRUCTURE OF THE EXAM
(Total time: 3 hours)

Section I (One hour)
50–60 multiple-choice questions based on 2 or 3 poems and 2 or 3 passages of fiction

45 percent of total score

Section II (Two hours)
3 essays

Essay 1: An analysis of a poem

Essay 2: An analysis of a prose passage from a work of fiction, a letter, or a speech in a play

Essay 3: An analytical essay on a novel or play of your choice

55 percent of total score

Note: The first two essay topics are reversed from time to time.

Considering the breadth and depth of the exam, successful completion of an AP English course or a regimen of independent study should enable you to earn a good score. Study this book in the months and weeks prior to the exam. Take the practice tests. Who knows—you may turn a good score into an even better one.

CHAPTER 2 Answering Multiple-Choice Questions

Answering the multiple-choice questions correctly demonstrates that you have what it takes to read, extract meaning from, and analyze poems and passages of prose fiction, including, on occasion, an excerpt from a play. The selections you'll find on the exam are taken from contemporary literature, as well as from the literature of previous eras. In most cases, the poets and authors are not identified, but the date, which is always given, may provide a clue to the work's historical context. Your knowledge of history is not being tested, of course, but if a sonnet is dated, say, around 1625, you might justifiably surmise that it is a Shakespearean sonnet with a prescribed structure and pattern of rhymes. Likewise, an allusion to a war in a 1920 piece, while not necessarily a reference to World War I, would at least enable you to discount every war fought since then.

Although the multiple-choice questions are not intended to mystify or thwart you, not everyone who takes the test is expected to answer every question correctly. Some questions are harder than others. Ninety-nine out of a hundred students may get some questions right, while other questions stump more than half the students taking a given exam. This is as it ought to be, since the test measures literary skills. If every student earned a perfect score, the AP test would be a test in name only. To increase the likelihood that you will earn the highest score of which you are capable, study the material that follows and practice the suggested techniques for answering the questions.

Tactics for Answering the Questions

Answer the questions in the order presented. Questions on the test are not arranged in order of difficulty but generally follow the progress of the poem or passage. It makes sense, therefore, to answer the questions as they are given. But don't be a slave to that order. If you come to a question you can't answer, don't agonize over it. Just go on to the next one and come back later if time permits.

Pace yourself. During the hour devoted to Section I, you must read four or five passages and poems and answer 50 to 60 questions. If you were to spend five minutes reading each passage and poem, you would have roughly 45 seconds for each question, more than sufficient time if you don't dawdle. Train yourself to work at the proper speed. Take the practice tests in this book under testing conditions. That is, find a quiet place, clear your desk of distractions, and allow yourself exactly one hour to complete the questions.

Guess if you must. If you can't answer a question, guess at the answer BUT only if you can eliminate one or more of the five choices. Here's why:

Multiple-choice questions are worth one point each. Each correct answer will add a point to your raw score (total number of correct responses). For every wrong answer, however, your raw score will be lowered by one-quarter point. An item left blank will neither increase nor decrease your score. Subtracting credit for wrong answers is meant to discourage blind guessing. So if you haven't a clue about how to answer a question, leave it blank. But if you can confidently eliminate one of the five choices, it pays to guess. The odds are four to one that you'll be right. Not terrific odds, but suppose that on four tough questions you can eliminate one wrong answer and you guess four times. If you guess right just once you will have earned a point and lost only three-quarters of a point, a net gain of one-quarter. If you leave all four blank you will gain nothing. True, it is a gamble because you could make four incorrect guesses, but the chances of losing every time are only one in four. And you could get lucky and hit two, three, or even four correct answers.

If a question gives you trouble, and you can't decide among, say, three choices, common wisdom says that you should go with your initial impulse. Testing experts and psychologists agree that there's a better than average chance of success if you trust your intuition. There are no guarantees, however, because the mind works in so many strange ways that relying on your first choice may not always work.

Another piece of folk wisdom is that if one choice is longer than the others, that's the one to choose. Don't believe it! Since economy of expression is a virtue in writing test questions as well as in most other places, the shorter choice may just as often be the correct answer.

Understand the test directions. If you know what the directions say before you walk into the exam room, you needn't waste precious seconds reading them. Here are the directions for Section I:

> "This section consists of selections from literary works and questions on their content, form, and style. After reading each passage or poem, choose the best answer to each question and then fill in the corresponding oval on the answer sheet."

Decide on a reading technique. The test directions above work for some people, but not necessarily for everyone—not necessarily for you. As you prepare for the exam, therefore, try to answer the questions in Practice Tests A through D using the various approaches described in the paragraphs below. Although each option carries gains and losses, give each one a chance before deciding which produces the best results for you.

Option A. Read the poem or passage carefully from start to finish. Don't try to recall every detail. As you read, ask yourself, "What is this poem or passage about?" The answer will often be evident within a few lines. When you have finished, state the point of the poem or passage in your own words. Even if your interpretation is vague, it will give you a starting point for answering the questions. Sometimes the questions themselves will shed light on the point of the poem or passage. Refer to the text as often as you wish while answering the questions.

This widely used technique takes longer at the start but allows you to make up the time later.

Option B. Skim the poem or passage for its general idea. Read faster than you normally would. At the same time, try to sense what the piece is saying. Read the poem or passage just intently enough to get an impression of what it's about. Don't expect to keep details in mind. Then, as you answer each question refer to the text.

This technique saves time at the start and keeps your mind free of needless details. At some point, however, you will be forced to scour the passage for specific answers to the questions.

Option C. Skim the poem or passage to get its general meaning; then go back and read it carefully. Two readings, one fast and one slow, enable you to grasp the piece better than if you read it only once. During the second reading, confirm that your first impressions were accurate. Then proceed to the questions, referring frequently to the text.

This technique takes the most time but offers you the firmest grip on the poem or passage.

Above all, avoid falling prey to the irresistible temptation to plunge into the questions without first reading the passage or poem at least once. Not only will you waste time, but you will be unable to answer questions pertaining to the overall intent or effect of the poem or passage.

Decide what to do with your #2 pencil. Consider the uses of the pencil in your hand. Use it to fill in the ovals on your answer sheet, of course, but use it also to highlight the key phrases and ideas in a poem or passage. When you come to something that seems important, quickly draw a line under it or put a checkmark next to it in the margin. Whatever you do, however, use your pencil sparingly or you may end up with every line marked or checked. Similarly, feel free to mark up the test questions, underlining key words or striking out obviously incorrect choices.

Read the questions carefully. This piece of advice is self-evident, but in the rush of taking the test it's easy to forget. Pay particular attention to the requirements of questions that contain the words NOT, LEAST, or EXCEPT (see sample #4 below). Answering such questions requires a rapid shift of your thought patterns. Instead of searching a poem or passage for what it says or implies, you must suddenly seek out what it fails to say or imply.

Sample Questions on Poetry with Practice Exercises

Although most of the poetry questions direct your attention to a small segment of the poem—perhaps to a particular phrase or a pair of lines—familiarity with the entire poem is usually a prerequisite for finding the correct answers.

SAMPLE # 1

The poem might best be described as
(A) a recollection of childhood.
(B) a series of epiphanies.
(C) a touching anecdote.
(D) a coming-of-age reminiscence.
(E) a sentimental journey.

To answer this question you must read the whole poem and then determine which choice describes it most accurately. Because a few of the choices are similar—(A) and (D), for example—you must choose the *best* description, a judgment that must be based on evidence in the poem, not on your intuition or feelings.

SAMPLE #2

The speaker in the poem views the city primarily in terms of
(A) sounds and smells.
(B) colors and shapes.
(C) dark and light.
(D) textures and patterns.
(E) youth and innocence.

This question asks you to identify the poem's prevailing images. To choose the best answer you must scan the poem, picking out images of sounds, smells, colors, and so forth. Frequency is a good criterion for deciding which images dominate the poem. But not always. If two sorts of images recur about equally, your decision must be based on a more subtle evidence such as the placement of images in the poem. Those that appear in the first and last lines of a stanza will probably stand out from those buried in the middle. Unfortunately, there are no hard and fast rules that apply to every poem. On the test, however, the question is sure to have a clear-cut answer.

SAMPLE #3

The title of the poem suggests that the poem is about

I. an ancient religious rite.
II. a historic site now overrun by visitors.
III. the scene of an unsolved murder.

(A) I only
(B) II only
(C) I and II only
(D) II and III only
(E) I, II, and III

Because ambiguity is a cornerstone of literature, you may be asked questions like this that offer one, two, or three correct answers. On the test, you may find two or three questions with this format. By itself the poem's title may not evoke a complex response, but once you have read the poem, the title may take on far greater significance. Titles are always included on the test and may help you unlock each poem's meaning.

SAMPLE # 4

Looking into the dark cave allows the speaker to experience all of the following EXCEPT

(A)   a surge of remorse for what he had done.

(B)   a sudden awareness of his own folly.

(C)   a rush of anger toward his former companions.

(D)   pride in overcoming the odds against him.

(E)   fear of what may be hiding inside the cave.

To respond to this question you must read the poem not for what it says but for what it doesn't say. That is, the correct answer is the one that states something inaccurate or false. A handful of questions on the exam may be of that type.

SAMPLE # 5

The primary rhetorical function of lines 21–23 is to

(A)   introduce a digression from the central theme of the poem.

(B)   extend the metaphor developed in lines 19–20.

(C)   illustrate the speaker's ambivalence toward the child.

(D)   contradict a point made previously.

(E)   develop a theme stated in the first stanza.

Although this question relates specifically to lines 21–23, it cannot be answered without revisiting the rest of the poem. To determine whether (A) is the best answer, you must reflect on the poem's main theme. Choices (B) and (D) require you to reread material that came before. Choice (C) forces you to assess the speaker's tone or point of view throughout the poem, and (E) obliges you to reread the first stanza.

Not all poetry questions on the exam are strictly intepretive. Some are more objective, calling for straightforward factual answers. Sample questions 6–8 are of this type.

SAMPLE # 6

Line 7 includes an example of

(A)   hyperbole.

(B)   oxymoron.

(C)   allegory.

(D)   consonance.

(E)   antithesis.

To answer this question you need to be acquainted with rhetorical terms. Then you must be able to identify which of these terms is exemplified in line 7 of the poem. In the Glossary of Literary and Rhetorical Terms, you'll find a brief definition of each term. For a more thorough discussion of poetic terminology see Chapter 4.

SAMPLE # 7
   The form and content of poem can best be described as that of
   (A)   an elegy.
   (B)   an ode.
   (C)   a lyrical ballad.
   (D)   a sestina.
   (E)   a sonnet.

To answer this question you must know some poetic terminology, more specifically the defining characteristics of an elegy, an ode, and other poetic forms. Chapter 4 and the Glossary at the end of this book contain the information you need.

SAMPLE # 8
   Grammatically, the word "demon" (line 14) functions as
   (A)   the direct object of "eats" (line 12).
   (B)   an appositive for "underbelly" (line 14).
   (C)   the subject of "Screams" (line 15).
   (D)   the direct object of "Screams" (line 15).
   (E)   the indirect object of "Screams" (line 15).

The test usually contains one question meant to test your knowledge of standard English grammar. It may appear as a poetry question or a question on a reading passage. If your grammar skills are rusty, a few enlightening hours spent in the company of a basic grammar textbook prior to the exam may serve you well.

For Practice:
A Poem and
Questions

To see how questions apply to a specific poem, carefully read "Sonnet—to Science" by Edgar Allen Poe. Then study the questions. Be sure to read the accompanying comments. They illustrate the kind of analytical thinking that leads to correct answers.

SONNET—TO SCIENCE

Science! true daughter of Old Time thou art!
   Who alterest all things with thy peering eyes.
Why preyest thou thus upon the poet's heart,
Line   Vulture, whose wings are dull realities?
(5) How should he love thee? or how deem thee wise,
   Who wouldst not leave him in his wandering
To seek for treasure in the jewelled skies,
   Albeit he soared with an undaunted wing?
Hast thou not dragged Diana[1] from her car?
(10)   And driven the Hamadryad[2] from the wood
To seek a shelter in some happier star?
   Hast thou not torn the Naiad[3] from her flood,
The Elfin[4] from the green grass, and from me
The summer dream beneath the tamarind tree?[5]

(1830)

---

[1]The huntress, a goddess of chastity. Her "car" is the moon.
[2]Wood nymph
[3]Water nymph
[4]Tiny creature residing in flowers
[5]A tropical tree with edible fruit and blossoms used for medicine

1. The speaker's attitude toward science is best described as
   (A) puzzled.
   (B) resentful.
   (C) mournful.
   (D) indifferent.
   (E) antagonistic.

Comment: This exemplifies the type of bread-and-butter question that appears—usually more than once—on every test. Read the phrase "speaker's attitude" as a synonym for "speaker's tone." Tone questions are ubiquitous on the AP exam because every piece of literature has an identifiable tone, and an analysis of a literary selection would hardly be complete without taking tone into account.

   To answer this question you must reflect on the intent of a speaker who decries the effects of science on poetry—not an uncommon theme at the dawn of the Darwinian Age when Edgar Allen Poe wrote this sonnet. Because the speaker asks several questions as the poem unfolds it may seem that Choice (A) could be the answer, but a scrutiny of those questions reveals that they are more rhetorical than inquisitive. Choice (C) suggests that poetry has died, but the very fact that this poem exists should put that idea to rest. Choice (D) is clearly wrong because the speaker attacks science with considerable verve. That leaves Choices (B) and (E) to consider. "Antagonistic" implies that the speaker would like to see science destroyed, while "resentful" is a more circumspect emotion. Knowing that it is unrealistic to expect science to dry up and go away, the speaker is chafing about the effects of science on poetry. The best answer, therefore, is Choice (B).

2. The effect of capitalizing the phrase "Old Time" in the first line is to
   (A) prove that the ancients were fascinated with science.
   (B) make the personification in line 1 more vivid.
   (C) suggest the stature of science.
   (D) imply that science is divinely inspired.
   (E) suggest that a true scientist must also be a kind of artist.

Comment: The question asks why the poet may have capitalized a phrase that would not ordinarily be capitalized. To determine the answer, consider the effects of the capitalization.

Choice (A) may state a truth about civilizations of antiquity but evidence in the poem cannot justify the idea. Choice (B) attempts to set up a rhetorical relationship that, alas, has no validity. Choice (D) may tempt you because references to divinity are often capitalized, but it is difficult to link "Old Time" to godliness. Choice (E) expresses a compelling idea but it can't be supported by the content of the poem. That leaves Choice (C), which is the best answer, not only because humans have practiced science for eons, but because science is revered and has long been a potent force in shaping the world.

3. The pronoun "he" in line 5 refers to
   (A) the vulture.
   (B) the scientist.
   (C) the poet.
   (D) God.
   (E) science.

Comment: Because poets often take liberties with English syntax and disregard conventions of grammar and style, readers are left to puzzle out just what the poet is saying. Poetry questions on the AP test, therefore, sometimes ask you to figure out the intent of certain usages, or in this case, a pronoun reference.

The second quatrain of a sonnet usually starts with a new sentence that may or may not refer directly to something in the first four lines. The antecedent of "he" in line 5 remains ambiguous unless you read on. The images in lines 6–8 reveal that "he" refers to the poet—Choice (C)—a figure who cannot love or respect science because, among other things, it has, like a predatory vulture, snatched away his freedom to wander and "seek for treasure in the jewelled skies."

4. In line 5, "should" is best interpreted as
  (A) can.
  (B) must.
  (C) is supposed to.
  (D) may.
  (E) might.

Comment: Because language and usage change constantly, it is hardly a surprise that a poem written nearly two centuries ago will contain diction that, while perfectly proper then, may now sound odd or archaic. The use of "should" in this context is a case in point.

To interpret its meaning you must read the entire sentence in which the word appears (lines 5–8). The sentence is a question in which the speaker asks how he can love something that has restricted his freedom or reined in his imagination. In context, then, "should" is not used in its usual sense, to suggest duty or obligation, but rather to express the conditional. To paraphrase the line loosely: How can you expect me to love you, if you treat me so badly? Choice (A), therefore, is the best answer. All the other choices miss the mark.

5. Which of the following stylistic features most significantly contributes to the poem's unity?
  (A) Numerous allusions to folklore and myth
  (B) A series of interrogative sentences
  (C) An extended metaphor
  (D) The use of alliteration
  (E) The pattern of end rhymes

Comment: A poem, an essay, a symphony, or any other work of art is unified when all its components—style, subject matter, structure, themes, composition, even technique—work together to create a harmonious whole. Unity of action, of form, of intent—these, along with dramatic unity, are principles that one might apply to a literary work. The concept of unity in literature is hard to pin down but easy to recognize when absent.

To answer the question, survey the poem for stylistic features listed in Choices (A) through (E). Because the poet used them all, your job is to determine which feature is "most significant" to the poem's unity. Since unity is derived from the overall effect of the work rather than from its individual parts, the best answer is (C), the central metaphor that compares science to a type of vulture. Throughout the poem, the speaker uses words and phrases that suggest the actions of a predatory bird, among them "preyest," "soared," "dragged," and "torn." In comparison to (C), the other choices fail to make the grade.

6. The speaker in the poem suggests all of the following EXCEPT
  (A) science is responsible for destroying the poet's capacity to dream.
  (B) science fails to value human emotions.
  (C) science reduces everything to observable facts.
  (D) science is the death knell of poetry.
  (E) a function of poetry and of science is to uncover reality.

Comment: Four of the five choices restate or paraphrase an idea found in the poem. Your task is to identify the one that doesn't. Choice (A) is suggested by the last two lines of the poem, Choice (B) by the idea that science preys on the poet's heart. Choice (C) is clearly stated in line 2, and Choice (E), while not stated directly, is implied by the notion that science is guided by "dull realities," and that poets find hidden realities in the moon, the sea, the grass, and other natural phenomena. Choice (D), the best answer, overstates the influence of science on poetry. While science may diminish poetry, its influence is not fatal. If science had the capacity to kill poetry, this particular poem, among others, would not have been written.

7. Which of the following is the best meaning of the phrase "not leave him" in line 6?
   (A) Leave him alone
   (B) Interfere
   (C) Abandon him
   (D) Take leave of him
   (E) Control him

Comment: Because poems often contain nonstandard idiom, AP questions frequently deal with the best paraphrases and interpretations of specific phrases such as this. The answer cannot usually be found in the phrase itself but only in its context. Therefore, you must read what comes before and after and determine, while taking into account the purpose and thrust of the poem, which choice makes the most sense. Then substitute each of the choices for the phrase "not leave him."

Characterizing science as a destructive force interested only in cold realities, the speaker finds himself unable to soar in fantasy, sit peacefully dreaming beneath a tree, or, as intimated in lines 6–7, wander in search of inspiring treasures. In other words, science has become the speaker's nemesis. It won't leave him alone to do his thing. Of the choices, only (D) represents what the speaker has in mind.

8. Line 8 ("Albeit . . . wing?") serves primarily to
   (A) suggest similarities between the speaker and the vulture.
   (B) contrast the poet before and after the coming of science.
   (C) show the magnitude of the poet's imagination.
   (D) reflect the speaker's ambivalence toward the poet.
   (E) undercut the speaker's emotional intensity.

Comment: Consider this a "function" question, that is, a question that can be answered only by figuring out not what the line says but its purpose in the poem. Structurally, the line is a subordinate clause tacked onto the end of a quatrain in which the speaker wonders aloud how he can be expected to do anything but loathe intrusive science. In line 8, the speaker briefly conjures an image of the way life used to be, when he "soared with an undaunted wing." Looking over the five choices, you'll see that only (B) comes close to describing the function of line 8.

9. Between lines 1–8 and 9–14 there is a shift from
    (A) optimism to pessimism.
    (B) emotionalism to rationality.
    (C) realism to fantasy.
    (D) inquiry to reproachfulness.
    (E) hatred to revulsion.

Comment: A point of view—the relation in which a speaker stands to the sub-ject matter—governs the overall character of most poems and other literary works. Speakers, being human, often digress, change their minds, insert asides, apostrophize, contradict themselves in the middle of whatever they have to say.

Because such a shift takes place within this poem, you are asked to identify the speaker's rhetorical stance toward science both before and after it occurs. As a result, you must compare and contrast the speaker's the viewpoint in lines 1–8 and in lines 9–14. Eliminate (A) as a possible answer because nowhere does the speaker show an iota of optimism. Choice (E) is not much better because there is hardly a difference between "hatred" and "revulsion." Choice (B) has potential because the speaker's voice is charged with emotion; there's not a hint of greater rationality in the last six lines. If anything, the tone is more antirational than before. With regard to (C), consider that the speaker compares science to a vul-ture—a poetic conceit inconsistent with a realist's way of thinking. That leaves (D) as the answer. Indeed, in lines 1–8 the speaker spews a series of questions about the deleterious effects of science. In the remainder of the poem, the questions become accusatory in nature. They castigate science for destroying the sensi-bilities of poets.

10. The contrast between science and poetry is best illustrated by which pair of phrases?
    (A) "from the wood" (line 10) and "from her car" (line 9)
    (B) "true daughter" (1) and "peering eyes" (2)
    (C) "jewelled skies" (7) and "tamarind tree" (14)
    (D) "undaunted wing" (8) and "happier star" (11)
    (E) "dull realities" (4) and "summer dream" (14)

Comment: To answer this question you might simply try studying the pairs of phrases and picking the one that suggests the conflict that lies at the heart of the poem. Choice (A) hints at a conflict between nature ("wood") and technology ("car") until you remember that the "car" is Diana's chariot, the moon. Choices (B), (C), and (D) contain pairs of phrases that contain no particular dichotomy. But (E) consists of two antithetical phrases, the first representing the speaker's view of science, the second a metaphor for the the poet's creativity.

11. According to the speaker, the most grievous effect of science has been to
    (A) replace emotions with cold, hard objectivity.
    (B) change man's perception of the universe.
    (C) distort the purposes of scientific investigation.
    (D) belittle nonscientists.
    (E) convince people to distrust their instincts.

Comment: Notice that the question begins with "According to the speaker," a telling phrase, suggesting that the answer will be not be found by reading between the lines of the poem but directly in the speaker's words. The phrase "most grievous" also obliges you to weigh each effect for its malignity. At the same time, you must ascertain that each effect listed in the five choices is mentioned in the poem

Choice (B) certainly qualifies as a malign effect but is neither implied nor discussed in the poem. Likewise, there is no evidence of (C) or (D) in the poem. There may be a hint of (E) in the speaker's words but the statement is overgeneralized since the poem focuses on the effects of science on poets and their work. Choice (A), therefore, is the correct answer because the speaker, using a variety of images and ideas, laments the intrusion of science into the life of the imagination. Science, with its dispassionate pursuit of facts, spoils the visions of the creative dreamer, ruins myth, and removes magic from the stars and storied constellations.

12. The speaker alludes to figures from myth and folklore in order to
   (A)   symbolize images that have long ignited the imagination of poets.
   (B)   endow the poem with a classical flavor.
   (C)   suggest how dramatically science has altered poetry.
   (D)   heighten the misunderstanding between poets and scientists.
   (E)   demonstrate the obsolescence of poetry.

Comment: Rather than ask you to explain allusions in the poem, this question asks you to identify the reason that Poe included them.

Choice (B) implies that Poe tossed allusions into the poem solely to show off, like a name-dropper at a cocktail party. Choices (C) and (D) restate themes in the poem but in no way account for the speaker's use of allusions. The suggestion that the allusions are meant to illustrate poetry's obsolescence makes Choice (E) an unlikely answer. Choice (A), on the other hand, goes to the heart of the poem's message: Science has shot the poet out of poetical skies and expelled some of the symbolic images that have inspired poets for ages and ages.

Sample Questions on Prose Fiction with Practice Exercise

Questions on prose fiction passages cover much of the same territory as the poetry questions: sentence structure, the effect of words and phrases in context, major themes, point of view, and so forth. In addition, they ask about narrative techniques, the interaction of characters, the development of ideas, and numerous other elements of literary analysis

A review of recent AP exams shows that some topics come up again and again: the tone of the passage, a shift in the speaker's rhetorical stance, the interpretation of a word, phrase, or sentence, the effect or purpose of a figure of speech, and the relationship between sentence structure and meaning. Because passages are usually excerpted from longer works, many exams include a question or two that asks you to make inferences about what may have preceded the events in the passage and what might reasonably follow.

Passages on the exam appear without titles, sources, and authors. Only a date of composition is given, information that may help you answer some of the questions. At the very least, the date may provide a clue to the meaning of an allusion or account for any unusual diction or the quirky style in which the text is written.

The samples below illustrate the types of questions most commonly found on the exam:

SAMPLE #1

The speaker's tone in the passage can best be described as
(A) satirical.
(B) despairing.
(C) contemptuous.
(D) irreverent.
(E) whimsical.

Tone is so vital an element in literary analysis that you can depend on seeing three or more tone questions on the exam. Tone questions come in a variety of guises. Some, like this one, are straightforward. Others are couched in words that don't mention tone at all, as in the following:

"In lines 12–15, the speaker's *attitude* toward Hortense can best be described as . . ."

"The speaker's *feelings* about the disaster are suggested by . . ."

"The speaker's *state of mind* is established predominently by . . ."

The diction may vary, but each italicized word or phrase is a synonym for tone or for the "speaker's rhetorical stance," a term that AP test writers like to use.

When a speaker's tone changes in mid-passage, you may be asked to identify two tones—before and after the change. Not all tone questions are about the entire passage. Some focus on the tone of a word, a phrase, or on any other component of the passage.

SAMPLE #2

The passage as a whole relies on all of the following contrasts EXCEPT
(A)   knowledge and ignorance.
(B)   elegance and bad taste.
(C)   sanity and madness.
(D)   urgency and leisure.
(E)   excitability and torpor.

Although you are not likely to be asked about the meaning of the entire passage, some questions, such as this one, can be answered only if you know what the whole passage says. The structure of this question obliges you to search the entire passage for various contrasts. If all goes well, you'll find four of the five listed in (A) through (E). The one you don't find is the answer to the question. You should anticipate two or three questions stuctured like this one on the exam.

Other questions that require familiarity with the whole passage may be phrased something like:

"The excerpt is chiefly concerned with a . . ."

"The change that Lou undergoes in the passage can best be characterized as . . ."

"By the end of the excerpt, Doc probably believed that Jesse had been . . ."

SAMPLE #3

The speaker implies in the first paragraph that the narrative that preceded the passage most likely included
(A) an altercation in the street.
(B) a reunion between two old friends.
(C) a description of Venice.
(D) a conversation between the shopkeeper and a policeman.
(E) the receipt of a shocking letter.

Almost certainly you'll be given a question that asks you to infer what might have occurred in the story before the passage begins or to speculate on what events might follow. Clues may appear almost anywhere in the passage. Sometimes before-and-after questions have more to do with style, characterization, setting, tone, or voice than with events in the story. Were a given passage to continue, for example, a tongue-in-cheek narrator would be more likely to say something funny than to tell a maudlin tale full of teary-eyed sentimentality.

SAMPLE #4

The phrase "cut her past away" in line 13 does which of the following?

I. It shifts the tone of the narrative from sentimentality to realism.
II. It introduces a strain of naturalism into the passage.
III. It foreshadows Mona's momentous decision.

(A) I only
(B) II only
(C) I and II only
(D) II and III only
(E) I, II, and III

On the exam you may expect several questions about the rhetorical function of a word, a phrase, a sentence, or an even lengthier piece of the passage, say, a description of the setting or a character sketch, for example. Asking a question about rhetorical function implies that the author chose language intended to create one or more effects. Your task is to identify those effects.

The format of this question indicates that the phrase "cut her past away" may have one, two, or three different functions. AP exams usually contain two or three questions formatted in this manner. Although you can't rely on past practice, more often than not a choice with two Roman numerals has been the correct answer.

SAMPLE #5

> In lines 4–8, the major effect of using a series of short compound sentences is to
> (A) create tension in the narrative.
> (B) indicate Mr. Herzog's state of mind.
> (C) emphasize the narrator's confusion.
> (D) prepare the reader for the tumultuous events that follow.
> (E) establish a mood of tranquillity.

This question, like others, relates to various effects of sentence structure. The structure of a sentence affects meaning, of course, but it may also alter the tone, slow or speed up the narrative, create suspense, and shape reader response in any number of other ways.

SAMPLE #6

> In the context of the passage, the phrase "remarkably sleek and plump clerks" (line 23) is used as a metaphor for the
> (A) indifference of the bureaucracy.
> (B) stylishness of the downtown area.
> (C) frenetic activity in the law office.
> (D) austerity of the courthouse.
> (E) judge's obsession.

This question comes as close to asking you to identify the meaning of a phrase as almost any question you'll find on the exam. Instead of asking you straight-forwardly what the phrase means, however, this question is couched in terms of interpreting a metaphor, which, all things considered, is just a sneaky way to assess your comprehension. Other questions meant to check how well you understand pieces of the passage may read as follows:

> "Which of the following is the primary meaning of the word 'love' as it is used in line 15?"
> "The best paraphrase of the sentence beginning in line 8 is . . . "
> "The speaker characterizes a 'farce' (line 19) as all of the following EXCEPT . . ."
> "The phrases 'gleamed like an eye below her room' (line 3) and 'rose in the distance like a moon' (line 5) imply a contrast between . . . "
> "From the context, the reader can infer that Robbins (line 40) works as a . . . "

SAMPLE #7

> In lines 34–39, the speaker makes use of all of the following EXCEPT
> (A) hyperbole.
> (B) equivocation.
> (C) dramatic irony.
> (D) nonsequitur.
> (E) pathos.

Two or more questions on the AP exam may test your recognition and understanding of terms common to literary analysis and criticism. No doubt you are already familiar with many of them, but to be sure, study the Glossary at the back of this book.

SAMPLE #8

Victor criticizes his son's performance (lines 37–39) because he

(A)   has unrealistic expectations.

(B)   hopes to make amends for his own failure.

(C)   wants to comfort Katherine.

(D)   expects to inspire the boy to try harder.

(E)   suffers from malevolence.

Because prose fiction passages are often about people, it's almost inevitable that a question or two may relate to characterization, to conflicts between characters, or to the influence of one character on another. In this question you are asked to analyze a character's motives.

For Practice: A Prose Passage and Questions   Carefully read the following passage, an excerpt from the British novel *Moll Flanders* by Daniel Defoe. Then answer the questions. The comments that follow each question explain the reasoning process that led to the correct answers.

I was very shy of shoplifting, especially among the mercers and drapers,[1] who are a set of fellows that have their eyes very much about them. I made a venture or two among the lace folks and the milliners, and particularly at one
Line
(5)   shop where two young women were newly set up and had not been bred in the trade. There I carried off a piece of bone-lace worth six or seven pounds, and a paper of thread. But this was but once; it was a trick that would not serve again.

It was always reckoned a safe job when we heard of a new shop, and especially when the people were such as were not bred to shops. Such may depend
(10)   upon it that they will be visited once or twice at their beginning, and they must be very sharp indeed if they can prevent it.

I made another adventure or two after this, but they were but trifles. Nothing considerable offering for a good while, I began to think that I must give over the trade in earnest; but my governess, who was not willing to lose
(15)   me and expected great things of me, brought me one day into company with a young woman and a fellow that went for her husband, though, as it appeared afterwards, she was not his wife, but they were partners in the trade they carried on, and in something else too. In short, they robbed together, lay together, were taken together, and at last were hanged together.

(20)   I came into a kind of league with these two by the help of my governess, and they carried me out into three or four adventures where I rather saw them commit some coarse and unhandy robberies in which nothing but a great stock of impudence on their side and gross negligence on the people's side who were robbed could have made them successful. So I resolved from that time forward
(25)   to be very cautious how I adventured with them; and indeed, when two or three unlucky projects were proposed by them, I declined the offer and per-

---

[1]types of fabric and clothing merchants

(30)

(35)

(40)

(45)

(50)

(55)

(60)

(65)

(70)

suaded them against it. One time they particularly proposed robbing a watchmaker of three gold watches, which they had eyed in the daytime, and found the place where he laid them. One of them had so many keys of all kinds that he made no question to open the place where the watchmaker had laid them; and so we made a kind of appointment. But when I came to look narrowly into the thing, I found they proposed breaking open the house, and this I would not embark in, so they went without me. They did get into the house by main force and broke up the locked place where the watches were but found but one of the gold watches and a silver one, which they took, and got out of the house again very clear. But the family being alarmed, cried out, "Thieves," and the man was pursued and taken. The young woman had got off, too, but unhappily was stopped at a distance and the watches found upon her. And thus I had a second escape, for they were convicted and both hanged, being old offenders, though but young people. And as I said before that they robbed together, so now they hanged together, and there ended my new partnership.

I began now to be very wary, having so narrowly escaped a scouring and having such an example before me. But I had a new tempter, who prompted me every day—I mean my governess; and now a prize presented, which as it came by her management, so she expected a good share of the booty. There was a good quantity of Flanders lace lodged in a private house where she had heard of it, and Flanders lace being prohibited, it was a good booty to any custom-house officer that could come at it. I had a full account from my governess, as well of the quantity as of the very place where it was concealed, and I went to a custom-house officer and told him I had a discovery to make to him, if he would assure me that I should have my due share of the reward. This was so just an offer that nothing could be fairer; so he agreed, and taking a constable and me with him, we beset the house. As I told him I could go directly to the place, he left it to me; and the hole being very dark, I squeezed myself into it with a candle in my hand, and so reached the pieces out to him, taking care as I gave him some so to secure as much about myself as I could conveniently dispose of. There was nearly 300 pounds worth of lace in the hole, and I secured about 50 pounds worth of it myself. The people in the house were not owners of the place, but a merchant who had entrusted them with it; so that they were not so surprised as I thought they would be.

I left the officer overjoyed with his prize and fully satisfied with what he had got and appointed to meet him at a house of his own directing, where I came after I had disposed of the cargo I had about me, of which he had not the least suspicion. When I came, he began to capitulate, believing I did not understand the right I had in the prize, and would fain have put me off with 20 pounds, but I let him know that I was not so ignorant as he supposed I was; and yet I was glad, too, that he offered to bring me to a certainty. I asked 100 pounds, and he rose up to 30 pounds; I fell to 80, and he rose again to 40. In a word he offered me 50 pounds, and I consented, only demanding a piece of lace, which I thought came to about 8 or 9 pounds, as if it had been for my own wear, and he agreed to it. So I got 50 pounds in money paid to me that same night, and made an end of the bargain. Nor did he ever know who I was or where to inquire for me, so that if it had been discovered that part of the goods were embezzled, he could have made no challenge upon me for it.

(1722)

1. In context, the phrase "not bred to shops" (line 9) is best interpreted to mean
   (A) unaccustomed to dealing with customers.
   (B) unable to market goods effectively.
   (C) unused to operating stores.
   (D) not considered skillful salespeople.
   (E) unaware of shopping protocol.

Comment: This question asks you to figure out the meaning of a phrase that may once have been common in everyday speech but is now all but obsolete. Indeed, the entire passage is packed with usage long out of fashion. What's more, the speaker, an uneducated young woman, uses English that was nonstandard even in her day. The correct answer can nevertheless be found by studying the context in which the phrase occurs.

In line 9 the subject under discussion is shoplifting. In particular, the speaker discusses which shops make the best targets. New shops are "safe" because people unaccustomed to being shopkeepers don't know enough to guard their wares against thieves. Choices (A), (B), (D), and (E) pertain generally to neophyte shopkeepers, but only (C) applies specifically to a trait that would pique the interest of a shoplifter. The best interpretation of "not bred to shops," therefore, is "unused to operating stores."

2. The structure of the sentence beginning in line 20 does which of the following?
   (A) It contradicts assertions made about the young couple in the previous paragraph.
   (B) It reflects the speaker's failure to make her own decisions.
   (C) It implies that the governess can't be trusted.
   (D) It attests to the speaker's ability to accurately assess the character of other people.
   (E) It makes light of the governess's efforts to help the speaker get ahead in her chosen career.

Comment: This question presumes a cause-and-effect relationship between the given sentence and some other aspect of the passage. The particulars of sentence structure actually count for little in working out the answer. What matters more is your ability to absorb what the sentence says and figure out its role.

At this point in the passage the speaker disparages her young associates, whose dumb luck rather than skill enabled them to pull off a robbery or two. Because the sentence contradicts nothing that came earlier, eliminate Choice (A). Disregard Choice (B) as well because the speaker's decisiveness is not an issue. Although the sentence vaguely impugns the judgment of the governess, Choice (C) is a stretch, and Choice (E) is irrelevant. Choice (D) correctly identifies the function of the sentence. Indeed, the speaker judges her two colleagues astutely. Her perspicacity is borne out by the couple's misadventures and ultimate demise.

3. In context, the word "impudence" (line 23) is best interpreted to mean
   (A) disrespect.
   (B) insolence.
   (C) indecency.
   (D) shamelessness.
   (E) boldness.

Comment: If a question asks you to interpret an everyday word such as "impudence," you can be sure that its conventional meaning isn't at issue. Look, therefore, for a secondary or more obscure meaning.

With that principle in mind, survey the five choices and eliminate the two common synonyms of "impudence" found in Choices (A) and (B). According to the speaker, the young couple's "impudence" helped them carry out a few robberies. Since neither "indecency" nor "shamelessness" can be construed as enabling traits of young freebooters, eliminate (C) and (D). That leaves (E), decisively the best answer.

4. The first three paragraphs suggest that the speaker believes all of the following to be true of shoplifting EXCEPT
   (A) it is more manageable with neophyte shopkeepers.
   (B) it can be a lucrative endeavor.
   (C) it will one day lead to her apprehension and punishment.
   (D) it is a trade like any other.
   (E) it involves a careful selection of prey.

Comment: The word EXCEPT is your cue to search through the passage for evidence of each of the five choices. Then select as your answer the item you can't find.

Eliminate (A) because the speaker says that she favors plying her trade in the shops of beginners (lines 6–8). That the work is lucrative—Choice (B)—is implied by lines 5–7. Choice (D) is suggested by the speaker's use of such words as "venture" (lines 2–3), "job" (line 8), and "trade" (line 14), and Choice (E) is discussed in both the first and second paragraphs. Only Choice (C) is missing from the passage. The speaker never discusses the possibility of her own apprehension and punishment.

5. In relating the story of the young couple (lines 20–41) the speaker's attitude toward her two former colleagues might best be described as
   (A) vindictive.
   (B) derisive.
   (C) despicable.
   (D) laudatory.
   (E) magnanimous.

Comment: This is a variation of a "tone" question. Read lines 20–41 with your sensors attuned to the speaker's opinion of her two former colleagues.

The fact that she keeps her distance from them (line 26) suggests that the two favorable adjectives—"laudatory" (D) and "magnanimous" (E)—should be eliminated. Because there is no evidence of vindictiveness in the speaker's words—after all, the couple never did her any harm—eliminate (A). Similarly, because the speaker has no reason to despise the pair, (C) is not a good answer. That leaves (B) as the only choice—a good answer considering the speaker's account of the bungled theft. The fact that the couple's trip to the gallows meant nothing more to the speaker than the end of her partnership, as stated in lines 40–41, indicate that she could never have thought very highly of the unfortunate pair.

6. The speaker in the passage reveals her character primarily through
  (A) her thoughts.
  (B) episodes she tells about.
  (C) her interaction with others.
  (D) physical descriptions.
  (E) her use of English idiom.

Comment: This question, about a crucial issue in any work of fiction, asks you to determine the manner in which the author develops the character. Because several techniques are used, choosing the predominant one is something of a challenge.

   Almost nothing in the passage supports (C) or (D) as the best choice. Choice (E) has some validity because the speaker's use of non-standard English reveals her background. But since the question asks about her character, (E) fails to hold up as the best answer. Choice (A) has promise because during the passage the speaker pours out her thoughts about shoplifting, about anxieties, ambitions, and so on. (B) is also a possibility because the passage is packed with vignettes of the speaker's life. As an answer to the question, (A) is arguably the better choice because a person's inner thoughts reveal character more tellingly than a person's experiences.

7. From the statement "I declined the offer and persuaded them against it" (lines 26–27), the reader may infer that
  (A) the speaker plans to reform and go straight.
  (B) the young couple's project is destined to fail.
  (C) the speaker feels guilty about spurning the young couple.
  (D) the speaker has been given good advice by the governess.
  (E) the young couple's project requires the speaker's participation.

Comment: Like other questions on the AP exam, this one requires you to infer the implication of a particular locution. To the speaker, the words merely report something she did. To a reader in search of meaning behind the meaning, however, the words signify more.

   By the time the speaker declines to participate in the couple's questionable ventures, the reader already knows from the previous paragraph that the pair was "taken together, and at last were hanged together" (line 19). The speaker calls their current schemes "unlucky," suggesting that no good could come of them. Consequently (B) is the best answer.

8. Which of the following best describes the speaker's use of language
  (A) Colloquial and unrefined
  (B) Informative and foul
  (C) Arrogant and self-serving
  (D) Personal and poetic
  (E) Pretentious and pompous

Comment: Had this passage been written recently, its use of language would be idiosyncratic to say the least. But the passage was composed in 1722. Would an eighteenth-century reader have found it equally eccentric? Answering that question puts your "ear" for language to the test.

By considering only the first adjective in each pair, you may quickly dispose of Choices (C) and (E). In no way is the speaker's language either "arrogant" or "pretentious." Now look at the second adjective in the remaining choices. Because there is no evidence of foul or obscene language, eliminate (B). Similarly, disregard (D) because there's hardly a poetic touch in the entire passage. To justify (A) as the only valid choice, consider such usages as "shy of shoplifting" (line 1), "a fellow that went for her husband" (line 16), and "that could come at it" (line 48)—all colloquial expressions that would not have passed the lips of a well-educated or discriminating speaker.

9.   The inclusion of the "custom-house officer" (lines 47–48) and the "constable" (line 53) in the speaker's narrative serves to

    I. demonstrate the speaker's cleverness in planning a theft.
    II. suggest that the keepers of law and order are as corruptible as anyone else.
    III. add an ironic twist to the account of the lace robbery.

(A)   II only
(B)   III only
(C)   I and II only
(D)   I and III only
(E)   I, II, and III

Comment: Recruiting a custom-house officer to help her steal a cache of Flanders lace attests to the speaker's foresight (Roman numeral I). That two men, both defenders of law and order, unwittingly aid in the commission of crime adds a nice ironic twist to the story (Roman numeral III). And since the corruptibility of the officer (Roman II) is questionable, (D) is the best answer to the question. If (E) were to be a better choice, the passage must contain evidence that the officer and the constable are not totally above board. Haggling with the speaker over her share of the reward may hint of illicit motives, but the officer's intentions are left in a cloud of ambiguity. As for the constable, he remains beyond reproach throughout the episode.

10.   The narrative that preceded the passage most likely consists of
(A)   a legal tract on penalties for shoplifting.
(B)   a summary of the speaker's experiences as a university student.
(C)   an analysis of the cycle of poverty.
(D)   a chronicle of the speaker's life of crime.
(E)   an attack on the social conditions of the time.

Comment: Readers expect that a novel or story be relatively consistent in subject matter, style, tone, voice, and and so forth. In fact, nonsequiturs and incongruities tend to diminish the pleasures of reading. By asking you to infer what may have preceded the passage, this question puts your sense of literary coherence on the line.

As the passage begins, the speaker explains the ins and outs of shoplifting. Later she turns to the subject of breaking and entering. This sequence suggests that these reminiscences of the speaker's experiences may be part of a longer piece about her journey to perdition. Then, considering the speaker's intellect and manner of speaking, only Choice (C) is a plausible answer to the question.

11.   The interaction between the speaker and the officer in lines 61–74 has the primary effect of
(A)   illustrating the officer's stubbornness.
(B)   indicating that the officer performs his duties beyond reproach.
(C)   confirming the speaker's self-assurance.
(D)   showing the speaker's gullibility.
(E)   emphasizing the success of the governess's original plan.

Comment: This question asks you to analyze the implications of the speaker's triumph over the custom-house officer.

Choice (A) has no merit because the officer shows flexibility in the face of the speaker's demands for a larger share of the reward money. Choice (B) is arguable because it's unclear whether the officer will pocket some of the money or return it to the custom-house. Choice (D) is indefensible, and while there is a smidgeon of truth in (E) it is a minor point, certainly less compelling than (C), the best answer.

12.   The shift in the speaker's state of mind that occurs between the beginning and end of the passage can best be described as one from
(A)   cautious to confident.
(B)   speculative to assertive.
(C)   passive to active.
(D)   determined to fatalistic.
(E)   selfish to altruistic.

Comment: Answering this question requires tracking the speaker's tone from the beginning to the end of the passage.

To determine the best answer, consider only the first adjective in each pair. Ask whether the speaker seems "cautious" (A), or "speculative" (B), or "passive" (C), etc. By weighing only the first adjective you save time and may quickly eliminate Choices (B), (C), and (E). Then turn to the second adjective of the remaining choices: "fatalistic" is not an accurate description of the speaker; on the other hand "confident" epitomizes her attitude once she has successfully stolen the Flanders lace and in the bargain hoodwinked the custom-house officer. Choice (A), then, is the best answer.

3 Answering Essay Questions

Section II of the AP exam, consisting of three essays to be written in two hours, has a dual purpose. First, it tests your facility with literary analysis, and second, it assesses your ability to write an analytical essay under the pressure of time. Of the two purposes, the first is more important, but frankly it would be hard for you to show off your command of analytical thinking without also being adept at organizing your thoughts and expressing them succinctly and coherently on paper.

Each essay is written in response to a different question, or "prompt," as test-makers like to call it: one on poetry, one on prose fiction, and one on a novel or play of your choice.

1. *The poetry question.* After reading a poem, you will be asked to write a well-organized essay that discusses how the poet's use of certain poetic techniques helps convey the meaning and effect of the poem. (A variation on this question is an essay on a pair of poems. Another possibility is an essay comparing a poem and a prose passage on the same subject.)

2. *Prose fiction question.* After reading a passage of prose fiction, you will be asked to write a well-organized essay on how the author's use of certain literary techniques helped to convey the contents and effect of the passage.

3. *Free-response question.* You will be asked to write a well-organized essay that discusses a literary issue or concept as it relates to a novel or play of your choice.

Questions from Previous Exams

What follows are synopses of essay questions given in recent years. Although the types of questions have remained the same, the order of questions 1 and 2 varies. That is, the question on poetry may precede or may follow the question on the prose passage. Invariably, however, the free-response question comes last. In any case, you may write the essays in any order you choose.

Because forty minutes is suggested for writing each essay, it is crucial that you apportion your time so that you'll finish all the essays. Guard against getting so wrapped up in the first or second essay that you'll have to rush through the third. It is better to submit three less-than-perfect essays than to write two dandy ones.

1994

1. Read a passage from "A White Heron," a short story by Sarah Orne Jewett. Then write an essay that shows how Jewett dramatizes the young heroine's adventure. Consider discussing diction, imagery, narrative pace, and point of view, among other literary elements.

2. After reading two short poems about Helen of Troy, write an essay that contrasts the two speakers' views of Helen. Consider elements such as diction, imagery, form, and tone.

3. Write an essay about a novel or play in which a character who appears briefly—or does not appear at all—is still a significant presence. Describe how the character functions in the work and how he or she affects such matters as action, theme, or development of other characters.

1995

1. After reading a poem by John Donne, write an essay that analyzes how the speaker uses imagery to show his attitude toward love.

2. Read "Eleven," a short story by Sandra Cisneros. Then write an essay that shows how the author uses literary techniques to characterize the main character, Rachel.

3. Write an essay about a play or novel that contains a character who is alienated from a culture or society because of gender, race, class, or creed. Show how that character's alienation reveals the values and assumptions of that culture or society.

1996

1. Read an excerpt from *The House of the Seven Gables* by Nathaniel Hawthorne. Then write an essay that analyzes how the narrator reveals the character of Judge Pyncheon. Emphasize any significant literary element, including tone, choice of detail, syntax, or point of view.

2. After reading a poem by Anne Bradstreet, write an essay that shows how the poem's primary metaphor conveys the attitude of the speaker.

3. Write an essay about a novel or play that ends with some kind of "spiritual reassessment or moral reconciliation." Identify the reassessment or reconciliation, and explain its significance to the work as a whole.

1997

1. After reading a poem by Richard Wilbur, write an essay that shows how such formal elements as structure, syntax, diction, and imagery reveal the speaker's reaction to the death of a toad.

2. Read a passage from Joy Kogawa's novel, *Obasan.* Then write an essay analyzing how changes in perspective and style mirror the narrator's attitude toward the past. Include such elements as point of view, structure, choice of detail, and figurative language.

3. Base an essay on a novel or play that includes a wedding, funeral, party, or other social event. Show how the event contributes to the meaning of the work as a whole.

1998

1. After reading "It's a Woman's World," a poem by Eavan Boland, write an essay that analyzes how the speaker reveals her conception of a "woman's world."

2. Read an excerpt from George Eliot's *Middlemarch.* Then write an essay that characterizes the narrator's attitude toward Dorothea Brooke, and explain the literary techniques used to convey this attitude.

3. After reading a brief assessment of literature by Thoreau, write an essay about a novel, play, or epic poem that you may initially have thought to be

conventional and tame but that you now value for its "uncivilized free and wild thinking." Explain why you value the work and how "uncivilized free and wild thinking" contributes to its value.

1999

1. After reading "Blackberry-Picking," a poem by Seamus Heaney, write an essay that explains how the intensity of the language conveys both the act of picking blackberries and the deeper meaning of the whole experience. Consider such elements as diction, imagery, metaphor, rhyme, rhythm, and form.
2. After reading about a dramatic experience in Cormac McCarthy's novel *The Crossing,* write an essay that shows how the author's techniques convey the impact of the experience on the main character.
3. Write an essay on a novel or play in which a character faces competing desires, ambitions, obligations, or influences. Identify the conflicting forces and explain how the conflict illuminates the work as a whole.

2000

1. First read an episode reprinted from Homer's *Odyssey,* then a contemporary poem that comments on the episode. In an essay compare the two works analyzing their points of view, diction, imagery, or other important literary elements.
2. After reading a passage by the eighteenth-century British satirist, Joseph Addison, analyze how the author achieves his satiric purpose. Consider such stylistic elements as choice of detail, repetition, and tone.
3. Write an essay about a novel or play that contains the investigation of a mystery. Identify the mystery and explain how the investigation contributes to the meaning of the work as a whole.

2001

1. After reading two poems, compare and contrast them. Then analyze the relationship between them.
2. Read an excerpt from *Tom Jones* by Henry Fielding. Then write an essay that analyzes the techniques that the author employed to characterize Mr. Allworthy and Mrs. Wilkins.
3. Write an essay about a novel or play in which a character's insanity or irrational mental state plays a crucial role. Explain the significance of the character's behavior to the work as a whole.

2002

1. After reading an excerpt from a modern British novel, write an essay analyzing how the author achieves a comic effect.
2. Read the given poem by Thomas Hardy. Then analyze how poetic devices, including the title, convey the speaker's attitude toward the sinking of a ship.
3. Write an essay about a novel or play in which a morally ambiguous character plays a significant part. Explain the character's moral ambiguity and in what respect it is significant to the work as a whole.

2003

1. Read two poems concerning Eros, written almost a century apart. Then compare and contrast the concepts of Eros and analyze the techniques used to create them.

2. After reading an excerpt from a recent short story by a Canadian writer, write an essay that explains how the author uses narrative voice and characterization to provide social commentary.

3. Write an essay about a novel or play in which a tragic figure functions as an instrument of suffering of others. Explain how the suffering brought upon others contributes to the tragic vision of the work as a whole.

Guidelines for Writing Essays

By this time in your school career, you've probably written reams of essays. Along the way you may have produced exemplary pieces of writing worthy of publication; at other times, you may have written essays fit only for the garbage. Regardless of your essay-writing history, no one expects you to produce three immortal pieces of prose during two hours of the AP exam. Instead, clearly organized, well-developed, and accurately written essays that answer the question will do. And if your essays also demonstrate a mastery of three fundamental writing goals—clarity, interest, and correctness—they should earn high scores.

Why those three? *Clarity* because your ideas probably need to be clear to you before you can make them clear to others. *Interest* because readers will abandon your essay if you bore them. *Correctness* because, whether it's fair or not, readers will judge you and your work according to how well you demonstrate the conventions of writing.

A full-scale review of essay-writing principles is beyond the scope of this book. But to remind you what to bear in mind as you write your AP essays, read through the following notes on essay writing.

1. *Study each topic closely.* Start with a meticulous reading of each question. Read it more than once, underscoring key words and ideas. If in doubt read it again, because an essay that misses the point of the question gets little or no credit on the exam.

    Here is a typical prompt for an essay on a poem or a passage of fiction:

    Read the following poem [or fiction passage] carefully, paying particular attention to the speaker's [or narrator's] <u>emotional vigor</u>. Then write a well-organized essay in which you explain <u>how the poet [or author] conveys not just a literal description of his encounter with a homeless vagrant</u> but a <u>deeper understanding of the whole experience</u>. You may wish to include an analysis of such elements as diction, imagery, metaphor, and form.

    The underscored sections lay out the task—to write an essay on how the poet or author conveys emotional vigor on both the literal level and on a deeper psychological or philosophical level. The absence of underscoring in the last sentence is deliberate. The phrase "You may wish" indicates that you are not required to discuss any of the four elements on the list. You are merely being given a suggestion. Accepting it, you might devote a paragraph of your essay to each of the elements. On the other hand, it could work to your advantage to choose your own literary devices. Including one or more relevant devices not listed in the prompt shows a measure of initiative and insight that may distinguish your essay from others and perhaps induce an AP reader to add a point or two to your score.

2. *Collect and organize ideas.* Because the prompt provides you with the essay's main idea—namely, that the writer's use of certain elements creates emotional vigor in the poem or passage—your first task is to scour the piece for evidence of "emotional vigor." Underline or encircle all the appropriate words, phrases, and ideas. Then arrange them in a logical, easy-to-follow sequence. Use the order in which they appear in the text, or organize them according to the literary elements you plan to discuss: metaphors in one group, images in a second group, and so on. In effect, you will have prepared a sketchy outline of your essay.

The order of ideas is important. What comes first? Second? Third? The best order is the clearest order, the arrangement that readers can follow with the least effort. The plan least likely to succeed is the aimless one, the one in which ideas are developed haphazardly or in the order they happened to pop into your head.

Try ranking your ideas in the order of importance. Ask, for example, which literary element is most influential in shaping the "emotional vigor" of the poem or passage. Which ranks second? Third? and so on. As you write the essay, save your best evidence for last. Giving it away at the start is self-defeating because everything that follows will be anticlimactic. In other words, work toward your best point, not away from it. An excellent way to plot three good ideas is to lead with your second best, save the best for the end, and sandwich the least powerful idea between the others. This structure recognizes that the end and the beginning of an essay are its most critical parts. A good opening draws the reader in and creates an all-important first impression, but a memorable ending, coming last, is what readers have fresh in their minds when they assign a grade.

3. *Follow the principles of good essay writing.* Let the opening of your essay tell readers what to expect. Get into the meat of your essay quickly. Don't fool around with an opening meant solely to entertain or grab the reader's attention—forty minutes doesn't give you much time for verbal flummery.

Once into your essay, develop your ideas fully with examples and details. Development indicates the depth of your thinking. Each paragraph should have a stated or implied topic sentence, and each sentence should contribute to the development of your main idea. If you are ever unsure whether all or part of a particular paragraph supports the thesis, trash it or revise it. Be merciless. Don't fall in love with an admirable idea or turn of phrase. Give it the boot if it doesn't help you make your case.

4. *Give your essay coherence.* Even if all your paragraphs are gems, they must somehow be tied together to give your essay coherence. Transitions, which establish relationships between one thought and the next, will help. Fortunately, our language is a cornucopia of transitional words and phrases such as, for example, *for example.* In addition, there is *in addition,*

furthermore, likewise, to be sure, accordingly, meanwhile, in other words, and many, many more. By using transitions, you do your readers a favor. You assure them a smooth trip through your essay. Without transitions, each sentence and paragraph stands like a disconnected link in a chain, causing readers to bump along and lose the point you are trying to make. Although not every sentence requires a transition, three or four sentences in succession without a link of some sort may leave readers doubting that this trip is worth taking.

5. *Use plain, simple words.* That's an admonition easy to say but hard to live by when you are trying to impress readers with your intellect and sophistication. Yet nothing, truly nothing, conveys your erudition better than ideas expressed in plain and simple language. AP essay readers are old hands at spotting pretentiousness. You'll get no extra credit for an essay crammed with exotic, multisyllabic words used for no other purpose than to sound exotic and multisyllabic. There's always a risk, in fact, that words that sound profound to you may seem pompous to others. Or worse, they could make you appear foolish.

6. *Watch your use of verbs.* Being human, AP readers favor those essays that are full of life. To inject life into your writing, pay close attention to your choice of verbs. Verbs, as you know, show action or state of being. *Active* verbs stimulate interest because they perform, stir things up, and move around. They excel over all other words in their power to energize sentences and, as a bonus, help you to write more economically. In contrast, *being* verbs such as *is, are, was, were, am, has been, had been,* and *will be* don't do much of anything except connect one thought to another. When used in sentences, each of these being verbs joins a subject to a predicate, and that's all. They act like verbal equal signs, as in "Joanie *is* a genius" (Joanie = genius). Because being verbs (and equal signs) show little life, use active verbs whenever possible.

  In addition to generating life, active verbs usually lead to more economical writing. In *Hamlet,* the old windbag Polonius knew what he was talking about when he said "Brevity is the soul of wit." What he meant, in brief, is that Brief is Better. Never use two words when one will do. Readers want to be told quickly and directly what you have to say. They value economy and resent reading more words than necessary. Excess verbiage is a pain in the neck. So cut out unnecessary words.

  Stop! Go back to the last paragraph. Did you notice that the last sentence is redundant? It's short, yes, but it merely adds fat to the paragraph. Sentences, like muscles, should be lean and tight. Because needless words are flabby, trim the fat.

7. *Vary your sentences.* While exercising your writing muscles, use them to vary your sentences. It's easy to fall into a rut by repeatedly using the same patterns. Because English is a pliant language, sentences can be endlessly revised until you've got a mix that works. Variety for its own sake, however, is hardly better than assembly-line production of identically structured sentences. But variety that clarifies meaning or accentuates ideas is another story.

  In essay writing, declarative sentences usually predominate. But you can create all sorts of fascinating effects with interrogative sentences or even occasional exclamatory and imperative sentences. What's more, you can write sentences interrupted in midstream by a dash—although some people claim that it's not proper to do so in formal prose—and you can use direct and indirect quotations. Again, though, don't deliberately scramble up sentence types just to cook up a sentence potpourri. Be guided always by what seems clearest and by what seems varied enough to hold reader interest.

In addition, pay attention to sentence length. A series of long sentences made up of subordinate clause after subordinate clause and a parade of short sentences make for equally dull reading. A balance is best. Take the trouble to dismember very long sentences when necessary and don't hesitate to combine a series of very short ones. But the simplest way to vary sentences is to practice using an array of sentence openings.

Start sentences with:

- prepositional phrases: *In the beginning, From the start, In the first place*
- adverbs and adverbial phrases: *Originally, At first, Initially*
- dependent clauses: *If you follow my lead, When you start with this*
- conjunctions: *And, But, Not only, Either, So, Yet*
- verbal infinitives: *To launch, To take the first step, To get going*
- adjectives and adjective phrases: *Fresh from, Introduced with, Headed by*
- participles: *Leading off, Starting off, Commencing with*
- inversions: *Unique is the essay that begins with . . .*

When you reach the end of each AP essay, you can simply lift your pen off the paper and be done with it. Readers of AP essays, knowing that you've had a time limit, won't penalize you for a brief or even a nonexistent conclusion. But some sort of ending helps readers feel they've arrived somewhere. It pleases both the heart and mind. Let whatever you write as a conclusion spring naturally from the essay's content. Above all, shun summary endings. They insult intelligent readers, who ought to be trusted to remember what you've told them in a few paragraphs of text.

8. *Follow the stylistic conventions of literary essays.* AP essays should follow the practices of scholarly writing. You're not expected to produce articles worthy of publication in a professional journal, but your essays should at least demonstrate that you know the basic conventions of the genre.

- Use standard English prose, as error-free as you can make it. (Try to leave time for editing and proofreading.)
- Place the titles of poems within quotation marks; underline the titles of novels and plays. (There is no need to give your essay a title.)
- Discuss poems and passages using the "literary present." In other words, write using present tense verbs, as in, "The speaker *declares* in the second stanza that he has finally arrived in Byzantium." Shift to other tenses only when it is necessary or logical to do so.
- Refer to the "speaker" or "narrator" of a poem or prose fiction passage, not the "author," because the voice you hear may not be the author's at all but that of an imaginary spokesperson.
- If the gender of the speaker is unknown, use either masculine or feminine pronouns—whichever you prefer. Stay away from "he or she," a pedantic and cumbersome usage.

- Keep yourself in the background. Avoid using first-person pronouns unless you absolutely must or if the topic invites you to write from your own observations or experience. Likewise, if you can, avoid addressing the reader with the second-person pronoun. In other words, a detached tone is the most appropriate one, but don't be a slave to it if another will serve you better.

- When quoting from poems or passages, copy the words and punctuation exactly as they appear in the text. If you must omit anything for grammatical purposes, indicate the omission with an ellipsis (. . .) consisting of three periods. Put into square brackets [ ] any words you insert into a quotation. Also, be sure to include line numbers either in parenthesis after the quotation or as part of your introduction to the quoted material. If you quote more than one line of a poem, use line breaks ("/") between each line. For example: "Had we but world enough, and time/ This coyness, lady, were no crime" (1–2). Instead of copying long quotations verbatim, save time by using an ellipsis between the first and last words, as in "Had . . . crime."

- Avoid using a quotation as a sentence all by itself. Rather, introduce the quotation in your own words, as in: *The speaker uses a paradox in line 13 when he says to God, "Except you enthrall me, never shall be free."* Likewise, quoted material should not be used as exposition in your essay. Use quotes only to illustrate what you have explained or to support what you plan to say.

- There is no specific length or word count to shoot for. Let your essay be long enough to cover the material and brief enough to remain interesting. An essay of a single paragraph may not develop your ideas sufficiently. On the other hand, an essay that rambles on page after page could lack focus.

- AP readers know the literature you are writing about. Therefore, it's not necessary to review it for them. Summarize texts only when it is necessary to explain or clarify an idea. Likewise, since readers know literary terminology, don't waste time explaining or defining technical terms.

How the Essays Are Scored

AP essays are read by two trained readers, each a high school or college English instructor or some other person well versed in literature. Each essay will receive a grade from 0 (worst) to 9 (best) based on the readers' judgment of the essay as a whole. High scores will be the reward for doing everything well. Exceptionally good writing may compensate for a mediocre analysis and raise the score from, say, a 6 to a 7, but a badly written essay is destined to earn a score no higher than 3 or 4. Should the grades assigned by the two evaluators differ by two or more points, the essay will be submitted to a third reader.

Because each question is different, the criteria for evaluating them are different, too. But the descriptions that follow apply generally to the three types of essays found on the exam.

BEST ESSAYS. SCORE 9–8.

These well-organized essays address the question astutely. The writer, using relevant and specific references to the text, convincingly develops a valid thesis. Perceptions of the literature are insightful and clearly expressed in language appropriate to literary criticism. The writer may also offer more than a single interpretation of a piece of literature or any of its parts. Although the essays may not be completely error-free, they demonstrate the writer's control of the elements of composition and the craft of analytical writing.

ABOVE-AVERAGE ESSAYS. SCORE 7–6.

These essays contain a solid, clearly expressed thesis, but the evidence provided for its development and support may fall short of excellence. The analysis of the literature, while thoughtful, may not be thorough or altogether precise. Or the discussion may lack the depth of insight or persuasiveness found in the very best essays. Although the essays give evidence of the student's ability to read and respond sensitively to literature, they are less mature, sophisticated, and controlled than papers that deserve ratings of 8 or 9.

MID-RANGE ESSAYS. SCORE 5.

These essays respond to the assignment but offer little more than pedestrian observations of the literature. Their analysis, while mostly accurate, may suffer from superficiality and a lack of conviction. Support of the thesis may be vague or limited. The text of these essays may accurately convey the students' thoughts but may contain a number of mechanical writing errors, none so severe, however, to obscure meaning.

BELOW-AVERAGE ESSAYS. SCORE 4–3.

Essays in this range often attempt to address the question but do so only marginally, possibly because the writer has either misread the literature or misunderstood the prescribed task. Essays may include a thesis, but supporting material drawn from the text is meager or inexact. As for literary analysis, it is vague and unconvincing, or it may rely largely on paraphrase. The writing in these essays is sufficiently clear to convey meaning, but it may suffer from lack of coherence, weak diction, faulty sentence structure, and a variety of mechanical errors.

WEAK ESSAYS. SCORE 2–1.

Failure to respond adequately to the question places an essay into this category. Thus, an essay consisting largely of plot summary may earn a 2. The same applies to essays in which confused or incoherent literary analysis demonstrates the writer's inability to comprehend the literature and to essays that reveal minimal understanding of composition and the conventions of standard written English. Essays that are particularly deficient in content, clarity, or the mechanics of writing are scored 1.

UNACCEPTABLE ESSAYS. SCORE 0.

No response or a response with no more than a reference to the task.

Based on the evaluations of three essays, you will earn a score between 0 and 27 in Section II of the exam. (Let's hope this book will help you skew your score toward the high end of the range.) The College Board won't report the score to you, to your school, or to any college. Rather, using a complicated formula, it will convert the score to a number on the AP five-point scale. The arithmetic calculations are of no compelling interest to most students, but if you're eager to know, check the "Technical Corner" of the web site: *www.collegeboard.org/ap.*

Student Essays

The Poetry Question

What you write in response to a question about a poem depends on the assigned task. Some questions direct you to discuss a single aspect of the poem such as its themes or its use of imagery. But more often, AP questions ask you to deal with several major elements of the poem and how they relate to each other and to the overall meaning and effect of the poem. In other words, you'll be explicating the poem, or explaining how poetic techniques contribute to its meaning.

What follows is an AP-type question on a poem accompanied by responses written by three students—Mark D, Tanya S, and Clarissa G. The essays are typed as written. After reading each essay, jot down your reactions and then compare your impressions with those of an AP reader.

Question: Read the following poem carefully. Then write a well-organized essay in which you analyze how the poet's language, along with such poetic devices as diction, sound, rhyme, and meter, conveys the speaker's attitude toward the taking of human life by hanging.

ON MOONLIT HEATH AND LONESOME BANK

On moonlit heath and lonesome bank
The sheep beside me graze;
And yon the gallows used to clank
Fast by the four cross ways.

Line
(5)   A careless shepherd once would keep
The flocks by moonlight there,[1]
And high amongst the glimmering sheep
The dead man stood on air.

They hang us now in Shrewsbury jail:
(10)   The whistles blow forlorn,
And trains all night groan on the rail
To men that die at morn.

There sleeps in Shrewsbury jail to-night,
Or wakes, as may betide,
(15)   A better lad, if things went right,
Than most that sleep outside.

And naked to the hangman's noose
The morning clocks will ring
A neck God made for other use
(20)   Than strangling with a string.

And sharp the link of life will snap,
And dead on air will stand
Heels that held up as straight a chap
As treads upon the land.

(25)   So here I'll watch the night and wait
To see the morning shine,
When he will hear the stroke of eight
And not the stroke of nine;

And wish my friend as sound a sleep
(30)   As lads' I did not know,
That shepherded the moonlit sheep
A hundred years ago.

—An excerpt from A. E. Houseman,
"A Shropshire Lad," 1896

---

[1]Poet's footnote: "Hanging in chains was called keeping sheep by moonlight."

Mark D's Essay
(Typed as it
was written)

By using a large number of contrasting images A.E. Houseman's poem "On Moonlit Heath and Lonesome Bank," illustrates the theme that the taking of human life by hanging is a cruel and violent act. In addition, the diction and tone help in making a deeper statement about life and death.

In the first stanza the speaker is on a peaceful moonlit heath among grazing sheep. Being there, where criminals once were hung, provides a contrast between the tranquil scene and violence that took place there. This contrast is emphasized when the peaceful imagery of lines 1 and 2 is broken by the "clank" of chains in line 3. This juxtaposition introduces a kind of duality that dominates the poem and is also reflected in the poet's footnote. To call hanging a man in chains "keeping sheep" is an ironic idea that appears to make the point that the hangmen of the past couldn't face the reality of what they were doing so made up a euphemism for their actions.

In stanza 2, the tranquil image of sheep in the moonlight is set against the eerie image of a hanged man who "stood on air." This contrast has a parallel in the speaker himself. Outwardly he's at peace, but inside he is mentally and emotionally wrought up. His language is plain and casual, but the clash of images implies that the speaker is intensely emotional. However, the reason for this intensity is not explained until the fourth stanza where he explains that a "lad," is waiting to be put to death in Shrewsbury jail. The speaker is disturbed about the impending execution of a boy who doesn't deserve it mainly because he is "better" than "most that sleep outside." (line 16).

Another contrast is set up in the third stanza by explaining that the site of hangings has been switched from the moonlit heath to the Shrewsbury jail. Hangings were once accompanied by the bleating of sheep but are now done where trains groan and whistles "blow forlorn," sounds that make the scene of the hangings even harsher and more grim.

In line 18 the speaker uses a pun on the word "ring." It may seem inappropriate to play word games in a poem about an execution, but since the poem uses many contrasts, the pun is consistent with speaker's double-sided view of the world. Likewise, the word "string" in line 20 is used for "rope," making light of something quite serious. One might argue that the poet used "string" for the sake of the rhyme with "ring," but "string" makes sense when you think of hangings as people "strung up" on the gallows. Therefore, "string" preserves the pattern of duality in the entire poem.

Wherever the hanging takes place—on the heath or at the jail—lines 21-22 return to the grusomeness of the act. The effects are the same regardless of the location—the "dead on air will stand"—an allusion to line 8 ("The dead man stood on air") that helps to unify the poem and supports the speaker's intent to portray hanging as an example of society's sick behavior.

Line 25 returns us to the moonlit heath of line 1, where the speaker will continue his vigil until morning shine. The emphasis on "shine" is poignant since it contrasts with the darkness that the lad must face, both in his last hours on earth and forever after. The casual reference to eight o'clock and nine o'clock signifies the passing of another typical hour, implying that the world goes on even though the lad will not. Incidentally, the speaker himself depends on euphemism here because he cannot face the fact of the lad's hanging. Instead of coming right out and saying that the lad will be executed, he softens the idea by saying "When he will hear the stroke of eight/And not the stroke of nine" (lines 27-28), leaving the reality of what happens unspoken.

In the last stanza the speaker refers to other men who tended sheep in the past. They, too, are dead, like the lad and like he himself will be one day. In a way, he is fatalistically accepts the future that all men face. Saying that we will all die is a fairly trite idea, but if you reconsider the footnote, that keeping sheep means the same as hanging by chains, a shocking element has suddenly been added to the poem. Basically, "keeping sheep" is really just a metaphor for "preparing to die." All of us in a sense are "keeping sheep," although we call it "going to school" or "applying to college," etc.

The subject of the poem is morbid, but Houseman won't let the style of writing be morbid. The use of a pun (explained above) and colloquial usage like "lad" and "chap" keeps the tone light, as do the short stanzas, brief lines, and consistent bouncy rhymes. The matter-of-fact informality of a poem that has a ponderous and grim theme give it a wry humor bordering on dark, or black humor, but the contrast between the light style and the dark subject is consistent with the main premise of the poem.

Maybe it is callous to treat death by hanging with a sense of humor. Giving the poet the benefit of the doubt, the subject is terribly painful for the speaker—almost too awful to contemplate. Therefore, he plays down the pain and uses a flippant tone to cover over his deep bitterness and sorrow. He gains artistically by doing that because it makes the impending execution more horrible.

Your impressions: _____

_____

_____

_____

Comment to Mark from an AP Reader

Although the essay is not perfect, its handful of stylistic soft spots (overuse of the verb *explain,* for instance, and writing *hung* instead of *hanged,* and the dubious assertion that Houseman uses "black humor") hardly detract from the perceptivity of your discussion of the poem. Your command of the language of literary criticism and analysis is demonstrated throughout the essay. You introduce sophisticated concepts such as the juxtaposition of images and the duality that underlies the structure of the poem.

Your expertise and ambition are apparent from the opening paragraph. Rather than follow the suggestion of the prompt, you focus on imagery. At the same time, however, you manage to work in cogent comments about the poem's tone, diction, sound, and rhyme.

As a writer, you appear committed to using details and incorporating quotations to support ideas. Your thorough dissection of just two words—"ring" and "string"—is impressive, largely because it is rare to find such precise and detailed analyses in AP essays. But more to the point, you avoid being pedantic; your analysis contributes a crucial piece of data in support of the argument that duality exists not only in the poem's content but in the speaker himself. Score: 8

Tanya S's Essay
(Typed as it was written)

Houseman's poem "On Moonlit Heath and Lonesome Bank" consists of eight separate stanzas telling the story of a man's feelings about the hanging of a boy he knows who is too good to experience such a terrible fate. The man who is the speaker in the poem is a shepherd taking care of his flock of sheep in the moonlight on a heath near a crossroads where "gallows used to clank" (line 3) and people were hung. He is waiting there for the boy to be hung the next morning in Shrewsbury jail.

The feelings of the man are conveyed through the poem's diction, sound, rhyme and meter. He speaks in affectionate terms about the boy, calling him a "lad" (15) and a "friend" (29). He obviously sympathizes with him because he uses phrases to show that the boy was unlucky in life—"if things went right" (15) he wouldn't be waiting to die, because he is "better . . . Than most that sleep outside" (15-16). He also adds that God made the boy's neck "for other use" (19) than having a noose put around it.

The speaker also talks about hanging in diction that indicates how terrible it is. He mentions the "dead man stood on air" (9) meaning swinging from a rope, and "strangling with a string" (20) as the man chokes to death. He uses the word "snap" (21) to create the sound that occurs when the body falls and the neck breaks. Even though he vividly describes hanging with such strong, tactile images, he stays calm about it, waiting patiently until the morning and refers to his friend's death as a sound sleep (29).

So basically, there is an ambiguous tone in the poem, partly violent and gross, partly calm and peaceful. It's like the speaker is sad but since he can't do anything about it he accepts the boy's fate as if it were God's plan.

That sense of a plan is also reflected in the sounds, rhymes and meter of the poem. It is all carefully laid out with a steady rhythm that remains the same from one stanza to the next. Each stanza is four lines. In each, the first and third lines and the second and fourth lines rhyme. There also are many uses of alliteration also. For example in "Fast by the four cross ways" (4) and "Than strangling with a string" (20). The poet also uses sound to support the meaning, as in "snap" (see above) and the onomatopoeia of "whistles <u>blow</u> forlorn" (10) and "trains all night <u>groan</u>" (11).

The kind of laid-back attitude portrayed by the speaker is natural for a shepherd, a man whose life is spent quietly taking care of sheep. An urban person might object to the hanging of the boy, but that is not in the lifestyle of a meek and humble shepherd. He accepts his own ate just as he accepts the fate of the boy.

Your impressions: _____

_____

_____

_____

Comment to Tanya from an AP Reader

Your analysis has a number of virtues, in particular the use of quoted material to illustrate and support assertions about the poem's tone. The point of the essay is clearly stated in the second paragraph, but you follow through with only a partial discussion of each poetic element. You provide examples of sound, but they are tenuously tied to the point you try to make about the speaker's feelings. You properly sense ambiguity in the poem but fail to explain its source with clarity and precision. Your discussion of rhyme and meter has no evident purpose other than to respond to the question. The entire analysis of the poem would have been far richer had you been able to show not only how rhyme and meter contribute to the meaning and effect of the poem, but how the elements work together.

Your use of "hung" instead of "hanged" is jarring, and the repetition of "also" suggests a need for more careful proofreading. You might also have chosen another word for the colloquialism "gross." To your credit, you make few other errors in English usage. I only wish that you had more fully fleshed out your ideas. Score: 5

Clarissa G's Essay
(Typed as it was written)

A.E. Houseman's poem <u>On Moonlit Heath and Lonesome Bank</u> expresses more than just a literal description of a young man's hanging. Using the structure of the poem, and the author's word choice and images, a more profound statement is being made. Since the boy will be put to death in the morning, the author concentrates on his feelings about hanging during the night before.

The poem is separated into eight stanzas. This structure allows Houseman to use three stanzas to describe the scene, including the "moonlit heath and lonesome bank" (line 1). In the next five stanzas he tells about the boy, including that he is a good boy who is

"A better lad, if things went right,
Than most that sleep outside."

Then the last stanza returns to the moonlit heath where the poem began.

The authors' word choice also contributes to the deeper message of the poem. He uses certain diction that conveys an opposition to hanging, such as "clank (line 3), naked (line 17), and strangling (line 20)." These words describe hanging as the most brutal, awful way to die. They show him being a sensitive person who shows empathy to the victim of the hanging and tries to convey his feelings about capital punishment in general.

These feelings are conveyed even more by the images that he uses. He talks about the dead man who "stood on air (line 8)", using a visual image, whistles "that blow" (line 10) using sound imagery, and the noose around the "neck made for other use' (line 19), a tactle image. Then, he returns to a visual and sound images associated with the hanging in lines 26-28, where he refers to seeing the "morning shine" and hearing the "stroke of eight/And not the stroke of nine."

Finally, I think Houseman was ahead of his time. He wrote the poem in 1896, but his arguments against cruel and unusual punishment are just as important to today's world, especially because DNA testing proves that many innocent men have been executed, or been put in jail, for crimes they didn't perfform. Therefore, the poem is just as relevent today, or maybe even moreso.

Your impressions: _____

_____

_____

_____

Comment to Clarissa from an AP Reader

You are to be commended for writing a five-paragraph essay that includes an introduction, three paragraphs of development, and a conclusion. Beyond the organizational effort, however, I find little to praise. Your main idea—that structure, word choice, and imagery add a measure of profundity to the literal meaning of the poem—could have merit had you provided solid supporting evidence. Citing examples of imagery and listing a few emotionally potent words adds little support to your interpretation of the poem. Basically, you fail to explain how these poetic elements relate to each other or to the speaker's attitude toward hanging. The evidence may hold promise, but it lacks direction and purpose.

The assumption that the "author" is also the speaker in the poem violates a basic principle of literary criticism, and the assertion that Houseman objected to capital punishment lacks credibility. Then, too, references to DNA and unjust sentences, while factually correct, step far beyond the bounds of the poem. Although you express yourself clearly, the mechanics of your writing are in dire need of repair. Score: 3

The Prose Fiction Question

Passages used for the prose fiction question usually consist of a roughly two-page excerpt from a novel or short story. What you are asked to write about depends on the passage but is most likely to relate to the author's narrative techniques. Some questions direct you to discuss character development, others the use of language. Still others raise issues of structure, tone, theme, or other literary elements.

Below is an AP-type question on a passage of fiction from a novel by Charles Dickens. This is followed by three student's essays, typed as they were written in response to the question. Read the essays and record your reactions in the space provided. Then read what an AP reader said about each essay.

Question: Carefully read the following excerpt from the first chapter of Dickens' novel *Dombey and Son,* in which the title characters are introduced. Observe the author's use of such elements as diction, syntax, figurative language, and tone. Then write an essay that analyzes how the author's use of language creates a vivid portrait of Dombey as a character.

Dombey sat in a corner of the darkened room in the great arm-chair by the bed-side, and Son lay tucked up warm in a little basket bedstead, carefully disposed on a low settee immediately in front of the fire and close to it, as if his constitution were analogous to that of a muffin, and it was essential to toast him brown while he was very new.

Line
(5)

Dombey was about eight-and-forty years of age. Son about eight-and-forty minutes. Dombey was rather bald, rather red, and though a handsome well-made man, too stern and pompous in appearance to be prepossessing. Son was very bald, and very red, and though (of course) an undeniably fine infant, somewhat crushed and spotty in his general effect, as yet. On the brow of Dombey, Time and his brother Care had set some marks, as on a tree that was to come down in good time—remorseless twins they are for striding through their human forests, notching as they go—while the countenance of Son was crossed and recrossed with a thousand little creases, which the same deceitful Time would take delight in smoothing out and wearing away with the flat part of his scythe, as preparation of the surface for his deeper operations.

(10)

(15)

Dombey, exulting in the long-looked-for event, jingled and jingled the heavy gold watch-chain that depended from below his trim blue coat, whereof the buttons sparkled phosphorescently in the feeble rays of the distant fire. Son, with his little fists curled up and clenched, seemed, in his feeble way, to be squaring at existence for having come upon him so unexpectedly.

(20)

"The house will once again, Mrs. Dombey," said Mr. Dombey, "be not only in name but in fact Dombey and Son; Dom-bey and Son!"

The words had such a softening influence, that he appended a term of endearment to Mrs. Dombey's name (though not without some hesitation, as being a man but little used to that form of address): and said, "Mrs. Dombey, my—my dear."

(25)

A transient flush of faint surprise overspread the sick lady's face as she raised her eyes towards him.

"He will be christened Paul, my—Mrs. Dombey—of course."

(30)

She feebly echoed, "Of course," or rather expressed it by the motion of her lips, and closed her eyes again.

"His father's name, Mrs. Dombey, and his grandfather's! I wish his grandfather was alive this day!" And again he said "Dom-bey and Son," in exactly the same tone as before.

(35)

Those three words conveyed the one idea of Mr. Dombey's life. The earth was made for Dombey and Son to trade in, and the sun and moon were made to give them light. Rivers and seas were formed to float their ships; rainbows gave them promise of fair weather; winds blew for or against their enterprises; stars and planets circled in their orbits, to preserve inviolate a system of which they were the center. Common abbreviations took new meanings in his eyes, and had sole reference to them: A. D. had no concern with anno Domini, but stood for anno Dombei—and Son.

(40)

He had risen, as his father had before him, in the course of life and death, from Son to Dombey, and for nearly twenty years had been the sole representative of the firm. Of those years he had been married, ten—married, as some said, to a lady with no heart to give him; whose happiness was in the past, and

(45)

(50)

(55)

(60)

who was content to bind her broken spirit to the dutiful and meek endurance of the present. Such idle talk was little likely to reach the ears of Mr. Dombey, whom it nearly concerned; and probably no one in the world would have received it with such utter incredulity as he, if it had reached him. Dombey and Son had so often dealt in hides, but never in hearts. They left that fancy ware to boys and girls, and boarding-schools and books. Mr. Dombey would have reasoned: That a matrimonial alliance with himself *must,* in the nature of things, be gratifying and honourable to any woman of common sense. That the hope of giving birth to a new partner in such a house, could not fail to awaken a glorious and stirring ambition in the breast of the least ambitious of her sex. That Mrs. Dombey had entered on that social contract of matrimony: almost necessarily part of a genteel and wealthy station, even without reference to the perpetuation of family firms: with her eyes fully open to these advantages. That Mrs. Dombey had daily practical knowledge of his position in society. That Mrs. Dombey had always sat at the head of the table, and done the honours of his house in a remarkably lady-like and becoming manner. That Mrs. Dombey must have been happy. That she couldn't help it.

Maribeth C's Essay
(Typed as it
was written)

The portrait of Mr. Dombey conveys a vivid impression of a self-important man. He is so wrapped up in himself that on the day of his son's birth his thoughts are not about the little baby but about the importance of the birth to his business. The author Dickens uses several literary devices to create this picture of a totally egotistical character, including sentence structure that emphasizes Dombey's thought processes, diction that exaggerates his lack of human warmth, and figurative language that suggests an obsession with business.

Using parallelism the author gives a physical description of both Dombey and his son. Dombey is 48 years old, bald, red, and too pompous looking to be attractive, the son is 48 minutes old, also bald, red, and "somewhat crushed and spotty." Dombey is also presented as a rigid person by being compared to a tree in the forest. Personifications of Time and Care have left marks on his face just like woodsmen notching trees. Similarly, the baby's skin is filled with "a thousand little wrinkles." This parallelism creates the effect that the son is a like a clone of his father and introduces Dombey's foregone conclusion that the baby will grow up to follow him into the business and carry on the company's name.

That is what pleases Dombey so much about the birth. He repeats the phrase Dombey and Son like a mantra and he exults in pleasure by jingling and jingling his heavy gold watch-chain, a symbol of the wealth he has earned in his business. By using additional figurative language Dickens informs the reader that Dombey is the archetypal business man. "Those three words [Dombey and Son] conveyed the one idea of Mr. Dombey's life." (line 36). In support of that hyperbole, he adds that in Mr. Dombey's view the sun and moon, the rivers and seas, even the whole universe exist only for the sake of the business (lines 36–41). In addition, Dombey translates "anno Domini" into "anno Dombei—and Son" giving it a sacred connotation by alluding to Jesus Christ. In the next line (44) the allusion is strenghtened by saying, "He had risen, as his father had before him. . . ." a clear reference to Jesus.

The only indication of what business Dombey and Son are engaged in comes in line 52. They "dealt in hides, but never in hearts." That's perfect for a man like Dombey, whose is dominated by skin-deep values and qualities. He is presented as incapable of expressing emotion because he has none that don't relate to his business. He is shown struggling to call his wife "my dear." His lack of emotion is further emphasized by the sentence structure in lines 53-64, where reasons why Mr. Dombey married and remained married to Mrs. Dombey are listed. Love had nothing to do with it. Their relationship is based on several reasons listed in a series of clauses beginning with "That," like in the clauses of a legal document.

Dombey's qualities are made known to the reader by his thoughts and actions. As a person, he is a pathetic character who is absorbed by business and his own grotesque self-righteousness. In spite of his flaws, Dickens intends to amuse the reader with this portrait of Dombey. His humerous tone becomes evident in the first paragraph, where he compares the newborn baby to a muffin set by the fire to be toasted. In a way, then Dombey is an object of derision; more a caricature than a character.

Your impressions: _____

_____

_____

_____

Comment to Maribeth from an AP Reader

The essay focuses clearly on Dickens' diverse techniques of character development. Your conclusion that Dombey is more caricature than character comes at the end of an astute and sensitive analysis of the text. My hat is off to you for avoiding the pitfall of paraphrasing or summarizing what happens in the passage. Following the plan laid out in your opening paragraph, you identify several telling examples of diction, sentence structure, and figures of speech that contribute to Dombey's portrait. A couple of spelling miscues, some punctuation errors, and a comma splice mar the essay, but the illuminating and precise explication of the passage is impressive. Few AP essays written in forty minutes contain such a variety of accurate and insightful observations. Score: 9

Alfonso R's Essay
(Typed as it
was written)

It is hard to know whether readers ought to chuckle at the character of Mr. Dombey in the novel <u>Dombey and Son</u>, or to despise him for being a selfish and vulgar egotist. Both qualities can be found in the portrait of him because of Dickens use of language, in particular his diction, syntax, and choice of details.

Looking at Dombey as a comical character, Dickens satirizes his obsession with his family business called Dombey and Son. For years he has been the sole proprieter of the business, yet it was still called Dombey and Son. Finally, he has a newborn son to give legitimacy to the name of the firm. He is thrilled with the idea and says to his wife, "The house will once again, Mrs Dombey, ...be not only in name but in fact Dombey and Son; Dom-bey and Son!" repeating the last name like someone who has fallen in love with it and can't get it out of their mind. All this takes place as he sits in an armchair by his wife's bedside less than an hour after the birth of his son, who is lying close to the fireplace for the sake of warmth. Dombey goes overboard about the business in another way, also. Dickens says that those three words (Dombey and Son) "conveyed the one idea of Mr. Dombey's life." His tunnel vision led him to believe that the whole solar system revolved around him and his business, as if Dombey and Son was really Dombey and the Sun. Furthermore, in Dombey's mind, the abbreviation A.D. (anno Domini) stands for "anno Dombei—and Son" according to lines 42 and 43. Obviously, Dickens is exaggerating for comic effect because a man of stature like Dombey could not be a totally out of touch with reality. He can't be insane and also run a good business that owns ships (line 38), be affluent enough to wear a "heavy gold watch-chain" and a trim blue coat with sparkling (gold??) buttons. Furthermore, he believes that Mrs. Dombey married him to be "part of a genteel and wealthy station." (59) So, readers could take Dickens creation of Dombey as someone who has many comical aspects to his character.

On the other hand, Dombey displays qualities that are far from funny or admirable. They are repulsive. For example, here is nothing funny about the way he treats his wife. While she is in bed suffering from post partum sickness, he surprises her by calling her "dear" to soften her up for his decision that the baby must be named after him and his grandfather—Paul. It's a fait accompli, and she has no voice in the matter. His insulting attitude toward his wife is more fully illustrated in the final paragraph of the passage where Mrs. Dombey's "broken spirit" is discussed. She is a dutiful and meek wife, but Mr. Dombey would have received such news with "utter incredulity" (line 51) since he practically ignores her and barely acknowledges her as a human being. Instead, he thinks of her as someone has helped by marrying her. In his view, to be married to him is an honor, and gives her social advantages and a higher position in society. And, based on the last lines of the passage, there is no question that a woman with a husband like Mr. Dombey must be happy. She couldn't help it. It's hard to imagine a more obnoxious attitude for a husband to have toward his wife.

This vivid portrait of Dombey is taken from the opening pages of Dickens' novel. Based on what he says, it is a toss-up whether in the rest of the story Dombey will turn out to be a hero or a villain. Probably he'll have elements of both. At this point in writing the novel, maybe Dickens himself didn't know, and so created a character full of ambiguities, like all human beings.

Your impressions: _____

_____

_____

_____

Comment to Alfonso from an AP Reader

Your opening paragraph pays lip service to the AP question. Dickens' diction, syntax, and choice of details, however, are subsumed by your real intent—to explore the two sides of Dombey's character. Whether to laugh at or be repulsed by Dombey constitutes a unique approach to the topic, and the essay masterfully balances the conflicting possibilities. Its conclusion, that Dickens himself may have been unsure, offers intriguing food for thought.

Your writing gives evidence of a sensitive reading of the passage and a grasp of subtleties that elude less perceptive readers. It also reflects your enthusiasm for probing into the text to find supporting details and quotations. Trying to be thorough, however, you devote too much of the essay to recounting and explaining events in the narrative. You might have trusted your readers to be familiar with the text and thus spent more time digging still deeper into the language of the passage. Your own diction, which is generally fresh and spirited, strengthens the overall effect of the essay and nudges the score from a solid 6 to a 7. Score: 7

Maury W's Essay
(Typed as it was written)

"Stern and pompous." Those words found in line 8 of the passage from <u>Dombey and Son</u> capture the essence of the title character of the Dickens novel. How Dickens conveys Dombey's stern and pompous personality can be seen in his use of such elements as sentence structure, diction, figurative language, and tone, all of which add to the character portrait of a proud man who takes himself very seriously but is not aware of what a comical image he projects.

As far as sentence structure is concerned, the passage begins with a paragraph made up of one long sentence setting the scene and introducing Mr. Dombey sitting in a great arm chair and his Son lying on a low settee in front of the fire. The next paragraph which begins to tell details starts with two short sentences describing basic similarites and differences between the father and son. The sentences get longer as the paragraph moves on, and the last sentence is a made up of several clauses and side comments, mainly because the subject matter is complex. It explains how "Time and his brother Care" (line 11) have left their marks on Mr. Dombey's brow. This pattern of short sentences for simple ideas and long sentences for more complex ideas continues throughout the passage and comes to an extreem at the end, where between lines 53 and 64, there are six sentences all beginning with the same word—"that."

The diction in the passage is typical of authors that use highly formal language to say simple things but can also use every day words. Therefor, when he says "countenance" for face (line 13) and "appended" for added (line 24), he is showing Dombey's pompousness. Dombey exemplifies sternness in the way he talks to his wife, instead of asking her what she thinks the baby's name should be, he tells her, "He will be christened Paul, . . . of course," obviously, he is not a type of man who will take no for an answer.

Figurative language is not as common as the diction in the passage, but Time and his brother Care are personifications in the second paragraph. Before that, the infant is compared to a muffin. And to illustrate Dombey's sternness, it says that Dombey and Son "often dealt in hides, but never in hearts," a metaphor for feelings.

The tone of the passage is basically a criticism of Dombey. I can find very little complimentary. The only thing that matters to him is Dombey and Son. He has a pompous attitude in thinking that "the sun and moon were made" to give Dombey and Son light and that "rivers and seas were formed to float their ships." It takes alot of chutzpah to think the whole world was made to serve you. Also, his wife doesn't mean anything to him. Her job is to take care of the house and he has done her a favor by marrying her because of the advantages he gave her.

Dombey is one of the most pompous fools in literature.

Your impressions: _____

_____

_____

_____

Comment to Maury from an AP Reader

Your strong feelings about the character of Dombey don't, unfortunately, add up to a strong essay. For one thing, the essay's premise is based on a faulty reading of the passage. The phrase "stern and pompous" pertains to Dombey's appearance, not to his personality, although a case could probably be made for a correlation between the two. The opening paragraph of the essay promises a discussion of four literary elements. Indeed, you dutifully devote a paragraph to each of them, but the discussion pertains only occasionally to Dombey's sternness and pomposity. The longest paragraph in the essay—about sentence structure—accurately describes Dicken's varied sentences, but entirely ignores the point of the essay. What's more, you try to show that Dombey's diction reflects pomposity, but as evidence pick two of the narrator's words, not Dombey's. You recover from this *faux pas,* however, by cogently showing how Dombey bullies his wife.

Although the essay contains numerous writing errors, your analysis of the passage is far from dull. You seem willing to take chances in interpretation and in use of language. How refreshing and rare it is to find the word "chutzpah," for example, in an AP essay. It's use as a synonym for arrogance, however, is slightly off the mark. Too bad that your essay lacks a precise and responsible analysis of the text. But don't despair; your effort is commendable. Score: 3

The Free-Response Question

The prompt introducing the free-response essay usually starts with a quotation or a broad statement about some aspect of literature. Most often it relates to the portrayal of character but may also refer to an element of plot or to a theme. Your task is to write an essay on a novel or play to which the general statement applies. Not every novel or play is an appropriate choice for every question, but the statement will no doubt be broad enough to include a great many of the works you have read and studied.

The test always lists twenty or more titles from which to choose. But you may pick your own, provided it is a novel or play "of similar quality" or "comparable literary merit"—vague phrases that mean a work taken from the so-called literary canon, a work worthy of study and analysis, one that contributes to a mature reader's understanding of life and the human condition. If the novel or play was written before the twentieth century and is still being read or performed on the stage, it would probably pass the test. More recent works that have won Pulitzer Prizes or National Book Awards would also qualify, as would works by highly-regarded contemporary authors such as Saul Bellow, William Trevor, Joyce Carol Oates, and Barbara Kingsolver. On the other hand, books by authors who appear regularly on best-seller lists—John Grisham, Jean M. Auel, Mary Higgins Clark, and Stephen King, for example, don't, although one could argue that not all of these authors' books are escapist pulp. No doubt an element of elitism governs the choices, but you probably wouldn't be taking the exam in the first place unless you more or less subscribed to the notion that some books are worthier than others.

Whatever your choice, be sure that you are very familiar with it. The question on the AP exam almost invariably asks you to discuss major events in the story or to write about characters. Therefore, you should know the plot intimately and be able to describe all the major and many of the minor events. You should also know the names and traits of the chief characters. The more you can say about the setting, the structure of the work, major themes, and the author's narrative techniques, the more you'll be able to demonstrate the depth of your reading and analytical skills. Above all, though, be conversant with the meaning of the work as a whole. That is, you should have a firm grasp of the author's main points.

That your essay will be evaluated by literate readers familiar with the work you chose to discuss may work either for you or against you. An informed reader could give you the benefit of the doubt if something you write is fuzzy or unclear. A reader who knows the work well, on the other hand, may penalize you for inaccuracies or omissions. Because AP readers cannot have read every novel or play ever published, don't be tempted to choose a very obscure title. Or even worse, don't invent one on the spot (don't laugh; it's been tried); it could work against you.

Because there is no way to predict the question you'll be asked, you should prepare an assortment of titles, some of which are reviewed in Chapter 5. Also, some works are so rich that they can be used for a broad range of questions. *Hamlet* may be one such work, along with *Great Expectations, Heart of Darkness,* and maybe *The Great Gatsby.* Knowing these works cold would be good preparation for answering just about any question the AP examiners could devise.

To give you an idea of how various other titles would serve to deal with topics from recent AP exams, the chart below recommends numerous possibilities taken from AP reading lists used in schools throughout the country. Rest assured that this is a limited list to which you can probably add many other equally appropriate titles. Use the blank spaces to suggest titles of your own.

Topic: A character opposed to or alienated from society

Carol Kennicott finds little joy in small-town life in *Main Street.*

Stephen Dedalus defies tradition to become a writer in *Portrait of the Artist.*

Holden Caulfield is repelled by society's hypocrisy and the compromises of adulthood in *The Catcher in the Rye.*

Joseph K in *The Trial,* when faced with incomprehensible accusations, discovers that he is truly alone in a world.

John Grady, a boy from Texas, can't adapt to Mexican culture in *All the Pretty Horses.*

_____

_____

_____

Topic: A character investigates a mystery

Oedipus uncovers the truth about his birth and destiny in *Oedipus Rex*.

Hamlet hopes to learn the truth about the death of his father in *Hamlet*.

Marlow attempts to unlock the mystery of Kurtz in *Heart of Darkness*.

Jaffrey in *House of the Seven Gables* seeks the vanished deeds to the house.

Several narrators search for the thief of a cursed jewel in *The Moonstone*.

_____

_____

_____

Topic: Ending with spiritual reassessment or moral reconciliation

Jim in *Lord Jim* makes up for an act of cowardice.

Wrongfully accused of murder, Jefferson in *A Lesson Before Dying* understands the simple heroism of resisting the inevitable.

Death creates an atmosphere of wonder and awe for the grieving characters in *A Death in the Family*.

Weak-willed and profligate, Father Mendez dies a Christ-like death to atone for his shortcomings in *The Power and the Glory*.

Becoming increasingly isolated and paranoid, Solness in *The Master Builder* finds that the enemy to his peace lies not outside himself but within.

_____

_____

_____

Topic: Suspenseful mental or psychological events

Othello is driven mad with jealousy by Iago's diabolical mind games in *Othello*.

Mrs. Pontelier in *The Awakening* suffers egregiously for betraying her family.

Captain Ahab in *Moby Dick* struggles against what he believes are malevolent forces in nature.

Defeated by a business rival, Michael Henchard pursues self-destructive revenge in *The Mayor of Casterbridge*.

Clarissa Dalloway and Septimus Smith lead seemingly separate but psychologically interconnected lives in *Mrs. Dalloway*.

_____

_____

_____

Topic: A significant social event

The ghost of Banquo shows up at Macbeth's banquet in *Macbeth*.

Romeo and Juliet meet and fall in love at the Capulets' ball in *Romeo and Juliet*.

During wedding festivities, Frankie in *Member of the Wedding* discovers a future different from the one she expected.

At a stag party for white men the protagonist of *Invisible Man* begins to understand his station in life.

In *One Flew Over the Cuckoo's Nest*, McMurphy throws a wild party with dire consequences for some of the guests.

_____

_____

_____

Topic: A character faces a dilemma created by competing forces

Frederick Henry in *A Farewell to Arms* volunteers to fight in the war but considers desertion after becoming disillusioned.

George in *Of Mice and Men* must decide whether to kill Lennie or let him be arrested and tried for murder.

The title character in *Ethan Frome* is caught between his marriage to a shrewish, sickly wife and his infatuation for a sweet young woman.

Obsessed with a desire for vengeance against her husband, the title character in *Medea* ignores law, culture, and her motherly instincts.

Arkady in *Fathers and Sons* is drawn to the progressive manners and attitudes of his friend Bazarov, but conventionality holds him back.

_____

_____

_____

Topic: A character harboring an important secret

Emma's secret discontent with her marriage ripens her for adulterous relationships in *Madame Bovary*.

Rochester in *Jane Eyre* cannot escape the mysterious disappearance of his wife.

Blanche in *A Streetcar Named Desire* conceals a sordid past.

A secret affair with Hester in *The Scarlet Letter* gnaws at Dimmesdale, who finds himself unable to make peace with himself or God.

Henry Fleming in *The Red Badge of Courage* knows that his award for valor was earned by fear of showing fear in battle.

_____

_____

_____

Topic: The effect of a minor or absent character on the protagonist

Ben in *Death of a Salesman* both inspires and plagues Willie Loman.

An unknown benefactor enables Pip to succeed in *Great Expectations.*

Tom in *The Glass Menagerie* follows in the footsteps of his absent father.

The memory of Ben in *Look Homeward, Angel* inspires Eugene to break away from his overbearing family.

Young Vladimir in *First Love* is tormented by an unknown rival for the affections of flirtatious Zinaida.

_____

_____

_____

Topic: Victim of prejudice

The young black, Bigger Thomas in *Native Son,* faces a future without hope.

The Okies in *The Grapes of Wrath* encounter abuse and oppression in California.

In *The Fixer,* Yakov Bok is wrongfully accused of a crime solely because he is a Jew.

At the trial of Kabio Miyamoto in *Snow Falling on Cedars,* bigotry left over from the war influences the proceedings.

In *Cry, the Beloved Country,* Stephen Kumalo and his son Absolom struggle against the injustices of South African apartheid.

_____

_____

_____

Topic: Character overcoming odds to succeed

Beset with poverty, crime, and despair, Jurgis in *The Jungle* finds a refuge in socialism.

The title character in *Jasmine* heroically casts off her poverty-ridden background in India to become a liberated American woman.

Pursued by the law for stealing a loaf of bread, Jean Valjean in *Les Misérables* redeems himself by helping downtrodden members of society.

Yuri in *Dr. Zhivago* preserves his identity in the face of revolution and a reign of terror meant to obliterate men's individuality.

Self-discipline enables the title character in *One Day in the Life of Ivan Denisovich* to endure ten years of harsh imprisonment in a labor camp.

_____

_____

_____

Topic: A rebel at odds with society

> Anna in *Anna Karenina,* pays with her life for transgressing the hypocritical moral codes of her society.
>
> Julien, a woodcutter's son in *The Red and the Black,* aims to make it big in the upper class but is vigorously rebuffed.
>
> John Proctor in *The Crucible* keeps his good name but is put to death by society for challenging its authority.
>
> Lily Bart in *The House of Mirth* is shunned by a society that rejects rebellious, iconoclastic women.
>
> Huck in *Huckleberry Finn* undertakes a voyage of discovery in a hostile world he cannot understand.

Questions and Student Essays

What follows is a free-response question and three student essays. After reading each essay, write your comments in the space provided, and then see what an AP evaluator thought.

Question: In literature, characters often find themselves torn between conflicting loyalties. In such cases, loyalty to friends or family or society may contend with such competing forces as morality, law, or personal conviction. Faced with dilemmas of this kind, characters may react in ways that might not otherwise have found expression. Therefore, they are more fully revealed to both the reader and to themselves.

Choose a novel or play of literary merit in which a major character encounters a conflict of loyalties, and in a well-organized essay, explain the conflict, how the character responds, and how the resolution of the conflict contributes to the meaning of the work as a whole. Please do not merely summarize the plot.

Feel free to select from the list below, or you may choose another work of comparable literary merit appropriate to the topic. Please do not write about a short story, poem, or film.

An American Tragedy	*One Flew Over the Cuckoo's Nest*
The Age of Innocence	*Othello*
As I Lay Dying	*Père Goriot*
Beloved	*The Picture of Dorian Gray*
Crime and Punishment	*Portrait of a Lady*
A Doll's House	*Pride and Prejudice*
Ethan Frome	*Romeo and Juliet*
Great Expectations	*Remains of the Day*
The Great Gatsby	*The Scarlet Letter*
Heart of Darkness	*A Streetcar Named Desire*
Miss Lonelyhearts	*Tess of the d'Urbervilles*
Madame Bovary	*Waiting for Godot*

Pat S's Essay
(Typed as it
was written)

Montana, 1948 is coming-of-age novel by Larry Watson. It tells the story of Wesley Hayden, the sheriff in Bentrock, a small town in rural Montana. He is facing a dilemma of whether to investigate rumors that that the doctor in the town, Dr. Frank Hayden, has sexually molested Native-American women and girls while performing medical examinations. Ordinarily, this would not be a problem, but in this case the doctor happens to be Wesley's brother. The situation is made worse by the fact that Frank is a well-loved war hero and the Haydens are the leading family in the town. Also, Wesley is kind of a bigot and neither likes nor trusts Indians, so he is torn about following up on their accusations. His wife, Gail, applies some pressure on him. She expects him to do his duty, partly because it's his job and partly because a Sioux girl, Marie Little Soldier, is a loyal live-in house-keeper in their home and claim that Dr. Frank has molested her. She and the other victims have said nothing in public because of preju-dice against Indians. They figured no one would believe their alle-gations, anyway.

The story is told through the eyes of twelve-year old David, the son of Wesley and Gail. David doesn't understand what is going on, but as the story develops, he overhears conversations, observes the actions of his parents, and more or less figures it out. He is actu-ally drawn into the action by chance because he sees Frank enter their house when no one is home but Marie, who is sick in bed. That after-noon, Marie is found dead, and David has a dilemma that parallels his father's dilemma. Should he tell what he saw or should he keep it to himself. All his life he has admired his Uncle Frank and he now real-izes that he has witnessed something that might destroy him and his family. Finally, he tells his father, which makes the conflict inside Wesley even more intense. His brother may be more than a rapist; he may also be a murderer.

It is then that the true character of Wesley emerges. He could look the other way and let Frank go free, since no one knows anything except his deputy, who is completely loyal to him. Wesley's father, the former sheriff, wants him to let Frank go, and sends four men to try and help Frank escape from Wesley's basement where he is tem-porarily incarcerated. Meanwhile, Gail is beginning to change her mind because he sees how the arrest is ruining her family life. When Wesley sees how little remorse Frank has over what he has done, however, he decides to resolve his dilemma by turning the case over to the pros-ecuting attorney of the county. He feels that the rules of society must be obeyed because they are more important than family ties. This realization is motivated partly by his own relationship with his father. Since old Mr. Hayden loves and favors Frank far more than Wesley, Wesley could be motivated by a desire for revenge against Frank for being the favorite son. In explaining his decision, Wesley tells his wife that a man must be guided by moral absolutes. He could not live with himself if he looked away, so Frank must be prosecuted and pay for his crimes.

The night before he is supposed to be turned in, Frank slits his wrists in the basement. To save the family name, Wesley says his death was an accident. But the family breaks apart anyway because old Mr. Hayden can't forgive Wesley for arresting Frank in the first place, and Frank's widow holds Wesley responsble for her husband's death.

This resolution relates closely to the novel's meaning as a whole because it is really the story of an important incident in David's boyhood. As a result of seeing how his family and others reacted to a tense situation, he grows up quickly. Before, he is just a little kid. Whenever his parents need to talk seriously, they send him to his room or concoct an errand for him. By the end, he has seen and learned so much about adult behavior that his innocence is lost. He is completely aware of adult hypocrisy and how adults hold grudges and make self-serving decisions. In an epilogue, David has grown up to be a history teacher. He admits that he is a cynic about what he teaches. After seeing how his father wavered about what to do and then swept the truth under the rug after Frank's death, David has no faith in the rule of law. He never tells his students that history contains stories about sexual abuse, murder, and suicide solves problem. Following in the footsteps of his father, he only pretends to tell the truth.

Your impressions: _____

_____

_____

_____

Comment to Pat from an AP Reader

Your gift for writing is obvious from the start. The novel that you chose to write about is an elegant choice for this essay, for conflicting loyalties is precisely its major theme. Your essay's praiseworthy introduction specifically lays out Wesley's dilemma. That you find a parallel between Wesley's quandary and David's adds a subtle dimension to the analysis of the story. Too bad, however, that you fail to capitalize on your insight, for David's decision to tell his father what he had seen marks a turning point in his youth. A child no longer, he has now in effect become responsible for his uncle's fate.

The essay concentrates on the dynamics within the Hayden family. Yet you assert that the novel is really about an important incident in David's life. Given more time than forty minutes, I suspect that you might have refocused the essay on David. But why quibble? You deserves a pat on the back for displaying a firm grasp of the novel and writing an essay worth celebrating. Score: 9

Sasha L's Essay
(Typed as it was written)

Tom Joad, the protagonist of John Steinbeck's <u>Grapes of Wrath</u>, is an tough ex-con just released on parole from an Oklahoma state penitentiary. He killed a man in a fight after the man accosted him with a knife. Self-defense was the defense at the trial, but he was ruled guilty. His conviction was unfair, but he had no choice and went to prison for five years of his sentence before being let out. The provisions of his parole are he has to stay out of trouble, required to obey the law, and required to remain inside Oklahoma. Upon his release, he intends to follow the provisions fully and he makes his way home to find his family.

At the farm, it is abandoned. A former neighbor Muley Graves tells Tom about the banks that owned the land in this part of Oklahoma which have kicked sharecroppers out of their houses and off their farms because they have been unable to grow enough crops as a result of the drought that has caused the Dust Bowl in that part of the country in the 1930s. The Joads, evicted from the land that they have lived on for centuries, have joined a mass migration westward along Route 66 to California where they think they can find jobs and created a new and happy life.

His family situation gives Tom a dilemma. Should he follow the rules of his parole, or should he take his chances and go with his family to California? Since he had unjustly been convicted of killing a man in self-defense, he has no allegiance to the government or its legal system. He also sees that the government has ignored his family just when they need protection from the money-hungry banks that kicked them off the land. Therefore, he decides that his family needs him in California more than the government needs him in Oklahoma. Loyalty to his family is far more important.

This turns out to be ironic. When they finally make it to California, he and the Joads are treated like "damn Okies," meaning lower than low. They are unwanted vagrants. One night Tom gets into a fight with an abusive deputy sheriff, killing him. All of a sudden he is made a fugitive. As a hunted man, he is danger to his family, who might be punished by never finding work again if they were caught harboring a cop-killer. To protect and save his family, he decides to leave them.

Tom's loyalty to his family shows that he is man willing to sacrifice himself for others, a decision is closely tied to the underlying base of the whole story. Steinbeck's book is socialist slant to it, telling a story with a message of how through collective action, oppression, and exploitation can be overcome. One man alone, or even one family alone doesn't have the power to resist the rich and powerful land owners from taking advantage of poor people like the Joads and thousands of others by paying them paltry wages and knowing that if they protest working for low wages there will always be others who will work for even less. Only by joining together, by organizing unions, and striking against the owners and thus letting the fruit wither and spoil on the trees, will the workers be able to survive and create respectable decent lives.

After the killing of the deputy, Tom would like to stay with his folks and help them, but he can't. When he leaves, he has the intentions of preaching like Preacher Casey did earlier. Casey believing that society was not made up of many individual souls but consisted of one great big "over-soul." Tom expects to finish the work Casey began by organizing the little people, getting them together to fight against the bosses, because he knows that in collectivization is where success lies. One he leaves on his mission, he leaves the book but his message stays behind to inspire his family to keep on going, to fight for a decent living and join with others to overcome poverty and exploitation. He is a symbol for "we, the people," as Ma says when Tom leaves. Just as Tom first got into trouble by defending himself from a knife attack, he wants the little people to defend themselves by fighting back against the owners of the farms and orchards of California.

Your impressions: _____

_____

_____

_____

Comment to Sasha from an AP Reader

Tom Joad isn't the most obvious candidate for a character torn between conflicting loyalties. After all, when faced with the choice of remaining with a family that needs him or following the provisions of his parole, his folks win hands down. Yet you clearly explain Tom's decision and its aftermath, paying particular attention to his transformation from hard-boiled ex-con to a self-sacrificing spokesman for the little people. Showing that Tom's actions represent Steinbeck's purpose and predilections reveals considerable insight. Where your essay falters is in its sometimes verbose and awkward expression and perhaps its overabundant recapitulation of the plot. Score: 7

Chris T's Essay
(Typed as it
was written)

Plays and novels often contain a character who is torn apart of conflicting loyalties, which conflict between what his family wants and what they feel they must do to lead a life that is self-satisfied. This case happens in "The Glass Managerie" the play by Arthur Miller in which Tom, the son in the Wingfeld family is pulled in two conflicting directions. He loves his younger sister, Laura, but despises for his single mother who was abandon by her husband, a "telephone man falling in love with long distance." Tom also hates his job and home life, in particular the constant nagging by his mother Amanda Wingfeld and can't wait to escape them both. He's looking for adventure, like his father did so he goes to the movies almost every night to have vicarious adventures. He also gets drunk to escape his drab life. His mother, of course wants Tom to support her and Laura and she pleads with Tom not to run away mainly because Laura is sickly and an introvert. She is so bashful that she won't go to secretarial school. Instead, she wanders around town when her mother thinks she's taking typing classes. At home, she plays with her collection of glass animals which is her way of escaping from reality. Then Amanda finds out that Laura is a truant from school and is very upset.

More upset comes after Tom agrees to stay around at least until Laura finds a man to marry. One day he invites a friend Jim from work to dinner and to meet Laura. Amanda is excited and practically redecorates the apartment to impress Jim, the one and only "gentleman caller" Laura ever had. Amanda uses her stories of gentlemen callers when she was growing up in the South. She naturally regrets winding up with the husband who ran off. Telling stories about her younger days as a southern bell is like her fantasy life and gives her a way to escape from her troubles.

Amanda fantasizes that Jim is going to be the family savior. He will marry Laura and free Amanda of life burdens. Then Tom can do whatever he wants and go wherever he wants to go. Only it turns out that Jim is engaged to be married. Laura is crushed, and Amanda goes ballistic at Tom. She yells at him and calls him names. Tom refuses to take it any more. He talks back to his mother and decides then and there that he's outta there, and he goes off by himself to join the marines and wander the earth in search of adventure.

He returns on stage as the narrator of the play and speaks to the audience and Laura, telling her that he couldn't help himself by running away and telling her that he still loves her in spite of it all.

Your impressions: _____

_____

_____

_____

Comment to Chris from an AP Reader

It's a stretch to consider this essay an adequate response to the question. Putting aside your mistaken attribution of *The Glass Menagerie* to Arthur Miller, there is regrettably little in the essay that deals directly with conflicting forces that weigh either on Tom or on any other character. Your essay holds promise at the start but soon evolves into little more than a synopsis of the play, with an emphasis on how the characters contrive to escape from unendurable lives. Your awareness that Tom functions as the narrator suggests that you've seen or read the play and perhaps been present when it was discussed in class, but from the experience you seem to have carried away little more than superficialities. The diction and writing style fall short of AP standards, and there is little in the essay to suggest that you are sufficiently acquainted with anything but the most elementary principles of literary criticism and analysis. I'm sorry to tell you that your essay cannot earn more than a minimal score. Score: 2

CHAPTER **4** What You Need to Know About Poetry

Poetry Overview

Whether you abhor poetry or eat it for breakfast, whether you think poetry is cool or hot, scintillating or dull—none of that really matters on the AP exam. When you take the test, you'll be handed two or maybe three poems accompanied by roughly twenty-five multiple-choice questions. In addition, you'll be asked to write an essay that analyzes one or more additional poems. If poetry is in your blood, you'll probably deal deftly with the poetry sections of the exam. However, if poetry is something you can live without, this chapter may not change your attitude, but it can prepare you to score high in the poetry sections of the exam.

Before reviewing what you need to know, let's quickly dispense with what you can do without. Rest assured that you won't be asked to identify the title of any poems or recall facts about a poet's life. Nor will you need to dredge up information concerning the history of poetry or expound on the various schools of poetic criticism that have long flourished in academia. Because highly technical aspects of poetry are generally off limits on the exam, you won't be expected to have mastered the intricacies of poetic metrics and its baffling vocabulary—although it could be advantageous to know both the meaning of such terms as *iambic pentameter* and *dactyl* and the function of a poetic *foot*. Also, because the AP exam will never ask you to expound on the esoterica of versification, rhyme, and the multitude of poetic forms, you won't need to know more than the rudiments of each.

Most literate people would probably argue that poetry should be read for pleasure. The poems on the AP exam, however, are not put there for your enjoyment or appreciation. With luck you may enjoy reading them, but you needn't praise their artistry or revel in their emotion. Your task will be more mundane— to read each poem, figure out its meaning, examine its structure, and analyze the effects of poetic techniques that the poet brought to bear. In short, you'll pore over the anatomy of each poem and respond to questions. In Section I, the multiple-choice questions themselves will steer you through the poems, pointing out important features. In Section II, for better or worse, you'll be left to find and discuss them on your own.

What you need to know. AP test takers are expected to have a reasonably firm grasp of poetic structure, form, sound, and the other elements that give poetry the power to move, entertain, and enlighten. To put it plainly, you should be able to answer the question *How does a poem convey meaning?* In your English classes these past years, while studying the fundamentals of diction, metaphor, rhyme, and the other components of poetry, chances are you've been developing the background and acquiring the know-how to answer that question insightfully.

How to Read a Poem

Ideally, poems should be read aloud. Poetry, after all, is an oral art akin to music. Its sounds, rhythms, and rhymes are meant to be heard. Regrettably, you can't declaim a poem during the AP exam or an irate proctor will take you away. So you'll have to settle for the next best thing: Read it aloud to yourself—a paradox, to be sure, but also a piece of advice that means pronouncing each word in your mind's ear, skipping not a single syllable or mark of punctuation, paying attention to built-in pauses and to line and stanza breaks. In short, listen to yourself reciting the poem just as the poet wrote it.

Easier said than done? Perhaps, because the poems pitched to you during the exam are a world away from "Roses are Red/Violets are Blue" or "Casey at the Bat"—ditties that may share the name *poem* with "In Memorium" and "The Lovesong of J. Alfred Prufrock" but can't compare in artistry or in the authentic expression of human experience. Because poems on the exam tend to be far from transparent, count on reading them two or three times. With each reading, a poem should start to reveal its meanings. And, as you begin to answer the questions, the poem should become clearer still. Don't forget to note the title. It may contain just the clue you need to crack open the world within the poem. Reading poetry well is a skill like any other, and the more you practice, the better you'll get. That's why the best thing you can do to prepare for the exam is to read scores of poems—many more than appear in this book—and for each one, have a go at it using the ten generic questions below:

1. *Who is talking?* What can you tell about the speaker's age, gender, station in life, opinions, and feelings? What, if anything does the poem reveal about the speaker's character?

    Some speakers take on a distinct personality. The speaker in Andrew Marvell's "To His Coy Mistress," for example, is urgently "on the make," citing reasons his sweetheart should go to bed with him. Other speakers simply reflect on a theme; in e. e. cummings' "in Just," the speaker pays tribute to the coming of spring. Aside from that, we learn nothing of his character. Likewise, the speaker in "Pied Beauty" by Gerard Manley Hopkins meditates on the magnificent colors, shapes, and textures of God's creations. Beyond that, there's little to say about him or her.

2. *To whom is the speaker talking?* To the reader only? To someone else? If so, to whom, and what is the listener's relationship to the speaker?

    Some poems, such as Shelley's "Ozymandias," are addressed only to the reader. Others, like Blake's "A Cradle Song" are directed at a third person but focus so intently on the subject of the poem that they reveal nothing about the speaker's connection to his audience. Still others are dramatic monologues—poems that resemble a speech in a play. In such monologues speakers address a specific person and often respond to the listener's unspoken reactions. Matthew Arnold's "Dover Beach" and Tennyson's "Ulysses" are examples.

3. *What is the background of the poem?* Is there a reason or occasion for the poem? Is there any evidence of a setting, a time, place, season, or situation?

    For lyric poems the answer will most likely be *no* to those questions. Narrative poems, dramatic monologues, ballads, and other poems that tell or imply stories often provide background that helps to shape the poem's effect and meaning. Frost's *"Out, Out—"* takes place on a farm during wood-cutting season. In Coleridge's "Rime of the Ancient Mariner," the speaker tells the story to guests at a wedding reception.

4. *What happens during the poem?* Do any events occur? Are they in the past or the present? Are they external or internal? Why are they important to the speaker or to a character in the poem? From what perspective does the speaker describe the events: as an omniscient narrator? as a participant? as an observer?

    The speaker in "The Twa Corbies," who happens to overhear two ravens talking about their next meal, has no vested interest in the conversation. In Wordsworth's "Composed upon Westminster Bridge," however, the speaker expresses his great affection for the city of London. Lyric poems, such as Keats's "Ode on a Grecian Urn," refer to no particular events, although it seems likely that the speaker is at that moment scrutinizing an ancient urn.

5. *What is the speaker's purpose and/or tone?* Does the speaker evince an attitude or bias regarding the subject matter of the poem? What imagery, diction, figures of speech, and choice of details contribute to the speaker's tone? Does the speaker use comparisons made via metaphors, similes, personification, or metonymy. Do you see any shifts in tone or perspective? Any contradictions?

    To understand a poem you must understand its tone. The tone of William Blake's "The Tyger" has long puzzled and intrigued readers. To this day, therefore, more than two centuries after it was written, the poem remains an enigma. In contrast, there's nothing elusive about the tone of "Counting-Out Rhyme" by Edna St. Vincent Millay and "Jabberwocky" by Lewis Carroll. Both poems are intended solely to entertain readers with collections of playful sounds. The types of poems you've studied in class as well as those that typically show up on AP tests fall somewhere between those two extremes.

6. *How does the language of the poem contribute to its meaning?* Is there anything distinctive about the poem's diction? Does the poet repeat words, sounds, phrases, and ideas? If so, to what purpose and effect? Which figures of speech and images are particularly potent? Do alliteration, assonance, consonance play a role in the poem?

    Since words are the lifeblood of poetry, look hard and long at the poem's language. Think of Macbeth's powerful words as he ponders his life: "Life's but a walking shadow . . . full of sound and fury, signifying nothing." Or consider a challenging poem like "Thirteen Ways of Looking at a Blackbird," in which Wallace Stevens embodies meaning in a series of intense, compact, and suggestive images. William Butler Yeats, spellbound by a fiercely independent woman, fills his love poem "No Second Troy" with language that alludes to Ireland's quest for freedom from England. Indeed, good poets bind language and meaning so tightly that altering a syllable would damage the poem's integrity.

7. *How is the poem organized?* Does it adhere to a closed form, such as a sonnet or villanelle? Or does it take liberties? Is it a free form? Does the verse structure contribute to meaning? Are the form and meaning related in some way? Does the ending contain some sort of resolution? How does organization contribute to the poem's meaning and effect?

The fourteen-line structure of a sonnet used by Shakespeare, Milton, Browning, and countless others has come to be considered the embodiment of human thought, just as the limerick seems just pithy enough to convey a whimsical idea with cleverly crafted rhymes. On the other hand, a more free-flowing organization is appropriate for "Ode to the Confederate Dead" by Allen Tate, a poem that takes place in the mind of a person wandering among the headstones in a Confederate cemetery and pondering the meaning of the soldiers' sacrifice.

8. *Do patterns of rhyme and rhythm contribute to the meaning and effect of the poem?* How does rhyme function in the poem? Are there patterns of sound that help to convey meaning or create effects? What does the meter contribute to the poem's meaning?

     Rhyme and rhythm that distract from the sense of a poem is a common flaw of second-rate poems. Thus, critics scorn Tennyson's "Charge of the Light Brigade" for its thundering hoof beats and repetitive rhymes that make the poem easy to remember but hard to take seriously. In high-quality poems, rhyme and meter are more than decorative features. They are a medium that subtlely enhances meaning and effect. Frequent shifts of meter in Shelley's "Ode to the West Wind," for example, suggest the wildness of the wind itself.

9. *What themes or motifs does the poem contain?* Are themes stated or are they implied? Can you draw a generalization about life or human nature from the poem?

     Poetic motifs are often vividly suggested or even stated outright. Anarchy, for instance, is evoked by a series of brief statements in William Butler Yeats' "The Second Coming": "The falcon cannot hear the falconer;/Things fall apart; the center cannot hold;/Mere anarchy is loosed upon the world."

     Themes, on the other hand, are rarely articulated. Instead, they must be inferred from the text. Sometimes a theme practically jumps off the page, as in the antiwar poems of Wilfred Owen (e.g., "Anthem for Doomed Youth"). In other poems, themes are less accessible. For example, "The Red Wheelbarrow" by William Carlos Williams consists of three visual images preceded by the words "so much depends/upon"—an altogether sparse amount of evidence from which to identify a theme. Yet it's sufficient. Williams' poem is about writing poetry. For him poems start with visual cues like "a red wheel /barrow" and "white/chickens."

10. *What was your initial response to the poem?* Did the poem speak to you? Touch you? Leave you cold? Confuse you? Anger you? Blow your mind? Cause you to pick up your cellphone and call a friend?

     More important, did your response change after reading the poem a second, third, or even a fourth time?

Ten meaty questions are far too many to keep in mind all at once. But they'll start to sink in as you use them over and over, and they can serve you well as you ready yourself for the AP exam.

First, however, find a poetry anthology such as *The Book of Living Verse* edited by Louis Untermeyer or *The Norton Anthology of Poetry*. Each contains a variety of poems—old, new, easy, hard, long, short. Taking your time, read a poem and run through the list of questions. Then read another and answer the questions again. Then read a few more, and then still more. Repeat the routine the following day and again the day after. Read whenever you have a few spare moments—while waiting for the bus, on the john, standing in the cafeteria line. Gradually, the questions will sink in, and as you continue to read poems, you'll start reading them more deeply. For every poem you read deeply, you'll learn something about reading the next one. In time it will become second nature to read poetry adroitly. Not that you'll breeze through every poem you encounter, but you will have at your command a number of strategies for insightfully drawing out a poem's effects and meanings.

To start you off, here is a Walt Whitman poem followed by the ten questions and some possible answers.

WHEN I HEARD THE LEARN'D ASTRONOMER

When I heard the learn'd astronomer;
When the proofs, the figures, were ranged in columns before me,
When I was shown the charts and the diagrams, to add, divide,
Line   and measure them,
(5)   When I, sitting, heard the astronomer, where he lectured with
        much applause in the lecture-room,
How soon, unaccountable, I became tired and sick,
Till, rising and gliding out, I wander'd off by myself,
In the mystical moist night-air, and from time to time,
(10)   Look'd up in perfect silence at the stars.

(1865)

1. *Who is talking?*
    The speaker may be a student or perhaps the poet himself. In either case, he is someone who attends lectures and has no stomach for pedantry. Before the lecture ends, he stalks out of the room repulsed by both the astronomer's presentation and the audience's response.
2. *To whom is the speaker talking?*
    He is talking to the reader and also to himself, perhaps to justify or make sense of his impulsiveness.
3. *What is the background of the poem?*
    The speaker attends a lecture on the heavens given by a learned astronomer.
4. *What happens during the poem?*
    Hard facts and mathematical problems dominate the astronomer's presentation. Disappointed in both the lecture and the audience's receptivity to it, the speaker leaves the lecture hall. Outside, as if awestruck, he occasionally looks up at the stars, saying nothing.
5. *What is the speaker's purpose and/or tone?*
    The speaker distances himself from the lecturer's scholarly, scientific perspective in favor of a more personal one. In fact, he appears to disavow science by assuming an almost disdainful, holier-than-thou attitude toward the astronomer. He also objects to the audience, whose applause pays unwarranted homage to the learned lecturer.
6. *How does the language of the poem contribute to its meaning?*
    The "facts" of astronomy are represented by a barrage of hard, clipped words: "proofs," "figures," "charts," "diagrams." The repeated use of "When"

at the beginning of successive clauses suggests the astronomer's plodding delivery as well as an absence of concern for anything other than getting the facts across to his audience. The repetition of "lecture" (line 6) further emphasizes the spiritlessness of the astronomer's presentation.

In contrast, the speaker's view of the stars is couched in poetic language including such sound-rich phrases as "off by myself,/In the mystical moist night-air."

In the last line the speaker feasts his eyes on stars "in perfect silence," suggesting that words are not only unnecessary but inadequate to describe the mystery of what he observes. The speaker's silence also contrasts with both the lecture and the applause it elicited.

7. *How is the poem organized?*

The poem is structured like a short story with a beginning (lines 1–4), middle (5–8), and end (9–10). The lecture serves as the stimulus for the speaker's response and escape from the lecture room. The episode is resolved as the speaker looks up at the stars in silence. All parts of the poem work together to tell a brief anecdote and to convey the speaker's disapproval of both the astronomer's approach to his subject and the audience's reaction.

8. *Do patterns of rhyme and rhythm contribute to the meaning and effect of the poem?*

As an example of "free verse," the poem ignores customary patterns of meter or rhyme. It creates its effect via the words, images, subtle variations in rhythm and length of the lines. The account of the lecture, for example, consists of lengthy, prosaic lines. Only at the end does the speaker's poetic voice reassert itself. For a poem about a person who rejects conventionality, free verse seems an appropriate choice.

9. *What themes or motifs does the poem contain?*

The speaker, a romantic, seems to believe that rationality robs nature of beauty and mystery. As someone with an antiscientific bent, he prefers to contemplate the stars in silence. On one level, the speaker's silence is literal, but it also implies a sense of isolation. While others in the audience applaud the astronomer, the speaker disapprovingly slinks out of the room to commune with the stars. Ironically, his silence is a sham because it is trumpeted loud and clear by this poem.

10. *What was your initial response to the poem?*

The answer to this question will vary from reader to reader.

Practice in Reading Poems

For practice in reading and dissecting poems, answer the questions accompanying each of the following three selections. Write your responses in the spaces provided, and compare your answers to those on pages 71–77.

POEM A

A POISON TREE

I was angry with my friend:
I told my wrath, my wrath did end.
I was angry with my foe:

Line   I told it not, my wrath did grow.

(5)   And I watered it in fears
Night and morning with my tears,
And I sunned it with smiles
And with soft deceitful wiles.

And it grew both day and night,
(10)   Til it bore an apple bright,
And my foe beheld it shine,
And he knew that it was mine—

And into my garden stole
When the night had veiled the pole;
(15)   In the morning, glad, I see
My foe outstretched beneath the tree.

(1794)

1. Who is talking?

_____

_____

_____

2. To whom is the speaker talking?

_____

_____

_____

3. What is the background of the poem?

_____

_____

_____

4.   *What happens during the poem?*

_____

_____

_____

5.   *What is the speaker's purpose and/or tone?*

_____

_____

_____

6.   *How does the language of the poem contribute to its meaning?*

_____

_____

_____

7.   *How is the poem organized?*

_____

_____

_____

8.   *Do patterns of rhyme and rhythm contribute to the meaning and effect of the poem?*

_____

_____

_____

9.   *What themes or motifs does the poem contain?*

_____

_____

_____

10. *What was your initial response to the poem?*

_____

_____

_____

POEM B

A SOLITARY REAPER

Behold her, single in the field,
Yon solitary highland lass!
Reaping and singing by herself;
Line   Stop here, or gently pass!
(5)   Alone she cuts and binds the grain,
And sings a melancholy strain;
O listen! for the vale profound
Is overflowing with the sound.

No Nightingale did ever chaunt
(10)   More welcome notes to weary bands
Of travelers in some shady haunt,
Among Arabian sands:
A voice so thrilling ne'er was heard
In spring-time from the cuckoo-bird,
(15)   Breaking the silence of the seas
Among the farthest Hebrides.

Will no one tell me what she sings?—
Perhaps the plaintive numbers flow
For old, unhappy, far-off things,
(20)   And battles long ago:
Or is it some more humble lay,
Familiar matter of to-day?
Some natural sorrow, loss, or pain,
That has been, and may be again?

(25)   Whate'er the theme, the Maiden sang
As if her song could have no ending;
I saw her singing at her work,
And o'er the sickle bending;—
I listen'd, motionless and still;
(30)   And, as I mounted up the hill
The music in my heart I bore,
Long after it was heard no more.

(1805)

1. *Who is talking?*

_____

_____

_____

2.   *To whom is the speaker talking?*

_____

_____

_____

3.   *What is the background of the poem?*

_____

_____

_____

4.   *What happens during the poem?*

_____

_____

_____

5.   *What is the speaker's purpose and/or tone?*

_____

_____

_____

6.   *How does the language of the poem contribute to its meaning?*

_____

_____

_____

7.   *How is the poem organized?*

_____

_____

_____

8. *Do patterns of rhyme and rhythm contribute to the meaning and effect of the poem?*

_____

_____

_____

9. *What themes or motifs does the poem contain?*

_____

_____

_____

10. *What was your initial response to the poem?*

_____

_____

_____

POEM C

THE CAMBRIDGE LADIES

the Cambridge ladies who live in furnished souls
are unbeautiful and have comfortable minds
(also, with the church's protestant blessings
Line   daughters, unscented shapeless spirited)
(5)   they believe in Christ and Longfellow, both dead,
are invariably interested in so many things—
at the present writing one still finds
delighted fingers knitting for the is it Poles?
perhaps. While permanent faces coyly bandy
(10)   scandal of Mrs. N and Professor D
. . . . the Cambridge ladies do not care, above
Cambridge if sometimes in its box of
sky lavender and cornerless, the
moon rattles like a fragment of angry candy

(1923)

1. *Who is talking?*

_____

_____

_____

2. *To whom is the speaker talking?*

_____

_____

_____

3. *What is the background of the poem?*

_____

_____

_____

4. *What happens during the poem?*

_____

_____

_____

5. *What is the speaker's purpose and/or tone?*

_____

_____

_____

6. *How does the language of the poem contribute to its meaning?*

_____

_____

_____

7. *How is the poem organized?*

_____

_____

_____

8.   *Do patterns of rhyme and rhythm contribute to the meaning and effect of the poem?*

_____

_____

_____

9.   *What themes or motifs does the poem contain?*

_____

_____

_____

10.   *What was your initial response to the poem?*

_____

_____

_____

Answers to Practice Questions

Some questions invite interpretation. Therefore, don't expect your answers to be precisely the same as those below. If any of your responses differ markedly from these, however, be sure that you can defend your position with specific evidence drawn from the poem.

POEM A "A Poison Tree" by William Blake

1.   *Who is talking?* The speaker may be the poet himself. Considering his villainy, however, he is more likely an invention of the poet's imagination.
2.   *To whom is the speaker talking?* First and foremost, he addresses the reader. His self-incriminating revelations suggest that he may be seeking forgiveness from some sort of father confessor. Either way, he has taken the audience into his confidence.
3.   *What is the background of the poem?* For an unspecified reason the speaker has been miffed by both a friend and a foe. He makes peace with the friend but not with the foe.
4.   *What happens during the poem?* The speaker comes to terms with his friend. But with respect to his foe, he keeps rage bottled up inside where it festers and grows into an obsession to kill. While feigning friendship, he hatches a plot to tempt his foe into stealing and eating a poison apple. Seeing the corpse of his foe sprawled beneath the apple tree gladdens the speaker's heart.
5.   *What is the speaker's purpose and/or tone?* The speaker describes two contrasting relationships, one with a friend, the other with a foe. In explaining the latter, he takes pride in how he disposed of his enemy

through guile and deceit. Lacking a trace of remorse, he appears unaware of his own malevolence.

6. *How does the language of the poem contribute to its meaning?* Simple and straightforward language, the kind that a friend might use to talk about everyday events, dominates the poem. An off-handed expression of deceit disguises the speaker's diabolical nature. The incongruity between his language and the subject matter underscores his callousness. The speaker's joy after killing his foe adds still another dimension to his perversity. Nothing the speaker says contains the slightest hint that he deserves sympathy or redemption. In that sense, he is no less a victim of evil impulses than his unfortunate foe.

   In relating his experience, the speaker alludes to an "apple" and a "garden," words that call to mind the biblical story of man's fall from innocence. The speaker tempts his foe just as Satan tempted Adam and Eve to eat the forbidden fruit.

7. *How is the poem organized?* Each stanza adds another dimension to the speaker's self-portrait. First the speaker represents himself as someone capable of both good and evil. But in the lines that follow, he flaunts only his maliciousness. At the end of the third stanza, the speaker briefly turns his attention to his foe's behavior, and in the last line we are shown the speaker at the height of his depravity, rejoicing at the consequences of his efforts.

8. *Do patterns of rhyme and rhythm contribute to the meaning and effect of the poem?* The poem's regular rhymes and steady, singsongy rhythm disguise its dark subject matter and imply the speaker's insensitivity to his own wickedness. Indeed, the incongruity between the speaker's message and the means by which it is delivered heightens the poem's emotional impact.

   Lines 1 and 3, in which the speaker expresses his anger, are trochaic. Lines 2 and 4, which tell of the speaker's action, are iambic, a sequence that sets up a brief dialogue between feelings and action. The only other all-iambic line is the last line, in which the speaker celebrates his deadly achievement. The change in rhythm intensifies the climax of the poem by setting it apart from the other lines in the stanza.

9. *What themes or motifs does the poem contain?* Biblical overtones expand the poem's meaning. By tempting an innocent to eat a poison apple, the speaker takes on Satan-like characteristics. At the same time, the speaker plays God by taking another's life. Paradoxically, then, he is an amalgam of evil and good, as he himself suggests early in the poem. Thereby, he represents humankind both before and after the fall from innocence.

   An altogether different interpretation is that the poem may be little more than a recipe for vengeance or a warning to readers against the dangers of insincerity.

10. *What was your initial response to the poem?* The answer will vary from reader to reader.

POEM B "A Solitary Reaper" by William Wordsworth

1. *Who is talking?* The speaker is a traveler on horseback passing by a field in the highlands. He is deeply moved by the singing of a country lass harvesting grain. His blasé allusions to far-off places (Arabia and the Hebrides) suggest he is well traveled, perhaps even weary of his aimless roaming

across deserts and oceans. As the poem begins, he is ready to be awakened to more profound aspects of both himself and the human condition.

2. *To whom is the speaker talking?* Unable to contain himself, the speaker must tell someone—the reader in this case—about the singing he heard in the highlands.

3. *What is the background of the poem?* Because the lass "cuts and binds the grain" (line 5), it is harvest time, presumably the late summer or fall.

4. *What happens during the poem?* Passing a field, a traveler hears a song being sung by a solitary peasant girl harvesting grain. Deciding to stop and listen rather than continue on his way, the speaker is struck by the beauty of the song. He compares it to other beautiful sounds—the song of a nightingale and the song of a cuckoo-bird. The speaker begins to muse on the possible meaning of the song but can discern only its sorrowful tone. Finally, he rides away haunted by the music he has heard.

5. *What is the speaker's purpose and/or tone?* The speaker tries to determine why he has been deeply touched by the melancholy strains of the girl's song. Recognizing only the song's plaintiveness (line 18) and its "sorrow, loss, or pain" (line 23), he carries the music away with him, harboring sorrow in his heart, even long after he can no longer hear the notes (line 32). His reaction seems to be a kind of epiphany, as though he has been suddenly awakened to his inner self and now understands the sorrows of others.

6. *How does the language of the poem contribute to its meaning?* Two exclamations (in lines 1–2 and in line 4) not only add drama to the opening of the poem but suggest that the speaker has been suddenly energized by the sound of the girl's singing. How deeply he has been affected, however, is not made clear until the third and fourth stanzas. By emphasizing solitude ("single in the field," "singing by herself," "alone she cuts . . ."), the speaker visually and emotionally keeps the girl at a distance, but by the end of the poem, she and her song have sunk into his soul. This shift from outside to inside the speaker begins with the word "melancholy" (line 6) and accelerates during the third stanza, nudged along by the girl's "plaintive," and "unhappy" song.

The poem's diction, like the peasant girl of the title, is generally plain and simple, but in the second stanza the speaker's words turn more exotic and fanciful: "chaunt," "shady haunt," "Arabian sands"—words and phrases befitting the stanza's more imaginative subject matter.

The use of the past tense in the last stanza signals the climax of the poem. The fading image of the girl contrasts to her song, which shall never end. The concluding lines show the traveler changed by his brief encounter with a mythic, symbolic figure. The music has awakened him to the universality of human woe, an artifact of which is now lodged in his heart.

The final couplet contains the simplest language in the poem. Almost entirely monosyllabic, it captures the essence of the speaker's transformation. His discovery that sorrow is a common aspect of everyday experience is conveyed in common, everyday words. Containing sounds that echo the sense, the words repeat a long *o* (b*o*re, l*o*ng, m*o*re) that resonates with the girl's music and reiterates the set of *o*-sounds that simulate the girl's song in lines 7–8. As the traveler continues on his way, a series of mellow *m*-sounds capture his subdued mood.

Calling the girl a "reaper" is an irony. Yes, she reaps grain, but the word is commonly associated with "grim reaper," the proverbial personification of death. Here, of course, the reaper is a young lass, a life-affirming figure, not a spectre of death. With her song, she unwittingly lays to rest some of the speaker's encrusted attitudes and endows him with new life, or at least with a new vision of the world.

7. *How is the poem organized?* Initially, the speaker confronts melancholy singing that sweeps through the valley. Next, he compares the music to the call of birds in far-off places, using images that awaken his desire to understand the meaning of the melody. Recognizing that sorrow can "have no ending" (line 26), he continues on his way with the music buried deep in his heart. All told, then, the poem begins with the speaker's external, sensual response to the music, goes on to explore his intellectual reactions, and concludes with a deeply felt self-realization.

These events, which occur at a confluence of two different worlds—that of a simple peasant girl and that of a worldly and superficially successful traveler—reflect the poem's symmetry. Each of four eight-line stanzas is composed of two quatrains, each devoted to a different aspect of the traveler's experience. The first four lines of the poem, for example, show what the man sees, the second four tell what he hears. This arrangement parallels the dramatic structure, for the poem is an account of a man's transformation. Before the change, he is an aimless, world-weary traveler. Afterwards, having realized not only that sorrow pervades the world but that he must share in that sorrow, he has become enlightened.

8. *Do patterns of rhyme and rhythm contribute to the meaning and effect of the poem?* Rhyme and meter support the poem's basic symmetry. The second and third stanzas contain identical rhyme schemes: *a-b-a-b-c-c-d-d*. The others differ only in the third line, an exception that softens the effects of a consistent and assertive rhyme. The pairs of rhyming couplets that end each stanza serve as a kind of coda that creates a climactic emotional surge.

Most lines are written in iambic tetrameter, a rhythm akin to everyday speech and appropriate to a poem about an ordinary country girl singing in the fields. With the occasional intrusion of dactyls such as *reaping* (line 3) and *breaking* (line 15), a rhythmic tension is created, a tension that reflects the state of the speaker's emotions. In addition, there are pauses, or caesuras, in mid-line, as in "Behold her" (line 1) and "Stop here" (line 4), suggestive of the pause taken by the traveler on his journey.

9. *What themes or motifs does the poem contain?* Two related motifs—solitude and melancholy—dominate the poem. The first is introduced by the title and by such references to the girl's isolation as "singing by herself" (line 3). From solitude it is a short step to melancholy, and the speaker dwells on images of sadness and sorrow. While these motifs are used to describe the girl and her song, the speaker, too, is a solitary figure, who, by listening to the music, becomes attuned to the melancholy nature of life.

While these motifs help to establish the mood of the poem, the third stanza, consisting largely of a series of questions, holds the key to the poem's main theme. Lines 21–24 ask what amounts to a rhetorical question about the nature of sorrow: Is it something that "has been, and may be again?" In a flash, the speaker realizes that sadness and pain "have no ending" (line 26). That is to say, suffering is part of the human nature. As he rides off, the traveler understands that private, internal events attest far more vividly to a man's humanity than such superficial experiences as globetrotting.

10. *What was your initial response to the poem?* This answer will vary from reader to reader.

POEM C "The Cambridge Ladies" by e. e. cummings

1. *Who is talking?* The speaker is either the poet or a spokesman for the poet. The phrase "at the present writing" (line 7) suggests that the speaker may be a journalist or a researcher-type preparing a sociological article or exposé.

2. *To whom is the speaker talking?* To the reader.

3. *What is the background of the poem?* Evidently, the speaker has had occasion to observe or to talk with this group of women he deprecatingly calls the "Cambridge ladies." Lacking individuality, they are given a collective persona that serves as an easy target for satire.

4. *What happens during the poem?* The speaker paints an unflattering portrait of the ladies' values, manners, and characteristics. He comments directly or indirectly on their hypocrisy, their conventional minds, their shallowness and superficiality. He also targets their banal efforts to help others, their tendency to gossip, and their mindless indifference to everything but keeping up appearances.

   Of all their faults, hypocrisy may arguably be the most egregious. The ladies pretend to be Protestants (note the lowercase *p,* implying the ladies' hollow piety). They act in un-Christianlike ways, unaware of their mean-spiritedness as they gossip "coyly" about the scandalous behavior of Mrs. N and Professor D, presumably two of their Cambridge neighbors. Also, because it is fashionable to do so, they "believe" in Christ and Longfellow, a pairing that both demeans Christ and elevates Longfellow. Regardless, the speaker pointedly declares them "both dead," not unlike the ladies' adherence to Christ's teachings and their comprehension of Longfellow's poetry. The ladies voluntarily knit for "is it the Poles?/perhaps." But their altruism is a sham, done to impress others rather than to help the needy.

5. *What is the speaker's purpose and/or tone?* The speaker intends to mock the women using satire and in-your-face sarcasm. Ultra-cynical, even destructive, he endows the ladies with not a single redeeming quality. In the last four lines, the speaker turns indignant, condemning the group for not caring about anything except their social standing. Even the moon, a symbol rich in meaning for people everywhere, means nothing to them. They view it as a piece of candy rattling around in a mostly empty (like the ladies themselves) lavender box.

6. *How does the language of the poem contribute to its meaning?* The language of the poem is off-beat. It takes liberties with syntax (". . . one still finds/delighted fingers knitting for the is it Poles?"), punctuation ("unscented shapeless spirited"), capitalization ("protestant"), and diction ("unbeautiful"). The quirkiness of the language stands in stark contrast to the ladies, who revere conventionality.

The phrase "furnished souls" (line 1), implying that the ladies are virtual automatons, introduces a concept built up and reinforced throughout the poem. The women possess "comfortable minds," that never question, think, or probe. Absent an imagination or dreams, and lacking both creativity and curiosity, they have been programmed by their provincial society to go to church, knit, and talk about other people. Meanwhile, they wear "permanent faces" and never consider what their various activities add up to. In effect, they are the living dead, a notion that bestows ironic overtones on the verb "live" in line 1.

Occasional fragments of conversation reveal still more about the ladies. Their claim to be "interested in so many things" (line 6) reflects their pedantry. The phrase "knitting for the is it Poles?" (line 8) indicates that their volunteer work is nothing more than a perfunctory duty.

7. *How is the poem organized?* In order to mock the ladies, the poet contrives an organization that mimics but fails to follow the conventions of the traditional sonnet. Like a sonnet, "The Cambridge Ladies" contains fourteen lines, but it ignores the customary arrangement of ideas. Very loosely, however, the initial eight lines (the octave) present a spuriously objective account of the ladies, while the last six lines (the sestet) are overtly judgmental. In fact, the speaker's undisguised scorn emerges in the final four lines.

Structurally, the poem, which begins with a general description of the ladies, becomes increasingly specific. Sweeping generalities in the first lines evolve into examples of the ladies' behavior, which abruptly give way to the speaker's perception of what goes on—or more accurately, what fails to go on—inside the ladies' heads.

8. *Do patterns of rhyme and rhythm contribute to the meaning and effect of the poem?* Playful patterns of rhyme and rhythm help cast the ladies in a comic light. There are no rhymes in the first six lines, but lines 7 and 8 rhyme with lines 2 and 1 respectively. The poet has rhymed the last six lines *g-g-f-f-g-g*, but in each couplet an unstressed syllable is paired with a stressed one, as in "bandy" and "Professor D." Instead of employing consistent end rhymes, then, the poet scatters internal rhymes throughout, relying on, among other techniques, alliteration and assonance. Line 6, for example, contains four instances of "in": "*in*variably *in*terested *in* so many th*in*gs—." Line 9 contains two words beginning with "per," and ends with a pair of similar words, "coyly bandy." In the following line, the consonants *n* and *d* in "scandal" are echoed in the names of "Mrs. N and Professor D." And in the poem's final line, the "rattle" of the moon is onomatopoetically represented by "a fragment of angry candy."

The poem's rhythms are equally capricious. Five-foot lines prevail, but the final quatrain contains two four-foot lines and a culminating six-footer. In other words, the poem is a kind of mischievous romp of sound and rhythm, its eccentricities contrasting vividly with its subject.

9. *What themes or motifs does the poem contain?* The main theme is the conventionality of the Cambridge ladies, whose lives follow a preordained pattern. Each of the ladies' flaws and foibles becomes a mini-theme in the poem. Thus, the allusion to Christ and Longfellow suggests that the ladies' values are skewed toward the dead, implying further that the ladies themselves are emotionally and intellectually insensible.

10.   *What was your initial response to the poem?* This answer will vary from reader to reader.

What to Listen for in Poetry

Here is a fact you *don't* need to know for the AP exam: Every pattern of rhyme and rhythm has a name.

Here's another fact, one that you *should* know for the exam: What is important in analyzing poems is not the names of various patterns of rhyme and rhythm, but that rhyme and rhythm contribute to the meaning and effect of a poem. If you can tell a slant rhyme from a spondee, more power to you, but what counts on the exam is your ability to describe the function of slant rhyme in a particular place or to explain the effect of a given spondee.

Because a feature of any good poem is unity, its sounds cannot be separated from its themes, structure, imagery, and so forth. That's why rhyme, rhythm, the use of repetition, and each of several other sound-related techniques are more than abstractions. They are integral to a poem's totality.

Rhyme

Rhyme is perhaps the most easily recognized characteristic of poetry, particularly *end rhyme,* the repetition of identical sounds at the end of successive lines, as illustrated by this excerpt from W. H. Auden's "It's No Use Raising a Shout":

> A long time ago I told my *mother*
> I was leaving home to find *another:*
> I never answered her *letter*
> But I never found a *better*
> Here am I, here are *you:*
> But what does it mean? What are we going to *do?*

Equally vivid end rhymes may occur in alternating lines, as in this fragment of Lord Byron's "She Walks in Beauty":

> She walks in beauty like the *night*
> Of cloudless climes and starry *skies*
> And all that's best of dark and *bright*
> Meet in her aspect and her *eyes:*

Another common rhyming pattern consists of end rhymes in only the second and fourth lines of a four-line stanza, illustrated in the anonymously written "The Dying Airman":

> Take the cylinders out of my kidneys,
> The connecting-rod out of my *brain,*
> Take the cam-shaft out of my backbone,
> And assemble the engine *again.*

Types of rhymes. Customarily, rhyme is produced by one syllable words (*fat/cat*) or by the final syllables of multisyllabic words (*prevail/entail; disclosure/ composure*).

Sounds that are close but not exact duplicates of one another are called, among other things, *slant* rhymes, *off* rhymes, and *near* rhymes (*seen/been; ill/all; summer/somewhere*). A major function of slant rhymes is to help avoid the monotony of repetitious conventional rhyme. The slant offers a change of pace, a small but welcome deviation, as in the concluding lines of this fragment from F. T. Prince's "To a Friend on His Marriage":

> A beautiful girl said something in your praise.
> And either because in a hundred ways
> I had heard of her great worth and had no *doubt*
> To find her lovelier than I *thought*
> And found her also cleverer, or *because*
> Although she had known you well it *was* . . .

Rhymes that end with accented syllables are *masculine (unloose/reduce; rehearse/perverse)*; those that end in unstressed syllables are *feminine (sleeping/leaping; center/tormenter)*. Words with two unstressed rhyming syllables are called *double feminine* rhymes (*monocle/chronicle*). Poets have occasionally been moved to use *triple* rhymes (*intellectual/henpecked you-all*) and *quadruple* rhymes (*Mephistopheles/with the most awful ease*),[1] but such linguistic contortions call so much attention to themselves that they are shunned by serious poets.

[1]Examples from John Ciardi and Miller Williams, *How Does a Poem Mean?* Houghton Mifflin, 1975, p. 138.

Sometimes, an individual line of poetry contains two or more words that rhyme. Examples of such an *internal rhyme* are found in Tennyson's "Blow, Bugle, Blow":

> The splendour *falls* on castle *walls*
> And snowy summits old in story:
> The long light *shakes* across the *lakes*
> And the wild cataract leaps in glory.

Poets may include internal rhymes for emphasis or additional unity. If used excessively, however, internal rhymes could create monotony rather than interest.

Rhyme scheme. A rhyme scheme is the pattern of rhyming words within a given stanza or poem. For convenience, each similar end rhyme is usually identified with a letter of the alphabet, here illustrated by Francis Cornford's "The Watch":

I wakened on my hot, hard bed,	*a*
Upon the pillow lay my head;	*a*
Beneath the pillow I could hear	*b*
My little watch was ticking clear.	*b*
I thought the throbbing of it went	*c*
Like my continual discontent,	*c*
I thought it said in every tick:	*d*
I am so sick, so sick, so sick;	*d*
O death, come quick, come quick, come quick,	*d*
Come quick, come quick, come quick, come quick.	*d*

This shorthand technique applies to rhymes in any poem. The rhyme scheme of "It's No Use Raising a Shout" is simply *a-a-b-b-c-c;* of "She Walks in Beauty": *a-b-a-b;* and of "The Dying Airman": *a-b-c-b.* On the AP exam, you are not likely to be asked about rhyme scheme unless it is germane to the effect or meaning of a particular poem. "The Watch," though hardly more than fluff, illustrates how rhyme can support and enhance meaning. By ending the poem with four rhyming lines, the speaker simulates the relentless and repetitive ticking of a mechanical timepiece.

Lines that come in pairs *(couplet)* often rhyme, as do three lines, or *triplets* (or *tercets*) as in Tennyson's "The Eagle":

> He clasps the crag with crooked *hands*;
> Close to the sun in lonely *lands*,
> Ringed with the azure world he *stands*, . . .

In a distinct group of four lines (sometimes called *quatrain,* or *stanza,* rhymes can vary enormously from a-a-a-a to a-b-a-b, a-b-c-b, and so on. And in stanzas of a greater number of lines, rhyming possibilities are virtually endless.

On the AP exam you're not likely to be required to describe the rhyme scheme or distinguish one type of rhyme from another, but when you write your essay on a given poem, it may be useful to discuss rhymes that contribute to the poem's meaning or effect.

Onomatopoeia. Using *onomatopoeia,* words that virtually replicate sound, poets often create vivid effects. Is there a more expressive word than *moan,* for example, to make the sound of . . . well, a moan? Likewise, *murmur* resembles the sound of a murmur. And numerous other words, too—*boom, buzz, clang, crack,* and so on—all echo their sense. Because sound can cause words to crawl or race, flow smoothly or stumble along, express beauty or ugliness, poets often choose words according to the effects they wish to create. Meaning ordinarily takes precedence over sound, but an astutely picked onomatopoetic word may add both sense and sensuality to an image or phrase, as in these lines by W. H. Auden:

> And the fenders grind and heave,
> And the derricks clack and grate, as the tackle hooks the crate,
> And the fall-ropes whine through the sheave . . .

Alexander Pope, in this verse from "An Essay on Criticism," encapsulates the use of onomatopoeia and other sounds in poetry:

'Tis not enough no harshness gives offense,
The sound must seem an echo to the sense:
Soft is the strain when Zephyr gently blows,
And smooth stream in smoother numbers flows;
But when the loud surges lash the sounding shore,
The hoarse, rough verse should like the torrent roar:
When Ajax strives some rock's vast weight to throw,
The line too labors, and the words move slow;

Other sound-related poetic techniques, more subtle than onomatopoeia, are those that involve repetition through alliteration, assonance, and consonance.

Alliteration. Alliteration is the repetition of initial sounds in words and syllables. Sometimes such repetition is merely ornamental, but skillful poets use it to intensify effects, add weight to an idea, and in the process make the verse easier to remember.

From Gerard Manley Hopkins's "Spring" come these alliterative lines emphasizing the beauty of the season:

Nothing is so beautiful as spring—
When weeds, in wheels, shoot long and lovely and lush;
Thrush's eggs look little low heavens, and thrush
Through the echoing timber does so rinse and wring
The ear, it strikes like lightning to hear him sing;

Overused, alliteration sounds silly, as in this deliberately exaggerated excerpt from Shakespeare's *A Midsummer Night's Dream*:

Whereat, with blade, with bloody blameful blade,
He bravely broach'd his boiling bloody breast;

Assonance. Assonance is the repetition of similar vowel sounds. It is generally ornamental, but because it can also create a near, or slant, rhyme, it may engender subtle poetic effects. Such rhymes include *earth* and *hearth, willow* and *yellow, peer* and *fur, little* and *beetle.*

Wilfred Owen relies heavily on assonance in the opening stanza of "Futility," a poem about a soldier fatally wounded in World War I:

Move him into the sun—
Gently its touch awoke him once,
At home, whispering of fields unsown.
Line Always it woke him, even in France,
(5) Until this morning and this snow.
If anything might rouse him now
The kind old sun will know.

The word "touch" in the second line is in assonance with "sun" (lines 1 and 7) and to "unsown," "once," and "Until." Also the "*o*" in "awoke" (line 2) is echoed in "unsown," "woke," "snow," "old," and "know."

Assonance is rarely as obvious as alliteration, but vowel sounds that resonate throughout a poem contribute a melodic effect and subtlely bind the lines to each other. Also, assonance combined with alliteration may produce engaging rhymes, such as "blossom" and "bosom" in these two lines from "Patterns" by Amy Lowell:

> For the lime-tree is in blossom
> And one small flower has dropped upon my bosom.

Similarly, observe the assonantal rhymes in lines 2 and 4 of this stanza from "Captain Carpenter" by John Crowe Ransom:

> Captain Carpenter mounted up one day
> And rode straight way into a stranger rogue
> That looked unchristian but be that as it may
> The Captain did not wait upon prologue.

Consonance. Consonance is the repetition of consonants appearing within a line or at the end of words. In combination with certain vowels, a series of similar sounds creates subtle harmonies. A few examples are *odds* and *ends*, *"struts* and *frets"* (Shakespeare), and the *"d"* and *"l"* sounds in this couplet from Gerard Manley Hopkins's "God's Grandeur":

> And all is seared with trade; bleared smeared with toil;
> And wears man's smudge and shares man's smell: the soil

Because the technique sometimes goes by such names as *dissonance, half rhyme,* and *oblique rhyme,* it creates considerable confusion among students of poetry. Not to fret, however. The odds are one in a million that you'd be asked about consonance on the AP exam.

Meter and Rhythm

Patterns of rhythm in poetry are based on *meter,* a word synonymous with "measure." Using the poetic *foot* as the unit of measurement, the meter of any line of poetry can be analyzed according to the number and arrangement of its stressed and unstressed syllables. Poetic *feet* may consist of two syllables (disyllabic) or three syllables (trisyllabic), and have names based on the order in which the syllables appear.

In analyzing meter, a vertical slash (/) is used to separate poetic feet. A ∪ represents an unstressed syllable, and a – stands for a stressed syllable.

- An *iamb* (∪ –) is a two-syllable foot, the first syllable unstressed, the second stressed. All of the following words are *iambic:* re-spect, ex-tent, e-nough, at-tack, mis-judge. In a line of poetry, however, the syllables of a multisyllabic word may belong to different feet, as in:

  From eve/ry room / descends/ the pain/ted face.

- A *trochee* (– ∪) is a two-syllable foot, the first syllable stressed, the second unstressed. The following words are *trochaic:* mit-ten, gun-shot, cryp-tic, aud-it, ap-ple. In a poem, two syllables of the same word may fall into different feet. In the couplet below *re/ceive* is such a word.

  Johnny/ Jones is/ laid to/ rest
  Earth re/ceive an/ honored/ guest;

- A *spondee* (– –) is a two-syllable foot consisting of two equally stressed syllables. Spondees are often found at the end of a poetic lines, as in:

  High on the shore sat the great god Pan.

- A *dactyl* (– ∪ ∪) is a three-syllable foot composed of a stressed syllable and two unstressed ones, as in pos-sib-le, crock-e-ry, crim-i-nal, trav-el-er. The following line contains three dactyls:

  Red were her/ lips as the / berry that/ grows. . .

- An *anapest* (∪ ∪ –) is a three-syllable foot containing two unstressed syllables followed by a stressed one, as in ling-er-ie, pal-is-ade, le-mon-ade, reg-u-late. All six feet in this line are anapests:

  At the top/ of the mount/ ain were ap/ ples, the big/ gest that ev/ er were seen/

  To help you remember the names and structure of poetic feet, here is a mneumonic device[1] using women's names:

  Irene in an iamb.
  Tanya is a trochee
  Sue-Ann is a spondee
  Deborah is a dactyl
  Antoinette is an anapest

[1]Contributed by English teacher Marti Kirschbaum, Falls Church, Virginia.

It happens that roughly ninety percent of poems in English use the iamb as the basic metrical unit, most probably because it best fits the structure, syntax, and rhythm of the language. You'll never be asked directly to name the characteristics of poetic feet on the AP exam, but do yourself a favor and develop the habit of *scanning* the poems you read. If you become adept at *scansion,* the process of analyzing meter, you can discuss in your essay how meter contributes to the meaning and effect of the poem in question. Hordes of students can accurately label metrical techniques, but only an elite few have the wherewithal to explain why poets use them. Your ability to insightfully interpret poetic meter will never fail to impress AP essay readers.

You've no doubt inferred by now that lines of poetry consist of one or more feet. A line of a single foot—a rarity in English verse—is called *monometer.* Two-foot lines are *dimeter,* followed by *trimeter, tetrameter, pentameter, hexameter* (sometimes called *alexandrines*), *heptameter,* and *octameter.* The bulk of poetry in English, including much of Chaucer, most works by Browning and Milton, and the plays of Shakespeare and Marlowe, is written in five-foot lines, or *pentameter.* For its flexibility and majesty, *iambic pentameter* is the most widely employed rhythmic pattern. This fact, however, won't take you far on the AP test. It's more important to know how meter can influence the tone, meaning, structure, and overall texture of a poem. Verses written in iambic pentameter are most likely to echo ordinary speech. A work, say, in dactylic dimeter or anapestic trimeter is apt to sound odd, as though written by someone in need of a cold shower. In the end, off-beat scansion best suits poems trying hard to make an off-beat statement.

While scanning poems, be aware of *elisions,* or unstressed syllables omitted for the sake of meter. Functioning as ordinary contractions, most elisions turn two-syllable words into words of a single syllable, as in *o'er* (over), *ne'er* (never), and *'ere* (before). Also note that poems would plod along monotonously like *Mary Had a Little Lamb* if they contained only one metric pattern. Attempting to animate their verse, poets often shift from one foot to another, thereby simulating the rhythms of speech. Rhythmic shifts also permit poets to pause, add asides, express emotions, speed up, slow down—in other words, give verse a human voice. Poets sometimes interweave a second rhythm, just as a musician may add counterpoint to a melody. If the poetic rhythms are too complex, however, or if they change too rapidly, the poem may end up sounding more like prose than poetry. In any case, don't frustrate yourself while scanning poems. Scansion is far from a precise science.

Caesura and enjambment. Some lines of poetry call for internal pauses, called *caesura,* that are usually indicated by a period, a semicolon, a dash, or other mark of punctuation. Such pauses mimic human speech, as in the first and third lines of this excerpt from James Stephens's "What Thomas An Buile Said in a Pub":

> I saw God. Do you doubt it?
> Do you dare to doubt it?
> I saw the Almighty Man. His hand
> *Line* Was resting on a mountain, and
> *(5)* He looked upon the World and all about it:
> I saw Him plainer than you see me now,
>   You mustn't doubt it.

Punctuation at the end of lines 1, 2, 5, and 6 also cues the reader to pause briefly before going on. Lines containing these so-called *end-stops* contrast with *enjambed* lines (3 and 4). *Enjambment,* often called *run-on,* is indicated by an absence of punctuation and eliminates the need to pause. Sentence structure most often determines enjambment, but a poet may deliberately use it to let words tumble uncontrollably perhaps to suggest the speaker's emotional state.

Still other effects can be achieved by changing the lengths of various lines. In *Dr. Faustus,* for example, Christopher Marlowe breaks up lines 3, 4, 5, and 6 with caesura and varies the accents to evoke the speaker's intense passion for the beauteous Helen of Troy:

> Was this the face that launched a thousand ships,
> And burnt the topless towers of Ilium? —
> Sweet Helen, make me immortal with a kiss, —
> *Line* Her lips suck forth my soul; see, where it flies!
> *(5)* Come, Helen, come, give me my soul again.
> Here will I dwell, for heaven is in these lips,
> And all is dross that is not Helena.

Free verse. As the name suggests, free verse ignores conventions of meter and rhythm. Poems in free verse may derive their effects from subtle variations of cadence, irregular length of line, and recurring imagery. Sound patterns such as alliteration, assonance, internal rhyme, and even a scattering of end-rhymes may also compensate for the absence of regular meter.

The following excerpt from Amy Lowell's "Lilacs" uses line breaks as a means to create rhetorical effect:

> Lilacs,
> False blue,
> White,
> Purple,
> Color of lilac,
> Your great puffs of flowers
> Are everywhere in this my New England.

Almost every line is an image that comes to a dead stop. Each stands more or less alone and receives equivalent emphasis.

Blank verse. Unlike free verse, blank verse, or unrhymed verse, incorporates conventional meter. It is often associated with the verse patterns in most of Shakespeare's plays and in Milton's *Paradise Lost,* a sample of which follows:

> The sun was sunk, and after him the star
> Of Hesperus, whose office is to bring
> Twilight upon the Earth, short arbiter
> *Line*   'Twixt day and night, and now from end to end
> *(5)*   Night's hemisphere had veiled the horizon round,
> When Satan, who late fled before the threats
> Of Gabriel out of Eden, now improved
> In meditated fraud and malice, bent
> On man's destruction, maugre, what might hap
> *(10)*   Of heavier on himself, fearless returned.

Notice that even without rhyme, Milton controls the texture of the verse with meter (iambic pentameter) and with alliteration (lines 1, 9–10), personification (2–3), and allusion (2, 6, 7). Perhaps you can detect additional poetic devices.

Stanzas. Foremost among structural patterns in poetry is the *stanza,* grouped lines of verse that serve as a poem's building blocks. Ordinarily, the structure of the first stanza sets the pattern for those that follow. If it consists of four lines, five feet per line, and a particular rhyme scheme, those qualities, perhaps with minor variations, will usually be repeated.

Variations between stanzas often enlarge a poem's meaning, but word-for-word repetition may have the same effect. Stanzas are described by the number of lines they contain: *couplet* (two lines), *tercet*—also called *terza rima* (three), *quatrain, cinquain, sestet,* and so on. In many poems, stanzas end with a *refrain* of lines or phrases, a pattern probably left over from the days when poetry was sung. Refrains, while often decorative, can also unify a poem or reiterate the poem's main theme.

The Language of Poetry

Diction—the poet's choice of words—is the living force of poetry. The words of a good poem carry meaning on both a literal and an abstract level. Literal meaning is what people agree a word stands for. Take, for instance, the everyday word *square*, the name of a four-sided polygon with 90-degree corners and equal sides. *Square* also stands for an open space in the middle of town, a kind of dance, a roofer's unit of measurement, and much more. A good dictionary may contain a dozen or more definitions, or denotative meanings, of the word. But all the definitions become useless when *square* is used as an adjective describing a person. Suddenly, *square* becomes an abstraction, connoting a respectable, law-abiding, tradition-bound personality. It may also evoke images of a stick-in-the-mud, old-fashioned, totally un-cool, nerdy individual—perhaps someone like you back in third grade. In short, *square*, along with countless other words, teems with meaning and when used in a poem may carry a good deal of weight. Not only does the poet's choice of words provide clues to the values, attitude, personality, and intent of the speaker, it may also reveal the speaker's background, education, time of life, gender, and more. On an elemental level, then, in diction lies the essence of poetry.

Think of a poem as you would a painting. Even the most realistic painting doesn't recreate or record reality. By selecting colors, devising shape, creating a composition, and applying paint in various ways, an artist interprets the subject, thereby expanding its meaning. Likewise, poets amplify the meaning of their works by choosing words that can be understood both on and below the surface.

In this poem by Emily Dickinson, observe how diction amplifies meaning far beyond its literal level:

THERE IS NO FRIGATE LIKE A BOOK

> There is no frigate like a book
> To take us lands away,
> Nor any coursers like a page
> Of prancing poetry.
> This traverse may the poorest take
> Without oppress of toll;
> How frugal is the chariot
> That bears the human soul.

(c.1875–80)

On the literal level, Dickinson compares reading books to traveling—hardly a unique idea. Her choice of conveyances, however, endows the poem with power. Instead of settling for ships and horses and coaches, the common forms of transportation in her day, she uses "frigate" and "coursers" and "chariot," words that conjure up images of romance and adventure, the very things readers often find in books.

But the poem contains still deeper dimensions. Notice the diction in the last four lines: "poorest," "oppress of toll," "frugal"—all money-related words meant to suggest the pecuniary benefits of vicarious travel. Finally, the speaker's reference to the "human soul" takes the poem to still another level of meaning. Although books are cheap, they not only excite and broaden our vision, they possess enough power to alter our very nature.

"There Is No Frigate Like a Book" reaches far greater depths than you might have guessed after one reading. The fact is that ambiguities keep most poems from revealing all they have to give during an initial encounter. By reading the same poems over and over, however, you create opportunities to mine profound and rewarding treasures lurking below the surface.

It is often said that poetry is written in a double language. One language turns on the intellect; the other fires up emotions and the imagination. Driven by the power of suggestion and the allure of ambiguity, poetry speaks in two tongues, evinced by its ample use of figurative language.

Figurative Language

When the poet writes, "The road is a ribbon of moonlight," he is neither telling the truth nor lying. Rather, he is making a comparison that gives the reader an artistic representation of the truth.

Comparisons, in fact, serve as the foundation of several figures of speech, or *tropes,* as they are sometimes called, especially the metaphor, the simile, and the symbol.

Metaphors and similes. Foremost among figures of speech are the metaphor and the simile, each an effective means to describe one thing in terms of another. It may seem asinine to say one thing when you mean another, but metaphors and similes are meant to communicate complex ideas in understandable, concrete terms. Besides, they often pump life into notions that might otherwise be a bore.

In such metaphors as "the lake was a quicksilver mirror," and "the girl wafted into the room," resemblances between disparate things are implied (lake/mirror, girl/airborne object). A simile makes the comparison more explicit by using *like* or *as:* "the lake was *like* a quicksilver mirror;" "the girl wafted into the room *like* a feather." Because similes merely join two disparate ideas or images, they are generally less fertile than metaphors, which can evoke additional and fresh shades of meaning.

Most simple metaphors and similes are easily understood. It's no stretch to imagine what Robert Burns had in mind when he compared his love to "a red, red rose." Why Robert Frost chose to compare drops of snowmelt in the sun to "silver lizards" is equally apparent. But metaphors that invite several interpretations require more effort. "He has wild stag's feet" suggests speed and grace, but also daring and the spirit of adventure. Shakespeare's "All the world's a stage" conjures up any number of possible implications, among them man's pretentiousness and the unreality of the world. In "The Love Song of J. Alfred Prufrock," T. S. Eliot writes "When the evening is spread out against the sky/ Like a patient etherized upon a table." The comparison may be striking but its meaning hardly jumps off the page. Once you read further into the poem, however, the simile not only makes sense but opens a window to the speaker's soul.

On the AP exam you may well find yourself dealing with a slew of metaphors and similes in both the multiple-choice section and the essay. You'll not only be asked to recognize such figures of speech but to interpret or explain their meaning. In the essay, in particular, you may wish to discuss why a poet included a particular simile or how a metaphor serves as an organic element in the poem. You may wish to comment on how a certain trope contributes to the poem's structure, or to its theme or tone. Keep in mind that simply identifying a metaphor or simile usually won't be enough. What matters is your ability to analyze and explain its function.

Some poems contain an array of similes and metaphors. On occasion, a single metaphor is developed at length—hence, the name *extended metaphor*. Sustaining a metaphor gives the poet an opportunity to dig deeply into apt and meaningful resemblances between literal and figurative meanings, as illustrated in "Uphill," Christina Rossetti's poem in which the speaker uses a "day's journey" as a metaphor for approaching death.

> Does the road wind uphill all the way?
> Yes, to the very end.
> Will the day's journey take the whole long day?
> *Line* From morn to night my friend.
>
> *(5)* But is there for the night a resting place?
> A roof for when the slow dark hours begin.
> May not the darkness hide it from my face?
> You cannot miss that inn.
>
> Shall I meet other wayfarers at night?
> *(10)* Those who have gone before.
> Then must I knock, or call when just in sight?
> They will not keep you standing at that door.
>
> Shall I find comfort, travel-sore and weak?
> Of labour you shall find the sum.
> *(15)* Will there be beds for me and all who seek?
> Yea, beds for all who come.

(1858)

The questioner in the poem seeks to learn what lies ahead in her journey. Her respondent assures her that she needn't worry. All will be well, for many others have gone before (line 10). No one who shows up at death's door will be turned away (line 12), and "beds"—i.e., graves—are plentiful (lines 15–16). Although the traveler seems to fret about the journey itself, her anxiety implies more profound misgivings, perhaps apprehension about the slumber that precedes salvation and entry into Heaven.

While preparing for the AP exam, you might look up other poems using extended metaphors, among them "Because I Could Not Stop for Death" by Emily Dickinson and "A Hillside Thaw" by Robert Frost. Notice that a sustained comparison works best when it is appropriate to the subject matter of the poem and to the poet's tone. A metaphor must also seem natural and unforced, as though the comparison it makes were virtually inevitable.

Because metaphors and similes are widely used not only in poetry but in prose and in everyday speech, any number of them have lost their original freshness and have become clichés. In addition, metaphors roll off tongues so readily and mindlessly that *mixed metaphors,* that is, usages that leap to two or more illogical, inconsistent, often grotesque resemblances, have become bred in the bones of the common herd. Now, that's a pretty kettle of fish—if you'll pardon the expression.

Sensitive to the pervasiveness of trite metaphors in love poetry, Shakespeare wrote "My Mistress' Eyes Are Nothing Like the Sun," a sonnet that parodies the emptiness of conventional declarations of love. As you read it, underline all the speaker's allusions to hackneyed poetic usage.

> My mistress' eyes are nothing like the sun;
> Coral is far more read than her lips' red:
> If snow be white, why then her breasts are dun;[1]
> If hairs be wires, black wires grow on her head.
> I have seen roses damasked,[2] red and white,
> But no such roses see I in her cheeks;
> And in some perfumes is there more delight
> Than in the breath that from my mistress reeks.
> I love to hear her speak, yet well I know
> That music hath a far more pleasing sound:
> I grant I never saw a goddess go,—
> My mistress, when she walks, treads on the ground.
>   And yet, by heaven, I think my love as rare
>   As any she belied with false compare.

---

[1]brownish-gray
[2]of different colors

Symbol. A symbol is a figure of speech that communicates a second meaning along with its literal meaning. To put it another way, a symbol represents itself as well as something other than itself. Take, for example an ordinary roadside marker. Literally it is a piece of sheet metal mounted on a pole. But it also stands as a warning to drivers to slow down for the slippery pavement or the curve ahead.

A traffic sign, because it conveys a single meaning, is one of the simpler symbols. But others, like the American flag, can stimulate all kinds of responses, some alike, some contradictory. To many Americans, the flag symbolizes a country that stretches from sea to shining sea, one nation indivisible . . . and all that. But even to the most ardent patriot, the flag may also evoke dismay over some harmful or destructive governmental policy or practice. And to an anti-American, the Stars and Stripes can symbolize everything evil in the world. In short, some symbols acquire a multitude of meanings, some widely shared, others idiosyncratic, some contradictory, some conflicted, some ambivalent. In effect, a symbol, like a rock dropped into a pond, may send ripples in all directions.

At the beginning of a poem a symbol that seems simple may by the end brim with meaning. Consider the albatross in Coleridge's "Rime of the Ancient Mariner" as a case in point. A mere bird, the albatross symbolizes nature at the start. As the narrative develops, it acquires additional meanings: torment, guilt, terror, the abandonment of humane values, and the Mariner's fall from grace. The slaying of the albatross is a symbolic event that gradually transforms Coleridge's literary ballad about an ocean voyage into a soul's journey through a purgatory of horrors. No wonder that in everyday parlance *albatross* has been given a bad rap and has become synonymous with an unwanted burden or a pain in the neck.

On the AP test, you won't go symbol-hunting for its own sake. Instead, you should be prepared to determine how symbols contribute to a poem's meaning and effect. Start with the assumption that poets have reasons for including symbols in their work. The more integrated the symbol, the better, especially if it is bound tightly to the poem's main theme.

A powerful symbol stands at the heart of the William Blake poem "The Sick Rose." Without it, in fact, there would be no poem at all.

THE SICK ROSE

O Rose, thou art sick!
The invisible worm
That flies in the night,
In the howling storm,

Has found out thy bed
Of crimson joy,
And his dark secret love
Does thy life destroy.

(1794)

For over two centuries this poem has baffled readers lacking a sense of symbolism. Once the rose is identified as a symbol of love, however, the poem opens wide. In poetry, as well as in song and fiction, a rose has long stood as a symbol for love and passion. Reading the poem, you must ask what force (here called an "invisible worm") flies in the night and can sicken, and ultimately destroy, love? (*Worm* is an apt choice, isn't it, since a worm can sap the life out of a rose.) But what unseen, intangible power can drain the life out of love? Boredom? Maybe. Complacency? Perhaps. Jealousy? Aha, that must be it. Jealousy (a "dark secret love") has stealthily crept into the rose's bed and snatched away the love residing there.

In "Sea-Shell Murmurs" by Eugene Lee-Hamilton (1845–1907) the sounds of the ocean that we pretend to hear echoing in seashells become symbolic of another common self-deception, the expectation of a life after death:

The hollow sea-shell which for years hath stood
On dusty shelves, when held against the ear
Proclaims its stormy parent; and we hear
The faint far murmur of the breaking flood.

We hear the sea. The sea? It is the blood
In our own veins, impetuous and near,
And pulses keeping pace with hope and fear
And with our feelings' every shifting mood.

Lo, in my heart I hear, as in a shell,
The murmur of a world beyond the grave
Distinct, distinct, though faint and far it be.

Thou fool; this echo is a cheat as well,—
The hum of earthly instincts; and we crave
A world unreal as the shell-heard sea.

(c. 1890)

Image. Images are words and phrases that refer to something that can be seen, heard, tasted, smelled, or touched. In other words, an image is a figure of speech evocative of the senses. From John Masefield's "The West Wind" comes the following stanza invoking at least three of the five senses:

> It's a warm wind, the west wind, full of birds' cries;
> I never hear the west wind but tears are in my eyes.
> For it comes from the west lands, the old brown hills,
> And April's in the west wind, and daffodils.

In Louise Bogan's "Putting to Sea," an image-filled stanza reads this way:

> Motion beneath us, fixity above.
> O, but you should rejoice! The course we steer
> Points to a beach bright to the rocks with love,
> Where, in hot calms, blades clatter on the ear;

Imagery often helps to establish the tone and meaning of a poem. Because images are usually quite literal and concrete, regardless of their connotative values, they differ markedly from symbols.

Personification. First cousin to metaphor, personification occurs when the poet assigns human characteristics to a nonhuman object or to an abstraction such as love, death, envy, victory, and so on.

In "Rime of the Ancient Mariner," Coleridge personifies the sun:

> The sun came up upon the left,
> Out of the sea came he!

Emily Dickinson not only endows insects with human personalities but gives them the ability to read and write:

> Bee, I'm expecting you!
> Was saying yesterday
> To somebody you know
> That you were due.
>
> The frogs got home last week,
> Are settled and at work,
> Birds mostly back,
> The clover warm and thick.
>
> You'll get my letter by
> The seventeenth; reply,
> Or better, be with me.
> Yours,
>   Fly.

Shakespeare personifies confusion when he has Macbeth say: "Confusion now hath made his masterpiece." And the speaker in e. e. cummings' "Gee I Like to Think of Dead" endows several objects with human characteristics:

> every
> old thing falls in rosebugs and jacknives and kittens and
> pennies they all sit there looking at each other having the
> fastest time because they've never met before

Poets' fondness for personification derives from the human tendency to ascribe human qualities to nonhuman objects. We project our emotions onto pets and other animals, we refer to cars and boats as "she," and assign human names to hurricanes. Through personification we breathe life into what might otherwise be lifeless and bestow on nonhuman objects a personality, willpower, the ability to think and feel and act in every way like a human being. While stimulating our imaginations, personification can also surprise us with insights.

Metonymy. A headline writer who says "White House Plans New Tax Cuts" uses metonymy, a figure of speech that substitutes a word or phrase that relates to a thing for the thing itself. In other words, the phrase" White House" stands not for the mansion on Pennsylvania Avenue but for its current occupants. The writer used one name with the intention that another be understood.

Shakespeare did it too: In saying "The crown will find an heir" he substituted "crown" for "king." In Houseman's "Is My Team Ploughing?" the speaker says "leather" when he means "a football":

> Is football playing
>   Along the river shore,
> With lads to chase the leather,
>   Now I stand up no more?

Although metonymy resembles metaphor, it implies both a literal meaning and something else. But unlike metaphor, it narrows rather than expands meaning. Yet, an aptly conceived metonymy is a treat. With a single word or phrase, the poet opens readers' eyes and stimulates their imagination.

Synechdoche. Synechdoche resembles metonymy so closely that differentiating them is akin to splitting hairs. Although you probably won't be asked to distinguish between them on the AP exam, keep in mind that a synechdoche substitutes a part for a whole. When a man is called a "suit" or a woman a "skirt," that's synechdoche. So is the word "summers" in "She was a lass of twenty summers," since the summer is part of a year. William Cowper uses synechdoche by substituting "wave" for "sea" in these lines:

> Toll for the brave!
>   The brave that are no more,
> All sunk beneath the wave . . .

In *Henry VI,* Shakespeare wrote "neck" as a synechdoche for "person," a particularly apt usage considering his subsequent reference to "yoke":

> Yield not thy neck
> To fortune's yoke, but let thy dauntless mind
> Still ride in triumph over all mischance.

Effective use of synechdoche can add a delightful and surprising aesthetic dimension to a poem.

Allusion. An allusion is a historical, literary, or cultural reference to a person, a place, or event. A well-chosen allusion can be enormously suggestive and richly symbolic, but only if the reader understands it. An allusion to Waterloo will be lost on someone clueless about Napoleon. On the other hand, an informed reader will make the connection between Waterloo and the notion of ultimate defeat and downfall. Because allusions can be drawn from anywhere, readiness to recognize them depends on familiarity with history, literature, the arts, and one's general fund of knowledge.

On the AP exam, instead of simply recognizing the source of an allusion, it may be more important for you to grasp its intent. For example, the title of Robert Frost's poem *"Out, Out—"* alludes to bitter words ("Out, out, brief candle, etc.") spoken by Macbeth following the untimely death of his wife. The poem's title prepares you for its subject matter: the death of a small boy. More importantly, though, Macbeth's words resonate through the poem's themes: the uncertainty of life, the waste of human potential, and the tragedy of a life suddenly snuffed out.

In *Doctor Faustus,* Christopher Marlowe asks:

> Was this the face that launched a thousand ships.
> And burnt the topless towers of Ilium?

This allusion contains a wealth of suggestiveness to one who knows the story of Helen and the fall of Troy. In a few words, Marlowe conveys the passion implicit in the tale of a woman whose beauty almost led to the destruction of a civilization.

Allegory. An allegory is a story or vignette that, like a metaphor, has both a literal and a figurative meaning. Many allegories use concrete images or characters to represent abstract ideas. To keep readers from missing the point, characters may actually bear the names of the ideas they stand for. For example, Good Deeds, Knowledge, Beauty, and Discretion are names in the *Dramatis Personae* of *Everyman,* a sixteenth-century allegorical play in verse by Anonymous. Other famous allegories include Spencer's "The Faerie Queen" and Tennyson's "Idylls of the King."

Oxymoron. An oxymoron is a phrase that seems self-contradictory or incompatible with reality: *eloquent silence, jumbo shrimp, free gift.* While oxymorons may be used just for fun, they are more frequently employed to suggest ambiguity or to develop a theme.

Paradox. A paradox is an apparently self-contradictory statement that under scrutiny makes perfect sense. It has the same effect as an oxymoron. Note the paradoxical quality of Hamlet's statement, "I must be cruel only to be kind," or Wallace Stevens's assertions in "Thirteen Ways of Looking at a Blackbird":

> It was evening all afternoon.
> It was snowing
> And it was going to snow.

Paradoxically, oxymorons and paradoxes contain both absurdity and truth at the same time. They invite the reader of a poem to cast aside conventional responses in favor of more whimsical interpretations. Should you find an oxymoron or paradox in a poem on the AP exam, start looking for the presence of subtexts and implied meanings.

Understatement. Understatement is a principal source of power in poetry. Think of Richard Cory, the eponymous character of Edwin Arlington Robinson's famous poem. Because no reason is given to explain why Cory put a bullet through his head, we are left to imagine the demons that drove him to it. Robinson, letting the action speak for itself, evidently understood the impact of understatement.

Another form of understatement is saying less than one means or using restraint in ironic contrast to what might be said. The speaker in "The Sum" by Paul Lawrence Dunbar, for example, attempts to capture several of life's momentous events in a brief phrase or two:

> A little dreaming by the way,
> A little toiling day by day;
> A little pain, a little strife
> A little joy,—and that is life.
>
> A little short-lived summer's morn,
> When joy seems all so newly born,
> When one day's sky is blue above,
> And one bird sings—and that is love.
>
> A little sickening of the years,
> The tribute of a few hot tears
> Two folded hands, and failing breath,
> And peace at last,—and that is death.
>
> Just dreaming, loving, dying so,
> The actors in the drama go—
> A flitting picture on a wall,
> Love, Death, the themes; but is that all?

One might argue that Dunbar's poem, with its singsongy rhythm and rhymes, trivializes life, but that may be just the point. Implying that we tend to exaggerate the gravity of everyday human experiences, the speaker aims to take a larger view—to be more circumspect. Yet, in the last line, he questions his own judgment, or at least allows that he could be understating the significance of life's defining themes.

Litotes. A teacher responding to your English essay by commenting "Not at all bad" is using litotes, a form of understatement in which a positive fact is stated by denying a negative one. You might retort with another litotes: "You are not a bad teacher."

In the funeral oration of *Julius Caesar,* Marc Antony uses litotes in "Not that I loved Caesar less . . ." The effect is to draw a sharp contrast with the second half of the statement, "but that I loved Rome more."

Writing about his birthday in "Anniversary," poet John Wain writes:

> As a little scarlet howling mammal,
> Crumpled and unformed, I depended entirely on someone
> Not very different from what I am to-day.

In the third line, the speaker makes the point that someone—presumably his mother—was much the same as he is today, but the sentiment, more emphatically expressed via litotes, is stated as a denial of its opposite.

Hyperbole or overstatement. Hyperbole is an exaggeration, a useful device for poets to intensify emotions, values, physical features, the weather, or virtually anything. W. H. Auden's "As I Walked Out One Evening," includes this hyperbolic declaration of love:

> I'll love you, dear, I'll love you
> Till China and Africa meet,
> And the river jumps over the mountain
> And the salmon sing in the street.

Macbeth, having murdered Duncan, uses hyperbole to express the horror he feels:

> Will all great Neptune's ocean wash this blood
> Clean from my hand? No. This my hand will rather
> The multitudinous seas incarnadine,
> Making the green one red.

Here's a piece of a folk ballad about a warrior. After being wounded in battle, the hero turns to his troops, and says hyperbolically:

> . . . "Fight on, my merry men all,
> And see that none of you be taine;
> For I will lie down and bleed awhile,
> And then I will rise and fight again."

Tone

Tone is the poet's or speaker's attitude toward the subject of the poem, toward the reader, or toward himself. Because tone derives from the sum total of the emotional and intellectual effects of a poem, comprehending the tone is tantamount to comprehending the whole thing. Tone carries so much weight in poetry explication, in fact, that it's virtually impossible to take the AP exam without having to deal with it, either in the multiple-choice questions or as a topic to discuss in an essay.

A single tone prevails in most poems, but a poet can't be stopped from changing his mind or altering the thrust of a poem in midstream. Therefore, the tone of many poems is multidimensional. This is as it should be. After all, feelings consist of an amalgam of impulses and reactions, sometimes ambivalent or contradictory.

What follows is an assortment of adjectives that might be used to describe the tone of various poems. No doubt you could expand the list many times over and perhaps cite examples from the repertoire of poems that you know well.

> brash, jovial, dour, playful, intimate, earnest, whimsical, grave, comic, urbane, fanciful, affected, rhapsodic, resigned, devotional, eulogistic, intemperate, fervent, elegaic, tender, sardonic, cynical, nostalgic, indignant, flippant, meditative, didactic, bitter, wry, sentimental, patronizing, extravagant

Because you can't hear the actual voice of the speaker in a poem, your interpretation of tone is a matter of decoding the evidence offered by the poem itself. Sometimes tone is most easily ascertained through figures of speech, at other times through rhymes and rhythms. Then, too, diction and word sounds may help you identify the tone of a poem. Unfortunately, there is no universal formula on which to rely. Because it takes the interaction of several ingredients, from imagery to structure, to create the tone of a poem, a thorough analysis works best to nail it down.

Using the following poem by Robert Browning, try your hand in determining tone:

MEETING AT NIGHT

> The grey sea and the long black land;
> And the yellow half-moon large and low;
> And the startled little waves that leap
> In fiery ringlets from their sleep,
> As I gain the cove with a pushing prow,
> And quench its speed i' the slushy sand.
>
> Then a mile of warm sea-scented beach;
> Three fields to cross till a farm appears;
> A tap at the pane, the quick sharp scratch
> And blue spurt of a lighted match,
> And a voice less loud, through its joys and fears,
> Than the two hearts beating each to each!

Line

(5)

(10)

Before deciding on the tone of "Meeting at Night," consider what happens in the poem: Night has fallen. The speaker, seemingly a romantic youth, is rushing to a tryst with his ladylove. The route, first on the water, then across the land, is long. Arriving outside her window, he taps on the glass, then enters her room where the lovers fall into an embrace.

Using a series of sensual images, the poet tracks the young man's progress toward his destination and conveys his growing eagerness to get there. Early images ("grey sea and the long black land") reflect the state of the young man's humor as he starts out. Soon, in accord with his improving mood, the images brighten: "yellow half-moon," "fiery ringlets." Finally, a "blue spurt of a lighted match" marks the climactic meeting of the two lovers.

The first stanza, in which the young man rows slowly to a distant beach, consists almost entirely of watery images. Just like the "startled little waves" awakening from their sleep, the young man's hormonal juices begin to flow. As his anticipation grows, the journey, as well as the poem, speeds up. In two lines (7 and 8) he races across a mile-wide beach and traverses three fields. In rapid sequence, a tap on the window and a burst of light bring the journey to a swift end. Abruptly, all motion ceases. Movement gives way to the two lovers' pounding hearts, the repetition of "each" vaguely simulating the sound of their heartbeats.

Diction throughout the poem underscores the speaker's fervor. The repeated use of "and" at the beginning of lines 2, 3, 6, 10, and 11 resounds with breathlessness. In lines 7 and 8 the words flow one into the other. Only in line 9 is there a caesura that briefly slows down the verbal deluge and prepares the reader for the young man's arrival in his lover's arms.

If the tone of "Meeting at Night" were to be reduced to a single word, *breathless* is a worthy choice. Throughout his journey, the speaker is portrayed as someone beside himself with love, and panting with fervor to reach his lover's arms.

From a speaker consumed by love, let's turn to one who sees the world from an entirely different perspective. Read Arthur Hugh Clough's "The Latest Decalogue."

THE LATEST DECALOGUE[1]

Thou shalt have one God only; who
Would be at the expense of two?
No graven images may be
Line   Worshipped, except the currency.
(5)   Swear not at all; for, for thy curse
Thine enemy is none the worse.
At church on Sunday to attend
Will serve to keep the world thy friend.
Honour thy parents; that is, all
(10)   From whom advancement may befall.
Thou shalt not kill; but need'st not strive
Officiously to keep alive.
Do not adultery commit;
Advantage rarely comes of it:
(15)   Thou shalt not steal; an empty feat,
When it's so lucrative to cheat.
Bear not false witness; let the lie
Have time on its own wings to fly.
Thou shalt not covet, but tradition
(20)   Approves all forms of competition.

(1862)

---
[1]The Ten Commandments

The speaker in this poem decries the morality of his time. He might simply have written a straightforward verse reproaching man's indifference to biblical teachings, but chose instead to express his disapproval through irony.

Even the title is ironic because the Ten Commandments are supposed to be a permanent, binding set of rules. To call them the "latest" suggests that modern men, while paying lip service to the word of God, adapt the rules for their convenience.

The poem devotes two lines, or two rhyming couplets, to each of the ten commandments ("Thou shalt not kill," "Thou shalt not steal," etc.). Each edict is undercut by a remark meant to show why the principle conflicts with the interests and values of contemporary society. In lines 19–20 ("Thou shalt not covet, but tradition/Approves all forms of competition") the speaker cynically declares that society's business has made quaint and obsolete what once was a guiding principle of moral behavior. Man's pursuit of money has forced each commandment to be cast aside or amended. Materialism is man's new religion. By implication, man worships Mammon (the god of money) instead of God, and the speaker doesn't like it.

Irony comes in many forms, from a chem teacher's sarcastic "Good work!" on a quiz you've flunked to an ironic twist of fate, such as the urban legend of the man who missed an airplane that crashed shortly after takeoff, but was killed on the highway during his drive home from the airport. A poet making use of irony is free to use any form, of course, but verbal irony is what poets seem to favor.

Basically verbal irony is an implicit contrast between what exists and what might be. Users of irony don't expect their words to be taken at face value. Rather, they hope that a reader will see the reality behind their pose. On the surface a poem may sound grave, but in actuality, the speaker may be poking fun at, say, a particular human foible or frailty. While lampooning hypocrisy, for example, the speaker may sound objective and emotionally uninvolved, but intense concern may underlie his posture. He may, in fact, feel so passionate or distraught about his topic that he cannot face it head on. He'd prefer to express his views indirectly, via irony, and thereby heighten the impact on the reader.

Poetic Styles and Forms

Below you will find a compilation of poetic terms that you should know for the AP exam. Although you won't be asked specifically to identify a sonnet or a villanelle or a dramatic monologue, knowing the basic characteristics of these and other poetic forms could give you a leg up in answering multiple-choice questions. As for writing an essay on poetry, a familiarity with basic terminology can give you a head start and as a bonus save you considerable time—time that could be spent polishing your essay instead of painstakingly describing a form that can be identified with a single word or phrase.

Narrative poem. True to its name, a narrative poem is a story. It adheres to no prescribed form, and while it may contain lyrical and descriptive passages, its primary purpose is to tell a tale. Epics such as *Gilgamesh, The Odyssey,* and *Sir Gawain and the Green Knight* are narrative poems, each about a heroic adventurer. While some narrative poems are book-length epics, others may be just a few lines, such as this one by Herman Melville:

THE FIGURE HEAD

The *Charles-and-Emma* seaward sped.
(Named from the carven pair at prow)
He so smart, and a curly head,
She tricked forth as a bride knows how:
  Pretty stem for the port, I trow!

But iron-rust and alum-spray
And chafing gear, and sun and dew
Vexed this lad and lassie gay,
Tears in their eyes, salt tears nor few;
  And the hug relaxed with the failing glue.

But came in end a dismal night,
With creaking beams and ribs that groan,
A black lee-shore and waters white:
Dropped on the reef, the pair lie prone:
  O, the breakers dance, but the winds they moan!

(1888)

In three brief stanzas the speaker relates the story of the *Charles-and-Emma,* a sailing ship with a striking wood carving—an attractive bride and groom clinging to each other—at its prow. In time, the figures deteriorate, the glue that binds them dissolves, and the ship is wrecked. The pair ends up on a reef battered by water and wind. The tale is simple, but its subtext suggests the inevitable erosion of youth, love, and life.

Lyric poem. Ballads, sonnets, elegies, odes, villanelles—these and many other poetic forms are lyric. In fact, any poem that is neither dramatic nor narrative is lyric. Lyric poems express an individual's thoughts and emotions. They can be mystical, didactic, satirical, reflective, mournful; indeed, the possibilities are endless.

What follows is a brief Robert Herrick lyric that may at first seem like a public-service message about fire but is actually an emotion-laden statement by a speaker in some serious amatory trouble:

THE SCARE-FIRE[1]

Water, water I desire,
Here's a house of flesh on fire;
Ope' the fountains and the springs,
And come all to bucketings.
What ye cannot quench, pull down,
Spoil a house to save a town:
Better 'tis that one should fall,
Than by one to hazard all.

(1648)

----

[1]A sudden conflagration

Another lyric poem, this one by Marianne Moore, conveys the speaker's feelings about the subject of this chapter. Once you've read it, please return to the poem's first four words and ask yourself whether Moore meant them to be taken seriously.

POETRY

I, too, dislike it: there are things that are important beyond all this fiddle.
Reading it, however, with a perfect contempt for it, one discovers in
it after all, a place for the genuine.

Line   Hands that can grasp, eyes
(5)   that can dilate, hair that can rise
if it must, these things are important not because a

high-sounding interpretation can be put upon them but because they are
useful. When they become so derivative as to become unintelligible,
the same thing may be said for all of us, that we
(10)   do not admire what
we cannot understand: the bat
holding on upside down or in quest of something to

eat, elephants pushing, a wild horse taking a roll, a tireless wolf under
a tree, the immovable critic twitching his skin like a horse that feels
a flea, the base—
(15)   ball fan, the statistician—
nor is it valid
to discriminate against "business documents and

school books"[1]; all these phenomena are important. One must make a
distinction
however: when dragged into prominence by half poets, the result is
not poetry,
(20)   nor till the poets among us can be
"literalists of
the imagination"[2]—above
insolence and triviality and can present

for inspection, "imaginary gardens with real toads in them," shall we have
(25)   it. In the meantime, if you demand on the one hand,
the raw material of poetry in
all its rawness and
that which is on the other hand
genuine, you are interested in poetry.

(1921)

----

[1]Poet's note from Tolstoy's journal: "Where the boundary between prose
and poetry lies, I shall never be able to understand. . . . Poetry is verse:
prose is not verse. Or else poetry is everything with the exception of
business documents and school books."
[2]Yeats said of Blake, "He was a too literal realist of the imagination."

The speaker, presumably the poet, doesn't dislike poetry at all. Rather, she takes a dim view of poems that can't be understood. In lines 2–8, she acknowledges that poems can be "useful," but not until line 24 is usefulness defined as a poetic quality that enables readers to see "'imaginary gardens with real toads in them.'"

In writing this lyric about poetry, Moore relies on rather prosaic language. Were the text reformatted as a prose passage, a reader probably couldn't tell it was a poem in mufti. The piece appears to be almost antipoetic not only in its sentiment but in its free verse style. Moore ignores many features of conventional poetry: it has no rhymes, no discernible rhythm, no end-stops. But to avoid formlessness, she divides the poem into stanzas and for no reason other than perhaps to assert her individuality uses nineteen syllables for the first line of each one.

Based on "Poetry," how do you regard Moore as a poet? Is she a "half poet," alluded to in the fourth stanza, or is she one of the "literalists of the imagination" (lines 21–22)?

Metaphysical poetry. The word "metaphysical" describes the lyric poems of certain seventeenth-century men—Donne, Marvell, Herbert, and others—who, like poet-psychologists, were fond of writing highly intellectual and philosophical verses on the nature of thought and feeling. Their work, which also concerns ethics, religion, and love, blends emotion with intellectual ingenuity in a manner that modern readers often find farfetched if not downright obscure. To illustrate, here are two short poems by Richard Crashaw about "Infant Martyrs," an allusion that Crashaw's biblically literate audience would instantly have understood even without benefit of a footnote.

TO THE INFANT MARTYRS[1]

Go, smiling souls, your new-built ages break,
In heaven you'll learn to sing, ere here to speak
Nor let the milky fonts that bathe your thirst
          Be your delay;
The place that calls you hence is, at the worst,
          Milk all the way.

UPON THE INFANT MARTYRS

To see both blended in one flood,
The mothers' milk, the children's blood,
Make me doubt[2] if heaven will gather
Roses hence, or lilies rather.

(1646)

---

[1]The Holy Innocents, the newborns of Bethlehem murdered by Herod in a vain attempt to destroy the one who, according to prophesy, would grow up to be the ruler of Israel.
[2]wonder

Although written separately, the two poems complement each other. The first addresses the dead children with words of solace and comfort. The second laments the children's murder.

Romantic poetry. In everyday usage, romantic poems are love poems, verses that declare poets' feelings for their sweethearts. In literary parlance, however, *romances* are carefully structured metrical poems that originated in medieval France and told stories of chivalrous knights undertaking perilous journeys to rescue damsels in distress.

Romantic poetry, on the other hand, refers to the literary movement that peaked in England during the nineteenth century. Wordsworth, Coleridge, Keats, Shelley, and Byron are often linked as the five luminaries of the romantic period (maybe add Tennyson to make it six), but their differences are no less pronounced than their likenesses. In general, their work constitutes a protest against the classic formalism that had long pervaded poetry. Therefore, their poems tend to focus on inner experience and feelings, including dreams and the subconscious. Their work also deals with cultures of nonclassic lands: with nature, particularly in its wilder moods, with the pleasures of the exotic, with the supernatural, and with Christianity and transcendentalism. Above all, romantic poetry lionizes the individual hero, often a young man consumed by melancholy and ennui or a firebrand rebelling against traditional society. The poetry itself reflects individuality. It breaks with convention and rules in favor of spontaneity and lyricism. Much of it is ponderously dreamy and given to reverie and reflection.

The following excerpt taken from Wordsworth's "Lines Composed a Few Miles Above Tintern Abbey" provides a glimpse of the kinds of moods and subjects that inspired not only Wordsworth but any number of his contemporaries:

> And now, with gleam of half-extinguished thought,
> With many recognitions dim and faint,
> And somewhat of a sad perplexity,
> The picture of the mind revives again:
> While here I stand, not only with the sense
> Of present pleasure, but with pleasing thoughts
> That in this moment there is life and food
> For future years. And so I dare to hope,
> Though changed, no doubt, from what I was when first
> I came among these hills; when like a roe
> I bounded o'er the mountains, by the sides
> Of the deep rivers, and the lonely streams,
> Wherever nature led—more like a man
> Flying from something that he dreads, than one
> Who sought the thing he loved.

The speaker has returned to the country after a long absence and reflects on his now-vanished youthful spirit. Notice his idealization of nature and his trancelike preoccupation with himself.

Ballad. Originally sung, folk ballads tell engrossing stories about life, death, heroism, and, as in "The Twa Corbies," love, murder, and betrayal:

THE TWA CORBIES

As I was walking all alane,[1]	[1]alone
I heard two corbies[2] making a mane;[3]	[2]two ravens; [3]moan
The tane[4] unto t'other say,	[4]one
"Where sall be gang[5] and dine today?"	[5]shall we go
"In behint yon auld fail dyke,[6]	[6]old turf wall
I wot[7] there lies a new-slain knight;	[7]know
And naebody kens[8] that he lies there,	[8]knows
But his hawk, his hound, and his lady fair.	
"His hound is to the hunting gane,	
His hawk to fetch the wild-fowl hame,	
His lady ta'en another mate	
So we may mak our dinner sweet.	
"Ye'll sit on his white hause-bane,[9]	[9]neck bone
And I'll pick out his bonny blue een;[10]	[10]eyes
Wi ae[11] lock o' his gowden hair	[11]With one
We'll theek[12] our nest when it grows bare.	[12]thatch
"Mony a one for him makes mane,	
But nane shall ken where he is gane;	
O'er his white banes when they are bare,	
The wind sall blaw for evermair."	

—Anon

The ravens in this ballad haven't a clue that they are telling us a tale of adultery and murder. They just have their eyes on a tasty meal.

The original authors of folk ballads remain anonymous, but literary ballads have known authors whose work may echo if not imitate the style and character of folk ballads. Coleridge's "Rime of the Ancient Mariner" is an example.

Cinquain. A five-line stanza or a five-line poem is called a cinquain, but *cinquain* is also the name of an idiosyncratic poetic form that is comprised of five lines that, respectively, are two, four, six, eight, and two syllables long.

Couplet. A couplet is made up of two rhymed lines, usually in the same meter, but not always, as illustrated by this two-line, slant-rhymed poem by Ezra Pound:

IN A STATION OF THE METRO

The apparition of these faces in the crowd;
Petals on a wet, black bough.

(1916)

Couplets rarely stand by themselves as complete poems. Rather, they are the building blocks of much longer works.

Heroic couplets, so called from their use in epics or heroic poetry, express a complete thought, with the second line often reinforcing the first. Because of this completeness, the couplet is said to be *closed* or *end-stopped.*

What follows is an excerpt from Alexander Pope's "Rape of the Lock." Belinda, the young heroine of the poem, has just been awakened by her personal maid and is about to have her makeup applied:

> And now, unveiled, the toilet stands displayed,
> Each silver vase in mystic order laid.
> First, robed in white, the nymph intent adores,
> *Line*   With head uncovered, the cosmetic powers.
> *(5)*   A heavenly image in the glass appears;
> To that she bends, to that her eyes she rears.
> The inferior priestess, at her altar's side,
> Trembling begins the sacred rites of pride.
> Unnumbered treasures ope and once, and here
> *(10)*   The various offerings of the world appear.
>
> (1712)

To avoid the monotony of regular rhymes and end-stopped lines, Pope varies his couplets with off-rhymes (lines 3–4) and enjambment (lines 9–10). He also breaks the steady rhythm of iambic pentameter with a short caesura in line 3. If you have been struck by the incongruity between the heroic tone of this excerpt and the triviality of its subject matter, that is just the point. "The Rape of the Lock" is a *mock epic.*

Dramatic monologue. A dramatic monologue is a poem spoken by one person to a listener who may influence the speaker with a look or an action, but says nothing. Although dramatic monologues differ from internal monologues and soliloquies, they can be equally effective in revealing the character of the speaker.

Robert Browning's dramatic monologues serve as models of the genre, including the one that follows:

MY LAST DUCHESS[1]

FERRARA

> That's my last duchess painted on the wall,
> Looking as if she were alive. I call
> That piece a wonder, now; Frà Pandolf's hands
> *Line*   Worked busily a day, and there she stands.
> *(5)*   Will't please you to sit and look at her? I said
> "Frà Pandolf" by design, for never read
> Strangers like you that pictured countenance,
> The depth and passion of its earnest glance,
> But to myself they turned (since none puts you by
> *(10)*   The curtain I have drawn for you, but I)
> And seemed as they would ask me, if they durst,
> How such a glance came there; so, not the first

(15)

Are you to turn and ask thus. Sir, 'twas not
Her husband's presence only, called that spot
Of joy into the Duchess' cheek: perhaps
Frà Pandolf chanced to say "Her mantle laps
Over my lady's wrist too much," or "Paint
Must never hope to reproduce the faint
Half-flush that dies along her throat." Such stuff

(20)

Was courtesy, she thought, and cause enough
For calling up that spot of joy. She had
A heart—how shall I say?—too soon made glad,
Too easily impressed; she liked whate'er
She looked on, and her looks went everywhere.

(25)

Sir, 'twas all one! My favor at her breast,
The dropping of the daylight in the west,
The bough of cherries some officious fool
Broke in the orchard for her, the white mule
She rode with round the terrace—all and each

(30)

Would draw from her alike the approving speech,
Or blush, at least. She thanked men—good! but thanked
Somehow—I know not how—as if she ranked
My gift of a nine-hundred-years-old name
With anybody's gift. Who'd stoop to blame

(35)

This sort of trifling? Even had you skill
In speech—(which I have not)—to make your will
Quite clear to such a one, and say, "Just this
Or that in you disgusts me; here you miss,
Or there exceed the mark"—and if she let

(40)

Herself be lessoned so, nor plainly set
Her wits to yours, forsooth, and made excuse,
—E'en then would be some stooping; and I choose
Never to stoop. Oh, sir, she smiled, no doubt,
Whene'er I passed her; but who passed without

(45)

Much the same smile? This grew; I gave commands;
Then all smiles stopped together. There she stands
As if alive. Will't please you rise? We'll meet
The company below, then. I repeat,
The Count your master's known munificence

(50)

Is ample warrant that no just pretense
Of mine dowry will be disallowed;
Though his fair daughter's self, as I avowed
At starting, is my object. Nay, we'll go
Together down, sir. Notice Neptune, though,

(55)

Which Claus of Innsbruck cast in bronze for me!

(1849)

---

[1]The poem, set in Ferrara during the Renaissance, is meant to reflect values and attitudes of the time. Names do not refer to specific people but to types.

In this monologue the Duke of Ferrara takes pains to favorably impress the envoy of an unnamed count whose daughter he wishes to marry. The duke escorts the gentleman around his villa, pointing out the artwork, dropping names, and bragging about his aristocratic lineage. But mostly he talks about the duchess. Through the duke's account of his late wife, we gain entrance into his mind, discovering that he is a jealous, possessive, and relentless martinet.

The use of heroic couplets in iambic pentameter—used in much heroic or epic poetry in English—attests to both the duke's pretentiousness and overblown self-esteem. Using a consistent rhyme scheme (a-a-b-b, etc.) he flaunts his expertise in language, undermining his self-effacing claim that he lacks skill in speech (lines 34–35). Intent on pumping himself up, the duke unwittingly lays bare his faults and foibles. Several instances of enjambment reveal an inability to reign in his emotions. His effort to flatter the envoy by saying that "none puts you by/The curtain I have drawn for you, but I," (lines 9–10) rings hollow. Although he stops short of explaining precisely how his late wife met her end, he is so convinced of his own rectitude that he recklessly hints that his "commands" (line 45) may have led to her demise. The envoy, seeing through the duke's lies and hypocrisy, attempts to take his leave (lines 53–54). Suspecting that the man will render an unfavorable report to his master, the duke in the last three lines of the poem shows off still more art and drops still another name in one last, desperate effort to win him over.

Elegy. An elegy, sometimes called a *dirge*, is a poem of mourning and meditation, usually about the death of a person but occasionally about other losses, such as lost love, lost strength, lost youth. Considering their subject matter, elegies are typically solemn and dignified.

The following elegy by the American author Ambrose Bierce, laments the death of President Ulysses S. Grant in 1885. Grant had made a name for himself as the victorious commanding general of the Union forces in the Civil War. As an eighteen-year-old, Bierce fought under Grant but left the army embittered, disillusioned, and virulently opposed to war. Twenty years later, however, he paid a prayerful tribute to his fallen leader:

THE DEATH OF GRANT

FATHER! whose hard and cruel law
Is part of thy compassion's plan,
Thy works presumptuously we scan

Line   For what the prophets say they saw.

(5)   Unbidden still, the awful slope
Walling us in, we climb to gain
Assurance of the shining plain
That faith has certified to hope.

In vain: beyond the circling hill
(10)   The shadow and the cloud abide;
Subdue the doubt, our spirits guide
To trust the Record and be still;

To trust it loyally as he
Who, heedful of his high design,
(15)   Ne'er raised a seeking eye to thine,
But wrought thy will unconsciously,

Disputing not of chance or fate,
Not questioning of cause or creed:
For anything but duty's deed
(20) To simply wise, too humbly great.

The cannon syllabled his name;
His shadow shifted o'er the land,
Portentous, as at his command
Successive cities sprang to flame!

(25) He fringed the continent with fire,
The rivers ran in lines of light!
Thy will be done on earth—if right
Or wrong he cared not to inquire.

His was the heavy hand, and his
(30) The service of the despot blade;
His the soft answer that allayed
War's giant animosities.

Let us have peace: our clouded eyes
Fill, Father, with another light,
(35) That we may see with clearer sight
Thy servant's soul in Paradise.

The speaker begins by addressing the Divinity, declaring his faith and trust in Him. Although he is grieved by Grant's death, he won't presume to fathom God's "hard and cruel law." Instead, he prays for the strength to remain faithful, hoping that, in spite of the "shadow and the cloud" that now hang over him, a "shining plain" (presumably a place in heaven) awaits those who subdue their doubt, keep quiet, and trust "the Record" (line 12) of God's ultimate goodness.

Having affirmed his faith, the speaker turns his attention to Grant, who rose above the doubts and concerns that beset ordinary mortals. Unlike the speaker, Grant sought no help from God, for he was blessed with godlike qualities and seemed divinely inspired to carry out God's will "unconsciously" (line 16). Accordingly, Grant, in the name of peace, plunged confidently into violent war ("The cannon syllabled his name;/His shadow shifted o'er the land/. . .He fringed the continent with fire,/The rivers ran in lines of light!"). Ever devoted to his "high design" (line 14), Grant, according to the speaker, never swerved from his duty, never wondered whether he did right or wrong, and by literally sticking to his guns, "allayed/War's giant animosities."

In the last stanza the speaker renews a prayerful attitude, beseeching God—as Grant never could or would—to give the general's soul a place in Paradise.

Limerick. Not considered a serious form of poetry, the limerick is one of the most popular lighter forms. Its simplicity—five lines built on two rhymes with the third and fourth lines shorter than the others—may explain why it is easy to recite and remember. Limericks often surprise readers with a curious rhyme or a pun in the last line, like this one by the ubiquitous Anon:

There was a young fellow named Hall,
Who fell in the spring in the fall;
   'Twould have been a sad thing
   If he'd died in the spring,
But he didn't—he died in the fall.

Ode. An ode, an ancient form of poetic song, is a celebratory poem. Highly lyrical or profoundly philosophical, odes pay homage to whatever the poet may hold dear—another person, a place, an object, an abstract idea.

The *Pindaric ode,* developed by and named after the Greek poet Pindar, has the following structure: The first stanza is called a *strophe,* the second an *antistrophe.* Both are structurally identical. Then comes an *epode,* with a different structure. This pattern—strophe, antistrophe, epode—once established may be repeated any number of times. Since Pindar's day, poets have taken great liberties with the form, writing what are now called *irregular* odes. In fact, none of the most widely read odes in English (Wordsworth's "Intimations of Immortality from Recollections of Early Childhood," and Keats's "Ode on a Grecian Urn" and "Ode to a Nightingale") is Pindaric. All employ an essentially uniform stanza throughout.

The same is true of the following ode by Alexander Pope:

ODE ON SOLITUDE

Happy the man whose wish and care
  A few paternal acres bound,
Content to breathe his native air,
     In his own ground.

Whose herds with milk, whose fields with bread,
  Whose flocks supply him with attire,
Whose trees in summer yield him shade,
     In winter fire.

Blest, who can unconcernedly find
 Hours, days, and years slide soft away,
In health of body, peace of mind
     Quiet by day,

Sound sleep by night; study and ease,
 Together mixed; sweet recreation;
And innocence, which most does please
     With mediation.

Thus let me live, unseen, unknown;
 Thus unlamented let me die;
Steal from the world, and not a stone
     Tell where I lie.

(c. 1709)

Any reader who ever longed to be left alone or wished to step away from the frenetic pace of modern life can appreciate Pope's heartfelt sentiment. The regular and consistent rhymes and rhythm, along with the plain diction and use of mellow sounds give the poem qualities resembling a pastoral or a lullaby.

On the AP exam you certainly won't be asked to recall the structure of a Pindaric ode. Should you be given an ode to read and dissect, however, at least you'll know its origins.

Sonnet. Sonnets come in many guises, but virtually all are fourteen-line lyric poems expressing one main thought or sentiment in iambic pentameter. The subject matter of sonnets ranges from love to politics. Any subject is fair game.

The *Italian sonnet,* developed by Petrarch and sometimes called the Petrarchian sonnet, is divided into two discrete units: an *octave,* consisting of the first eight lines rhymed *a-b-b-a a-b-b-a,* and a *sestet*—the remaining six lines commonly but not always rhymed *c-d-c-d-c-d* or *c-d-e-c-d-e.* The rhyme scheme usually corresponds with the progress of thought in that particular sonnet. In other words, the poet uses the octave to present a problem, question, story, or idea. The sestet resolves, contrasts with, or comments on the contents of the octave. If truth be told, when it comes to sonnets, nothing is truly fixed. Variations abound, especially in the sestet that tends to be more emotionally charged than the octave. The sonnet's malleability may explain why poets have turned to the form over and over as though drawn by an irresistible force.

How closely does the following sonnet by Milton resembles the Italian model?

ON HIS BLINDNESS[1]

When I consider how my light is spent
Ere half my days, in this dark world and wide,
And that one talent which is death to hide
Line   Lodged with me useless, though my soul more bent
(5)   To serve therewith my Maker, and present
My true account, lest he returning chide;
"Doth God exact day-labor, light denied?"
I fondly[2] ask: but Patience to prevent
That murmur, soon replies, "God doth not need
(10)   Either man's work or his own gifts; who best
Bear his mild yoke, they serve him best. His state
Is kingly. Thousands at his bidding speed
And post o'er land and ocean without rest:
They also serve who only stand and wait."

(1652)

---

[1]By 1651, at age 43, Milton had completely lost his sight.
[2]foolishly

Early in Milton's sonnet, the speaker, presumably the poet himself, reflects on his untimely loss of sight. Being unable to see is devastating, but being unable to write is tantamount to death, and because his soul demands that he serve God by using his writing talents, he despairs over being deficient in the eyes of God. (Milton is alluding to the biblical parable of the talents in the book of *Matthew,* in which a servant is cast "into outer darkness" as punishment for burying his one God-given talent.) In an instant of spiritual blindness paralleling his physical blindness, the speaker verges on asking his "Maker" whether as a blind man, he is expected to continue doing God's work. Patience, personified, holds the speaker back, assuring him that those who bear their burdens in silence serve God best. Besides, God has legions to do His bidding. Comforting the speaker still further, Patience affirms that "They also serve who only stand and wait."

"On His Blindness" adheres to the rhyme scheme of the Italian sonnet but ignores the customary break between the octave and sestet. Having already begun a response to the concerns expressed in the opening lines, Milton uses enjambment at the end of line 8. He also deviates from the Italian pattern by embedding a short but independent sentence into the sestet (lines 11–12). Thus, "On His Blindness" borders on the traditional Italian form but doesn't quite make it. Milton's variation, used frequently by other poets, is called as you might expect, the *Miltonian sonnet.*

The structure of the *English,* or *Shakespearean* sonnet differs still more from the Italian form. Instead of an octave and sestet as its basic building blocks, it consists of three quatrains and a climactic couplet with a new rhyme. Its typical rhyme scheme is *a-b-a-b-c-d-d-c-e-f-e-f-g-g,* a pattern that obliges the poet to look for seven different rhyming pairs. Since Shakespeare's time poets have changed and adapted the form to suit themselves. They've shortened or lengthened lines and occasionally scrapped iambic pentameter in favor of some other meter.

The following sonnet by Shakespeare, however, follows to the letter the form that bears his name. Three discrete quatrains end with periods. A concluding couplet clinches the poem's theme. Every line is five feet, or ten syllables long. Each rhyme is exact—no slant rhymes in sight. In other words, Shakespeare plays it straight in this sonnet, shunning deviations that could distract readers from enjoying his intricate word play.

SONNET 138

When my love swears that she is made of truth,
I do believe her, though I know she lies,
That she might think me some untutored youth,
Line   Unlearnéd in the world's false subtleties.
(5)   Thus vainly thinking that she thinks me young,
Although she knows my days are past the best,
Simply I credit her false-speaking tongue:
On both sides thus is simple truth suppressed.
But wherefore says she not she is unjust?
(10)   And wherefore say not I that I am old?
Oh, love's best habit is in seeming trust,
And age in love loves not to have years told.
Therefore I lie with her and she with me,
And in our faults by lies we flattered be.

Villanelle. A villanelle is a nineteen-line poem with five three-line stanzas and a concluding quatrain. It is usually light in tone and is based on only two rhymes. Here is a villanelle by W. E. Henley about villanelles:

VILLANELLE

A dainty thing's the Villanelle.
Sly, musical, a jewel in rhyme,
It serves its purpose passing well.

Line   A double-clappered silver bell
(5)   That must be made to clink and chime,
A dainty thing's the Villanelle.

And if you wish to flute a spell,
Or ask a meeting 'neath the lime,
It serves its purpose passing well.

(10)   You must not ask of it the spell,
Of organs grandiose and sublime—
A dainty thing's the Villanelle.

And filled with sweetness, as a shell
Is filled with sound, and launched in time,
(15)   It serves its purpose passing well.

Still fair to see and good to smell
As in the quaintness of its prime,
A dainty thing's the Villanelle.
It serves its purpose passing well.

If you don't already know it, find and read Dylan Thomas's "Do Not Go Gentle into That Good Night." It's probably the best-known villanelle in modern English.

5 What You Need to Know About Fiction

The AP exam asks more questions about fiction than about any other genre. Two of the essay questions and at least half of the multiple-choice questions pertain to passages of fiction. Most passages come from novels and short stories. On occasion, the passage is an entire short story, hardly more than a page or two in length. The multiple-choice questions range from broad to narrow—from the meaning of the passage to the use of a single word or phrase. You may be asked about themes, structure, character, setting, tone, purpose, language. In fact, every aspect of the passage is fair game for the multiple-choice questions.

The fictional passage in the essay section of the exam will also be an excerpt from a longer work or a short story printed in its entirety. After you have read the passage, you are expected to write a well-organized essay that analyzes the story. In most cases, the question will suggest the aspects of the passage on which to focus your essay—usually such elements as tone, imagery, use of language, choice of details, and so on. Your analysis is then supposed to show how such elements are used to contribute to the meaning or effect of the passage.

The open-ended essay question invariably instructs you to choose a novel or a play about which to write an essay. Although novels and plays are drastically different creatures, the question makes no distinction between them. Both are "works of literature," with such common characteristics as plot, structure, conflict, settings, themes, major and minor characters, and some sort of resolution.

The present chapter reviews the elements of fiction. In addition, several works of literature are analyzed in detail in order to familiarize you with the sort of literary analysis expected of you on the AP exam. You probably have studied some of the works in school. In such cases, you will become reacquainted with their form and substance. If a work is new to you, however, perhaps you will be inspired to go out and read it.

Reading and Responding to Literature

Elements of Literary Interpretation

As an AP English student you are expected to respond to a short story, a play, or a novel with something more substantial than "It's good," or "I didn't like it." Not that a snap judgment about a piece of literature is wrong, but you might render the same verdict about a song by Elton John or a dish of pudding. A piece of literature on which an author toiled, sometimes for years, deserves more than a simple thumbs up or thumbs down. The next several pages explain and illustrate what thoughtful people think about when they read fiction or go to the theater. By studying this material, your repertoire of responses to literature should grow broader and more piquant. As you prepare for the AP English exam, that's a goal worth striving for.

Subjective, or visceral, responses. Typically, an initial response to a work of literature is emotional. It comes from your heart rather than your head. Perhaps the beauty of the language has moved you, the author's passion has stirred your soul, or you've been struck by the force of a new idea. Perhaps you identify with a character, or the story is so compellingly presented that you lose yourself in the work and must exert some effort to jolt yourself back into reality. Do you recall the gripping scene early in Herman Hesse's *Siddhartha,* when the young Siddhartha, hoping to exact his father's permission to leave home to join the wandering Samanas, stands waiting silently all through the night? Siddhartha's vigil proves to his father how desperately his son wishes to leave. Whether you empathize with the young man on the verge of adulthood or feel pity for his hapless father who wants to protect his only son from harm, or even if you don't take sides at all, it's hard to resist being caught up in the timeless and universal conflict between generations that the incident epitomizes.

No doubt you can think of other scenes from literature that for a time drew you away from the world of reality into the world of fiction. During those moments you literally gave yourself up to the world of the book or story. How, you might ask, does a work elicit such a hypnotic response? The answer, of course, lies partly within you. As a reader, you are willing to surrender yourself to the world created by the author. More specifically, your sensibilities are stimulated by esthetic and psychological forces that a skillful author marshals through use of language, style, form, rhythmic patterns, allusions, figurative expression, and much, much more.

Basically the intensity of an emotional response to a piece of literature is measured by how thoroughly you become immersed in it. When you give yourself completely, you tend to like, even to love, the work. When you can't get into it, or the work holds you at arm's length, your response will be unfavorable or, at best, indifferent.

Sometimes, when the totality of the work leaves a reader cold, analyzing its component parts may inject it with a life. (On the other hand, a thorough analysis could kill it forever. No doubt you've often heard—and maybe even felt—that too much analysis can kill a book and that English teachers, despite their good intentions, have spoiled many good books.) But you probably wouldn't be preparing for this AP test in literature unless you are pretty good at literary analysis and your past experience at dissecting literature hasn't been altogether a waste of your time. At the very least, the fact that you are reading these paragraphs suggests that you are open to the possibility that serious fiction may not only be a means to understanding yourself and the world, but that it provides access to rewards and pleasures that ignorance and self-delusion do not.

Analytical reading takes work, but those who have learned to do it usually find it worth the effort. Examining a text and studying how it was created turn the simple act of reading into an opportunity to stimulate thinking and deepen understanding.

In any case, the intent of this essay on reading literature is to help you become a more observant and appreciative reader. No doubt you are familiar with most of the components of fiction already—such matters as plot, setting, character, structure, and theme. By reviewing how authors use these techniques you may start to observe beauty in works that, initially, you may not have seen.

A word about rereading. Initially, most readers focus on the story, gaining a relatively superficial impression of the whole work. A single reading provides one kind of experience; repeated readings extend the first experience into something more complex, more satisfying, more lasting. As you discover more intricate relationships among all the elements of the work, you experience those elements more fully. Reexamination in no way diminishes your responses; it rather obviously enhances them, emotionally, imaginatively, intellectually. It heightens what is commonly called "appreciation," a vague concept that amounts to what a character in Jane Austen's *Northanger Abbey* insightfully calls ". . . the most thorough knowledge of human nature, the happiest delineation of its varieties, the liveliest effusions of wit and humour . . . conveyed to the world in the best chosen language."

Plot

In common parlance, the words *plot* and *story* are used interchangeably, as though they were synonymns. Literary experts, however, like to distinguish between the two. By *story* they mean the narrative—the unfolding of events that concludes on the last page and makes the question *What happens next?* irrelevant.

When they talk of *plot*, on the other hand, they mean the story *plus* the complex interconnections between events. When a plot "thickens," events of the story become more intricate. Conflicts develop, characters face new dilemmas, a resolution grows farther away and harder to discern. Think, for instance, of Steinbeck's *Of Mice and Men*, the tale of George, an itinerant farmhand, and his retarded sidekick Lennie. Toward the end of the novel, an event occurs that leads to the denoument, or climax, of the story. Lennie, unable to control his brute strength, has accidentally broken the neck of a woman who had playfully come on to him. As a posse hunts for the killer, George must decide what to do with Lennie, who is unaware that he has erred. George could let Lennie be caught and hanged for murder, or he could destroy Lennie himself, thereby sparing his longtime companion much pain and confusion. Those events comprise the *story*. The *plot*, however, teems with nuances about George and Lennie's interdependence. Lennie trusts George implicitly. Should George betray that trust? Is George's obligation to Lennie greater than his obligation to society and the rule of law? George's dilemma brims with moral, emotional, psychological, social, and legal implications.

Some readers regard plot as the most compelling component in a work of fiction. It's a thing that they expect to find when they sit down to read, and it keeps them turning the pages. In one form or other the plot they encounter can be charted roughly as follows:

- *Exposition:* Acquaints readers with the setting of the story (time and place) and introduces the characters.
- *Conflict:* The primary obstacle that prevents the protagonist (main character) from reaching his or her goal. The most common conflicts are man vs. man, man vs. nature, man vs. society, and man vs. himself.
- *Rising action:* The complications that develop and prolong the central conflict.
- *Climax:* The point of greatest tension in a story; the point of no return.
- *Falling action:* The result of the conflict.
- *Denouement:* A resolution that ties up loose ends.

Although the concept of plot connotes a formal, relatively inflexible structure, not unlike that of a sonnet or a five-act play, few plots follow this formula to the letter. Variations abound, but almost always, the conflict is what gives a story its allure. Conflict raises interest and keeps readers engrossed because they want to know how it turns out.

The conflict, or problem, serves as the backbone of the story and means basically that two forces of relatively equal strength are at odds with each other. To create tension, the face-off must be vital to the parties involved and not easily resolved. A protagonist may clash with an antagonist, with all the variations that that suggests. The struggle may be internal and consist of a dilemma that offers a choice between two equally desirable or undesirable alternatives. Whatever the choices, undesirable alternatives are infinitely superior for heightening drama. Trivial or frivolous choices are . . . well, trivial and frivolous. But forcing a character to choose the lesser of two significant evils—as George does when he shoots Lennie in the head, or as Othello does when he smothers Desdemona, or as Sidney Carton does when he steps up to the guillotine—builds tension, magnifies pathos, and reveals the true nature of the chooser as nothing else can.

A good plot should also be unified. That is, everything in the story, from conflict to character, from theme to point of view, is related to the story's basic purpose or effect. If any element is incongruent, the entire work suffers. For example, if a demure character suddenly turns weird, the reason for the change must be motivated and sooner or later made perfectly clear. Any event that fails to follow plausibly from preceding developments also dilutes the effectiveness of the plot. That doesn't necessarily require that the story be told chronologically but that harmony exists between the unfurling of events and the meaning and intent of the narrative. If an author wants to create suspense, the action will almost certainly be organized chronologically. Before the twentieth century, except for inserting occasional flashbacks to fill in background, novelists rarely structured plots in any other way. Over time, however, authors experimented wildly and often rearranged time beyond recognition. James Joyce, among others, devised plots in which past, present, and future exist simultaneously, as they do in a person's thoughts. Today, a narrative that adheres faithfully to a time sequence is considered almost quaint.

Finally, to fully understand the meaning of a novel or play, you must read it to the end. Because an AP essay question may ask you to discuss how the plot of a novel or play relates to the meaning of the whole work, don't even think of writing about a work you haven't read to its conclusion. Last pages often provide clues to the author's purpose. A story in which the protagonist emerges victorious—call it a "Hollywood ending"—says one thing. A tragic ending says something else. A story that ends with a tainted victory expresses still another meaning, as does a story in which the conflict remains wholly or partly unresolved. In fact, final paragraphs and sentences, like aphorisms, may contain a world of profundity, or at least provide closure by giving you the literary equivalent of a party favor, a thought to carry away. Recall how Fitzgerald ends *The Great Gatsby*: "So we beat on, boats against the current, borne back ceaselessly into the past"—fourteen pithy words that sum up Nick's experience. (Nick, along with Gatsby, longed for a better, simpler, and nobler time. Nick knows the past cannot be reclaimed but he can't stop trying.) Or consider how the last two sentences of *Huckleberry Finn* capture the very essence of young Huck: "But I reckon I got to light out for the territory ahead of the rest, because Aunt Sally she's going to adopt me and civilize me, and I can't stand it. I been there before."

Here is something for you to try: Reread the last page of any novel you've read. See if your memory isn't jogged and if you are not inspired to think about the meaning of the work as a whole.

Setting

Understanding the "world of the work." Like strangers arriving in a town for the first time, readers try to get their bearings when they enter a fictional world. They want to know almost immediately where they are, what kind of place it is, and what sort of people they should expect to meet. Broadly speaking, they need to make sense of the "world of the work" in which they find themselves, and from the first page seek such information as: In what kind of community does the action occur? What are the customs, the beliefs, the values of the community? What is sacred in this society and what is held in scorn? What forms of behavior and response are expected from those who live within its boundaries? What are the patterns of daily life, what patterns of faith are typical, and what patterns are considered atypical and therefore suspect? What institutions exist in this society, and how effectively are they functioning? What causes tension among the different members of this society? Are there conflicts and disagreements? What forms do they take? Are they open or secret?

With a profusion of details, some of which may at first strike you as trivial and unnecessary, authors often present a full-blown portrait of a society to their readers. In *War and Peace,* Tolstoy, never one to skimp on words, piles facts on facts and details on details to help readers understand what it meant to be a Russian noble at the time of Napoleon's ill-fated attempt to conquer Russia in the early 1800s. Likewise, Thomas Mann in *Buddenbrooks* draws a well-rounded picture of middle-class life—the births, christenings, marriages, divorces, deaths, the commercial successes and failures—all the commonplace happenings in the lives of four generations of a wealthy burgher family in Germany during the nineteenth century. And William Faulkner, in his fourteen Yoknapatawpha novels and many stories, creates a fictional county in northern Mississippi with a long social history, a culture, and a population of 6,298 whites and 9,313 blacks. Some readers are impatient with long passages of background material. They skim over matters that describe the setting, the social and cultural milieu, and the history of a place in order to get to the meat and potatoes of the story. Try to avoid doing that.

Indeed, some novels won't let you escape the social milieu. What would *Pride and Prejudice* be if you ignored the social customs that govern the behavior of the Bennet family and their circle of friends and relatives? In some novels such as Virginia Woolf's *Mrs. Dalloway*, the social setting *is* the book. We are shown a segment of 1920s London society through the eyes of the title character as she prepares for a party that she will host that evening. Mrs. D's thoughts during the day and the gathering itself capture the entire lives of several middle-aged characters, most of whom have outlived the possibilities of their youth. The lively, glittering party portrays a social reality poised on the brink of its own demise. As we are drawn to the bittersweet quality of the people who fill the room, we also cringe at their capacity for shallow insensitivity.

Because surroundings profoundly influence the thoughts, emotions, and actions of the characters, a place can be as significant to a story as any of the people in it. If you accustom yourself to carefully reading the descriptions of setting and other background matters, your experience with the book will be that much richer, and you will soon grow aware of the reasons for the selection of details.

As you read a work of literature and become involved in its world, you can hardly avoid making judgments about it, first in terms of your own values and then in terms of the esthetic, philosophical, and moral values that prevail in your own culture and society. When you enter the world of Franz Kafka's *The Castle,* for example, you are suddenly transported to a weirdly illogical place where the individual struggles against ubiquitous, elusive, and anonymous powers. As someone accustomed to a degree of freedom and autonomy, you are likely to be repelled by the world Kafka has created. Yet, you read on because the story of "K," the novel's protagonist, resonates with you and perhaps causes you to reflect on the pathos of a place where human isolation is the norm and an individual's quest for freedom and responsibility never succeeds. Certainly you wouldn't choose to live in a world such as Kafka's. In fact, you couldn't even if you wanted to. His world doesn't exist except in the pages of his novel, but in spite of knowing that fact, readers suspend their disbelief, even their rationality at times, and go along with the illusion. Thus, the worlds of Oedipus's Thebes, Hamlet's Elsinore, Ethan Frome's Starkfield, and Madame Bovary's Rouen seem as real to readers as their own home towns—more real, perhaps, while the folks next door, not to mention members of your own family, can be forever strangers.

The conclusions that readers draw about the world of the work usually are the most enduring. Readers may soon forget the names of characters, subplots, elements of form and structure, twists and turns of the story, and stylistic conceits. What remains embedded in the mind is that which gives a piece of literature its general identity. Thus, the world of Hemingway's *The Sun Also Rises* is the American expatriate subculture drifting through Europe after World War I. The world of Dickens's *A Tale of Two Cities* is London and Paris during the time of the French Revolution and the Reign of Terror. Flaubert's *Madame Bovary* depicts the plight of a middle-class woman in nineteenth-century France.

Character

Responding to characters. While the "world of the work" helps to identify a piece of literature, what attracts most readers to a story, novel, or play is usually its cast of characters. After all, literature is about people, and in literature you meet such interesting and unusual types, from monsters to heroes, from losers to people you'd die to know in real life. Unless you are a self-centered, antisocial, reclusive egomaniac, you probably have an abiding curiosity about other people—how they live, what they think, and most of all, what they are like. That may explain why so much of one's daily conversation and thinking are about other people, and also why character analysis is often the most agreeable aspect of literary criticism.

In books, characters' innermost lives are often revealed as they rarely are in life. You are privy to others' desires and dreams and to secrets that would be virtually impossible to know if the character actually existed. In *Moby Dick,* for instance, you learn in the very first paragraph that Ishmael is subject to bouts of depression, that he follows funerals, pauses in front of coffin warehouses, and has a hard time resisting the urge to knock people's hats off. You learn too that "whenever it is a damp, drizzly November" in Ishmael's soul, he casts off his anger and spleen by going to the ocean and boarding a ship to see "the watery part of the world." Were Ishmael a fellow you just met on a bus, how long would it take to learn so many intimate facts about him?

At the start of *Crime and Punishment,* you learn that the protagonist, Raskolnikov, is a "crushingly poor" student, that he is frightened by his landlady, to whom he owes money, and that he's got murder on his mind. In fact, when you meet him, he's going out to rehearse the murder he soon expects to commit. Because would-be killers usually don't advertise their intentions, you know something about Raskolnikov that would never be revealed to you in real life.

On the other hand, in a work of literature not everything about a character is presented. You see only that portion of a person the author chooses to show, sometimes a more circumscribed and limited view than you might see in reality. This is necessary because people are multidimensional, and there are countless elements of a character's behavior, speech, emotional life, and personality that are extraneous to the author's purpose. To include what Romeo liked to eat for breakfast or how often Richard III took a bath might thrill a gossip-hound but would only befuddle Shakespeare's aims. Even though you see only part of a character's whole being, however, an author's skill can transmute the selected elements we are given into a revelation of the entire person. Functioning like a metonymy, the parts you see provide a pretty accurate picture of the whole character. Thus you can easily speculate that, given the choice of staying home and reading a book on Friday night or going bowling with the gang, Elizabeth Bennet in *Pride and Prejudice* would sit in the parlor and read, and McMurphy in *One Flew Over the Cuckoo's Nest* would end up at Bowl-o-Rama.

Like people in real life, characters in literature reflect the world in which they live. Because they have been shaped by the customs, beliefs, and values of their time and place, their thoughts and actions shed light on the world of the work and may reveal aspects of their society that might otherwise remain hidden. For example, Macbeth first resists murdering the king because Duncan is his overnight guest at Inverness. Macbeth's thoughts reveal the sanctity of the relationship between a monarch and his subjects as well as his particular responsibility to keep his guests safe from harm. Knowing that by murdering Duncan, Macbeth violates a "double trust," you can more fully understand why guilt drives him to ruin later in the play. In *A Tale of Two Cities,* the actions of memorable Madame Defarge embody the anger and resentment of the French lower classes against the aristocracy at the time of the Revolution. In Richard Wright's novel, *Native Son,* Bigger Thomas, for all practical purposes, represents the victimization of blacks in America during the 1950s. Such characters, while having distinctive and discrete personalities, function also as docents to their unique worlds. In a sense, they reveal the lay of the land and show you around.

In any work of literature, you are likely to meet an assortment of minor characters who show up once or twice in a play or novel, help to move the story along or add local color to the world of the work. They are not throwaway characters. Pay attention to them, especially when they touch the lives of the main, more fully developed people in the story. In Steinbeck's *The Grapes of Wrath,* the Joad family, en route to California, meets scores of minor characters, among them a one-eyed junk dealer, portrayed as a pathetic and defeated loser whose chief joy in life is to feel sorry for himself. Why give the man more than a glance? On the surface, he is just another hapless victim of the Depression and Dust Bowl of the 1930s. His presence in the book, however, serves another function: to contrast vividly with Tom Joad, whose troubles are no less burdensome than the junk dealer's. Yet Tom won't be defeated. He endures, and when you consider how easy it was succumb to self-pity, Tom's fortitude is all the more impressive.

Fully comprehending fictional characters takes time and vision. Examine not only their individual personalities but their relationships with one another, their actions and thoughts in response to the demands of these relationships, and their behavior in response to the demands of the community. Like a detective, seek motives for their actions, especially in terms of what the characters presently are and what they hope to be or to achieve. Ask how they see themselves and how they are seen by others, and try to determine how the narrator or author wishes you to see them.

In general, look for information about characters in three main places.

1. *What the author or narrator tells you.* What you learn about a character is determined, of course, by what the author wishes to tell you. Thus, the author wields great power in influencing your attitude toward a character. In *Crime and Punishment,* Dostoevsky describes the old pawnbroker this way: "She was a tiny dried-up scrap of a creature, about sixty years old, with sharp, malicious little eyes and a small sharp nose. . . Her fair hair, just beginning to go grey, was thick with grease. A strip of flannel was twisted round her long thin neck, which was wrinkled and yellow like a hen's legs . . . ." Perhaps you'll agree that Dostoevsky was trying to stack the cards against the old lady. He seems to want the reader to feel repulsed by her appearance, just as Raskolnikov is, and to feel, as Raskolnikov and others do, that her death will be no great loss to society. Descriptions such as that of the pawnbroker not only help to define characters but sometimes provide clues to the author's overall purpose. In part, *Crime and Punishment* attacks the nihilists of mid-nineteenth-century Russia, who rejected all traditional moral values. To Dostoevsky, a nihilist had no right to take another's life, even if the victim were a wretched old hag.

2. *What other characters say.* When information comes from other characters, you must be more circumspect. Don't accept the information at face value, not at the outset, at least. Like people in real life, characters in literature have hidden motives, vested interests, propensities to distort the truth or to exaggerate—all qualities that keep them from describing others with complete accuracy and objectivity. After you're familiar with an informant's background and personality, you'll then be in a somewhat better position to judge the validity of the information given to you. Better still, try to define the relationship between the speaker and the character about whom he or she is talking, as well as the dynamics between speaker and listener. Each of these relationships may subtly alter what the speaker says. When, for instance, Mr. Collins in *Pride and Prejudice* first describes his patroness, Lady Catherine de Bourgh, in a letter to the Bennets, you might well believe that the honorable lady has a kind, benevolent soul. After meeting Mr. Collins in person, however, and hearing from Jane Austen that he is "not a sensible man," but rather a "mixture of pride and obsequiousness, self-importance and humility," your preconceptions of Lady Catherine's bounty must be cast aside. Why does Mr. Collins present Lady Catherine as an exalted figure when, in fact, she is a rancorous shrew? In the answer lies a clue to Mr. Collins's personality and values. Consider also the works of Joseph Conrad. Does Marlow's view of Jim in *Lord Jim* and of Kurtz in *Heart of Darkness* coincide with the actual characters? Or is Marlow's vision slightly blurry? If Marlow is not seeing Jim and Kurtz clearly, why not?

Before drawing your conclusions about characters, it pays to identify the sources of your information and weigh the validity of the evidence. Are the sources reliable? Is there any reason to believe that the sources themselves have been misled or that shading or distorting the truth is in their own best interest?

3. *What characters say and how they act.* The words and actions of characters are probably the surest indicators of who they truly are. Nevertheless, proceed cautiously in making definitive character analyses because fictional people, like those in real life, often lie, put on airs, wear masks, and disguise their true nature in countless other ways. Stories told in first person are particularly resistant to easy analysis because narrators will often be very selective in choosing what to reveal about themselves. At the beginning, any judgments you make should be extremely tentative. Through much of *Huckleberry Finn,* Huck, the narrator, calls himself "ornery" and "low down." In other words, he doesn't think much of himself because no one has ever thought much of him. By the end of the book, though, you realize that Huck has many admirable qualities—basic kindness, loyalty, love of life, and a well-tuned sense of right and wrong. In short, don't be swayed by everything that characters say about themselves. Only after reading the last page should you feel reasonably sure that you fully grasp what makes a character tick.

Whether the old observation that "actions speak louder than words" applies to analysis of characters in literature is a question worth pondering. Do actions or do words provide more helpful clues? Hamlet has customarily been seen as confused and contemplative. In soliloquies and speeches, he grieves at his own inability to act decisively. Yet, as the play goes on, Hamlet adopts an "antic disposition," writes some lines for the traveling players, kills Polonius, plots against Rosenkrantz and Guildenstern, fights Laertes, and more. He may be more of a man of action than he claims to be.

When analyzing a character it is equally important to take into account who is telling the story. The narrator or speaker will deeply affect your perceptions. In the short story by Willa Cather, "Paul's Case," Paul, a troublesome teenager, is someone people loved to hate. Had the tale of his adventures been told from his own viewpoint, however, he might have explained and justified his delinquent behavior, causing you to judge him less harshly. But had his bitterly disappointed father told the story, Paul would probably lack a single redeeming trait. Since Cather assumes the role of omniscient narrator, you get all the facts about Paul but no cues as to the way you should feel about the facts. Therefore, your attitude toward Paul is likely to fall somewhere between scorn and pity.

Of all the characters in a play, novel or story, those that require the most careful scrutiny are the protagonist and the antagonist. The protagonist particularly deserves your attention because that person very often bears messages from the author. Consider such characters as King Lear, Elizabeth Bennet (*Pride and Prejudice*), and Lieutenant Frederic Henry (*A Farewell to Arms*). Lear's division of his kingdom unleashes the forces that lead ultimately to the catastrophic ending of the play. Shakespeare uses Lear to show the consequences of upsetting the natural order that Elizabethans held dear. Through Elizabeth Bennet, Jane Austen comments on issues of marriage and the burdens borne by single women in the polite society of her time, and Lieutenant Henry's life and experience vividly illustrate the loss of innocence and the disillusionment that Hemingway means to convey in his story of love and death in World War I.

Usually it is quite clear who the protagonist is in a work of fiction. Occasionally, however, especially when the conflict pits two equally "good" forces against each other, or when two appealing personalities clash, it is not so easy. Generally a case can be made for either character. Is it Phaedra or Hippolytus who is the protagonist of Euripides' *Hippolytus*? Is it Antigone or Creon who is the protagonist of Sophocles' *Antigone*? Who is the protagonist of Conrad's *Heart of Darkness*? Is it Marlow, the narrator, who receives from Kurtz's experience a revelation of the potential for evil in man? Or is it Kurtz, who is destroyed by the baleful consequences of living in the tropics and acquiring supreme power over the natives of the region?

Identifying the true protagonist is not necessarily a critical issue, of course, but it often forces you to think deeply about the characters, events, and themes in a work of literature. In that sense, it is a valuable exercise in literary analysis. Similarly, the identity of the antagonist, the force that opposes the protagonist, is worth pondering. Antagonists range from individual adversaries, who for various reasons seek to thwart the protagonist, to inner psychological demons that threaten or even destroy him. Consider Akaky Akakievich, the protagonist of Gogol's "The Overcoat." He falls prey to his associates at work, to the Russian bureacracy, to the frigid St. Petersburg winter, and to the muggers who steal the coat. All seem to conspire to defeat Akaky, but he is really brought down by an internal nemesis, his inability to cope with the slings and arrows of workaday life. The protagonist of Eugene O'Neill's play *The Emperor Jones* is pursued through the jungle by rebel tribesmen who seek to dethrone him, but it remains unclear whether he is finally subdued by the hunters or by the accumulated horrors of his life that appear in his mind's eye as he tries to avoid capture. Hamlet must overcome the thinking that "puzzles the will" before he can move to avenge the murder of his father. Othello falls prey to jealousy, the "green-eyed monster." In both *Hamlet* and *Othello*, the protagonists face physical adversaries (Claudius, among others, and Iago), but the main sources of their tragedies lie within themselves.

In many works, protagonists encounter forces that are other than human. Nature and God can also deal a cruel hand. The central conflicts in Ole Rolvaag's *Giants in the Earth*, Willa Cather's *My Antonia*, and Pearl Buck's *The Good Earth* find humans struggling against nature. Per Hansa, the Shimerda family, and Wang Lung face unrelenting hardships while scraping a living from the land or trying to survive in the face of nature's freakish, seemingly antagonistic, behavior. Opposition from the gods often comes in the form of fate that, for good or ill, determines human destiny. In the works of Thomas Hardy, fate invariably shapes the lives of the characters. No matter how hard she tries to pick herself up from despair, Tess, the protagonist of *Tess of the d'Urbervilles*, experiences one setback after another. Her destiny is to suffer and die. Fate plays a crucial role in classical Greek drama. Oedipus, Antigone, Agamemnon, Clytemnestra, and Orestes cannot avert the disasters that the oracles decree for them. Like Hamlet, Othello, and King Lear, they also suffer from a personal flaw that to a large extent contributes to their fate.

Economic, social, and political forces also serve as the grist of literature. How people cope with poverty and hunger, oppression and greed, is the theme of works like John Steinbeck's *The Grapes of Wrath,* Emile Zola's *Germinal,* and Upton Sinclair's *The Jungle.* How people of color respond to prejudice and alienation is dealt with in novels like Ralph Ellison's *Invisible Man,* Toni Morrison's *Beloved,* and David Guterson's *Snow Falling on Cedars.* The laws and institutions that a society establishes to maintain order sometimes produce injustice that overwhelms innocent members of the society. Such situations occur in John Galsworthy's *Justice,* Victor Hugo's *Les Miserables,* and Theodore Dreiser's *An American Tragedy.* Frequently also, idealists—those who see flaws in society and try to fix them—run headlong into the opposition of vested interests who want to preserve the status quo. Such confrontations are the stuff of Hendrick Ibsen's *An Enemy of the People,* George Bernard Shaw's *Saint Joan,* and Ernest Hemingway's *For Whom the Bell Tolls.*

In the end, the crux of a work of literature, and the very reason you are apt to keep reading, is the struggle between the protagonist and the antagonist. A story ends in either victory or defeat, but it could just as well end in a stalemate. Victory leads most often to a happy ending, defeat to a tragic one, although many works end ambiguously by balancing a bit of both. With the human condition being so subtle and the human personality so complex, it is not surprising that what sometimes appears as disaster may be a triumph, particularly when an assertion of moral force accompanies the fall or when the protagonist's collapse is accompanied by the promise of a resurrection of good. As *Wuthering Heights* draws to a close, for instance, Heathcliff's fury is spent. Heathcliff joins his beloved Catherine in death, and the tempests subside. Young Catherine and Hareton now can find tranquility in a world cleansed of the passionate extremes of love and hate. Oedipus blinds himself after he discovers the truth about the murder of Laius. The act, however, restores clarity to his vision of himself. Yes, he was wronged by the casual and wanton actions of the gods, but he sees clearly that his quest for power and his arrogance have caused his downfall. He paid the price of thinking that he was an equal of the gods. In disaster he finds the peace that had eluded him throughout his life.

Narrative Voice or Point of View

Hearing the voice of the author. Every piece of literature has a narrator or speaker. Sometimes, as in essay and biography, it is the author's voice you hear. In fiction and poetry, on the other hand, the identity of the narrator may not be so apparent. In order to fully appreciate the piece, however, you should try to figure out who is speaking. It is not always easy to do so. It takes practice to examine the language and imagery, the characters and conflicts, the themes and plots—virtually every aspect of a literary work—to discover whether the narrator or speaker is the author, a surrogate assigned to speak for the author, or an invented voice whose beliefs and values differ from the author's. Because an author's views are often signaled in the tone of a work, you must be alert for clues to the narrator's attitude. By scrutinizing language you will detect satire, irony, humor, sentimentality, detachment, foreboding, melancholy, anger, and countless other states of the narrator's mind and feelings.

Gustave Flaubert uses *Madame Bovary,* in part, to express disapproval of the treatment of women in France in the 1850s. Moreover, the novel's focus on Emma's inner life—her memories, dreams, and fantasies—might very well reflect Flaubert's own obsessions with love, sexuality, and art. Because straight-laced

Germans of the early 1900s spurned romantic writers, Herman Hesse wrote the novel *Steppenwolf* to tell the reading public of his displeasure about how artists and intellectuals felt ostracized. Some critics consider *The Grapes of Wrath* a piece of literary propaganda that Steinbeck wrote to espouse his socialist views. *Women in Love* by D. H. Lawrence has a pervasive note of gloom that undoubtedly reflects the author's response to World War I. Novels like *Johnny Got His Gun* by Dalton Trumbo and *All Quiet on the Western Front* by Erich Maria Remarque are statements that passionately convey their authors' antiwar positions.

When a story is told in first person, the narrator may or may not represent the author's views. The narrator in "Family Happiness," a story by Tolstoy, is Masha, an innocent young woman from the country who falls in love with and marries an older man. Masha is swept up by the social whirl when her new husband introduces her to big city life. In every way, she's a world apart from Tolstoy himself, who was well over fifty and firmly entrenched in his country estate when he wrote the story. In *Wuthering Heights,* several narrators, including Lockwood, Catherine, Ellen Dean, Heathcliff, and Isabella, tell the story. None of them speaks for Emily Brontë, the author. Nick Carraway narrates *The Great Gatsby,* but he is not F. Scott Fitzgerald, although they both came from Minnesota and attended Ivy League colleges. (If anything, Jay Gatsby is more like Fitzgerald.) Similarly, David Copperfield is not Charles Dickens, nor is Ishmael Herman Melville in *Moby Dick,* although some parallels exist between the lives of the characters and the lives of the authors. Poetry offers the same kinds of ambiguities as prose fiction. Shakespeare's sonnets are assumed to express the poet's love for the so-called dark lady, but you can't be sure. The poems of the romantics (Wordsworth, Keats, Shelley, and Coleridge) seem also to have been written straight from the heart, but there are exceptions. One certainty, however, is that in dramatic monologues, such as "My Last Duchess" by Robert Browning, the speaker is always someone other than the poet. In drama, except when a playwright deliberately uses a narrator, as in *Our Town* and *A Man for All Seasons,* there seems to be no omniscient narrator, although one or more characters in a play may very well represent and express the author's views.

Third-person narrators are often trickier to pin down, for authors are wont to invent voices completely different from their own. The narrator may be the author, but often is not, and there is a danger of misinterpretation in ascribing to the author the views and attitudes of the narrator. Would it be fair to say that the author of *Studs Lonigan,* James T. Farrell, is anti-Catholic or anti-Irish because he presents a critical portrait of Irish-Catholic life in Chicago? Is Philip Roth of *Goodbye, Columbus* fame antisemitic because so many of the Jewish characters in his novels behave badly? Are James Joyce's views of Catholicism in *Portrait of the Artist as a Young Man* the same as those of his protagonist Stephen Dedalus? Contrary to what many readers think, Jonathan Swift, the author of *Gulliver's Travels,* did not accept entirely the beliefs by which the Houyhnhnms governed their lives. Nor did Voltaire, who wrote *Candide,* find perfection and the answer to the ills of mankind in the values of El Dorado.

Omniscient narrators complicate the task of identifying the author's views because they move in and out of characters' minds, know everything about everybody and may even pause occasionally to editorialize on the story they are telling you. In order to thoughtfully judge the psychological and social connection between authors and narrators, study carefully the manner in which narrators tell the story and the range and completeness of their knowledge of characters and events. Do they know all about the characters' lives and background? Who is their source? Do they know what characters are thinking and dreaming? Are they privy to confidential information? Is the narrator a character in the story or just an observer? Answers to such questions help to unravel the tone of a story. Edith Wharton's *Ethan Frome* is narrated by a young man who hears the story from Ethan himself twenty-four years after the events occurred. Since memory is highly selective, readers should not unquestioningly accept everything in the account of Ethan's love affair with Mattie Silver as the absolute truth. Similarly, because *First Love* by Ivan Turgenev is a story of sixteen-year-old Vladimir's first brush with love told by Vladimir in middle age, distortions and semitruths are bound to occur.

In brief, readers should be aware of the distance between the narrator and the events in the story. They should also try to ascertain the distance between the narrator and the author. In calculating this distance, it may be tempting to read a life story of the author in search of traces of autobiography in the fiction. Perceptive readers ordinarily eschew such aid because they are able to find sufficient evidence in the text itself to draw reasonable conclusions about the purpose and meaning of the work—conclusions, that is, about what the author thinks.

But no simple formula or prescription will provide a technique for determining the author's point of view. Works of literature are often too complex and subtly written to yield easy answers. As you know, a work of literature frequently may be read or interpreted in various ways. One reader may draw from the content, form, and language a valid meaning amply supported by evidence in the text, while another reader may find an equally valid alternate meaning. The threat of being dead wrong is real, but feeling strongly about an interpretation and wishing that it were valid won't make it so. Whenever you have doubts, go back to the text to look for supporting evidence. A careful rereading may either strengthen your position or expose its weaknesses.

Structure

Responding to the art of literature. Although it is often said that literature imitates life, it doesn't. Authors select experiences from the vast context of life and redesign them to suit their purposes. By doing so, authors abstract life and give it a form and a semblance of order rarely found in the chaotic universe in which we lead our lives. The result is often a unified and coherent literary work. All its parts—the world of the work, the action, the characters, the theme, the language, the imagery—combine to produce a pleasing artistic structure.

Structure, in fact, applies to all the arts. A medieval cathedral, for example, has a specific floor plan, usually in the shape of a cross. It has a central nave, side aisles, transepts, an apse, and three entrances, symbolizing the Holy Trinity. Huge pillars, surrounded by smaller satellite pillars, hold up the heavy slate roof using a system of rib vaults. Flying buttresses transfer structural forces to strong outer walls. Stained glass windows and a large centrally located rose window permit a wash of iridescent light throughout the dim interior. Tall towers reach toward the heavens. In its composition, the cathedral is a harmonious work of art, its pieces, when taken as a whole, reflecting a coherent faith in God.

This kind of organic unity is a characteristic of good literature, too. As a student of literature, you should be aware that individual elements work together to create a sense of unity in a novel, story, play, or poem. If you focus on only one element (the characters, for example), you'd find yourself in the position of the blind men and the elephant, using only a small piece of evidence to generalize about the whole thing. Determining how individual parts blend with each other to achieve organic unity is not always easy to pin down or to articulate. Yet you know organic unity when you see it and miss it when it's not there. Of course, no one says, "Okay, I'm going to read this book for its organic unity." Rather, a reader's intuition or sense of harmony and balance will serve as a guide. You know that neon lights don't belong in a cathedral, nor a rumble seat on a sleek new Porsche. Likewise, an incongruous turn of events, trite ideas, senseless sequences, a character's inconsistent or impossible behavior, figurative language that seems forced, dialogue that is stylized and artificial, as well as many other writing sins tend to tear organic unity apart.

Unity is achieved partly through the structure of a work. For instance, the Italian sonnet, discussed earlier in this book (pages 108–109), consists of two parts. The first part, the octave, develops a question, a story, or an idea. The second section, the sestet, offers an answer, a comment, or a proposition. If either part were missing or out of synch with the other, the coherence and unity of the piece would be lost. Similarly, plays, discussed in detail in a previous chapter, are often constructed like a pyramid, the moment of their greatest tension at the apex. A play with a too early climax would flop. Because novels are often long and far-ranging, discovering their structure takes time and practice.

One simply structured work is Conrad's "The Secret Sharer." Like its style of writing, the tale is straightforward, with no shifts in time and space. The story's structure consists simply of a character's movement from ignorance to knowledge. By the end of the story the young captain knows himself more thoroughly. As a consequence, he is a better leader than he was at the start. You'll find a more complex structure in *The Great Gatsby.* Fitzgerald begins the story in the present, using the first three chapters to describe the novel's four main locales: Daisy's house, the valley of ashes, New York City, and Gatsby's house. The plot of the novel is developed in the next several chapters. Only toward the middle of the book, when he is pretty sure that the reader will be curious about the enigmatic Gatsby, does Fitzgerald begin to tell the story of Gatsby's past. In the climactic last chapter, the past and the present come together. This design seems to suit the novel perfectly because Fitzgerald reveals information as Nick Carraway gets it, in bits and pieces over a period of time. As the story approaches its climax, the reader learns more and more about Gatsby so that by the end, Gatsby's motivation and behavior are thoroughly understandable. The technique that Fitzgerald employs—first-person narrative combined with gradual revelation of the past—works well and endows the novel with unity and coherence.

The unifying structure of Joyce's *Portrait of the Artist as a Young Man* invites several interpretations, the simplest being that each of the book's five chapters represents a stage in Stephen Dedalus's growth from childhood to maturity. The book has also been thought to have a three-part structure that reflects the three phases of Stephen's increasing self-awareness. An alternate view is that the book is structured as a series of rhythmic waves. Each chapter moves from a trough of Stephen's self-doubt to a peak of triumph. Since the action rises slowly, only to fall at the start of the next chapter, the pattern has also been likened to the myth of Daedalus, Stephen's mythic namesake. Each chapter recounts Stephen's attempt to break away, and at each chapter's end, he breaks another link in the chain that binds him to his roots. Finally, at the book's climax, Stephen leaves for good. Whether he will succeed in the world like Daedalus or fall like Icarus remains unclear.

In general, unity achieved through the structure of a work plays subtly on a reader's response. Far more direct is storytelling technique. Readers are perpetually aware of *how* the story is told. Because there are innumerable ways to tell a tale, no one method is superior to another. What counts is whether the manner of storytelling fits the point and purpose of the story being told. The most elementary way, of course, is chronological. What happens first is told first, what happens next is told next, and so on. Children's stories are usually told chronologically, as are picaresque novels like Cervantes's *Don Quixote* and Henry Fielding's *Tom Jones,* in which a central character undergoes numerous adventures, one after another. Most chronological works, however, refer to things past, often to give readers background for comprehending what comes next. For example, Homer's *The Odyssey* begins with Telemachus's decision to journey forth to seek news of his absentee father. Why the young man undertakes the search is not made clear until Homer goes back in time to tell the story of Odysseus's adventures after the Trojan War. In almost all of Shakespeare's plays, as well as in dramas by Ibsen and others, early dialogue informs the audience of the events that occurred before the curtain rose.

A backward look can also provide a window into a character. When Billy Budd, the title character of Melville's story, is impressed into His Majesty's navy, the captain of Billy's ship explains to the British lieutenant (and to the reader) that Billy is no ordinary sailor. He's "the best man . . . the jewel of 'em," the crewmember whose presence turned the ship from a "rat-pit of quarrels" to a place of peace and good will. This description accounts for Billy's subsequent actions and makes his tragic fate all the more poignant. Then, too, Jay Gatsby is a more intriguing character because we are told that long ago he may have been not only a crook, a bootlegger, and a companion of criminals, but also a German spy and a killer. Similarly, in *Candide,* characters frequently stop to relate tales of their past misfortunes. Still other stories, such as Melville's "Bartleby the Scrivener" and Turgenev's "First Love," begin with a narrator in the present recalling events of long ago, another popular storytelling device.

Conrad's *Lord Jim,* Faulkner's *As I Lay Dying,* and Toni Morrison's *Beloved* use another narrative technique for relating the story. Each of these novels depends for its effectiveness on the compatibility between the content and form. In other words, their form follows their function. Events are recounted by multiple voices that move forward and backward in time. Because the voices change repeatedly, we are told of the same events again and again, but each time from a different perspective. In *Beloved,* for example, we hear of Paul D's arrival in Cincinnati related first from Denver's point of view, then later by Sethe and then by Paul D. Some readers react negatively to this kind of storytelling, claiming that it's too repetitive and confusing, or that the author's virtuosity as an artist seems to overshadow the point of the book itself. To a point, such responses may be valid. (Certainly they're valid for those readers.) On the other hand, life is often like a Gordion knot: disorderly, chaotic, and too complex to unravel easily, and in order to be faithful to reality, stories should not oversimplify human experience.

Clearly, a piece of literature need not be realistic to reflect real life. Even the most improbable stories can mirror reality. Think of the fantastical occurrences in works by authors from Hawthorne to Hesse, the absurdist plays of Ionesco, Albee, and Becket, and the remarkable story by Nikolai Gogol, "The Nose," in which a man discovers one morning that his nose has vanished from his face, only to have it show up in the breakfast muffin of his barber, who lives across town. Literature is filled with unnatural events and supernatural beings. The story of Hamlet is launched by the appearance of a ghost, the setting of *Beloved* is haunted by the spirit of a dead child, and Gulliver for a time is taken prisoner by a horde of people no taller than his thumb. Does this mean that Shakespeare, Morrison, and Swift and their fellow authors have a distorted sense of reality? No, it means that they give expression to reality rather than recreate it. Having apprehended reality, authors transmute it and give it a shape and a clarity by focusing on meticulously selected elements that depict their vision sharply and truthfully. Artistic license permits authors to shuffle sequences, omit or enlarge happenings, change and combine characters, spin the world in any way they like, but there are limits to their freedom. On the whole, unless there is an artistic reason for doing so, they should not introduce implausible psychological distortions in human response or behavior. If an incident could not happen in any world, real or imagined, or if a character with a certain personality acts inconsistently, or if historical anomalies creep into the work (e.g., the use of jet planes in World War II) the author may well have betrayed the truth, misrepresented reality, and written a flawed work—but not always.

Before you can respond somewhat intelligently to a work of literature, therefore, it helps to be a little dry behind the ears, that is, to have tasted a little bit of life, either in person or vicariously. If you didn't know anything about individual freedom, for example, reading Kafka's *The Castle* would be a totally meaningless exercise, or if you had no understanding of religion, it would be pointless to read, say, *Portrait of the Artist as a Young Man.* In other words, responses to books involve assessing how effectively authors have remolded the raw material of life into works of art. It takes a passion for real life to react passionately to the life in books. You can't be out to lunch and also appreciate good literature.

Narrative Style

Perhaps the feature of a work of literature that you're apt to notice first is writing style. After a few paragraphs you'll know whether the language is poetic or plain, flowery or simple, lofty or down-to-earth, figurative or literal. Almost from the outset you can tell whether the narrator is humorous or serious, bitter or cheerful, proud or humble, hard-boiled or romantic. Sentence length and structure, word choice, figures of speech, allusions, use of dialogue—with all of these the author establishes a mood and tone. More important than simply recognizing the components of a writer's style, however, is determining whether the language is appropriate for the purpose of the work and assessing whether the language contributes to the work's impact on the reader, decisions that you can't make until you've read most of the work. Hemingway's distinctive style of writing is a case in point. You probably know that Hemingway wrote simple, spare, journalistic prose, full of sensory detail. In a way, his style resembles his characters—tough, terse, and not given to wearing emotions on their sleeves. Frederic Henry, the protagonist in *A Farewell to Arms,* distrusts abstract concepts like *patriotism* and *honor.* His wound in battle has nothing to do with bravery or glory. His leg hurts; that's all that matters. Hemingway's writing has a hard edge to it. Using short, concrete, tangible words and phrases (a glass of wine, hot bath, soft bed) rather than multisyllabic, abstract words, he captures the more-or-less macho personalities of men and women caught up in the conflicts of war, the bull ring, the sea, and the big game hunt.

James Joyce's style is a world away from Hemingway's. Using all the resources of the English language, Joyce sets a mood, creates a tone, and captures the essence of the characters. In *Portrait of the Artist as a Young Man,* he portrays Stephen Dedalus and his world by taking liberties with language that might give an English teacher fits. He coins words, expands meanings, plays with rhythms and sounds, spells whimsically, ignores punctuation when it suits him, and pours his thoughts into streams of consciousness, apparently not giving a hoot whether the reader will understand or not. Much of the language is meant to suggest the confused state of young Stephen's emotions, the boy's inner turmoil. The style changes with Stephen's age, starting with the short, choppy sentences of a tot, developing complexity as Stephen grows to manhood. In his inimitable way, Joyce integrates language with the meaning and purpose of his novel.

At some point you'll probably run into authors who employ a style that seems antithetical to the content of the work. For example, murder and suicide are pretty grim topics. Yet they can be given a light touch or written about in poetic language of great beauty. Likewise, violent and painful death can be described with the detachment of a scientist taking lab notes, and an everyday occurrence like spreading cream cheese on a bagel can be related in ornate, bombastic, grandiloquent words. Such oppositions between language and content or between style or form and content are called *tensions,* created for a humorous, satirical, or in some cases, a bitterly ironic effect. When Jonathan Swift, in "A Modest Proposal," advances the idea of eating babies to put an end to lower-class starvation, he uses a no-nonsense, objective style of writing. The contrast between the horror of his culinary idea and its cool, impersonal presentation makes the piece one of the most enduring satirical essays ever written. In his many stories and novels, Franz Kafka records bizarre and frightening experiences—waking up to discover yourself turned into a cockroach, for one—in simple, direct, deceptively innocent language. Alexander Pope's poem "The Rape of the Lock" focuses on an attractive young woman about to have a lock of hair snipped from her head. Written in the style of a grand epic worthy of Homer or Virgil, the piece is known aptly as a "mock" epic. By using inflated language, Pope has trivialized (i.e., mocked) the event.

Figurative language also adds dimension to a piece of literature. Broadly defined, figurative language is a way of saying something in other than the ordinary way. Authors get mileage (a metaphor) by using allusions, similes, personifications, tropes, or any other of 250 separate figures that have been identified. (See What You Need to Know About Poetry [Chapter 4] for definitions and examples.) In poetry as well as prose, nothing enriches and broadens meaning like a fresh and original figure of speech.

Two figures, perhaps, deserve your particular attention: the metaphor and the metonymy. Both extend objects, people, and experiences into innumerable imaginative and symbolic forms. Simply stated, a metaphor compares two essentially unlike things. A metaphor such as "All the world's a stage" evokes, among other things, the thought that our lives are fleeting dramas, that life from birth to death is a performance that succeeds or fails according to our skill as actors. The parallels can be extended much farther. By thinking of what it takes to mount a play from its birth to final curtain, and thinking then of what it takes to make a life, the power of Shakespeare's metaphor is bound to become obvious. Metonymy, the use of a closely related idea for the idea itself, is also a comparison. In the phrase "The pen is mightier than the sword," *pen* stands for the writer, *sword* for the warrior. The sentiment (that a writer wields more power with words than a warrior with arms) is conveyed vividly and is actually a living example of its meaning.

Metaphor and metonymy provide access to a deeper meaning in many works of literature. A modern work rooted in a biblical tale or in ancient Greek myth or drama can be viewed as a metaphor for its source. *East of Eden* by John Steinbeck, for one, is a modern adaptation of the story of Cain and his brother Abel. *The Grapes of Wrath* has numerous parallels to the Old Testament's account of the Israelites' search for the promised land. In reading modern literature, you can hardly go far without running into Christ-like figures, people who sacrifice themselves to save others from death or indignity, like Sonia in *Crime and Punishment,* McMurphy in *One Flew Over the Cuckoo's Nest,* and the hero of *The Informer* by Liam O'Flaherty. No doubt you can think of stories and novels in which a parent, acceding to a higher moral duty, gives up a child. Chances are those works are metaphors for the story of Abraham's obedience to God's command to sacrifice his son Isaac. If you have read tales of children defying their parents, it's likely that they are metaphorical adaptations of the parable of the prodigal son.

Greek myth and drama have also served as the source of modern works. A story in which a child slays a parent alludes metaphorically to Oedipus. Antigone's compulsion to bury her brother in defiance of the law serves as the basis for works in which family loyalty takes precedence over loyalty to the state. Much of Clytemnestra is to be found in such modern characters as Ibsen's Hedda Gabler. James Joyce's mammoth novel *Ulysses* is a latter-day transmutation of *The Odyssey,* in which the hero, instead of wandering around the waters and isles of the ancient Mediterranean, roams the streets and sites of modern Dublin.

Finally, consider the metonymic significance of certain literary characters; Arthur Miller's Willy Loman (*Death of a Salesman*) as the modern worker lost in changing economic times; Kafka's Joseph K. (*The Trial*) as the modern citizen lost in the bureaucratic maze; Beckett's Didi and Gogo (*Waiting for Godot*) as modern man lost in a meaningless existence.

Authors rarely limit themselves to story telling. They write novels and shorter works to inform, entertain, or enlighten readers. But the best of them don't let the story get in the way of conveying an idea they want to pass along to readers about the state of society, the plight of the world, or any aspect of the human condition they have on their minds. When Melville's *Moby Dick* was first published, critics dismissed it as a story about whaling. Over time, though, readers began to see that Melville's book had things to say beyond its "story." What seemed a realistic account of a whaling voyage was also an allegorical exploration of the conflict between man and his fate and the nature of good and evil. In other words, underneath the story lay profound philosophical themes. Because a theme is an *idea* that the author wants to explore and communicate, it should not be confused with the subject matter of the work. For example, the subject of Toni Morrison's *Beloved* is slavery, but its theme is what Morrison has to say about slavery. Even though the story is set in 1873, a decade after slavery was declared illegal in the United States, Morrison's premise is that time cannot separate former slaves from the horror of their experiences nor undo its effects. Sethe, the main character, in fact, wears permanent scars of slavery on her back, and she is perpetually deluged with nightmarish visions of Sweet Home, the plantation on which she had been enslaved.

Similarly, the subject of *War and Peace* is what the title indicates, but Tolstoy's themes reflect his thinking about how men find purpose in their lives. The nihilist Andrei, one of the primary characters, despairs of identifying a purpose until, ironically, he lies on his deathbed after suffering a wound in combat. Pierre, whose experiences on the field of battle and on the home front make up the bulk of the novel, is moved by an out-of-the-ordinary belief in life's possibilities. In the clash of life and death, he discovers reasons for carrying on. In fact, all the important characters in the novel are to some degree engaged in a quest for happiness and for the satisfaction of knowing that their days on earth will add up to something more than a shapeless gray blur.

Generally, themes express big ideas, too sweeping and elusive to summarize in just a catch phrase or two. Attaching a label such as "man's inhumanity to man" or "the triumph of good over evil," may be a convenient way to identify a theme, but it usually fails to do justice to the author's vision. Besides, themes are often multidimensional, too complex to be readily pigeonholed.

That's one reason that a theme should not be confused with the *moral* of a story. A moral such as *Hard work pays off* is a platitude unambiguously conveyed, for example, by the famous fable of the ant and the grasshopper. Although a serious piece of literature may deal with issues of rectitude and virtue, by and large it isn't going to preach at you. Nor will it contain a theme quite so obvious and banal as that in Aesop's story. Knowing that art is a faithful mirror of what goes on in the human psyche and that human experience is too complex to be reduced to a Sunday-school maxim, good authors devise themes that reflect reality as they see it.

No thoughtful novelist would propose that a given generalization is always true; rather, it may be true only under certain conditions. For example, the sentiment that hard work pays off won't apply to a frail old man with a heart condition and a long driveway to shovel after a blizzard. In addition, themes are often ambiguous and subject to modification. Good is never totally good, nor evil totally evil. Even such personifications of depravity like Iago and Lady Macbeth have a redeeming quality or two. Because a theme won't apply to everyone at all times, it must be tempered to take into account the rich variation that makes up the world.

The presence of significant themes in literature—at least in the kind of literature usually studied in AP classes—separates so-called literary classics from escapist potboilers that keep readers entertained but have little enduring value. To be sure, the lines between "classic" and "pop," or "pulp," fiction, are not always apparent. But one distinct difference is that high-quality works offer readers ideas to think about, while pop fiction ordinarily emphasizes plot above all else. People read novels by John Grisham and Tom Clancy, for instance, mainly to find out what happens. Does the hero win the girl? Who has sex with whom? How is the villain defeated?. . . and so on. These are all titillating questions, but they lack the power to lift readers out of themselves, stimulate readers' imagination, or provide anything resembling an intellectual or transcendent experience.

To be fair, some authors of pop fiction infuse themes into their works, but the themes are generally mundane, unambiguous, or both. Stephen King's novels and stories are known for recurring themes that pertain to malevolent, goosebumpy forces abroad in the land. Although King introduces themes into his riveting plots, his work is not taken seriously. Why this is so raises questions about the nature of literature.

Truly, there is no litmus test to determine whether a work is "literary" or pulp. The literary canon (novels and plays deemed worthy of study in AP classes and elsewhere) is always in flux. Authors come and go based on many factors. Sinclair Lewis, author of *Main Street, Babbitt,* and many other novels, was awarded a Nobel Prize for Literature in 1930. Afterward, he fell from grace, but early in the twenty-first century enjoyed a partial rebirth in literary circles after a reappraisal of his work in a well-received biography by Richard R. Lingeman. For decades, *The Awakening* by Kate Chopin was regarded as a pop novel. With the advent of feminism in the 1960s, however, it was rediscovered and made part of the canon.

Authors rarely state their themes outright. Rather they communicate themes through plot, character, setting, point of view, symbols, language, and all other basic literary elements. Indeed, questions on the AP exam sometimes ask students to write about the interrelationship between theme and other aspects of a novel. A several-hundred page novel may contain scores of characters, descriptive passages, background material, and long chains of events, some more significant than others. Drawing a theme out of such a work takes practice, patience, and insight. It requires a knack for finding meaning under the surface of things, for weaving a single impression out of a series of diverse episodes, and conferring a sense of wholeness and integrity on what initially may seem fragmented and chaotic. Clues are there, but they must be found and interpreted.

A work of fiction is not a math problem for which there is only one correct answer. Different readers have different responses. Authors select and arrange material to express certain themes. Your interpretation may coincide with the author's intent or it may be far afield. Either way it is neither wrong nor right. Rather, because literary criticism isn't a free-for-all, the validity of your interpretation depends on the evidence that can be drawn from the text to support your views. On the AP exam, you must always be prepared to back up your opinions with specific references to the plot, characters, language, setting, and so forth. If your interpretation of a novel is contradicted by details in the story, back off, reconsider, and change course.

Analyses of Selected Novels

In the next section of this book you will find discussions of several novels often studied in AP English classes. All of the titles, representing a cross section of works from the literary canon, are suitable for the free-response essay (Question #3) that you must write on the exam.

Chances are you have already read one or more of these works. If so, the material that follows will refresh your memory of each title's story, characters, themes, style, and so forth. By no means is each treatment complete. You can't expect a few pages of text to do more than hit some highlights. These discussions cannot—repeat *cannot*—be equivalent to reading the book itself. There is no substitute for immersing yourself in a book's pages and experiencing the world created by the author. Anything less is like perusing the menu posted outside a fine restaurant; you'll see what's being served but for sure it won't satisfy your hunger.

As you read through discussions of the character, narrative style, symbolism, and themes, notice the repeated references to events in the story. Observe how generalizations are supported by specific evidence drawn from the novel being analyzed. Scrutinize the diction, syntax ,tone, and the amount of development needed to make a convincing case. Notice how one sentence leads to the next, and how paragraphs are often tied together with transitions. In other words, use the material as a model of the writing techniques that you would do well to follow when you write essays on the AP exam. You have your own unique style of writing, of course, so it serves no purpose to imitate someone else's, but the material illustrates any number of approaches to writing literary essays. In addition, it contains the kinds of ideas and concepts that you will be expected to discuss on the exam.

Pride and Prejudice by Jane Austen

Background

Pride and Prejudice is one of the most popular works read in AP English classes. What makes it endure is not its humorous portrait of an obsolete society, although it contains much to make readers laugh. Rather, the book lives on because Austen's subject is basic to human experience. The process of courtship and marriage has changed since the early 1800s, but the emotions surrounding the search for a partner and falling in love remain the same. Like the novel's characters, we, too, are subject to pride and to prejudice of all kinds. Such failings, in fact, color much of what we do and say every day. We are apt, therefore, to find much of ourselves in the adventures of Elizabeth, Darcy, and the other characters. What's more, Austen tells a whopping good story. At the outset we might sense that Elizabeth and Darcy will some day get together, that their antipathy will somehow turn to mutual respect and love. How that happens after their rocky, spite-filled start keeps readers turning the pages.

Most of the novel takes place in Hertfordshire, an area of small villages and large estates outside of London. It tells the story of the Bennets, a family with a problem. Because Mr. and Mrs. Bennet have five daughters and no sons, their estate, Longbourn, is "entailed," which means that, upon Mr. Bennet's death Longbourn will be inherited by his closest male relative, a distant cousin, Mr. William Collins. Therefore, it's crucial for the daughters, whose ages range from sixteen to twenty-three, to find good, preferably wealthy, husbands. How some of the Bennet girls go about this task is the subject of the novel.

A typical romantic novel might show each of the daughters meeting a rich young man, falling in love, enduring some sort of conflict, marrying, and living happily ever after. Although there are such elements in the novel, Austen was not inclined to write a run-of-the-mill romance. When her two major characters, Charles Darcy and Elizabeth Bennet, meet, they don't fall in love. On the contrary, they clash, insult each other, and develop deep-seated, long-lasting animosity.

Although Longbourn and the other Hertfordshire estates are imaginary places, Austen paints a realistic portrait of the landed gentry of her day. Social stratification and rank, determined by pedigree and the size of the family fortune, are terribly important. Families engage in an active social life governed by a strict etiquette that by today's standards seems absurd. Some of the rules must have seemed absurd to Austen, too, for she ridicules many of the customs and those who practice them.

> *Pride and Prejudice* is applicable to any number of essay questions, including those relating to 1) family conflict, 2) social stratification, 3) the conflict between reason and passion, 4) the hazards of first impressions, and 5) the dimensions of satire.

Synopsis

News that Netherfield, a neighboring estate, has been leased by Mr. Bingley, a rich young bachelor, sends Mrs. Bennet into a tizzy, a response derived from her obsession to marry off her five daughters posthaste. Mrs. Bennet beseeches her husband to pay a call on the new tenant, thereby initiating a social relationship that will lead to the marriage of one of her girls. Mr. Bennet obliges but not before ridiculing his wife for prematurely counting her chickens.

Bingley shows up at the next ball held in Meryton and proves to be a lively, agreeable gentleman who dances with many girls but seems to have his head turned by Jane, one of the Bennet sisters. In contrast to Bingley, his friend Mr. Darcy, another wealthy bachelor, offends the crowd with aloof manners and rude remarks, one of which is directed at Elizabeth Bennet.

During subsequent social occasions, Darcy begins to notice Elizabeth's attributes—her wit, her intelligence, her refreshing personality, even her attractive eyes. Elizabeth, on the other hand, is put off by Darcy's behavior, however curious she is about the unusual attention he seems to pay her. She notices him eavesdropping on her conversations with others, for instance. Meanwhile, Bingley's sister Caroline seems to have developed more than a passing romantic interest in Darcy.

To the delight of Kitty and Lydia, the youngest of the Bennet sisters, a military regiment arrives in nearby Meryton for the winter, promising them a lively social season in the company of young officers.

Jane receives a dinner invitation from Caroline Bingley. Mrs. Bennet, hoping that Jane might be asked to spend the night at Netherfield, sends Jane on horseback rather than by carriage. En route Jane is soaked in the rain and develops a bad cold and fever, forcing her into bed. The next day Elizabeth, worried about Jane, walks the three miles to Netherfield to visit her ailing sister. Her appearance upon arrival—damp, muddy, and disheveled—earns the scorn of Caroline and her sister, Mrs. Hurst, who disapprove of young women trekking unaccompanied around the countryside. Jane has taken a turn for the worse, obliging Elizabeth to prolong her visit. The extended stay allows the characters to interact at length and to take each other's measure. Elizabeth decides that the Bingley sisters' excessive interest in Jane's condition rings hollow and hypocritical, while Bingley himself shows genuine concern. Caroline views Elizabeth as a rival for Darcy and Darcy shows signs of being won over by Elizabeth, who engages him in several bouts of verbal one-upmanship. Each tries to outwit the other with cleverly expressed views, always spoken with utmost courtesy. Their verbal sparring usually ends in a tie.

Mrs. Bennet arrives to see Jane and declares her too sick to go home. Boorishly, she promotes Jane's good qualities to Bingley, who is unfailingly polite. His sisters, on the other hand, are repulsed by her pushiness and gauche manners. Mrs. Bennett wants Jane to stay at Netherfield as long as possible, but Elizabeth can't wait to escape.

After their return to Longbourn, Mr. Bennet tells the family that a Mr. William Collins will be dining with them that evening. Collins, a distant cousin whom Mr. Bennet has never met, stands to inherit Longbourn after Mr. Bennet dies. The very thought of Collins upsets Mrs. Bennet, but the letter announcing his weeks-long visit is conciliatory and exceedingly polite. Elizabeth notes the excessive pomposity of Collins's writing style and his exaggerated deference to Lady Catherine de Bourgh, his benefactor and patron. During the visit, Collins lavishes praise on everyone and everything, impressing Mrs. Bennet while repulsing Mr. Bennet and Elizabeth. It soon becomes clear that Collins has been dispatched to Longbourn by Lady Catherine in order to claim one of the Bennet sisters as a wife.

Out walking one day, the Bennet girls encounter Mr. Denny, an officer acquainted with Kitty and Lydia Bennet, and another officer, Mr. Wickham. As the group chats, Bingley and Darcy happen along on horseback. While greetings are being exchanged Elizabeth notices an odd look, but no words, passing between Darcy and Wickham. One gentleman turns white, the other red, suggesting some sort of previous relationship between them.

During a subsequent dinner party Wickham discloses to Elizabeth that his late father worked as steward at Pemberly, the Darcy estate. Darcy's father, now dead, had generously left a sum of money to Wickham be used for education. But young Darcy, jealous of his late father's affection for Wickham, gave the money to someone else, depriving Wickham of his future livelihood. Wickham attributes Darcy's contempt to excessive pride, and Elizabeth, no fan of Darcy's, enthusiastically concurs. From Wickham she also learns that Lady Catherine is Darcy's aunt and plans to combine her fortune with his by having him marry her daughter, a bit of gossip that, in light of Caroline Bingley's avid pursuit of Darcy, amuses Elizabeth no end.

Wickham, unable to tolerate being near Darcy for any length of time, fails to attend the ball at Netherfield. Disappointed, Elizabeth dances with Darcy. Their conversation consists of caustic but politely phrased put-downs. They also discuss Wickham. Darcy makes it clear that he resents Wickham's arrival in the local area. Miss Bingley tells Elizabeth that Wickham's story about Darcy is untrue, but Elizabeth is not persuaded.

During the ball, Collins inflicts himself on Elizabeth for the first two dances. His unwelcome attention sounds the alarm that he has selected her to be his bride. She anticipates that her refusal will profoundly upset some members of her family. As expected, Collins proposes the next day, laying out the reasons why the match would be a suitable one. Elizabeth declines, and Mrs. Bennet, hearing that Elizabeth turned down an offer of marriage, entreats her husband to talk sense to Elizabeth. Mr. Bennet, of course, won't let his favorite daughter marry such an irksome, disagreeable booby.

Undeterred in his effort to find a wife, Collins asks Charlotte Lucas, who, to the astonishment of nearly everyone, accepts, thereby putting herself in line to one day become the mistress of Longbourn.

Meanwhile, Jane is dismayed to hear that Bingley and his sisters have suddenly decamped to London for the winter. The news arrives in a letter from Caroline Bingley, who speculates that her brother may soon marry Darcy's sister, Georgiana. Elizabeth tries to reassure Jane that Bingley loves no one but her. She adds that Caroline wants her brother to marry Georgiana to improve her own chances of snaring Mr. Darcy for herself. To Jane, unable to think ill of anyone, Elizabeth's explanation is preposterous. Soon after, Jane, hoping to renew her friendship with Caroline Bingley, accepts an invitation to spend time in London with her aunt, Mrs. Gardiner. She and Caroline exchange visits but Jane feels that Caroline has turned decidedly cool toward her. She grants that Elizabeth's assessment of Caroline's motives may be valid, but she also conjectures that Caroline must be very anxious about her brother's welfare.

Letters from Charlotte tell Elizabeth all is well in her marriage to Mr. Collins. Elizabeth is skeptical but changes her view during a lengthy visit to their home, Hunsford. During her stay, she and her hosts are invited next door to dine at Rosings with Lady Catherine, whose idea of dinnertime conversation is to state strong opinions on every conceivable subject. During Elizabeth's stay at the parsonage, Darcy and his cousin Colonel Fitzwilliam visit Rosings. Elizabeth asks Darcy whether he has seen Jane in London. (She knows that he hasn't but hopes to learn from his response whether Bingley and Jane have seen each other. Evidently they haven't. Elizabeth also hopes to observe whether Darcy has any particular affection for Miss de Burgh, Lady Catherine's daughter. Evidently he doesn't.)

At Rosings, Darcy and Elizabeth, who've been apart for months, resume trading witty remarks. A day or so later Darcy drops in at Hunsford, finding Elizabeth home alone. Their conversation consists of small talk, but a nit-picky semantic disagreement generates palpable tension between them. Charlotte, after hearing that Darcy had visited Elizabeth so casually, speculates that he must be in love with her. Elizabeth doubts it but Darcy repeatedly encounters Elizabeth accidentally-on-purpose during her frequent walks in the park.

Colonel Fitzwilliam passes an offhand remark to Elizabeth that Darcy recently kept a good friend from making an imprudent marriage. Assuming that he is alluding to Bingley and Jane, Elizabeth is overwrought, having thought all the while that Caroline was responsible for keeping Bingley and Jane apart. Unwilling to face Darcy again, she begs off going to dinner at Rosings that evening. Her solitude is broken, however, by a knock on the door. It is Darcy, come to declare, in spite of his better judgment, his ardent love and desire to marry her. Elizabeth is dumfounded. Once she regains her composure, she turns him down, citing, among other reasons, that Darcy has destroyed Jane's chances for happiness as Bingley's wife and that he has unfairly and cruelly condemned Wickham to a life of poverty. Darcy barely replies and scurries out the door.

The next morning Darcy hands Elizabeth a long letter in which he justifies his actions with respect to Bingley and Jane. Basically, he believed Jane to be less enamored of Bingley than Bingley was of her, and he intervened only to stop his friend from marrying a woman whose love was questionable. He also wanted to keep Bingley from becoming entangled with the Bennet family, particularly with Mrs. Bennet and her two youngest daughters, whose uncouth behavior demeans the family name. With regard to Wickham's allegations, Darcy writes that he's been falsely accused. What happened in fact is that he gave Wickham three times the amount left to him by the elder Darcy, but instead of using it to educate himself, Wickham squandered it. When asked for more money—this time to study for the clergy—Darcy refused. To exact revenge, Wickham convinced Georgiana, Darcy's fifteen-year-old sister, to elope with him. But his plot was foiled when Georgiana got cold feet.

After reading the letter, Elizabeth reflects on Jane's laid-back, undemonstrative manner and sees how Darcy might have mistaken Jane's insouciance for lack of affection. She also acknowledges that her mother and sisters are beyond hope. Ruminating on Wickham's personality and behavior, she concedes that Darcy's version of events could be valid. Finally, Elizabeth begins to regret having so vehemently upbraided Darcy.

Elizabeth returns to Longbourn, picking up Jane in London on the way. At home they find Lydia and Kitty upset that the troops billeted in Meryton are to be redeployed, thus putting an end to their active social schedule. However, Mrs. Forster, the young wife of the regimental colonel, invites Lydia to go with her to Brighton, a seaside town where the officers are to be stationed. Lydia is overjoyed. Kitty, left out, is not. Elizabeth, fearing that Lydia is too flighty to be let off the family leash, urges her father to prevent Lydia from going, but Mr. Bennet declines. In fact, he'll be relieved to have Lydia out of the house for a while.

Elizabeth accompanies her aunt and uncle, the Gardiners, on a vacation trip to Derbyshire, the area in which Pemberly, Darcy's home, is located. Fearing an encounter with Darcy, Elizabeth agrees to visit Pemberly only after learning that Darcy is away. Impressed with the beauty and elegance of the place, she is overwhelmed by the praise that the housekeeper, Mrs. Reynolds, heaps on the master of the house. According to Mrs. Reynolds, Darcy's generosity, kindness, and affability are legendary among the servants and the local people. Elizabeth can hardly believe her ears.

When Darcy unexpectedly shows up at Pemberly, Elizabeth blushes. Darcy, astonished to find her there, proves to be a model of good manners and gentleness, showing a side of himself that Elizabeth had never seen. To both her and the Gardiners he is exceedingly attentive. He compliments Elizabeth and asks her to meet his sister, due to arrive the next day. The Gardiners perceive that there is more to Elizabeth and Darcy's relationship than they thought. Their hunch is confirmed when Darcy and Georgiana and even Mr. Bingley exchange visits. Elizabeth soon realizes that she is actually in love with Darcy and wonders whether, after all the rotten things she said to him the last time they met, he might ever renew his marriage proposal. Observing Bingley and Georgiana together, Elizabeth infers that there is nothing romantic between them and sees in fact that Bingley, eight months after his departure from Netherfield, is still stuck on Jane.

A letter arrives from Jane containing the news of a terrible scandal: Lydia has run off from Brighton with Wickham. Distraught, Elizabeth blames herself for her sister's ruin because she had concealed the facts about Wickham's shady past from her family. Darcy tries to console her but fails, and Elizabeth hurries home to be with her distressed family. Meanwhile, Mr. Bennet has gone to search for Lydia, leaving his agitated wife worrying that Wickham will fight and kill him. Mr. Gardiner joins the hunt for Lydia and soon sends news that he has found her and Wickham in London and has exacted a promise from Wickham to marry her promptly in exchange for her share of the Bennet estate, about a thousand pounds, and a small annual allowance. This solution satisfies the Bennets until it occurs to them that Mr. Gardiner must have bought Wickham off with as much as ten thousand pounds, a sum far larger than anything they could afford to repay. What's more, the marital agreement specifies that Wickham, after having his gambling debts paid, will be commissioned in the army and stationed in the north of England far from Hertfordshire. Only Mrs. Bennet disapproves of the plan; she had so looked forward to having a married child living close by. Elizabeth realizes that with Wickham as her brother-in-law, she has irrevocably lost a chance to marry Darcy, who would never deign to affiliate himself with a family of which Wickham is a member.

Lydia and her new husband visit Longbourn. In telling Elizabeth about the wedding, Lydia lets slip a secret—that Darcy had been present at the ceremony. Amazed, Elizabeth sends a letter to Mrs. Gardiner for an explanation. The reply says that it had been Darcy and not Mr. Gardiner who had prevailed upon Wickham to marry Lydia. Not only had Darcy paid Wickham's debts, he also bought Wickham's commission, and gave him a thousand pounds in Lydia's name. Mrs. Gardiner adds that she and Mr. Gardiner had allowed Darcy to become involved in the matter because of what she calls "*another interest* in the affair," presumably Darcy's regard for Elizabeth. The recognition that Darcy had acted unselfishly in her behalf lifts Elizabeth's spirits and moves her deeply.

Word soon comes that Bingley, with Darcy in tow, is about to return to Netherfield. Jane claims indifference to the news, but when Bingley pays his respects at Longbourn, it is obvious that he and Jane still love each other deeply and will soon marry. Darcy, on the other hand, shows no sign of special feelings for Elizabeth. Never suspecting that Darcy is her family's benefactor, Mrs. Bennet treats him abominably, much to Elizabeth's discomfort. To add to Elizabeth's woes, Lady Catherine, as insolent and disagreeable as ever, shows up at Longbourn to warn Elizabeth to keep hands off Darcy, whom she has reserved for her own daughter. Elizabeth won't be intimidated by such bullying and declares in effect that Lady Catherine should take a hike.

When Darcy next visits Longbourn Elizabeth thanks him on behalf of her family for his generosity toward Lydia. Darcy, surprised that Elizabeth knows of his largesse (it was meant to be kept secret), says that what he did was not for her family but only for *her*, adding that he feels no less drawn to her than he had been last April when he asked her to marry him. Having found the opening she'd been waiting for, Elizabeth declares that she now feels similarly about him. Darcy responds with heartfelt glee and delight. What follows is a long walk during which the happy pair explain their past behavior toward one another. They clear up any leftover misunderstandings and apologize for whatever pain each may have caused the other.

Virtually everyone is astonished over the sudden engagement of Elizabeth and Darcy. Mr. Bennet, in particular, needs assurance that Elizabeth, whom he understood to be an avowed Darcy-hater, has not lost her mind. Convinced finally that all is well, he gives his consent. The marriage is celebrated, and over time, even Lady Catherine and Miss Bingley come to terms with it.

Cast of Characters

The characters in *Pride and Prejudice* come mainly from the society's upper crust. Although all are affluent, gradations exist among them. The better families, such as the Darcys, are richer and hence more esteemed than others. Because Bingley comes from great wealth, he is said to "condescend" in order to marry Jane, whose family's relative penury is compounded by having their home, Longbourn, "entailed." Wealth, though, seems to have no bearing on manners. The vulgarity of superrich Lady Catherine de Bourgh defies belief. Although Bingley is polite and charming, his sister Caroline is a snake. It is fascinating to observe how people from different families treat and interrelate with one another according to their rank.

The Bennet Family

Elizabeth is the Bennets' second daughter and the book's main character. Critics say that she represents the *prejudice* of the book's title. Opinionated and assertive, she often jumps to conclusions but lacks the pride that often forces stubborn people to cling to faulty views. Whatever her weaknesses—her fast and sometimes caustic tongue, a propensity to fall for affable gentlemen (i.e., Wickham), little tolerance for others' faults and foibles—they are far outweighed by her many virtues. It's hard not to think the world of her. She is the strongest, brightest, and most admirable character in the book, although some readers might choose Darcy for that distinction.

Not as physically radiant as her sister Jane, Elizabeth is nevertheless fine-figured and blessed with beautiful eyes, an aptly chosen feature considering how perceptive she is. Her wit and intelligence are obvious. Austen tells us at the start that Elizabeth has "a lively, playful disposition which delighted in anything ridiculous," and then provides a social scene bristling with things to deride, from the inanity of her mother and younger sisters to Mr. Darcy's aloofness. "I hope I never ridicule what is wise or good," says Elizabeth to Darcy. "Follies and nonsense, whims and inconsistencies do divert me, I own, and I laugh at them whenever I can." Elizabeth is refreshingly frank, but not ill-mannered enough to hurt others' feelings. She usually keeps her thoughts private until she can share a good laugh with her confidante, Jane, or sometimes with her father. Only those as callous as Lady Catherine or boorish as Mr. Collins bear the brunt of Elizabeth's disdain face to face.

Elizabeth's natural, unaffected manner sets her apart from most other women in the novel and is the very quality that attracts and ultimately beguiles Darcy. She doesn't flirt, feign false modesty, or pretend to be excited by clothes and dances and tea parties. Ordinarily immune to the charm and good looks of young officers, she is quite taken by Wickham, however, and this in spite of Mrs. Gardiner's warning that she oughtn't fall in love with a man who lacks a sizeable fortune. Innocently, she swallows Wickham's story of Darcy's perfidy, an error fueled by her disposition to view Darcy in the worst possible light. Even after Wickham jilts her in favor of a wealthier woman, it doesn't occur to her to doubt his veracity.

In the wake Wickham's egress, Elizabeth turns cynical about all men, even about her own father, whom she loves but also judges harshly for having chosen an unsuitable wife. She blames men for being arrogant and women for being so desperate they'll marry anyone. Unlike her friend Charlotte Lucas, she is determined to marry only for love. The strength of her conviction is put to the test when Darcy proposes. A less principled woman might have jumped at the chance to marry a man of such wealth, but Elizabeth won't compromise. Besides, when Darcy declares his love to her, he already has three strikes against him: Elizabeth abhors him for treating Wickham cruelly, she despises him for persuading Bingley not to marry Jane, and she considers him a contemptible, supercilious boor.

In spite of Elizabeth's keen ability to size up other people, she has misjudged Darcy. Perhaps he is too complex or too mysterious to be easily appraised. At first, Elizabeth is put off by his rudeness. But until Darcy stepped into her life, Elizabeth had never met a man as clever. She seems to enjoy the challenge of exchanging witty insults with him. Their banter is basically light but contains enough vitriol to keep it interesting.

Elizabeth's misjudgment of Darcy, of course, is important to the development of her character and crucial to the story's dramatic tension. She must judge him harshly at the beginning in order to undergo a change of heart at the end. As she learns about him—mostly through his letter to her and via the testimony of others—she becomes more circumspect. Her capacity for reflection improves. She reconsiders her views, acknowledging that her antipathy may have led her to draw hasty conclusions. As evidence mounts that Darcy is kinder, nobler, and more generous than she had ever imagined, her prejudices erode. And when it turns out that Darcy's largesse rescued both Lydia and the Bennet family from a world-class social scandal, she sees just how wrong she has been. Darcy opens her eyes and shames her into admitting that until then, in spite of her intelligence and perspicacity, she never truly knew herself.

Jane is the oldest and prettiest daughter. In contrast to Elizabeth, she is blind to malice and the follies of others. For example, she thinks of Caroline Bingley as a friend, when the truth is that Caroline disdains her and is determined to keep Bingley from courting and marrying her. Later Jane refuses to accept the story Wickham tells about Darcy's infamy, preferring to believe that both he and Darcy are being maligned in some way. She also tries to defend Charlotte Lucas's decision to marry Mr. Collins.

Critics have pointed out that Jane is a Cinderella figure, inasmuch as she and Bingley, her "prince," fall in love almost instantly and that their mutual love eventually overcomes the obstacles that stand between them. Jane and Bingley ignore Caroline's objections to their marriage and prove to Darcy, who suspects that Jane doesn't love Bingley as much as Bingley loves her, that he has misconstrued Jane's undemonstrative nature.

Mary, the plainest and oddest of the sisters, likes to read and make pronouncements of what she has derived from her books. Since she reads without reflection, however, she comes across as a pedantic pseudointellectual, making irrelevant or erroneous assertions to her family and friends. She plays the piano and sings pitifully but remains oblivious to her lack of talent.

Kitty (Catherine) and *Lydia*, the youngest of the sisters, are flighty, vacuous lasses totally absorbed in clothes, flirting with officers, and other fluff. Their father considers Lydia and Kitty "two of the silliest girls in the country." Of the two, Lydia, fifteen, is the more high-spirited and ditzy. She urges Bingley to hold the ball at Netherfield. She buys an ugly bonnet so that she can take it home and fix it up. Unmindful of the consequences to her family, she runs off with Wickham, then proudly returns as the first of the Bennet daughters to be married. Through a curious chain of events, Lydia's impulsiveness leads Elizabeth to appreciate Darcy's generosity and goodwill.

Mrs. Bennet has a one-track mind focused on finding husbands for each of her five daughters. Austen says that she is a "woman of mean understanding, little information, and uncertain temper." High-strung and nervous, Mrs. B is clueless about her effect on others. She epitomizes shallowness and superficiality, values that she has passed on to her two youngest daughters. To be fair, however, she has a good reason to see her daughters married well. The Bennets' home, Longbourn, is "entailed" to her husband's nearest male relative, meaning that when Mr. Bennet dies, she and her family could find themselves out on the street.

Mr. Bennet is a witty, sarcastic, and antisocial country gentleman. Refusing to be drawn into the social whirl around his house, he habitually withdraws to his library where he can enjoy books and solitude. Mr. Bennet has nothing but disdain for his wife and thinks that two of his daughters, Kitty and Lydia, are the most air-headed girls in England. Elizabeth is his favorite child because, unlike others in the family, she is sensible and intelligent.

It is like him to retreat from adversity. All his life he has avoided unpleasantness, including the need to save money for his daughters' future. Now his family bears the brunt of his laxity. Knowing that his family's reputation has been put on the line by Lydia's escapade with Wickham, Mr. Bennet is spurred into uncharacteristic action. He rushes off to seek the whereabouts of his giddiest daughter.

Mr. Bingley

Bingley is a well-to-do, handsome young bachelor with an easy, unaffected manner. He is smitten by Jane Bennet almost immediately after taking up residence in Netherfield. His sister, however, tries to convince him that Jane would not make a proper wife. His dearest friend Darcy, who leads him around by the nose, adds that pursuing Jane would be a lost cause because Jane shows no sign of a particular regard for him. Months later, after he learns that Jane has indeed been in love with him from the beginning, he asks for her hand, and to the delight of everyone but his shrewish sister, becomes Jane's husband.

Miss Caroline Bingley

Miss Bingley lives with her brother and serves as lady of the house at Netherfield. Supposedly well bred, Caroline is a pompous, vulgar, and cruel social climber. She finds fault at every turn with Elizabeth, Jane, and all the other Bennets. She opposes a marriage between her brother and Jane, preferring that he marry Miss Darcy instead. The Darcys are filthy rich, and a marriage between her brother and Georgiana Darcy would substantially improve her own chances of snaring Mr. Darcy for herself. Darcy's attraction to Elizabeth grates on Caroline no end.

Mr. Fitzwilliam Darcy

Darcy is rich and rather handsome in a mysterious, brooding sort of way. Because he declines to conform to traditional etiquette, he appears aloof and arrogant. Accompanying his friend Bingley to soirees and other social events, he manages to offend everyone, especially Elizabeth Bennet, with his rudeness. But the more he insults Elizabeth and banters with her, the more he is attracted to her. Before long, he finds himself "bewitched" by her cleverness, forthrightness, and superior intellect. He can't bring himself to admit it, though, because Elizabeth's family is socially inferior to his.

As a social maverick, it seems inevitable that he will fall in love with Elizabeth. Before that happens, however, he succeeds admirably in turning her against him. But rather than end their relationship, he leaves the door open a crack, hoping, subconsciously perhaps, that something will develop between them. And when his emotions get the better of him, he asks her to marry him. Considering himself a prime catch, he is thunderstruck to be turned down cold. In fact, Elizabeth really lets him have it, listing all his faults and reciting a list of reasons why she'd never want to be Mrs. Darcy. Rattled by the vehemence of her response, he writes a long letter hoping to explain his past behavior and to correct Elizabeth's misapprehensions. Keeping an open mind, Elizabeth gradually recognizes the truth of Darcy's claims. It was he, after all, not Wickham who had been betrayed. Jane does, in fact, project indifference toward Bingley; some of the Bennets indeed are pretty gauche characters. It also seems plausible that Darcy's pride and haughty manner might very well mask a reserved disposition.

In the end Darcy emerges as a man of integrity, wedded to the truth and to Elizabeth. As an honest fellow, he says what he thinks regardless of the impression his words may leave on others, a quality he shares with Elizabeth. His kindness and sensitivity are legendary among the servants at Pemberly and others who know him well. One could argue that Darcy buys Elizabeth's heart with his vast wealth, for it was his fortune that brought the Lydia-Wickham episode to a happy conclusion, and thereby saved the Bennets from social ostracism. Because he claims to have done it for Elizabeth and not for her family, however, any prejudices that Elizabeth may still harbor about his character are thrown to the wind.

Lady and Sir William Lucas

The Lucases are wealthy neighbors of the Bennets. Sir William is an old-time and obsolete aristocrat, enamored of his rank and title, and portrayed as an empty-headed old geezer.

Charlotte Lucas

Elizabeth's friend, Charlotte is considered sensible and intelligent until she startles Elizabeth by accepting a proposal of marriage from Mr. Collins. "I am not romantic, you know. I never was. I ask only a comfortable home," she says by way of explaining her extraordinary decision. It is easy to criticize Charlotte for her choice of husband, but later in the novel, she is depicted as being a secure and contented wife, suggesting that Austen respects Charlotte for having the courage of her convictions regardless of what others may think.

Mr. William Collins

A clergyman, Mr. Collins is Mr. Bennet's closest male relative. As a consequence, Longbourn is entailed to him, a frightening prospect made worse by his grotesque politeness. He is so oily and unctuous that it's impossible to confuse him with a real person. He slavishly worships his patron, Lady Catherine de Bourgh. At her behest he visits Longbourn in order to choose a wife from among the Bennet sisters. Lighting upon Elizabeth, who considers him a pathetic fool, he is rebuffed and turns instead to Charlotte Lucas, who accepts his proposal in order to secure a comfortable future.

Although Collins is notable for his exaggerated courtesy, beneath his respectful veneer lurks a vindictive spirit, best exemplified by his tactless letter of condolence to the Bennets in which he writes, after Lydia's elopement with

Wickham, that it's a darn good thing that Elizabeth refused to marry him because he would never wish to have been affiliated with a scandal-tainted family.

Lady Catherine de Bourgh

Lady Catherine, a self-important, autocratic *grande dame*, regards herself as an authority on every topic known to man or woman. She lords it over everyone, especially over Mr. Collins, who owes his ministry to her and in return acts the ultimate sycophant, humbly paying obeisance and catering to her every wish.

Because she is the aunt of Mr. Darcy, she assumes the right to determine his marital plans. When she demands that Elizabeth keep hands off her nephew, Elizabeth stands up to her bluster and intimidation.

Mr. and Mrs. Gardiner

The Gardiners are uncle and aunt to the Bennet girls. Mrs. Gardner serves as a kind of surrogate mother to Elizabeth, often advising her niece about affairs of the heart. She and Mr. Gardiner invite Elizabeth on a trip to Derbyshire, during which they visit Darcy's estate, Pemberly. There they observe that Elizabeth and Darcy's relationship has greater depth than they had suspected. Afterward, Mr. Gardiner involves himself in the search for Lydia and Wickham and brokers the deal that leads to their marriage.

Mr. Wickham

Wickham is a handsome and extremely gallant officer with a knack for charming young women. As son of the late steward at Pemberly, Wickham knows the Darcy family well and tells Elizabeth a story of how his prospects were ruined by Darcy who deprived him of a large amount of money left to him by Darcy's late father. Although the story is untrue, Elizabeth readily accepts it and adds it to her growing list of reasons to detest Darcy.

But Wickham, a liar, a gambler, and a fraud, squandered the money he received and now holds a grudge against Darcy for refusing to give him more. Wickham is also fond of trying to seduce rich young girls, including Georgiana, Darcy's sister, whose virtue is saved in the nick of time. Later, Wickham gets Lydia Bennet to run away with him from Brighton, hardly a challenging conquest considering her fickleness.

Structure

Told chronologically, the story takes place over the course of twelve months. Most of the plot focuses on Elizabeth's prickly relationship and ultimate *rapprochement* with Darcy. Three subplots, each involving events leading to a wedding, tend to keep the two main characters apart but also, at the end of the book, bring them together.

1. Both Darcy and Elizabeth affect the course of the first subplot—about Jane and Bingley. Darcy feels compelled to save his friend from marrying a woman who appears not to love him. He persuades Bingley to put the romance on hold for a while, devastating Jane and angering Elizabeth, who suffers along with her sister.

2. By telling slanderous lies, Wickham, the male half of the second subplot, adds to Elizabeth's distaste for Darcy. Later Darcy comes to the aid of Elizabeth's family by paying Wickham to marry Lydia Bennet, an act of generosity that convinces Elizabeth that she has completely misjudged him.

3. In the third subplot Mr. Collins, spurned by Elizabeth, marries Charlotte Lucas, giving Elizabeth an opportunity to reflect on happiness in marriage. The Collins home later serves as the setting for Darcy's proposal of marriage to Elizabeth.

In spite of intricate connections between the various plot lines and a maze of relationships among the characters, Austen flawlessly fits the pieces together. Her control of the book's structure becomes most evident in the second half of the novel where readers find that, as one event follows the next, the depth of the story grows. What may appear on the surface to be inconsequential bits of dialogue are often pregnant with meaning. At Pemberly, for example, Elizabeth pays a return call to Miss Darcy and is confronted by Miss Bingley's comment, "Pray, Miss Eliza, are not the _____ shire Militia removed from Meryton? They must be a great loss to *your* family."

This is not polite small talk but a spiteful put-down in the form of a question. It is so full of insinuation that the narrator requires half a page to lay it all out. Each person in the room, including Darcy and Bingley, is touched differently by the comment, and each character, especially Elizabeth, is aware of its effect on the others. The single word *your*, for instance, is meant not only to put Elizabeth in her place but to remind Darcy that Elizabeth comes from a socially inferior family. It also reveals Miss Bingley's disdain for the Bennets and cautions her brother to avoid becoming entangled with Jane. For Elizabeth, the remark painfully calls to mind Darcy's aversion to her mother and sister.

Themes and Motifs

Social Etiquette

Austen depicts a society overstocked with rules and customs worthy of ridicule: formal balls and social protocols and obligations. In the guise of comedy, Austen conveys serious messages pertaining mostly to pressures on every young woman to find a mate. Among other things, it was generally assumed that every girl wished to be married in order to avoid the dreary life of a spinster. Also, although Lydia Bennet disregards the custom, daughters in the same family were to be married in the order of their birth. (By breaking tradition, Lydia blights the reputation of both herself and her family. Lydia's waywardness might ordinarily diminish her sisters' prospects for finding good husbands but in this instance it indirectly brings Elizabeth and Darcy together.)

Austen's satirical attitude toward social conventions is made evident by assigning Mr. Collins the role of spokesman for social propriety. Collins is a laughable figure, and nowhere more hypocritical and ridiculous than when he proposes to Elizabeth. Following a formula, he first professes the violence of his affection for her—an empty gesture if ever there was one. Then he declines to accept Elizabeth's refusal, interpreting it as a form of coquetry expected by elegant females.

By adding Lady Catherine to her depiction of polite society, Austen lampoons upper class narrow-mindedness. A self appointed goddess, Lady Catherine dictates to others what is right and wrong, what is proper, acceptable, customary, and so on. She finds it impossible to believe, for example, that a girl can grow up without a governess.

It's easy for Austen to mock social conventions. But mocking conventions and the people who mindlessly observe them is not enough. Once the conventions are derided, what shall replace them? One can't build a civil society on Mr. Bennet's brand of cynicism nor on Lydia's sort of recklessness. Because

Austen is no anarchist, she values a balance between convention and freedom, best exemplified by Elizabeth, who appreciates the importance of rules but knows that it is damaging to follow them slavishly. Elizabeth is usually a model of decorum and respectability but rarely passes up opportunities to express her opinion, as, for example, when she unequivocally tells Darcy what she thinks of his startling marriage proposal. Feminist readers of *Pride and Prejudice* have long adopted Elizabeth as a kind of ideal woman. She stands up for her gender, sticks to her principles, and thinks for herself. Unwilling to be passive and dutiful or to spend her days pouring tea and cultivating feminine charms, Elizabeth, a thoroughly progressive and assertive woman, represents Austen's view of society at its best.

Reason vs. Passion

Rationality guides the behavior of many but not all the characters in *Pride and Prejudice*. Lydia Bennet, for one, is driven by desire for anyone in pants, and consequences be damned. Her recklessness almost leads to her loss of virtue and the destruction of her family's reputation. Charlotte Lucas, on the other hand, represents rationality taken to extremes. Passion has no role in her decision to wed. In exchange for a life of security and comfort, she marries the unendurable Mr. Collins.

Elizabeth, falling somewhere between Lydia and Charlotte, takes a dim view of both extremes. She cannot imagine being content in a marriage based on security, nor does she believe that happiness comes to a match born in passion. Her own parents, she believes, married thoughtlessly and have made a mockery of married life. Whatever passions may have driven them together faded long ago. Mrs. Bennet now lives vicariously through her two youngest daughters, and Mr. Bennet, stuck forever with a woman he scorns, escapes to his library.

In her own love life, Elizabeth avoids making a similar mistake. She doesn't fall wildly for her man. In fact, she despises him at first. But as she gradually discovers his virtues, her affection for Darcy grows. Likewise, Darcy's love evolves out of his increasing respect for Elizabeth's wit and intellect. At the end, Elizabeth's view of a happy and wise marriage consists of balancing passion and reason.

Pride, Prejudice

Displays of both pride and prejudice recur throughout the novel. Darcy, the embodiment of pride, antagonizes virtually everyone at Bingley's ball. Charlotte Lucas and the Bennet sisters can't get over Darcy's egoism, although Charlotte springs to his defense, noting that his wealth gives him the right to be proud. Mary Bennett observes that pride is a common failing, and then lectures pedantically on differences between pride and vanity, thereby exemplifying the very attributes she is trying to define.

Darcy's pride, which repulses Elizabeth, creates a huge barrier between them that gradually fades away. Initially, though, Darcy's pride is evident in almost everything he says and does. Elizabeth's pride is more subtle and is used defensively, when, for example, Darcy insults her. Even though Darcy intrigues her more than any man she has ever met, Elizabeth is too proud to give in to him. She sees something of herself in Darcy's habit of trying always to eschew hypocrisy and pretense. Yet, pride keeps her from admitting that Darcy may be just as honest, intelligent, and witty as she is.

The social milieu of the novel is dominated by prejudice derived largely from wealth. Affluence seems to entitle rich people to look down at those less well off. Lady Catherine, for one, assumes that the size of her fortune gives her the right to pass judgment on everyone and everything.

A more subtle, and therefore more insidious, kind of prejudice is embodied by Elizabeth. Usually a keen a judge of character, she is sometimes blinded by her biases. She is completely sucked in by Wickham's lies about Darcy, for example, because of her predisposition to judge Darcy negatively. Prejudice also keeps her from believing Caroline Bingley's assertion that Wickham's story is a pack of lies. At Rosings, Elizabeth, catching a glimpse of Miss de Bourgh, a thin, small, sickly, and cross-looking young woman, rejects her out of hand. Knowing that this girl may someday marry Darcy, Elizabeth says sarcastically, "Yes, she will do for him very well. She will make him a very proper wife."

Prejudice initially prevents Elizabeth from accepting Darcy's account of Wickham's behavior. Later, after realizing the truth of Darcy's allegations, she regrets having spoken harshly to Darcy and acknowledges that prejudice made her do it.

By the end of the book, Elizabeth has changed. Not that all her prejudice has vanished, but she is more aware of how it has for a long time undermined her happiness. Whether falling in love and marrying Darcy will purge prejudice from her heart we will never know, but the novel's conclusion implies that it will.

Flaws and Foibles
Pride and Prejudice includes several portrayals of men, almost all unflattering, at least in part. Darcy, although he turns out all right at the end, suffers from an excess of *hubris*. Mr. Bennett, while clever and witty, is basically an isolated and unhappy man. Mr. Collins is a buffoon and Wickham, a rogue. Bingley, despite his charm, appears to be a milquetoast, manipulated easily by Darcy and by his sisters. Only Mr. Gardiner, a minor character, emerges free of blemish.

The women in the novel are equally flawed, perhaps even more so. Think of Mrs. Bennet, Lydia, Mary, Charlotte, Lady Catherine, Miss Bingley, and Jane. Even Elizabeth, the most admirable woman in the book, suffers from both pride and prejudice. In spite of the characters' various flaws and foibles, however, Austen in no way conveys a misanthropic message. Rather, she portrays people as they are, mixed bags of good and bad qualities, often out of balance. As a consequence, ordinarily sensible, sober-minded people sometimes act foolishly, and rarely more so when it comes to the rituals of love and marriage.

The young women in the novel tirelessly pursue flawed men and hope to marry them in spite of their defects. Charlotte, who views men as unfeeling simpletons, claims that love is a question of communicating feelings. To her, happiness in marriage is a matter of chance. After being jilted by Wickham, Elizabeth becomes cynical about love and marriage. Having seen no happy marriages, including that of her parents, she condemns men for their arrogance and women for being tolerant of cads and bounders. Elizabeth's experiences with men—from Darcy to Bingley to Wickham—have embittered her. Thinking of her forthcoming visit to Charlotte, she says "Stupid men are the only ones worth knowing, after all."

Narrative Style/Language

"It is a truth universally acknowledged, that a single man in possession of good fortune must be in want of a wife." Readers encountering this opening line of Chapter 1 for the first time may suspect that it is silly, but will require several more lines to grasp the full extent of its silliness. The generalization is a "truth" fixed only in the mind of Mrs. Bennet and other ridiculous characters like her.

At the very start, then, Jane Austen provides a glimpse of her attitude toward the society she portrays in the novel. As early scenes unfold, such as Mr. Bennet's mockery of Mrs. Bennet for jumping to conclusions about Mr. Bingley's marital plans, Austen's intent becomes clear. She means to point out the self-delusion and absurd conventions of a small segment of the English upper class.

Although Austen tells the story as an omniscient narrator, she sometimes steps out of her role. When, for example, Elizabeth and the Gardiners are touring in Derbyshire, Austen says directly to the reader, "It is not the object of this work to give a description of Derbyshire, nor of any of the remarkable places through which their route thither lay; Oxford, Blenheim, . . .etc., are sufficiently known." Most of what we learn about the characters, however, comes from their own words and actions. (Many long passages consist almost entirely of dialogue—Chapter 1, for instance.) We are also privy to the generally sensible and astute observations made by Elizabeth, whose point of view controls the story. Through Elizabeth, readers come to see what Austen thinks of courtship and marriage, the effects of wealth and privilege, the complexity of interpersonal relationships.

Austen generally gives readers a quick take on her characters and then lets the characters speak for themselves. Chapter 15, for example, begins, "Mr. Collins was not a sensible man. . . ." The narration that follows contains a concise review of Collins's life. Then, after Austen removes herself from the story, we see Collins in action and hear him converse. With the help of Elizabeth, Mr. Bennet, and others, we are then left to draw our own conclusions about his character and substance.

When Elizabeth arrives at Rosings for the first time, we are told that Lady Catherine's "air was not conciliating, nor was her manner of receiving them [her guests] such as to make her visitors forget their inferior rank." This is the narrator's view, but it is also Elizabeth's and soon, as Elizabeth observes Lady Catherine more fully, it also becomes the reader's. We are privy to Elizabeth's thoughts about her hostess: "She was not rendered formidable by silence, but whatever she said was spoken in so authoritative a tone as marked her self-importance and brought Mr. Wickham immediately to Elizabeth's mind." Later in the evening, Elizabeth (i.e., Austen) can't help passing a witty comment about the *grande dame*'s pomposity: "The party gathered around the fire to hear Lady Catherine determine what weather they were to have on the morrow."

Indeed, Austen never tires of revealing her ironic sense of humor. Sometimes, she pokes fun at the characters. Referring to Mrs. Bennet's preparations for a dinner party: nothing "less than two courses could be good enough for a man . . . who had ten thousand a year." At other times, characters pass ironic remarks to each other. Mr. Bennet sends Kitty weeping with the threat: "And you are never to stir out of doors till you can prove that you have spent ten minutes of every day in a rational manner." The irony goes over the girl's head, but Mr. Bennet doesn't stop trying. Seeing Kitty in tears, he adds, "Well, well, do not make yourself unhappy. If you are a good girl for the next ten years, I will take you to a review [a show] at the end of them." Not one to let an opportunity pass without a witticism, Mr. Bennet targets the follies of other characters. Having been advised by Mr. Collins to never permit Lydia and Wickham in his sight or allow their names to be uttered in his hearing, he exclaims, "*That is his notion of Christian forgiveness!*"

Humor helps readers become involved in a novel that might be considered quaint, perhaps even out of date. The world of the book is remote in time and place. Austen's style of expression, although streamlined for early nineteenth-century writers, is still by modern standards elegant and ornate. Its formality, emphasized in part by customs of address—even married couples call each other Mr. and Mrs.—may keep us at arm's length, but only briefly. Distance diminishes as we come to know the characters. Their problems may differ in detail from ours but they pertain to us as directly as they do to the lives of the fictional people in Hertfordshire. They, like us, are caught up in family concerns and in issues of honesty, social acceptance, love and marriage, and finding the best route to decent and satisfying lives.

Questions for Writing and Discussion

1. Is there any evidence before Darcy's proposal to suggest that he has a special affection for Elizabeth, or that she has affection for him? Does their relationship go through stages, or does his proposal come as a complete surprise?

2. *Pride and Prejudice* reflects the values and customs of a small segment of British society during a particular historical era. One critic accuses Austen of "writing dull stories about ordinary people." Yet *Pride and Prejudice* endures as a classic of English literature. How might its longevity be explained?

3. In traditional interpretations of the novel Elizabeth stands for prejudice, Darcy for pride. Some critics maintain that such a dichotomy oversimplifies the book and its main characters. Do you agree? To what extent, if any, might the two protagonists exemplify *both* pride and prejudice?

4. To what extent does the notion of "opposites attract" pertain to the relationships between various couples, married and otherwise, in *Pride and Prejudice*?

5. In what ways does Austen's narrative style contribute to the overall effect of the novel on readers? Consider any relevant aspects of the narration, including tone, use of language, dialogue, point of view.

The Red and the Black by Stendahl

Background

An illicit love affair between a young man and a married woman lies at the core of both Stendahl's *The Red and the Black* and Flaubert's *Madame Bovary*, the other romantic nineteenth-century French novel read widely in AP English classes.

Published in 1830, Stendahl's novel tells the story of Julien Sorel, son of a small-town sawmill owner. It follows Julien's journey from the provinces to a seminary where he studies for the priesthood, and then to the socially prominent salons of Paris. Although the story focuses on one individual, it is also a portrait of French society—its strict social stratification, its politics, economics, and religion. It takes place during the Restoration, a period of relative peace and prosperity between the Napoleonic era and the Revolution of 1830. Stendahl diagnoses the multiple ills of the period and provides an astute, if not always impartial, rendering of various classes and professional groups, including merchants, judges, the military, the clergy, the liberals, and the ultraroyalists who support the despotic King Charles X.

The title of the book has long been a puzzle. Some readers conjecture that the title symbolizes the red of love and the black of death. Others think that the title alludes to the colors of a roulette wheel, suggesting that Julien's quest for fame and fortune is akin to a game of chance. Still other readers assert that the colors refer to a chess board, as if to say that Julien is like a pawn being manipulated toward ultimate victory or defeat by forces he can't control. The most common interpretation, however, is that the two colors represent Julien's choice of careers: the *Red* referring to uniforms worn by Napoleon's army, the *Black* to the traditional garb worn by men of the church. A generation earlier Julien would probably have joined the army to make his fortune. In his own times—the late 1820s—his future lies in the priesthood, the only career that would allow him to climb into a higher social class. It couldn't be accidental that Stendahl alludes to the color of clothing instead of to great ideas of the Revolution or Rousseau in his title. Stendahl portrays a society steeped in superficiality, as well as in pretense, hypocrisy, and dissimulation. Hardly a character in the book is not in some way warped by shallowness, greed, or stupidity. Even Julien, the book's hero, while engaging in a bitter struggle against philistinism and the despotism of the upper classes, is often prey for Stendahl's satirical invective.

The Red and the Black is more than satire, however. It's also a kind of prophesy. It foreshadows the historic struggle between the classes that rocked France and the rest of Europe from the early 1800s into the twentieth century. Stendahl was one of the first European novelists to contemplate what happens when excessive power resides in the hands of an elite few. That the lower classes will suffer at the hands of the nobility is a given, but a kind of tyranny infects the aristocracy as well. Far from leading a carefree life of wealth, the upper crust finds itself as constrained as citizens in a police state.

Use *The Red and the Black* for an essay on any of the following topics: 1) a young protagonist trying to succeed in a hostile world, 2) a young man's ambition, 3) class discrimination, 4) social stratification, 5) social satire, 6) the novel as history, or 7) the varieties of love.

Synopsis

The story is long and complicated, full of twists, turns, and surprises. Here are some of its highlights:

Part I

Chapter 1 begins with an account of the little French mountain town of Verrières on the banks of the Doubs River. Verrières is a mill town that manufactures painted tiles, nails, and a cotton cloth known as Mulhouse. Business is good. Money, in fact, drives the town, and the pursuit of more money is the obsession of three-fourths of its inhabitants, including members of the clergy, who seem more concerned about getting rich than about saving souls. The idyllic peacefulness of Verrières is slightly undercut by the existence of old "fortifications," once used to used to keep out armed invaders. The walls are now in ruins, suggesting that invaders—if indeed there are any—will be of another kind, perhaps from within the town's population.

The mayor of Verrières, Monsieur de Rênal, epitomizes the town's privileged class. A conservative royalist supporting the restoration of the Bourbon monarchy, Rênal is an aristocrat fallen into hard times. At present he is trying to beat his way back up the social scale via business and financial dealings. On the other end of the ideological spectrum stands Rênal's rival and nemesis M.Valenod, a militant liberal representing the rising bourgeoisie.

Like others of his class, Rênal is engaged in a perpetual struggle against the less privileged residents of his town. One adversary is Père Sorel, a stern, obstinate peasant who runs a sawmill and overcharges Rênal for a parcel of land that the mayor wants for a walled garden that he hopes will enhance his social stature. To bolster his reputation still further Rênal also plans to engage a tutor for his three children and picks Sorel's son Julien, a young man known in Verrières for his mastery of Latin. The fact is that Julien's Latin is limited to a knack for reciting from memory long passages of the New Testament, but Rênal regards hiring Julien as a kind of social coup. He gloats about having outfoxed Valenod, who, according to the rumor mill, has had his eye on Julien as a tutor for his own children.

At first Julien balks. He claims an interest in the priesthood, a career that will propel him up the social ladder, not the job of a lowly servant. But Madame de Rênal, indifferent to the niceties of social rank, calls him "sir" and treats him far more courteously than he expected. Besides, Madame de Rênal is shapely, beautiful, and much younger than her husband. She suggests "ideas of sweet voluptuous pleasure." Julien is attracted and immediately starts to flirt with her. Bored with life and ignored by her husband, she is flattered by Julien's attentions. She blushes like a schoolgirl in his company, gives him gifts, and begins to pays closer attention to her clothes and makeup.

Julien's presence in the Rênal household arouses intense feeling among his fellow staff members. All resent him, except for Elisa, Madame Rênal's maid, who falls in love with Julien and asks him to marry her. To Madame de Rênal's relief Julien turns down the proposal, but from then on Elisa, a spurned and vengeful lover, misses no opportunity to note moments of tenderness between Julien and Madame de Rênal. At times Julien suspects that Madame de Rênal is toying with him, as though he were a pet or favorite knickknack. As a callow youth, he is tongue-tied in her presence, unable to carry on a simple conversation. The reason is that much of what he knows has come from books instead of experience. Books have taught him to idolize Napoleon but he knows better than to praise the former emperor in front of the Rênals. Expressing liberal views would hurt his chances of social success.

Monsieur Rênal is not always satisfied with Julien's performance as a tutor. He chides Julien for coddling the children but quickly regrets it, thinking that he may drive Julien away. When Julien asks whether Rênal might prefer another tutor, Rênal suspects that Julien is planning to work for Valenod and immediately raises the boy's salary.

Julien, in a fit of self-confidence, launches a personal campaign to seduce Madame de Rênal, not because he loves her but because he thinks it is his duty, something that Napoleon would have done in similar circumstances. In plain sight of her husband, he holds hands with Madame de Rênal, but Rênal is so wrapped up in business affairs, that he remains oblivious to the hanky-panky occurring right in front of his nose.

The Rênal children adore Julien. At times he returns their affection, but at other times finds them as repugnant as the Rênals' crowd of pretentious, boorish, and hypocritical friends and relatives. Yet, Julien's hopes for ascending the social ladder depend on his ability to please and emulate them. Therefore, he swallows his pride and decides to master the art of hypocrisy, rationalizing that, as a disciple of Napoleon, he must allow his ends to justify his means. If he must lie and deceive to gain entree into the aristocracy, so be it—he'll lie and deceive.

One day Julien goes walking alone in the hills surrounding Verrières. At a high elevation he pauses on top of a huge rock. His physical position suggests to him the moral position he yearns to attain. He also spies a powerful hawk. Impressed with its strength and isolation, he draws an analogy between the powerful bird and Napoleon's destiny. Will such a destiny someday be my own? he asks himself.

Julien sets out to visit Fouqué, a timber merchant friend in the mountains. En route, he feels as happy and free as he's ever been and daydreams of future grandeur in Paris. When Fouqué offers him a lucrative job in the timber trade, Julien turns it down. The work would put an end to his dreams of glory. By rejecting the job Julien, in effect, rejects the life of the bourgeoisie and commits himself to achieving success in loftier circles. Back in town, he renews his campaign to seduce Madame de Rênal with increased vigor and finally draws her into adultery. Repeated triumphs in bed heighten his sense that he is inching up the social ladder. After each sexual encounter, however, he feels silly and awkward, thinking that the anticipation was more exciting than the reward. When all is said and done, he'd just as soon stay in his own room reading about Napoleon. But he steels himself for repeated visits to Madame de Rênal. Although nocturnal dalliances with this desirable and noble woman become routine, his ambition to raise himself socially remains stronger than ever.

The king's visit to Verrières serves as a stepping-stone. Madame de Rênal, grown increasingly lovesick for Julien, who has begun to make up excuses to stay away from her, arranges a position for him in the honor guard for the king. Dressed in military garb Julien fantasizes that he's Napoleon's *aide de camp* and feels closer to his idol than at any other time in his life. Afterward, he dons the robe of a cleric to participate in church services held in the king's honor. Impressed by the Bishop of Agde—like Napoleon, the bishop acquired power at a young age—Julien assures himself that the church offers him the most direct route to social prominence. Madame de Rênal, picturing Julien as an eminent figure in the church, supports his decision.

A week later the serious illness of Stanislaus, the Rênals' youngest son, convinces Madame de Rênal that God is punishing her for violating her marriage vows. She is about to confess to her husband when Julien stops her, arguing that a scandal will not only ruin her life but will keep M. de Rênal from membership in the Chamber of Deputies. Persuaded, she once more declares her love for Julien, who responds in kind. Seething with jealousy, Elisa informs M. Valenod about the affair. Valenod, happy to cause trouble for Rênal, writes him an anonymous letter describing his wife's infidelity. Julien and Madame de Rênal, however, conspire to discredit the allegations by writing a fake letter from an anonymous source and addressing it to her. The bogus letter asserts that Valenod had written the first letter in order to embarrass Rênal and to improve his own chances of seducing Madame de Rênal. To prove that Valenod is capable of such licentiousness, Julien and Madame de Rênal arrange for Rênal to come across a packet of Valenod's love letters written long ago. Convinced of his wife's innocence, Rênal is relieved that a costly scandal has been avoided. What's more, he decides that Valenod's letter was meant to trick him into firing Julien, who then would be free to tutor the Valenod children.

During a social evening at the Valenods, Julien is the life of the party. A gracious guest, he compliments the hosts and their children, demonstrates his knowledge of Latin, and shows off his wit. But his performance is an exercise in hypocrisy. The truth is that he is repulsed by the Valenods' bourgeois obsession with money. Realizing that his sensibilities are more refined and genteel than theirs, he resolves once more to gain greater prestige and power via the church. With Father Chélan's help, Julian gains admission to the seminary at Besançon. Madame de Rênal, devastated by her lover's imminent departure, gives him a lock of her hair, but he, at the threshold of a new career, finds that his ardor for her has cooled.

Besançon, in contrast to Verrières, strikes Julien as a vibrant and bustling town. But he is less enthusiastic about the seminary. Father Pirard, the director, initially treats him with disdain but soon recognizes his quick mind and assigns him to a private room as a mark of special distinction. Other students resent Julien's academic success, his hypocritical piety, eloquence, and free thinking. Julian, in return, scorns their ignorance and lack of refinement. Because Julien seems to foment ill will at the seminary, some of the faculty wish to expel him. Pirard defends him, however, and promotes him to a quasi-teaching position, causing disgruntled priests to put the screws to Julien in their classes. Fed up with the politics of the seminary, Pirard resigns. Offered a job in Paris as the personal secretary to Marquis de la Mole, a wealthy nobleman, Pirard declines but recommends Julien for the position. Before relocating to Paris Julien hastens back to Verrières for one more tryst with Madame de Rênal.

Part 2

A life in Paris is Julien's dream come true. Overwhelmed by the luxury and opulence of the marquis's residence, the Hôtel de la Mole, Julien hobnobs with the superrich and acquires many of their airs and affectations. He learns to fence, shoot, and ride horses—sometimes with comical results. He goes riding with Norbert, the marquis's son, and falls from the horse. His trendy new clothes raise eyebrows in the marquis's salon. After an altercation in a café, Julien fights a duel of honor and gets a bullet in the arm. His opponent, a M. de Beauvoisis, is red-faced to learn that he has dueled with a lowborn carpenter's son and spreads a rumor that Julien is really the illegitimate son of a nobleman.

Satisfied with Julien's performance on the job, the marquis becomes his mentor, trusted friend, and surrogate father, showing him the way into Parisian society. The deeper his involvement, however, the more Julien perceives that the glamour of the elite is tainted by their utter boredom. Bored with themselves and with each other, they welcome Julien, a new face, into their midst like a breath of fresh air.

Before long Julien and the marquis's daughter Mathilde are drawn to each other. Julien is attracted by her good looks and free spirit. As one who shuns the petty conversation and social etiquette of her class, Mathilde is fascinated by Julien's humble birth and his intellect. To counteract the boredom of her life, she reads novels set in the days of chivalry and romance. In fact, she has developed a quirky attachment to one of her own ancestors, Boniface de la Mole, a revolutionary figure decapitated in 1574. On the anniversary of his death,

Mathilde wears black. Confiding in each other, Julien and Mathilde also discover that they both revere Napoleon.

Several young noblemen court Mathilde, but she is intrigued by Julien, whose lower-class origins make him different from the others and feed her romantic fantasies. She is excited by the idea of making Julien her lover. Julien is equally eager. To seduce her would be like a battle won against Mathilde's suitors.

After a night of passion, each suffers uncertainty about the other's feelings. Mathilde's arrogance keeps Julien at arm's length; Julien's timidity prevents him from asserting himself. The winds of love blow hot and cold between them, causing each to suffer unbearably. They treat each other cruelly and play psychological mind games that leave them full of hate and full of longing for each other at the same time.

Because of his extraordinary memory, Julien is sent by Marquis de la Mole on a secret mission around the country to deliver a message to various members of a conspiracy that supports the restoration of the monarchy. In Strasbourg he runs into an acquaintance, Prince Korasov, to whom he confides the story of his stormy relationship with Mathilde. Korasov, a veteran in affairs of the heart, gives Julien a prescription for making Mathilde jealous and thereby capturing her love. He instructs Julien to feign interest in another woman and provides him with copies of over fifty fake love letters to send to his alleged paramour. Back in Paris, Julien successfully carries out the plan, using a family friend, Madame de Fervaques, as his foil. Mathilde, overcome with jealousy, berates Julien for treating her badly, and Julien, unable to sustain the ruse, confesses his love for her.

Without passing Go, the pair fly into bed, and before long Mathilde finds herself pregnant. She and Julien plan an escape to Switzerland. Via a letter, she asks her father for forgiveness, explaining that it was her fault for seducing Julien, not vice-versa. But the marquis furiously rebukes Julien for betraying his trust and for exploiting his position in the Hôtel de la Mole. Father Pirard advises the marquis that anything but a public marriage would be a crime in the eyes of God. The marquis, desperate to prevent his daughter from marrying a man so far beneath her, would like to have Julien killed "accidentally." But he realizes that Julien could have a brilliant career and reluctantly grants a piece of property and a generous sum of money to him and Mathilde. To save Mathilde from being stuck with a commoner's name—Madame Sorel—the marquis also arranges for Julien to receive both a military commission and the name of an aristocrat, de La Vernaye. Julian rejoices, having finally reached the status he has sought.

As wedding arrangements gear up, the marquis suddenly withdraws his consent to the marriage, however. The mail has brought a letter from Madame de Rênal denouncing Julien as a fraud, a seducer, a fortune hunter, and a complete hypocrite, providing the marquis with just the excuse he needs to prevent the match from taking place.

Thunderstruck, Julien impulsively sets out for Verrières. He finds Madame de Rênal in the church, takes aim, and shoots her with a pistol.

In prison Julien celebrates the news that Madame de Rênal survived his attack. Nevertheless, as a commoner who nearly took the life of a noblewoman, he is charged with murder and fully expects to be guillotined. Content to remain in prison for the remaining five or six weeks of his life, Julien rejects his friend Fouqué's proposal to arrange an escape by bribing the jailer.

In a letter he once again declares his love for Mathilde and urges her to marry one of her suitors, M. de Croisenois, after he is gone. Mathilde, disguised as a peasant, visits him. Attempting to arrange Julien's release, she pulls strings and drops names in official circles, but her efforts fail. Meanwhile, Julien begins make peace with himself. His ambition for high status, a craving that drove him all his life, lies dead in his heart. He regrets betraying the marquis, loving Mathilde, and wounding Madame de Rênal, who, during a visit to his cell, reiterates her love and explains that her confessor had actually written and then forced her to send the damaging letter to the marquis. Hoping to save Julien, Madame de Rênal urges the jury appointed to hear Julien's case to acquit him. Killing him, she asserts, will destroy two lives, his and hers. Because Valenod, the foreman, still smarts with jealousy about Julien's affair with Madame de Rênal—rumors abound that Valenod had once unsuccessfully tried to seduce her—her pleas are certain to be ignored

At his trial, Julien addresses the jury, not a jury of his peers, but an assemblage of noblemen. Acknowledging his guilt, he ironically convinces them that they must put him to death. Their duty, he says, is to discourage other lowborn young men from securing a good education and boldly mingling with so-called good society.

After Valenod announces the verdict, Julien sits on death row prepared to die in three days. He forbids Mathilde to appeal his case. But when Madame de Rênal offers to make the appeal for a stay of execution, Julien realizes after all that she is the woman he loves and agrees to sign the papers provided that she promises to visit him every day he remains in jail. She vows to do so, but after a few days M. de Rênal gets wind of the situation and commands her to stop.

Julien's case has made him a public figure, a kind of romantic folk hero. A holy man visits Julien in his cell. He comes not to bring comfort, however, but to generate publicity for himself. A certain M. de Frilair, thinking it would be useful to his own ambitions to be Julien's successor in the de la Mole household, interviews the condemned man. Even Julien's father pays a call, not to say good-bye to his son but to insist that Julien bequeath his money to his brothers and himself. In Julien's final hours, a confessor priest comes to exploit the doomed prisoner. If Julien would only convert to Jansenism, he would give a much-needed boost to religion.

During his last days, dark and cynical thoughts crowd Julien's mind. He ponders the absurdity of "natural law" that sets one class of men above others and meditates on the hypocrisy and charlatanism of even the greatest and most virtuous men. Feeling isolated and abandoned by a God that has deprived him of Madame de Rênal, the woman he loves, Julien at age twenty-three is ready to die. Just before death, he hears that Marquis de Croisenois has been killed in a duel and urges Mathilde to marry another suitor, M. de Luz.

After the execution Mathilde kisses Julien's severed head and buries it with her very own hands, just as Queen Margot had done with the head of her own lover, Boniface de la Mole, back in 1574. Three days later Madame de Rênal dies, presumably from a broken heart.

Cast of Characters   A crew of smug, petty, and mostly unsavory men and women populate the pages of *The Red and the Black*. Some are caricatures; others are aristocratic types that frequent the salons of Verrières and Paris. Members of the clergy are often meddling do-gooders, sycophants, or petty tyrants. The bourgeoisie is represented by a cadre of unprincipled scoundrels enslaved by greed and driven by ambition.

One character who doesn't appear in the novel but is never far from events in the story is Napoleon. Dead since 1821, his legacy inspires and propels Julien through life. Julien emulates Napoleon, aspiring to achieve equivalent glory and grandeur.

Julien Sorel

The youngest son of a provincial sawyer, Julien is the novel's central character. From his earliest years he is fueled by a desire to reach the upper echelons of French society. When readers first lay eyes on him Julien is eighteen and seated high on a roof beam in his father's sawmill. Instead of supervising the work below he is reading a book about Napoleon. Julien's lofty perch says it all. Physically, intellectually, emotionally—in every way he is obsessed with escaping the life into which he was born.

Julien breaches the wall separating the working class from the bourgeoisie quite by chance. M. de Rênal hires him to tutor his children and Julien, lukewarm at first, begins to seize opportunities for advancement, especially by endearing himself to Madame de Renal, the lady of the house. Later in the book we see Julien standing alone on a mountain peak, exulting over his climb both literally and figuratively out of the stifling existence of working-class Verrières.

Father Pirard, one of Julien's mentors, notices something troubling in Julien's character. He predicts that his young friend will either succeed admirably in life or fall flat on his face. For Julien there is no middle way. He'll either turn himself into a second Napoleon or be executed as a common criminal. Extremes are evident in Julien's behavior. One moment paralyzed by fear and self-doubt, in the next he is the picture of courage and confidence. At one point he endlessly weighs the pros and cons of placing a ladder under Mathilde's bedroom window; at another time he rushes off hell-bent on shooting a bullet into Madame de Rênal. While discussing the Bible and classical literature with seminary priests, Julien seems a paragon of sophistication and scholarship. In other circumstances he acts like a tongue-tied rustic, unable to hold up his end of a simple conversation.

Such flipflops stem partly from the conflict that rages within Julien himself. He can't decide which path to follow to fame and fortune. Should he be a soldier or a priest? Wear the red or the black? He daydreams of being the next Napoleon. He also envisions himself holding a very high office in the church hierarchy. What he ultimately chooses won't be based on rational thought, however, but on what happens to be fashionable at the moment. That is, he'll pick the career that promises to be more socially advantageous.

Julien's relentless desire to rise above his present station in life controls almost everything he thinks and feels. Whatever affection he has for Madame de Rênal, for example, is tainted by his ambition. Loving her is a tactical move, rather like a stratagem used by Napoleon on the battlefield. He equates making love with doing his duty. There are times, however, when he feels truly smitten by Madame de Rênal. But as he courts her, he's hardly a lover in thrall to his beloved. He pursues her like a robot programmed to follow protocols of courtship and romance.

Despite his efforts to earn a place in society, Julien is destined to fail. He's an outsider, a spiritual orphan. Having walked away from his roots, he's no longer a peasant, but adopting the trappings of gentility in no way assures him a place in the fashionable world he yearns to join. He remains adrift. Julien's alienation is more than a social term; it is also psychological. He is at odds with himself because the tension between his passions and his rationality tears him to pieces. He would like to love freely, but can't. Nor can he enjoy the rewards of his efforts. Quite the contrary, he is repulsed by the corruption and hypocrisy that taint the life he observes in the drawing rooms of the aristocracy.

Julien's sharp mind alienates him still further. Society has no room for his kind of genius. He has the wit to overcome his peasant background but not the subtlety to place it in proper perspective. He is bookish in an elegant but philistine world where his mind is admired not for its depth but for its trivial qualities. Julien has an uncanny knack for memorization. To prove his qualifications to teach Latin to the Rênal children, Julien recites long passages from scripture, rather like a performing monkey. His intellect impresses others, but those it impresses are mainly fools.

Julien is something of a fool himself. Despite his loathing of the hypocrisy that pervades the upper classes, he himself consciously practices hypocrisy. He cheats and lies, endures boredom, and pours all his craft and strength into ascending the social ladder. At one point he comes across a document left behind in a room by the Marquis de la Mole. The paper is a petition from an underling seeking favors from the marquis. Julien slips it into his pocket, thinking that it might come in handy as a model to follow when he himself may need help.

Julien's Machiavellian obsession with social status steers him from Verrières to the seminary at Besançon, then to the Hôtel de la Mole, and finally, to prison. This physical journey is also a journey of Julien's mind. Each stop deepens him spiritually and intellectually. Locked in a cell, Julien thinks more clearly and feels freer than at any time in his life. As he faces execution, he surrenders himself to reverie. The outer world loses importance. Action shifts to the world within. He loses the will to carry on and rejects both escape and acquittal. Perhaps he wishes for death, desires martyrdom. Or maybe he's simply exhausted from trying to live at a far greater pitch of intensity than the general run of men. Hypocrisy may have taken its toll. His last wish is to die heroically, just as he had hoped to live heroically.

Père Sorel

Julien's father is a sawmill owner in Verrières. A shrewd businessman, he outwits M. Rênal by selling him a piece of property for more than it's worth. Then, hoping to cash in on Julien's position as a tutor, he persuades Rênal to raise Julien's salary. Otherwise, he has no use for Julien, who'd rather read books than work in the mill, a preference that Père Sorel cannot understand.

Monsieur Chélan

Chélan, the priest of Verrières, takes Julien under his wing and hopes to steer his young charge toward a career as a clergyman. He teaches Julien Latin and helps him memorize the New Testament. At various points in the novel, Julien goes to Chélan for advice and comfort.

Monsieur de Rênal

Rênal, the mayor of Verrières, is a conservative aristocrat who has recently lost much of his fortune and is clawing his way back to wealth as a businessman.

Stendahl portrays him as a status-seeking, money-loving, egoistic boor, as well as something of a buffoon. Père Sorel, Julien's father, dupes him into paying too much for a piece of property. Rênal hires Julien as a tutor for his children, mainly to enhance his social standing in the town. Blind to almost everything except his position and rank, Rênal is oblivious to the illicit goings-on between Julien and Madame de Rênal. When he learns of Madame de Rênal's secret offer to pay for Julien's new clothes, a plan that Julien declines, he is outraged, not by the subterfuge, but by the impropriety of allowing a lowly servant to say no to the mistress of the house.

When Rênal receives an anonymous letter alleging an affair between his wife and Julien, he turns briefly introspective, bemoaning his inattentiveness to Madame de Rênal. He considers killing her, but after realizing that his good name will be destroyed, he changes his mind. Madame de Rênal soon restores his faith in her with a fake letter implicating Valenod as a jealous troublemaker bent on undermining the Rênals' marriage. She even insists that Julien be sent away, knowing full well that her husband would never consent to do so. Poor Rênal is completely hoodwinked but also much relieved that he has managed to avoid a ruinous family scandal.

Madame de Rênal

The glamorous wife of the mayor of Verrières, ditzy Madame de Rênal falls for Julien and allows herself to be seduced. At the same time, she is concerned about keeping up appearances. She insists that Julien dress appropriately for his role as the tutor of her children. She frets about his lax approach to teaching because it will reflect badly on her. In spite of such pathetic concerns, however, she lacks the complete hypocrisy and pretence that define others in her social circle. Rather, she stands for a kind of innocent purity.

During her affair with Julien her moods swing from bliss to self-loathing. She's plagued by jealousy and can't control her carnal desires. Guilt tears her apart. When her little boy falls ill, she thinks God is punishing her. She is bereft when Julien leaves Verrières to study at the seminary.

Hearing the news that Julien plans to marry Mathilde, she sends a letter to the marquis accusing Julien of fraud and fortune-hunting, allegations that cause the marquis to cancel the wedding. In a fury Julien shoots Madame de Rênal in the shoulder. Still hungering for his love, however, she forgives him and pleads with the authorities to spare his life. Three days after he is put to death, Madame de Rênal herself expires, apparently of a broken heart.

Monsieur Valenod

Valenod is a neighbor of the Rênals. He runs both the local poorhouse and the jail and secures a steady income by bilking the least fortunate citizens of Verrières of their hard-earned cash. Rênal's arch-rival, he is rumored to have designs on the mayoralty of the town. Having been informed of Madame de Rênal's affair with Julien, Valenod delights in informing Rênal that he is being cuckolded.

Later, serving as jury foreman at Julien's trial, he enthusiastically condemns the accused to death. A political liberal at the beginning of the novel, he is a staunch royalist at the end. Taken altogether, he is as unprincipled and corrupt as they come, a quality that assures his social and financial success.

Elisa

Elisa, Madame de Rênal's maid, falls in love with Julien, who gives her a cold shoulder. Jealousy drives her to inform Valenod that Julien and her mistress have become an item.

Fouqué

Fouqué, a longtime and loyal friend of Julien, works in the lumber business in the mountains. Julien complains to him about the intrigues and problems of in-town life. Fouqué offers him a job but Julien turns it down, knowing that Fouqué has no social clout. Julien is too ambitious, too restless, too enamored of power to be satisfied with a bourgeois life in the country

Monsieur Pirard

Monsieur Pirard is the director of the seminary at Besançon, where Julien studies theology. As a Jansenist, he endures persecution and the criticism of the church establishment and resigns his position. (Unlike the Jesuits, Jansenists believe in predestination, a heretical doctrine in Roman Catholicism.)

Pirard serves as Julien's mentor, advisor, and agent. He promotes Julien in the seminary and recommends him for a position in the Hôtel de la Mole.

Marquis de la Mole

The marquis, Julien's employer in Paris, symbolizes France's fading aristocracy. Aware of his young aide's aptitude, he doles out increasingly important jobs to him, including tasks in support of a conspiracy to restore the Bourbon monarchy to France.

Enraged by Julien's affair with Mathilde, he nevertheless gives him a piece of property, a commission in the military, and the consent to marry his daughter. After reading Madame de Rênal's letter that describes his future son-in-law's shady past, however, the marquis forbids Mathilde ever to see Julien again.

Mathilde de la Mole

The nineteen-year-old daughter of the marquis, Mathilde is bored by her social life and refuses to play the role expected of her. She has an attitude toward almost everyone in her entourage of family, friends, and suitors. Like a brat, she insults others and says whatever she wants. To stimulate her mind and escape boredom, Mathilde reads books, but her taste in reading is confined to historical romances about the exploits of her sixteenth-century ancestors.

Mathilde strikes up a friendship with Julien, attracted to him for being different from the young men who constantly buzz around her. Their mutually friendly feelings evolve into a secret affair, full of discord and emotional stress. Because Julien and Mathilde are rarely in the same mood at the same time, they clash repeatedly, taking turns as the pursuer and pursued, the oppressor and the victim. This conflict-ridden, on-and-off relationship frustrates them both. After Mathilde finds herself pregnant, they plan to marry. Although circumstances interfere, Mathilde remains loyal to Julien until the end. When last seen, she is kissing Julien's disembodied head before burying it with her own hands.

Narrative Techniques   The novel's omniscient narrator is neither detached nor objective. Like a Greek chorus he expresses strong, often irreverent opinions about almost everything: the characters, the setting, the events in the story, the moral and social climate of the time. Unavoidably, the narrator's frequent editorial asides shape readers' responses.

That Stendahl enjoys drawing readers into a state of complicity is suggested by the epigraphs that precede each chapter. Some of the epigraphs relate hardly at all to the chapters they introduce, and many of them are specious, wholly invented by Stendahl but attributed to poets, writers, philosophers, and other men of letters, ancient and modern. Why Stendahl bothers with counterfeit quotations may be explained by a desire to create a bond between himself and the savvy reader. If he can get readers to laugh with him, he has established contact and can take them into his confidence.

If readers miss Stendahl's impishness in the epigraphs they'll surely recognize Stendahl's cunning in the text itself. After telling us about Verrières and its industrious mayor, for example, he comments on despotism in small towns: "The tyranny of public opinion—and what public opinion!—is as stupid in the small towns of France as it is in the United States of America." The allusion to small French towns reiterates what he has already told us, that nonconformists in Verrières are "damned forever in the eyes of the wise and sober people who dole out public esteem." The specifically American phenomenon that Stendahl has in mind remains less clear, but he obviously likes to take pokes at conventionality wherever it appears. He also lampoons many of his characters by portraying them as dolts and knaves. Some characters are little more than caricatures. He dismisses a whole group of Julien's seminary classmates, for example, with a scathing generality:

> The remainder of the three hundred twenty-one students were only coarse creatures who were not too sure of the meaning of the Latin words they repeated all day long. They were nearly all sons of peasants, and they preferred to earn their living by reciting a few Latin words, rather than by tilling the soil.

Stendahl likes to mock people's fakery, pretense, and self-delusion. Monsieur de Rênal, for one, is an archetype of a hypocritical, self-absorbed buffoon. The author treats Rênal's rival, M. Valenod, with equivalent disdain. Valenod wears bushy side whiskers, an enormous quantity of hair, embroidered slippers, gold chains that cross his chest in all directions. With all the trappings of a provincial financier who regards himself as a ladies' man, Valenod, according to the narrator, deserves a good beating. When Julien shows up at his house for dinner, he finds Valenod at his desk "displaying his importance in the midst of a large number of cardboard folders."

Such irony typifies the tone of the entire narrative, which brims with humor. Julien's bedroom trysts with Madame de Rênal border on farce: husband rapping on the locked door, Julien hiding under the sofa (but leaving his hat on the chair), Madame feigning a headache, Julien leaping into the garden to escape. As silly as such episodes seem, they are not frivolous. Stendahl, a sworn enemy of clichés and sentimentalism, is waging a serious war on cant and conventionality. Almost nothing escapes his vitriol: not the Church, not politics, and certainly not the social structure and customs of his day.

It would be a mistake to conclude that Stendahl's sole purpose is to tear everything apart, however. His point of view is more complex than that, more quixotically ambiguous. He values honesty, kindness, sincerity, and a host of other virtues, and he treats affectionately such upright characters as Father Chélan, Madame de Rênal (at times), and Julien's pal, Fouqués. On balance, though, his cynicism and disenchantment overshadow idealism and affirmation.

Readers of Stendahl often are more impressed with the tone and rhythm of his work than with the plot and characters. Indeed, what often lingers in the mind is the cumulative effect of literally hundreds of events and countless details that seem to rush by like cars on a highway. A careful reading reveals that Stendahl has a knack for contrast and nuance, for sly, subversive winks at the reader. At the beginning of the novel, for example, with a hypothetical Parisian traveler-narrator as our guide, we enter the town of Verrières, survey its clean white houses, the river Doubs, and lovely mountain setting. In no time, however, Stendahl undercuts the portrait of this charming provincial town by introducing not only the ruins of the Spanish fortifications, suggesting Verrières's less than peaceful past, but the deafening roar of the town's nail factory. He further heightens the contrast between beauty and harsh reality by telling us that "fresh, pretty girls" work the monstrous machines that turn sheets of iron into nails.

Stendahl's prose continually twists and turns in this manner. It changes directions repeatedly, thereby producing startling effects and juxtapositions.

Take, for instance, the following passage about Julien's days at the seminary:

> It was at about this time that Julien decided he could improve his standing among his fellow students by making use of Monsieur de Maistre's book, *Du Pape.* He did, in fact, astonish them, but this was only one more misfortune for him. He displeased them by expressing their opinions better than they could themselves.

The first sentence describes Julien's intention to impress his fellow students. We learn subsequently that he succeeds. But since his success backfires, did he succeed or did he fail? It's hard to tell. The answer is probably *both* and *neither* because the upshot of Julien's effort moves in two contrasting directions at the same time. Stendahl, in effect, touches us simultaneously in different places. He builds tension and keeps us off balance.

Stendahl sustains a climate of ambiguity by leading readers on, first by giving them a body of information and then introducing elements that change whatever impressions his readers may have formed. At one point we are told that Julien would risk a thousand deaths rather than fail to make his fortune. Our concept of Julien's combative spirit is quickly altered, however, by the discovery that victory for Julien means nothing more than getting away from Verrières. Similar inversions—one critic aptly calls them "somersaults of irony"—enrich the narrative and force readers to stay on their toes.

Julien himself helps to creates a similar kind of ambiguity. He habitually makes sense of things through contrasts and comparisons. "What a difference . . . " is one of his favorite expressions: "What a difference with Madame de Rênal's eyes," "What a difference with what was fourteen months ago." Seeing the world through its divergencies lies at the heart of Julien's growth as a person. He despises and yet adores Madame de Rênal at the same. He scorns hypocrisy in others but turns himself into a world-class hypocrite. According to the narrator, Julien's "distrustful nature made him rarely responsive to any memories save those which are evoked by contrasts, but such memories moved him to tears . . . ." The title of the novel itself contains the very same ambiguousness that reaches into all aspects of Julien's character.

To deepen his characters, Stendahl uses another distinctive technique—conditional constructions. That is, characters often think hypothetically: If such and such were so, then . . . etc. At one point M. Rênal, who values his social status above all else, wonders to what extent his reputation might suffer if Julien remained in Verrières and tutored the Valenod children. Later, Madame de Rênal, displaying a pessimistic streak, ponders the potential consequences of a duel between her husband and Julien: "I might be left a widow . . . . If I don't prevent that duel then I'll be guilty of murdering my husband." At Besançon, Julien's mind is full of *ifs*: *if* he fights a duel, his ecclesiastical career will be ruined; *if* only he knew how to express his anger by some means other than a slap; *if* the argument had turned physical, he would have been beaten and left lying on the floor. By providing samples of characters' inner thoughts, Stendahl nudges us closer to the essence of each person. These *might have beens* also prepare readers for future action.

Sometimes, when the narrator himself uses a conditional construction, we learn what no one else, not even the characters themselves, know. Madame de Rênal, the narrator tells us, is quite a beauty: tall, shapely, and suggestive of "sweet voluptuous pleasure." Stendahl then adds hypothetically, "If she had been aware of her success in this direction, she would have been deeply ashamed," an observation that, although we have just met her, gives us a peek at her privacy and a look at sensual qualities of which she herself is apparently unaware. In other words, Stendahl's use of the conditional form gives us access to places deep inside the minds and souls of his characters.

Only an author attuned to human nature and well versed in psychology could show us features hidden under the masks of his characters. Critics make the case that Julien's actions are somewhat Oedipal. Early in the story, he sits on a rafter in the paternal sawmill, symbolically high above his father. Julien's sexual relationship with Madame de Rênal, an older woman, perhaps a mother figure, adds credence to the theory.

More than anything, the novel navigates the landscape of love. Several seduction scenes, which blend tenderness and irony, bring out the author's insight into the conflicting and contradictory feelings related to love and sex. Both Julien and his paramours are ruled not by consistent passion but by oscillation between desire and apathy. At various times Julien is infatuated and then repulsed by Madame de Rênal or by Mathilde. Sometimes, he feigns love but suspects he is being used for some ulterior motive. Both women are also torn by antithetical emotions. Each is certain that Julien loves her, then equally sure that he doesn't. At one point Mathilde loathes Julien and later desires nothing more than to be his slave.

Themes and Motifs

Several interrelated themes help Stendahl point out the flaws and foibles of society, in particular, how the social structure affects people's values and behavior.

Society's Walls

Verrières embodies the social barriers typical of class-conscious societies. Aside from its factories, the town's most noteworthy feature is its walls, ramparts that separate the world of the privileged from the world of the unprivileged. The walls, by constraining movement, symbolically protect the bourgeoisie from encroachment by workers and peasants such as Julien Sorel. Clipped and pruned trees inside walled gardens reflect a spirit of conformity and symbolize the pervasive tyranny of social convention. The walls are high and hard to climb. By all rights, Julien ought to stay put, but congenitally unable to accept his lot in life, he leaps over the walls, only to find on the other side that freedom is restricted by an equally confining set of social constraints. Ultimately, he loses his struggle for freedom and winds up incarcerated behind real walls of impenetrable stone.

The Class Struggle

The upper class finds itself in a state of siege. It is being invaded by social climbers, newly rich members of the bourgeoisie, typified by uppity Valenod types who in their unashamed baseness can talk about nothing but the weather and money. Many members of the aristocracy—the young, in particular—aware that their status is being vitiated, can no longer remain loyal to what their class has long represented.

Into this state of quasi-decay steps Julien Sorel, a young upstart status-seeker. Julien penetrates the walls of the Rênal estate, passes through the gates of the seminary, and makes his way into the Hôtel de la Mole. But in the end society puts its foot down. It casts Julien off, shuts him behind prison walls and executes him, not for slaying or attempting to slay one of its members but for trying to usurp its privileges. The ironic thing about Julien's climb is that he didn't set out seeking social advancement. Rather, he was recruited to work in the Rênal household. Once inside, he naïvely began to take advantage of the opportunities he found there.

Boredom

Changes brought on first by the Revolution and then by Napoleon are anathema in the drawing rooms and salons of Paris and the provinces. Subsequent efforts by the Bourbon regime to restore conditions of the past create a stultifying atmosphere marked by convention, limitation, constraint, and lack of freedom. Etiquette forbids talk about controversial issues of politics and religion. Piety replaces pleasure, and boredom sets in. Boredom, in fact, becomes ideologically characteristic of the Restoration period.

Stendahl portrays people so lacking in *joi de vivre* that they resort to entertaining themselves by ridiculing and insulting others, by playing practical jokes and making sarcastic remarks. Julien, after falling from a horse, becomes a butt of ridicule in the marquis's salon. Madame de Rênal fights boredom by taking a lover. Marquis de la Mole fills time by leading a conspiracy to restore the monarchy. Mathilde keeps boredom at bay by retreating into the distant past, fantasizing romantically about her long-dead ancestor Boniface de la Mole.

Julien's discovery that it is chic to be bored shatters his dream of a glamorous and scintillating life in the upper class. Nevertheless, he tries to assume the requisite mannerisms and attitudes, but not always successfully.

Politics

After Napoleon, France found itself divided between conservative monarchists and liberals. When *The Red and the Black* takes place the lines between them have blurred. Aristocrats like M. de Rênal have fallen on hard times and become bourgeois businessmen. On the other hand, M. Valenod, originally a civil servant and a liberal, gradually acquires wealth and power. By the end of the novel he has assumed the trappings, if not the grace, of the upper class.

Into this political muddle Stendahl places Julien, a Janus-faced social climber who fails to identify himself with either ideology. He speaks up for liberals and for conservatives alike, whichever will work to his advantage. Stendahl's point is that political allegiance, passionately intense during the Revolution and the Napoleonic era, has turned into a farce.

The church, as a microcosm of society, is also beset with politics. The clergy is divided among class lines. Priests vie for power and stab each other in the back. Students at the seminary lack piety and plan to use the church as a means to make money. There are strong ties between the church and aristocracy. The marquis asks Pirard to work with him on a court case. He needs the priest not for his insights or strength of character but because the presence of a clergyman will lend *gravitas* to his position.

Pursuit of Happiness

Stendahl portrays a tyrannical society that forces humbly born people to think not of fulfilling dreams of happiness but of simply making a living. Julien is an exception. He is blessed with talents that enable him to earn his daily bread and at the same time pursue his private dreams. He drives himself so hard, however, that he rarely enjoys himself. He learns quickly, for instance, that to succeed in high society he must conceal his true opinions and pay lip service to the beliefs of others. He decides to become a hypocrite, a role that he perfects. Although he is not a believer, he relies on the church to enhance his social standing. Still, happiness and contentment elude him.

In spite of mastering the art of dissimulation, Julien is stung by the charge in Madame de Rênal's letter to the marquis that he is a social-climbing hypocrite. The allegation, in fact, unhinges him. Provoked by painful truth, he charges off to find Madame de Rênal and shoot her. Only after being locked away is he granted a glimpse of the happiness that he has sought. Behind bars, paradoxically, he feels freer than ever before. His cell grants him salvation from the insidious hypocrisy that has sullied his character and corrupted his life. Prison offers him a private purifying dreamworld where he can meditate on death and escape from himself. His only complaint is that his door won't lock from the inside.

Superficiality

The old saw that clothes make the man is carried to extremes in *The Red and the Black*. People often define and value each other according to their clothing. Julien in a blue suit evokes a different response from the marquis than Julien in black. Eyeing Mathilde, Julien enjoys "the contrast between the simplicity of her present attire and her elegant splendor of the night before." Such superficiality reaches even into the church. Clergymen takes pains to maintain a proper appearance. At one point the young bishop asks Julien to assess the cut of his figure. He wants to be certain that he looks the way a bishop ought to look. During the service Julien is impressed not with the bishop's spirituality but with his charming manners and style of praying.

Love

Any reader who's been in love will understand why Julien's affairs of the heart follow a rocky course. A careless word, an odd look, an ill-timed gesture, turn ecstasy into doubt, pain, and distress, even, in extreme cases, into thoughts of suicide. Young love is complicated enough, but Stendahl tangles it further by tying it constantly to love triangles. Virtually every love affair in the book involves a third party. Madame de Rênal 's love for Julien, for instance, is intensified by Elisa, who also loves Julien. Meanwhile, Julien's love of Madame de Rênal is adulterated by his affection for Napoleon. Mathilde de la Mole aims to seduce Julien, not because she adores him but because she views him as a latter-day Boniface, a romantic hero who will risk everything for his lover.

Madame de Rênal loves Julien from the heart, Mathilde, who lets her heart be moved only when she has a good reason for doing so, loves him from the head. In the end, Julien recognizes that Madame de Rênal's love is truer, more enduring.

Questions for Writing and Discussion

1. Why do you suppose the author decided to kill off his hero at the end of the book? What are some implications of having Julien die?
2. Do you agree or disagree with the critic who said the following: Stendahl's main concern in *The Red and the Black* is the dilemma of how an elite heart and mind can protect itself against encroachments of any form of despotism without abdicating its values and surrendering to absolutes?
3. Using such literary devices as ironic intrusions, commentaries, pretense at being surprised, and denigrating the hero at the very moment he enjoys him most, the narrator is very much in evidence throughout the book. What, specifically, does his presence add? Please cite examples. Does his presence weaken the book in any way?
4. Stendahl seems to take a dim view of society—its corruption, its philistinism, its hypocrisy, and so forth. Yet he doesn't despair. In what aspects of the novel do you find glimmers of hope that not all is lost and not everything is for the worst?
5. Julien has both admirable qualities and a great many flaws. On balance, is he more a hero or more a rogue? Justify your responses with specific examples taken from various stages in Julien's journey through life.

Crime and Punishment by Fyodor Dostoyevski

Background

Even if the reading list in your AP English class does not include *Crime and Punishment,* you should read it on your own. But be forewarned—Dostoyevski's famous novel is not a quick and easy read like, say, *Harry Potter.* It is long and complex and written in prose so tightly packed that you can quickly lose your way, especially if you let your mind wander. To prevent this from happening, read it when you are alert, when your powers of concentration are at their best. Then you should reread the book, twice, three times, or more. You'll be rewarded for your effort—guaranteed!

Written in the mid 1860s, *Crime and Punishment* is a murder story, but not a *whodunit.* Rather, it is a psychological account of a crime. Decades before Freud and other analysts of the human psyche, Dostoyevsky studied the depths of the criminal mind and in doing so raised big moral and social questions about values, fate, and the human condition, all ageless issues for readers to ponder and, as luck would have it, to write about on AP English exams.

Although the book makes you grapple with profound thoughts, *Crime and Punishment* is hardly an abstract, philosophical tale. Rather it's the highly realistic and intense story about a gifted young university student forced by poverty to drop out of school. With time on his hands to contemplate the value of human life, he contrives a radical theory that goads him into committing a murder. Because the killing takes place early in the story, the bulk of the novel focuses on the aftermath of his crime.

Use *Crime and Punishment* as the subject for an essay on 1) a character in conflict with himself, 2) fate vs. free will, 3) the effects of poverty, 4) sin and redemption, 5) the power of dreams, 6) man's depravity, 7) moral ambiguities, and many other topics.

Synopsis

Rodya Romanovich Raskolnikov, an impoverished ex-student in St. Petersburg, plans to rob and murder Alëna Ivanovna, an old pawnbroker. As the story opens Raskolnikov is rehearsing the crime, determining among other things the number of steps between his room and Alëna's flat. (There are 730.) He knocks on Alëna's door ostensibly to pawn a watch but really to stake out the site and establish himself as a regular customer. Deep down, Raskolnikov can't be positive that he'll actually implement his plan.

Tormented by self-loathing over his evil intent, he stops at a pub on his way home and encounters Marmeladov, a down-at-heels alcoholic and former civil servant. In a drunken tirade Marmeladov laments his own wretchedness and admits to absconding with his starving family's food money in order to buy vodka. He also regrets allowing Sonya, his seventeen-year-old daughter, to become a prostitute. Yet, Marmeladov believes in a forgiving God and expects one day to be accepted into heaven. His belief interests Raskolnikov, who may soon need forgiveness himself. After helping Marmeladov back to his squalid rooms, Raskolnikov meets the family—Marmeladov's consumptive wife Katerina Ivanovna and his three tattered stepchildren. On his way out, he leaves them a handful of coins, an act of charity he can ill afford.

A letter from his mother, Pulkheria, contains news that Dunya, his sister, is engaged to be married. Because her fiancé is Luzhin, a civil counselor, family finances are looking up and Rodya might soon expect to return to school. The letter explains that the engagement came about while Dunya was working as a governess. It seems that her employer, Mr. Svidrigaylov, attempted to hit upon her, but his wife Marfa Petrovna, thinking that Dunya had made the first move, immediately fired her and spread word throughout the district that Dunya was a whore. Remorseful, Svidrigaylov showed Marfa a letter proving Dunya's innocence. Marfa apologized for jumping to conclusions and to make up went out of her way to praise the girl. Intrigued, Peter Petrovich Luzhin, Marfa's distant cousin, proposed to Dunya, and she, ignoring Luzhin's overbearing and harsh manners, agreed to marry him. Pulkheria further informs Raskolnikov that Luzhin is about to arrive in St. Petersburg and to pay him a visit. Also, she and Dunya plan to come to town in a day or two.

Raskolnikov smells a rat. To him Luzhin sounds like a loser, a hypocrite who pretends to be big-hearted but is basically an arrogant, calculating penny pincher. Raskolnikov resolves to prevent Dunya from sacrificing herself on his behalf. He isn't worth it, and besides, he's already hatched a plan to acquire enough money to resume his studies.

Upset and distracted, he wanders the city and comes upon a teenage girl being accosted and propositioned by an older man, whom Raskolnikov impulsively calls "Svidrigaylov." To save the girl, he punches the man but a policeman intervenes. Raskolnikov gives the girl a few copecks and urges her to leave in a cab, but she continues to walk. Seeing the man follow her, Raskolnikov ruminates on the depths to which humans can sink.

After stopping for a glass of vodka and a pastry, Raskolnikov falls asleep in some bushes on a parklike island. He dreams "a terrible dream" about himself as a young boy witnessing the fatal beating of a helpless old horse. The dream suggests that Raskolnikov has violence and bloodshed on his mind.

Next Raskolnikov finds himself in the Haymarket. By chance he overhears Lizaveta Ivanovna, Alëna's sister, make a business appointment with a dealer for the following evening at seven. Knowing when Alëna will be home alone, Raskolnikov chooses that time to do his dirty deed. The episode reminds him of another conversation he recently overheard in a tavern: a student was telling an officer that Alëna planned to bequeath her wealth to a monastery in order to pay monks to pray for the "eternal repose of her soul." The young man joked that he could "kill that damned old woman and rob her, without a single twinge of conscience." Turning somber, he added that Alëna's death might be justified if her money promoted the common good, perhaps saving hundreds or thousands of people from beggary, ruin, and corruption. Raskolnikov, startled because he himself has had similar thoughts, interprets the coincidence as a sign that he was meant to carry out his deadly plan.

The next afternoon, concealing inside his jacket an axe "borrowed" from the porter's woodpile, he goes to Alëna's flat. As the old woman unties a knot on the package he has brought, he raises the axe and strikes her head with the butt end. She falls. Panicked, he hits her again and again, imagining that she has survived. From a cord around her neck he takes keys, a religious medal, two crucifixes, and a small purse. While rifling a trunk in her bedroom, he hears a footstep behind him. It is her sister Lizaveta. In a panic he kills her, too. Suddenly, he notices that the apartment door is still ajar. Terror-stricken, he shuts and locks the door just as the sound of voices and footsteps reaches him from downstairs. Two men, Koch and Pestryakov, knock on the door. Receiving no reply they try to open it. Finding it bolted they suspect something is amiss. Raskolnikov nearly passes out from fright. Pestryakov goes for help, and Koch follows moments later, allowing Raskolnikov to escape. In the stairway below he hears two men arguing—we learn later they are house painters, Mitya and Mikolay—and hides behind the open door of an unoccupied apartment. After Koch, Pestyakov, and a porter climb back upstairs Raskolnikov slips out, returns the axe, and hurries back to his room.

Upon awakening from a long sleep he cuts a bloodied cuff off his trousers and discards it in the stove along with a blood-soaked sock. He also hides the handful of items he stole from Alëna into a niche in the wall under a flap of wallpaper. After more sleep Natasya the servant girl awakens him with a summons to police headquarters. Terrifed, Raskolnikov can't believe how quickly he's been found. But at the station house, Zametov, the chief clerk, tells Raskolnikov that his landlady has reported him for failing to pay his rent.

Although relieved, Raskolnikov starts to feel the weight of his heinous crime. He feels lonely, estranged, and tormented as the police chief, Fomich, discusses Alëna's murder with Zametov. Then and there he considers falling to his knees and confessing. He imagines that the police know he did it and at that very moment are searching his room for evidence. He resolves to get rid of the loot as soon as he can, and later, without ever opening Alëna 's purse to see what he had stolen, stashes the goods under a large stone at a construction site.

Raskolnikov begins to despise himself for lying and for cringing with fear at the police station. In a feverish delirium he confuses dreams and reality. He projects his self-hatred onto others including his friend Razumikhin, whom he insults during a brief visit. Razumikhin calls Doctor Zosimov for help. Slipping in and out of sleep, Raskolnikov perks up only when his friend and the doctor begin to discuss the murder of the old pawnbroker and her sister. For now, the prime suspect is Mikolay, the house painter, implicated by his attempt to pay a tavern bill with gold earrings belonging to Alëna. Claiming that he had found the earrings in the street, Mikolay later admitted that he had picked them up behind the door of an empty apartment in Alëna's building. (Apparently, Raskolnikov had dropped them there.) Razumikhin and Zosimov doubt Mikolay's guilt, however, because just after the killings he had been seen joking and laughing with Mitka, engaging in altogether incongruous behavior for a murderer.

The arrival of Luzhin ends the conversation. Pompously, Luzhin introduces himself and informs Raskolnikov that he has arranged housing for Dunya and her mother in a hotel that Razumikhin declares to be a flophouse. Luzhin himself is staying with his ward Lebezyatnikov, who rents rooms at Mrs. Lippewechsel's establishment, also the home of the Marmeladovs. Raskolnikov accuses Luzhin of treating Dunya shabbily. Luzhin snaps back by insulting Raskolnikov's mother. Raskolnikov threatens Luzhin, who quickly withdraws. Having witnessed the exchange, Razumikhin and Zosimov realize that Raskolnikov is not himself. He seems indifferent to everything except the story of the murder.

From a bank representative Raskolnikov receives thirty-five rubles sent by his mother. On the mend, Raskolnikov roams the city, as though looking for someone to whom he can tell his dark secret. In a pub, he finds Zametov and virtually confesses his crime. But he retreats, claiming to be kidding around. But Zametov notes Raskolnikov's behavior and finds it odd that Raskolnikov suddenly has a pocket full of money.

Continuing to roam, Raskolnikov sees a woman attempt suicide by jumping into a canal. He considers doing the same as a way to end his suffering. Soon he finds himself in front of Alëna's building and climbs the stairs to her apartment, which is being refurbished. He steps from room to room commenting on the murder. Struck by his intimate knowledge of the crime, the workmen chase him off and threaten to call the police.

Entering a crowd gathered around a hit-and-run victim lying in the street, Raskolnikov sees it is Marmeladov. He helps carry the bloody Marmeladov home. A doctor, paid for by Raskolnikov, declares that there's no hope. A priest administers last rites, and Marmeladov dies in the arms of Sonya after begging forgiveness for what he has done to her. Katerina Ivanovna is relieved that her no-good husband is dead. Chief Fomich, on the scene to investigate the accident, observes that Raskolnikov's vest is bloodsoaked (it is Marmeladov's blood), to which Raskolnikov replies, "I am all over blood stains!" a double entendre that Fomich misses.

Before hurrying off, Raskolnikov gives Katerina Ivanovna twenty rubles for funeral expenses. Sonya sends her little sister Polenka to thank Raskolnikov. The girl throws her arms around his neck and vows to pray for him. The encounter lifts Raskolnikov's spirits. Polenka's unsolicited love has rekindled his desire to live.

Returning to his room, he finds Dunya and Pulkheria waiting. They are thrilled to see him but joy soon turns to conflict over Luzhin. Raskolnikov, threatening to disown his sister if she doesn't break her engagement, declares "It is either me or Luzhin!" Meanwhile, Razumikhin has taken a fancy to Dunya.

Later Dunya and her mother receive a note in which Luzhin denounces Raskolnikov, accusing him of giving twenty-five rubles to Sonya, "a notoriously ill-conducted female," an allegation that Raskolnikov later refutes. Luzhin also demands that Raskolnikov not be present when he comes to call. Forced to make the choice between her fiance and her brother, Dunya urges Raskolnikov to be there. She reasons that if Luzhin truly values her, Raskolnikov's presence won't matter.

Sonya suddenly enters Raskolnikov's room. Timidly, she invites Raskolnikov to attend her father's funeral and the the dinner afterward. Her modest mien, not at all that of a "notoriously ill-conducted female," favorably impresses Dunya and Pulkheria. On her way home, Sonya is followed by a tall, stout, older man. He turns out to reside in the room adjacent to hers. Later we discover that he is Svidrigaylov.

Razumikhin brings Raskolnikov up to date on the murder investigation. Porfiry Petrovich, the chief investigator, has asked all of Alëna's customers to redeem their pledges, i.e., their pawn tickets. Because Raskolnikov hasn't done so, Razumikhin escorts him to Porfiry's office. Entering, they laugh out loud over Razumikhin's crush on Dunya. To Raskolnikov, the laughter is a ruse meant to show that he has nothing to fear. Yet he secretly wonders whether Porfiry knows of his recent visit to the crime scene.

Raskolnikov is wary. It occurs to him that the detective suspects him and could be laying a trap, concealing what he knows behind a veil of banter and light conversation. Porfiry is savvy. He feigns naïveté, puts words in Raskolnikov's mouth. He even cites a published article of Raskolnikov's that divides humanity into two classes, the "ordinary" and the "extraordinary." Porfiry is particularly intrigued by Raskolnikov's thesis that extraordinary men possess the right to commit crimes because laws that apply to ordinary men don't apply equally to them. Defending his idea, Raskolnikov asserts that extraordinary people aren't required to commit offenses, but they have the moral authority to do so for the betterment of mankind. Alarmed by Porfiry's rhetorical question whether an "extraordinary" individual might have dispatched Alëna, Raskolnikov leaves the interview convinced that Pofiry suspects him of murder.

Walking home, Raskolnikov encounters an odd little man who glares at him and calls him "murderer." (The sudden appearance of the man startles Raskolnikov, not to mention the reader. Who is this fellow? Where did he come from? Raskolnikov speculates later that he might simply have imagined the episode, although he subsequently learns not only that the man is real but that he had observed him being chased from the murder site by the workmen in Alëna's flat. Putting two and two together, the little man concluded that Raskolnikov was the killer.)

Downhearted as never before, Raskolnikov is reduced to calling himself "a louse," a creature lower than vermin. In a dream, he relives the murder of Alëna, but this time the old woman, instead of falling to the floor after being axed, just sits and laughs at him, implying that his victim not only remains very much alive within his mind but will forever mock and haunt him.

Upon awakening, Raskolnikov finds a stranger in his room. It is Svidrigaylov, hoping to induce Raskolnikov to let him to see Dunya again. He plans to offer Dunya ten thousand rubles to break up with Luzhin and assures Raskolnikov that he no longer has a lascivious interest in his sister. In fact, he is engaged to another young woman, and what's more, he adds cryptically, he may soon "undertake a certain . . . journey." Svidrigaylov also tells Raskolnikov that Marfa, his late wife, has left Dunya three thousand rubles in her will. Despite their generally amiable conversation, Raskolnikov doesn't trust Svidrigaylov to keep his word.

When Luzhin comes to call, Dunya tries to mediate between her fiancé and her brother, but Luzhin won't bend. He demands that Dunya give up her brother for him, arguing that love for one's husband should surpass love for one's brother. Dunya won't be bullied, however, and the visit turns contentious. In the end, Dunya breaks her engagement and Luzhin storms out, determined to exact some kind of revenge for being discarded. On the other hand, Razumikhin is gladdened by this turn of events and brightens the day by proposing that he and Raskolnikov become partners in a small publishing business. Dismissing the idea, Raskolnikov suddenly rises and declares that he may never see any of them again. As he hurries out he gives Razumikhin a strange look, a look that conveys his terrible and monstrous secret. Razumikhin gets the message. Finally grasping that his friend is the murderer, he grows pale as a corpse.

In his misery, Raskolnikov seeks out Sonya in her room. They talk about her life and family. Raskolnikov is astounded by her "almost *insatiable* compassion" for Katerina Ivanovna, at whose urging Sonya had prostituted herself. Instead of condemning her stepmother, Sonya grieves for the woman's poor health and unhappiness. Raskolnikov wonders aloud about the future of Katerina's children. If their mother dies, they will be destitute. Sweet Polenka may be forced into prostitution. Sonya protests, insisting that God will protect the innocent little girl. When Raskolnikov questions the existence of God, Sonya is horrified, not at his sacrilege but by the intensity of his despair. To Sonya a life without faith in God is unfathomable.

In awe that Sonya has retained such goodness of heart despite her suffering, Raskolnikov falls down and kisses her foot. When he learns that she and Lizaveta had been friends who prayed and read the Bible together, he asks her to read the story of Lazarus to him. Moved by Lazarus's resurrection, Raskolnikov feels an urge to confess to Sonya. As a pure and saintly figure, she'll forgive rather than condemn him for his crime. Before taking his leave, Raskolnikov announces to Sonya that if he comes back tomorrow he'll tell her who killed Lizaveta. Then we learn that Svidrigaylov, next door, has overhead the entire conversation.

Raskolnikov takes his pledge to Porfiry, who explains his investigative method. Basically, he uses psychology to outwit suspected perpetrators. A criminal, he says, is always conscious of being a suspect. Afraid that he may tip his hand, a guilty person carries a burden that will ultimately undo him. Porfiry hints that Raskolnikov's actions, such as visiting the murder site, implicate him, causing Raskolnikov to ask angrily why Porfiry doesn't arrest him on the spot. But Porfiry is not ready to make an arrest. In fact, he throws Raskolnikov off by denying that he suspects Raskolnikov. The truth, however, is that Porfiry is waiting for Raskolnikov to contradict himself or to make a slip of the tongue, to make some sort of mistake that will reveal his guilt. Porfiry rattles Raskolnikov still further by promising a little "surprise."

Suddenly, Nikolay the painter bursts into the room and admits to slaying Alëna and Lizaveta. Porfiry is skeptical since Nikolay can add nothing new to the account of the murder. (Conscience-stricken, Raskolnikov will later refuse to let Nikolay take the rap for him.) On his way out, Raskolnikov again encounters the little man who had called him "murderer." In view of Nikolay's confession, the man apologizes to Raskolnikov, explaining also that he been the "surprise," planted behind a screen in Porfiry's office to eavesdrop on the conversation.

The scene shifts to Lebezyatnikov's rooms where Luzhin regrets having been so hasty with Dunya. He consoles himself by counting out substantial wads of his beloved bank notes and discussing with his ward the latest progressive ideas concerning women and marriage. Luzhin, in the meantime, has asked Sonya to visit him and informs her that he won't attend her father's funeral dinner but that he would like to initiate a "subscription"—i.e., take up a collection—for her destitute family. He contributes a ten-ruble note but asks her to keep its source a secret.

Katerina Ivanovna has invited a throng to the funeral dinner but only the rabble has shown up to gorge on food and drink. Tense and irritable, she trades insults with her landlady, Amalia, who loses her cool and evicts Katerina from the house. The melee that follows is interrupted by the sudden appearance of Luzhin, who accuses Sonya of stealing a hundred rubles from him. Sonya denies it but a search of her pockets reveals a hundred-ruble note. Luzhin offers to forgive and forget if Sonya confesses, but Lebezyatnikov steps forward and declares that he had earlier seen Luzhin slip the note into Sonya's pocket. Thinking at the time that Luzhin was being charitable he kept silent, but now he realizes Luzhin meant to play a deceitful trick on Sonya. Raskolnikov rises to explain, saying that he himself is the reason that Luzhin has tried to discredit Sonya. Luzhin has an account to settle with Raskolnikov for undermining his plan to marry Dunya. By debasing Sonya, Luzhin also intended to show that Dunya and her mother had themselves been debased, for they had allowed Raskolnikov to bring Sonya, a prostitute and thief, into their company as though she were socially on a par with them.

Back in Sonya's room Raskolnikov confesses to killing Lizaveta. Sonya embraces him and asks, "What have you done to yourself ?. . . There is no one, no one, unhappier than you in the whole world." He implores her never to forsake him. Trying to explain his motive, Raskolnikov summarizes the theoretical article he had written, but all his talking points ring hollow. Sonya can't understand them, anyway. All she cares about is that he has strayed from God and that he must begin the process of redemption. She urges him to confess and to suffer the consequences. Through suffering he will achieve atonement. Raskolnikov refuses, but his resolve begins to waver when Sonya offers to suffer with him. Their conversation ends when Lebezyatnikov comes to inform Sonya that Katerina Ivanovna has gone berserk. Sonya rushes off to find Katerina in the street, banging frying pans and forcing her children to sing and dance for alms. Soon Katerina spits blood, collapses, and is carried to Sonya's room to die.

Svidrigaylov pulls Raskolnikov aside to say that he'll fund both Katerina's funeral and her children's care in an orphanage. The money will come from the ten-thousand rubles he intended to give to Dunya. Svidrigaylov's generosity puzzles Raskolnikov, who suspects less than altruistic motives. Svidrigaylov also reveals that he had overheard Raskolnikov confess to Sonya and therefore feels confident that Raskolnikov will do whatever he asks of him.

The pressure on Raskolnikov mounts. He feels trapped. Svidrigaylov asserts that "every man needs air, air, air! . . . More than anything," a sentiment echoed later by Porfiry during a second interrogation. Porfiry also reveals his knowledge of Raskolnikov's motives, the theories that guided him, and how he went about committing the murder. Aware of Raskolnikov's current state of mind, Porfiry encourages him to ease his conscience by f'essing up, but Raskolnikov refuses, insisting that Porfiry file charges and arrest him. Porfiry declines, however, because he lacks sufficient evidence to link Raskolnikov with the crime. Finally, he asks Raskolnikov to do him a favor: if he decides to kill himself, he should leave a note behind telling where he hid the loot. All the while Raskolnikov is troubled by the possibility that Svidrigaylov has betrayed him to the police.

During a chance encounter in a tavern, Svidrigaylov tells Raskolnikov the story of his marriage to Marfa. He also explains how Dunya came into his life, and how he now intends to marry a sixteen-year-old girl. Reading between the lines, Raskolnikov senses that Svidrigaylov still has designs on Dunya. Indeed, using his knowledge of Raskolnikov's crime as leverage, Svidrigaylov soon prevails on Dunya to meet him. In his room he offers her money and a passport to help Raskolnikov escape. He also guarantees financial security to her if she consents to a relationship with him. Alarmed at his growing passion, Dunya tries to flee but the door is locked. She pulls a revolver from her pocket. The danger raises his ardor still more. She shoots, grazing his scalp. Svidrigaylov won't give up. The gun misfires. When she declares as forcefully as she can that she will never love him, he finally gets the message and allows her to leave.

In despair, Svidrigaylov first bids adieu to Sonya and then to his young fiancee, claiming that he must go on a long trip. He gives them sums of money. That night he dreams about finding a small abandoned girl in a hallway and putting her to bed. Suddenly, the face of the child morphs into the face of a whore, her arms seductively stretching out to him. At that moment, he awakens, horrified at his own debauchery. Soon, he embarks on his "certain journey" by stepping outside and putting a bullet into his head.

Meanwhile Raskolnikov has decided to turn himself in. He makes the rounds, bidding good-bye to Dunya and to his mother, who has remained unaware of what he's been up to. Although he still believes that ridding the world of a person like Alëna was not really a crime, he knows that society regards him as a scoundrel who deserves to be punished. He asks Sonya for the crucifix given to her by Lizaveta. On his way to police headquarters, he pauses at the crossroad, falls to his knees and announces his guilt to the world. At the police station, he experiences a momentary change of heart after hearing that Svidrigaylov, who could have testified against him, is dead. He starts to run away but seeing Sonya waiting outside he turns back.

In an epilogue, Dostoyevsky reviews the legal proceedings following Raskolnikov's confession and the reasons he received a rather light eight-year prison term. The court found that Raskolnikov suffered from "temporary mental derangement." Additional evidence showed that Raskolnikov had great kindness in him, that he had done a series of charitable acts, and had once saved the lives of two little children in a burning house. These and other factors persuade the judge to be lenient.

In prison Raskolnikov broods about his past and falls ill. True to her word, Sonya follows him to Siberia and helps him recover. In a dream, occurring near Easter, the time of resurrection, he envisions the consequences of the chaos that would ensue if all men were free to ignore society's laws. The world would suffer the worst kind of anarchy and be ravaged as though by a deadly plague. With Sonya's help Raskolnikov concludes that there was something profoundly false within himself and his beliefs and that he had no right to do what he had done.

When Sonia also falls ill, Raskolnikov experiences a new sensation. For the first time he worries about another person's well-being. As she recovers, he weeps, kneels before her, and pledges his love to her. She embraces him. Like Lazarus, they have been raised from the dead and given a chance for a new love-filled life together.

Cast of Characters

Readers of nineteenth-century Russian novels often need a scorecard to keep the characters straight. That's because many of the characters have three, and sometimes more, names: a given name, a middle name (called a *patronymic*), and a surname. Raskolnikov, for example, is often called *Rodya*, the familiar form of *Rodion*. Most often he goes by his last name, *Raskolnikov*, but is sometimes addressed by both his first name and patronymic: *Rodion Romanovich*. A patronymic is based on the first name of one's father. Since the given name of Rodya's father was Roman, Rodya's patronymic is *Romanovich*, meaning "son of Roman." The patronymic of Roman's daughter (Dunya) is *Romanovna* because *ovna* or sometimes *evna* is the feminine ending. Family names of women are also given feminine endings, as in Sonya's last name, *Marmeladovna*.

Diminutive or familiar names are also added to the mix. Thus, Dmitri is also called *Mitya* and *Mitka*; Polenka can be *Polya* or *Polechka*, and so forth.

Rodion Romanovich Raskolnikov (Rodya)

Raskolnikov may not be someone you'd invite home to dinner, but he has many endearing qualities, his propensity to commit murder notwithstanding. He is good-looking, literate, and bright enough to have written an article published in a scholarly journal. He is sufficiently savvy to have read between the lines of his mother's letter about Dunya's engagement and resolute in preventing Dunya from marrying Luzhin. Later, he insightfully figures out why Luzhin has accused Sonya of theft. Raskolnikov also has a compassionate side, especially for abused and downtrodden people like the Marmeladovs and a poor young girl in the street about to be hit on by an old lecher. Although he can ill afford it, he gives them money to weather personal crises.

At the same time, however, he dehumanizes himself by subscribing to his "extraordinary man" theory and committing the most heinous of crimes. Indeed, the dual nature of his personality may be his most striking feature. Two opposing and contradictory impulses seem to guide his action. In the book's opening scene, for example, he is intimidated by his landlady at the very moment he contemplates murdering someone else. Poverty drives him to kill for money, but he gives sums away to the needy. He steals the pawnbroker's purse but hides it under a stone without once looking inside. After the crime, desperate to avoid capture, he leaves a trail of incriminating evidence. Talking to Dunya and Pulkheria, Razumikhin encapsulates him: "Really, it is as if he had two separate personalities, each dominating him alternately."

At the start Raskolnikov has monumental hubris, regarding himself as a superior being on a par with Napoleon. As such, he is exempt from common morality. In fact, he considers it a duty to defy conventionality for the benefit of mankind. Once his ax has fallen on his victims, however, he realizes that life will never again be the same. The sickness in his mind manifests itself in spells of fever and delirium. Nightmares torment him. He becomes isolated, wracked with guilt, and preoccupied with concealing his crime. While he may be *in* the world he is no longer *of* it. In effect, he has died in all ways except physically.

Sonya helps him understand that he can be restored to life by confessing and accepting his punishment. Inspired by the story of Lazarus, Raskolnikov recognizes that he has sinned against both man and God and takes the first steps toward redemption.

Alëna Ivanovna

Alëna is the old and repulsive pawnbroker whom Raskolnikov kills with an ax. Her job is lending money to impoverished people, taking as collateral whatever possessions they are willing to part with and charging big interest on the loan. Some readers argue in Alëna's behalf that she performs a necessary service for desperate people, but others say she is a profiteer, exploiting the poor for selfish gain.

Lizaveta Ivanovna

Alëna's younger half sister, Lizaveta earns her keep by keeping their apartment spotless. Bad timing rewards her with a whack in the head from Raskolnikov's ax. An autopsy shows that she was pregnant, compounding the heinousness of Raskolnikov's crime.

Sëmen Zacharovich Marmeladov

Marmeladov is a hapless drunk, the epitome of misery. Seated in a pub with Raskolnikov, he describes the depths to which he has sunk. Among other things, he has permitted his daughter to become a prostitute and then used her earnings to buy vodka. Listening to Marmeladov's story, Raskolnikov concludes that men are basically scoundrels who can endure every shame, a thought that helps to erase his lingering doubts about killing Alëna. Marmeladov has faith that God will ultimately forgive him, however, while Raskolnikov remains a skeptic until Sonya convinces him of God's benevolence.

Katerina Ivanovna

Katerina is Marmeladov's consumptive second wife and the stepmother of Sonya. To save her family, she urges Sonya into prostitution. While claiming roots in an upper-class family fallen on hard times, undoubtedly a stretch of the truth, she aspires someday to be the mistress of a school for young ladies. After being evicted from her flat, she begs in the street with her children and dies soon thereafter.

Sonya (Sonechka, Sofya Semenovna Marmeladovna)

Sonya is the teenage daughter of Marmeladov. Pushed into prostitution in order to save her family, she earned thirty rubles for her virtue, an allusion to the thirty pieces of silver Judas received for betraying Jesus, although in this case Sonya is the person being betrayed. Her self-sacrifice, in effect, makes Sonya a Christ figure, willing to suffer for the sake of others. Dostoyevsky idealizes her, portraying her as a saintly, Madonna-like figure almost too pure to be true.

Eternally optimistic, she has faith that God will see her through. Sonya serves as Raskolnikov's savior. Knowing that redemption is possible even for a murderer, she convinces Rodya to confess his sin and accept his punishment.

Pulkheria Alexandrovna

Pulkheria is Raskolnikov's devoted mother. "Everything you do is right," she says to him at one point. "Don't be too sure," he responds. Pulkheria encourages her daughter to make an unsuitable marriage for the sake of helping Raskolnikov make his way in the world. News of his crime is kept from her, but she may know more than she lets on. She dies near the end, probably of a broken heart.

Dunya Romanovna (Avdotya, Dunechka)

Dunya is Raskolnikov's sister. Expecting to marry Luzhin, she changes her mind after coming to St. Petersburg. She is pretty, so attractive to Svidrigaylov, her former employer, that he follows her to the big city and won't stop pursuing her until she almost shoots him dead. In the end she marries Razumikhin.

Peter Petrovich Luzhin

Luzhin, a civil servant, aspires to a career in the law. He chooses Dunya to be his wife because she is poor and, therefore, will always be indebted to him for lifting her out of poverty. His warped ways of thinking also lead him to babble the latest ideas being espoused by Lebezyatnikov and other young progressives in St. Petersburg. At one point Razumikhin mocks Luzhin for reciting pseudointellectual platitudes and catch phrases.

From the first, Raskolnikov pegs him as an arrogant and self-absorbed martinet. At a meeting with Dunya and her family, Luzhin demands that Dunya break off relations with her brother. When she refuses, he becomes testy and still more ill-tempered. Seeing him for what he is, Dunya breaks off her engagement and sends him packing. To exact revenge on Raskolnikov and his family, he later plants a one-hundred ruble note in Sonya's pocket and accuses her of stealing it.

Arkady Ivanovich Svidrigaylov

Svidrigaylov employed Dunya as a governess. Smitten by her youth and beauty, he follows her to St. Petersburg after the death of his wife, Marfa Petrovna. Rumor has it that he did Marfa in, but he admits only to hitting her twice with riding switch. In addition to being an occasional wife beater, Svidrigaylov is a gambler. He married Marfa because she bailed him out of a thirty-thousand-ruble debt.

Svidrigaylov asks Raskolnikov to arrange a meeting with Dunya. He promises to give her ten thousand rubles to break her engagement, but Raskolnikov mistrusts him. When Svidrigaylov calls Raskolnikov a kindred spirit, he has a point. Like Raskolnikov, he is slightly mad, he sees ghosts (Marfa has appeared to him three times since her death), and has nightmarish dreams. Both men have engaged in violence against women, and both have a particular interest in Dunya, although Svidrigaylov's interest is more lascivious than brotherly. Both men tend to give away their money, although in vastly different amounts, and both abhor Luzhin.

Later in the story Svidrigaylov overhears Raskolnikov confess his crime to Sonya and threatens to blackmail him unless he gets his way. To save her brother, Dunya agrees to see Svidrigaylov briefly. With the aid of a pistol, she finally convinces him that she wants no part of him. Dejected, Svidrigaylov dreams about molesting a young girl, and then, recognizing his own depravity, shoots himself in the head.

Andrey Semënovich Lebezyatnikov

A young progressive, Lebezyatnikov is Luzhin's former ward. He witnesses Luzhin slip money into Sonya's pocket and denounces him at Marmeladov's funeral dinner.

Dmitri Prokofich Razumikhin

Raskolnikov's only friend, Razumikhin is a charming and good-humored fellow. When Raskolnikov falls ill, Razumikhin takes care of him. While serving as a buffer between Raskolnikov and his sister and mother, he falls in love with Dunya. He foresees a bright future for all of them if Raskolnikov would agree to help him set up a small publishing business.

Raskolnikov confides in Razumikhin about the murder but with words so cryptic that Razumikhin, while catching their drift, can scarcely believe them.

Porfiry Petrovich

Porfiry, the chief investigator, understands human nature and the mind of the criminal. Suspecting Raskolnikov early on, he cleverly uses banter and verbal tricks to disarm his prey. By being patient and playing mind games, Porfiry makes Raskolnikov suffer. Eventually, Raskolnikov can't take it anymore and turns himself in.

Nikolay (Mikolay, Mikolka)

Nikolay is the housepainter who arouses suspicion because he tried to pay his tavern bill with a pair of earrings taken from Alëna's apartment. After claiming that he found them in the street, he admits to picking them up behind the door of the empty flat that he and Mitka had painted. Scared, Nikolay tries to hang himself. Later he confesses to the murder. But since he and Mitka were observed laughing and engaging in horseplay just after the murder, Porfiry and others can't take the confession seriously, attributing it to Nikolay's self-delusion. Also, Nikolay is a religious zealot who believes that suffering is necessary to find God's grace.

Minor Characters

Nastasya is a kindly servant girl employed in the house where Raskolnikov lives. She brings him tea and soup.

Praskovya Pavlovna Zarnitsyna (Pashenka) is Raskolnikov's landlady. At one time Raskolnikov had been engaged to her sickly daughter, Natalya.

Koch and *Pestryakov* show up immediately after the murder and discover Alëna's door bolted. They go for help and, because the door is ajar when they return, instantly become suspects.

Zametov is the chief police clerk. Raskolnikov virtually confesses the murder to him but then says he was joking. Zametov is not so sure, however.

Zosimov is the physician who tends to Raskolnikov during his illness.

Polenka (Polya, Polechka) is Sonya's ten-year-old sister. Raskolnikov's spirits are briefly buoyed by Polenka's promise to pray for him.

Amalia Ivanovna Lippewechsel is the Marmeladovs' landlady. An ill-tempered and proud German, she threatens and fights with her tenants but gladly takes their money.

Structure

Crime and Punishment was written in installments for a St. Petersburg newspaper. To keep readers coming back, Dostoyevsky regularly suspended the action at a crucial moment in the story. At the end of Part 2, for example, Dunya and Pulkheria have just come to town. Because readers know that Raskolnikov intends to stop Dunya from marrying Luzhin, we are curious to see how he'll do it. At the very end of Part 3, Svidrigaylov, whose unsavory reputation precedes him, enters the story. His presence is bound to create tension that will likely steer the plot in unexpected directions in Part 4.

As a work of literature, *Crime and Punishment* has a distinct beginning, middle, and end. The first section introduces most of the characters, by name at least, and includes the murder of Alëna and her sister. Parts 2 to 6 deal with the aftermath of the crime, showing Raskolnikov's emotional and physical response to what he has done. Part 7, occurring several months later, consists of two epilogues that review the legal proceedings after Raskolnikov's confession and then show Raskolnikov undergoing a spiritual rebirth while incarcerated in Siberia.

Structurally, the novel is also made up of three separate but interlocking stories. The first concerns the murder and its consequences. The second story consists of the Raskolnikov family's experience, and the third deals with the relationship between Raskolnikov and Sonya. Raskolnikov's presence unifies the three stories and gradually blurs the lines between them.

Another kind of structure is built on several contrasting conceits implied not only in the book's title, but by Raskolnikov's dual personality. Raskolnikov is driven by both good and evil impulses. He is poor but gives away money. He contemplates murder but goes out of his way to protect a young woman from abuse. He does not want to be caught but carelessly leaves a trail of incriminating evidence. Such dualities are echoed by pairs of parallel events in the story. For one, Dunya is prepared to sacrifice her happiness for her brother just as Sonya sacrifices her virtue for her family. Svidrigaylov's revealing question, "Am I a monster or am I myself a victim?" could also have been uttered by Raskolnikov. Indeed, there are startling parallels between the two men, not the least being their mutual desire to make amends for past transgressions. In the end they choose opposite paths, however. Svidrigaylov ends his life while Raskolnikov, with Sonya's help, strives to create a new one.

Themes

Coincidence and Fate

Happenstance plays a major role in the unfolding of Raskolnikov's story. On the verge of killing and robbing Alëna, for example, he receives word from his mother that the family's financial woes are just about over. Purely by chance, while crossing the Haymarket he overhears Lizaveta make an appointment with a dealer for the next day. Another coincidence finds Raskolnikov in a tavern eavesdropping on a discussion in which an officer and a student talk hypothetically about killing Alëna, an idea that has been festering in Raskolnikov's mind for several weeks. It's a matter of fate, too, that Svidrigaylov takes a room adjacent to Sonya's and by chance listens to Raskolnikov tell Sonya that he killed Lizaveta. The confession turns out to be just what Svidrigaylov had been waiting for—a free ticket to talk to Dunya.

Poverty

Money, or, more accurately, a lack of it, underlies every event in the novel and determines the fate of virtually every character. Raskolnikov's poverty leads him to kill Alëna. Poverty pushes Dunya into a relationship with Luzhin and brings her to St. Petersburg. The rubles that Marfa wills to Dunya—money "fallen from heaven," says Pulkheria Alexandrovna—later frees Dunya to turn her fiancé Luzhin into her ex-fiancé. The impoverishment of the Marmeladovs forces Sonya into prostitution and Katerina Ivanovna into the street with her children. Because Raskolnikov gives a few coins to the Marmeladovs, he gets to befriend Sonya, a fateful relationship that ultimately leads him to come clean and admit his guilt. Without Sonya to buoy his spirits, Raskolnikov's self-loathing might well have led to self-destruction instead.

Duality

Raskolnikov personifies the kind of duality denoted both by the book's title and by events in the story. His dual personality is introduced on the very first page when he steps out of his room contemplating murder but at the same time fearing an encounter with his landlady. Raskolnikov can think like a cold-blooded killer, but he also has a heart of gold. Think of how he rescues a young girl on the street from the clutches of a lecherous old man. Or consider his generosity toward the Marmeladov family and his concern for Dunya's future. Through much of the book Raskolnikov fears being caught for his crime but leaves a wake of incriminating evidence, from virtually confessing to Zametov in the tavern to revisiting Alëna's apartment.

Sonya also has a dual nature. She commits a sin by selling her body, but the reason she does so preserves her honor and good name. By saving her family from ruin and never losing her faith in God, she redeems herself. Add to that her concern for Raskolnikov and her overall goodness of heart, and Sonya emerges as nothing short of a saint.

The Power of Dreams

Several dreams reveal Raskolnikov's violent tendencies and emotional turmoil both before and after the murder. In a nightmare that foreshadows his crime, he envisions himself as a young boy witnessing a brutal and bloody destruction of a helpless old horse. After the murder of the pawnbroker, he dreams that his landlady is being savagely beaten by a policeman—a sign perhaps of his fear of arrest. In another particularly telling dream, he hits Alëna with an ax again and again. But instead of dying, she laughs at him, as if to say that in spite of being physically dead, she will ever be alive in his conscience. Toward the end of the book, in Siberia, he dreams about a society wracked with anarchy and disease. Afterward, realizing that his warped view of the world leads only to mayhem and destruction, he vows to make amends.

Like Raskolnikov, Svidrigaylov also has powerful dreams. The final dream of his life, about the seduction of a young girl, reveals to him his own depravity and leads him to commit suicide.

Sin and Redemption

Sin, according to church dogma, leads to suffering, and suffering to ennoblement and redemption. The possibility of redeeming oneself through suffering is illustrated by Sonya's story. Sonya has every right to despair but remains optimistic about the future. She is confident, for example, that Katerina Ivanovna's children will somehow endure in spite of their mother's death, a conviction that comes from her belief in God. Because she has suffered for a noble purpose—to save her family—she has the moral authority to convince Raskolnikov to turn himself in. She believes that he must be punished for his crime but knows that in being punished he will redeem himself in God's eyes.

Lazarus, a biblical figure brought back to life by Jesus, serves as Sonya's (and ultimately Raskolnikov's) inspiration. By committing murder Raskolnikov has died spiritually. The prospect of being forgiven and returned to life keeps him going and persuades him to yield to Sonya's entreaties to confess.

Punishment

Punishment wears various guises. Immediately after the murder, Raskolnikov is overcome with fear, panic, and confusion. During his interview at police headquarters, aware that he harbors a terrible secret, he begins to be tormented by "eternal loneliness and estrangement." Never again can he feel free or be intimate with another person. In effect, he has become a prisoner within himself. He is also plagued by the thought that the police already suspect him of murder and that they have summoned him to the station in order to search his room for evidence.

Punishment comes also as a form of self-loathing. He hates himself for lying, for fawning, and for cringing from fear. Despising himself, he soon starts to despise others, including his mother and sister, the people who love him most. His agony is as much a punishment as a term in prison.

Raskolnikov's suffering abates only when he realizes, with Sonya's assistance, that rehabilitation is possible through faith.

Narrative Style/Language

An omniscient narrator tells Raskolnikov's story chronologically but with occasional flashbacks. Reference is made, for example, to Raskolnikov's previous association with his landlady's invalid daughter. We also hear that some time ago Raskolnikov dashed into a burning building and rescued two children.

Characters in the book often talk about the past, too. Marmeladov tells the tale of his pathetic career as a civil servant, and Pulkheria's long letter to her son explains the Dunya-Svidrigaylov affair and Dunya's engagement to

Luzhin. Raskolnikov recollects conversations he has overheard, and Porfiry, during an interrogation, recalls Raskolnikov's article published in a scholarly journal.

When introducing characters the author provides vivid thumbnail sketches, with one major exception. Raskolnikov is disposed of in a single parenthetical sentence: "He was, by the way, a strikingly handsome young man, with fine dark eyes, brown hair, and a slender well-knit figure, taller than the average." Other portraits are richer and include details meant to shape readers' opinions of the characters. Dunya, for one, is almost irresistible. The narrator tells us that she is "remarkably good-looking, tall, extremely well made, strong, self-assured, as her every gesture showed, without in the least detracting from the grace and tenderness of her movements." The sketch of Dunya concludes with an account of her generosity and good nature.

In contrast, the narrator stacks the cards against Alëna. He describes her as Raskolnikov sees her: "a tiny dried-up scrap of a creature, about sixty years old, with sharp, malicious little eyes and a small sharp nose. She was bare-headed and her fair hair, just beginning to go grey, was thick with grease. A strip of flannel was twisted around her long thin neck, which was wrinkled and yellow like a hen's legs . . . ." Her repulsive appearance and personality remove any sympathy we might have for her. Not that we condone her murder, but she seems about as dispensable as a person can be.

St. Petersburg serves as a suitable backdrop for the events in the story. The city is filled with seedy, rundown characters residing in seedy, rundown places, from Raskolnikov's hovel to the Marmeladovs' flat. The streets are hot, dirty, smelly, and crowded with people who reflect their surroundings. The denizens of the city are disheveled, raggedy, corrupt, and emotionally degenerate. To convey an overall sense of decay and decrepitude, the narrator relies heavily on the color yellow, not a bright cheerful yellow, but a faded yellow-gray, like a hen's legs. Alëna's scarf and jacket are yellow with age, as is the wallpaper in Raskolnikov's room.

Such attention to physical details is balanced by spiritual concerns. References to religion and the Bible abound. Sonya talks about God incessantly. Porfiry asks Raskolnikov about his religious beliefs and discusses the tale of Lazarus, a man that Jesus raised from the dead. The reference is apt, for Raskolnikov, by committing murder, has in essence joined the ranks of the living dead. From the moment the ax falls, the story follows his restoration, or resurrection, to a full and useful life. In another biblical allusion, Sonya, like Judas who betrayed Christ for thirty pieces of silver, sells herself for thirty rubles. But unlike the traitor, Sonya acts not to enrich herself but to help others. Her sacrifice is soon acknowledged by her stepmother, Katerina Ivanovna, who kisses Sonya's feet in appreciation and treats her like a savior.

Questions for Writing and Discussion

1. Raskolnikov cites several reasons to justify his crime. Which, if any, are valid? Can you think of any other justification for killing Alëna?

2. Does Raskolnikov's punishment fit the crime he has committed? Does he suffer enough to pay for his transgression?

3. When Raskolnikov goes out to rehearse his crime he wants to be as inconspicuous as possible, but a passerby yells at him about the high round hat he is wearing. Raskolnikov berates himself for overlooking such a "trifle," as he calls it. Such a mistake could cause his undoing on

the day of the murder. Yet he seems bent on self-destruction. What reasons are there to explain this aspect of his character?

4. What, if anything, do the settings contribute to the meaning of the novel as a whole?

5. To what extent does Raskolnikov exercise his free will? To what extent is he controlled by outside forces? Where does Dostoyevsky stand on the issue of free will vs. fate?

Portrait of the Artist as a Young Man
by James Joyce

Background

Portrait of the Artist as a Young Man, often called *Portrait of the Artist*, or even more economically, *Portrait*, has long been a staple of AP English courses. Why do teachers and AP curriculum writers choose it? Explanations vary, of course, but one reason is almost universal: The author, James Joyce, is one of the superlative stylists of the twentieth century. His inventive writing style takes getting used to, but once readers catch on, they're usually hooked.

Neither all fact nor all fiction, *Portrait of the Artist* fuses the two. In recounting his first twenty years, James Joyce calls himself Stephen Dedalus and chronicles the emotional and intellectual adventures that shaped his personality and molded his values. The novel—although it's also an autobiography—details the social milieu and psychological factors that drove the young protagonist, a sensitive and thoughtful boy, to look inward, to turn away from his family and church, and ultimately to leave Ireland to become a writer.

Because of parallels between Joyce's life and events in *Portrait*, many readers view the book as an accurate portrayal of the author's childhood. But Joyce wrote the book decades after the events occurred. Besides, he never claimed to be writing a factual account of his youth. Just as any casual storyteller may embellish the truth to make a tale more dramatic and compelling, Joyce selectively altered the truth by reconstituting people, places, and events for the sake of achieving his artistic vision. He also made generous use of artistic license to heighten the intensity of Stephen's despair. He magnified the quirks and qualities of the characters and turned mild disagreements into life-altering conflicts.

> You should find *Portrait of the Artist as a Young Man* applicable for an essay on any of the following: 1) psychological realism, 2) a misunderstood rebel, 3) the power of religion, 4) father-son relationships, and 5) a young man's sexuality.

Synopsis

The book begins with Stephen as an infant, a creature of the senses. He sees his father's "hairy face," hears the story of the "moocow coming down along the road," smells the queer odor of the oilsheet, feels his wet bed ("first it is warm then it gets cold"), and tastes "lemon platt," a delectable kind of candy. At this point the significant people in Stephen's life include his parents; Dante, the governess; and Eileen, the neighbor's daughter.

Suddenly the setting shifts from the Dedalus home to Clongowes Wood College—the equivalent of an elementary and middle school—where Stephen begins his formal education at about age six. Stephen is a good student, except in math, and also a social outcast. Bullies pick on him. An older boy named Wells throws him into a cesspool, resulting in an illness serious enough to put Stephen in the infirmary. The incident colors Stephen's attitude toward being at the school. In Stephen's view, everything at Clongowes is cold and slimy, damp and wet—from the chilly corridors to the soggy and limp tablecloths in the refectory. Joyce makes the place seem physically uncomfortable, which certainly reflects Stephen's emotional attitude toward it as well. During the first term he longs for his family and counts the days until he can go home for Christmas.

Home for the holidays, Stephen witnesses a heated conversation among the adults gathered for Christmas dinner. They argue about Parnell,[1] whose immoral actions have divided the Irish population. Dante sides with the Church, while the gentlemen at the table idolize Parnell. Stephen is unconsciously caught in a dilemma to choose between his father's way or Dante's way—between allegiance to the secular view or the religious view, a conflict that haunts Stephen for the remainder of his youth.

A hurtful incident back at Clongowes raises doubts in the boy's mind about the rectitude of the priests who run the school. Having broken his eyeglasses, Stephen has sent home for a new pair. Father Dolan, the prefect of studies, accuses Stephen of being a slacker and hits him with a pandybat, a leather instrument used for corporal punishment. Stephen smarts with pain and grieves over the injustice. At the urging of other boys, he informs the rector, Father Conmee, who treats Stephen kindly. But some time later the boy learns from his own father that Dolan and Conmee had enjoyed a good laugh over Stephen's behavior. The incident drives a wedge between Stephen and the Church.

Chapter 2 covers roughly five years of Stephen's life, from age nine to fourteen. Naive and innocent at the start, by the end Stephen has been initiated into adulthood. In between he becomes increasingly troubled about the path his life is taking. On the outside he is the picture of a dutiful son, an excellent student, a good lad in every way. But secretly he seethes with anxiety because of thoughts and feelings that he believes good boys are not supposed to have.

During a pleasant summer in suburban Blackrock, Stephen fantasizes a good deal about his future. In his imagination he is a great lover, sweeping women off their feet and enjoying moments of passion. In reality, Stephen is angry with himself for being young and having such foolish thoughts.

---

[1]Charles Stewart Parnell and his associate Michael Davitt were heroes of a movement that fought successfully for land reforms at the end of the nineteenth century. Until then, most Irish land was owned by English and Scottish landlords who kept the Irish tenant farmers impoverished. The Land Act of 1881, called the Magna Charta of the Irish farmer, fixed a fair rent for tenants and provided loans for farmers to buy their own land. Parnell in particular, was lionized as a champion of liberty, Ireland's uncrowned king, and a Moses figure leading the Irish people to the promised land. He was elected to Parliament, but in 1904 word got out that he was having an affair with a married woman, Kitty O'Shea. The Church condemned Parnell, priests denounced him, and the population of Ireland was torn between their allegiance to the Church and their adulation of Parnell.

In the fall, Simon Dedalus finds himself in financial straits, forcing the family to take up residence in a drab Dublin neighborhood. Stephen is sent to Belvedere, a less prestigious school than Clongowes. He continues to be a top student with a bent toward literature, particularly the poetry of Byron. One day, after developing a crush on E.C., a girl he met at a party, he writes her a love poem in Byronic style but doesn't send it.

Moved to try writing more poems, he fails. But Stephen is charmed by the mystery of creating beauty in words. At school he excels at essay writing. On one occasion he writes an essay that his teacher regards as heretical—much to the delight of Stephen's classmates who are glad to see the top boy stumble. Adding further insult, a handful of boys rough Stephen up for favoring Byron over their own favorite poet, Tennyson. Strangely, Stephen bears no malice. He regards the beating as just another attempt to force him into conformity, hardly different from parental pressure to be a gentleman and a good Catholic.

That year Stephen accompanies his father on a trip to Cork, where Simon had spent his youth and now hopes to sell some family property. Observing Simon on the train and in the pubs of Cork surrounded by the cronies of his past, Stephen is repulsed. The visit heightens Stephen's sense of detachment from his father and strenghtens his resolve to become his own person.

For writing a fine essay and scoring high on a national exam, Stephen wins a prize of thirty-three pounds—a considerable sum in those days. Stephen spends his winnings freely on food, clothing, and merrymaking. When the money runs out, his general malaise returns. He again finds solace in sexual fantasies. Wandering the streets of Dublin, he encounters a prostitute, and letting his desires overcome his fear of sin, he allows himself to be seduced.

Chapter 3 takes Stephen on a nightmarish journey into sin, guilt, and repentance. Stephen knows that eternal damnation awaits his soul, but he is possessed by lust. While steeped in mortal sin, he takes perverse pride in his debauchery, as though yearning for his soul's destruction. Although he stops going to Mass, Stephen continues as the leader of his school's devotional society, the Sodality of the Blessed Virgin Mary. While finding fault with most church doctrine, he is strangely moved by the Virgin's gentleness and at times considers repenting for his sins.

When the rector of Belvedere announces a three-day religious retreat to "examine the state of our conscience," Stephen, guilt-ridden about his behavior, grows fearful of facing the truth about what he has become. His former teacher, Father Arnall, presides at the retreat, causing Stephen to reflect on the innocent days he spent at Clongowes. With powerful sermons meant to strike terror into his impressionable young audience, Arnall describes the ghastly punishments that await sinners in hell. Stephen imagines that Arnall's words have been directed specifically at him and can't imagine why God had not already struck him dead.

After a terrifying nightmare, Stephen obeys voices that urge him to "confess, confess!" He finds a church, enters the confessional, and spills out his story of sin and self-degradation to the priest. Absolved of his sins, Stephen leaves the church "holy and happy."

The start of Chapter 4 finds Stephen making amends for his past sins. Practicing religion like a fanatic, he prays, goes to Mass daily, says his rosaries, does more than necessary to fulfill his devotional duties. To bolster his resistance to temptation, he punishes himself. He fasts, averts his eyes from women, sits in uncomfortable positions, subjects himself to the smell of stale urine—trying as best he can to share the suffering of the saints, in particular his namesake, the martyr St. Stephen. Nevertheless, guilt continues to gnaw at him, and he falls prey to petty irritations like the sound of his mother's sneeze and the twitching mouths of his teachers.

Having observed his apparent piety, the director of Belvedere urges Stephen to study for the priesthood. At first Stephen is excited. He had often daydreamed about being a priest, and his mother would be thrilled. But he is also terrified by the awful assumption of powers that ordination entails. As he reflects more seriously on becoming a priest he is repelled by the grave, orderly, and passionless life of a Jesuit. He values freedom too highly to conform to a religious or social order.

Against his mother's wishes, Stephen enrolls in the university to study literature. One afternoon a solitary walk along the shore unexpectedly leads him to his life's vocation. Hearing his name shouted by some university friends in the distance, he is suddenly connected in spirit to Daedalus, the fabulous artificer of myth, and realizes that his calling in life is to art, namely the art of writing. Like the birds he sees circling between the sea and sky, and like "a hawklike man [Daedalus] flying sunward above the sea," his soul soars in an ecstasy of flight. A new wild life sings in his veins. The moment marks a transition from boyhood to manhood. This is Stephen's deliverance, the pivotal point in his life. When he observes a girl standing in the water, he likens her to a lovely seabird, a metaphor for physical freedom. To Stephen, she is also an "angel of mortal youth and beauty," perhaps symbolic of both the sensual and the creative life that awaits him.

Chapter 5 shows Stephen as a student in the university, immersed in literature and other intellectual pursuits. Although family life stifles his youthful spirit, Stephen continues to live at home. As he walks to class his mind dances with ideas inspired by books he has read. He also thinks about his cronies, among them McCann, the idealistic democrat; Lynch, a crude down-to-earth type; Cranly, naïve, conservative, but also Stephen's closest confidante; and Davin, first and foremost an Irish nationalist. Davin has told Stephen an intriguing story about a recent escapade out in the country: Stopping at a small cottage to ask for a drink of water, he was greeted by a half-dressed young woman who hands him a mug of milk and immediately invites him to spend the night. But Davin declines and makes a quick getaway. The incident reminds Stephen of his own past profligacy and leads him to contemplate the current decadence of Ireland. The alienation he feels pushes him toward the decision to flee his native land.

Additional episodes weaken Stephen's ties to his past. A conversation with the dean of studies about the difference between practical arts and liberal arts nudges Stephen further from the Church. He regards the dean, who is a priest, as an "unlit lamp," a closed-minded phony. Asked by friends to sign a petition for world peace and to participate in causes that benefit society, Stephen refuses, unwilling to divert his energy away from art. Davin urges him to be one of the boys, to "be a poet or mystic later." But Stephen remains aloof, wrapped up in a complex set of beliefs about art and about the nature of beauty and truth. Stephen articulates his beliefs to his friends, whose humorous responses tend to deflate some of his esoteric ideas. At times Stephen's theories seem borderline pretentious, but they also illustrate the depth of his extraordinary intellect.

Putting theory into practice, Stephen composes a passionate love poem to "E-C-" (Emma), the girl who has resided in his thoughts for years and has returned full force after a chance encounter near the campus library. The poem, a villanelle, encapsulates a variety of conflicting emotions that Stephen had felt about his attraction to Emma as well as to women in general.

From the steps of the library Stephen observes numerous birds in flight. Prophetically, he is again reminded of the hawklike Daedalus, soaring freely into the sky. From then on Stephen focuses largely on preparing himself for escape from friends, family, church, and country. He turns his back on Cranly, suspecting that his friend has betrayed him by secretly seeing Emma. At the same time, however, Cranly expresses a fear of loneliness that carries overtones of homosexuality. During his final conversation with Cranly, Stephen confides that a quarrel with his mother about attending Easter Mass and taking Communion has upset him. But Cranly's advice—to oblige his mother—increases Stephen's determination to go his own way and pursue the "unfettered freedom" of a creative life. Stephen makes clear his willingness to sacrifice himself for art, saying, in effect, that he's willing to risk eternal damnation, if necessary, to follow his beliefs.

The last pages are fragments from Stephen's diary or journal which reveal his state of mind and tie up loose ends before his emancipation. Stephen still longs for Emma, but tries to cast away his feelings: "Give it up, old chap!" he says. "Sleep it off!" Recorded in the next to last entry is his mother's wish that he "may learn . . . what the heart is and what it feels," as if to say that Stephen's life heretofore has been marred by a lack of compassion. Eyes focused only on the future, he writes, "Welcome, O life! I go to encounter for the millionth time the reality of experience and to forge in the smithy of my soul the uncreated conscience of my race."

Cast of Characters   *Stephen Dedalus*
Stephen, from whose point of view the novel is written, crowds out other characters, most of whom drift in and out of the story and often serve as foils to set off aspects of Stephen's personality. Stephen's caustic view of family, friends, and members of the clergy is not surprising. After all, in order to justify his flight at the end of the book, Stephen must show that no one in Ireland—not even his mother or Emma—has a sufficient emotional hold on him to keep him from fleeing.

As a character Stephen is bright and acutely observant at times. His eyesight may be poor, but he is sensitive and perceptive enough to peer into his own soul. In his early years Stephen is sharply differentiated from his environment. The richness of his inner experience is continually played off against the grim reality of the external world. Raised in an intensely Irish and devoutly Catholic household, the boy struggles for intellectual and emotional freedom. At home and at school, while steeped in the ritual and orthodoxy of the Church, he often finds himself at odds with his surroundings. Inner impulses and desires consistently rebel against tradition. Anguish comes from feeling stifled and from observing contradictions between what the Church says and what his emotions and intellect tell him. In his family, he regards himself as a pariah, a foster child with alien blood flowing through his veins.

In many ways Stephen is a bundle of inconsistencies. Timid, homesick, and fearful at Clongowes, he's also courageous enough to report being unjustly punished by the school's prefect of studies, Father Dolan. Early in his teens, he shies away from romance but is driven to satisfy his sexual urges with a prostitute. Afterward, he is frightened about spending eternity in hell but cannot resist sin. He toys with the idea of becoming a priest but can't abide the tyranny of the Church. These and other contradictions epitomize Stephen's emotional turmoil. Once Stephen pledges himself to life as an artist, however, his internal conflicts seem to work themselves out, or at least he refuses to let them continue pushing him around. Intuitively he knows that someday he will transcend the joyless, depressing world in which he lives. By the end of the book, he has grown into a confident, even haughty, young man, about to break his ties to family, faith, and country in order to pursue the unfettered life of a writer.

Mrs. Dedalus

A shadowy, long-suffering character, Stephen's mother is a rigid religious zealot struggling to maintain a secure home for her family. In his mind Stephen sometimes links her with the Virgin Mary. His love for her, however, can't keep him in Ireland. When he rejects the Church and leaves Dublin, his mother is shattered.

Simon Dedalus

Simon, Stephen's father, is a more well-rounded character than Mrs. Dedalus. To the infant Stephen, he is a "hairy face." A big talker, a cheerful, back-slapping sort of fellow, he loves Ireland to a fault and grows nostalgic over the days of his youth. Because he drinks heavily and finds himself increasingly overwhelmed with the responsibilities of being a father and breadwinner, he slowly drags his large family into poverty. While envying his father's charming manner, Stephen can hardly endure the old man's superficiality and hypocrisy. The misrule and confusion of Simon's house come to stand in Stephen's mind for the plight of Ireland. Simon worships Parnell like a god and during a scene at Christmas dinner ends up weeping about his recent death.

Charles

Charles, a great-uncle, is like a grandfather to Stephen, who accepts the old man's eccentricities and enjoys the summer they spend together in Blackrock. Charles's descent into senility parallels both the decline of Ireland and the fall of the Dedalus family fortunes.

Dante Riordan

Stephen's governess is a devout Catholic and an ardent Irish nationalist. In the Parnell case, where politics clashes with religion, she sides with the Church.

John Casey

Casey, a family friend, epitomizes the Irish loyalist. He has been jailed for his involvement in political demonstrations. In spite of the Church's condemnation of Parnell, however, he remains a good Catholic.

School Friends

None of Stephen's school chums leaves an indelible mark on his development. Yet their personalities and beliefs help Stephen to define himself. They figure largely as interlocutors to draw him out on various themes. Cranly, for instance, represents conventional thinking and the voice of conscience. He questions

Stephen's motives for wanting to leave Ireland and become a writer. During long conversations with Cranly, Stephen articulates his resolve to follow his wayward nature. Lynch and others serve as an audience for Stephen's lengthy, convoluted explanation of his artistic theories. Stephen sometimes feels he is casting pearls before swine because his friends respond with lewd jokes and indifference.

Of all his university friends, only McCann stands as Stephen's intellectual equal. But McCann's concerns are political. He speaks of such global matters as equality and one-world government while self-indulgent Stephen contemplates his navel.

Members of the Clergy

Of all the characters in Stephen's story, he clergy come off the worst. Father Dolan, the prefect of studies at Clongowes, personifies petty cruelty. He punishes Stephen unjustly and plants the thought in Stephen's mind that priests can be just as flawed as the rest of us. Father Arnall is no better. He fails to stand up for Stephen against Father Dolan. To scare impressionable young boys into behaving themselves, he preaches a searing sermon about sinners burning forever in the fires of hell. Priests provide Stephen's schooling, but he comes to regard them condescendingly as "men who washed their bodies briskly with cold water and wore clean cold linen."

Structure

Each of the book's five chapters is loosely devoted to a stage in Stephen Dedalus's journey to manhood. Although the tale unfolds more or less chronologically, neither the past nor the future is far out of sight. Allusions to earlier incidents recur repeatedly. Visiting Cork with his father, for example, the budding adolescent Stephen overcomes a momentary spell of childish insecurity by quickly reviewing his early life. He defines himself as a boy who "had been taught geography by an old woman [Dante Riordon, his governess] who kept two brushes in her wardrobe." A girl, variously named Emma and E.C., slips in and out of Stephen's consciousness, appearing when sexual longings occupy his thoughts. Bittersweet memories of Clongowes, his first school, return again and again. Indeed, there are few major events in Stephen's early life that fail to be reprised at least fleetingly as the story progresses.

At the same time, the story is fertile with foreshadowing. During the summer at Blackrock, for instance, young Stephen, then about seven years old, memorizes words that adults use, sensing that through them he may catch glimpses of his future, namely the world of the writer. Furtively he has begun to prepare himself "for the great part which he felt awaited him the nature of which he only dimly apprehended." It's hardly unexpected at the end of the book that Stephen leaves Ireland and goes off on his own. As you read *Portrait*, you'll no doubt notice many more instances of foreshadowing.

By blending past, present, and future, Joyce may be suggesting that we are all made up of the totality of our experiences. There's nothing particularly profound in that, but it's indicative of Joyce's effort to describe life not as a discrete series of disconnected events but a fluid succession of present moments. Some readers consider the technique the linguistic equivalent of a cinematic montage.

Each chapter of the book finds Stephen coping, for better or worse, with the circumstances of his life. As chapters end, however, Stephen experiences moments of joy, triumph, or contentment. Chapter 1, for instance, closes with Stephen being hailed as a hero by his schoolmates for reporting sadistic Father Dolan to the rector of Clongowes. Like Parnell, Stephen is briefly a symbol of justice restored over force and violence. This is followed in Chapter 2 by the Christmas dinner scene, during which a fierce argument among the adults ends in tears. For the first time, in a kind of fall from innocence, Stephen sees his elders' faults and foibles. Stephen's letdown is compounded by a sudden awareness of his family's money problems and the gradual awakening of unsatisfied pubescent longings. The chapter is brought to a close when Stephen, in the throes of sexual arousal, experiences physical ecstasy in the bed of a prostitute.

Template-like, the pattern repeats itself in the next chapter, which begins with Stephen in a state of postcoital guilt and remorse, and ends with Stephen, having been purged of his sins during confession to a Capuchin priest, anticipating a "life of grace and virtue and happiness." Stephen is anything but happy at the beginning of the next chapter, however. Rather, he has been numbed by a brutal self-imposed regimen of worship and religious ritual.

And so it goes—a consummate high followed by a low. Readers have observed that this rhythm imitates the swooping up-and-down flight of Daedalus, of birds in the air, and of emotional fluctuations typical of adolescence.

In any case, Joyce is fond of juxtaposing opposites, not only between chapters but within them. Pairings like *wet-dry, cold-hot,* and *dark-light* occur with unusual frequency throughout the novel. For instance, words such as *gloomy, dark, dull,* and *cold* proliferate in the account of Stephen's nightly adventures prowling the red-light district of Dublin. Such words reflect both the city streets and Stephen's state of mind. Dark words are later replaced by references to brightness—*white pudding, pale candle flames, white flowers*—clean images that embody Stephen's return to piety. The repeated pairing of opposites, while conveying Stephen's various moods and conflicts, also functions to unify the story.

The novel's disjointedness leaves room for multiple interpretations of its structure. Its five-chapter organization invites the view that each chapter covers a different stage of Stephen's development. Some critics argue that the writing style matures from chapter to chapter as Stephen grows up. Others prefer to divide the book into thirds—one third showing Stephen's coming of age, another his development as a writer, and a final section detailing his decision to leave Ireland. Another analysis compares the book to the process of birth. Like a human embryo Stephen is barely formed at the start. Subsequent chapters show the fetus developing a heart, entering the birth canal, and ultimately being born, that is, leaving the "womb" of family, Church, and homeland.

However ambiguous the structure, there's no question that Joyce has chosen to tell Stephen's story through a series of important episodes in the boy's life. These episodes, often called *epiphanies*, a term borrowed from Church ritual, are experiences that embody meaning in a single moment. They are basically intense moments of discovery or heightened awareness. Stephen's mystical encounter with the bird/girl at Bull Island is one of the most obvious examples. While strolling along the shore, Stephen realizes the connection between his name, Dedalus, and the destiny that awaits him. Like the "hawklike man flying sunward above the sea," Stephen must be a "great artificer," a creator: "To live, to err, to fall, to triumph, to recreate life out of life!"

Other epiphanies may lack the theatrics of this one, but they nevertheless serve to jolt Stephen awake to the nature of the world. An unjust punishment in Latin class rocks his naïve belief in the beneficence of priests; evidently men of the cloth can be as malicious as other men. Later, he is shocked at news of the "hearty laugh" that his father shared with Father Dolan over the pandybat incident. What Stephen once regarded as an important triumph of his boyhood—reporting Dolan to the rector—turns out to be nothing more than an amusing trifle.

As Stephen matures, he makes additional discoveries. He recognizes his father's failures. He realizes the emptiness of promiscuity, and he also comes to acknowledge the hypocrisy of practicing piety without curbing his sensual desires. Finally, on the eve of his departure from Ireland, he abandons a long-held impression that women are either fodder for erotic fantasies or prostitutes meant to relieve his sexual appetite. Following a brief encounter with Emma, he has come to realize that women are human beings after all. While reading *Portrait*, you'll undoubtedly run into other moments of awareness. (Some critics have counted up to twenty epiphanies.)

Narrative Style

In *Portrait* Joyce relies heavily on interior monologue or stream of consciousness. Thoughts tumble onto the page as they occur in Stephen Dedalus's mind—shifting illogically, compulsively, without benefit of transitions. Because the human mind works in uncontrollable ways and associations come as they will, Joyce's prose is celebrated for his psychological realism. Some readers relish the opportunity to crawl inside the author's head while others detest it, quickly tire of it, or simply just don't get the point. (Upon publication, *Portrait* was hailed as a revolutionary piece of literature, but it also received a number of chilly reviews. One critic thought it "too discursive, formless, unrestrained. . . too unconventional. . . . [Joyce's] pen and his thoughts seem to have run away with him.") It's true that episodes often seem unconnected and disjointed, but a careful reading of the book reveals considerable artistic unity, derived from both thematic material and Joyce's use of language.

It is telling that the distinctive style of *Portrait of the Artist* has inspired more comment, both positive and negative, than virtually any other aspect of the novel. Joyce revels in language. He confers on words a kind of "magical potency," as one critic says, using allusions and artifice to recreate lifelike feelings, sensations, and impressions. By and large, authors employ straightforward narrative and descriptive techniques to tell a story. Joyce, on the other hand, aims to create dreamlike effects, using unexpected leaps through space and time, indirection, and the power of suggestion. As an author Joyce is credited with a number of stylistic innovations. In *Portrait of the Artist* these include the coining of words, in particular, compound adjectives such as *darkwindowed, indiarubber, fowlwise, rainfragrant*. He takes liberties with standard syntax, writing incomplete sentences, violating rules of punctuation—all manner of things that drive English teachers up the wall. That Joyce's prose is idiosyncratic registers Stephen's cleavage with his family, with the Church, and with Ireland. Stephen deviates from the straight and narrow in his conduct just as Joyce deviates from the ordinary in his writing. By being deviant, the prose reflects the rifts between Stephen and others. In short, the style is symbolic of the story.

Joyce is fond of shifting styles and modes of writing, from lush verse (love poems) to dry scholarly pontification (Stephen's theories of art and beauty). For descriptions of people and the outside world, he uses precise, often scathing exposition that derives its strength from its imagery, symbolism, sound, and unremitting attention to documentary realism. (As you read the following brief excerpt, for instance, listen to the hard, dry words: "A field of stiff weeds and thistles and tufted nettlebunches. Thick among the tufts of rank stiff growth lay battered cannisters and clots and coils of solid excrement.")

Numerous passages demonstrate Joyce's mastery of ordinary straightforward narration and of writing realistic dialogue. Many of the book's strongest and most memorable scenes are conversations, such as the unforgettable Christmas dinner and Stephen's talk with Belvedere's director of studies about the possibility of becoming a priest. These exchanges could easily have been scenes lifted verbatim from the script of a play.

Interpolated into the mix of styles are a number of purple passages, heavy on emotion and overloaded with evocative adjectives. Like many autobiographers, Joyce tends to overstate, amplify, and embroider the reality of his youth, more to create an effect than to tell the truth. For example, after Father Dolan strikes Stephen on the hand,

> Stephen drew back his maimed and quivering right arm and held out his left hand. The soutane sleeve swished again as the pandybat was lifted and a loud crashing sound and a fierce maddening tingling burning pain made his hand shrink together with the palms and fingers in a livid quivering mass. The scalding water burst forth from his eyes and, burning with shame and agony and fear, he drew back his shaking arm in terror and burst out into a whine of pain. His body shook with a palsy of fright and in shame and rage he felt the scalding cry come from his throat and the scalding tears falling out of his eyes and down his flaming cheeks.

Later, Stephen's sexual initiation is presented in the purplest of purple prose:

> It was too much for him. He closed his eyes, surrendering himself to her, body and mind, conscious of nothing in the world but the dark pressure of her softly parting lips. They pressed upon his brain as upon his lips as though they were the vehicle of a vague speech; and between them he felt an unknown and timid pressure, darker than the swoon of sin, softer than sound or odour.

Tastes, sounds, smells, the feel of things on his skin—Joyce crowds the book with sensual imagery rich with symbolic meaning. The very fact of Stephen's poor eyesight—he wears glasses at an early age—symbolizes powerlessness and punishment, as in the pandybat incident. Yet Stephen has the power to peer into his own soul.

Some readers claim that Joyce often views his protagonist with irony. That is, the author tries to maintain a certain distance from his former self. At times Joyce clearly admires Stephen, but at other times he seems to mock him or satirize his reactions in trying circumstances. No doubt young Steven was hurt by Father Dolan's pandybat, certainly he was tormented by Father Arnall's sermon, but the melodramatic tone used to recount these episodes suggests that readers shouldn't take Stephen's exaggerated reactions at face value. It's not that Joyce intends to ridicule Stephen's boyishness but rather to suggest that early in his life the author probably took himself too seriously.

Themes and Symbolism

We first meet Stephen as a very small child being told a story of a moocow (a symbol for Ireland) and a baby (Stephen himself) named "tuckoo." In relating young Stephen's earliest memories, Joyce seeds the book's one-and-a-half-page prelude with a number of references that will later grow into the major themes of Stephen's life. For one, the boy relishes his father's stories, which may be a negligible fact at first but one that anticipates Stephen's interest in language and literature. Stephen also notices differences between his mother and his father—she smells nicer than he does. Eventually, his regard for each of his parents comes to differ dramatically: She is instrumental in Stephen's religious training while his father, something of a hard-drinking, irresponsible roustabout, serves first as a standard against whom Stephen measures himself and later becomes a model for him either to emulate or reject.

Stephen observes that Dante Riordan, his governess, owns two brushes, one with a "green velvet back for Parnell," another with a "maroon velvet back for Michael Davitt." This allusion to Irish politics evolves into a topic of abiding interest to the Dedalus family and to several of Stephen's college friends.

As the prelude ends, Dante recites a verse about apologizing. Precisely what Stephen is told to apologize for remains unspecified, but gradually the notion of seeking forgiveness develops into the full-fledged theme in Stephen's religiosity. More specifically, the confession and absolution from sin, a cardinal principle of Roman Catholicism, comes to dominate Stephen's view of life. It turns out that Dante is a devout Catholic. Her threat that the eagles will come and pull out Stephen's eyes not only induces a fear of sin into the little boy, but introduces a general reference to birds that evolves gradually into a symbol of Stephen's freedom (as free as a bird) and taking flight from Ireland. What's more, Dante's admonition to "*apologize*" resonates whenever Stephen is pressured to *admit, repent, submit, conform,* and *confess*.

Although the themes at first may seem discrete, the lines between them gradually blur, each theme becoming entangled with others. In its way, it is like hypertext; everything links to everything else. You can't separate Stephen's Catholic upbringing from his carnal adventures. Numerous dalliances with prostitutes bring out guilt and fear of burning in hell. Stephen's attraction to Eileen's cool, creamy hands and blonde hair make him think of "Tower of Ivory" and "House of Gold," phrases in a prayer to the Virgin Mary. Images of the Virgin are often linked to young Stephen's sexuality. He notices in a likeness of the Virgin hanging on his bedroom wall "a strange light glowing faintly upon her frail flesh." He yearns to serve the Virgin as a knight serves his lady. Murmuring her name feels like a taste of a "lewd kiss." Stephen's inability to curb his sexual appetites contributes to his eventual break from the Church, a breach that further separates him from his mother and leads directly to his decision to forsake Ireland.

Stephen's Love of Language

Joyce's extravagance with words has prompted readers to observe that language itself is one of the book's main concerns. Truly, Joyce seems to call attention to his art. He writes with a fluid succession of prose styles corresponding to Stephen's maturing consciousness.

The opening is almost primitive. Prelinguisitic, a pastiche of childish language, it is made up of sensations and devoted to puzzling out ordinary facts about the nature of the world, such as whether a real boy ought to kiss his mother goodnight. During Stephen's days at Clongowes and Belvedere the text is filled with the slang of youth ("fecked," "scut," "smugging") and schoolboy jingles (*"It can't be helped;/ It must be done./ So down with your breeches/ And out with your bum."*).

From an early age, the boy is fascinated with words. At Clongowes he enjoys the "nice sentences" in the spelling book and reflects on the "queer" sound of the word *suck*. Throughout his youth he reads prolifically, in part because reading not only lets him escape from drab reality but feeds his fantasies. He falls for Mercedes, the fictional heroine of *The Count of Monte Cristo* and longs to meet a real girl like her. The best he can do, however, is to idolize a distant figure, E.C., to whom he composes love poems. One of the essays he writes for school wins a large sum of money that gives Stephen his first taste of independence from his family. Until the money runs out, he lifts his family's spirits by spending freely on food and clothing. Another of his essays, however, earns him both the censure of his teacher, for its heretical content, and a beating from his schoolfellows.

While the lure of vicarious adventure originally leads Stephen to books, writing offers boundless opportunities for self-expression. But Stephen is constrained by his family and the Church. His mother and the priests who are his teachers, claiming to have the best interests of Stephen's soul in mind, plead with him to adhere to Catholicism, to become a priest. Stephen refuses, unwilling to plug up his creativity and cease his free-thinking. He views himself potentially as a "priest of the eternal imagination."

Throughout his youth, Stephen notices the speech of others. Cranly's, for instance, "unlike that of Davin, had neither rare phrases of Elizabethan English nor quaintly turned versions of Irish idioms. Its drawl was an echo of the quays of Dublin . . . ." As Stephen matures, the narration grows more lyrical. In the last chapter Stephen, influenced by years of language study, talks the talk of literary theory, influenced by Aquinas and Aristotle. Prior to scuttling off into exile as a writer, he contrives an elaborate aesthetic theory that stands as a kind of credo for his art. To his college mates he delivers a lecture in which he explores questions of literary merit. Concerned with artistic beauty, among other things, and the relationship between tragedy and the emotions, Stephen takes the position that beauty in art must possess *wholeness, harmony*, and *radiance*, terms that Stephen carefully defines to his various listeners, who are more impressed with the fact that he has actually thought out such matters than with the substance of his ideas.

Exile from Ireland

The misrule and confusion in the Dedalus household comes to stand in Stephen's mind for the plight of Ireland. Repulsed by intellectual stagnation and slavish adherence to the Church, Stephen dreams of escape. "Ireland is the old sow that eats her farrow," says Stephen to his friend Davin, alluding to his feeling of being devoured by the tyranny of Irish tradition. Davin, the archnationalist, accuses Stephen of being a "born sneerer," and tells his friend, "In your heart you are an Irishman but your pride is too powerful." But Stephen won't be dissuaded. "You talk to me of nationality, language, religion," he says. "I shall try to fly by those nets."

Stephen's eventual flight from Ireland is foreshadowed long before he decides to escape. Even the name that Joyce chose for his hero proclaims that Stephen will one day flee the country. As Joyce puts it when Stephen hears friends shout "Dedalus" in ersatz Greek ("Stephanos Deadlos!" etc.) across the water of Dublin Bay, "his strange name seemed to him a prophesy," namely "a symbol of the artist forging anew in his workshop out of the sluggish matter of the earth a new soaring impalpable imperishable being." Joyce adopted Stephen's given name from the first martyr of the Catholic Church, suggesting that young Stephen's martyrdom to art echoes St. Stephen's martyrdom to the faith. The name Dedalus has still richer connotations. It derives from the mythic and priestly figure of Daedalus, known as the builder of wings and the architect of the famous labyrinth. Stephen invokes his namesake as both "the hawklike man" and "the fabulous artificer." Like Daedalus, Stephen aspires to fly from entrapment, escaping Dublin on wings of art.

But Stephen also bears a likeness to Daedalus's son, Icarus, whose ill-fated and rebellious spirit caused him to ignore his father's warning not to fly too high. When the hot sun melts the wax on his wings, Icarus falls to his death in the sea. Is Icarus's fall a prophetic symbol for Stephen? We don't know, for the book ends as Stephen's flight is about to begin.

Religion

The Church pervades Stephen's life from the day he is born. Stephen's break from the Church, therefore, is a courageous act. His decision not to become a priest represents the turning point of his story. Until then Stephen loves God and possesses a childish faith in his religion. As he matures, repulsed by God's ministers, he defects. Priests in Stephen's mind are despots and usurpers. In repudiating the Church, however, Stephen doesn't relinquish his faith in God. He merely gives faith a personal slant. As a lifelong Catholic, though, Stephen cannot completely shake a burden of guilt inspired by his rejection of the Church and his concomitant rejection of his mother.

Water and Wetness

Joyce drenches his prose with images of wetness. From urine to holy water, from tears to the sea, liquids of all kinds flow through the book. The first chapter overflows with references to water and dampness, from Stephen's wetting the bed to hearing the far-off sound of cricket bats—"pick, pack, pock, puck: little drops of water in a fountain slowly falling in the brimming bowl." Just as life on earth evolved out of some primordial soup, Stephen's early days, while he is still "wet behind the ears," so to speak, are dominated by watery images, many of them cold, slimy, and repellent. By the end of the book, however, the sea, which Stephen soon will cross to begin a new life, has become a thing of beauty, symbolizing Stephen's renewed life.

Stephen's climactic epiphany, the vision of himself as an artist, takes place while he walks along the water's edge. At the height of his ecstasy, he sees a lovely girl wading in the shallows, like a "strange and beautiful sea bird." Exhausted and emotionally spent, Stephen falls asleep by the water and wakes up to find the tide "flowing in fast to the land with a low whisper of her waves, islanding a few last figures in the distant pools."

Joyce's obsessive attention to liquids may be rooted in the ritual of baptism, one of the principal rites of the Church. If you agree with the premise that *Portrait* is the story of Stephen's coming into the world, the wet, moist, dark images that crowd the book's pages suggest Stephen's womblike existence. The culmination comes near the end of Chapter 4 when Stephen's soul greets life in "an outburst of profane joy." No longer swimming in darkness, his soul emerges into air, the new metaphor being *flight*.

Sexuality

Stephen lives basically in an all-male world. He attends boys' schools run by rigid, authoritarian, and celibate priests who serve as role models. The notion of equality of the sexes is alien in this setting. In fact, women are remote, barely human figures. Eileen, Emma (E.C.), and even Stephen's mother remain shadowy background characters.

Nevertheless Stephen feels the sexual urges common to young boys. To him women are erotic creatures that fill his nighttime fantasies. He tries to suppress his impulses but can't, and then feels guilty about it, especially after his sexual initiation with a prostitute. Having committed sins of the flesh, the equivalent of Adam falling from God's grace, Stephen tries to repent. His failure to do so thrusts him back into the world of the senses, enables him to turn away from the Church, and ultimately releases his creative powers. By the time Stephen flees Ireland, he has a more circumspect view of women.

Questions for Writing and Discussion

1. At end of the book, Stephen tells his friend Cranly that he is planning to leave Dublin. "I have to go," says Stephen. "I will try to express myself in some mode of life or art as freely as I can, using for my defence the only arms I allow myself to use—silence, exile, and cunning." Why does he specify *silence, exile,* and *cunning*? Why can't he just settle down in Dublin among his friends and family and be an artist? Must an artist go into exile to pursue his craft?

2. Davin tells Stephen, "In your heart you are an Irishman but your pride is too powerful." Is this an accurate assessment of Stephen?

3. Many artists have incorporated politics into their works. Why is Stephen different? Why does he believe that the artist must remain separate from politics?

4. Is Stephen a likeable character? Which qualities do you find favorable? Which turn you off? On balance, is the book a positive or a negative portrait of Stephen?

5. Although Stephen dominates the book, which other character is a significant presence in the story? Explore how that character functions in the book and how he or she affects the plot, the themes, or Stephen's development as a person.

Their Eyes Were Watching God by Zora Neale Hurston

Background

Written in 1937, *Their Eyes Were Watching God* was sharply condemned by other writers, most famously by Richard Wright, who considered it a degrading piece of trash, as insulting to blacks as an old-time minstrel show. Soon after publication, the book went out of print. In the 1970s, however, the American author Alice Walker rescued it from oblivion, and ever since, the novel has been firmly lodged in AP English reading lists and in college curricula throughout the country.

Walker apparently realized that during the 1930s, male-dominated, black folk-culture would not embrace a strong and daring female like Janie, the protagonist of *Their Eyes Were Watching God*. But decades later, as male attitudes toward women began to change, readers could readily accept her as a heroic figure. A widespread reassessment of the novel also revealed that Hurston, far from maligning black culture, celebrated it, especially the black oral tradition. Some critics observe that Hurston's writing is a literary counterpart to that staple of African-American culture, the "blues," and that Hurston represents the first serious black female voice in American literature.

As you might expect, black culture pervades the story. It shapes the characters, provides the setting, plots the events, and determines the language in the novel. But unlike many other mid-twentieth-century black authors, Zora Neale Hurston never intended to use her art as a form of social protest. She says more about the reality of black women's lives than about the problems of racial prejudice. Her book, in essence, recounts the quest of Janie Crawford to find a voice and create a meaningful life—a theme that transcends time, place, race, and gender.

> Use *Their Eyes Were Watching God* as the subject for an essay on 1) a hero's search for identity, 2) gender roles, 3) the influence of nature on men's lives, 4) the effects of prejudice, 5) the power of words, and 6) a protagonist at odds with the established culture.

Synopsis

The novel opens with the return home of forty-year-old Janie Crawford after an eighteen-month absence. She had gone away with a younger man, whose name we subsequently learn was Tea Cake and who has recently died "down in the Everglades there, down on the muck." The townspeople assume that Janie has been jilted and agree that she got what she deserved for her unseemly behavior. They are curious to know exactly what happened, just as the reader is, but are too proud to ask.

Janie's friend Pheoby stands up for her, welcoming her back with a good meal. Janie appreciates Pheoby's generosity and willingly tells her the story, beginning with her childhood in West Florida where Janie was raised by her grandma, Nanny, on the farm of a white family, the Washburns. As a small girl, Janie didn't realize she was black but discovered her skin color by seeing her image in a photograph.

As Janie blooms into an attractive young woman, Logan Killicks, a much older but "good man," who owns sixty acres, asks Nanny about the possibility of marrying the girl. Hoping to see her granddaughter settled before she dies, Nanny convinces Janie to accept Logan's offer, even though Janie, then only sixteen, has no feelings for him. Nanny tells Janie that she'll learn to love him, and besides, marriage to Logan will keep her from a life of hardship. Nanny knows what hardship is: She had been born a slave and was raped by her master. After the man left for the war, his wife threatened to whip Nanny and sell the baby, named Leafy, but Nanny ran away. Nanny dreamed that her daughter would grow up be a schoolteacher but at seventeen Leafy, too, was raped and afterward gave birth to Janie.

Not long after marrying Logan, Janie complains that she cannot love her husband. Angry, Nanny scolds her for being an ingrate. Janie is particularly upset because Logan expects her to do considerable heavy work around the house and farm. On a day when Logan is out buying a mule for Janie to use in the fields,

Jody Starks, a stylishly dressed Georgian gent passes by and flirts with Janie. Swayed by his sweet talk and the promise of a more glamorous life, Janie forsakes Logan and marries Jody.

The newlyweds head to Eatonville, a new, all-black Florida town. It is a fleabag of a place, just a few houses scattered on the dunes, but Jody has ambition and begins to organize the place. He rents a house, gets himself elected mayor, sets up a general store and a post office, brings in streetlights, and instructs the people about how to make the town thrive. Many of the citizens resent Jody's control, which they equate with the power of the white man. As the mayor's wife, Janie is respected by the townspeople but not by her own husband, who becomes increasingly domineering. He keeps Janie at home or minding the store while he goes off to do the town's business. Feeling lonely, Janie is distracted by the men who gather each day on the porch of the store, but Jody, who regards the group as trash, forbids Janie to participate in their chatter. When his mule dies, Jody presides at the beast's funeral, but he won't let Janie attend. As Janie becomes increasingly sullen and resentful, Jody thinks she lacks appreciation for the social status he has bestowed on her.

Year by year their loveless marriage slowly dissolves. One day, after he slaps her for serving a bad meal, Janie's reserve snaps. For the first time, Janie thrusts herself into the conversation on the porch and berates the men for denouncing a certain Mrs. Robbins, a woman in rebellion against her overbearing husband. In spite of her loneliness and emotional malaise, Janie evidently still has a good deal of pluck. At age thirty-five, she fantasizes about fleeing from Jody. Serving a customer in the store one day, she makes a mistake while cutting chewing tobacco. Jody ridicules her in front of the others, but she refuses to tolerate his abuse. She talks back, alluding to his lack of sexual prowess. Their exchange of insults draws a laugh from the others in the store, but Jody, tasting his own medicine for a change, is humiliated. In a rage he strikes Janie hard.

In effect, the blow ends their marriage. Janie and Jody occupy the same house but lead separate lives. Jody starts to take his meals elsewhere, and refuses the soup that Janie makes for him. Distraught, Janie talks to Pheoby about her troubles. Jody loses his health, and growing weaker by the day, takes to his bed. Just before he dies of kidney failure, Janie tells him off good and proper. She accuses him of selfishness and indifference, and leaving her emotionally scarred.

Jody's death releases Janie to do whatever she chooses for the first time in her life. As months pass, she continues to run the store. Various suitors, who assume that Janie needs a man, attempt to court her. But she rejects them all, basking in freedom too precious to give up for a man.

One day, however, a stranger comes into the store. He banters with Janie, treats her courteously, and teaches her to play checkers, until then a pastime reserved for men. Janie glows with pleasure and catches on quickly. Finally, the man introduces himself as Tea Cake, a name that makes Janie laugh. She jests with him about his sweetness. Later, Tea Cake helps Janie close the shop for the day.

Although Tea Cake charms her, she remains suspicious. Maybe he's trying to take advantage of her. During his next visit, they play checkers again and that night go fishing in the dark. Janie begins to feel young again. But still cynical after her experience with Jody, she resists Tea Cake's sweet talk. Tea Cake apologizes for having overstepped his bounds. Aware of their increasing fondness for each other, they soon discuss their burgeoning relationship. Tea Cake claims not to care that he is twelve years younger, but Janie can't shake her ambivalence about his age. By inviting her to the Sunday School picnic, however, he finally relieves her doubts.

The townspeople are aghast that Mayor Starks's widow has let a worthless lout like Tea Cake latch onto her. They are positive that he'll bilk Janie of her money. Pheoby reports what the rumor mill is saying, but Janie assures her friend that she knows what she's doing. In fact, she soon plans to sell the store, marry Tea Cake, and go somewhere to start a new life together. Pheoby warns that she's taking an awful chance.

After their wedding in Jacksonville, Janie and Tea Cake celebrate for weeks, but one morning he goes out, taking with him $200, Janie's secret supply of emergency money. When he fails to return on time, Janie is beside herself. She recalls hearing about a fifty-two-year old widow, Annie Tyler, who squandered all her money on a younger man, found herself jilted, and died soon thereafter. Janie fears a similar fate. But Tea Cake returns the next day bringing a new guitar and an account of how he had spent Janie's money: He had thrown a big party for some railroad workers, folks he knew were socially beneath Janie, which explains why he neglected to invite her. Janie forgives Tea Cake but insists that she be included in all his future adventures. He promises, but immediately breaks his vow by making a plan to win the money back by shooting craps. Because his fellow-gamblers are rough customers, he thinks Janie ought to stay away from the game. After practicing with dice and buying a switchblade, Tea Cake goes off, leaving Janie behind. She frets about Tea Cake but rationalizes that gambling is really no worse than the sins of other men.

Tea Cake comes back with knife wounds and $320 in winnings. He promises that, once healed, he and Janie will head down "on de muck," meaning the Everglades, where they'll have fun and make good money by working in the annual bean harvest. Janie's love for Tea Cake deepens.

Near Lake Okeechobee in south Florida, the happy couple move into a house. He plays his guitar and teaches Janie to hunt with a rifle. She is a good shot. As other bean pickers pour into the area, Tea Cake and Janie's house becomes the center of a small social community. Evenings find the men gathered there, shooting craps, and occasionally getting into arguments. During the day Tea Cake picks beans while Jane tends the house. After a time, he asks her to work with him. One day in the fields, Janie observes a young woman named Nunkie flirting with Tea Cake. Janie grows jealous, a sign that she has not yet lost her doubts about Tea Cake's fidelity. He reiterates his loyalty, however, and tries to overpower Janie with love.

During the off season Janie becomes acquainted with Mrs. Turner, a light-skinned black with a virulent hatred for common, dark-skinned blacks. She can't believe that Janie, whose skin is the color of coffee and cream, could love a dark-hued man like Tea Cake. Mrs. Turner brazenly suggests that her brother would make Janie a more suitable husband. Having overheard her diatribe, Tea Cake urges Janie to stay away from Mrs. Turner, and when the brother shows up, Tea Cake, sensing trouble, gives Janie a whipping, not out of jealousy but to show her and the Turners who is boss.

A hurricane heads toward the Everglades. Fearing a flood, cautious residents head to high ground. Janie and Tea Cake, however, along with several of their companions, such as Motor Boat, ignore the warnings, determined to match their might against God's, and stay put. Commenting on the risk of defying nature's fury, the narrator says, "They seemed to be staring at the dark, but their eyes were watching God." Before long the wind rises and the lake begins to act up. The dike breaks and sends a tidal wave of water down on them. Motor Boat refuses to move, but Tea Cake and Janie attempt to rescue themselves. Outside, Janie latches onto a piece of roofing that acts like a sail in the wind and throws her into the water. To keep from drowning, she holds onto the tail of a swimming cow with an angry dog perched on its back. Tea Cake rushes to the rescue and attempts to climb onto the cow. The dog bites Tea Cake on the cheek but is quickly dispatched by Tea Cake's switchblade. The cow then ferries both him and Janie to safety.

After the storm, Tea Cake wanders out to survey the devastation. Some white policemen force him to join crews clearing wreckage and burying the dead. Tea Cake observes that white corpses are buried in coffins, the blacks just thrown into the ground and covered with quicklime.

Two weeks after the storm Tea Cake falls ill. He feels as though he's being choked to death and believes that Janie may be giving him impure water to drink. The doctor says that Tea Cake has an incurable disease, presumably rabies, caused by the bite from the mad dog. He also tells Janie to stay away from Tea Cake during his violent spells, for if he should happen to bite her, she too will be infected.

Janie's suggestion that Tea Cake go to the hospital convinces him that Mrs. Turner's brother and Janie are conspiring to kill him. Under his pillow he hides a half-loaded pistol. While Tea Cake is briefly out of bed, Janie turns the gun's cylinder to prevent shots from being fired the first three times the trigger is pulled. This will give her time to escape if Tea Cake should attack her. In delirium, Tea Cake decides to frighten Janie with his pistol. Three times he pulls the trigger. Nothing happens. Janie grabs a hunting rifle and in the ensuing struggle both Tea Cake and Janie fire their weapons. His bullet hits the wall but Janie's strikes and kills Tea Cake, but not before he has sunk his teeth into her arm—in effect, mortally wounding her.

Janie, in a stupor, is arrested and brought to trial for murder. On the witness stand, she tells her story to the judge and all-white jury. What she fears most is not the death sentence but rather being misunderstood—the major problem of her life. The trial as well as Janie's story ends with her acquittal.

Back in Eatonville, where the book began, Janie defines the lesson she has drawn from her adventures. She tells Pheoby that " . . . you got to *go* there to *know* there." That is, you've got to experience life and not be held down or told by others how things are.

To Janie, Tea Cake is not dead. He will live in her heart as long as she herself breathes the air. How long that will be is uncertain. We don't know whether she has been infected by Tea Cake's bite or whether she has been saved. The book leaves Janie at an ambiguous crossroads. The narrator says that "she pulled in her horizon like a great fish-net," as though to suggest that Janie's life is over. Janie, it appears, may have seen all that she's going to see.

Cast of Characters   Hurston fills her novel with a crowd of distinctive personalities each with a role to play in the life of Janie Crawford.

The narrator's opening parable serves as a prelude:

> Ships at a distance have every man's wish on board. For some they come in with the tide. For others they sail forever on the horizon, never out of sight of landing until the Watcher turns his eyes away in resignation, his dreams mocked to death by Time. That is the life of men.
>
> Now, women forget all those things they don't want to remember, and remember everything they don't want to forget. The dream is the truth. Then they act and do things accordingly.

Men apparently dream big but do nothing but wait for their proverbial ship to come in. In contrast, women take steps to reach their dreams. Whether these assertions will be borne out in the story remains to be seen. At first, Janie seems to watch passively as life goes by. She, like other women, accepts her role. Whatever happens will happen. Men, on the other hand, do what they want, although not always successfully.

As the story develops, gender roles are turned topsy-turvy. Janie, and to some extent Pheoby, undergo a transformation. They learn from experience and pay attention to their inner lives, where change takes place. In contrast, Janie's three husbands—Logan, Jody, and Tea Cake—are static characters. They remain basically unaltered from beginning to end.

Janie Crawford

Janie is the novel's major character. Her struggle for identity from childhood to middle age is marked by relationships with three men, each adding another dimension to the person she eventually becomes. At an early age Janie senses that she is destined to transcend the drab and isolated existence of a rural black farm wife. At age sixteen she wants "flower dust and springtime sprinkled over everything." Although she is moved by an irrepressible spirit, she doesn't know what to do about it, not until Jody happens by and lures her away from Logan, her first husband. Her new life turns out no more satisfying than the first, but the small-town setting gives her an opportunity to observe, if not participate in, the activities of a community. As before, she works tirelessly to serve her man, but she is hardly more content than before.

The author endows Janie with unusual sensuality. She is attractive to men, partly because of her light skin (she is a quadroon) and a full head of long hair that Jody, out of jealousy, forces her to tie up in a head rag. Much of her life she plays the role expected of her—a subservient, passive woman, who allows herself to be tyrannized first by her grandmother and then by her husbands. With age, however, comes increasing confidence. She grows bolder and more assertive, standing up to Jody's abuse. Widowed at about forty, Janie is self-reliant, powerful, outspoken. Yet, she is still plagued by a sense that her life is incomplete. Offered friendship and love by Tea Cake, she accepts, rather tentatively at first because he's a younger man and a smooth talker, but eventually, all the way. As the narrator says, "her soul crawled out from its hiding place."

Much of Janie's self-actualization comes through her increasing ability to articulate what she believes. At her trial after Tea Cake's death, Janie speaks out, determined to make the world understand the meaning of her life with Tea

Cake. Critics have made much of the fact that we don't hear the actual words that Janie speaks but only a report of what she says. Is Hurston undercutting Janie's newfound autonomy, suggesting perhaps that the society of her time could not yet deal with a fully liberated woman?

Certainly the author wants us to regard Janie as a hero. She sets Janie on a path toward the sort of self-reliance and power usually associated with men. Janie dresses in men's overalls, works in the fields, becomes a skillful shot with a rifle. By rejecting the traditional woman's role she becomes her own person. As a literary character, Janie represents more than a heroic woman declaring her independence. Janie's story might be read allegorically. Her life reflects a mode of living that exemplifies what it takes to live fully and deeply. Near the end of the book, Janie says, "'Ah done been tuh de horizon and back and now Ah kin sit heah in mah house and live by comparisons.'" In other words, she has seen the world and now, without regret, can sit back and evaluate what the pursuit of her dream has meant, savoring the important experiences and casting the others out of her mind.

Nanny

Nanny is Janie's grandmother. Born a slave and mirroring a slave's mentality, Nanny still talks about "Massa Jesus," as though the relationship of slave and master is all she understands. Were Janie to follow Nanny, she would accept her fate, work nonstop, and aspire to a station in life no higher than that of a mule.

Nanny's experience has taught her that male treachery knows no bounds. As a young woman, she was forced to have sex with her white master. She bears a child with gray eyes and blond hair—Janie's mother, who at age seventeen is also raped.

As Janie matures, Nanny is alarmed by the girl's growing sexuality and hopes to live long enough to see Janie "safe in life," meaning that Janie would avoid being sexually exploited. Yet all she can do is place her faith in God to provide Janie with a husband. Her prayers are answered by Logan Killicks, an older man pledged to protect and take care of Janie.

Years afterward, in the wake of Jody's death, Janie realizes that she hates Nanny for leaving her with a long legacy that in the guise of love had actually kept her down and out. Seeing herself whole for the first time, Janie discards Nanny's prescription for life and from then on improvises one of her own.

Logan Killicks

Logan, Janie's first husband, is a widower with sixty acres and a desire to marry someone who'll keep house and help him farm his land. He vows to be a respectful husband but he also expects his wife to plow the fields, plant seeds, haul manure, and have sex with him whenever he has the urge. Logan's view of marriage differs from Janie's. She envisions something more tender and romantic. When Jody Starks happens by and promises her a more glamorous life, she jumps at the chance to escape her loveless marriage.

Jody Starks

With his fancy talk, silk shirts, suspenders, and a look in his eyes that speaks of far horizons, Jody lures Janie away from her first husband. Driven by ambition, he is a take-charge guy, representing the values and definition of success derived from white society. In Eatonville, Jody gets the town up and running.

As the power-hungry mayor, he lords it over his constituents, looks down on the trashy element, and laughs at them behind their backs. Ever the politician, though, he participates in their life in order to keep their support. Many of the townsfolk resent his ruthlessness.

Jody forbids Janie to mingle with the citizenry of Eatonville, claiming that the mayor's wife must remain above the riffraff. Bitterly, Janie realizes that Jody is busy living his dream while she wastes away as a clerk, cook, and housekeeper. He argues that his being a big shot makes a big woman out of her, but she resents Jody's presumption to speak for her. Moreover, he demeans her in public and forces her to spend long hours laboring in the general store he owns. As Jody lies on his deathbed, Janie lashes out at him, confronting him with painful truths about their twenty-year marriage. Her attack is not gratuitously cruel but is an essential step toward her self-reclamation. The episode is a dramatic break from her past and brings her a measure of relief. From then on she is a different person.

Tea Cake

Tea Cake enters Janie's life soon after Jody dies. Although he is a fighter and an incorrigible gambler, he is polite, engaging, and considerate. (Critic Henry Louis Gates points out that Tea Cake's first name, "Verigible," is a vernacular form of *veritable*, meaning genuine, or truthful. Tea Cake lives up to his name; unlike Jody, he is honest and open in his relationship with Janie. Lacking pretense and shame, he feels deeply and says what's on his mind.) Tea Cake treats Janie like an equal, teaching her how to play checkers, to fish, and to shoot a hunting rifle. By encouraging Janie to join him at work in the fields, Tea Cake strengthens their marriage and enables Janie to bond with the community of workers in the Florida Everglades.

Of all the men Janie has known, Tea Cake is the least hung up on being a strong, dominant male. Power and position mean little to him. Money is not a status symbol but something meant to be enjoyed. Tea Cake easily accepts who and what he is; he's an elemental, natural man. Offering nothing but his love and companionship, Tea Cake enables Janie to know herself as never before. For a time she is not sure whether to trust him. Because he is younger than she, Janie fears his motives. But when, after returning from a spree paid for with Janie's money, he agrees to include her in every aspect of his life from then on, he wins her over. Soon after, however, the tables are turned. He falls sick and begins to suspect, mistakenly, that Janie may have put the hex on him so that she can take up with another man.

Pheoby

Janie's closest friend and confidante, Pheoby brings word to Janie that the community disapproves of her involvement with Tea Cake on the heels of Jody's death. As a traditional woman, she also reflects the town's widespread skepticism about Tea Cake's motives.

Pheoby also serves as the audience for Janie's story and is changed by it, declaring, "Lawd! Ah done growed ten feet higher from jus' listenin' tuh you, Janie." Inspired by Janie's transformation, Pheoby expresses a spirit and hope for a new kind of community based not on male dominance, as in the past, but on sisterhood.

Mrs. Turner

Mrs. Turner is an opinionated, hate-filled woman, representing white, elitist, racist values. She runs a restaurant serving black workers but has no use for them personally. She tries to convince Janie that her marriage to Tea Cake is unnatural, speculating that he may have hypnotized her. She also tries to convince Janie that her (Mrs. Turner's) light-skinned brother would be a more suitable husband for her than Tea Cake. Janie remains unmoved by Mrs. Turner's attitudes, but Tea Cake lashes out with uncharacteristic violence, beating Janie just to show the world that he's in charge. Mrs. Turner's outspokenness drives a wedge between Janie and Tea Cake and disturbs their marital happiness.

Structure

As the book opens, Pheoby welcomes Janie home after a long absence. Their conversation evolves into Janie's chronological account of her life since childhood, dwelling mainly on the months since she left town in the company of Tea Cake. Janie's story is presented within the frame of her visit with Pheoby.

The story is built around Janie's lifelong search for identity. For most of her years, Janie's ambition consists of vague, dreamlike longings. Rather than articulate her hopes, she remains mute, in part because nothing in the culture encourages her either to speak out or to pursue her dreams. Contentment is not an issue. Her society simply expects black women to accept their station in life unquestioningly.

Janie's marriages add new dimensions to her personality and contribute to the person she ultimately becomes. During her short-lived marriage to Logan, she feels sad and unloved. At the first opportunity, she gives up material security and marries Jody. No less stifled as Jody's wife, however, she begins bit by bit to gain perspective on her life. Jody's death twenty years later frees her to wed yet again. Married to Tea Cake, Janie relishes the goodness of life for the first time, although her current home is but a modest shack down in the muck of the Everglades. Janie mingles with crowds of friends who shoot dice on the floor. She listens to their chatter, laughs and talks as much as she wants, even feels free to "signify."

In a word, life with Tea Cake brings Janie to the brink of self-awareness. But she doesn't become fully conscious of herself until her trial for murder. With her life in jeopardy, Janie defends her actions and explains to a group of white strangers who and what she is. Janie's ultimate self-discovery, it seems, coincides with her mastery of oral language. Whenever she speaks her mind, first to Nanny, then to each of her husbands, and finally to the jury, she is taking steps toward liberation. In her courtroom defense Janie reaches the pinnacle of her growth and attains her identity as a person.

The author's use of language also implies the book's structure. Hurston's imagery reflects Janie's preoccupations and state of mind at each stage of life. Feeling her budding sexuality Janie is likened to a pear tree blossom in the spring. The image returns much later in the story when she falls in love with Tea Cake. During her marriages to Logan and to Jody, numerous images relate to hearth and home. While she resides and works in the Everglades, the prevailing images come from nature.

Critic Henry Louis Gates has observed that another structural element of the novel relates to the various locales in which Janie finds herself: From childhood Janie comes to occupy progressively grander quarters: first Nanny's small cabin on the Washburn land, then Logan's sixty acres, finally Jody's expansive white mansion. Yet, as Janie moves from place to place, she becomes increasingly confined. Only when she relinquishes material possessions and moves to the "muck" of the Everglades with Tea Cake does she begin to draw beauty from life and see her dreams come true.

Themes and Motifs

The Black Woman

Janie goes from country waif to strong, self-actualized woman during a decades-long physical and spiritual journey. To achieve her selfhood, she must discard the customary definition of "woman" passed on to her by old Nanny, who believed that women are the mules of the world, ciphers obliged to work hard and do their husbands' bidding. Janie, while married to Logan, learns firsthand that Nanny had a point and decides to run away with Jody Starks.

Jody promises to show her new horizons, but he's really no more enlightened than Logan. He keeps Janie in semibondage, insisting that she keep house and work long hours at the general store. All the while, he disparages her in front of others, saying among other things, that playing checkers "wuz too heavy" for her brain and that Janie is unable to speak coherently, a canard of the first order considering how eloquently she defends herself at her murder trial years later.

Jody is convinced that as a man he's got the responsibility "to think for women and chillun and chickens and cows. I gog, they sho don't think none for theirselves." His patronizing attitude typifies black men's view of women in the novel. Men, except for Tea Cake, throw their weight around, exercising power, perhaps to compensate for their impotence in the society at large. Big talk is a smokescreen that hides weakness and pain, a defense against showing their "interiority," as critic Mary Helen Washington calls it.

Nanny's concept of the oppressed black woman is difficult for Janie to shake off. It weighs on her. She struggles with the burden of trying to reconcile what others expect of her and what she feels inside. Nanny counts on Janie to grow fond of Logan, for example, but Janie soon realizes she can't. The traditional stereotype of a married woman who loves, honors, and obeys her husband doesn't apply to her.

Jody's increasingly cruel taunts call to mind the town's treatment of Matt Bonner's yellow mule, a hapless creature abused by its master and teased by the townspeople. Jody buys the mule to let it die in peace and presides over its elaborate mock funeral. Janie, naturally sensitive and kind, abhors the proceedings, her repulsion rooted in sympathy for downtrodden creatures like herself. The incident provokes Janie to break out of her submissiveness and leads to her first public utterance, ironically in praise of Jody's decision to free the mule just as Lincoln freed the slaves. Her sudden outspokenness turns out to be the first step in the dissolution of her marriage to Jody.

Finding the strength to speak with a voice of her own, Janie bit by bit transforms herself into a self-assured, self-actualized woman. Janie's experience gives the lie to the notion that black women are weaklings, the mules of the world. In the end, Janie takes control of her own life. Considering the way that both Jody and Tea Cake turn against her during their last hours, Hurston implies that neither Janie nor any other woman can expect help from men to fully realize themselves. But by sharing her story with Pheoby, Janie declares that her kind of transformation is available to all women in the same situation.

Prejudice

Among blacks a pecking order based on skin color puts light skin ahead of dark skin. Light-skinned, thin-lipped Mrs. Turner, a "milky sort," takes a dim view of dark-skinned people with typically Negroid facial features. "'Ah can't stand black niggers,'" she says. "'Ah don't blame de white folks from hatin' 'em 'cause Ah can't stand 'em mahself.'" Drawn to Janie because of her coffee-and-cream color, Mrs. Turner thinks she has found a companion and soul mate. She urges Janie to forsake her dark-skinned, hence trashy, husband, Tea Cake.

A similar hierarchy exists within the larger framework of a prejudicial society, but Hurston generally skirts issues of racial prejudice in her novel. Janie herself claims not to have thought much about the issue. To her, class difference is far more significant than skin color. White society rarely intrudes into the novel except in the aftermath of the hurricane when Tea Cake reports that white men have forced him to help in the cleanup and that, unlike the storm's black victims, white bodies are being given respectful funerals. Yet, it is a white doctor who administers to Tea Cake and who puts in a good word for Janie to the all-white jury at her trial.

Rather than racial prejudice, gender discrimination plagues Janie throughout her life. Men, especially her first two husbands, deny her right to make autonomous decisions. Tea Cake helps to liberate her, but after his death Janie still faces a world that imposes restrictions on women.

Although victimized at times, Janie herself is not free of prejudice. The Florida hurricane is predicted by the Seminole Indians, who scramble for high ground. But Janie, thinking that the "Indians are dumb," ignores the warning. Antipathy toward the Indians has dire consequences for her and Tea Cake.

Hoodoo (Voodoo)

An anthropologist by training, Hurston frequently alludes to hoodoo, or voodoo, which she learned about while studying various Caribbean folk cultures.

During the hurricane, for example, Tea Cake contracts rabies from the bite of a mad dog. No ordinary dog, this one "growled like a lion, stiff-standing hackles, stiff muscles, teeth uncovered as he lashed up his fury." Tea Cake attributes his illness to poison administered by some outside force and tells Janie that during the night, "somethin jumped on me . . . and choked me." Janie replies, "Maybe it was a witch" and tells Tea Cake that she'll search for mustard seed, a traditional folk remedy.

That Tea Cake uses the word "demon" to describe his ailment may be partly metaphorical, but it also expresses his fear that demonic forces have infected his body. Such a notion grows out of a faith in hoodoo (commonly called voodoo), a belief in the influence of mystic, often demonic, powers. Along with his body, Tea Cake's mind is possessed. In his delirium he suspects that Janie is out to kill him. Finally, the "fiend" within forces him to attack Janie with a pistol. Just before Janie shoots him dead, Tea Cake's eyes look ferocious, like those of the rabid dog that bit him. Janie regards Tea Cake's fatal illness as her illness, too. The mad dog is killing her through Tea Cake and it is too much to bear.

Despite the influence of hoodoo, Janie and Tea Cake also surrender their fate to a Christian God. Overtones of Christianity echo in their speech and actions. During the hurricane, rather than escape the storm's fury, they follow their customary passivity and wait to see what God has in store for them. The book derives its title from their behavior.

The Power of Words

All her life Janie resides among highly verbal people. Their way with words determines the course of the story and also delineates each character. Nanny, for one, is an accomplished storyteller, a skilled slave narrator, who recounts her past life in vivid, moving detail. She uses her way with words to convince Janie to marry Logan Killicks. Although Nanny's voice is as powerful as a preacher's, and she uses metaphors that fuse the biblical and the domestic in arresting ways, her words carry no farther than Janie's ears.

Both Jody and Tea Cake win Janie over by their gift of gab. Both are glib talkers, Jody especially. As mayor of Eatonville he uses prodigious oratorical skills to sway the townspeople to follow his lead. Tea Cake's agile tongue steers him through life, but when Sod tells him of rumors that Janie, in cahoots with Mrs. Turner's light-skinned brother, may have conjured him, Tea Cake finds that his tongue lies "cold and heavy like a dead lizard between his jaws." In other words Tea Cake is suddenly deprived of his customary rhetorical powers.

Janie can turn a phrase herself but she is gagged by menfolk, especially by Jody, who declares in public that Janie isn't capable of "speechifying." When she finally speaks up about the dead mule she delights the crowd with her use of words. Jody, feeling threatened by his wife's sudden rhetorical savvy, berates her and even slaps her face. Janie's speech foreshadows an event in the next chapter when Janie impugns Jody's manhood, a blow from which he never recovers. Humiliated, he soon falls ill and loses his desire to live. Later, on trial for the murder of Tea Cake, Janie, observing the crowd of colored people in the courtroom, realizes that their only power to change the outcome of the proceedings resides in their tongues, which are "cocked and loaded." She regards language as a weapon, the only killing tool that weak folks are allowed to use in the presence of whites. At the end Janie's way with words wins her acquittal. (Oddly, the author only tells readers what Janie says instead of letting us hear Janie's words, prompting some critics to suggest that Janie may not have found her genuine voice, after all.)

As a narrator, Janie demonstrates an acute sensitivity to words. In childhood she listens to "the words of the trees and the wind." Running off with Jody, she senses that old thoughts were going to come in handy now but that new words would have to be made and said to fit them. Later, widowhood rekindles her awareness that a new life requires new thoughts to be thought and new words to be said. Telling Pheoby about Tea Cake, she says, "He done taught me de maiden language all over." At each stage in her life, Janie recognizes the need for new words. And from the beginning of the novel, Janie struggles to find a voice in a culture that places a premium on speaking. Gradually, she grows into an articulate heroine, confirmed by the novel's prologue, when Pheoby listens to her story in rapt attention.

The oral tradition of black culture is most apparent in the characters' regular use of "signifying," or word play. Signifying, a contest of hyperbole, is part of everyday life, particularly among the men. One form of signifying is "Playing the Dozens," in which participants try to outdo each other with extravagantly imaginative claims of superiority. The game often consists of a series of insults that, because they are so outrageous, cannot be taken seriously. Sometimes, the game consists of hyperbolic statements about love and affection. One evening on the Starks' porch, the men participate in "acting-out courtship" with Daisy, the town beauty. Each tries to "prove" the depth of his love with exaggerations. One brags that he would buy a passenger train as a gift for Daisy. Another would buy her a steamship and a crew of men to run it; still another would clean out the whole Atlantic Ocean for her. Some observers note that black men participate in signifying as an escape from the drab reality of their lives. Their rhetorical rivalry doesn't express truth nor is it meant to, but it helps to relieve their pain. It also gives them a power and articulateness they don't ordinarily have, a chance to "talk big" by showing off rhetorically without the requirement to "act big."

As a woman, Janie is excluded from this porch talk, which sometimes consists of telling stories, folk stories mostly, often about crows, buzzards, and mules. Matt Bonner's yellow mule inspires considerable conversation and "big picture" talking. Janie listens, of course, but is free to speak only at home among female friends. Her narrative is fueled by "that oldest human longing—self revelation" and is urged on by Pheoby's "hungry listening." By telling her personal story, Janie finds her voice and takes her place as an individual in the black community.

Narrative Style/Language	*Voice*

Two distinct voices dominate the text. The first, that of an omniscient third-person narrator, sets various scenes, moves the story along, and occasionally provides commentary on the characters, much like the chorus in a Greek drama. This so-called "free direct discourse" is unusually poetic and allusive, suffused with similes, metaphors, and the rhythms of black vernacular. As a girl Janie sees her life as "a great tree in leaf . . . . Dawn and doom was in the branches." Janie's growing awareness of her sexual longings at age sixteen is described in sensual terms:

> She was stretched on her back beneath the pear tree soaking in the alto chant of the visiting bees, the gold of the sun and the panting breath of the breeze when the inaudible voice of it all came to her. She saw a dust-bearing bee sink into the sanctum of a bloom; the thousand sister-calyxes arch to meet the love embrace and the ecstatic shiver of the trees from root to tiniest branch creaming in every blossom and frothing with delight.

Janie adopts the image of the pear tree as the rhetorical centerpiece for her life. "Oh to be a pear tree—*any* tree in bloom" she thinks. This trope, bees pollinating the blossoms of a pear tree, recurs when Janie finds herself attracted to Jody and later to Tea Cake. When her relationship with Jody begins to fall apart, Janie has "no more blossomy openings dusting pollen over her man." Having met Tea Cake, Janie reflects that he "could be a bee to a blossom—a pear tree blossom in the spring." As she matures, Janie sees her life like a "great tree in leaf with the things suffered, things enjoyed, things done and undone. Dawn and doom was in its branches," as though to say that she accepts all parts as contributions to the wholesome black woman whom she ultimately becomes.

While Jody is dying the narrator personifies Death, "that strange being with the huge square toes who lived away in the West," and by extending the metaphor, endows Death with mythic dimensions:

> The great one who lived in the straight house like a platform without sides to it, and without a roof. What need has Death for cover, and what winds can blow against him? He stands in his high house that overlooks the world. Stands watchful and motionless all day with his sword drawn back, waiting for the messenger to bid him come.

The narrator is also fond of lyrical language that leaves readers with no more than an impression of what is occurring:

> The years took all the fight out of Janie's face. For a while she thought it was gone from her soul. No matter what Jody did, she said nothing. She had learned how to talk some and leave some. She was a rut in the road. Plenty of life beneath the surface but it was kept beaten down by the wheels. . . . But mostly she lived between her hat and her heels, with her emotional disturbances like shade patterns in the woods—come and gone with the sun.

Here, as in numerous other passages, readers are left to fill in the details.

A counterweight to the omniscient narrator is Janie, telling her story in the vernacular of southern blacks. By shuttling between the two, readers become creative and active partners in the story. The words are no less poetic than the free direct discourse, but at first glance may seem nearly illiterate because of phonetic spelling. Yet the idiom conveys a wealth of wit and wisdom. While creating a measure of verisimilitude, it also shows the characters' natural affinity for poetic expression. Talking about the impact of Jody Starks, for example, the men of Eatonville say, "You kin feel a switch in his hand when he's talkin' to yuh" and "Speakin' of winds, he's de wind and we'se de grass. We bend which ever way he blows." Says one of the porch denizens, "My old woman . . . get her good and mad and she'll wade through rock up to her hip pockets." To Jody on his deathbed, Janie laments, "Listen, Jody, you ain't de Jody ah run off down de road wid. You'se whut's left after he died. . . . Mah own mind had tuh be squeezed and crowded out tuh make room for yours in me." Virtually every page contains a profusion of equally delicious locutions.

The language of the novel does double duty. It tells the reader the story but also contributes to one of the novel's major themes. The author depicts men sitting around the store entertaining themselves by telling stories, signifying, and play acting. Because Janie is excluded from the delights of verbal sparring, she feels increasingly alienated and alone. But Janie's way with words gradually lifts her out of her rut, and as she becomes more articulate she grows as a person. Oddly, in the trial scene Hurston uses the omniscient third-person narrator to tell what happens, thereby depriving Janie of a chance to demonstrate the power of her oratory.

Imagery

Domestic images abound in the novel because the women spend most of their lives in the home and kitchen. Nanny calls herself "a cracked plate," an image that suggests her hard life, her fragile condition, and an awareness that she has outlived her usefulness. Hoping that young Janie's life will be better than hers, Nanny says that she can't stand the thought that white or black menfolk will make a "spit cup," a vessel for spitting tobacco juice, out of her granddaughter. Nanny's wish comes true but not before Jody provides a communal spittoon for the entourage gathered on his Eatonville porch.

Other homey images include the look of Daisy's hair: "the piece of string out of a ham," and Mrs. Turner's reference to "flies in the buttermilk." Janie in conflict with Jody is said to be ready to eat out of a long-handled spoon, an allusion to the cook being relegated to the kitchen while respectable people eat with regular utensils. As his health deteriorates, Jody starts to sag "like bags hanging from an ironing board," and after his death, Janie, about to step out on her own for the first time, "starches and irons" her face.

The natural world spawns a multitude of images associated with flora and fauna. When Janie and Jody arrive in Eatonville, they are struck by the palmetto roots, the live oaks, rattlesnakes, alligators, buzzards, and sandspurs. Down on the muck of the Everglades Janie observes the sugarcane, the rich soil, outsized vegetation, palm trees, sand dunes, alligators, birds, and other wildlife. The trope of bees pollinating a pear tree is introduced early in the novel and repeated throughout. It can't be accidental that Tea Cake's surname is *Woods* and that the name of Janie's mother is *Leafy*.

Nature helps Janie define herself, to situate herself in the world. Through nature, says one critic, Janie and Tea Cake "conjure their own true being from the elements." The culminating event in their lives is the hurricane, a fierce natural phenomenon that indirectly kills Tea Cake and at least for a time destroys Janie's well-being.

Questions for Writing and Discussion

1. To what extent is *Their Eyes Were Watching God* a feminist tract? Or is it a misreading of the book to consider it mainly a work meant to further feminist causes?

2. Based on the depiction of the relationship between husbands and wives in the novel, what conclusions can you draw about the author's view of marriage?

3. Please read the following excerpt from Chapter 2 of *Their Eyes Were Watching God:*

   "Ah was wid dem white chillun so much till Ah didn't know Ah wusn't white till Ah was round six years old. Wouldn't have found it out then, but a man come long takin' pictures and without askin' anybody, Shelby, dat was de oldest boy, he told him to take us. Round a week later de man brought de picture for Mis' Washburn to see and pay him which she did, then give us all a good lickin'.

   "So when we looked at de picture and everybody got pointed out there wasn't nobody left except a real dark little girl with long hair standing by Eleanor. Dat's where Ah wuz s'posed to be, but Ah couldn't recognize dat dark chile as me. So Ah ast, 'where is me? Ah don't see me.'

   "Everybody laughed, even Mr. Washburn. Miss Nellie, de Mama of de chillun who come back home after her husband dead, she pointed to de dark one and said, 'Dat's you, Alphabet, don't you know yo' ownself?'"

   Now analyze how Janie's account of this childhood experience either foreshadows what she becomes as an adult or reveals differences between Janie as a child and Janie as a mature woman.

4. Discuss how the reception Janie receives in her hometown after Tea Cake's death contributes to the meaning of *Their Eyes Were Watching God* as a whole.

5. Choose any social event that occurs in *Their Eyes Were Watching God* (wedding, funeral, party, gathering, rendezvous, etc.) and discuss how the event contributes to the development of a character or to one of the novel's themes.

Invisible Man by Ralph Ellison

Background

Since its publication in 1952, *Invisible Man* has become ubiquitous on AP English and college-level reading lists. Although some readers regard Ralph Ellison's novel as an indictment of racial bigotry in America, Ellison asserted that he never intended to write "an attack upon white society!" Rather, he meant to illustrate the plight of one man growing up black in America. *Invisible Man* is full of violence, cruelty, bitterness, suffering, and anger. At every turn the hero is disabused of his ideals. Nevertheless, he rejects cynicism and in the end embraces a philosophy of hope. Despite his invisibility, he fully intends to be a player in a world of "infinite possibilities."

Invisible Man tells the story of a young man's struggle to find his identity in mid-twentieth century America. Published during the heyday of racial segregation, the novel documents some of the effects of discrimination during the 1940s. The race riot near the end of the book is based on events in Harlem in 1943. It also anticipates the turmoil that rocked many American cities during the Civil Rights movement in the late 1950s and thereafter.

The unnamed protagonist of the book—the eponymous "invisible man" and the narrator of his own story—is born and reared in the South. At his all-black college he dreams of achieving success through hard work and humility, a doctrine instilled in him at school and by the culture at large. When the college president expels him for a minor *faux pas*, the boy heads for New York City, where most of the book's action takes place.

The narrator's experience in the North is strikingly like the saga of countless other Negroes (the term used by the author of the book) in the 1930s and 1940s who left the South in search of jobs and a better life. Not that every black boy from Georgia or the Carolinas journeyed specifically to New York, scrambled to find work, joined a Brotherhood resembling the Communist Party, and underwent one frustrating disillusionment after another. Nor, like the main character in *Invisible Man*, did they all end up living underground in the coal storage room of a whites-only apartment building. But stories of young Negroes newly arrived in the big city, while differing in the details, are often startlingly alike.

> Use *Invisible Man* as the subject for an essay on 1) a character alienated from society, 2) a character's loss of innocence, 3) a character torn between conflicting forces, 4) the influence of an absent character on the protagonist, and 5) the significance of a particular social event on the meaning of the work.

Synopsis

In a prologue, the narrator, a forty-year-old black, introduces himself as "invisible man." How he became invisible is a story that began more than twenty years earlier at the deathbed of his grandfather. Chapter 1 opens with an anecdote about the old man's dying words, a cryptic message to his family: ". . . our life is a war and I have been a traitor all my born days, a spy in the enemy's country. . . . Live with your head in the lion's mouth. I want you to overcome 'em with yeses, undermine 'em with grins, agree 'em to death and destruction, let 'em swaller you till they vomit or bust wide open." The words puzzle the narrator, and when he is praised by the "lily-white men of the town" for being a good boy who knows his place, he wonders whether he, too, is being a traitor.

As an adolescent, the narrator, along with several of his black schoolmates, is invited to attend a white men's stag party. They don't know it, but the boys themselves are to be the entertainment: Before donning blindfolds and taking part in a free-for-all mêlée called a *battle royal*, they are made to watch a voluptuous naked blonde dance among them. Then the boys are forced to scuffle for brass tokens scattered on an electrified rug. Afterward, the narrator, his mouth bloodied in the fracas, is called upon to repeat the valedictorian's speech he had recently delivered at his high school graduation, a speech that advocated humility as the essence of progress. Rattled by drunk and boisterous hecklers, he accidentally says "equality" when he means to say "responsibility." The slip of the tongue angers the white audience. They think the boy may be putting on airs unbefitting a member of his race. But he corrects the mistake and in the end receives a leather briefcase containing a scholarship to the state college for Negroes.

In college the boy is a model student. But on Founder's Day he innocently chauffeurs Mr. Norton, a northern white trustee of the college, to visit a black sharecropper, Jim Trueblood, who willingly tells the story of his incestuous affair with his daughter. Shocked by the story, Norton gives Trueblood a hundred dollars and asks the narrator to drive him somewhere for a drink to calm his nerves. The closest place is the Golden Day, a seedy gin mill/brothel where Norton drinks whiskey, is propositioned by a prostitute, and is overwhelmed by the other patrons, most of them war vets from the nearby mental hospital. When Dr. Bledsoe, the president of the college, hears of Norton's adventures, he blames the narrator for exposing a trustee to such seaminess and immediately cancels his scholarship and expels him from college.

The young man, expecting to be reinstated the next term, heads to New York to earn tuition money, carrying what he believes are seven sealed letters of recommendation from Dr. Bledsoe addressed to prospective employers in New York. Upon arrival in Harlem, he is astonished by the sight of large numbers of black people peacefully going about their lives. He is impressed that an angry black man can harangue an audience of blacks on a street corner without being arrested and that black traffic cops can tell white drivers what to do. New York is like a dream to him, a place where the rules and customs of the South apparently don't apply.

The letters in the narrator's briefcase fail to land him a job. The reason is that Bledsoe has betrayed him. Each letter describes the boy's infamy and says that he'll never be readmitted to the college. But the homosexual son of the last recipient, himself an outcast, takes pity on the narrator, reveals the contents of the letter, and steers him to a job in a paint factory, where, unbeknownst to the narrator, the workforce is out on strike. Caught between the pressure of the union and the nonunion bosses, the narrator tries to please his employer but makes honest mistakes. He clashes with one of his supervisors, Brockway, who exacts revenge by rigging a boiler to explode. The "accident" sends the narrator first to the hospital and then into the ranks of the unemployed. Although he's broke, a kindly woman named Mary Rambo takes pity on him and permits him to live in her rooming house rent-free while he regains his health.

Wandering the streets of Harlem, he witnesses the unjust eviction of a poor old couple from their apartment. Enraged by the black men and women who stand silently by and watch, he speaks out against the inhumanity of the landlords. His eloquence and passion catch the eye of Brother Jack, the leader of the Brotherhood, an organization that espouses social equality. Recruited to join the organization, the narrator becomes the group's chief spokesman in Harlem. As a member of the Brotherhood, he earns a regular salary and resides in his own apartment. Membership also brings him new clothes, a cadre of associates, women fawning over him, and best of all, "more human" feelings about himself. Soon he strikes up a friendship with Tod Clifton, also an up-and-coming member of the Brotherhood. One day, walking with Tod, they encounter Ras the Exhorter and his followers. Ras, a militant black, calls Tod a traitor for joining the Brotherhood, which is run by whites. Angered, Tod knocks Ras to the ground and walks away.

The narrator dedicates himself to the mission of the Brotherhood. He's good at his job and makes a name for himself in the Harlem community. He's so good, in fact, that a magazine reporter interviews him for a feature story. When Wrestrum, a jealous member of the Brotherhood, accuses him of opportunism, the narrator is removed from his Harlem assignment and demoted to speak instead about the "Woman Question." Following his first speech about the persecution of women, he allows himself to be seduced by a white woman who feigns fascination with his ideas but is truly more attracted to his body.

Tod Clifton is reported missing. Concerned, the narrator searches the community and finds him on a street corner selling dancing Sambo dolls made of folded paper. He is stunned by Clifton's actions and disgusted by the dolls. He wants to intervene but a white policeman comes to arrest Clifton for doing business without a permit. The cop is rough and abusive, and when Clifton hits back the officer shoots him dead.

At Clifton's funeral, the narrator delivers a eulogy meant to recall his friend's good works on behalf of Harlem's youth. Reflecting on Clifton's life and death, the narrator decides that he no longer needs the Brotherhood to give him an identity and sense of purpose. What's more, he's been soured by the Brotherhood's secretive and dictatorial leaders, particularly by Brother Jack and Brother Tobitt.

On a Harlem street he sees a crowd being stirred up by Ras the Exhorter. Ras is attacking the Brotherhood for its meek response to the killing of Clifton by a white police officer. After an argument with Ras, the narrator scurries away but is grabbed and punched by two of Ras's goons. He is saved by the intervention of a doorman. To keep himself from further harm, the narrator tries to disguise himself with sunglasses and a broad-brimmed hat. Walking along, he is amazed that people mistake him for someone named "Rinehart." Gradually, he discovers that Rinehart has multiple identities: numbers runner, pimp, preacher, and ladies' man.

The narrator's relationship with the Brotherhood worsens when Brother Hambro tells him that the Brotherhood has decided to concede control of Harlem to Ras. In other words, Harlem is being written off, and the promises he once made to Harlem's people that the Brotherhood will stand by them are about to be broken. Feeling betrayed, the narrator resolves to undermine the Brotherhood by playing the yes-man. He has closed in on the meaning of his grandfather's dying words and begins to agree with everything the leaders do and say. He also plots to dig out damaging inside information about the Brotherhood from Sybil, a lonely white woman and the wife of George, a Brotherhood big shot. Sybil responds eagerly, but during a tryst in the narrator's apartment he discovers that she knows nothing. He immediately backs off, unwilling to serve as the object of Sybil's sexual fantasies.

Later that night Harlem explodes into violence and bloodshed. Trying to make his way to Mary's, the narrator sees four looters wheeling a stolen safe down the street. He is grazed by a stray bullet from the gun of a pursuing policeman. The men who tend to his slight wound set a tenement building afire. Men with baseball bats chase the narrator through the streets. He escapes by falling into a manhole, landing in a pitch-black coal cellar. For light, he ignites the contents of his briefcase, thus symbolically destroying his past. Soon he falls asleep. His dreams are crowded with many of the hostile people he's encountered in his life, including Brother Jack, who castrates him while the others watch. Awake again, the narrator realizes he's transcended his past life and rid himself of illusion. "I couldn't return to Mary's, or to any part of my old life. . . . I had been as invisible to Mary as I had been to the Brotherhood," he says. Living in his dark underground hole, however, will give him a chance to think things out.

In the Epilogue, the narrator reflects on what he has learned from writing his story. Part of him remains angry at the world, but aware that unbridled hate is harmful to one's humanity, he resolves to love the world, especially the opportunities it has to offer. "I denounce and I defend and I hate and I love," he says. In the end, he expects to come out of his "hibernation" and, despite being "invisible," try to assume the role of a socially responsible citizen.

Cast of Characters

Except for the narrator, most characters in the novel have bit parts, slipping into the story for a few pages and then out again. In a way they function like an ensemble of jazz musicians, taking brief turns in the spotlight while improvising a solo. Some characters return to the story fleetingly, either in person like Mr. Norton or, in the narrator's memory, like Grandfather and Dr. Bledsoe.

The characters who most influence the narrator during his youth in the South include his grandfather, Norton, Trueblood, the vet, The Founder, and Dr. Bledsoe.

Important New York characters include Ras, Emerson, Brockway, Mary Rambo, Rinehart, and people affiliated with the Brotherhood: Jack, Hambro, Tarp, Wrestrum, Tod Clifton, and Sybil.

The Narrator

The nameless main character is given many opportunities to reveal his name to the reader, but Ellison chooses to leave him anonymous to emphasize his invisibility.

Despite his anonymity, though, we learn that he's a "ginger-colored" grandson of slaves. Growing up in the segregated South, the boy is timid, compliant, and naive. He attends a white men's stag party anticipating the receipt of a college scholarship. He considers himself superior to the other boys, and endures the indignity of the battle royal by focusing on what comes afterwards—delivering his speech.

In college he shows great promise but is expelled after innocently allowing a northern white donor to speak to a poor black sharecropper and visit a rural gin mill. Hoping to find success in New York, the young man would like to shed his rural southern demeanor in favor of something more northern, more sophisticated. Although he is discontent with who he is, it's difficult to cast ingrained attitudes aside. He works briefly in a paint factory and becomes a soapbox speaker for the Brotherhood, a group that purports to follow a kind of Marxist egalitarianism. He is good at his job, so good that he becomes a Harlem celebrity, causing the Brotherhood's leaders to denounce him for selfishly putting his own interests before the interests of the people. The accusation is dead wrong, however, for time and again the narrator has demonstrated compassion for others. At one point he tries to help an old couple on the verge of being evicted from their apartment. He also feels compelled to help ease Mary Rambo's financial strain.

The narrator is shocked to realize that he has been manipulated and lied to by the Brotherhood. Because cooperation with the white world has gotten him nowhere, he abandons his naïveté and finally makes peace with his blackness. Recalling his grandfather's dying words, he begins to undermine the Brotherhood. During a riot in Harlem, the narrator stumbles into a manhole where he reflects on his invisibility.

Grandfather
The narrator's grandfather appears in the book only in a brief anecdote. Yet the old man's dying words, a confession that he has been a traitor to his race, haunt the narrator throughout his life. Raised to go along in order to get along and succeed in life, the boy rarely disrespects authority. But he is ambivalent about it. Only toward the end of the book, after years of disillusionment, does he finally accept his grandfather's advice to "overcome 'em with yeses." The grandfather's words recall the legacy of slavery and resonate powerfully during the battle royal when white men abuse and belittle a group of helpless black boys. The battle itself symbolizes the social and political power struggle depicted throughout the novel.

Norton
A rich white New Englander, Norton is a trustee of the college in which the narrator is enrolled. Although he gives money to the college, he is patronizing and supercilious toward blacks. En route to meet Trueblood and then get a drink at the Golden Day, Norton tells the narrator cryptically that their two destinies are intertwined, in part because his donations to the college are made in memory of his lovely daughter, dead at an early age. Near the end of the novel the narrator and Norton meet by chance in the subway. Norton neither recognizes the narrator nor remembers anything about their intertwined destinies.

Trueblood
Initially, Trueblood seems like some kind of untamed beast. In telling his story, however, he shatters the image. Trueblood plays the poor ignorant darkie to gain Norton's sympathy and, incidentally, a hundred-dollar "reward," but he is truly a God-fearing, hard-working, loving, and sensitive family man.

The Vet
The vet, one of the shellshocked patrons of the Golden Day, refuses to be servile to whites. Considered an incorrigible menace by his white attendants, he is shipped to a mental hospital in Washington, D.C.

"The Founder"
A statue of the Founder stands on the campus of the narrator's college. It has been placed there to inspire students to believe that hard work and a cooperative attitude will help them achieve success despite their humble beginnings. Booker T. Washington is the prototype for "The Founder."

Dr. Bledsoe

Bledsoe, the college president, poses as the natural successor of the Founder. He excels at fund-raising and public relations. His motives, however, are self-serving. With the college's white trustees he is a sanctimonious and sycophantic prig. With blacks, he can be arrogant and malicious. As the narrator says, "He was our coal black daddy of whom we were afraid." Threatened by the actions of the narrator on Founder's Day, Bledsoe expels the boy and sends him off with a batch of fake letters of recommendation.

Ras the Exhorter

Ras is haranguing a street-corner crowd when the narrator first arrives in Harlem. A black nationalist, Ras espouses black power and is repulsed by the Brotherhood's message of equality for both blacks and whites. He wants to destroy the Brotherhood and tries to convince Tod Clifton that he has been a traitor to blacks by joining it. Assuming the name "Ras the Destroyer," he is determined to fight for black people's rights. He instigates the riot at the end of the book. In his final scene Ras appears on a horse, dressed in the costume of an Abyssinian chieftain, carrying a shield and wildly flinging a spear. Retrieving the spear, the narrator aims it at Ras. The tip hits Ras's jaw, making it impossible for him to speak, symbolically silencing the strident and vociferous rabble-rouser.

Emerson

Emerson interviews the narrator for a job. As a gay man, he is also an outcast. Sympathizing with the narrator, he reveals the contents of Bledsoe's alleged "letter of recommendation." Based on Emerson's suggestion, the narrator applies for a job in a paint factory.

Brockway

Brockway supervises the mixing of paints at the factory. Although he is black, he originated the company's suggestively racist slogan: "If It's Optic White, It's the Right White." To save his job after the narrator makes a costly mistake, he arranges an "accidental" explosion that sends the narrator to the hospital.

Mary Rambo

Mary owns a Harlem rooming house. Although the narrator is broke, Mary gives him a place to stay, an indication of her compassion and humanity. Indebted to Mary, the narrator hesitates to leave her house after he lands a lucrative job with the Brotherhood. At Mary's house the narrator finds a cast-iron savings bank in the shape of a degrading black figure. The narrator tries to dispose of it, but can't. Finally, he puts it in his briefcase with other items that represent various aspects of the black experience.

Brother Jack

Brother Jack, the leader of the Brotherhood, is an idealogue. That is, he is totally committed to the ideals of the organization. He is prepared to sacrifice himself and others to help the Brotherhood reach its goals. Consequently, he has lost much of his humanity, although it comes through occasionally, when, for example, he introduces the narrator to cheesecake. Jack is the author of an anonymous letter warning the narrator to slow down. In a "white man's world," the letter says, they will "cut you down if you go too fast." Realizing who wrote the letter, the narrator feels betrayed because Jack seemed to encourage and support his efforts. Jack has one glass eye, suggesting that he cannot see beyond his own narrow interests.

Additional Characters in the Brotherhood

Brother Tarp, one of the narrator's mentors, is a fugitive from justice. Having been imprisoned for almost twenty years for saying "No" to a white man, Tarp escaped by sawing his chains. As a token of his esteem for the narrator, Tarp presents him with a hunk of metal that came from a link in the chain. The narrator displays the gift on his desk, a symbol not only of Tarp's escape but of freedom from slavery and injustice

Brother Wrestrum, a white man, finds the link offensive. To him it symbolizes the differences between blacks and whites and, therefore, is inappropriate in the offices of the Brotherhood, an organization whose purpose is to unite all victims of oppression. Soon after, when a magazine runs a story about the narrator's work, Wrestrum accuses the narrator of opportunism, of putting his own individual interests above those of the Brotherhood.

Emma, who briefly flirts with the narrator, is Jack's mistress.

Brother Hambro helps train the narrator to be an effective speaker for the Brotherhood.

Tod Clifton is a good-looking, polite, and princely young member of the Brotherhood. He quickly wins the narrator's friendship and affection. Later, he inexplicably abandons the Brotherhood and disappears. Before long the narrator finds him selling tissue-paper Sambo dolls on the street. Trying to make sense of such demeaning behavior, the narrator decides that Clifton must think that society despised him and therefore surrendered himself to the most loathsome work he could find. In a willful act of self-destruction, Clifton hits an abusive cop and is shot dead.

Sibyl is the wife of a Brotherhood member. The narrator hopes to use her to get inside information about the Brotherhood, but she knows nothing. She tries to seduce the narrator but he thinks the better of it and resists her advances.

Rinehart

Rinehart himself doesn't actually appear in the book. The narrator discovers his existence when he dons a pair of dark glasses and a hat and is repeatedly mistaken for Rinehart. He deduces that Rinehart is a man of many identities: a lover, a gambler, a numbers runner, a crook, and a minister. The narrator, who has been seeking an identity for himself, is fascinated by Rinehart's multiple identities and the possibilities it offers. But he is reluctant to emulate Rinehart. When he sets out to undermine the Brotherhood, however, he realizes that a Rinehart-type disguise can be useful.

Structure

The novel's twenty-five chapters are framed between a prologue and an epilogue. The prologue, which begins "I am an invisible man," hints broadly at the consequences of being invisible ("people refuse to see me . . . . When they approach me they see only my surroundings, themselves, or figments of their imagination . . ."). Not until you read the epilogue, however, does the meaning of *invisibility* become completely clear. Chronologically the epilogue occurs before the prologue. The chapters between the prologue and epilogue describe the events that bring the narrator to the prologue. The narrator's story, literally *his-story*, concludes with the words, "The end was in the beginning."

Clarifying the novel's structure, Ellison once wrote, "I began it with a chart of the three part division. It was a conceptual frame. The three parts represent the narrative's movement from, using Kenneth Burke's terms, purpose to passion to perception." Each section covers a stage in the narrator's growth: At first, he is a college student, driven to play the role expected of him for the purpose of getting ahead. During the second section—the bulk of the novel—he starts to make his way in the world and rallies to the causes of the Brotherhood. Finally, after he perceives the disingenuousness of the Brotherhood's program, he becomes aware of his invisibility and is permanently transformed. To put it another way, the novel records the experiences of the narrator as he moves from country to city, from naïveté to disenchantment, and ultimately from confusion to clarity.

Like many other novels, *Invisible Man* is also structured like a *bildungsroman*, a novel constructed as a series of adventures. At times the adventures may seem unrelated, but they are linked by the hero's reactions and thoughts. *Don Quixote, Tom Jones*, *Gulliver's Travels*, and numerous other books, including *The Odyssey* are examples. In fact, Ellison might well have had *The Odyssey* in mind while writing *Invisible Man*. While Odysseus sails the sea in search of home, he survives one peril after another. Similarly, the invisible man, in pursuit of his destiny, finds himself in one perilous situation after the next. Odysseus fights with the Cyclops, a one-eyed monster; our narrator tangles with Brother Jack, also a one-eyed villain whose glass eye pops from his head in the heat of argument. During his voyage, Odysseus is tempted by the beautiful sirens, one of whom is Sybil, the name given to the white woman who tries to seduce the hero of *Invisible Man*. Rinehart, a man of many identities, parallels Odysseus, disguised as a beggar upon his arrival home. If you are familiar with *The Odyssey*, you'll no doubt find additional similarities.

Parallels within the novel itself provide a structural balance and unity. Events occurring early in the book are often echoed later on. For example, the narrator's expulsion from college reverberates in his expulsion from the Brotherhood. Then, too, Bledsoe's deceitful letters of recommendation are mirrored by the anonymous letter of warning written by Brother Jack. Indeed, Bledsoe and Brother Jack are equally malevolent characters. Both betray the narrator after winning his trust. Bledsoe's behavior also parallels the behavior of Brother Tod Clifton. By calling the narrator "nigger," Bledsoe reveals a vicious hatred of blacks, including himself. Tod, who demeans himself by selling Sambo dolls in the street, also demonstrates a destructive self-hatred. The book ends with rioting and looting in the streets of Harlem. The violence of the incident calls to mind the chaotic and bloody battle royal that took place during the narrator's boyhood.

Narrative Style/Language

Told in the first person from the limited point of view of a single narrator, *Invisible Man* overflows with the idiom and rhetoric of African-American culture: of urban streets, of the rural South, the church, and the jazz band. It also combines the language of academia, business, the laboratory, the factory, the union hall, and politics with the language of poetry. The narrator, in effect, is an astute listener, a linguistic sponge, and a stylist of the first order. He celebrates the rhythm and music of words and delights in playing with multilevel meanings and with metaphors, puns, allusions, alliteration, even ono-matopoeia. (Consider characters' names, for example: Rinehart—the rind and heart—a complete person, self-sufficient and whole. Or Trueblood, perhaps the most honest person in the book, and Tod Clifton, whose given name is the German word for *dead*.) At one point the narrator describes himself as "*the bungling bugler of words, imitating the trumpet and the trombone's timbre, playing thematic variations like a baritone horn. Hey! old connoisseur of voice sounds, of voices without messages, of newsless winds, listen to the vowel sounds and the crackling dentals . . . .*"

Ellison records sights and sounds in telling detail and replicates real-life speech and dialogue. Take Trueblood's tale of how he seduced his own daughter. Trueblood's language is electric. He uses a sharecropper's words but masterfully tells a tragic, comic, thoughtful, and highly poetic story. In Barbee's sermon about the Founder we hear the cadences and rhetoric of countless preachers trying to inspire their flocks. In the angry shouts of Ras the Exhorter we hear the inflammatory strains of black nationalism, in the words of white policemen we hear scorn, in the hoots of Harlem rioters we hear discord and confusion, in the pious words of Brother Jack we hear platitudes about brotherly love. Among other things, we also hear folk songs, Harlem street jive, physicians discussing a case, and the pleas of a West Indian woman encouraging her man to resist eviction.

Regardless of tape-recorder renderings of human speech, much of *Invisible Man* is surprisingly antirealistic. The unexpected is always happening. Even the book's basic premise—that the protagonist is invisible and lives underground—is a conceit from the world of fantasy. The blend of realism with fantasy endows characters and events with grotesque qualities. Many characters represent types, or better still, archetypes: Norton, the self-absorbed do-gooder; Bledsoe, the sanctimonius snake; Mary Rambo, the loving mother figure; and so forth. Accordingly, many critics view *Invisible Man* as an allegory, a story in which a second meaning is to be read beneath the surface.

People, places, and events throughout the novel are rarely what they appear to be. The ceremony held to award a college scholarship to the narrator turns out to be redneck entertainment. Bledsoe, feigning kindness, writes phony letters of recommendation. The Brotherhood preaches equality but acts despotically. And the narrator, believing that he has opportunities to be a functioning member of society, discovers that he is "invisible."

Because the narrator habitually daydreams of the past and fantasizes about the future, several sequences have dreamlike qualities: The grandfather's death scene returns to the narrator time and again. On the verge of a prestigious career as a spokesman for the Brotherhood, the narrator is reminded of his modest roots and is humbled by a fleeting whiff of carbolic acid. In his mind's eye he looks "past a Hooverville shanty of packing cases and bent tin signs to a railroad yard that lay beyond" and envisions "a syphilitic who lived alone in the shanty . . . coming to beg money for food and disinfectant with which to soak his rags" on a hand from which the fingers had been eaten away. En route to New York, the narrator fantasizes about the successes he hopes to find in the big city. Harlem impresses him as a city of dreams, where black traffic cops tell white drivers what to do and black girls work as store clerks.

Frightening, nightmarish dreams besiege the narrator's mind during various spells of semiconsciousness. Hooked to a machine in the paint factory hospital, the narrator is convinced that he himself is a machine, born from a machine mother. For a time, he thinks of himself as an accordian being played by two doctors, a understandable reaction to electroshock therapy and to overhearing a pair of white physicians discussing his case with callous indifference.

Long after, while flailing about in the dark of the coal pile, the narrator collapses. In a state "neither of dreaming nor of waking, but somewhere in between," he imagines being taken prisoner by an assemblage of his previous tormenters—Norton, Bledsoe, Emerson, Brother Jack, and others—and being castrated. This grisly nightmare serves as a turning point. By losing his "parts," the narrator feels suddenly free of the illusions that have dominated his life. Upon waking he ironically feels "whole" for the first time and realizes that as a changed man he can no longer return to any part of his old life. "I could only move ahead," he writes, "or stay here, underground," where at last he has a peaceful place in which to think things out and plan his future.

Themes and Motifs

White vs. Black

Contrasts of white and black (also light and dark) pervade the novel. Images such as white cloth blindfolds wrapped around black heads, white snow on Harlem's dark streets, soot-flecked snow, black drops of pigment added to pure white paint, the black coal cellar of a whites-only building—these and many more white-black images keep the division between blacks and whites on center stage.

In general, white prevails over black. Drops of black mixed into the Optic White paint quickly disappear when the paint is stirred. In the hospital, the narrator is trapped in "clinical whiteness." A "clinging white mist" befogs his mind. Wired to a machine, he can't separate his black body from the white world around him. Unable to remember his own name, he plunges into the black recesses of his mind and finds nothing but pain. That white often masks or prevails over black symbolizes race relationships in America. In the author's view, the plight of blacks is generally ignored by white society. Certainly it can be argued that until the Civil Rights movement, American racism was a condition that had largely been kept under the rug.

Other Colors

In addition to black and white, Ellison threads several other colors through the narrative. Gray, a mixture of black and white, for example, conveys blandness. En route to his first Brotherhood party, an event where blacks and whites intermingle, the narrator observes the "gray mist and gray silence" of the city. Because gold has always symbolized wealth and prosperity, naming the run-down roadside tavern the Golden Day is ironic. On the other hand, for the inmates of the mental hospital an outing at the Golden Day is a glorious adventure. Note also that during the men's smoker the boys scramble for gold coins that turn out to be worthless brass tokens, giving the black boys a foretaste of false hopes and disillusionment. Blue connotes sadness and hardship—the message conveyed by notable singers of the blues such as Billie Holiday, a figure often mentioned in the novel. While most blues songs are about unhappy love, others are responses to frustration and general malaise. Red is traditionally associated with blood, rage, passion, danger, and love. Brother Jack's red hair hints at his malevolence. The red faces of the men at the stag smoker suggest a kind of savagery, even a bloodlust in forcing hapless black boys to fight it out during the battle royal.

As you read or reread *Invisible Man* stay alert to many more references to colors, including green (the color of money) and red, white, and blue, often an ironic allusion to the flag that is supposed to symbolize freedom.

Freedom/Lack of Freedom

The legacy of slavery is woven through the fabric of the novel. Note that the main character himself is the grandson of an ex-slave and that the grandfather's dying words are never far from the narrator's consciousness. During the eviction of the Provo family, the narrator finds papers freeing Primus Provo from slavery in 1859. The document moves him deeply and evokes bitter memories of his early boyhood in the South.

Through much of the novel the narrator lacks the rights ordinarily enjoyed by citizens in a free society. In his youth he follows rules that a powerful white society has imposed on him. He has been led to believe that if he does what is expected, he will succeed in life. In that sense, he is a slave to disillusionment as well as to his own ambitions. In college, Dr. Bledsoe and the values espoused by the institution keep him in his place. In New York, he is similarly controlled. As an employee in the paint factory, he is told to follow directions meticulously. The one time he makes a decision on his own, the results are disastrous. Hospitalized by an explosion, he is subjected to punishing electric shock treatment (an echo of the electrified rug during the battle royal episode).

As a member of the Brotherhood, he is given a new name, a place to live, and a specific work assignment. His attempts at independent initiative irk the leaders. Instead of being rewarded, he is chastised and told that he is not being paid to think. Much of the time he is intent on escaping his southern roots and casting off his black attitudes, but to do so is harder than he expected. For example, he wants to discard the pieces of the savings bank he smashed in his room at Mary's but is repeatedly foiled. Finally, he puts the bundle of shards in his briefcase with the metal link of Brother Tarp's chain and other mementos of oppression.

Although the narrator refuses to order the "special" southern-style breakfast that consists of grits, pork chops, and hot biscuits, he ultimately caves in and devours several portions of baked yams. Eating yams is a turning point, a declaration of freedom. For once in his life, he has broken the white man's grip on him and eaten food that he enjoyed in his youth.

His emancipation is furthered by a Rinehart-type disguise. Masked, he is at liberty to do almost anything he pleases. Then, after he lands in his underground quarters the narrator relishes the taste of freedom as never before.

Invisibility

The full meaning of the term *invisibility* is not apparent until the epilogue, in which the narrator realizes that he has never been seen as a real flesh-and-blood human being. But the concept of invisibility is developed throughout the book largely by allusions to various visual afflictions: Reverend Barbee's blindness, Brother Jack's glass eye, Rinehart's dark glasses, the glaze in Mr. Norton's eyes after hearing Trueblood's story of incest. All are meant to suggest an inability to see either themselves or others. Norton regards himself as a humanist, a charitable do-gooder when in fact he is a patronizing racist. He has no sense of blacks as people; rather they are a cause that needs his money. Norton sees Trueblood as a poor, sex-driven beast, a stereotypical view that blinds him to Trueblood's humanity.

With his eyes wide shut, the narrator himself fails to see who he is, what others are doing to him, and what he has become. During the battle royal, for instance, he is violently degraded, but he just doesn't get it; he's too anxious to please his white audience. Vet, speaking to Norton at the Golden Day, perceptively confirms the narrator's lack of self-awareness: "He believes in you as he believes in the beat of his heart. He believes in that great false wisdom taught slaves and pragmatists alike, that white is right. I can tell you his destiny. He'll do your bidding, and for that his blindness is his chief asset." Only when he is betrayed by Bledsoe do the narrator's eyes pop open. He discerns that Bledsoe, the respected educator, is in reality a sycophantic and malevolent tyrant. But it still takes most of the novel for the narrator to appreciate the extent of his own visual infirmities. For a long time he repeatedly misjudges others and allows himself to be misled. In the end, however, it takes a cataclysm to knock the truth into him that, while he may not have seen others clearly, others have not seen him at all. In effect, he has been invisible.

Because the novel is the story of a man's search for an identity, the narrator's namelessness contributes to his invisibility. A man without a name is hard to identify. During his quest he plays various roles—southern black, class valedictorian, worker in a paint factory, member of the Brotherhood, Rinehart look-alike, and so on—but all these are labels that have been forced upon him by others. His tendency to accept others' opinions of him and to act according to what others tell him clouds his vision and keeps him from discovering his true self.

Questions for Writing and Discussion

1. Although the narrator is the only well-rounded character in *Invisible Man*, he is profoundly influenced by minor characters or even characters who never appear bodily in the pages of the book. Does this shortage of major, fully drawn characters strengthen or weaken the portrayal of the narrator, or does it have no particular effect?

2. Will the narrator ultimately emerge from his underground hole? What suggests that he will? What suggests that he won't?

3. One of the conditions that make things happen in *Invisible Man* is racial conflict and tension. In what respect do other factors such as social class, wealth, education, power, or morals influence events in the book?

4. The narrator tells us in the prologue that he is neither complaining nor protesting his invisibility. Then he adds, "It is sometimes advantageous to be unseen, although it is most often rather wearing on the nerves." Does the narrator illustrate the "advantages" of being unseen in the remainder of his story? Does invisibility wear on his nerves, as he claims?

5. In literature, as in life, people often take poses, pretend to be what they are not. (Hamlet and Macbeth come immediately to mind). Consider the characters in *Invisible Man.* Choose three characters who wear disguises or play roles other than himself or herself. Discuss the reasons for and the effects of their pretense.

All the Pretty Horses by Cormac McCarthy

Background

Readers find that *All the Pretty Horses* transcends the formulaic western novel. Its depth of insight, luscious prose, and characterizations elevate it far above the cliché-ridden horsey narratives that give the "western" genre its pulpy reputation. Consequently, it is one of the few contemporary American novels that is becoming a standard in AP English classes as well as in university and college English courses.

In 1949, when the story takes place, the American frontier had long been but a memory. But the frontier mystique lingers in the novel and is embodied in the three young men who are the book's protagonists. John Grady Cole, the main character, and two cohorts, Lacey Rawlins and Jimmy Blevins, all teenagers, call to mind the cowboys and gunslingers of the Old West.

A quest for adventure takes the three boys south of the Texas border into Mexico. Driven by naïveté and improbable dreams, they are energetic and resourceful. Setting out on a lark, they are bold and full of hope. Each is a talented horseman, handy with guns, self-reliant, and able to fend for himself in the wilderness. As the trio wanders in the mountains and across arid, desolate flatlands, they begin to encounter challenges that test their mettle. They do battle with thieves and bandits, with sheepherders and policemen, and sometimes with themselves. Their most virulent adversary, however, is Mexico itself. Their ignorance and misreading of the people and culture lead to clashes that nearly destroy all of them.

All the Pretty Horses is a coming-of-age story about love—love of nature, love of life, love of freedom, and also romantic love. It's also about friendship, loyalty, and inescapable evil. En route to adulthood John Grady, from whose point of view the story is told, emerges as warrior-hero, but he is beset by antiheroic, self-destructive traits such as stubbornness, pride, and naïveté. In the end, after enduring a series of harrowing life-changing moments, John Grady achieves an adult awareness. By the time he returns to Texas, he has recognized just who he is and what he might expect to be for the rest of his life.

> Use *All the Pretty Horses* as the subject for an essay on 1) coming of age, 2) a fall from innocence, 3) the clash of cultures, 4) friendship and loyalty, 5) a young protagonist at odds with an established culture, 6) a hero's quest, and 7) the conflict between free will and fate.

Synopsis

In 1948, John Grady Cole's grandfather dies, bequeathing the family's ranch, where John Grady grew up, to his daughter. Mrs. Cole, John Grady's mother, however, is an occasional actress divorced from John Grady's father and has no interest in ranching. She plans to sell the property, leaving John Grady, at age sixteen, without a home and without any real prospects for the future. Both John Grady and a buddy, Lacey Rawlins, feel they've come to the end of possibilities in Texas and decide to take off on horseback on an ill-defined quest across the border in Mexico. Before they go John Grady, as though to confirm that there's nothing to hold him in San Angelo, bids good-bye to his ex-girlfriend Mary Catherine who has dumped him in favor of a boy with a car, and to his father, a drifter psychologically damaged in the war and deteriorating physically.

Riding south, John Grady and Rawlins traverse desolate and forbidding country. Parts of it are wild and beautiful. The boys forage for food and live off the land. Rawlins shoots a rabbit for their dinner. Near the Rio Grande, they hook up with another runaway, Jimmy Blevins, a thirteen-year-old raggedy kid on a handsome bay horse. Blevins talks big, has a hot temper, and is unpredictable. His manner irritates Rawlins, who wants to ditch him, but John Grady tolerates him well enough. By moonlight they cross the river into Mexico, where the pastoral land is free of fences and highways. Mexico is also a world that the boys don't completely understand. Crisscrossing the land, they meet other riders, sheepherders, peasants, and migrant traders but can't always read their actions or interpret the looks in their eyes. During a terrific thunderstorm, Blevins panics, strips so he won't attract lightning, and loses his bay horse, his gun, and his clothing except for skivvies and one boot. Afterward, in a small town, they contrive to steal back Blevins' horse, but branded as thieves they are pursued by armed men. On the run they elude their pursuers but get separated from Blevins.

John Grady and Rawlins get jobs as wranglers at the Hacienda de Nuestra Señora de la Purisima Concepción. The boys' skills make them valued employees, especially John Grady, whose knack for taming wild horses turns heads. Impressed, Don Hector Rocha y Villareal, the wealthy hacienda owner, talks with John Grady about horses and horse breeding. One day he asks John Grady whether he rode all the way from Texas. "Yessir," John Grady says.

"Just the two of you?"

"Yessir . . . Just me and him"—he replies, deliberately omitting a reference to Blevins and concealing the fact that they are wanted as accomplices in a horse theft. He says instead that he's in Mexico only to see the country. Don Hector probably knows it is a lie but says nothing. Quizzing him further, Don Hector asks his age. The answer—"sixteen"—surprises Don Hector for he recalls his own youth when he often added years to his own age. John Grady's truthfulness wins Don Hector's respect but he can't totally forgive John Grady for the larger indiscretion.

Trouble starts for John Grady after he and Alejandra, Rocha's teenage daughter, fall for each other. Late at night, the starry-eyed pair secretly ride her father's prized sire into the nearby mountains. Dueña Alfonsa, Alejandra's great-aunt, gets wind of the romance and warns John Grady to stop seeing Alejandra, whose reputation is being sullied. He is not easily put off, however. Nor is Alejandra, whose desires drive her to John Grady's bed for nine nights running. Then she returns to school in Mexico City.

Soon thereafter, Rocha finds out about their affair. The police arrest John Grady and Rawlins and haul them to jail in Encantada. Blevins is already incarcerated there, accused of killing three Mexicans while trying to reclaim the gun he lost during the thunderstorm. John Grady and Rawlins suspect that Blevins turned them in to save himself, but he denies it. A brutal police captain interrogates the boys further, brushing off John Grady's and Rawlins's protestations of innocence. Blevins, whose guilt is undeniable, is finally led off into the trees and shot dead. John Grady and Rawlins are transported to Saltillo, a prison where inmates prey on each other and often fight to the death in order to protect their turf or prove their manhood. Rawlins is savagely beaten. Emilio Pérez, Saltillo's presiding official, explains the perils of Saltillo and offers to free the boys for a price. But they are virtually broke. Then, says Pérez, they should expect to be killed. Using a few pesos left to him by Blevins, John Grady buys a switchblade knife from another inmate. The weapon saves his life, for he is presently set upon by a fellow prisoner. During the fight, John Grady is wounded but manages to stab and kill his attacker.

To their surprise, days later, John Grady and Rawlins are handed a bit of money and released from Saltillo. Rawlins lights out for Texas, but John Grady, determined to find Alejandra, returns to the hacienda. Alejandra is gone, sent to school in Mexico City. Dueña Alfonsa warns him that he and Alejandra must not see each other again. Alejandra has agreed to the end of their affair in exchange for having Dueña Alfonsa save John Grady's life by bailing him out of Saltillo. What's more, a match between John Grady and Alejandra is impossible; they come from two different worlds.

John Grady mounts his horse, Redbo, grabs Rawlins's horse, Junior, and leaves the hacienda. He telephones Alejandra, and arranges a rendezvous in Zacatecas. Their farewell meeting, a twenty-four-hour love fest, ends when Alejandra declines to elope with him. She loves him but is too firmly tied to her family to break away.

Saddened, John Grady returns to Encantada where he locates Blevin's horse. He captures the beast and boldly takes a hostage, the police captain who shot Blevins. Heading north toward the Texas border, he escapes the posse but he and the captain are accosted by brigands with a score to settle with the captain. In the scuffle, a bullet pierces John Grady's leg. Later, he cauterizes the wound with the red-hot pistol barrel and releases the weakened, sniveling captain to his fate with the mountain people.

John Grady had left Texas as a boy. Roughly six months later, he returns a man and has the wounds to prove it. Losing Alejandra had been painful. He is conscious-stricken about having killed a man in prison. He is troubled by his own cruelty toward the police captain. He feels like a man without a country, alienated from the land of his youth. His detachment is exacerbated by the news that both his father and Abuela, his childhood nurse and substitute mother, have died during his sojourn in Mexico.

John Grady intends to return Blevins's horse to Blevins's family, but can't locate them. After finding another Jimmy Blevins, a radio evangelist from whom the dead boy presumably borrowed a name, John Grady accepts that he'll never find the horse's rightful owner. Before long, however, three men claim ownership. At a judge's hearing, after John Grady tells the true story of the horse and of his Mexican adventures, he is awarded legal rights to the horse. That night, John Grady visits the judge, hoping to sort out the moral ambiguities of killing his attacker in prison. The judge assures John Grady that he had not acted immorally. Considering that he had had no choice, violence was justified.

Relieved, John Grady rides away, a solitary figure, a wandering horseman bound for no particular destination. Like his father, he is essentially a drifter, but better prepared to handle the challenges around the bend. In a concluding vignette, he rides past a group of Indians who watch him go by but say nothing. In a sense, John Grady represents the transcience of man. A defeated rider on the old Comanche road, he vanishes into the darkening landscape like "the ghost of a nation passing."

The Cast of Characters　The protagonists in most narratives of the Old West often assume mythic roles—playing the part of real men whose image is built not so much on historical accuracy but on readers' associations with such archetypes as Billy the

Kid, Wyatt Earp, and the Marlboro Man. All are rugged, self-sufficient cowboys who thrive on an honest day's work, a well-bred horse, a blanket roll, and a campfire in the mountains. Gunplay and horsemanship are the standards by which their bravery and skill are measured.

Female characters in many western novels are *femmes fatales*, idealized sexual objects. The most beautiful damsel in the group may fall for the hero, but the society may not trust or accept him. Sometimes a jealous suitor attempts to undermine the budding romance. In the end, the hero could win the girl's heart, but just as often he rides away alone, sadder but wiser, from the experience.

To what extent these simplified thumbnail sketches define the characters in *All the Pretty Horses* is arguable. Certainly some of the supporting cast in the novel are one-dimensional stereotypes, but the major characters are much more like real people with multidimensional personalities.

John Grady Cole

John Grady, a sixteen-year old Texan, is an expert horseman. He's also a fine chess player and can hold his own around a pool table. At the beginning of the novel he has no particular goals or responsibilities—no college plans, no AP exams; he doesn't even go to school anymore.

Early on, he contemplates the wilderness and the wildness within himself. But as the story progresses, he develops gravitas beyond his years. He adheres to a kind of cowboy code of honor and exhibits enviable moral stamina. He is determined to see justice done and to find answers to the questions of life.

In the book's opening scene John Grady observes his grandfather's corpse in a casket. Saddened by the death of his hero, the only role model of his life, John Grady finds himself inspired by the old man's pioneering exploits and dreams of replicating his grandfather's adventurous life. He would gladly continue living on the ranch but his mother can't unload the place quickly enough. The sale marks the end of John Grady's childhood. Having been deprived of the ranch on which he grew up and rejected by both his girlfriend and his mother, John Grady replaces his broken family with the comradeship of Rawlins and, by chance, Blevins. Long rides with his father convince him that his destiny is in the saddle. The "faint trace" of the Comanche road beckons him to Mexico. Suddenly the future, represented by a strong horse, Denbo, and a new saddle, the only tangible legacy left to him by his father, opens wide with possibilities.

John Grady sits on a horse "not only as if he'd been born to it which he was but as if he were begot by malice or mischance into some queer land where horses never were he would have found them anyway." Dreaming of a meaningful life, he relies on Denbo to carry him on his quest for meaningfulness. In time, John Grady's skill at roping and horse-breaking earns him a job at the hacienda. With Rawlins's help, he breaks sixteen wild horses in four days, a feat that impresses even the old *caballeros* and brings him to the attention of the hacendado, Don Hector, who confides in the young vaquero, telling him of his dream to breed mares with a great stallion.

Horses dwell in John Grady's thoughts and dreams. Wounded in a prison fight, he lies in bed for three days with his mind fastened on horses, believing that "they were always the right thing to think about." At night he dreams of running freely with young mares and fillies over the plains as though he himself is part equine. Released from prison he continues to have horses on his mind. But the images have turned dark. The unrestrained joy of his earlier musing is tempered by the disorder, death, and sadness that have been thrust into his consciousness by Blevins's execution and its aftermath.

For most of the book, John Grady's behavior is governed by a romantic, high-minded idealism. When Rawlins proposes to ditch Blevins, he refuses. Blevins, after all, is an American and a soul mate on a quest of his own, a quest that John Grady fully understands. What's more, he feels responsible for this younger double of himself. John Grady's romanticism contrasts with Rawlins's grating practicality and reasonableness. John Grady has had reason up to here from his mother and the lawyer. If he'd listened to them, he'd be going to high school in Texas instead of living it up in Mexico. At the hacienda Dueña Alfonsa tries to reason with John Grady, too, warning him to stay away from Alejandra. Quite correctly she says, "In the end we all come to be cured of our sentiments. Those whom life does not cure death will. The world is quite ruthless in selecting between the dream and the reality, even where we will not." Her words fall on deaf ears, however, for John Grady's romantic impulses won't let him give up Alejandra easily.

As Don Hector's hireling, he earns his keep by caring for horses. His job description does not include courting Don Hector's beautiful daughter, but he can't rein in his emotions nor see past his inalienable right to pursue happiness any way he sees fit. Warned that his pursuit of Alejandra will lead to trouble, he can't worry about it. An incorrigible optimist, he is unmoved by mundane truths and feels immune to threats from above. He's gutsy and willing to risk danger in pursuit of romantic ends. If he gets into trouble, he figures there'll always be a way out.

The difficulty is that crossing the Mexican border has taken John Grady into a complex world that he doesn't fully understand. South of the Rio Grande, good mixes with evil, fate merges with free will, and rationality often turns out to be ludicrously irrational. The ambiguity of Mexico is nowhere more apparent than in his dealings with Dueña Alfonsa, whose statements and personal history attest to a rebellious nature but whose actions adhere to the traditions and values of the landed aristocracy. In this setting, John Grady's moral code fails to bring about the results he desires and expects.

His crush on Alejandra is a case in point. Unable to see beyond the all-encompassing present of his beautiful dream girl, John Grady remains unfazed by Dueña Alfonsa's admonition to keep his distance. In falling for Don Hector's daughter he ignores decorum and the long and proud history of her family. Like a hyperromantic adolescent, he believes that love conquers all. He is blind to the power of custom and tradition, an ironic shortcoming considering that he himself embodies a traditional figure of myth and legend, namely the adventuresome and fearless two-fisted rebel in love with horses and the hardscrabble life of a working cowboy. He pays dearly for his recklessness. Once Don Hector gets wind of their romance, John Grady is arrested and incarcerated. Critics have noted that John Grady is an American Adam, suffering from the sin of pride and defiantly reaching for forbidden fruit. Tempted by the Eve-like Alejandra, he must be expelled from the mini-paradise he had found at the hacienda and suffer a swift fall from innocence.

The John Grady who goes to prison differs from the John Grady who comes out. At first, even the harsh reality of a Mexican prison can't break his stubborn independence. He unhesitatingly talks back to the police and the prison authorities when his rights are violated. Blevins's death and a brutal fight with a would-be assassin shock him into recognizing both the malevolence of the world and his own limitations. His failure to act on the brink of Blevins's execution torments him. He also suffers guilt for knifing to death the inmate who attacked him. After Alejandra jilts him—the *coup-de-grâce* of his fall from innocence—John Grady steals back Blevins's horse and, in what seems like an act of both revenge and self-flagellation, takes the police captain hostage.

John Grady's journey back to Texas leaves him wiser, sadder, and alone. He remains essentially a restless drifter, unyielding in his determination to see his dream, however vague, fulfilled. Still, out of his heartbreak there emerges a resilient man with a right to claim his niche in the world.

Mr. Grady

A pathetic man, John Grady's father is emotionally and physically ill. Long divorced from John Grady's mother, he tries to act fatherly but is too weak and ineffectual. His vacuity and aimlessness are suggested by details such as his ill-fitting clothes, his pointless small talk about the child movie star Shirley Temple, and his habit of stirring black coffee with a spoon. Years back he taught John Grady to play chess. "He was about the best I ever saw," John Grady says later. But, he has nothing of value to pass on to his son except a new Hamley Formfitter saddle, a gift that John Grady appreciatively straps onto his horse's back. The old man's parting words to his son reflect his overall diffidence: "People dont feel safe no more. . . . We're like the Comanches was two hundred years ago. We dont know what's goin to show up here come daylight. We dont even know what color they'll be."

John Grady, the opposite of his father, doesn't know his limits. He gorges on life. At times he thinks that there is nothing he can't be or do. As the son of an ineffectual father he occasionally seeks help and counsel from surrogate fathers—older men such as Mr. Franklin, his mother's lawyer. He also talks horses with Don Hector, and near the end of the book visits the judge to talk over the guilt gnawing inside him.

Mrs. Grady

John Grady's mother is not much of a parent. In order to pursue an acting career, she selfishly turns her back on John Grady and on her war-damaged husband. She ridicules John Grady's desire to manage the ranch after the death of her father. "You have to go to school," she tells him and promptly puts the place on the market, effectively leaving John Grady without a home. Prior to setting out on his journey, John Grady hitchhikes to San Antonio to see his mother perform in a play. He watches intensely hoping that it can teach him something about life, but it doesn't. He is disappointed further when he observes his mother in a hotel lobby on the arm of her current lover, a man in a suit and topcoat.

Lacey Rawlins

Rawlins is John Grady's seventeen-year-old buddy and sidekick in Mexico. By temperament, he balances John Grady's dreamy idealism. Intolerant of ambiguity, Rawlins is a pragmatist. He thinks concretely and respects facts. He questions the meaning of song lyrics and asks, "Do you think they got vienna sausages in Mexico?" In some ways, he is like a kid brother to John Grady, asking him questions and looking for guidance. Rawlins is impatient with Blevins and would like get rid of him. He hounds John Grady with reasons: Blevins is arrogant, unstable, and likely to get their little group into trouble. Once Blevins is gone, Rawlins tells John Grady that Blevins had a "loose wingnut." Later he predicts that John Grady's involvement with Alejandra will lead to no good. When the boys are arrested, Rawlins, as a realist, figures that it would be to their benefit to cooperate with the authorities. "Just shut the hell up," he tells John Grady, who can't resist shooting off his mouth.

In prison, Rawlins endures a severe beating. Upon release, he hurries back to Texas, unable to cope with Mexico's irrationality. At home, at least he knows what's what and why's why. John Grady's visit near the end of the book prompts Rawlins to say about his familiar surroundings, "This is still good country." John Grady concurs but adds that "it ain't my country."

Jimmy Blevins

Blevins, a runaway boy from Texas, latches on to John Grady and Rawlins near the Mexican border. He may or may not be thirteen years old. It's unclear because he takes liberties with the truth. He may rightfully own the big bay horse he rides, or then again, he may have stolen it. His skill with a pistol is a certainty, however. Given the chance to validate himself as a marksman, he puts a hole dead center into a wallet tossed into the air. Blevins has a hot temper and a loud mouth. Rawlins wants to ditch him, but John Grady not only tolerates him more easily but views him as a soul mate. Like John Grady, Blevins has ridden into Mexico secure in his right to exist on his own terms in a foreign country, expecting to devise rules of his own choosing and without regard to Mexican law or customs. Blevins loses his horse in a thunderstorm but feels free to steal it back from a stable. Later, for shooting and killing a Mexican officer, he is imprisoned. John Grady and Rawlins, implicated as Blevins's accomplices, are also arrested. After questioning, Blevins is executed by a police captain. Some time afterward, John Grady tries to return the bay horse to Blevins's relatives back in Texas but can't locate them. He surmises that "Jimmy Blevins" was not the boy's name at all but a pseudonym borrowed from a radio evangelist.

Don Hector Rocha y Villareal

The wealthy haciendado of La Purisma and father of Alejandra, Don Hector owns a thousand head of cattle and flies his own airplane. Because he hopes to breed wild mountain horses with his own stock, he is glad to have Rawlins and especially John Grady among his vaqueros. While he admires John Grady's work with horses, he opposes John Grady's courtship of his daughter. Too polite to confront John Grady directly, Don Hector veils his disapproval in remarks made during a game of billiards. He points out his family's long history, emphasizing the strength of tradition and the power of family loyalty, concepts alien to John Grady's recent experience.

Alejandra

Alejandra is Don Hector's daughter. Portrayed in the novel as an ideal young woman, she remains a fairly remote character. We know that she's the only child of a wealthy family, that she goes to a private school in the city, is outfitted in expensive clothes, and rides a beautiful horse. She also has blue eyes, black hair, and is a knockout. She is flirtatious and seductive and instantly drives John Grady crazy with desire.

In taking up with John Grady, she rebels against her family, her culture, and her society, but in the end she won't be swayed into eloping with him. She has already suffered from the loss of her father's love, which she needs more than she needs John Grady. Moreover, she is rooted solidly in Mexico. While walking with John Grady one last time she points out the place where her grandfather died in the Revolution. In effect, she abandons her romantic, defiant posture, trades love for history, and seems destined to become another Dueña Alfonsa.

Dueña Alfonsa

Alejandra's godmother and *grande dame* of the hacienda, Dueña Alfonsa functions as the protector of Rocha family traditions. In her youth she was an idealist not unlike John Grady, but now she has become set in her ways and defends the intractable society she once despised. She warns John Grady away from Alejandra, informing him that Don Hector will never allow his daughter to marry a poor American. To make sure that such a union never takes place, she later bails John Grady out of prison after exacting a promise from Alejandra never to see him again. Freeing John Grady may seem like an altruistic thing to do, but its underlying motives are self-serving and tyrannical.

Dueña Alfonsa functions in the novel as more than just a spoiler of romance, however. She also embodies her country's history and speaks on behalf of the values treasured by Mexico's landed aristocracy. Ironically, Dueña Alfonsa claims to have been an early-day feminist espousing reformist causes. Yet her behavior belies her past. She acquiesces to Don Hector's wishes and denies Alejandra the right to make her own decisions. Speaking from experience, she challenges John Grady's idealism, telling him that in the end reality will cure him of pie-in-the-sky fantasies. In a long monologue she tells John Grady of her experiences with power, ignorance, and evil. She relates the story of the Mexican Revolution and how the people's dreams of freedom turned into tragedy and bloodshed. She explains social divisions that have long racked Mexico and talks of her passionate love for a man killed by a mob after he'd helped depose the dictator Diaz.

At the hacienda she invites John Grady to play chess. The game proves to be a metaphor for her need to exert control over others. John Grady wins the first two games. Once she sees his skill, she resolves to beat him. In the third game Dueña Alfonsa uses an opening he'd never seen before and wipes him out easily. She has toyed with her victim before destroying him.

Waxing philosophical, she wonders aloud about the interrelationships between free will and fate. She envisions a puppet show as a key to understanding human actions. A puppet in her youth, she's now the puppeteer, pulling the strings of Alejandra's life. She bends the girl to her will and changes her destiny by taking advantage of the opportunity to save John Grady's life.

The Captain

The captain, an imperious and ruthless sadist, epitomizes villainy. When John Grady, Rawlins, and Blevins are imprisoned, he strips them and insists on knowing why they are in Mexico. He doubts their answers, brands Blevins an assassin, and executes him in cold blood. John Grady, on the other hand, intrigues him. In the boy's defiance, he recognizes a bit of himself. Explaining his willpower, he relates an anecdote from his youth about being rejected by a whore and laughed at by other boys. Obsessed by shame, he vows to make sure that no one will ever laugh at him again.

John Grady will later take him hostage, the ultimate humiliation for the proud and domineering captain. John Grady leaves him to his fate with the mountain people. Mexican lawlessness will destroy the captain as surely as he exploited the country's lawlessness to destroy others.

Emilio Pérez

Pérez presides over Saltillo. He takes a dim view of Americans: They are not only impractical, he says, but their minds are closed. He also believes that men need to prove their manhood over and over. Thus, he allows his prisoners to maim and kill each other. Pérez exemplifies still another gap between Mexican and American society.

The Horses

Technically, horses are not characters, but they do have personalities and they steer the plot of *All the Pretty Horses* as forcibly as any human character except perhaps John Grady. Their presence contributes to the mythic quality of the novel. Horses link John Grady and the other boys not only to the frontier but to earlier eras when knights on horseback quested after adventure and other goals. To be sure, Redbo, Junior, and Blevins's bay horse are innocent beasts, but they transport John Grady and his buddies south of the border. It is the loss of the bay horse that leads to Blevins's arrest and death and to John Grady and Rawlins's employment at the hacienda. John Grady's skill with horses allows him to stay on and to develop a relationship with Alejandra and with her father. After his release from prison, John Grady returns to the heart of Mexico where he reclaims not only Redbo but the horses belonging to Rawlins and Blevins. Seizing Blevins's horse leads to kidnapping the captain and to the long and painful journey home.

Structure

All the Pretty Horses fits easily into the category of a *Bildungsroman*, an on-the-road story of a hero's quest. Typically, a young, starry-eyed hero sets out in search of love, adventure, or some other undefined goal. Along the way he endures numerous perils and passes several tests of strength and character. He may suffer a slight wound, however—just to keep him humble—but he soon recovers and emerges from his journey a wiser and more mature individual. Although John Grady's journey resembles that of literary heroes from Odysseus to Huck Finn, his quest ends without a neat resolution. Rather, John Grady rides out of town still seeking the secrets of life and ready for additional adventures. (The novel *Cities of the Plain*, also by Cormac McCarthy, continues the saga of John Grady.)

The story in *All the Pretty Horses* is largely chronological and divided into four sections: The first chapter sets the scene and finds John Grady leaving home and heading to Mexico. The second chapter covers his wanderings in Mexico and his stint at the hacienda where he breaks horses and manages simultaneously to fall in love and out of favor. Taken to prison during the third chapter, and having learned a good deal about cruelty and evil, John Grady comes of age. In the last chapter, beaten down but far from broken, he returns to Texas, the starting point of his adventures. Upon returning, he attends the funeral of Abuela, the nurse who reared him. Just as the death of his grandfather at the beginning of the book launches John Grady on his journey away from childhood, Abuela's death severs his last flimsy ties with his youth.

Cormac McCarthy is fond of using such parallels, which not only heighten contrasts but serve to unify the story. The contrast between Alejandra and John Grady, for example, strikingly suggests why the young lovers must ultimately go their separate ways. Alejandra comes from wealth, John Grady from modest means. Don Hector is accomplished and strong-minded; John Grady's father is weak and ineffectual. The intrusive Dueña Alfonsa, Alejandra's mother-protector, is precisely the opposite of John Grady's indifferent mother.

Early in the novel the author shows us the hallway in the Grady family home. It is dimly lit and hung with portraits of John Grady's forebears. John Grady barely knows who they are. At Don Hector's La Purisma, ancestral portraits also line the walls, but there everyone knows the hacienda's proud one-hundred-and-seventy-year history, implying that John Grady, a rootless stranger, doesn't belong there. As an outsider, and a poor one at that, he can't enter the hacienda's world and culture. Nor can he draw Alejandra away from it. He is doomed to fail in both endeavors.

The Rio Grande not only separates the United States and Mexico, it represents a divide between two ways of life—Alejandra's and John Grady's. Crossing the border sets into motion opposing forces such as civilization and wilderness, the individual and the community, free will and fate, present and past, poverty and wealth, and numerous other tensions central to the novel. Indeed, these dichotomies keep John Grady forever a stranger in Mexico. When the story takes place, the United States is nearly two hundred years old. Mexico has traditions dating back two thousand years.

The differences between the two countries is nowhere more evident than in the book's portrayal of the law. Early in the book the lawyer Franklin advises John Grady that he's too young to run the family's ranch. At the end a judge upholds his claim to Blevins's horse. In one instance the law denies; in the other it yields. But win or lose, John Grady can depend on the law to be fair and just. Contrast this to the application of laws in Mexico, where jurisprudence is chaotic and capricious. Laws are made and broken at will. Although he's underage and has had no trial, Blevins is executed in cold blood. Anarchy rules at the prison at Saltillo. Perez solicits bribes to release prisoners, and inmates are out of control.

Themes and Motifs

Coming of Age

The death of John Grady's grandfather portends the loss of family, ranch, and a traditional way of life. Only a boy at the time, John Grady feels like a man who's "come to the end of something." What that something is he discovers during his dangerous and harrowing journey into the beautiful and foreign world that is Mexico. The journey covers more than geography, however. It covers the distance from childhood to adulthood, innocence to experience. In other words, John Grady's adventures in Mexico amount to a rite of passage into adulthood.

Until then John Grady lived on the stuff of dreams, thrived on challenges, boldly confronted authority. Romantic impulses served him well, especially in competitive or dangerous situations, but he is undone by an affair of the heart. The climactic moment occurs while he fights for his life and stabs a fellow prisoner to death. The killing awakens him both to the evils of the world and to the evil residing within himself. His experiences from then on—in prison, while vainly pursuing Alejandra, and during his painful return to Texas—shock and sadden him. He bears a burden of remorse for not taking action when the captain walked Blevins out in the trees and shot him. He grieves over his thwarted love and is overcome with hatred for the captain. When he returns from Mexico he sits naked on his horse in the falling rain, thinks about his dead father, and weeps. But the tears are not only for his father. Rather, he weeps for his failed dreams and his lost youth. Ironically, he has returned to Texas on Thanksgiving Day, but the day means nothing to him. He has little to be thankful for.

A Clash of Cultures

In traditional western stories, heroes roam the American wilderness, occasionally paying a visit to rustic ranches and small towns. But John Grady and his chums venture south into Mexico in search of an Old West that they can no longer find in Texas. It is the wrong move, for Old Mexico is an inhospitable place crowded with bandits and desperados. (This view may strike you as grossly biased, but in the mid-twentieth century, when the story takes place, political correctness was unheard of.) Perhaps nowhere in the world are two neighboring countries as different as Mexico and United States. The contrast is startling. The clash of cultural differences literally kills Blevins and sends Rawlins scooting for home as quickly he can. Only John Grady, fueled by his infatuation for Alejandra, tries to take on the country. He loses of course. Separated by language, religion, race, philosophy, and history, a solitary American, however resilient, doesn't stand a chance against a several thousand-years-old culture still clinging to its past.

Paradise Lost

As John Grady and his companions leave civilization and ride into the mountains of Mexico, Rawlins asks, "Where do you reckon paradise is at?" The answer for John Grady is La Purisma.

The land around the hacienda is a mini-paradise on earth, described in lush prose:

> The grasslands lay in a deep violet haze and to the west thin flights of waterfowl were moving north before the sunset in the deep red galleries under the cloudbanks like schoolfish in a burning sea and on the foreland plain they saw vaqueros driving cattle before them through a gauze of golden dust.

John Grady, doing work he adores, riding horses, and secretly courting Alejandra, could not be more content. But when he ignores the warnings of Dueña Alfonsa and conceals the truth from Don Hector about his connection to the alleged horse thief Blevins, his fall from innocence begins. Once Alejandra (an Eve-like temptress) entices him to reach for the forbidden fruit (their love affair), John Grady, an American Adam, slides into sin, is arrested, and finally expelled from the "garden." With his cowboy's paradise lost, he is initiated into harsh reality.

Fate vs. Free Will

Attitudes toward fate and free will create tension in the novel and help to differentiate the Mexican character from the American. Dueña Alfonsa, using a metaphor of puppets who control puppets who control puppets *ad infinitum*, argues for a kind of predestination. Since her rebellious youth, she has mellowed. Now she invests the hacienda with old world ties, with antiquity and tradition. She sees the interconnectedness of things, in particular how historical events cannot be forgotten or ignored. Her missing finger reminds her of the reality of the past. As an aging woman, she accepts the fate that culture has given her.

Her fatalism contrasts with John Grady's and Rawlins's faith in their capacity to determine what they do and when they do it. Deciding for themselves is their inalienable right. Rawlins, the pragmatist, says "ever dumb thing I ever done in my life there was a decision I made before that got me into it. It was never the dumb thing. It was always some choice I'd made before it."

One could argue that they misapprehend the extent of their freedom to choose. After all, they had no real control over the events that shaped their lives. Nor to any great extent do they have a say about what happens to them in Mexico. John Grady's acceptance of his limitations contributes to his eventual fall from innocence.

Illusion and Reality

The theme of illusion and reality is sounded in the novel's opening paragraphs. Repeated images of illusion occur as John Grady comes to view the body of his grandfather and sees the flickering candle flame in the mirror. As he studies the corpse, all dolled up for the funeral, he says to it, "You never combed your hair that way in your life." Here, in the semidarkness John Grady is perceptive enough not to be fooled by illusion. But many of his experiences thereafter show that he's more than susceptible to its wiles. He thinks that he can run a ranch until the law tells him he's too young. He deludes himself into believing that he can break open Mexican society and draw out the girl he loves. His misapprehension, however, sets into motion a series of events that end in sorrow and disillusionment.

It might have done John Grady good to listen to the aged cook who accompanies him and Rawlins the first time they go to the mountains to catch wild horses. The old man tells the boys of his exploits in the cavalry, of how horses had been killed under him, and that horses love war just as men do. He believes that horses have souls, and that if you can understand the soul of one horse you understand them all. But, he adds, to understand the soul of a man is just an illusion.

A Code of Honor

John Grady pledges to himself instead of to a higher authority to live by the revered values of the Old West: courage, determination, ingenuity, loyalty. His actions are governed by the code of a cowboy/warrior—to fight with tenacious nobility and maintain a defiant idealism even in the face of death. Thus, we find John Grady standing heroically firm against an assortment of sinister characters, including the brutal police captain and the waxcamp workers who offer to buy Blevins.

To John Grady it is a matter of personal honor to stand by his countrymen. For no reason other than Blevins is American, John Grady allows the boy to join him and Rawlins as they set out for Mexico. The code of honor dictates that he lend a hand to his brother horseman.

In Mexico, John Grady can hardly face himself after he has stood passively by when Blevins is taken out and shot. Inaction at a time of peril amounts to an egregious violation of the code.

John Grady's cowboy code ultimately collides with Dueña Alfonsa's feminine matriarch's code—the code that prescribes whom Alejandra will marry. It also fails to mesh with Alejandra's code of loyalty to her own family and the customs of her country. In spite of his code's failure to bring about desired results, John Grady remains true to its dictates. Even when he fails to get the girl, he holds fast to the code's provisions, nowhere more evident than in his use of a red-hot pistol barrel to cauterize a bullet wound in his leg.

But the code demands more than an ability to endure pain. Back in Texas, it also compels him to seek absolution from a kindly judge to whom John Grady confesses two moral lapses: his failure to stand by Blevins and the knifing of his assailant in prison.

Narrative Style/Language

You can't read more than a page of *All the Pretty Horses* without being struck by Cormac McCarthy's virtuosic writing style, a style that has earned him a place of honor among contemporary American authors. In particular, his writing is distinctive for realistic unpunctuated dialogue, lyrical passages of unparalleled beauty, vivid imagery, the liberal use of Spanish, long and rolling sentences that recall Faulkner, and a spare use of language reminiscent of Hemingway and Raymond Carver.

McCarthy relies on unpunctuated realism to accelerate dialogue and action. The drama of numerous sequences is heightened by rapid-fire give-and-take between the characters. Look, for example, at the long exchange in the Eagle Café between John Grady and his father. The two bat clipped sentences back and forth. Their way of speaking not only reveals something of their rough-hewn personalities, it reflects a degree of the tension between father and son. The words that describe action are equally terse: "The boy nodded. He ate. His father looked around." All told, the writing is a kind of macho vernacular that integrates character and language.

Juxtaposing staccato dialogue against passages of evocative beauty and power, McCarthy uses a stylistic conceit perhaps derived from Faulkner, who often combined ungrammatical utterances with highly literary language. One night in the hills near the hacienda John Grady and Rawlins have the following exchange:

You ain't sorry you come down here are you?
Not yet.
He nodded. Rawlins rose.
You want your fish or you aim to just set there in the rain?
I'll get it.
I got it.
They sat hooded under the slickers. They spoke out of the hoods as if addressing the night.
I know the old man likes you, said Rawlins. But that dont mean he'll set still for you courtin his daughter.
Yeah, I know.
I dont see you holdin no aces.
Yeah.
What I see is you fixin to get us fired and run off the place.

The boys speak in a precisely rendered dialect—the way you'd expect two teenage boys to speak as they stare into the fire. The narration that follows,

however, suggests that the characters are more attuned to their physical surroundings than they are to the nuances of refined speech:

> They watched the fire. The wire that had burned out of the fenceposts
> lay in garbled shapes about the ground and coils of it stood in the fire
> and coils of it pulsed red hot deep in the coals. The horses had come in
> out of the darkness and stood at the edge of the firelight in the falling
> rain dark and sleek with their red eyes burning in the night.

McCarthy often uses visual motifs associated with people sitting around
campfires. Typically, they stare at the flames while sparks sweep up into the
black void. In fact, McCarthy's imagery regularly lifts the readers' gaze to the
sky, to the stars, moon, or blood-red sun. The effect is cinematic and suggests
our primal beginnings and mankind's remote isolation in the vast cosmos.

At times you find hyperpoetic passages embedded into the narrative. Using
a voice pitched at a rhetorical level that some readers have called biblical or
oratorical, the narrator makes pronouncements on the order of what Job heard
from the whirlwind. Here is John Grady in the wake of his breakup with
Alejandra:

> He slept that night in a field far from any town. He built no fire. He lay
> listening to the horse crop the grass at his stakerope and he listened to
> the wind in the emptiness and watched the stars trace the arc of the
> hemisphere and die in the darkness at the edge of the world and as he
> lay there the agony in his heart was like a stake. He imagined the pain
> of the world to be like some formless parasitic being seeking out the
> warmth of human souls wherein to incubate and he thought he knew
> what made one liable to its visitations. What he had not known was that
> it was mindless and so had no way to know the limits of those souls and
> what he feared was that there might be no limits.

Some readers find such passages a distraction. Others say they add to the
novel's emotional impact. Either way, the writing is rich and evocative and
often suggests the author's striving for deeper significance.

McCarthy's high prose style consists of sonorous tones, long rhythmic sentences, repetition of conjunctions, and a demanding vocabulary. McCarthy piles
up details using compound sentences joined by *and,* causing each event in a
series to be equally important, as in:

> There were storms to the south and masses of clouds that moved slowly
> along the horizon with their long dark tendrils trailing in the rain. . . .
> Crossing the plain the next morning they came upon standing water in
> the bajadas and they watered the horses and drank rainwater from
> the rocks and they climbed steadily into the deepening cool of the
> mountains . . . .

This sort of elegaic narrative is used primarily to describe the landscape and
to chronicle events that take place in the wide open spaces of Texas and
Mexico. McCarthy's style shifts, however, when the characters return to civilization. In town, he emphasizes tawdriness—the filth and ugliness of streets
and buildings. Here, for instance, is the town of Los Picos:

A single mud street rutted from the recent rains. A squalid alameda where there stood a rotting brushwood gazebo and a few old iron benches. The trees in the alameda had been freshly whitewashed and the upper trunks were lost in the dark above the light of a few lamps yet burning so that they looked like plaster stagetrees new from the mold.

Such contrasts between country and town may suggest McCarthy's own biases. But it also echoes his hero's experiences. John Grady thrives in the wilderness. The whole purpose of his sojourn in Mexico is to revive the Comanche legacy, when men, like trees and rocks, were inseparable from land. When John Grady returns to civilized places, trouble starts, hopes fade, and thoughts turn dark. It's no accident that Alejandra breaks up with John Grady in the town of Zacatecas. Listen, too, to the malaise in the words of the Los Picos café owner as he stares at the wedding party on the town square: . . . it is "a good thing that God kept the truths of life from the young as they were starting out or else they'd have no heart at all."

Much has been made of McCarthy's extensive use of Spanish. Although use of a foreign tongue may inconvenience some readers, it autheticates the locale and imparts a verisimilitude to the novel. It also gives readers a taste of what the boys are experiencing. Both Rawlins and Blevins remain out of touch with the country. They feel alienated, like strangers in a strange land. Although John Grady comprehends the language, his misadventures reveal that knowing the words is not the same as understanding the culture.

Questions for Writing and Discussion

1. To what extent is the history, culture, and society of Mexico a force in the novel? In which ways does it influence John Grady's actions. In which ways does it determine the behavior of other characters?
2. *All the Pretty Horses* is commonly thought to be a coming-of-age story. That is, John Grady grows up pretty quickly during his time in Mexico. Describe the ways in which he is different when he returns to Texas. In what ways, if any, are his character and personality unchanged?
3. Describe the differences between Mexican and American values as portrayed in the novel. Which events illustrate the differences most vividly?
4. In what ways is John Grady a typical teenager? In what ways is he unusual or larger than life?
5. *All the Pretty Horses* takes place in the middle of the twentieth century. Aside from allusions to World War II and occasional references to technology such as airplanes and radio, are there any reasons it could not have been set during another time—in the nineteenth century, for example, or today, early in the twenty-first century? In other words, does the novel transcend the time and place in which it is set?

6 What You Need to Know About Drama

Analyses of Selected Plays

For the third essay of Section 2 on the exam, you are offered the option of choosing either a novel or a play as your subject.

Reading a Play vs. Reading Fiction

Chances are that a play you write about on the AP exam will be one you have read and studied. Having done so, you will probably know that reading a play is a far different experience from reading a novel. The vast majority of plays are more compact than novels, and unless you stop now and then to reflect on what you've read, can be finished more quickly. Some novelists, particularly those using an omniscient narrator, fill their work with more facts and details than any reader can remember. A novel may contain scores of chapters, hundreds of scenes, numerous narrative passages, page after page of description, and more. Playwrights, on the other hand, work within stricter constraints: a few acts (five in a Shakespearean play; fewer in most modern works), at most, a handful scenes per act, and that's it. Although some playwrights meticulously describe sets, music, costumes, lighting, and the appearance of characters, dialogue is the primary means of communication. Behind the relatively few things a character says and does there is a whole universe to which we are not privy. Good playwrights, however, will give us glimpses of the unknowable. To do so, they must exclude everything that is not essential, leaving the audience of readers (or viewers) to infer what has been left out. As a consequence, whatever a good playwright puts into a drama has a peculiar prominence. Nothing may be taken for granted. In a well-crafted play, that which appears in the text is like the visible part of an iceberg. The bulk of it remains hidden below the surface.

Like readers of fiction, readers of plays draw inferences about the meaning of the work from the words on the page. In effect, the author or playwright speaks directly to the reader. On stage the dynamic is far different. A third party, the actor, functions as a go-between, an interpreter of the writer's words and ideas. Then, too, a character seen through the personality of one actor may be vastly different from the same character rendered by a second actor and still more different from the character you meet on the printed page. What's more, an actor's portrayal may change from one performance to the next, depending on his mood, the interplay of other actors, the personality of the audience, the lighting, and a host of other variables. Add to that the influence of a director and the character we see on stage may be virtually unrecognizable from the person we know only through words we have read.

Although drama differs from fiction in countless ways, for purposes of the AP exam consider it simply as another form of imaginative literature. The special techniques that set a play apart from all other literary forms make little difference as you write your essay. Therefore, many of the comments in the previous chapter that pertain to fiction apply equally to drama.

For example, a play is usually written in a style that creates certain effects and that contributes to the meaning of the work as a whole. In addition, it has a setting, major and minor characters, events that take place within a time frame, a plot, primary and secondary themes, and other elements suitable for you to expound upon in an AP essay.

The remainder of this chapter consists of discussions of three plays often read and studied in AP English classes. The first—*Medea* by Euripides—comes from the theater of ancient Greece; the next, *Hedda Gabler* by Henrik Ibsen, is a nineteenth-century drama; and the third play, *A Streetcar Named Desire* by Tennessee Williams, although more than half a century old, is considered a "contemporary" work.

All three would be suitable subjects for the free-response essay. If you have seen or read any of these plays, you'll have your memory refreshed by brief summaries of characters, themes, style, and so forth. If you don't know the plays, perhaps you'll be inspired to read them in preparation for the AP exam.

Note that these are full-length plays, the sort you are expected to choose for your essay. Be sure to steer clear of short dramatic sketches and brief one-act plays.

Medea by Euripides

Background

First presented in 431 B.C., *Medea* shows the effects of a powerful love gone bad. The title character is a strange, barbaric princess and sorceress, hideously repellent and totally fascinating at the same time. The mother of two young boys, you'll see that she's not your everyday soccer mom.

Before the play opens her husband Jason has done her wrong, and Medea lusts for revenge. As the play unfolds, her passions run shockingly amok. Whether Euripides condones her fury or condemns it remains uncertain. While reading the text or attending a performance of *Medea*, you'll have to make up your own mind, just as audiences have done for the past 2,500 years.

> Use *Medea* as the subject for an essay on how extremes of human passion (love, hatred, vengeance) can overwhelm reason, law, culture, self-esteem, and basic human instincts. An essay on the play might also discuss issues of family loyalty, physical and/or psychological violence, and the eternal conflict between men and women.

Synopsis

If you're familiar with the classic myth of Jason and the Golden Fleece, you may recall that Medea, a barbarian princess and a sorceress, comes from Colchis where her father King Aeetes, son of Helios the sun god, kept an enviable and priceless sheepskin called the Golden Fleece. You may also remember that when Jason, intent on plundering the treasure, descends on Colchis, Medea falls in love with him and after a quick courtship helps him snatch the valued object from her family. In doing so she murders her own brother and chops up the poor fellow before dumping his body parts into the sea. In pursuit of the thief, Aeetes's fleet stops to pick up the pieces, allowing Jason and Medea to escape to Iolchus where Jason's aging uncle, Pelias, cheats him of his rights to the throne. Unwilling to tolerate an affront to her husband, Medea contrives a plan for revenge. She convinces Pelias's daughters to let her rejuvenate their father by using her magic powers. All they need to do is cut him up in pieces and boil them in a pot, which they do, realizing too late that they've been duped. Meanwhile, Medea and Jason, now the parents of two boys, flee to exile in Corinth.

And that brings us to the start of Euripides's play. At the beginning, Medea's nurse stands alone on stage. She briefly reviews the story of the Golden Fleece and brings the audience up to date about the family. Evidently, Medea has sunk into a depression brought on by Jason's disloyalty. On an impulse, Jason has cast Medea aside and married Creusa, the daughter of King Creon of Corinth. In her grief, Medea won't eat. She weeps constantly and loathes the sight of her children. She has vengeance in mind, not only against Jason and his new bride but against Creon. Knowing Medea's bent for violence, the nurse suspects that her mistress, in dealing a blow to Jason, may harm her two young sons and then do away with herself. The nurse's mournful foreboding sets the scene and prepares the audience for what is to come.

The nurse's suspicions are confirmed when Medea enters, cursing her children and their father and exclaiming, "Let the whole house crash!" Wishing to comfort Medea, a group of Corinthian women—called the "chorus"—assemble in front of Medea's house. But Medea won't be consoled. Instead, she utters threats to destroy Jason and Creon as well as herself. Calling women "unfortunate creatures," she catalogs the ills that afflict herself and other members of her sex.

Creon arrives with an edict that banishes Medea and her children from Corinth. Medea may not stay put because she poses too much of a threat to the royal family. Shaken by the decree but still set on revenge, Medea pleads for a one-day reprieve to prepare for the journey. Against his better judgment Creon agrees but vows to execute her if she misses the deadline.

Medea must act fast. Invoking Hecate, mistress of the underworld, she swears to poison Jason, Creusa, and Creon before she leaves. In case fate interferes, she has an alternate plan: she'll simply stab them all to death.

Jason enters and blames Medea for her own banishment. Had she kept still, she might have lived happily ever after in Corinth. Furthermore, she ought to be grateful that Creon chose to banish her rather than kill her for her nonstop griping. In spite of her peevishness, however, Jason will make sure that she and the children don't go into exile penniless.

In response, Medea launches into Jason with accusations of cowardice and ingratitude. Hadn't she helped him steal the Golden Fleece? Hadn't she betrayed her kin and given up her homeland for him? And now because of his treachery she must go into exile alone and friendless.

Jason sees it otherwise. Medea should thank him for rescuing her from barbarism and for introducing her to civil society. Besides, Jason claims, he married the king's daughter to gain access to the royal fortune so that he could provide Medea and the children with a secure and comfortable life in Corinth

Medea doesn't believe a word of it. She berates Jason for acting without discussing his motives beforehand. As for his offer to help, Medea won't take it. She refuses to accept a gift from anyone as base as he. Jason calls her obstinate and says that she'll live to regret it.

Soon, an old friend, Aegeus, the king of Athens, pays a call on Medea. He has stopped in Corinth en route home from the oracle of Pheobus where he had inquired how children might be born to him and his barren wife. Medea tells Aegeus about Jason's infidelity and about her imminent exile. She begs him for refuge in Athens and in exchange offers to mix the drugs that she knows are used to beget children. Aegeus agrees but only if Medea can make her way to Athens on her own. Because of his friendship with Creon, it would be impolitic to take her with him. Medea accepts Aegeus's condition and also exacts his pledge never to cast her out once she has arrived in Athens.

With refuge assured, Medea readies her plans for revenge. After swearing the chorus to secrecy Medea discloses that she will send her children to Creusa bearing gifts—an elegant dress and a golden diadem that contain the power to kill anyone who touches them. Afterward, she will slay the boys and escape to Athens. Don't harm the children, pleads the chorus, but Medea ignores them. She must murder the boys because their death will devastate Jason, who'll suffer and grow old without lover, children, or friends.

The chorus again urges her to change her mind, warning that the beautiful city of Athens will turn her away if she destroys her own children. But Medea won't budge.

She summons Jason and, masking her real intentions, apologizes for her earlier diatribe. To make up, she wishes to send gifts to his bride. Jason expresses pleasure at Medea's contrition and praises her for seeing things his way. Medea also asks Jason to persuade Creon not to banish the children. Jason says he'll try but doubts that he'll succeed.

After presenting the gifts, the boys return with their tutor who tells Medea that the boys' banishment has been lifted. Instead of rejoicing at the news, Medea feels heartbroken, for she must now carry out the next step of her sinister plan. She struggles with her conscience, wavering back and forth, weighing her love for them against her hatred for their father. Meanwhile, the chorus argues to spare the children, but the barbarian part of her nature triumphs.

Suddenly, a messenger arrives, warning Medea to flee. Both Creon and his daughter have perished, just as Medea had hoped. Creusa had donned her new dress and the golden crown, but moments later staggered and fell. White foam escaped from her mouth. Flames engulfed her hair and head. Trying to save her, Creon was attacked by the fire and died in agony.

As far as Medea is concerned, that seals the boys' fate. If she doesn't kill them herself, Creon's followers will slaughter them for their role in the murder of the king and his daughter. She rushes into the house, bars the door behind her, and slays the two lads with a sword. Outside, the appalled chorus shrieks in despair, unable to stop the carnage.

Jason dashes in, concerned for the safety of the children. Told of the boys' fate, he almost collapses with grief and vows to punish Medea. But Medea is beyond his grasp. She and her sons' corpses appear above the house aboard a chariot drawn by winged dragons sent by Helios, her grandfather. Jason, realizing his utter ruin, curses Medea and calls her a "monster, murderess of children." Medea blames Jason for the boys' death. His betrayal set her against them. Medea and Jason exchange charges and countercharges. In the end, she brushes off Jason's request to bury his sons' bodies, telling him to go bury Creusa instead.

(*Note*: The play has no epilogue, but in subsequent stories Medea buries the children in the mountain temple of the goddess Hera and then sets out for Athens. There, according to Euripides's subsequent play *Aegeus*, Medea honors her commitment to help Aegeus beget children. But rather than brewing up a magic potion, she bears them herself.)

Cast of Characters

Medea, Princess of Colchis and Wife of Jason

Medea's family tree contains the name of Helios, the sun god, a blood tie to divinity that may account for her legendary expertise in black magic and sorcery. Among her other qualities is the ability to cause major mayhem. During one infamous episode in Colchis, she slew her brother and helped Jason steal the Golden Fleece from her father. Later, she contrived the dismemberment of Jason's uncle, Pelias, a deed that pales next to the crimes she commits after arriving in Corinth.

One could argue that Medea's troublemaking talent qualifies her as one of the most notorious characters in all of literature, but in spite of her foibles she often evokes a mixed emotional response from audiences. Some see her as a hapless victim of forces beyond her control. She is, after all, a single parent raising two small boys whom she adores. She is a foreigner in Corinth forever cut off from her roots and unaccustomed to local manners and mores. As a princess in Colchis she once wielded power and prestige but now resorts to cunning to make her way in the world. Destitute and alone in a strange place, she is a desperate woman on the brink of suicide.

Medea earns the most compassion, however, for being stuck with a traitorous husband. Jason's treachery, exacerbated by Creon's cruelty, has piled grievous problems onto her. She burns with a fierce but justifiable desire to pay Jason back for jilting her. But before she can exact revenge, she must make several interrelated decisions—where to go into exile, for one, a problem solved with the help of Aegeus. Then she must ponder the best way to dispatch Creon and Creusa. She knows that poison would do the job but chooses her specialty, the famous lethal garment technique. Finally, she must figure out how to inflict maximum damage on Jason without actually taking his life, a problem that leads to the most horrific question of all—whether to kill her children. Tremble though she does at the thought, it is a sacrifice that must be made to punish Jason adequately. That she hesitates, ruminates, and wavers before she actually does the deed saves her from being a cold-blooded murderer. Or does it?

Evidently, Euripides declined to portray Medea as a total monster. The fact is that he gives her qualities that deserve some recognition if not admiration. Medea has brains, exotic beauty, and enough sympathy to have won the devotion and support of a group of Corinthian women, a.k.a. the chorus. As the play proceeds, Medea heroically takes on and overcomes powerful forces that harbor ill will against her. She consistently shows strong resolve and emotional strength under trying circumstances. Think about how she handles Creon, Jason, and Aegeus. Knowing that Creon is pure bluster, she squeezes an extra day in Corinth out of him. She fools Jason completely by feigning repentance. She also persuades Aegeus to provide her asylum. Had Aegeus realized that Medea was scheming to destroy the royal house of Corinth, he might not have promised to take her in, but at that point in the play, Medea deserves more pity than reproof.

The passion that rules Medea makes her both sub- and superhuman. Certainly, she is larger than life. She swears by Hecate, mistress of the underworld, to destroy both Creon and Jason. As daughter of a king and granddaughter of a god, she refuses to be made an object of scorn by men of lesser rank. Her revenge inspires awe and dread. After butchering her boys, remorse, if any, quickly vanishes. In the afterglow of her triumph over Jason, she adopts the attitudes and language of a god. At the end she finds herself perched beyond Jason's reach high above the house in a magic chariot provided by Helios. She has become something beyond mortal, transcending humanity as she escapes in her dragon-drawn rig. She has become a dangerous yet irresistible force of nature—female, barbaric, violent, destructive—a figure who, like a volcano or an earthquake, cannot be judged according to ordinary moral standards.

Jason

As head of the renowned Golden Fleece expedition, Jason ought to rank among the great adventurers of ancient mythology. In *Medea*, however, Euripides's up-close portrait of Jason presents him not as a legendary hero but as a spineless husband and an indifferent father. His putative heroism takes a beating, too, for it appears that his quest for the Golden Fleece would have failed miserably had Medea not kept him out of harm's way and helped him escape from Colchis. Now, years later, Jason has forgotten his indebtedness to Medea and without the slightest pang of conscience has discarded her like a soiled old rag.

Not only is he totally unheroic, he is in most respects a mean-spirited, self-centered, money-grubbing scoundrel. Why Medea had been blind to his true nature is a mystery. Surely she must have recognized that Jason's quest for the Golden Fleece, an escapade no more noble than a poorly planned bank heist, had been driven by greed and avarice. Naïvete, perhaps, kept her from seeing that this suave young warrior hungered more for loot than for love. To her regret, she also learned that Jason welcomed the results of the crimes she committed, but neither accepted culpability nor showed the slightest gratitude for the risks she took for him.

Jason's words and deeds throughout the play reveal his basic infamy. In addition to lusting for wealth, he craves power and will do whatever it takes to get it, including cheat on his wife and then toss her aside to marry Creusa, the king's daughter. When Medea accuses him of betraying her, Jason tries to justify his behavior by asserting that he married Creusa only to provide comfort and security for Medea and the children. In other words, he abandoned his wife and children to give them access to the social and financial benefits that accrue to those with connections to the king. Whether Jason actually believes this whopper remains unclear, but because arrogance is a form of self-delusion, he may well think that he is telling the truth. In any case, he can't understand why his betrayal bothers Medea. She and their children will be better off in the long run.

Medea then reminds Jason that she once saved his life. Curtly he replies that she rescued him only to satisfy her own lust. What's more, he's already returned the favor by wresting her from barbaric Colchis and bringing her here to Corinth, an eminently more civilized, law-abiding place.

Jason's self-serving attitude ultimately backfires. Pleased with himself when Medea apologizes for accusing him of treason, he fails to discern her ruse and becomes putty in her hands. He'll try to get Creusa to talk to her father about exempting the children from banishment. In appreciation, Medea proposes to send Creusa two magnificent gifts—a finely woven dress and a golden diadem. Jason, always aware of the value of things, says they are too fine and costly to give away, but Medea persists. By acquiescing, Jason unwittingly becomes a participant in Medea's deadly scheme. That he fell for her subterfuge suggests just how self-absorbed he has become.

To be fair, however, Jason isn't wrapped up totally in himself. To his credit, he volunteers to provide for Medea and the children in exile. He graciously accepts Medea's apologies and ungrudgingly agrees to help block the children's banishment. Then, after the murder of Creusa and Creon, he shows concern for his sons by rushing to protect them from the wrath of Creon's followers.

That he arrives too late to save them from their mother is not his fault. Their deaths crush Jason, who instantly resolves to punish Medea. But again he's too late. Medea is out of reach, perched in her dragon-drawn chariot. Jason's obvious frustration suggests that he never really stood a chance competing with a wife blessed with godlike powers. Like Medea, he now faces a future bereft of a spouse, of children, and of friends, and he'll be forever possessed by the same kind of hatred and fury that fueled Medea's unquenchable fire.

Creon, King of Corinth

Appearing on stage only briefly, Creon is an autocrat with a human touch. Stern and decisive when banishing Medea, he listens sympathetically to her plea to let her stay in Corinth one more day. Although he distrusts her—rightly so!—and avows that he has made mistakes in the past, he grants her request. Ironically, his act of kindness leads to his and his daughter's death.

Aegeus, King of Athens

Medea claims Aegeus as a friend, but uses him indifferently. She persuades him to grant her asylum but conveniently forgets to tell him of her intention to commit a murder or two on her way out of Corinth. His willingness to take her in serves as a turning point in the play, for once Medea is assured of a safe haven, she feels free to implement her plan for revenge. Aegeus's heartsickness at being childless inspires Medea to render Jason childless, too.

Medea's Nurse

Along with her mistress, the nurse decries and resents Jason's treachery. Highly emotional, she is a doom-and-gloom monger whose laments to heaven and earth are charged with foreboding about Medea and the children. She fears for the boys' safety and questions why they must suffer for their father's crime. As a servant, she grieves for her high-born mistress. Speaking for herself, she'd prefer poverty and peace in old age to the wealth and turmoil of high birth.

Chorus of Corinthian Women

The chorus observes and comments on the action in the play. Made up of women who empathize with Medea and support her plan to seek revenge, the chorus feels that Medea's plight could be their own and that Medea speaks not just for them but for downtrodden women everywhere. When Medea asserts that Jason's death will also mean the death of Creon and his daughter, they raise no objections. On the contrary, they sing an ode exalting Medea for the honor she is about to bring to the female sex. The chorus calls on the goddess Themis to see that justice will be done.

Like loyal co-conspirators, the chorus says nothing when Medea entraps Jason with feigned humility. But the women cannot condone Medea's use of her children to deliver fatal gifts to Creusa. Instead, they weep and wail over the children's fate and cry out against their grisly mission. In response to the messenger's account of Creusa's and Creon's death, however, the women thank heaven for giving Jason the comeuppance he deserves.

When Medea rushes inside to kill her children, the chorus, overcome by the pathos of her murderous rampage, beats on the locked doors of the house, but to no avail.

Dramatic Structure

When Medea first appears onstage she is the image of a wronged woman. Her litany of woes captures the sympathy of both the chorus and the audience, which roots for her to exact the revenge she's entitled to. Support for her erodes, however, as the blood begins to flow. By the final curtain, after Medea's desire for revenge overpowers her maternal instincts, Medea has been demonized beyond redemption. Compassion for her has been supplanted by horror. How this change occurs constitutes the structure of the play.

In the opening sequence, as the nurse explains Medea's background and warns of calamity ahead, the notion of child murder is introduced. The tutor reinforces the sense of foreboding that pervades the play by spreading the rumor that Medea, who is already deep in a funk, shall soon be exiled. Medea enters to face an audience that already knows what she doesn't about her future—a compelling piece of dramatic irony that reverberates at the end of the play when Jason, ignorant of his children's fate, arrives to save the boys from harm.

At first, killing the children is just an evanescent idea, but each event in the play fuels its inevitablilty. Medea curses her children whose innocence reminds her of Jason's perfidy and bolsters her urge to seek revenge. Creon's decision to exile her intensifies the urge even further. When Medea perceives how child-lessness torments Aegeus, she takes still another step closer toward giving Jason a taste of the same torment. (Notice another structural irony here: Aegeus's hope to create children bolsters Medea's plan to destroy hers.)

Medea's conversation with Aegeus is pivotal in still another respect. Having extracted Aegeus's promise to provide a refuge, Medea ignores her lingering doubts for the time being and swings Operation Revenge into action. Her speech following Aegeus's departure is in effect a prologue for the second half of the play. "Now, friends," she announces to the chorus, "has come the time of my triumph over/My enemies. . . Now I am confident they will pay the penalty."

Medea reaches a point of no return after dispatching the children to Creusa carrying lethal gifts. The boys' unwitting complicity in Creusa's murder can mean only one thing—that they are irrevocably doomed. For Medea, an intense struggle within her soul is about to begin. Shall she let Creon's lieutenants kill her children, or does she have the stomach to do it herself?

A desire for revenge that seemed perfectly understandable at the beginning of the play has evolved into something deplorable. But only when she has slain Creusa and Creon does she fully realize the awfulness of her course. Momentarily, she considers spiriting the boys away into exile, but she fears that her enemies will pursue and harm them. In her confusion and wrath, she makes the ungodly decision that ignores good judgment and repudiates every mother's instincts. With a final bloodbath the play reaches its climax, bringing Medea's conflicts—one within herself, the other with her ex-husband—to an end.

Themes and Motifs

The Nature of Revenge

Vengeance arises out of terrible suffering. Behind a sufferer's impulse to seek revenge lies a desire to create identical agony in the person who caused it. To be effective, revenge must be final, complete, and worth the price that the sufferer pays for achieving it.

Is Medea's retaliation against Jason a success? To be sure, her actions prove devastating to Jason and give him a taste of the agony he caused her. Jason is pitiful at the end of the play, a victim of his own infidelity and baseness. What's more, Medea has every right to be pleased that she plotted and carried out a course of revenge in the face of considerable opposition from the nurse, the chorus, and her own conscience. But was the loss of her sons and the spectre of a lifetime of remorse worth it? Although everyone may hold an opinion on the matter, it is a question that only Medea can answer.

The Power of Passion

Medea's highly charged passions come to a head during her monologue after the children have returned from Creusa. It is then that she realizes that the boys' fate has been irrevocably decided. But how they will meet their doom remains a question. Initially, Medea resolves to kill them herself, but beset by second thoughts and undermined by the monstrousness of her design, she wavers.

Reason and passion duke it out within her. As the duel continues, reason sometimes prevails: "You must not do these things," she says to herself. But at other times passion, fueled by her hatred of Jason, cannot be contained.

Some critics claim that, although the adversaries may seem evenly matched, the conflict is a sham. Medea's passion for revenge will inevitably prove the stronger combatant because it is part of her nature. She literally cannot hold herself back from killing her offspring as the most effective means to repay Jason for his perfidy. It's a *fait accompli*, but she goes through the motions of a struggle anyway, in order to justify her decision.

Another view is that the voices Medea hears within come not from two opposing wills but from a simple longing for happiness. Medea's real enemy is a destiny that forces her to perform deeds of superhuman proportion, deeds expected of gods but not of ordinary mortals.

The Place of Women in Society

The enmity between Jason and Medea can be read as the clash between reason and passion, civilization and barbarism, man and nature. But lodged at the core of their antagonism is the age-old tension between men and women.

As a woman, Medea might have expected to marry, rear children, obey her husband, and sacrifice her brains, energy, and other gifts to the greater glory of the male. At first, she willingly plays the part and gives her all to Jason. She saves his life in Colchis, she murders Pelias for him, and even gives up her native land, where she could have reigned as queen

Jason's betrayal changes the ground rules of their relationship, however. Wounded to her marrow, Medea diverts her abundant energies away from helping Jason to inflicting severe damage not only on him but on Creusa and Creon. Feeling intimidated, Creon distrusts her, as he might any other agitator. That his adversary is a woman, though, exacerbates the threat. To Creon, a clever woman is a devil who must be dispatched or expelled. In response to banishment, Medea quickly becomes an even more lethal force, running circles around Creon, Jason, and Aegeus. In short, Medea knows how to defy and outsmart all the oppressive males that stand in her way.

In the end Medea emerges victorious but not unscathed from the conflict. While overpowering Jason and getting the better of both Creon and, to some extent, Aegeus, she suffers the loss of her children. In the process, she also loses her humanity. But her loss is but trifle, considering her larger-than-life, godlike aura.

Although a female protagonist triumphs over the males at the end of the play, Euripides was no feminist. His intent is not to reform society but to dramatize a chain of tragic events that show forces of human nature in violent conflict. Whatever violence exists in men also exists in women. Medea, an enlightened woman, explains:

> "What they [men] say of us is that we have a peaceful time
> Living at home, while they do the fighting in war.
> How wrong they are! I would very much rather stand
> Three times in the front of battle than bear one child."

Her protestations apparently echo the sentiments of other women. The chorus, stirred by Medea's words, recites a great ode that hails the coming of a new and glorious day for the female sex.

Black Magic and Sorcery

Even before the play starts, Medea is an acclaimed sorceress. Her reputation of performing black magic enables her to trick the daughters of Pelias into believing that she can rejuvenate their father. That she fails to do so after they chop him up and put him in a kettle is not a sign of Medea's incompetence but of her mendacity. Aegeus also knows of Medea's proficiency in sorcery and grants her asylum on the strength of her promise to cook up a brew that will enable him to beget children. Medea's ultimate feat of sorcery is a pivotal event in the play. As a gift for Creusa, she fabricates a lethal dress that kills both its recipient and her father.

As though the plot weren't supernatural enough, at the end of the play Medea finds herself perched in a dragon-drawn getaway chariot, literally a god-send from her grandfather, Helios. Without it, Medea would likely fall prey to the wrath of Jason. With it, she escapes unharmed and pours salt in Jason's wounds before liftoff by denying his final request to kiss their dead children good-bye. Some critics liken Medea to a witch riding off on a broomstick. Others regard her as a newly annointed god, doing what gods like to do. A good case can be made for both points of view.

Medea doesn't defeat Jason on her own. Magic helps, but so do the gods. In fact, she never doubts that her calls for help will be answered. She appeals to Themis (ancestral law) and to Artemis (woman's help in childbirth) to witness Jason's unjust action; she invokes the name of Zeus, whom she blames for her plight, and she swears revenge in the name of Hecate, calling her "the mistress I revere above all others, my chosen helpmate." Because all her prayers are answered, the gods must approve her gruesome plan. Near the end, Medea says to the tutor, "The gods and I,/ I in a kind of madness, have contrived all this," suggesting that she is both the gods' instrument and their associate.

Language

Medea dominates and holds the stage virtually throughout the play. She struggles heroically against obstacles, advice, and threats. Her resolve to get revenge is uncompromising. "The deed must be done," she says; "I must dare, I shall kill"; "No other soul can hold so many thoughts of blood." The same ominous words again and again: *kill, die, blood, murder.* The language brooks no uncertainty.

Medea's mind is made up. After Creusa and Creon have met their doom, she says "My task is fixed; as quickly as I may/To kill my children, and start away from this land." No equivocation, no hesitation.

As the time draws near to do the deed, however, Medea's language reflects ambivalence: "Oh, Oh, what can I do? My spirit is gone from me . . . I cannot bear to do it. I renounce my plans/I had before . . . Ah, what is wrong with me?" Finally, of course, Medea's grim heroic resolve triumphs over her deepest maternal feelings, but the fact that she has had doubts may save her from being a complete monster.

Governed by passions such as anger, wrath, daring, rashness, temper, isolation, despair, Medea wears her heart on her sleeve. Jason has "broken my heart," she tells the chorus, adding "I am finished. I let go/All my life's joy." To Creon she says, "Oh, this is the end for me. I am utterly lost." Disclosing her plot to kill Creusa, she utters "I weep to think of what a deed I have to do/Next after that; for I shall kill my own children."

Although Medea states her moods and feelings unambiguously, she also uses language to trick and mislead. She is totally honest only with the chorus. Addressing Creon, Aegeus, and Jason, however, her words often cover up her real motives. Medea's bogus apology to Jason is a model of deception. "Now I give in, and admit that then I was wrong," she tells him in words that sound sincere but contrast with her usual purposefulness. Clueless that Medea's capitulation is part of her plot to kill Creusa, Jason congratulates her on seeing the light.

Earlier in the play, Medea begs Creon for one more day in Corinth in order to consider where to live in exile and to provide for her children. Creon, unaware that Medea is really seeking time for a killing spree, consents. The language in the scene is revealing. Creon comes to Medea's house having made up his mind. Mincing no words, he says, "Medea, I order you to leave my territories." But moments later, softened by Medea's piteous cries, he shows his soft, pliable side: "What you say sounds gentle enough. Still in my heart/I greatly dread that you are plotting some evil." After reconsidering, he comes back full of vigor again: "No. You must go. No need for more/Speeches. The thing is fixed. By no manner of means/Shall you, an enemy of mind, stay in my country." But Medea sees through Creon's swagger and convinces him to let her stay—and this just after he has declared, "Your words are wasted. You will never persuade me."

Questions for Writing and Discussion	1. In spite of Medea's monstrous actions, some observers perceive her as mostly, if not entirely, human. Her grief, her anger, her cleverness in taking revenge upon her enemies, her ploy to get Creon to delay her exile—these and other things attest to her humanity. To what extent do you agree or disagree?

1. In spite of Medea's monstrous actions, some observers perceive her as mostly, if not entirely, human. Her grief, her anger, her cleverness in taking revenge upon her enemies, her ploy to get Creon to delay her exile—these and other things attest to her humanity. To what extent do you agree or disagree?

2. Could Medea have spared her children, or is the matter out of her hands because of her nature and the circumstances of her life?

3. If you have studied *Oedipus Rex* by Sophocles, compare Medea and Oedipus. Are they both tragic heroes? Are their tragic flaws comparable? Is one more ignoble than the other? Are they both driven by fate?

4. As her campaign for revenge nears its end, Medea faces a colossal dilemma—whether or not to kill her children. What are the pros and cons she must consider? In what ways does her final decision contribute to the meaning of the play as a whole?

5. Does Jason warrant any sympathy? Or is he simply an arch-villain who gets what he deserves?

Hedda Gabler by Henrik Ibsen

Background

Hedda Gabler Tesman engages in a private struggle against the stifling conventions of the bourgeois world in which she is trapped. At age twenty-nine, in anguish, she discerns nothing ahead but years of dullness and boredom.

Hedda's problems, however, are not initiated by the forces of an indifferent society. Rather, she is wracked with torment from within. She can't cope with the emptiness of her existence and as a result lashes out against others and finally against herself. In short, the play *Hedda Gabler* is the portrait of a woman's psychological turmoil.

Written in 1890, *Hedda Gabler* broke fresh ground for the playwright Henrik Ibsen. For the first time a female protagonist suffers frustrations that had previously been consigned to Ibsen's male characters. Vivid insights into Hedda's agonized personality constitute the purpose and meaning of the play.

> Use *Hedda Gabbler* as the subject for an essay on the psychological make up of a character who is part victim, part victimizer. Other topics germane to the play include 1) the vagaries of love, 2) a protagonist seemingly devoid of redeeming virtues, 3) the nature of power, and 4) the age-old conflict between individualism and conformity.

Synopsis

The entire play takes place in the home of George and Hedda Tesman located in an unspecified Norwegian city late in the nineteenth century. It is autumn.

Act 1

The opening of the play finds recently wedded George and Hedda Tesman just back from a six-month honeymoon trip. The curtain rises on the interior of an elegant house that George had bought for his bride as a wedding gift. Berte, the housekeeper, is talking to Juliane Tesman, George's aunt, in the drawing room. A former employee of Juliane, Berte is worried about meeting the exacting standards of her new mistress.

Juliane has arrived early to greet her nephew and his wife. When George enters, she inquires about the honeymoon and asks him whether he has any "expectations" to tell her about; that is, she wants to know whether Hedda is pregnant. George misses his aunt's point entirely and instead says that he expects soon to be given a prestigious and lucrative university professorship. He adds that his honeymoon trip had been exceedingly productive. At every stop, he visited libraries in search of material on his specialty, the history of civilization, and he has brought home a suitcase full of notes.

Hedda enters. She is the daughter of the late General Gabler, whose portrait hangs in the room. In spite of numerous suitors, she surprised everyone in her circle by marrying George, a rather dull, pedantic type. But at twenty-nine, Hedda consented be his wife partly because he offered to buy her the high-end villa they now occupy. To sweeten the deal, George also pledged to spare no expense in furnishing the house and provide Hedda a footman, a horse, and the opportunity to lavishly entertain crowds of sophisticated, scintillating guests. Hedda doesn't know it, but Juliane helped her nephew pay for their new residence.

Greeted warmly by Juliane, Hedda is decidedly aloof. She is equally cold to her husband and finds fault with the house, with Berte, with an open window, and even with a new hat that Juliane had left lying on a table. If he is aware of her dissatisfaction, George doesn't show it but tries unsuccessfully to cater to her every wish and whim. After Juliane leaves, he implores Hedda, as a new member of the family, to try harder to be more affectionate to Juliane.

Berte announces the arrival of a surprise visitor. It is Mrs. Thea Elvsted, a long-time acquaintance of the Tesmans. Years ago she had briefly been a sweetheart of George's, and Hedda recalls that Thea, then Miss Rysing, had been a schoolmate of hers. Thea has come to seek the Tesman's help and advice. She doesn't make clear exactly what she wants of them but relates a long, sad story of life with her husband, a sheriff in a remote area far from the city. Originally, she had been a housekeeper and a governess for the Elvsted children. Five years ago, after the first Mrs. Elvsted died, Thea married Mr. Elvsted, a man twenty years her senior and with whom she has nothing in common. To tutor her husband's children, they hired a certain Ejlert Lövborg. Thea goes on to explain that, while working for the Elvsteds, Lövborg lived in the house and spent two years writing a book that deals with the history of civilization, George's very field of expertise. George, in fact, knows Lövborg slightly but doesn't think much of him as a person or as a scholar. The book, however, has been highly praised by the critics and is selling well.

Thea tells George and Hedda that Lövborg is in town and that she is afraid that he may get into trouble. Why he is prone to trouble is not made clear until later, but both the Tesmans understand Lövborg's past difficulties. Thea implores the Tesmans to be kind to him if he should come to call. Hedda asks George to immediately write a letter inviting him to their home that evening.

With George out of the room, Hedda tries to warm up to Thea by nostalgically recalling their days at school. Startled, because as a girl Hedda used to bully and threaten her, Thea explains her attachment to Lövborg, who enlisted her help in writing his book and in the process treated her like a "comrade," had taught her a great deal, and made a thinker out of her. Their relationship might have developed further, but as Thea observes, a "woman's shadow" came between them. That is, Lövborg was still emotionally attached to a woman he knew long ago, someone who had threatened to shoot him with a pistol. Thea suspects that her rival is a certain red-headed cabaret singer, and Hedda, who shows an inexplicable interest in the story, readily concurs. Clearly, Hedda has an ulterior motive in quizzing Thea about Lövborg, but the precise reason remains a mystery.

As Thea takes her leave, the next visitor, Judge Brack, enters. Brack is a distinguished gentleman, once Hedda's suitor and now the Tesmans' personal and business advisor. Among other things, he recently arranged the finances for George to buy the house. Brack tells the Tesmans that Lövborg is in town and that his brilliant new book has made him a minor celebrity. George politely feigns pleasure at Lövborg's achievement but predicts that success will be fleeting, for Lövborg will soon regress to his former ways.

The main purpose of Brack's visit, however, is to advise the Tesmans to spend less money. The lucrative position that George expected has been offered to Lövborg. Dismayed, George tells Hedda that for the time being she'll get no footman, no saddle horse, nor any of the costly luxuries she had been promised.

In disgust, Hedda distracts herself by playing with a collection of firearms left to her by her late father. George begs her to refrain, but she ignores him.

Act II

Brack plans to throw a bachelor party that evening and returns to pick up George. Only Hedda is at home, George having been summoned to Juliane's home where his other aunt, Rina, lies on her deathbed. As Brack enters, Hedda scares him with a pistol shot. Brack seems unperturbed and uses the opportunity to have a no-holds-barred conversation with Hedda about her life and marriage.

Hedda makes clear that she is unhappy and discontent. On her honeymoon, George spent days in libraries, leaving her alone and bored. For nearly six months she talked to almost no one else but her plodding husband. When Brack suggests that she must love her husband, anyway, Hedda denies it, saying that the word "love" revolts her. Hedda's reaction leads Brack to raise the possibility of including a third party in her relationship with George; in other words, he's propositioning her. Hedda, talking hypothetically, says that such an arrangement would be a welcome relief, but she turns him down.

George returns, carrying Lövborg's book. Unable to tear himself away from it, he goes off to continue reading, while Hedda explains to Brack that she married George almost by chance. One day as she and George passed the villa that is now their home, Hedda remarked jokingly that she'd like to live there. George took her words to heart, proposed to marry her and buy the house for her. Although she cared even less for the house than for George, Hedda accepted, and now as its mistress dwells there in misery.

To brighten her marriage, Hedda thinks that George ought to go into politics. Brack is dubious—George can't afford to run for office. Hedda replies that "genteel poverty is what makes life so hideous." She also claims never to have been emotionally stirred. When Brack alludes to a future "responsibility," meaning motherhood, Hedda denies that possibility. I'm not good for anything, she insists, except "boring myself to death."

George returns dressed for Brack's party. Soon Lövborg enters and exchanges polite and cordial greetings with his old acquaintances. He attributes the success of his book to its inoffensive contents and informs the group that he has written a sequel, a work about the future, that is currently in manuscript form. With his new book, he expects to be offered a position at the university, but to George's relief, he won't accept. Lövborg wants only a moral victory, the recognition that he might have had the job if he wanted it.

As George and Brack go off to get a drink, Hedda and Lövborg speak intimately about their past. They had once been lovers. Together, they recall the excitement of their secret relationship, full of passion and frenzy, drinking and madness. Although she adored Lövborg's zest for life, Hedda chose to play it safe in the end. Because of Lövborg's uncertain future and his profligate impulses, she threw him over and threatened to shoot him for pursuing her relentlessly. But too cowardly to keep her word, she failed to follow through.

Now, years later, Hedda is angry not only at herself for turning her back on Lövborg, but at Thea for possessing what she had lacked the courage to keep for herself. At this moment she may not have a mind to destroy the relationship between Thea and Lövborg, but circumstances soon play into her hands.

Thea arrives to spend the evening, happy to be reunited with Lövborg. Unlike Hedda, Thea has had the courage to defy convention and social ignominy by following her heart. To work with Lövborg, she has abandoned her husband. Hedda turns the conversation to the concerns that Thea expressed to her in confidence that morning. Lövborg is shocked by the disclosure that Thea had come to town to keep an eye on him. Insulted by her apparent lack of trust, he suffers a setback. Out of spite he accepts a glass of wine. Then, goaded by Hedda, he decides to go with George to Brack's party, secretly craving to drink himself silly but telling Hedda and Thea that he's going along only in order to read sections of his book to George.

Thea and Hedda wait for Lövborg to return. Hedda urges Thea not to despair, assuring her that Lövborg will come back with renewed confidence and wearing vine leaves in his hair, a symbol of his defiance and free spirit. Asked why she has such faith in Lövborg, Hedda answers cryptically that for once in her life she feels "the power to shape a human destiny."

Act III

Early the next morning, neither George nor Lövborg has returned. George soon appears, however, to tell Hedda the story of the previous evening. Lövborg had read him excerpts of his magnificent book. He had also lauded the woman who inspired him, presumably Thea. After the party, they started walking home accompanied by Brack. Enroute, Lövborg, in a drunken stupor, dropped the parcel containing the manuscript of his book. Lagging behind, George picked it up from the sidewalk and has now brought it home. He plans to return it promptly, but Hedda, sensing an opportunity to shape human destiny, says not to, claiming she'd like to read it first. George insists that it be returned, anticipating that Lövborg would be shattered to discover the loss of the only extant manuscript.

A moment later, George, having read a letter from Juliane delivered to him that morning, rushes off to the deathbed of his other aunt, Rina. As Brack arrives, Hedda hastily hides Lövborg's manuscript in the bookcase. Last night's party, Brack tells Hedda, had turned quite wild, and Lövborg had ended the evening at a brothel run by Mlle Diana, a notorious red-haired singer—apparently the redhead whom Thea suspects as the "other woman" in Lövborg's life. The visit ended badly, however, because Lövborg accused Diana and her friends of stealing the notebook containing his manuscript. Accusations led to a row that brought police to the scene. Lövborg was arrested and charged with disorderly conduct.

Brack, worried that his reputation will be sullied, needs to conceal the fact that Lövborg had been his guest before going to Diana's. He warns Hedda that Lövborg may wish to use her house as a cover for his illicit relationship with Thea. Because Lövborg's presence may be interpreted as evidence of her involvement in a love triangle, Brack urges Hedda to keep her distance. But Hedda sees Brack's ulterior motive. With Lövborg on the premises, Brack would feel obliged to keep his lecherous hands to himself. More or less mockingly Hedda calls Brack a "cock-of-the-walk," meaning the best man, the one who emerges unscathed from the battle. Brack concurs; he is dead serious about protecting himself.

Brack leaves and Lövborg enters looking distraught and confused. Thea comes in, also, to hear Lövborg announce that he no longer has any use for her, that he will no longer do any scholarly work. Thea protests, saying that she must be involved in the publication of the book on which they worked together. There will be no book, he replies, for he has torn it up, an act that Thea, beside herself with grief, likens to killing their child.

After Thea goes off like a bereaved mother, Lövborg explains to Hedda that his life has changed. Hedda is startled that inconsequential Thea, "a pretty little fool," could have influenced a man's destiny. Lövborg then admits that he hadn't destroyed the manuscript. He had spent the night drinking and had lost it at Diana's obscene and loathsome house. Because Thea had virtually given her soul to the book, Lövborg had chosen to lie, thereby saving Thea from the pain of knowing the awful truth. Desperately, Lövborg says he has reached his end and can no longer go on.

Hedda takes Lövborg's story as a cue to intervene—to indeed help shape another person's life, or in this case, another person's death. She urges Lövborg to make it a beautiful end, meaning an honorable death from a self-inflicted bullet into the temple. To help him along, she hands him one of her father's pistols, emphasizing again that he must let his death be beautiful.

Pistol in hand, Lövborg goes out. Hedda then takes the manuscript from its hiding place and throws it piece by piece into the fire.

Act IV

That evening, George learns that Hedda has burned Lövborg's manuscript. He is appalled but also flattered because he thinks Hedda did it for him as an act of love. On an impulse, she almost tells him of her pregnancy but stops halfway through. He guesses what she intended to say, however, and is overjoyed. At the same time, however, George realizes his wife has committed a crime that must be kept a secret.

Thea returns, worried about Lövborg. Brack steps in to deliver the news that Lövborg is dying in the hospital after shooting himself. Hedda, rejoicing at her success, assumes that he had put a bullet into his head. But Brack knows better. Lövborg didn't intend to kill himself but got into a fight and shot himself accidentally.

Thea divulges that Lövborg had destroyed the manuscript. Brack is puzzled because he knows that Lövborg, convinced that the manuscript had been stolen at Diana's, had returned there to claim it. In the ensuing altercation, Lövborg shot himself in the abdomen.

Remorseful about Lövborg's tragic end, George hopes to honor his memory by rewriting Lövborg's book. Thea will help. She still has Lövborg's notes and will inspire George just as she had inspired Lövborg.

Alone with Hedda once again, Brack discloses the real circumstances of Lövborg's death. He knows that it was Hedda's pistol that killed him, and if word of that got around, she'd be scandalized. Aware that Brack has her at his mercy, Hedda throws herself at his feet. He can do with her whatever he wishes, even make her his mistress if he chooses to. Brack vows not to exert his power over her, however.

Hedda realizes once and for all that indeed she has no power over anyone. All her hopes for beauty in life and the world are gone. Defeated, she retreats to the bedroom, plays a wild dance on the piano, and then shoots herself in the temple with the other pistol of the pair.

Cast of Characters

Hedda Gabler Tesman

Hedda stands at the center of the drama, always in the spotlight and portrayed far more vividly than the play's other characters, who function largely as dramatic foils. That is, George and Brack and the others "play against" Hedda, presenting opposing views or contrasting sets of motives that induce Hedda to act in ways that might not otherwise find expression. Hedda responds to the Lövborg-Thea alliance, for instance, by unveiling a neurotic compulsion to destroy. Rather than share Lövborg with Thea or with anyone else for that matter, she crushes him.

At age twenty-nine, Hedda suffers from a persistent malaise. At one time, she had a cadre of suitors to cheer her up, but having danced herself "tired," as she admits to Brack, Hedda settled for George, fully expecting her new husband to provide a glamorous life, complete with a footman, a horse, a grand piano, and an upscale circle of friends. But during a six-month honeymoon trip she grew to despise him, and upon their return, the promise of a grand and beautiful lifestyle proved to be a mirage. The best George can do is try to make her comfortably middle-class—quite a comedown for the daughter of the aristocratic General Gabler and for Hedda a fate akin to a life sentence without parole.

As the wife of a bourgeois academician, Hedda is expected to do little more than tend to domestic affairs, be loyal to her husband, and, if the occasion arose, be a good mother. But Hedda is too intelligent, selfish, and strong-willed to cheerfully accept her assigned lot. At every turn, she vents her frustration and lusts for power over others. Consider, for example, how she ravages her ex-lover, the reformed alcoholic, Lövborg: Although it had been her own timidity that ended their brief affair, she abuses him vengefully. Knowing the fragility of his ego, she discloses that Thea lacks faith in his ability to resist a drink. Aware of his weakness for alcohol, she offers him wine and urges him to attend Brack's bacchanalia. The next morning she hides the hapless man's misplaced manuscript and then in a fit of depravity sets it ablaze. When her victim claims to have lost his will to live, she hands him a loaded pistol and encourages him to make his death an act of beauty.

Hedda treats George almost as wretchedly. Not for nothing is the play called *Hedda Gabler* instead of Hedda Tesman: Hedda is married only in name. She loathes George and forbids him to use the word "we" to describe the two of them. Her repulsion extends even to George's aunt Juliane, whom she treats with utter contempt. Hedda's aversion for the Tesmans leads her to ignore her pregnancy because bearing George's baby binds her irrevocably to him and his detestable family. Rather than celebrate her impending motherhood, Hedda prefers to cling to the illusion that she is still the beautiful daughter of General Gabler. Acknowledging her condition is also tantamount to giving up her individuality and yielding to femininity, which she equates with powerlessness. Indeed, Hedda often grieves that she lacks the power to determine the destiny of another human being, and being pregnant suggests that she has lost control even of her own body. To compensate for the loss, she manipulates others and takes up typically masculine endeavors. She occupies herself with guns, a legacy left to her by her aristocratic father, whose portrait on the wall not only attests to Hedda's affection but inspires her will to power.

Hedda bullies and destroys others not for pleasure but to deprive them of what they have created. She burns Lövborg's manuscript, then orchestrates his demise first by trying to dismantle his relationship with Thea and then by urging him to commit suicide. Her actions deprive Thea of a mentor, an idol, perhaps a lover as well. Ironically, those who survive Hedda's venom live on, guided by ideals of self-sacrifice. George plans to devote himself to reconstructing Lövborg's book; Juliane plans to open her house to an invalid in need of help. Hedda sacrifices herself, too, but for different reasons. She pulls the trigger because she prefers an efficient death to a messy, scandal-ridden life. Besides, she can no longer live with the truth of what she has become.

Her preoccupation with pistols dramatizes the chasm that separates Hedda from the bourgeois world in which she finds herself. Unable to create a life of beauty, she can think of only one way to escape. Indeed, death fascinates her, especially in contrast to her worthless life. She calls suicide "a free and courageous action . . . that shimmers with spontaneous beauty." In other words, it's a glorious way to go. Hoping to die with the kind of honor of which her father would approve, she shoots herself in the head.

Hedda's death usually evokes mixed responses among audiences and readers. Some, convinced that Hedda finally had the gumption to do "one free and courageous action," consider it Hedda's victory. For once, she has escaped from her stultifying bourgeois life and gone out in glory, like the aristocrat she always wanted to be. You may recall that in *Macbeth*, young Malcolm says of the original Thane of Cawdor, "Nothing in his life/Became him like the leaving it." So it is with Hedda.

Hedda's death strikes other observers as a pathetic end to a pathetic life. Although Hedda tries to die beautifully, there is nothing pretty or noble about finishing yourself off with a bullet in the head. Consequently, Hedda's suicide is no less wasteful than her days on earth. She squandered herself, vainly trying to control the fate of others. In response to her failure, she pursued a course of destruction, dragging down everyone she could, including herself. Unlike the demise of a genuinely tragic hero, Hedda's death arouses neither terror nor pity.

George (Jörgen)Tesman

George Tesman blundered when he chose Hedda to be his wife. Completely distracted by his scholarly but pedantic work and research, he naïvely assumes that he and Hedda have a great deal in common, that she will be content as a housewife, and that she will be a loyal and supportive companion. When his university professorship fails to materialize, he blithely predicts that Hedda will easily adapt to a middle-class lifestyle.

None of George's assumptions about Hedda are valid. He has no clue that Hedda is an emotional cripple—not unlike himself—and that she despises him and his family. Oblivious to the reasons Hedda consented to marry him in the first place, George considers himself lucky to have won a trophy wife. He means well and aims to please by providing material pleasures, but he is out of his element when it comes to dealing with Hedda's emotional needs.

In contrast to Lövborg, George is a second-rate scholar, mired in the obscure trivia of "domestic handicrafts in Medieval Brabant." Unable to generate original ideas, he collects a suitcase full of notes from library sources. At the end of the play he pounces on the chance to redo Lövborg's book rather than write one of his own.

Juliane Tesman

George's aunt is a do-gooder devoted to helping others and making people happy. She raised George after his parents died, and unbeknownst to Hedda, helped George pay for his expensive new house. She sends her housekeeper Berte to work for George and Hedda. For many years she has nursed her invalid sister, and after Rina dies plans to take in another invalid in need of help.

As far as Hedda is concerned, however, Juliane is an intrusive pest. Juliane tries to welcome Hedda into the Tesman family but Hedda rebuffs her. Juliane offers to sew things for Hedda's baby, but Hedda won't even admit she's pregnant. It could be argued that Juliane's selflessness springs from a need to control the lives of others, and in that regard she may have more in common with Hedda than meets the eye. But on the surface, her altruism stands out vividly against Hedda's malignity.

Mrs. Thea Elvsted

Thea is a virtual opposite of Hedda. Sensitive, insecure, and frumpy, Thea lacks Hedda's good looks and sophisticated demeanor. Also unlike Hedda, whose cowardice aborted her affair with Lövborg, Thea bravely follows her heart and conscience. She even casts her husband aside to be with Lövborg, despite the opprobrium that's sure to follow.

Thea inadvertently contributes to Lövborg's decline and fall. In order to protect Lövborg from himself, she reigns in his free spirit and stifles his genius. Visiting Hedda, she innocently confides her attachment to Lövborg, a revelation that spurs Hedda's attempt to drive a wedge between them. Hedda can't accept losing her ex-lover to a woman she considers beneath her. Hedda fails at the start because Lövborg, grateful to Thea for all she has done for him, won't turn his back on a woman who idolizes him. To Lövborg, Thea is almost saintly—too noble and pure, in fact, to be told the next day that he lost the precious manuscript in a brothel. His inability to tell her the truth plays directly into Hedda's deviousness and ultimately causes Lövborg's demise.

Regardless of her naïveté, Thea possesses an inner strength that Hedda lacks. After Lövborg dies, she shows surprising resilience, hanging onto life and using the power he instilled in her by assisting George to recreate Lövborg's book.

Eilert Lövborg

Before the play begins, Lövborg has put aside his past profligacy and been reborn. Once a ne'er-do-well who squandered his intellect and talent in drink and debauchery, he now enjoys acclaim as a brilliant author and scholar. A new book, presently in manuscript form, promises him still greater rewards, including the offer of a university professorship. Lövborg plans to reject the offer, however, because holding down an academic job goes against his nature. It's too mundane, too constricting. Freedom is what he craves.

Lövborg owes his recovery from alcoholism to the Elvsteds, particularly to Thea, who engaged him as a tutor, encouraged him to write, and stabilized his life. Yet, he can't forget the excitement of a long-ago romance with Hedda Tesman. Together they had love and a thirst for life that now has faded. Neither Lövborg nor Hedda can extinguish the memory, and when Lövborg sees Hedda again, he can't resist trying to rekindle their former passion. In spite of his respect for Thea, he tells Hedda that his internal fire hasn't been quenched. Hedda reads his desire as a weakness and resolves to exploit it by poisoning his relationship with Thea.

During a dissolute night on the town, Lövborg loses his manuscript. Overcome with remorse, he impulsively rushes off to accuse Diana and her associates of stealing it. In the ensuing struggle he shoots himself in the abdomen—a decidedly inelegant way to go when compared to the beautiful and heroic death that Hedda had in mind for him.

As the prime target of Hedda's malevolence, Lövborg is a weak and pitiable character. He's done nothing to deserve an ignominious fate. If only he been endowed with more self-confidence and a stronger will, he might have resisted an enemy determined to bring him down.

Judge Brack

A representative of society's establishment, Brack is ostensibly an advisor and friend of the Tesmans. But he proves to be an unsavory, calculating manipulator, as ruthless in his world as Hedda is in hers. Hedda recognizes Brack as a soul mate and confides in him about her loveless marriage. Brack uses Hedda's discontent as an opportunity to proposition her. In the abstract, she agrees that having an affair might add zest to a dismal life, but Hedda won't stoop to adultery.

As a judge with a reputation to uphold, Brack is willing risk taking a lover, but as he admits to Hedda, he also fears a scandal. When Lövborg is arrested, Brack backs away, making sure to disassociate himself from the drunken troublemaker. Hedda understands his motives perfectly.

Once Lövborg has shot himself, Brack figures out he used Hedda's pistol. Hedda will do anything—even yield to Brack's lust—to avoid being implicated. Brack vows not to reveal her secret nor to blackmail her, but his predatory nature raises doubts he'll keep his word.

After Hedda shoots herself, Brack says, "Good God—but—people don't do such things!" a remark that both demonstrates his hypocritical concern for propriety and epitomizes his callousness.

Dramatic Structure

Each of the play's four acts adds dimensions to the complex personality of the title character.

Act I is largely exposition, commonly called "retrospective action," a device that enables the dramatist to reveal events that precede present action. Ibsen brings Hedda and George back after a long absence. As they summarize for other characters what they've been up to for six months, the audience is also brought up to date. George talks mostly to his aunt, while Hedda reveals much of her past during a *tête-à-tête* with Brack. Before the act ends, all the characters but Lövborg have appeared on stage, but from both Thea and Brack we have learned about Lövborg and anticipate his arrival.

By the end of Act I Hedda has revealed aspects of her personality as well. To Juliane she has shown contempt, to George disdain, and to Thea, an arrogance disguised as sincerity. In the meantime, she has also outwitted her husband and has scored a victory over Thea by wrenching from her the true story of her relationship with Lövborg. Playing with pistols at the end of the act is an ominous foreshadowing of events to come.

In Act II Hedda has a true story extracted from her. Brack listens intently as she tells about her hopeless marriage. Lövborg's arrival reveals still more about Hedda. At one point she and Lövborg had been lovers, but Hedda, lacking the courage to continue, had ended their affair. Hedda still wields power over Lövborg and induces him to go to Brack's party—this, despite her claim that she is powerless to shape the destiny of another human being.

Act III contains the turning point. George gives Lövborg's manuscript to Hedda, who burns it after sending Lövborg off to do himself in.

Act IV settles tensions between Hedda and the other characters and resolves the conflict within Hedda herself. After Lövborg is killed Hedda finds herself at the mercy of Brack, who knows that it was Hedda's pistol that fired the fatal shot. George and Thea resolve to piece together Lövborg's book and Hedda, seeing the dissolution of her power and influence over others, takes her own life. Before pulling the trigger, she plays a "frenzied dance melody" on the piano, a symbolic representation of her inner turmoil.

Themes and Motifs

Each theme in *Hedda Gabler* warrants a separate discussion, but Hedda, the dominant figure in the play, more or less embodies them all as she evolves from self-indulgent child to bride to dangerous and despairing woman.

Search for Identity

In contrast to Hedda, the other characters in the play coast through life pursuing their goals. Through their work they derive satisfaction, earn recognition, and gain a measure of success. Lövborg, in fact, regards his work as the lifeblood of his existence. The disappearance of his manuscript amounts to a death sentence.

Hedda's struggle for self-realization, on the other hand, is all frustration and rage. It is telling that Berte and Juliane never mention Hedda by name. She is the "General's daughter" or "George's bride," suggesting that Hedda is not an individual in her own right, but merely an appendage. Neither marriage nor motherhood does it for Hedda. She longs for something nobler, but doesn't know what or how to get it.

Initially Hedda hoped to live in the lofty style of her late father, but marriage to George undercuts that possibility. Directionless, she flounders, unable to steer her angst toward any positive goal. Insecurity turns to hardheartedness and an appetite for destroying those who, for better or worse, have created an identity for themselves.

Quest for Power

One source of Hedda's discontent is the accident of her birth as a female. Cursed with a man's impulses, she rejects virtually everything that bourgeois society expects of women—motherhood, domesticity, social grace—which explains in part why she can't abide Juliane, whose outward manner exemplifies the family-oriented, nurturing woman. Behind Juliane's facade may lie an urge to control others, including George, and a need to be depended on, but she hides these selfish impulses under a veneer of good deeds.

Hedda lacks both the subtlety of mind and the spirit to play Juliane's deceptive game. Envious of men, she states outright to Brack that she craves the power to determine the fate of others. Imposing her will on others would be to assert her identity and importance in the world.

Some people use their power to do good. Hedda uses hers to exploit and destroy others. She jumps at the chance to badger George, to abuse Thea, and to lord it over Lövborg. Unable to overcome her sense of impotence, at the end of the play Hedda turns her destructive impulses toward herself. Her use of firearms, typically the domain of men, symbolizes the depth of her frustration and sense of failure. That the pistol once belonged to her father underscores General Gabler's hold on Hedda. Barred from replicating his aristocratic lifestyle, she uses his weapon as a means of escape from her personal prison.

Individualism vs. Conformity

George naïvely expects a wife to be . . . well, wifely. That is, he wants her to conform to the expectations of society. If he has any inkling that Hedda is incapable of conformity, he denies it, or at least he avoids coping with her impudence by escaping into bibliographic research.

In the meantime, society embraces Juliane for her apparent selflessness. It rewards George for following the career path expected of academicians, and it approves of Brack, a figure of authority, who freely flouts society's rules while maintaining an image of respectability.

Lövborg is another story. Ordinarily, society scorns off-the-wall eccentricity, but because Lövborg is a brilliant author, he can get away with it. As for Hedda, she yearns to be her own person and do whatever she wants regardless of the consequences—but at scandal she draws the line. She'd rather commit adultery with Brack than be humiliated by a police investigation into her complicity in Lövborg's death.

Selfishness

Selfishness to some extent taints all the characters in the play. Even Juliane, a model of concern for others, shows signs of doing good primarily to please herself. Her altruism, for instance, keeps George under her thumb, feeling beholden to her for rearing him and lending him money. Her kindness also contributes to the rift between George and Hedda.

George epitomizes self-indulgence. He devotes himself to collecting trivial facts in libraries, then marries Hedda not out of love but because she is a beautiful collector's item, one who would boost his ego and enhance his stature in the community.

Thea, to satisfy her longings, leaves her husband to be with Lövborg, whose behavior also suggests a preoccupation with himself. He applies for a university professorship not because he wants it but to gratify his ego.

Brack—self-confident, ruthless, impressed with his ability to manipulate others—is a virtual egomaniac. His reaction to Lövborg's arrest says it all: Fearing that his good name may be tarnished, Brack refuses to help.

Hedda's selfishness is open to question. One could argue that almost everything she does is motivated by greed and a desire to please herself. On the other hand, she is also a victim of circumstance. Lacking private insight, she appears to use people, but may exploit them more out of naïvete than cold calculation. In that sense, she lacks awareness of her own influence and power and therefore ought not to be branded a mercenary.

Language

The language of the upper class prevails in *Hedda Gabler*. In the original Norwegian, characters speak even more formally than they do in most English translations of the play. Yet, Ibsen intended the dialogue to reflect the everyday speech found in the salons and drawing rooms of the educated, literate, and well-heeled members of nineteenth-century Norwegian society.

To create verisimilitude, no character is given long speeches or monologues. The pace is quick. Characters interrupt each other in mid-sentence. To mimic everyday parlance, Ibsen slips in "hmmm's" and "eh's," the equivalent of today's "uh's" and "ya know's." The characters also stumble and occasionally misspeak. George repeatedly addresses Thea as Mrs. Rysing. Using her maiden name indicates that he knew her long ago, but his slip of the tongue has Freudian overtones. Perhaps George hasn't yet fully recovered from his romantic interest in Thea.

The longest passages in the play are Ibsen's stage directions, often depicting the appearance of characters. Although he proves himself a scoundrel and a hypocrite, Judge Brack is described as "*a man of forty-five. Thick-set but well built and supple in his movements. His face is rounded and his profile aristocratic . . .*" and so on. In every detail he looks like a distinguished jurist. His appearance belies his character, however, which is exactly why Ibsen ironically dresses him in smart clothes and a monocle, which he lets drop from time to time.

Ibsen decorates and furnishes the Tesmans' drawing room in bold, realistic detail: "*dark colors,*" "*folding door,*" "*small sofa.*" He includes everything from "*two étagères with terra-cotta and majolica ornaments*" to the view of "*autumn foliage*" outside the windows. The setting contributes thematic overtones to the play. It represents prevailing middle-class taste, precisely the aesthetic that Hedda deplores. The fall colors presage the arrival of winter. "They're so yellow—so withered," says Hedda, unwittingly foreshadowing her own decline. Behind the drawing room where the action takes place is a small, dark room, perhaps the embodiment of Hedda's subconcious. It's the place to which Hedda retreats to shoot herself.

The entire play is a metaphor for, among other things, a domineering society. The text is crowded with language meant to enrich the dramatic experience for the audience. A few samples:

Diana, the red-haired floozy, alludes to the mythic goddess Diana, the huntress. In this case, Diana's prey is not deer or ducks, but libidinous men.

George's slippers allude to the debt that George owes to Juliane, not just for taking him in and raising him after the death of his parents but the money he owes his aunt for helping to finance his house.

The metaphorical *crown of vine leaves* that Hedda urges Lövborg to wear in his hair refers to a custom of classical antiquity. Heros, rulers, and other godlike figures often wore leafy headpieces to distinguish them from ordinary mortals.

The *wild dance* that Hedda plays on the piano in the final scene reflects the chaos in her mind.

Questions for Writing and Discussion

1. To what extent is *Hedda Gabler* an indictment of stuffy middle-class society and values?

2. Do you consider Hedda's death a triumph or an inevitable defeat, or does it contain elements of both? Does she die as beautifully as she might have hoped, or does she die ignominiously? Please explain.

3. By introducing Hedda's pistols in the first act, Ibsen foreshadows future events. Can you find other examples of foreshadowing as the play unfolds? How important is foreshadowing in *Hedda Gabler*?

4. Critic Theodore Jorgenson comments: "Hedda would have made a marvelous queen . . . . She understood what might bring any man or woman in line with her desires." Do you wholly agree or wholly disagree with this assessment? Or does your view fall somewhere between these two extremes? Please explain.

5. Do you agree that under other circumstances Hedda might have been quite a different person? What if she had been surrounded by beauty, culture, and wealth?

A Streetcar Named Desire
by Tennessee Williams

Background

Produced on Broadway in 1947, *A Streetcar Name Desire* captured the Critics' Circle Award, won the Pulitzer Prize, and vaulted Tennessee Williams into the front rank of twentieth-century American playwrights.

Williams found the stuff of *Streetcar* and his other plays in the agonies of his own life. Places where he had lived became settings, plots were drawn from life's experiences. He barely disguised his parents, his sister, and himself when he cast them as characters on the stage. If you combine Williams's mother, a genteel and prudish southern lady, with his fragile sister Rose, you get Blanche Dubois, the central character in *Streetcar*. Stanley Kowalski, Blanche's nemesis, is a brute like Williams's father. When Stanley clashes with Blanche, the fireworks come straight out of brutal, pitched battles that Williams witnessed at home. Few artists have ever left behind a more personal and intense legacy.

Use A *Streetcar Named Desire* as the subject for an essay on 1) the pangs of loneliness, 2) the triumph of savagery over civility, 3) illusion vs. reality, or 4) various forms of love. In addition, any of the main characters would serve as the subject for a case study of irrational behavior.

Synopsis

May in New Orleans is warm but not yet stifling with summer heat. Flowers bloom, people's voices and the sounds of jazz fill the air. The smells are sweet from cargoes of coffee and bananas in freighters along the river. Even the tawdry quarter of town between the railroad tracks and the waterfront has its charms. There, in a rickety apartment building on a street ironically named Elysian Fields—an allusion to a Club Med sort of place straight out of Greek mythology—is where the Kowalskis make their home.

Stanley comes onstage first, walking with his friend Mitch. He is a hulk of a man carrying a package of bloody meat that he heaves to his wife Stella standing on the first floor landing. Williams wants you to perceive Stanley as a modern caveman, returning to his mate with the kill for the day. Instead of wearing a leopard skin, however, he carries a bowling jacket. Stanley tells Stella that he's on his way to bowl, and she, his faithful mate, follows him to the alley.

Moments later, Blanche Dubois, just arriving in town with her suitcase, hesitantly walks down Elysian Fields to visit her sister, Stella, and brother-in-law, Stanley. She looks and acts out of place. Refinement and good breeding show in all she says and does, at least until her mask is stripped away later in the play. Blanche, a high school English teacher in Laurel, Mississippi, is recovering from a nervous breakdown, and Stella has agreed to put her up for a while. Greeting her sister, Stella explains that the apartment is tiny and that Stanley's rough and undignified manners may take some getting used to.

Soon, Blanche reveals that Belle Rêve, the old family plantation in Laurel, has been lost to creditors. The loss troubles Stanley, who distrusts Blanche and accuses her of having sold the place to buy furs and jewelry. When Blanche denies wrongdoing, Stanley ransacks her belongings looking for a bill of sale. He tears open a packet of letters and poems written by Blanche's husband, who committed suicide years ago. Stella tries unsuccessfully to protect her fragile sister from Stanley's fury.

That night Stella takes Blanche to the movies while Stanley and his cronies play poker and drink. When they return, Blanche is introduced to Mitch, whose courteous manners set him apart from the other men. Blanche flirts with Mitch and has no trouble winning him over. Upset that the poker game has been interrupted, Stanley explodes in a drunken furor. He hurls a radio out the window and strikes Stella. To prevent him from again assaulting his pregnant wife, Stanley's friends drag him into the shower. Meanwhile, Stella and Blanche escape to a neighbor's apartment upstairs.

Dripping wet, Stanley emerges into the street. Like an animal crying for his mate, he calls out for Stella until she comes down and allows herself to be carried off to bed. Later Mitch returns and apologizes to Blanche for Stanley's barbarity. Blanche would like to leave, but she has no other refuge. She invents a story about a rich suitor named Shep Huntleigh who might take her away, and she pleads with Stella to flee with her. Stella, who pledges love for Stanley regardless of his brutality, won't be swayed.

Meanwhile, Mitch, a lonely man seeking a wife, starts to court Blanche. But Stanley has acquired some information about her that would probably destroy the relationship. A trucker who often passes through Laurel has told him that Blanche is an infamous whore. She denies it, of course, but soon after, when she comes on to a young newspaper boy, the rumor gains credibility.

Mitch talks of marriage. Blanche discloses the tragic story of her earlier marriage to Allan, who turned out to be gay. When Blanche rejected him, Allan destroyed himself. Now Blanche can't erase from her memory the image of his bloody corpse or the sound of the fatal gunshot. Profoundly moved, Mitch embraces Blanche.

Stanley has learned more about Blanche's past. She hasn't taken leave from her teaching job, after all, but has been fired for seducing one of her students. What's more, she was kicked out of Laurel for entertaining soldiers from a nearby base night after night.

Stanley tells Mitch. As Stella prepares a birthday party for her sister, Stanley tells her, too. Shocked, Stella implores Stanley to be gentle with Blanche. Before the party begins, Stanley gives Blanche a cruel present, a one-way bus ticket back to Laurel. Stella rebukes Stanley for his heartlessness, but he reminds her that their marriage has liberated her from a life of phony gentility. Suddenly Stella feels labor pains and Stanley rushes her to the hospital.

That evening, Mitch visits Blanche. Highly agitated, he tells her about Stanley's allegations. Admitting that she has been intimate with men in the wake of Allan's death, she pleads for understanding. Her confession arouses Mitch, who wants sex. As he begins to assault her, she resists and shouts "Fire!" out the window.

Late that night Stanley returns to find Blanche dressed in fine traveling clothes. She tells Stanley that Shep Huntleigh has invited her on a cruise and that Mitch has apologized for absenting himself from her birthday party. Stanley calls her a liar and approaches her seductively. She tries to fight him off with a bottle, but too weak to resist, she collapses at his feet. Stanley picks her up, then carries her off to be raped.

Weeks later Stella is packing Blanche's belongings. Blanche thinks she is going to the country, but Stella has arranged for Blanche's commitment to a mental hospital. Stella wonders whether she'd done the right thing. To preserve her marriage, however, she had decided to dismiss the story of the rape as just another of Blanche's fictions. While dressing, Blanche talks of cruises and romantic adventures with Shep. Shortly, Stella leads her sister out to meet the doctor and nurse from the hospital. Blanche balks at the sight of them. The nurse begins to overpower her with a straitjacket, but the doctor intervenes. He talks politely, as though he is the gentleman caller she's been expecting. Calmed by the doctor's gentleness, Blanche says, "I have always depended on the kindness of strangers." Taking the doctor's arm, she walks to the waiting ambulance.

Cast of Characters

The script of *Streetcar* describes the set, the appearance of the characters, the sound and light need to create moods, and so forth, but it doesn't tell you how to view the characters. It is clear, however, that Blanche Dubois stands apart as the play's central figure. No one else ever appears on stage alone. Minor characters like the newspaper boy and the flower peddler are interesting only insofar as they touch Blanche. By the end of the play, audiences know Blanche better than any other character. They probably understand why she acts as she does and appreciate what has happened to her. That doesn't mean they cherish her, but she merits their compassion, for she is a tragic figure who has lost her way in life.

Blanche Dubois

If you ever had an English teacher like Blanche, you'd never forget her. She's one of a kind. Shortly before the play begins, she has lost her job, fired not for incompetence but for being "morally unfit," according to the school superintendent's letter. That's probably a valid assessment of a teacher who seduced one of the seventeen-year-old boys in her class and whose other extracurricular activities so outraged the good people of Laurel, Mississippi, that they threw her out of town.

At first, you don't know these facts about Blanche's past. She seems just a high-strung but refined woman visiting her sister in New Orleans. But as the play unfolds, her past is revealed piece by piece. At the end, she is undone, fit only for the asylum. Nevertheless, you never see her humbled by defeat. She maintains ladylike dignity even after being raped. Perhaps she's not as crazy as she appears.

As an ambiguous character, Blanche arouses compassion and disapproval simultaneously. She is a symbol of a decaying way of life engaged in a losing struggle against modern commercialism. She came to Elysian Fields seeking love and help, but found only hostility and rejection. She has been scarred by her husband's suicide and by the loss of her family's ancestral home. She's too old to depend on good looks to attract men. No wonder she flirts and prefers dimly lit places.

To compensate for loneliness and despair, Blanche creates illusions. She clings to the manners and speech of dying southern gentility. She favors pretense over hard truth. Deception is half of a lady's charm, she says. Unfortunately, though, she is caught in a situation with Stanley Kowalski, who not only abhors her superior airs but is bent on destroying her for them. Why he finds Blanche such a threat is worth thinking about.

Some people consider Blanche not a tragic victim but an immoral woman who deserves what she gets. Blanche tells so many lies that she herself can't remember them all. Some lies may be harmless, but others are destructive. Mitch, for one, is crushed by her untruthfulness.

Because of her past—town whore, liar, sexual deviate—you may agree with critics who say that Blanche is an object of derision, too degenerate to be taken seriously. On the other hand, her past behavior can be explained and maybe even defended. If you appreciate what has happened to her in life, you may understand why she acts as she does.

In the end you may see Blanche as an advocate of civilized values. She alone speaks up for humanity, for achievement in the arts, for progress made by civilization. Perhaps it is odd that uplifting words come from the mouth of an ex-prostitute, but remember that Blanche often confuses truth and illusion. Perhaps Williams is implying that society's most illustrious accomplishments are illusions, too, and that the brutish Stanley more accurately represents our true nature.

Stanley Kowalski

You always know where you stand with Stanley. He speaks plainly, never hides his feelings, and hates affectations of any kind. Yet in some respects he is a mystery. Why is he so intent on destroying Blanche? What makes him so aggressive? What was he like as a young man? How did he get to meet and court Stella? How does a man as animal-like as he succeed in business as a traveling representative of his company? In short, is there more to Stanley than meets the eye?

You can only speculate. But sparse as the evidence is, you know he's a sturdy man of Polish descent who likes to drink, play poker, and bowl. His greatest pleasure is sex. He also has a violent streak. He strikes Stella, hurls a radio out the window, throws dishes, shouts, and in uncontrollable fury, he rapes Blanche. In spite of his brutishness, however, he has surprising appeal. He can make you laugh with his earthy wit. His frankness is refreshing. There's no doubt that he has a charismatic personality. He's always going to extremes, from his adoration of Stella to his self-centered pleasures.

Stanley's efforts to destroy Blanche reveal still other dimensions of his personality. Blanche not only interferes with his sex life, she attempts to lure Stella away from him. So his hatred of Blanche is quick and unrelenting. Perhaps you can respect Stanley for trying to defend his cave by annihilating the intruder. But do you ravage a person merely for getting under your skin and cramping your style? Has Blanche consciously done anything to provoke Stanley's venom? Did she rob him of Belle Rêve as he believes? Maybe Stanley just can't bear the thought of being taken advantage of. If that's the case, he may mean no harm; he merely wants to protect his fragile ego and his way of life.

A further explanation of Stanley's malice toward Blanche may lie in the fact that he is male and she is female. As a virile hunk, Stanley is used to having his way with women, and Blanche won't give him his way. But his discovery that she's been a whore is his ticket to tear away her pretences, rape her, and bring her down to his level once and for all.

Stella Kowalski

Stella grew up with Blanche at Belle Rêve. Then she left for New Orleans, where she met and married Stanley. Had she remained in Mississippi she could well have turned out like Blanche, futilely maintaining appearances and faking her way through life. Perhaps she would still be tied to the shabby gentility of the Old South. But as Stanley likes to say, he "pulled [her] down off them columns" on the plantation.

Gentle, level-headed, and affectionate, she's an unlikely mate for a brutal husband. Sex and bowling are the only interests she shares with him. When he plays poker, she goes to the movies. She accepts his tantrums, abuses, and coarse manners as the price for having him as a husband and sex partner.

She seems to have the patience of a saint. When Blanche insults her, Stella often listens unperturbed, as though she is insensitive. It's puzzling that she rarely fights back, as though she has no grounds for a defense. Or perhaps Blanche's criticism is too close to the painful truth. As Blanche berates her, an unconscious hostility may be growing inside, something that could have begun years ago when the sisters were young. Stella's decision to commit Blanche to an asylum could be her ultimate expression of antagonism toward her older sister.

On the other hand, Stella may send Blanche away for her own good, preferring to believe Blanche is insane rather than facing the truth about Stanley. In effect, Stella chooses to sacrifice her sister to preserve her marriage. Whether Stella knows that Stanley raped Blanche remains uncertain. If she knows and closes her eyes to the fact, however, she is behaving true to form. Stella has learned one useful lesson from her older sister—how to deceive oneself to avoid coping with painful reality.

Mitch

When Blanche meets Mitch, she is desperate to be treated like a lady. Mitch's sense of propriety, in contrast to the other men in Stanley's poker-playing crowd of slobs, makes him stand out like a prince. He's good-hearted and honest and treats Blanche respectfully. Ordinarily, Blanche would have her eye out for a rich and courtly gentleman like the legendary Shep Huntleigh, but she overlooks Mitch's short supply of intellect, wit, and looks because he is courteous and he is a bachelor. He also happens to be lonely and is looking for someone to love.

Mitch is enthralled by Blanche the moment he lays eyes on her. She is clearly more refined, charming, and intelligent than the women he's used to. He also knows that his mother would approve, an important criterion because Mitch is something of a mama's boy. He rarely speaks without mentioning his mother. In his view, Blanche would be a good substitute for his mother. She is domineering. She leads him about like a puppy on a leash. He won't even kiss her without permission.

Mitch is not onstage when Stanley reveals details about Blanche's sordid past, but you might imagine his grief and shock. In an instant, his relationship with Blanche suffers a mortal blow. Later, when Mitch arrives unshaven and dressed in work clothes, he shows a side of him Blanche has never seen. Assertive for the first time, he accuses Blanche of deceit and tears the paper lantern off the light in order to get a good look at her. He remains unmoved by heartbreaking stories about her past. Instead, he declares that he wants Blanche to give him what she's denied him all summer—her body. He advances, intent on raping her, but Blanche scares him off by rushing to the window shouting "Fire! Fire! Fire!"

Eunice and Steve Hubbell

Eunice and her husband Steve live in the apartment above the Kowalskis. Eunice pries into the daily lives of Stella and Stanley, and like a big sister helps

Stella whenever she's distressed. Eunice gives her refuge, for example, when Stanley goes on a rampage. Steve is one of Stanley's poker and drinking cronies, crass and inelegant. He fights with Eunice, throws dishes at her, and later slinks back apologetically.

The sounds that come from the Hubbells' apartment add to the junglelike ambience of Elysian Fields and reveal that fighting and lovemaking are not restricted to the street floor of the building. Eunice's comment to Stella about the rape of Blanche illustrates how Eunice, whose instincts are generally tender, has come to terms with the unspeakable vulgarity around her: "Don't ever believe it. Life has to go on. No matter what happens, you've got to keep on going."

A Young Collector

When the boy comes to collect for the newspaper delivery, he gets paid with a kiss from Blanche. The encounter calls to mind two other boys in her experience: her young husband and the student in her English class whom she seduced.

Nurse and Doctor

Having come to take Blanche to the asylum, the nurse, or matron, is just about to stuff Blanche into a straitjacket when the doctor, recognizing the need for a gentle hand, steps in. Blanche rewards the doctor with thanks.

Dramatic Structure

Instead of acts, *Streetcar* consists of eleven scenes in chronological order between May and September of an unspecified year. In most productions of the play, intermissions occur at natural breaks in the action, as, for example, after Scene 4, in which Stanley has won his first major victory over Blanche. A second break sometimes comes after Scene 6, when Blanche has won Mitch's love. Thus, the first third of the play ends with a defeat for Blanche, the second with a triumph, and the final scenes follow Blanche's decline into permanent defeat.

The structure of the play, then, pulsates like a heartbeat, and is made up of short episodes often containing a conflict and a resolution: Stanley and Stella have a row, then make up; Eunice and Steve fight, then make up. Blanche, as usual, is out of step with the others. She establishes a liason with Mitch, then breaks up. The regularity of the pattern suggests the rhythm of passion, which reaches a climax in the rape scene. It also parallels the up-and-down state of Blanche's emotional and mental health.

The turning point in the play comes when Stanley discovers the truth about Blanche's past. Until then Stanley and Blanche are adversaries competing for space and for Stella's allegiance. After the discovery, as Stanley handily destroys Blanche, it's no longer a contest. Stanley's triumph also puts an end to the blossoming relationship between Blanche and Mitch. Until Mitch learns Blanche's history, he aspires to marry her. Once he knows, he rejects her except as a sex object.

Themes and Motifs

The Triumph of the Apes

In one of her impassioned speeches to Stella, Blanche depicts Stanley as an ape. Indeed, from the first moments in the play when he arrives home lugging a package of bloody meat, he resembles a primate. Dialogue throughout the play alludes to the subhuman quality of life in Elysian Fields. Sometimes the place is described as a jungle. Shrieks and groans pierce the night air. Mitch is depicted as a bear, the women are called "hens." Stanley and Stella emit "low, animal moans."

Only Blanche champions civilization. "Don't hang back with the brutes," she exhorts Stella. Yet, in the end, the brutes destroy her. The values she espouses prove useless in a savage world.

Loneliness

Look at what loneliness has done to Blanche. Bereft after her husband's suicide, she became a prostitute to fill her emptiness. She molested young boys and constructed a web of pretense to delude herself and others that she is a charming, sophisticated woman. She often refers to a gentleman friend, Shep Huntleigh, whose existence, whether imaginary or real, comforts her and keeps her hope alive that she'll someday be rescued from loneliness.

Pangs of loneliness bring Blanche and Mitch together. Blanche would prefer a more debonair man, but rather than remain a lonely spinster, she's willing to compromise. Mitch, too, hopes to find a woman to replace his ailing mother, who will soon die.

Imagining a Beautiful Past

Hardly a character in the play is immune from looking at the past through rose-colored glasses. Blanche's manners and speech suggest that the sort of past she has lodged in her memory is grand and genteel. Her tale of Belle Rêve's decline, however, shatters the image of Old South *noblesse oblige*. Stella, too, fondly recalls the white-columned plantation. Her ties to the place must have been tenuous, however, for she left at an early age. The name *Belle Rêve* (beautiful dream) indicates that both Blanche and Stella believe in an illusion.

Reality vs. Illusion

Symbolically, the conflict between Stanley and Blanche pits reality against illusion. To Stanley reality is what can be touched and seen. Stanley feels right at home among real people, the kind who act natural and say what they think and feel. Stanley believes humans are animals and therefore, should behave accordingly. To put on airs, to deny one's instincts, to hide one's feelings—these are dishonest acts.

In contrast, Blanche rejects reality in favor of illusion. Reality has treated her unkindly. Too much truthfulness destroyed her marriage. Taking refuge in dreams and illusions, she plays a perpetual game of let's pretend. She values what *ought* to be true, not what *is* true.

Stanley can't tolerate idealists like Blanche. What she calls "magic" he calls "lies." Losing her way entirely at the end of the play, Blanche can no longer distinguish illusion from reality, so she goes to an asylum, where such distinctions don't count.

Sexual Violence

Sexual hostilities rage throughout the play. On one side, Blanche is a veteran of considerable sexual give-and-take. She lures the newspaper boy into her arms but thinks the better of it and frees him after one kiss. She wins Mitch's affection but claims "high ideals" to keep him at a distance. When Mitch discovers that he's been fooled, he tries to rape her, but Blanche wards him off like a seasoned warrior.

Only Stanley is unconquerable. He sees through Blanche's sexual pretenses. At the end of his war with Blanche, he rapes her, proving that in sexual combat he is the winner and still champion.

Language

Streetcar, a play about people trapped in frightful conditions, brims with poetry. A poem doesn't require elegant words. In fact, the inelegant denizens of Elysian Fields speak in the blunt, straightforward idiom of common people. Only Blanche's speech soars above the ordinary. Figures of speech gush naturally from her lips. She tells Mitch, for example, how life's joys have been extinguished: "And then the searchlight which had been turned on the world was turned off again and never for one moment since has there been any light that's stronger than this—kitchen—candle . . . ." Why did Tennessee Williams give Blanche the gift of poetic speech? She's an English teacher, to be sure, but her eloquence also widens the gap between her and the other characters, especially the gigantic maw between her and Stanley.

Poetic language, rich with imagery, pervades the play's stage directions. *"The houses [of New Orleans] are mostly white frame, weathered grey, with rickety outside stairs and galleries and quaintly ornamented gables."* To help create the mood of the play, Williams prescribes the sound of a *"tinny piano being played with the infatuated fluency of brown fingers."* To vividly explain characters, Williams calls Stanley a *"gaudy seed bearer"* and a *"richly feathered male bird among hens."* Blanche's uncertain manner, as well as her white clothes, suggest *"a moth."*

Apes, hens, moths—Williams's images make up a menagerie that serve as a constant reminder of the tension between man's civilized impulses and his beastlike instincts. They also highlight the symbolic clash between Stanley and Blanche—that is, the conflict between civilization and primitivism, the collision between the dreamer and the realist.

Even the names of people and places carry symbolic weight. The streetcars, "Desire" and "Cemetery," evoke, among other things, Blanche's need for love and her fear of death. Other names reveal Williams's irony and humor: he assigns the name "Elysian Fields," a paradise in ancient mythology, to a cheerless street in a shabby neighborhood. "Blanche" means white, the color signifying purity. "Stella," the earthy sister, means star. And "Belle Rêve," of course, means "beautiful dream."

Questions for Writing and Discussion

1. In which ways is the conflict between Stanley and Blanche more than mere disagreement between two incompatible people? Does their mutual antipathy have symbolic overtones?
2. How does *Streetcar* compare to a classical Greek tragedy?
3. Regardless of her past, why is Blanche a generally sympathetic figure?
4. Is Williams's portrayal of the world totally pessimistic, or does he leave room for at least a little optimism? Defend your answer.
5. *Streetcar* is a play in which insanity or irrational behavior plays a crucial role. Explain the significance of any character's behavior in terms of the meaning of the entire work.

PART TWO

PRACTICE AP ENGLISH LITERATURE AND COMPOSITION TESTS

Answer Sheet for Practice Test A

Section I

1. Ⓐ Ⓑ Ⓒ Ⓓ Ⓔ	21. Ⓐ Ⓑ Ⓒ Ⓓ Ⓔ	41. Ⓐ Ⓑ Ⓒ Ⓓ Ⓔ
2. Ⓐ Ⓑ Ⓒ Ⓓ Ⓔ	22. Ⓐ Ⓑ Ⓒ Ⓓ Ⓔ	42. Ⓐ Ⓑ Ⓒ Ⓓ Ⓔ
3. Ⓐ Ⓑ Ⓒ Ⓓ Ⓔ	23. Ⓐ Ⓑ Ⓒ Ⓓ Ⓔ	43. Ⓐ Ⓑ Ⓒ Ⓓ Ⓔ
4. Ⓐ Ⓑ Ⓒ Ⓓ Ⓔ	24. Ⓐ Ⓑ Ⓒ Ⓓ Ⓔ	44. Ⓐ Ⓑ Ⓒ Ⓓ Ⓔ
5. Ⓐ Ⓑ Ⓒ Ⓓ Ⓔ	25. Ⓐ Ⓑ Ⓒ Ⓓ Ⓔ	45. Ⓐ Ⓑ Ⓒ Ⓓ Ⓔ
6. Ⓐ Ⓑ Ⓒ Ⓓ Ⓔ	26. Ⓐ Ⓑ Ⓒ Ⓓ Ⓔ	46. Ⓐ Ⓑ Ⓒ Ⓓ Ⓔ
7. Ⓐ Ⓑ Ⓒ Ⓓ Ⓔ	27. Ⓐ Ⓑ Ⓒ Ⓓ Ⓔ	47. Ⓐ Ⓑ Ⓒ Ⓓ Ⓔ
8. Ⓐ Ⓑ Ⓒ Ⓓ Ⓔ	28. Ⓐ Ⓑ Ⓒ Ⓓ Ⓔ	48. Ⓐ Ⓑ Ⓒ Ⓓ Ⓔ
9. Ⓐ Ⓑ Ⓒ Ⓓ Ⓔ	29. Ⓐ Ⓑ Ⓒ Ⓓ Ⓔ	49. Ⓐ Ⓑ Ⓒ Ⓓ Ⓔ
10. Ⓐ Ⓑ Ⓒ Ⓓ Ⓔ	30. Ⓐ Ⓑ Ⓒ Ⓓ Ⓔ	50. Ⓐ Ⓑ Ⓒ Ⓓ Ⓔ
11. Ⓐ Ⓑ Ⓒ Ⓓ Ⓔ	31. Ⓐ Ⓑ Ⓒ Ⓓ Ⓔ	51. Ⓐ Ⓑ Ⓒ Ⓓ Ⓔ
12. Ⓐ Ⓑ Ⓒ Ⓓ Ⓔ	32. Ⓐ Ⓑ Ⓒ Ⓓ Ⓔ	52. Ⓐ Ⓑ Ⓒ Ⓓ Ⓔ
13. Ⓐ Ⓑ Ⓒ Ⓓ Ⓔ	33. Ⓐ Ⓑ Ⓒ Ⓓ Ⓔ	53. Ⓐ Ⓑ Ⓒ Ⓓ Ⓔ
14. Ⓐ Ⓑ Ⓒ Ⓓ Ⓔ	34. Ⓐ Ⓑ Ⓒ Ⓓ Ⓔ	54. Ⓐ Ⓑ Ⓒ Ⓓ Ⓔ
15. Ⓐ Ⓑ Ⓒ Ⓓ Ⓔ	35. Ⓐ Ⓑ Ⓒ Ⓓ Ⓔ	55. Ⓐ Ⓑ Ⓒ Ⓓ Ⓔ
16. Ⓐ Ⓑ Ⓒ Ⓓ Ⓔ	36. Ⓐ Ⓑ Ⓒ Ⓓ Ⓔ	
17. Ⓐ Ⓑ Ⓒ Ⓓ Ⓔ	37. Ⓐ Ⓑ Ⓒ Ⓓ Ⓔ	
18. Ⓐ Ⓑ Ⓒ Ⓓ Ⓔ	38. Ⓐ Ⓑ Ⓒ Ⓓ Ⓔ	
19. Ⓐ Ⓑ Ⓒ Ⓓ Ⓔ	39. Ⓐ Ⓑ Ⓒ Ⓓ Ⓔ	
20. Ⓐ Ⓑ Ⓒ Ⓓ Ⓔ	40. Ⓐ Ⓑ Ⓒ Ⓓ Ⓔ	

A English Literature and Composition

SECTION I

Multiple-choice questions

Time—1 hour

Percent of total grade on the exam: 45 percent

Instructions: This section of the exam consists of 55 questions on the content, form, and style of several literary selections, both prose and poetry. Please record your answers on the answer sheet provided.

<u>Questions 1–15</u>. Read the following passage carefully before you decide on your answers to the questions.

The sun (for he keeps very good hours at this time of the year) had been some time retired to rest when Sophia arose greatly refreshed by her sleep, which, short as it was, nothing but her extreme fatigue could have occasioned; for though she had told her
Line maid and, perhaps herself too that she was perfectly easy when she left Upton, yet
(5) it is certain her mind was a little affected with that malady which is attended with all the restless symptoms of a fever and is, perhaps, the very distemper which physicians mean (if they mean anything) by the fever of the spirits.

Mrs. Fitzpatrick likewise left her bed at the same time and, having summoned her maid, immediately dressed herself. She was really a very pretty woman and, had
(10) she been in any other company but that of Sophia, might have been thought beautiful, but when Mrs. Honour of her own accord attended (for her mistress would not suffer her to be waked) and had equipped our heroine, the charms of Mrs. Fitzpatrick, who had performed the office of the morning star and had preceded greater glories, shared the fate of that star and were totally eclipsed the moment those glories shone
(15) forth.

Perhaps Sophia never looked more beautiful than she did at this instant. We ought not therefore to condemn the maid of the inn for her hyperbole, who when she descended after having lighted a fire declared, and ratified it with an oath, that if ever there was an angel upon the earth, she was now above-stairs.

(20) Sophia had acquainted her cousin with her design to go to London, and Mrs. Fitzpatrick had agreed to accompany her; for the arrival of her husband at Upton had put an end to her design of going to Bath or to her aunt Western. They had therefore no sooner finished their tea than Sophia proposed to set out, the moon then shining extremely bright, and as for the frost, she defied it; nor had she any of those apprehen-
(25) sions which many young ladies would have felt at travelling by night, for she had, as we have before observed, some little degree of natural courage, and this her present sensations, which bordered somewhat on despair, greatly increased. Besides, as she had already travelled twice with safety by the light of the moon, she was the better emboldened to trust it a third time.

(30) The disposition of Mrs. Fitzpatrick was more timorous; for though the greater terrors had conquered the less, and the presence of her husband had driven her away

(35) at so unseasonable an hour from Upton, yet being now arrived at a place where she thought herself safe from his pursuit, these lesser terrors of I know not what operated so strongly that she earnestly entreated her cousin to stay till the next morning and not expose herself to the dangers of travelling by night.

(40) Sophia, who was yielding to an excess, when she could neither laugh nor reason her cousin out of the apprehensions, at last gave way to them. Perhaps, indeed, had she known of her father's arrival in Upton, it might have been more difficult to have persuaded her, for as to Jones, she had, I am afraid, no greater horror at the thoughts of being overtaken by him; nay, to confess the truth, I believe she rather wished than feared it, though I might honestly enough have concealed this wish from the reader, as it was one of those secret, spontaneous emotions of the soul to which the reason is often a stranger.

(45) When our young ladies had determined to remain all that evening in their inn, they were attended by the landlady, who desired to know what their ladyships would be pleased to eat. Such charms were there in the voice, in the manner, and in the affable deportment of Sophia that she ravished the landlady to the highest degree, and that good woman, concluding that she had attended Jenny Cameron,[1] became in a moment a staunch Jacobite and wished heartily well to the Young Pretender's cause

(50) from the great sweetness and affability with which she had been treated by his supposed mistress.

(1749)

1. The opening paragraph suggests that this passage was most probably preceded by
    (A) a sleepless night.
    (B) a dispute with "Jones."
    (C) an upsetting incident.
    (D) a doctor's visit.
    (E) an unidentified illness.

2. The narrator provides the parenthetical remark "if they mean anything" (line 7) most probably as a comment on
    (A) the pretentiousness of doctors.
    (B) Sophia's lack of medical knowledge.
    (C) the seriousness of Sophia's malady.
    (D) physicians' incompetence.
    (E) the arrogance of some physicians.

3. In lines 11–12, "her mistress would not suffer her to be waked" is meant to suggest that
    (A) Mrs. Honour has a short temper.
    (B) Mrs. Honour is devoted to her mistress.
    (C) Sophia has a kindly disposition.
    (D) Sophia lacks respect for her maid.
    (E) Sophia is unusually self-sufficient.

---

[1]The legendary mistress of Scotland's Bonnie Prince Charlie, who led the Jacobite rebellion against England in 1745 and pretended to (i.e., claimed) Great Britain's throne.

4. In line 12, "equipped" might best be interpreted to mean
    (A) prepared.
    (B) supported.
    (C) served.
    (D) provided for.
    (E) dressed.

5. By attributing Sophia's "extreme fatigue" (line 3) to a so-called "fever of
    the spirits" (line 7), the narrator provides the motivation for Sophia's
    (A) desire to get dressed without a maid's help.
    (B) request for a fire in her room.
    (C) desire to make haste to London.
    (D) willingness to yield to Mrs. Fitzpatrick.
    (E) effort to pass herself off as Jenny Cameron.

6. The primary effect of the imagery and figures of speech in lines 9–19 is to
    (A) affirm the luxury and glamor of Sophia's lifestyle.
    (B) emphasize the characters' spirituality.
    (C) suggest the social status of Sophia and Mrs. Fitzpatrick.
    (D) create an impression of Sophia's radiant beauty.
    (E) contrast exterior darkness with interior brightness.

7. In lines 30–31, the reference to "greater" terrors and "less" terrors serves
    chiefly to show that Mrs. Fitzpatrick
    (A) would rather travel in the dark than displease Sophia.
    (B) was paralyzed by a variety of fears.
    (C) feared her husband more than she feared traveling in the dark.
    (D) was torn between going with Sophia and remaining safe at the inn.
    (E) would rather ignore her husband than defy Sophia.

8. The structure of the sentence (lines 30–35) does all of the following
    EXCEPT
    (A) emphasize Mrs. Fitzpatrick's apprehensiveness.
    (B) imply that some of Mrs. Fitzpatrick's behavior is difficult for an
         observer to understand.
    (C) suggest that one mustn't believe all that Mrs. Fitzpatrick says.
    (D) support the narrator's view that Mrs. Fitzpatrick lacks Sophia's self-
         assurance.
    (E) provide evidence of Mrs. Fitzpatrick's indecisiveness.

9. In line 36, "an excess" refers to
    (A) Sophia's determination.
    (B) Sophia's softheartedness.
    (C) Mrs. Fitzpatrick's plea to spend the night at the inn.
    (D) Mrs. Fitzpatrick's unwillingness to travel in the dark.
    (E) Mrs. Fitzpatrick's inexplicable fears.

10. The passage indicates that the speaker believes which of the following to be true of Sophia?

(A) She has deliberately developed charm and affability in order to attract men.

(B) She has a secret affection for Mrs. Fitzpatrick's husband.

(C) She has grown weary of her cousin's company.

(D) She has a mean streak hidden beneath her charm.

(E) She does not know her own mind when it comes to Jones.

11. During their visit to the inn, Sophia and Mrs. Fitzpatrick's state of mind can best be characterized by their

(A) dissatisfaction with their surroundings.

(B) uncertainty about what to do next.

(C) impatience with each other.

(D) preoccupation with feeling safe and secure.

(E) anxiety over offending other travelers.

12. In line 47, "ravished" is best interpreted to mean

(A) transformed.

(B) enthralled.

(C) hypnotized.

(D) impressed.

(E) devastated.

13. The narrator's allusions to Jenny Cameron and the Young Pretender (lines 48–49) serve primarily to

(A) imply the landlady's capacity for self-delusion.

(B) illustrate Sophia's tendency to flaunt her charms.

(C) exaggerate the effects of Sophia's personality.

(D) capture the intensity of Sophia's ambition to raise her social status.

(E) demonstrate that Sophia had recovered from her earlier "distemper" (line 6).

14. The function of the narrator of the passage can best be described as

(A) an omniscient observer.

(B) a participant observer.

(C) an involved spectator.

(D) a disinterested bystander.

(E) a concerned participant.

15. The main concern of the passage is

(A) Sophia's trials and tribulations.

(B) the impression Sophia creates on others.

(C) Sophia's relationship with Mrs. Fitzpatrick.

(D) Sophia's manner and appearance.

(E) the differences between Sophia and Mrs. Fitzpatrick.

Questions 16–26. Read the following poem carefully before you decide on your answers to the questions.

DOVER BEACH

The sea is calm tonight,
The tide is full, the moon lies fair
Upon the straits;—on the French coast the light
Line Gleams and is gone; the cliffs of England stand,
(5) Glimmering and vast, out in the tranquil bay.
Come to the window, sweet is the night-air!
Only, from the long line of spray
Where the sea meets the moon-blanched land,
Listen! you hear the grating roar
(10) Of pebbles which the waves draw back, and fling,
At their return, up the high strand,
Begin, and cease, and then again begin,
With tremulous cadence slow, and bring
The eternal note of sadness in.

(15) Sophocles long ago
Heard it on the Aegean, and it brought
Into his mind the turbid ebb and flow
Of human misery;[1] we
Find also in the sound a thought,
(20) Hearing it by this distant northern sea.

The Sea of Faith
Was once, too, at the full, and round earth's shore
Lay like the folds of a bright girdle furled.
But now I only hear
(25) Its melancholy, long, withdrawing roar,
Retreating, to the breath
Of the night-wind, down the vast edges drear
And naked shingles of the world.

Ah, love, let us be true
(30) To one another! for the world, which seems
To lie before us like a land of dreams,
So various, so beautiful, so new,
Hath really neither joy, nor love, nor light,
Nor certitude, nor peace, nor help for pain;
(35) And we are here as on a darkling[2] plain
Swept with confused alarms of struggle and flight,
Where ignorant armies clash by night.

— Matthew Arnold, c. 1850

[1]An allusion to Sophocles' Antigone
[2]dark, deeply shadowed

16. The poem's mood can best be described as
    (A) rancorous.
    (B) mournful.
    (C) mysterious.
    (D) elegiac.
    (E) caustic.

17. In lines 1–14, all of the following stylistic techniques contribute to the poet's rendering of the sea EXCEPT
    (A) assonance.
    (B) rhythm.
    (C) diction.
    (D) imagery.
    (E) end rhyme.

18. In the poem, the sea is depicted primarily through its
    (A) colors.
    (B) movement.
    (C) sounds.
    (D) smells.
    (E) tides.

19. The allusion to Sophocles (lines 15–20) serves

    I.   To universalize the speaker's experience.
    II. To indicate the timelessness of human suffering.
    III. To compare the ancient world with contemporary England.

    (A) I only
    (B) II only
    (C) I and II only
    (D) II and III only
    (E) I, II, and III

20. In the third stanza, the speaker's analogy compares
    (A) the effects of high tide to the effects of low tide.
    (B) diminishing religious faith to the ebbing tide.
    (C) the sound of the waves to the sound of breathing.
    (D) the wind at night to the rise and fall of the sea.
    (E) the shoreline to a piece of clothing.

21. In line 22, "at the full" is best interpreted as
    (A) completely saturated.
    (B) loud and forceful.
    (C) overflowing.
    (D) at its maximum height.
    (E) abundant.

22. Between lines 28 and 29, there is a shift from
    (A) loathing to jubilation.
    (B) apathy to gusto.
    (C) discontent to satisfaction.
    (D) annoyance to pleasure.
    (E) dejection to solace.

23. The phrase "land of dreams" (line 31) serves primarily to support the notion that
    (A) idealists will inevitably be disappointed.
    (B) hopefulness comes from having strong faith.
    (C) goodness in the world is an illusion.
    (D) optimism serves as a defense against a hostile world.
    (E) love blinds one to reality.

24. What is the subject of the verb "Hath" (line 33)?
    (A) "love" (line 29).
    (B) "world" (line 30).
    (C) "land" (line 31).
    (D) "dreams" (line 31).
    (E) "joy" (line 33).

25. The poem can best be described as
    (A) a villanelle.
    (B) a narrative.
    (C) an ode.
    (D) a prose poem.
    (E) a dramatic monologue.

26. The poem derives its unity mainly from
    (A) a comparison between the past and the present.
    (B) the contrast between the peacefulness of nature and the tumult of battle.
    (C) a description of the sea.
    (D) the symbolism of The Sea of Faith.
    (E) the speaker's disenchantment with the world.

Questions 27–41. Read the following passage carefully before you decide on your answers to the questions.

Animals talk to each other, of course. There can be no question about that; but I suppose there are very few people who can understand them. I never knew but one man who could. I knew he could, however, because he told me so himself. He was a

Line middle-aged, simple-hearted miner who had lived in a lonely corner of California,
(5) among the woods and mountains, a good many years, and had studied the ways of his only neighbors, the beasts and the birds, until he believed he could accurately translate any remark which they made. This was Jim Baker. According to Jim Baker, some animals have only a limited education, and use only very simple words, and scarcely ever a comparison or a flowery figure; whereas, certain other animals have a large
(10) vocabulary, a fine command of language and a ready and fluent delivery; consequently

these latter talk a great deal; they like it; they are conscious of their talent, and they enjoy "showing off." Baker said, that after long and careful observation, he had come to the conclusion that the bluejays were the best talkers he had found among the birds and beasts. Said he:

(15)   "There's more *to* a bluejay than any other creature. He has got more moods, and more different kinds of feelings than other creatures; and, mind you, whatever a blue-jay feels, he can put into language. And no mere commonplace language, either, but rattling, out-and-out book-talk—and bristling with metaphor, too—just bristling! And as for command of language—why *you* never see a bluejay get stuck for a word.

(20)   No man ever did. They just boil out of him! And another thing: I've noticed a good deal, and there's no bird, or cow, or anything that uses as good grammar as a blue-jay. You may say a cat uses good grammar. Well, a cat does—but you let a cat get excited once; you let a cat get to pulling fur with another cat on a shed, nights, and you'll hear grammar that will give you lockjaw. Ignorant people think it's the

(25)   *noise* which fighting cats make that is so aggravating, but it ain't so; it's the sickening grammar they use. Now I've never heard a jay use bad grammar but very seldom; and when they do, they are as ashamed as a human; they shut right down and leave.

   "You may call a jay a bird. Well, so he is, in a measure—because he's got feathers on

(30)   him, and don't belong to no church, perhaps; but otherwise he is just as much a human as you be. And I'll tell you for why. A jay's gifts, and instincts, and feelings, and inter-ests, cover the whole ground. A jay hasn't got any more principle than a Congressman. A jay will lie, a jay will steal, a jay will deceive, a jay will betray; and four times out of five, a jay will go back on his solemnest promise. The sacredness of an obligation is

(35)   a thing which you can't cram into no bluejay's head. Now, on top of all this, there's another thing a jay can outswear any gentleman in the mines. You think a cat can swear. Well, a cat can; but you give a bluejay a subject that calls for his reserve-powers, and where is your cat? Don't talk to *me*—I know too much about this thing. And there's yet another thing; in the one little particular of scolding—just good, clean,

(40)   out-and-out scolding—a bluejay can lay over anything, human or divine. Yes, sir, a jay is everything a man is. A jay can cry, a jay can laugh, a jay can feel shame, a jay can reason and plan and discuss, a jay likes gossip and scandal, a jay has got a sense of humor, a jay knows when he is an ass just as well as you do—maybe better. If a jay ain't human, he better take in his sign, that's all. Now I'm going to tell you a perfectly

(45)   true fact about some bluejays.

   "When I first begun to understand jay language correctly, there was a little incident happened here. Seven years ago, the last man in this region but me moved away. There stands his house—been empty ever since; a log house, with a plank roof—just one big room, and no more; no ceiling—nothing between the rafters and the floor. Well, one

(50)   Sunday morning I was sitting out here in front of my cabin, with my cat, taking the sun, and looking at the blue hills, and listening to the leaves rustling so lonely in the trees, and thinking of the home away yonder in the states, that I hadn't heard from in thirteen years, when a bluejay lit on that house, with an acorn in his mouth, and says, 'Hello, I reckon I've struck something.' When he spoke, the acorn dropped out of his

(55)   mouth and rolled down the roof, of course, but he didn't care; his mind was all on the thing he struck. It was a knot-hole in the roof. He cocked his head to one side, shut one eye and put the other one to the hole, like a possum looking down a jug; then he glanced up with his bright eyes, gave a wink or two with his wings—which signifies gratification, you understand—and says, 'It looks like a hole, it's located like a hole—

(60)   blamed if I don't believe it *is* a hole!'"

(1880)

27. In the first paragraph, the author establishes the predominant tone for the rest of the passage primarily by
    (A) comparing illiterate animals to animals with a good education.
    (B) overstating Jim Baker's qualifications to speak on the subject.
    (C) feigning a serious attitude toward a nonsensical subject.
    (D) making a generalization based on one piece of evidence.
    (E) exaggerating the naïveté of the speaker.

28. The structure of the sentence beginning in line 3 ("He was . . .") does which of the following?

    I. It calls into question the straightforward assertions made in line 1.
    II. It implies the gullibility of the speaker.
    III. It raises doubts about the soundness of the speaker's judgment.

    (A) I only
    (B) II only
    (C) I and II only
    (D) II and III only
    (E) I, II, and III

29. The allusion to "certain other animals" (line 9) is an indirect reference to
    (A) trained animals.
    (B) mythical animals.
    (C) domestic animals.
    (D) human beings.
    (E) purebred animals with pedigrees.

30. Jim Baker's attitude toward cats (lines 23–28) might best be described as
    (A) grim indifference.
    (B) bogus pity.
    (C) avid hostility.
    (D) feigned disdain.
    (E) bitter resentment.

31. The second, third, and fourth paragraphs of the passage differ stylistically from the first paragraph in all of the following ways EXCEPT
    (A) they contain passive sentences.
    (B) they include colloquialisms.
    (C) they address the reader directly.
    (D) they make use of repetition.
    (E) they contain instances of nonstandard usage.

32. The discussion of poor grammar (lines 23–28) includes which of the following grammatical mistakes?
    (A) Faulty parallelism
    (B) Dangling modifier
    (C) Lack of agreement between subject and verb
    (D) Lack of agreement between pronoun and antecedent
    (E) Ambiguous pronoun reference

33. In the context of the passage, the phrase "cover the whole ground" (line 32) is used as a metaphor for
(A)   come in a great many varieties.
(B)   range from the best to the worst.
(C)   match those of any human being.
(D)   tend to remain hidden from human observers.
(E)   are hard to define clearly.

34. The speaker's allusion to "a Congressman" (line 32) is meant primarily to
(A)   imply the speaker's underlying dissatisfaction with all politicians.
(B)   express disapproval of the bluejay's personality and character.
(C)   introduce material intended to disparage members of Congress.
(D)   compare the loquacity of both bluejays and Congressmen.
(E)   emphasize the deceptiveness of bluejays.

35. In context, "and where is your cat?" (line 38) can best be paraphrased to read
(A)   and you'll be dumbfounded.
(B)   and where do you think the cat will go?
(C)   and the cat will hide from shame.
(D)   and a cat will run away.
(E)   and a cat doesn't stand a chance.

36. The use of the phrase "maybe better" (line 43) indicates that the speaker
(A)   holds humans in low regard.
(B)   wishes to tease his listener.
(C)   believes that bluejays are almost as smart as people.
(D)   fears that the listener may doubt his word.
(E)   knows that some bluejays tend to be stupid.

37. The reader can infer that the "perfectly true fact" (lines 44–45) that follows will most likely be about
(A)   the humanlike qualities of bluejays.
(B)   the bluejay's sense of humor.
(C)   a foolish bluejay.
(D)   a bluejay that behaved scandalously.
(E)   a gossipy bluejay.

38. The sentence that begins in line 46 signals a change in the speaker's
(A)   tone from critical to sentimental.
(B)   use of rhetoric from generalizations to specific examples.
(C)   use of language from informal to sedate.
(D)   point of view from dispassionate to personal.
(E)   purpose from persuasive to argumentative.

39. Jim Baker relates the anecdote in lines 46–60 in order to
  (A) further inform his listener about the habits of bluejays.
  (B) impress the listener by demonstrating his comprehension of bluejay language.
  (C) reiterate his assertion that bluejays are virtually human.
  (D) illustrate the bluejay's intelligence.
  (E) provide evidence to support his previous claims regarding bluejays.

40. Jim's description of his life (lines 47–53) has the primary effect of
  (A) suggesting his discontent.
  (B) indicating his perverse way of thinking.
  (C) emphasizing his reclusiveness.
  (D) criticizing his antisocial attitudes.
  (E) reflecting his bizarre behavior.

41. The speaker's overall tone in the passage can best be described as
  (A) whimsical.
  (B) unrefined.
  (C) smug.
  (D) mock heroic.
  (E) discreet.

Questions 42–55. Read the following poem carefully before you decide on your answers to the questions

SNAKE

A snake came to my water-trough
On a hot, hot day, and I in pyjamas for the heat,
To drink there.

Line	In the deep, strange-scented shade of the great dark carob-tree
(5)	I came down the steps with my pitcher
	And must wait, must stand and wait, for there he was at the trough before me.

He reached down from a fissure in the earth-wall in the gloom
And trailed his yellow-brown slackness soft-bellied down, over the edge of
(10) the stone trough
And rested his throat upon the stone bottom,
And where the water had dripped from the tap, in a small clearness,
He sipped with his straight mouth,
Softly drank through his straight gums, into his slack long body,
(15) Silently.

Someone was before me at my water-trough,
And I, like a second comer, waiting.

He lifted his head from his drinking, as cattle do,
And looked at me vaguely, as drinking cattle do,
(20) And flickered his two-forked tongue from his lips, and mused a moment,
And stooped and drank a little more,
Being earth-brown, earth-golden from the burning bowels of the earth
On the day of Sicilian July, with Etna[1] smoking.

The voice of my education said to me
(25) He must be killed,
For in Sicily the black, black snakes are innocent, the gold are venomous.

And voices in me said, If you were a man
You would take a stick and break him now, and finish him off.

But must I confess how I liked him,
(30) How glad I was he had come like a guest in quiet, to drink at my water-trough

And depart peaceful, pacified, and thankless,
Into the burning bowels of this earth?

Was it cowardice, that I dared not kill him?
Was it perversity, that I longed to talk to him?
(35) Was it humility, to feel so honoured?
I felt so honoured.

And yet those voices:
If you were not afraid, you would kill him!

And truly I was afraid, I was most afraid, But even so, honoured still more
(40) That he should seek my hospitality
From out the dark door of the secret earth.

He drank enough
And lifted his head, dreamily, as one who has drunken,
And flickered his tongue like a forked night on the air, so black,
(45) Seeming to lick his lips,
And looked around like a god, unseeing, into the air,
And slowly turned his head,
And slowly, very slowly, as if thrice adream,
Proceeded to draw his slow length curving round
(50) And climb again the broken bank of my wall-face.

And as he put his head into that dreadful hole,
And as he slowly drew up, snake-easing his shoulders, and entered farther,
A sort of horror, a sort of protest against his withdrawing into that horrid black
hole,
(55) Deliberately going into the blackness, and slowly drawing himself after,
Overcame me now his back was turned.

I looked round, I put down my pitcher,
I picked up a clumsy log
And threw it at the water-trough with a clatter.

---

[1]a volcano in Sicily

(60)   I think it did not hit him,
        But suddenly that part of him that was left behind convulsed in undignified
              haste.
        Writhed like lightning, and was gone
        Into the black hole, the earth-lipped fissure in the wall-front,
(65)   At which, in the intense still noon, I stared with fascination.

        And immediately I regretted it.
        I thought how paltry, how vulgar, what a mean act!
        I despised myself and the voices of my accursed human education.

        And I thought of the albatross[2]
(70)   And I wished he would come back, my snake.

        For he seemed to me again like a king,
        Like a king in exile, uncrowned in the underworld,
        Now due to be crowned again.

        And so, I missed my chance with one of the lords
(75)   Of life.
        And I have something to expiate:
        A pettiness.

                                        — *Taormina, 1923*

42. The speaker's experience in the poem is best described as
    (A) an unresolved conflict with Mother Nature.
    (B) an escape from routine that causes remorse.
    (C) an adventure in stalking a wild creature.
    (D) an event leading to self-revelation.
    (E) a spiritual awakening.

43. After finding the snake, the speaker behaves as though he
    (A) has no prior claim on the water-trough.
    (B) lacks the means with which to chase the snake away.
    (C) is accustomed to waiting his turn at the trough.
    (D) takes pride in his composure.
    (E) feels threatened.

44. The speaker provides the detail "and I in my pyjamas" (line 2) most
    probably as
    (A) an indication of the time of day.
    (B) a subtle manifestation of his state of mind.
    (C) an aside that reveals an important dimension of his personality.
    (D) a hint about his less-than-perfect health.
    (E) an omen for something unusual.

---

[2]The Ancient Mariner in Coleridge's poem is forever plagued by the albatross he thoughtlessly killed.

45. Which of the following best describes the prevailing poetic technique used in lines 8–15?
(A) Hyperbole that stresses the snake's malevolence
(B) Personification that endows the snake with a human personality
(C) Imagery that captures the snake's intimidating appearance
(D) Onomatopoetic words that replicate snake sounds
(E) Diction that suggests the snake's slithering movement

46. Lines 18–21 imply that the foremost characteristic of the snake is its
(A) awareness of potential dangers.
(B) indifference to the observer.
(C) similarity to other creatures.
(D) unquenchable thirst.
(E) unpredictable movement.

47. The snake's origins, as described by the speaker, suggest that the snake
(A) represents Satan or some other evil force.
(B) symbolizes the dark side of man.
(C) foreshadows the coming of the apocalypse.
(D) stands for temptation.
(E) indicates the innocence of the speaker.

48. In line 24 and line 68, "education" is best interpreted to mean
(A) the speaker's natural impulses.
(B) a code of ethical behavior.
(C) the things taught in school.
(D) society's beliefs and expectations.
(E) acquired inhibitions.

49. In lines 27–32, the speaker conveys that he
(A) resents competing with the snake for access to the water-trough.
(B) feels torn between his instinct and his education.
(C) both admires and fears the snake.
(D) has doubts about his own masculinity.
(E) regards the snake as welcome distraction from his usual routine.

50. For the speaker, the snake is most like
(A) a stroke of luck.
(B) an unexpected gift.
(C) a bothersome intruder.
(D) an univited guest.
(E) a welcome visitor.

51. The questions that the speaker asks in lines 33–35 serve to

    I. illustrate conflicting feelings clashing inside him.
    II. indirectly reveal his intention to harm the snake.
    III. reveal that he identifies with the snake.

    (A) I only
    (B) II only
    (C) II and III only
    (D) I and III only
    (E) I, II, and III

52. Which of the following adjectives best describes the speaker's action in lines 51–59?
    (A) Instinctive
    (B) Premeditated
    (C) Reckless
    (D) Devious
    (E) Impulsive

53. The allusion to "the albatross" (line 69) most strongly conveys the speaker's
    (A) alienation from nature.
    (B) disenchantment with his education.
    (C) repentance for his action.
    (D) affection for the snake.
    (E) feelings of confusion.

54. The word, "again" in "he seemed to me again like a king" (line 71) refers back to all of the following EXCEPT
    (A) "He lifted his head from his drinking . . ./And looked at me vaguely" (lines 18–19)
    (B) "flickered his two-forked tongue from his lips, and mused a moment" (line 20)
    (C) "Being earth-brown, earth golden" (line 22)
    (D) "honored still more/That he should seek my hospitality" (lines 39–40)
    (E) "And looked around . . . unseeing, into the air" (line 46)

55. At the end of the poem the speaker regards his encounter with the snake as
    (A) a cherished moment.
    (B) a memorable experience.
    (C) an unfulfilled opportunity.
    (D) an unwanted diversion.
    (E) an inspirational event.

SECTION II
Three essay questions
Total time—2 hours
Suggested time for each essay—40 minutes
Percent of total grade on the exam: 55 percent

Instructions: This section of the exam consists of three questions that require responses in essay form. You may write the essays in any order you wish and return to work on a completed essay if time permits. Although it is suggested that you spend roughly 40 minutes on each essay, you may apportion your time as you see fit.

Each essay will be evaluated according to its clarity, effectiveness in dealing with the topics, and the overall quality of your writing. If you have the time, go over each essay, checking its punctuation, spelling, and diction. Unless plenty of time remains, try to avoid major revisions. In the end, the quality of each essay counts more than its quantity.

For Question 3, please choose a novel or play of at least the same literary merit as the works you have been assigned in your AP English course.

Essays should be written in pen, preferably with black or dark blue ink. Use lined paper and write as legibly as you can. Do not skip lines. Cross out any errors you make. Feel free to make notes and plan your essay on a piece of scrap paper. Please number your essays and begin each one on a new sheet of paper. Good luck.

Essay Question 1
(Suggested time—40 minutes. This question counts as one-third of your score for Section II of the exam.)

The setting of the following narrative poem, written by the eighteenth-century British poet Robert Southey, is near the site of the Battle of Blenheim, in Bavaria. Read the poem carefully and then, in a well-organized essay analyze how the speaker conveys his attitude toward the battle and the effects of war on the characters. Take into account tone, word choice, rhyme, meter, imagery, or any other relevant poetic elements.

AFTER BLENHEIM

It was a summer evening,
Old Kaspar's work was done,
And he before his cottage door
(Line)　　Was sitting in the sun;
(5)　　And by him sported on the green
His little grandchild Wilhelmine.

She saw her brother Peterkin
Ross something large and round
Which he beside the rivulet
(10)　　In playing there had found;
He came to ask what he had found
That was so large and smooth and round.

Old Kaspar took it from the boy,
Who stood expectant by;
(15)　　And then the old man shook his head,
And with a natural sigh,
"'Tis some poor fellow's skull," said he,
"Who fell in the great victory."

"I find them in the garden,
(20)　　For there's many here about;
And often, when I go to plough,
The ploughshare turns them out;
For many thousand men," said he,
"Were slain in that great victory."

(25)　　"Now tell us what 'twas all about,"
Young Peterkin he cries;
And little Wilhelmine looks up
With wonder-waiting eyes;
"Now tell us all about the war,
(30)　　And what they fought each other for."

"It was the English," Kaspar cried,
"Who put the French to rout;
But what they fought each other for
I could not well make out.
(35)　　But everybody said," quoth he,
"That 'twas a famous victory.

"My father lived at Blenheim then,
Yon little stream hard by;
They burnt his dwelling to the ground,
(40)　　And he was forced to fly:
So with his wife and child he fled,
Nor had he where to rest his head.

"With fire and sword the country round
Was wasted far and wide,
(45) And many childing mother then
    And newborn baby died;
But things like that, you know, must be
At every famous victory.

"They say it was a shocking sight
(50) After the field was won;
For many thousand bodies here
    Lay rotting in the sun;
But things like that, you know, must be
After a famous victory.

(55) "Great praise the Duke of Marlboro' won,
And our good Prince Eugene,"
"Why 'twas a very wicked thing!"
    Said little Wilhelmine.
"Nay . . . nay . . . my little girl," quoth he,
(60) "It was a famous victory.

"And everybody praised the Duke
Who this great fight did win."
"But what good came of it at last?"
    Quoth little Peterkin.
(65) "Why that I cannot tell," said he,
"But 'twas a famous victory."

(1798)

Essay Question 2

(Suggested time—40 minutes. This question counts as one-third of your score for Section II of the exam.)

The following passage comes from the opening of "New Year's Day" (1924), a short story by Edith Wharton set in upper-class social circles of New York City early in the twentieth century. Read the passage carefully. Then, in a well-organized essay, analyze the literary devices Wharton uses to show that social values and customs of the day had changed since days gone by. You may wish to consider the structure of the excerpt as well as its diction, tone, or any other relevant literary element.

"She was *bad* . . . always. They used to meet at the Fifth Avenue Hotel," said my mother, as if the scene of the offence added to the guilt of the couple whose past she was revealing. Her spectacles slanted on her knitting, she dropped the words in a hiss
Line that might have singed the snowy baby-blanket which engaged her indefatigable
(5) fingers. (It was typical of my mother to be always employed in benevolent actions while she uttered uncharitable words.)
    "They used to meet at the Fifth Avenue Hotel"; how the precision of the phrase characterized my old New York! A generation later, people would have said, in reporting an affair such as Lizzie Hazeldean's with Henry Prest: "They met in

(10)   hotels"—and today who but a few superannuated spinsters, still feeding on the
venom secreted in their youth, would take any interest in the tracing of such
topographies?

Life has become too telegraphic for curiosity to linger on any given point in a sentimental relation; as old Sillerton Jackson, in response to my mother, grumbled through
(15)   his perfect "china set": "Fifth Avenue Hotel? They might meet in the middle of Fifth
Avenue nowadays, for all that anybody cares."

But what a flood of light my mother's tart phrase had suddenly focussed on an
unremarked incident of my boyhood!

The Fifth Avenue Hotel . . . Mrs. Hazeldean and Henry Prest . . . the conjunction
(20)   of these names had arrested her darting talk on a single point of my memory, as a
search-light, suddenly checked in its gyrations, is held motionless while one notes
each of the unnaturally sharp and lustrous images it picks out. At the time I was
a boy of twelve, at home from school for the holidays. My mother's mother,
Grandmamma Parrett, still lived in the house in West Twenty-third Street which
(25)   Grandpapa had built in his pioneering youth, in days when people shuddered at
the perils of living north of Union Square—days that Grandmamma and my parents
looked back to with a joking incredulity as the years passed and the new houses
advanced steadily Park-ward, outstripping the Thirtieth Streets, taking the Reservoir
at a bound, and leaving us in what, in my school-days, was already a dullish
(30)   back-water between Aristocracy to the south and Money to the north.

Even then fashion moved quickly in New York, and my infantile memory barely
reached back to the time when Grandmamma, in lace lappers and creaking *"moire,"*[1]
used to receive on New Year's day, supported by her handsome married daughters.
As for old Sillerton Jackson, who, once a social custom had dropped into disuse,
(35)   always affected never to have observed it, he stoutly maintained that the New Year's
day ceremonial had never been taken seriously except among families of Dutch
descent, and that that was why Mrs. Henry van der Luyden had clung to it, in a reluctant half-apologetic way, long after her friends had closed their doors on the first of
January, and the date had been chosen for those out-of-town parties which are so often
(40)   used as a pretext for absence when the unfashionable are celebrating their rites.

Grandmamma, of course, no longer received. But it would have seemed to her an
exceedingly odd thing to go out of town in winter, especially now that the New York
houses were luxuriously warmed by the new hot-air furnaces, and searchingly illumi-
nated by gas chandeliers. No, thank you—no country winters for the chilblained
(45)   generation of prunella[2] sandals and low-necked sarcenet,[3] the generation brought up
in unwarmed and unlit houses, and shipped off to die in Italy when they proved
unequal to the struggle of living in New York! Therefore Grandmamma, like most of
her contemporaries, remained in town on the first of January, and marked the day by a
family reunion, a kind of supplementary Christmas—though to us juniors the absence
(50)   of presents and plum-pudding made it but a pale and moonlike reflection of the Feast.

---

[1]garments made of stylish, elegant fabric
[2]a silk fabric
[3]a dress made of soft, thin silky fabric

Essay Question 3

(Suggested time—40 minutes. This question counts as one-third of your score for Section II of the exam.)

Many novels and plays focus on individuals involved in a struggle to find themselves or to seek a purpose in life. Sometimes the effort pays off; sometimes it doesn't.

Choose a novel or play of literary merit in which a character (not necessarily the protagonist) engages in a search for meaning or personal identity. In a well-organized essay, explain the search or struggle, assess to what extent it succeeds, and analyze how it contributes to the meaning of the work as a whole. You may use one of the works listed below or choose one of your own. Do not merely summarize the plot.

The Adventures of Augie March
The Adventures of Huckleberry Finn
The Awakening
Death of a Salesman
Dr. Faustus
A Farewell to Arms
Great Expectations
The Great Gatsby
The Glass Menagerie
Hamlet
Heart of Darkness
House of Mirth
Joseph Andrews
The Jungle
Madame Bovary
Main Street
Moby Dick
Oedipus Rex
A Portrait of the Artist as a Young Man
The Red and the Black
Sister Carrie
Tess of the d'Urbervilles

END OF PRACTICE TEST A

Answer Key for Practice Test A—Section I

1.	C	12.	B	23.	C	34.	C	45.	E
2.	A	13.	C	24.	B	35.	E	46.	B
3.	C	14.	C	25.	E	36.	A	47.	A
4.	E	15.	D	26.	E	37.	A	48.	D
5.	C	16.	B	27.	C	38.	B	49.	B
6.	D	17.	A	28.	E	39.	E	50.	E
7.	C	18.	C	29.	D	40.	C	51.	A
8.	C	19.	C	30.	D	41.	A	52.	E
9.	E	20.	B	31.	A	42.	D	53.	C
10.	E	21.	D	32.	D	43.	A	54.	B
11.	B	22.	E	33.	C	44.	B	55.	C

Summary of Answers in Section I Multiple-Choice

Number of correct answers _____

Number of incorrect answers _____

Number of questions not answered _____

Use this information when you calculate your score on this exam. See page 296.

Answer Explanations

SECTION I

1. **C** Sophia's fatigue and fever of the spirit seem to have been occasioned by an untoward—and unspecified—happening in Upton.

2. **A** The narrator evidently has no confidence in physicians, who cover their ignorance with high-sounding words and phrases that mean virtually nothing.

3. **C** By pointing out that Sophia lets Mrs. Honour, her maid, remain asleep, the narrator adds to the list of Sophia's virtues, in this case, her consideration for others.

4. **E** According to the passage, Sophia acquires radiant beauty when Mrs. Honour helps her get dressed.

5. **C** Suffering fatigue, a "fever of the spirits," and feelings "bordering on despair" (lines 26–27), Sophia resolves to set out to London that night.

6. **D** Radiant beauty is conveyed not only by the reference to Sophia's "greater glories" (line 13) but by the maid's description of Sophia as "an angel upon the earth" (line 19).

7. C By fleeing from Upton at an "unseasonable" (line 32) hour, Mrs. Fitzpatrick shows that she fears her husband more than she fears traveling by night.

8. C As described in lines 30–35, Mrs. Fitzpatrick is plagued with various fears that make her seem irresolute and uncertain, particularly in comparison to Sophia. The narrator admits in lines 33–34 that he doesn't grasp the nature of Mrs. F's "lesser terrors." There is no hint in lines 30–35 that she lacks credibility.

9. E The reference is to Mrs. Fitzpatrick's terrors. Sophia, by agreeing to stay the night at the inn, apparently recognizes their existence, although she'd be hard put to explain them.

10. E Although she claims to recoil at the thought of being overtaken by Jones (lines 39–40), the narrator thinks that "she rather wished than feared it" (lines 40–41). The narrator attributes the discrepancy between what she says and what she feels to "those secret, spontaneous emotions of the soul to which the reason is often a stranger" (lines 42–43).

11. B Mrs. Fitzpatrick won't go to Bath after hearing that her husband had arrived in Upton. Sophia hopes to avoid her father, also newly arrived in Upton. She also wishes to stay away from "Jones" (line 39), although the narrator is not so sure (lines 40–41). In brief, the two women alter the itinerary according to their likes and dislikes, their whims and fears.

12. B The landlady is so enchanted by Sophia's sweetness and affability that she decides to become a Jacobite.

13. C The landlady's outlandish fantasy is reported to have been spawned by Sophia's "great sweetness and affability" (line 50).

14. C Evidence of the narrator's viewpoint appears in short asides and comments, such as "I know not what" (line 33) and "I am afraid" (line 39), among others. The narrator's use of "our heroine" (line 12) and "We ought not . . ." (lines 16–17) reveals his concern for the characters. Thus, the narrator is a spectator but is far from an indifferent one.

15. D The narrator pays most attention to Sophia's charm and good looks.

16. B Such phrases as "eternal note of sadness" (line 14), "human misery" (line 18) and "Its melancholy, long, withdrawing roar" (line 25) turn the poem into a lament about the condition of the world.

17. A All except assonance (the repetition of vowel sounds) help to render an impression of the sea.

18. C In line 9, the speaker says, "Listen!" and then cites such sounds as the "roar of pebbles," and the "tremulous cadence" of the sea. Further on, the speaker finds "in the sound a thought" (line 19) and says that "now I only hear/Its melancholy, long, withdrawing roar" (lines 24–25).

19. C Recalling that the Aegean Sea evoked in Sophocles what the straits between England and France evoke in him, the speaker both universalizes the experience and suggests that human misery has existed for a long, long time.

20. B Reflecting on the ebbing of the sea, the speaker is reminded of the decline in religious faith.

21. D The speaker compares the Sea of Faith with the sea observed in lines 1–2. In both the tide is "full," or high.

22. E In the third stanza the speaker is troubled by the diminution of faith in the world. As the next stanza begins, he aspires to use love as a possible antidote for the sadness and indifference that pervade the world.

23. C The phrase describes the appearance of the world as seen from a distance. What follows is a depiction of the world as it really is.

24. B The grammatical subject is "world." Because the other nouns are either in the predicate or in a subordinate clause, they may not serve as the subject.

25. E A villanelle is a tightly structured nineteen-line poem with a prescribed pattern of rhymes. A narrative poem tells a story. An ode comes in various forms but usually glorifies a dignified or lofty subject. A prose poem is a piece of prose written in poetic language. A dramatic monologue consists of the words of a single person speaking to a listener who does not respond in words but may nevertheless influence the speaker.

26. E The poem is dominated by the speaker's melancholy over the state of the world, especially the loss of religious faith. In the final stanza, love may provide solace, but overall, the poem is suffused with references to human misery and sadness.

27. C The author creates humor by taking an absurd premise and dealing with it in a serious, respectful manner. In effect, the author, like many good comedians, keeps a straight face while being funny.

28. E The speaker's informant is a "simple-hearted miner" living alone in the woods who "believed" that he could understand animal talk. To rely on such questionable authority raises doubts about the speaker's judgment. While the sentence beginning in line 3 doesn't disprove the assertion that animals talk, it tends to call it into question.

29. D The narrator of the passage reports what Jim Baker told him. The author, however, who speaks to the reader through the narrator, has human beings in mind, in particular big, puffed-up talkers who try to impress others with their command of language.

30. D Jim adopts a scornful tone while discussing cats but not because he despises them. Rather, he takes a disdainful stance only to prove that, compared to bluejays, cats are grammatical disasters.

31. A The first paragraph contains no colloquial expressions such as "grammar that will give you lockjaw" (line 24). Nor does it speak directly to the reader using second-person pronouns like "you." It contains no repetition like "bristling with metaphor, too—just bristling" (line 18). It also lacks usages that violate conventional English grammar, such as "ain't" (line 25) and "use bad grammar but very seldom" (line 26). Choice (A) is correct because nowhere in the passage does the author use passive sentence structure.

32. D In line 27, the plural pronoun "they" refers to the singular antecedent "jay." While you may find additional grammatical flaws in lines 22–28, none of them appears in the list of choices.

33. C The speaker uses the phrase while trying to prove that a jay is endowed with human qualities, that is, a bluejay "is just as much a human" as the listener.

34. C Just prior to making the allusion, the speaker likens bluejays to humans. Once "a Congressman" is mentioned, however, the speaker begins indirectly to charge members of Congress with lying, stealing, deceiving, and so forth.

35. E The speaker is saying that when it comes to swearing, a cat can't hold a candle to a bluejay.

36. A The phrase is supposed to get a laugh, but behind the humor lurks a misanthropic notion.

37. A Trying to make the case that a jay is everything a man is, Jim is about to cite a "perfectly true fact" to prove his point. All the other choices—(B) to (E)—are too specific to be inferred.

38. B Prior to line 46, Jim Baker's description of the bluejay's talents is full of generalities. After line 46, Jim tells about a specific bluejay in a specific place and time.

39. E While the anecdote doesn't actually prove that Jim comprehends bluejay talk, it tells of a specific time when he claims to have translated what a bluejay said.

40. C The details included in the description—from the empty house to the "leaves rustling so lonely in the trees" (line 51)—stress Jim's hermit-like existence.

41. A The speaker seems to revel in the fanciful notion of animals speaking articulately and following the rules of grammar.

42. D During his encounter with the snake the speaker allows his "education" to prevail over his instincts. Suddenly, he realizes that he has erred and must atone for his "pettiness."

43. A The speaker, surprised to find the snake at the trough, waits patiently while the snake drinks its fill. He acts as though the snake has no less a right to drink there than he does.

44. B Ostensibly, the speaker wears pyjamas "for the heat," but also to imply that he meets the snake with an open mind, "undressed" as it were, or unencumbered by the ordinary contraints of society.

45. E Smooth-sounding phrases such as "yellow-brown slackness soft-bellied down" (line 9) and "slack long body,/Silently" (lines 14–15) recreate the sinuous flow of the snake over the ground.

46. B The snake seems to ignore the observer. It is intent on getting its fill of water.

47. A   According to the speaker, the snake comes from and returns to "the burning bowels of the earth" (lines 22 and 32). It also writhes into the "black hole" (line 64), and seems like the king "of the underworld" (line 72). In that respect, the snake is, or at least stands for, Satan.

48. D   The speaker's mind resounds with the voices of a society that fears snakes and destroys them without compunction.

49. B   The lines portray a man in conflict. One side of him says kill the snake, the other side appreciates the snake's visit.

50. E   In line 30, the speaker says, "How glad I was he had come like a guest."

51. A   Each of the questions sets up an either/or dichotomy, providing evidence of the ambivalence raging inside the speaker. Although he hurls a log at the snake later in the poem and also shows signs of empathy toward the snake, the questions do not relate to either II or III.

52. E   The speaker's action is precipitated by an ill-defined "sort of horror, a sort of protest" (line 53). Without knowing exactly why, he impulsively throws the log at the water-trough.

53. C   In *Rime of the Ancient Mariner*, the title character, after killing an albatross, is burdened by remorse and guilt. Even if you are not familiar with Coleridge's poem, the speaker's regret for attacking the snake is evident in lines 66–68 and also in lines 74–77.

54. B   All the quotations except that in Choice B suggest regal bearing, regal appearance, or an ordinary man's response to a regal presence.

55. C   In lines 74–75, the speaker laments, "I missed my chance with one of the lords/Of life."

SECTION II

Although answers to essay questions will vary greatly, the following descriptions suggest an approach to each question and contain ideas that could be used in a response. Perhaps your essay contains many of the same ideas. If not, don't be alarmed. Your ideas may be at least as valid as those presented below.

Note: Don't mistake these descriptions for complete essays; essays written for the exam should be full-length, well organized, and fully developed. For an overview of how essays are graded, turn to "How Essays Are Scored," on page 35.

Essay Question 1

"After Blenheim" is a narrative poem that describes a conversation between Old Kaspar and his two grandchildren, Peterkin and Wilhelmine. The first stanzas set the scene, introduce the characters, and present circumstances that inspire Kaspar to acquaint the children with the tale of the Battle of Blenheim, fought nearby during his boyhood. Stanzas in the middle of the poem consist of the old man's account of the battle. Kaspar's narration and responses to the children's questions about the purpose of the battle imply the poem's main theme—the mindless brutality of war.

This theme is also evident in the poem's structure and language. Composed of six-line iambic stanzas, each with an *a-b-c-b-d-d* pattern of rhymes, the poem has a consistency emphasized by Kaspar's repeated assertion that England had won a "great" or a "famous" victory at Blenheim. Kaspar's tag line, which appears at the end of seven of the poem's eleven stanzas, suggests that the old man is mouthing a stock response to the events that took place on the battle-field. He has had no thoughts of his own about the battle but merely repeats what "everybody said" (line 35). In fact, he seems inured to the horrors captured by such images as a "thousand bodies . . . rotting in the sun" (lines 51–52), to the fires ravaging the country (line 43), and to the death of "many a childing mother" and their newborn infants (lines 45–46). He remains equally unmoved about his own family's flight from their burning home.

Kaspar's indifference to slaughter and suffering is tempered only by inter-mittent bursts of patriotic fervor in which he praises both the Duke of Marlborough and "good Prince Eugene" (lines 55–56), and mindlessly repeats the same old cliché. Wilhelmine innocently—and wisely—concludes that the battle must have been a "a very wicked thing!" (line 57), but Kaspar sets the lit-tle girl straight: "'Nay . . . nay . . ./It was a famous victory'" (lines 59–60). The boy, "little Peterkin," a name no doubt chosen to reflect the lad's youth and naiveté, wonders "what good came of it at last" (line 63). Stumped by the ques-tion, Kaspar once more resorts to his customary words about the "famous vic-tory" (line 66).

Essay Question 2

To construct the passage, Wharton uses the words of a gentleman recalling his youth, a technique that allows the speaker to compare the past and the present. The narrator's remembrances of things past are triggered by a disapproving comment made by his aging mother about a promiscuous couple who once held trysts at the "Fifth Avenue Hotel," a location that suggests the epitome of high-class extravagance.

Scornfully, the narrator likens his mother's indictment of the couple to that of a snake's "hiss" (line 3), a notion developed later with a simile comparing his "superannuated" mother's remark to secretions of "venom" (line 11). All told, the narrator, who reflects contemporary values, has little stomach for the old-fashioned judgments issuing from his mother. He supports the view of Sillerton Jackson, an old gentleman grumbling through his false teeth—a "perfect 'china set'" (line 15)—that these days nobody cares about such so-called scandalous behavior (lines 15–16).

While rejecting his mother's outdated values, however, the narrator can't arrest the flood of his boyhood memories. Thinking back, he adopts a slightly mocking tone that says, in effect, how straight-laced and rigid his family's life had been. Among other things, he cites the perceived "perils of living north of Union Square" (line 26), implying that the perils were more a threat to one's social standing than to one's physical well-being. He also cites the example of his grandmother, who, attired in clothing that bespoke of her social status, reli-giously followed the now-obsolete custom of receiving visitors on New Year's day. These days, the narrator maintains, fashionable people leave town in the winter.

Essay Question 3

Any of the titles listed after the prompt would be an appropriate work on which to base an essay about a character's search for meaning and fullfullment.

An essay on *The Awakening* by Kate Chopin would most likely focus on Edna Pontellier, a wife and mother who has reached a point in life when she can no longer tolerate her respectable, upper middle-class existence. Nothing pleases her more than doing what she chooses to do when she chooses to do it. Her gradual "awakening" includes letting go of some lifelong inhibitions, briefly taking a lover, falling in love, starting to paint, and leaving her husband. At one point she almost drowns while learning to swim, symbolizing inevitable difficulties encountered during journeys to self-fullfillment. Along the way, Edna realizes that virtually every decision she makes affects others, including her two children. Willing to risk social ostracism for herself, she can't let go of her maternal obligations. Because she refuses to live in misery, she sees death by drowning as her only path of escape. Before diving into the sea, she stands naked on the beach feeling reborn. Although she is about to destroy herself, for once she feels completely free to determine her own fate.

Fate is also the issue in Sophocles' play *Oedipus Rex*. In order to free Thebes of a deadly pestilence, the title character struggles to identify the murderer of Laius, his late father. After the blind seer, Tiresias, names Oedipus himself as the guilty party, Oedipus's efforts turn into a pursuit of self-knowledge As events unfold, Oedipus discovers that he had inadvertently fullfilled an ancient prophesy, not only by killing his own father but marrying his mother. Horrified, Jocasta hangs herself and Oedipus gouges out his eyes and goes into exile. Oedipus's effort to know himself and his origins obviously has tragic consequences. Finding the truth, instead of setting him free, destroys him. Events in the play suggest the inexorable power of fate and the tragic destiny that awaits those who fail to exercise moral self-restraint. Oedipus's downfall results not so much from preordained action, however, as from his uncontrollable pride (hubris), which figuratively and then literally blinds him.

Another work in which a character searches for meaning and fails tragically is *Death of a Salesman* by Arthur Miller. The hero, Willy Loman, devotes his life to building what may be called a typical American Dream: security, a successful career, a loving and happy family. But as hard as he tries, Willy can't make it. Too many social and economic barriers stand in his way. Even more, his own personality and temperament work against him. Unable to face his own shortcomings, he contrives fantasies to stave off the reality of his failures. He tries in vain to create an image of himself as a successful salesman but everyone, his sons included, sees through his posturing. Shattered after being fired from his job, Willy realizes that his life insurance makes him worth more dead than alive. Accordingly, he commits suicide. Willy represents a malaise that infects vast numbers in our society, and *Death of a Salesman* can be viewed as an implicit indictment of capitalism as a way of life.

Self-Scoring Guide for Practice Test A

Scoring Section 2   ESSAYS

After referring to "How Essays Are Scored," on page 35 of this book, use this guide to help you evaluate each essay. Do your best to evaluate your performance in each category by using the criteria spelled out below. Because it is hard to achieve objectivity when assessing your own writing, you may improve the validity of your score by having a trusted and well-informed friend or experienced teacher read and rate your essay.

On the following Rating Chart, enter a number (from 1 to 6) that you think represents your level of performance in each category (A–F).

Category A: OVERALL PURPOSE/MAIN IDEA
  6   extremely well-defined and insightful
  5   clearly defined and generally insightful
  4   mostly clear
  3   somewhat clear but occasionally confusing
  2   generally unclear and confusing
  1   virtually incomprehensible

Category B: HANDLING OF THE PROMPT
  6   self-evident or extremely clear throughout
  5   mostly clear
  4   somewhat clear
  3   somewhat unclear
  2   generally unclear or ambiguous
  1   confusing or nonexistent

Category C: ORGANIZATION AND DEVELOPMENT
  6   insightfully organized; fully developed with excellent supporting evidence
  5   reasonably well organized; developed with appropriate supporting material
  4   appropriately organized; developed with some relevant material
  3   inadequately organized; weak development
  2   poorly organized; little or no development
  1   no discernible organization; no relevant development

Category D: SENTENCE STRUCTURE
  6   varied and engaging
  5   sufficiently varied to create interest
  4   some variety
  3   little variety; minor sentence errors
  2   frequent sentence errors that interfere with meaning
  1   serious sentence errors that obscure meaning

Category E: USE OF LANGUAGE

6   precise and effective word choice
5   competent word choice
4   conventional word choice; mostly correct
3   some errors in diction or idiom
2   frequent errors in diction or idiom
1   meaning obscured by word choice

Category F: GRAMMAR AND USAGE

6   error-free or virtually error-free
5   occasional minor errors
4   basically correct but with several minor errors
3   meaning somewhat obscured by errors
2   meaning frequently obscured by errors
1   meaning blocked by several major errors

RATING CHART

Rate your essay:	Essay 1	Essay 2	Essay 3
Overall Purpose/Main Idea	____	____	____
Handling of the Prompt	____	____	____
Organization and Development	____	____	____
Sentence Structure	____	____	____
Use of Language	____	____	____
Grammar and Usage	____	____	____
Composite Scores (Sum of each column)	____	____	____

By using the following chart, in which composite scores are converted to the 9-point AP rating scale, you may determine the final score for each essay:

Composite Score	AP Essay Score
33–36	9
29–32	8
25–28	7
21–24	6
18–20	5
15–17	4
10–14	3
7–9	2
6 or below	1

AP Essay Scores   Essay 1 _____   Essay 2 _____   Essay 3 _____

Calculating Your AP Score on Practice Test A

The scores you have earned on the multiple-choice and essay sections of the exam may now be converted to the AP 5-point scale by doing the following calculations:

I.   Determine your score for Section I (Multiple-Choice)
Step A: Number of correct answers _____
Step B: Number of wrong answers _____ (Note: Do not count unanswered questions.)
Step C: Multiply the number of wrong answers by .250 and enter the figure here _____
Step D: Subtract the figure in Step C from the figure in Step A _____
Step E: Multiply the figure in Step D by 1.2500 to find your Multiple-Choice Score _____ (if less than zero, enter zero)

II. Determine your score for Section II (Essays)[1]
Step A: Enter your score for Essay 1 (out of 9) _____
Step B: Enter your score for Essay 2 (out of 9) _____
Step C: Enter your score for Essay 3 (out of 9) _____
Step D: Add the figures in Steps A, B, and C _____
Step E: Multiply the figure in Step D by 3.0556 _____ (Do not round). This is your Essay Score.

III. Determine Your Total Score
Add the scores for I and II to find your composite score _____ .

To convert your composite score to the AP 5-point scale, use the chart below. The range of scores only approximates what you would earn on the actual test because the exact figures may vary from test to test. Be aware, therefore, that your score on this test, as well as on other tests in this book, may differ slightly from your score on an actual AP exam.

Composite Score	AP Grade
108–150	5
93–107	4
72–92	3
43–71	2
0–42	1

---

[1]After the AP exam, essays are judged in relation to other essays written on the same topic at the same time. Therefore, the score you assign yourself for an essay may not be the same as the score you would earn on an actual exam.

Answer Sheet for Practice Test B

Section I

1. Ⓐ Ⓑ Ⓒ Ⓓ Ⓔ
2. Ⓐ Ⓑ Ⓒ Ⓓ Ⓔ
3. Ⓐ Ⓑ Ⓒ Ⓓ Ⓔ
4. Ⓐ Ⓑ Ⓒ Ⓓ Ⓔ
5. Ⓐ Ⓑ Ⓒ Ⓓ Ⓔ
6. Ⓐ Ⓑ Ⓒ Ⓓ Ⓔ
7. Ⓐ Ⓑ Ⓒ Ⓓ Ⓔ
8. Ⓐ Ⓑ Ⓒ Ⓓ Ⓔ
9. Ⓐ Ⓑ Ⓒ Ⓓ Ⓔ
10. Ⓐ Ⓑ Ⓒ Ⓓ Ⓔ
11. Ⓐ Ⓑ Ⓒ Ⓓ Ⓔ
12. Ⓐ Ⓑ Ⓒ Ⓓ Ⓔ
13. Ⓐ Ⓑ Ⓒ Ⓓ Ⓔ
14. Ⓐ Ⓑ Ⓒ Ⓓ Ⓔ
15. Ⓐ Ⓑ Ⓒ Ⓓ Ⓔ
16. Ⓐ Ⓑ Ⓒ Ⓓ Ⓔ
17. Ⓐ Ⓑ Ⓒ Ⓓ Ⓔ
18. Ⓐ Ⓑ Ⓒ Ⓓ Ⓔ
19. Ⓐ Ⓑ Ⓒ Ⓓ Ⓔ
20. Ⓐ Ⓑ Ⓒ Ⓓ Ⓔ

21. Ⓐ Ⓑ Ⓒ Ⓓ Ⓔ
22. Ⓐ Ⓑ Ⓒ Ⓓ Ⓔ
23. Ⓐ Ⓑ Ⓒ Ⓓ Ⓔ
24. Ⓐ Ⓑ Ⓒ Ⓓ Ⓔ
25. Ⓐ Ⓑ Ⓒ Ⓓ Ⓔ
26. Ⓐ Ⓑ Ⓒ Ⓓ Ⓔ
27. Ⓐ Ⓑ Ⓒ Ⓓ Ⓔ
28. Ⓐ Ⓑ Ⓒ Ⓓ Ⓔ
29. Ⓐ Ⓑ Ⓒ Ⓓ Ⓔ
30. Ⓐ Ⓑ Ⓒ Ⓓ Ⓔ
31. Ⓐ Ⓑ Ⓒ Ⓓ Ⓔ
32. Ⓐ Ⓑ Ⓒ Ⓓ Ⓔ
33. Ⓐ Ⓑ Ⓒ Ⓓ Ⓔ
34. Ⓐ Ⓑ Ⓒ Ⓓ Ⓔ
35. Ⓐ Ⓑ Ⓒ Ⓓ Ⓔ
36. Ⓐ Ⓑ Ⓒ Ⓓ Ⓔ
37. Ⓐ Ⓑ Ⓒ Ⓓ Ⓔ
38. Ⓐ Ⓑ Ⓒ Ⓓ Ⓔ
39. Ⓐ Ⓑ Ⓒ Ⓓ Ⓔ
40. Ⓐ Ⓑ Ⓒ Ⓓ Ⓔ

41. Ⓐ Ⓑ Ⓒ Ⓓ Ⓔ
42. Ⓐ Ⓑ Ⓒ Ⓓ Ⓔ
43. Ⓐ Ⓑ Ⓒ Ⓓ Ⓔ
44. Ⓐ Ⓑ Ⓒ Ⓓ Ⓔ
45. Ⓐ Ⓑ Ⓒ Ⓓ Ⓔ
46. Ⓐ Ⓑ Ⓒ Ⓓ Ⓔ
47. Ⓐ Ⓑ Ⓒ Ⓓ Ⓔ
48. Ⓐ Ⓑ Ⓒ Ⓓ Ⓔ
49. Ⓐ Ⓑ Ⓒ Ⓓ Ⓔ
50. Ⓐ Ⓑ Ⓒ Ⓓ Ⓔ
51. Ⓐ Ⓑ Ⓒ Ⓓ Ⓔ
52. Ⓐ Ⓑ Ⓒ Ⓓ Ⓔ
53. Ⓐ Ⓑ Ⓒ Ⓓ Ⓔ
54. Ⓐ Ⓑ Ⓒ Ⓓ Ⓔ
55. Ⓐ Ⓑ Ⓒ Ⓓ Ⓔ

B English Literature and Composition

SECTION I
Multiple-choice questions
Time—1 hour
Percent of total grade on the exam: 45 percent

Instructions: This section of the exam consists of 55 questions about the content, form, and style of several literary selections, both prose and poetry. Please record your answers on the answer sheet provided.

<u>Questions 1–11</u>. Read the following poem carefully before you decide on your answers to the questions.

LA BELLE DAME SANS MERCI[1]

O what can ail thee, Knight-at-arms,
   Alone and palely loitering?
The sedge[2] is withered from the Lake,
   And no birds sing!

Line
(5)   O what can ail thee, Knight-at-arms,
   So haggard and so woebegone?
The Squirrel's granary is full,
   And the harvest's done.

I see a lily on thy brow,
(10)   With anguish moist and fever dew;
And on thy cheek a fading rose
   Fast withereth too.

"I met a Lady in the Meads,[3]
   Full beautiful, a faery's child;
(15)   Her hair was long, her foot was light,
   And her eyes were wild.

"I made a Garland for her head,
   And bracelets too, and fragrant Zone;[4]
She looked at me as she did love,
(20)   And made sweet moan

---

[1]The Beautiful Woman Without Mercy
[2]grassy marsh plant
[3]meadows
[4]a belt of flowers

"I set her on my pacing steed,
  And nothing else saw all day long,
For sidelong would she bend and sing
  A faery's song.

(25)   "She found me roots of relish sweet,
  And honey wild, and manna dew;
And sure in language strange she said—
  'I love thee true.'

"She took me to her elfin grot,[5]
(30)   And there she wept and sighed full sore,
And there I shut her wild wild eyes
  With kisses four.

"And there she lullèd me asleep
  And there I dreamed—Ah woe betide!
(35)   The latest dream I ever dreamt
  On the cold hill side.

"I saw pale Kings, and Princes too,
  Pale warriors, death-pale were they all;
They cried—'La Belle Dame sans Merci
(40)   Hath thee in thrall!'

"I saw their starved lips in the gloam,
  With horrid warning gapèd wide,
And I awoke, and found me here
  On the cold hill's side.

(45)   "And this is why I sojourn here,
  Alone and palely loitering;
Though the sedge is wither'd from the Lake,
  And no birds sing."

            —John Keats
            (1819)

1. The narrator in the poem observes the autumn season primarily through
    (A)   tastes and feelings.
    (B)   light and dark.
    (C)   odors and colors.
    (D)   sights and sounds.
    (E)   land and sky.

2. The significant shift in the poem's structure occurs between lines
    (A)   4 and 5.
    (B)   12 and 13.
    (C)   24 and 25.
    (D)   32 and 33.
    (E)   46 and 47.

---

[5]grotto

3. By setting the poem in autumn the poet

    I. draws a parallel between the season and knight's state of mind.
   II. establishes a mood of loss and loneliness.
  III. creates an atmosphere of sickness and death.

    (A) I only
    (B) I and II only
    (C) I and III only
    (D) II and III only
    (E) I, II, and III

4. The tone of the poem can be described by all of the following EXCEPT
    (A) melancholic.
    (B) despairing.
    (C) horrifying.
    (D) mysterious.
    (E) magical.

5. Which of the following literary techniques most significantly contributes to the poem's unity?
    (A) Its pattern of rhymes
    (B) The capitalization of certain words
    (C) The use of figurative language
    (D) Its blend of the setting and mood
    (E) Its repetition of sounds

6. The metaphors in lines 9–12 are meant to
    (A) contrast the hues in the flowers with the absence of color in the countryside.
    (B) suggest the religious affiliation of the knight.
    (C) show that the knight is behaving strangely.
    (D) imply that the knight has been on a romantic quest.
    (E) depict the pallor of the knight's face.

7. In line 19, "as she did love" means
    (A) trying to love.
    (B) as though she loved.
    (C) when she was loved.
    (D) like someone craving love.
    (E) experienced in the art of love.

8. Which of the following best paraphrases the meaning of line 22?
    (A) And rode on with my eyes closed
    (B) And she blocked my vision
    (C) And was preoccupied by my horse
    (D) And could think of nothing else for the rest of the day
    (E) And was blinded by love

9. The phrase "Ah woe betide!" (line 34) serves primarily to
    (A) overstate the knight's compassion.
    (B) indicate the knight's awareness that he has made a mistake.
    (C) heighten the emotional intensity of the knight's story.
    (D) change the spirit established by "lullèd me asleep" in line 33.
    (E) suggest the conflict going on in the knight's mind.

10. The pronoun "this" in line 45 refers to
    (A) awakening alone on the cold hillside instead of in the lady's grotto.
    (B) the deathly pale warriors, kings, and princes.
    (C) words that he heard uttered in his dream.
    (D) the lady's declaration of love for the knight.
    (E) the loss of the knight's horse.

11. Which of the following describes the main theme of the poem?
    (A) Untrustworthy women
    (B) The power of dreams to foretell the future
    (C) Unrequited love
    (D) How time heals wounds
    (E) The consequences of hypocrisy

Questions 12–20. Read the following dialogue carefully before you decide on your answers to the questions.

RAMSDEN [*very deliberately*] Mr. Tanner: you are the most impudent person I have ever met.

TANNER [*seriously*] I know it, Ramsden. Yet even I cannot wholly conquer
Line   shame. We live in an atmosphere of shame. We are ashamed of everything that is
(5)   real about us; ashamed of ourselves, of our relatives, of our incomes, of our accents,
        of our opinions, of our experience, just as we are ashamed of our naked skins. Good
        Lord, my dear Ramsden, we are ashamed to walk, ashamed to ride in an omnibus,
        ashamed to hire a hansom instead of keeping a carriage, ashamed of keeping one horse
        instead of two and a groom-gardener instead of a coachman and footman. The more
(10)   things a man is ashamed of, the more respectable he is. Why, you're ashamed to buy
        my book, ashamed to read it: the only thing you're not ashamed of is to judge me for
        it without having read it; and even that only means that you're ashamed to have
        heterodox opinions. Look at the effect I produce because my fairy godmother
        withheld from me this gift of shame. I have every possible virtue that a man
(15)   can have except—

RAMSDEN. I am glad you think so well of yourself.

TANNER. All you mean by that is that you think I ought to be ashamed of talking
        about my virtues. You don't mean that I haven't got them: you know perfectly well that
        I am as sober and honest a citizen as yourself, as truthful personally, and much more
(20)   truthful politically and morally.

RAMSDEN [*touched on his most sensitive point*] I deny that. I will not allow you or
        any man to treat me as if I were a mere member of the British public. I detest its
        prejudices; I scorn its narrowness; I demand the right to think for myself. You

(25)   pose as an advanced man. Let me tell you that I was an advanced man before you were born.

TANNER. I knew it was a long time ago.

RAMSDEN. I am as advanced as ever I was. I defy you to prove that I have ever hauled down the flag. I am *more* advanced than ever I was. I grow more advanced every day.

TANNER. More advanced in years, Polonius.[1]

(30)   RAMSDEN. Polonius! So you are Hamlet, I suppose.

TANNER. No: I am only the most impudent person you've ever met. That's your notion of a thoroughly bad character. When you want to give me a piece of your mind, you ask yourself, as a just and upright man, what is the worst you can fairly say to me. Thief, liar, forger, adulterer, perjurer, glutton, drunkard? Not one of these names fits

(35)   me. You have to fall back on my deficiency in shame. Well, I admit it. I even congratulate myself; for if I were ashamed of my real self, I should cut as stupid a figure as any of the rest of you. Cultivate a little impudence, Ramsden; and you will become quite a remarkable man.

RAMSDEN. I have no—

(40)   TANNER. You have no desire for that sort of notoriety. Bless you, I knew that answer would come as well as I know that a box of matches will come out of an automatic machine when I put a penny in the slot: you would be ashamed to say anything else.

(1903)

12. Which of the following adjectives best describes the tone of the conversation?
     (A) Flippant
     (B) Pretentious
     (C) Contentious
     (D) Humorous
     (E) Pragmatic

13. Ramsden's characterization of Tanner in lines 1–2 is borne out in the remainder of the dialogue by all of the following EXCEPT
     (A) Tanner's assessment of himself.
     (B) Tanner's advice to Ramsden.
     (C) Tanner's overall arrogance.
     (D) Tanner's remark, "More advanced in years, Polonius" (line 29).
     (E) Tanner's appearance.

14. The sentiment expressed in lines 9–10, "The more things . . . is," is an example of which of the following?
     (A) An analogy
     (B) An understatement
     (C) A mixed metaphor
     (D) A metonymy
     (E) A paradox

---

[1]A character in *Hamlet* known for verbosity and deviousness

306 Practice Test B

15. The repeated use of "ashamed" in lines 3–15 indicates that Tanner
(A) wishes to emphasize the pervasiveness of shame.
(B) hopes to provoke Ramsden into an argument.
(C) expects Ramsden to take back his nasty remark about Tanner's impudence.
(D) doubts that Ramsden can readily absorb the message.
(E) wants to impress his listener with the breadth and depth of his thinking about the issue.

16. Tanner's allusion to "my fairy godmother" (line 13) serves to
(A) add a spiritual dimension to his thinking.
(B) lighten the tone of his remarks.
(C) turn the style of the passage from argumentative to analytical.
(D) assert the sincerity of his beliefs.
(E) provide evidence that his theory of human behavior is correct.

17. Ramsden's reference to "a mere member of the British public" (line 22) does which of the following?

   I. Identifies him as a member of the upper class
  II. Reveals a degree of snobbishness
 III. Exposes a major difference between himself and Tanner

(A) I only
(B) III only
(C) I and II only
(D) I and III only
(E) I, II, and III

18. In lines 27–29 "advanced" is used in the sense of
(A) tolerant of others.
(B) experienced.
(C) progressive.
(D) ahead of his time.
(E) aged.

19. The metaphor in lines 27–28, "hauled down the flag," is best interpreted to mean
(A) retreated into the past.
(B) accepted less than the best.
(C) insulted my colleagues.
(D) violated my principles.
(E) surrendered.

20. By comparing Ramsden to an "automatic machine" (lines 40–42), Tanner suggests Ramsden's
(A) equanimity.
(B) conservatism.
(C) callousness.
(D) conventionality.
(E) lack of judgment.

<u>Questions 21–35.</u> Read the following passage carefully before you decide on your answers.

I am a rather elderly man. The nature of my avocations, for the last thirty years, has brought me into more than ordinary contact with what would seem an interesting and somewhat singular set of men, of whom, as yet, nothing, that I know of, has ever

Line
(5)

been written—I mean, the law-copyists, or scriveners.[1] I have known very many of them, professionally and privately, and, if I pleased, could relate diverse histories, at which good-natured gentlemen might smile, and sentimental souls might weep. But I waive the biographies of all other scriveners, for a few passages in the life of Bartleby, who was a scrivener, the strangest I ever saw, or heard of. While, of other law-copyists, I might write the complete life, of Bartleby nothing of that sort can

(10)

be done. I believe that no materials exist for a full and satisfactory biography of this man. It is an irreparable loss to literature. Bartleby was one of those beings of whom nothing is ascertainable, except from the original sources, and, in his case, those are very small. What my own astonished eyes saw of Bartleby, *that* is all I know of him, except, indeed, one vague report, which will appear in the sequel.

(15)

Ere introducing the scrivener, as he first appeared to me, it is fit I make some mention of myself, my employees, my business, my chambers, and general surroundings; because some such description is indispensable to an adequate understanding of the chief character about to be presented. Imprimis:[2] I am a man who, from his youth upwards, has been filled with a profound conviction that the

(20)

easiest way of life is the best. Hence, though I belong to a profession proverbially energetic and nervous, even to turbulence, at times, yet nothing of that sort have I ever suffered to invade my peace. I am one of those unambitious lawyers who never addresses a jury, or in any way draws down public applause; but, in the cool tranquillity of a snug retreat, do a snug business among rich men's bonds, and

(25)

mortgages, and title-deeds. All who know me, consider me an eminently *safe* man. The late John Jacob Astor,[3] a personage little given to poetic enthusiasm, had no hesitation in pronouncing my first grand point to be prudence; my next, method. I do not speak it in vanity, but simply record the fact, that I was not unemployed in my profession by the late John Jacob Astor; a name which, I

(30)

admit, I love to repeat; for it hath a rounded and orbicular sound to it, and rings like unto bullion. I will freely add, that I was not insensible to the late John Jacob Astor's good opinion.

Some time prior to the period at which this little history begins, my avocations had been largely increased. The good old office, now extinct in the State of

(35)

New York, of a Master in Chancery,[4] had been conferred upon me. It was not a very arduous office, but very pleasantly remunerative. I seldom lose my temper; much more seldom indulge in dangerous indignation at wrongs and outrages; but, I must be permitted to be rash here, and declare that I consider the sudden and violent abrogation of the office of Master in Chancery, by the new

(40)

Constitution, as a—premature act; inasmuch as I had counted upon a life-lease of the profits, whereas I only received those of a few short years. But this is by the way.

My chambers were up stairs, at No.——Wall Street. At one end, they looked upon the white wall of the interior of a spacious skylight shaft, penetrating the building

(45)

from top to bottom.

This view might have been considered rather tame than otherwise, deficient in what landscape painters call "life." But, if so, the view from the other end of my chambers offered, at least, a contrast, if nothing more. In that direction, my

---

[1]Clerks whose job was to copy documents by hand
[2]A legal term meaning "in the first place"
[3]In the mid-nineteenth century Astor was one of America's wealthiest men
[4]A type of court that handled issues of fairness; abolished in New York in 1846

(50)   windows commanded an unobstructed view of a lofty brick wall, black by age
and everlasting shade; which wall required no spyglass to bring out its lurking
beauties, but, for the benefit of all near-sighted spectators, was pushed up to
within ten feet of my window panes. Owing to the great height of the surrounding
buildings, and my chambers being on the second floor, the interval between this
wall and mine not a little resembled a huge square cistern.

(1853)

21. On the whole, the passage is about
    (A) the narrator's qualifications to write Bartleby's story.
    (B) the narrator's background.
    (C) the setting in which the story takes place.
    (D) practicing law in New York.
    (E) Bartleby's eccentricities.

22. The relationship between the narrator and Bartleby can best be described
    as
    (A) distant.
    (B) alienated.
    (C) bitter.
    (D) sentimental.
    (E) easygoing.

23. Grammatically, the phrase "law-copyists, or scriveners" (line 4) functions
    as
    (A) an objective complement.
    (B) a comparison.
    (C) a direct object.
    (D) a predicate nominative.
    (E) an appositive modifier.

24. The major effect of the narrative in lines 7–14 is to

    I. spur the reader's curiosity about Bartleby.
    II. surprise readers about the author's inability to find material on
        Bartleby.
    III. give readers the impression that the speaker is a renowned author.

    (A) I only
    (B) II only
    (C) III only
    (D) I and II only
    (E) I, II, and III

25. The sentence starting in line 10 does which of the following?
   (A) It contradicts an opinion expressed by the narrator in the previous sentence.
   (B) It introduces the thought that literature has suffered an "irreparable loss."
   (C) It explains the assertion made in the previous sentence.
   (D) It develops the statement that Bartleby was the strangest of all scriveners.
   (E) It functions as a transition between the preceding and following sentences.

26. The phrase "original sources" (line 12) can best be understood to mean
   (A) material written in Bartleby's hand.
   (B) documents pertaining to Bartleby's life.
   (C) stories told by Bartleby's friends and colleagues.
   (D) information provided by Bartleby himself.
   (E) sketches and drawings.

27. Lines 18–25 serve mainly to show that the narrator
   (A) came into his profession late in life.
   (B) reveres people with money.
   (C) takes a dim view of attorneys.
   (D) prefers not to work very hard.
   (E) adheres to a set of strong beliefs and principles.

28. In lines 20–32, the narrator uses all of the following stylistic devices EXCEPT
   (A) apostrophe.
   (B) alliteration.
   (C) litotes.
   (D) simile.
   (E) repetition.

29. In its context, "suffered" (line 22) can best be interpreted to mean
   (A) endured.
   (B) agonized.
   (C) permitted.
   (D) damaged.
   (E) forced.

30. Which of the following best characterizes the narrator's style?
   (A) Flippant and condescending
   (B) Didactic and detached
   (C) Patronizing and pompous
   (D) Personal and low-key
   (E) Opinionated and contentious

31.   The narrator chooses the phrase "a—premature act" (line 40) most probably
    (A)   as a euphemism for something that galls him.
    (B)   to express disapproval of the new Constitution.
    (C)   to use a familiar term of legal jargon.
    (D)   to characterize an injustice once done to him.
    (E)   as an understatement meant to ridicule New York attorneys.

32.   As used in line 25, the word "*safe*" means which of the following?
    (A)   Secure and conscientious
    (B)   Honest and reputable
    (C)   Unbiased and discreet
    (D)   Well-informed and dependable
    (E)   Circumspect and competent

33.   The allusion to the late John Jacob Astor (line 26) serves mainly to
    (A)   illustrate the narrator's affection for money.
    (B)   indicate the prestige of the narrator's law practice.
    (C)   show that the narrator pursued clients from the upper reaches of
          society.
    (D)   suggest why the narrator located his office on Wall Street.
    (E)   exemplify the level of client that the narrator typically served.

34.   The shift in the narrator's rhetorical stance between lines 43–45 and lines
    46–54 can best be described as one from
    (A)   subjective to objective.
    (B)   factual to whimsical.
    (C)   critical to nurturing.
    (D)   effusive to reserved.
    (E)   confident to uncertain.

35.   The narrator establishes the tone of the last paragraph (lines 46–54),
    primarily by
    (A)   using the language of aesthetics to describe the views from his office
          windows.
    (B)   emphasizing black and white visual images.
    (C)   comparing the narrow shaft outside his window with a "huge square
          cistern" (line 54).
    (D)   exaggerating the size of the surrounding structures.
    (E)   contrasting the view from windows at opposite ends of his office.

Questions 36–45. Read the following poem carefully before you decide on your answers to the questions.

THE BROKEN HEART

He is stark mad, whoever says,
    That he hath been in love an hour,
Yet not that love so soon decays,
Line   But that it can ten in less space devour;
(5) Who will believe me, if I swear
That I have had the plague a year?
    Who would not laugh at me, if I should say
    I saw a flash of powder burn a day?

Ah, what a trifle is a heart,
(10)   If once into love's hands it come!
All other griefs allow a part
    To other griefs, and ask themselves but some;
They come to us, but us love draws;
He swallows us and never chaws;
(15)   By him, as by chain'd shot, whole ranks do die;
    He is the tyrant pike, our hearts the fry.[1]

If 'twere not so, what did become
    Of my heart when I first saw thee?
I brought a heart into the room,
(20)   But from the room I carried none with me;
If it had gone to thee, I know
Mine would have taught thine heart to show
    More pity unto me ; but Love, alas!
    At one first blow did shiver[2] it as glass.

(25) Yet nothing can to nothing fall,
    Nor any place be empty quite;
Therefore I think my breast hath all
    Those pieces still, though they be not unite;
And now, as broken glasses show
(30) A hundred lesser faces, so
    My rags of heart can like, wish, and adore,
    But after one such love, can love no more.

—John Donne, 1633

---

[1]small fish, easily devoured
[2]shatter

36. The speaker in the poem would most likely characterize his experience in love as
    (A) annoying.
    (B) tedious.
    (C) lamentable.
    (D) pointless.
    (E) odious.

37. The purpose of the first stanza (lines 1–8) is primarily to
    (A) reveal the speed and potency of love.
    (B) compare being in love with being "stark mad."
    (C) caution readers about the hazards of love.
    (D) suggest that love is infectious as the plague.
    (E) pity anyone who falls in love.

38. Line 10 includes an example of
    (A) a conceit.
    (B) a paradox.
    (C) irony.
    (D) personification.
    (E) an oxymoron.

39. The imagery in the poem is dominated by
    (A) references to rationality and madness.
    (B) allusions to violence and destruction.
    (C) the use of anatomical language.
    (D) references to grief and mourning.
    (E) an emphasis on stealth and secrecy.

40. Which sentence best paraphrases line 13?
    (A) Distress comes in many forms, but none lasts as long as heartache.
    (B) Emotions can damage us, but none as severely as love.
    (C) Love tends to grab us and never let go.
    (D) We fall in love easily, but no one knows why.
    (E) Unbidden pains afflict us, but lovesickness pulls us to it.

41. The metaphors in lines 14–16 are meant to suggest all of the following about love EXCEPT that
    (A) love is beyond man's control.
    (B) love is ruthless.
    (C) love is like a force of nature.
    (D) love is a predatory beast.
    (E) love is malicious.

42. Which of the following best describes the function(s) of lines 21–26?

   I. They condemn the damaging effects on the speaker's heart.
   II. They reconsider the validity of the speaker's account of what had happened to him.
   III. They show the speaker applying logic to explain a highly emotional event.

   (A) I only
   (B) II only
   (C) I and III only
   (D) II and III only
   (E) I, II, and III

43. The literary device that most significantly contributes to the poem's unity is the
   (A) rhyme scheme.
   (B) use of alliteration.
   (C) repetition of words and sounds.
   (D) archaic diction.
   (E) use of the first person.

44. Lines 31–32 most strongly express the speaker's
   (A) acknowledgment of a weakness in his personality.
   (B) urge to "like, wish, and adore," but not fall in love.
   (C) desire to fall in love again.
   (D) awareness of his lost capacity to love.
   (E) hopes to keep himself from falling recklessly in love again.

45. Which of the following best describes the development of the poem?
   (A) Past to present
   (B) Abstract to specific
   (C) Idealistic to realistic
   (D) Subjective to objective
   (E) Conjectural to assertive

Questions 46–55. Read the following passage carefully before you decide on your answers to the questions.

After their marriage they busied themselves, with marked success, in enlarging the circle of their acquaintance. Thirty people knew them by sight; twenty more with smiling demonstrations tolerated their occasional presence within hospitable thresholds;

Line
(5)
at least fifty others became aware of their existence. They moved in their enlarged world amongst perfectly delightful men and women who feared emotion, enthusiasm, or failure, more than fire, war, or moral disease; who tolerated only the commonest formulas of commonest thoughts, and recognized only profitable facts. It was an extremely charming sphere, the abode of all the virtues, where nothing is realized and where all joys and sorrows are cautiously toned down into pleasures and

(10)
annoyances. In that serene region, then, where noble sentiments are cultivated in sufficient profusion to conceal the pitiless materialism of thoughts and aspirations Alvan Hervey and his wife spent five years of prudent bliss unclouded by any doubt as to the moral propriety of their existence. She, to give her individuality fair play, took up all manner of philanthropic work and became a member of various rescuing

(15)
and reforming societies patronized or presided over by ladies of title. He took an active interest in politics; and having met quite by chance a literary man—who nevertheless was related to an earl—he was induced to finance a moribund society paper. It was a semi-political, and wholly scandalous publication, redeemed by excessive dulness [sic]; and as it was utterly faithless, as it contained no new thought, as it never by

(20)
any chance had a flash of wit, satire, or indignation in its pages, he judged it respectable enough, at first sight. Afterwards, when it paid, he promptly perceived that upon the whole it was a virtuous undertaking. It paved the way of his ambition; and he enjoyed also the special kind of importance he derived from this connection with what he imagined to be literature.

(25)
This connection still further enlarged their world. Men who wrote or drew prettily for the public came at times to their house, and his editor came very often. He thought him rather an ass because he had such big front teeth (the proper thing is to have small, even teeth) and wore his hair a trifle longer than most men do. However, some dukes wear their hair long, and the fellow indubitably knew his business. The

(30)
worst was that his gravity, though perfectly portentous, could not be trusted. He sat, elegant and bulky, in the drawing-room, the head of his stick hovering in front of his big teeth, and talked for hours with a thick-lipped smile (he said nothing that could be considered objectionable and not quite the thing), talked in an unusual manner— not obviously—irritatingly. His forehead was too lofty—unusually so—and under it

(35)
there was a straight nose, lost between the hairless cheeks, that in a smooth curve ran into a chin shaped like the end of a snow-shoe. And in this face that resembled the face of a fat and fiendishly knowing baby there glinted a pair of clever, peering, unbelieving black eyes. He wrote verses too. Rather an ass. But the band of men who trailed at the skirts of his monumental frock-coat seemed to perceive wonderful

(40)
things in what he said. Alvan Hervey put it down to affectation. Those artist chaps, upon the whole, were so affected. Still, all this was highly proper—very useful to him—and his wife seemed to like it—as if she also had derived some distinct and secret advantage from this intellectual connection. She received her mixed and decorous guests with a kind of tall, ponderous grace, peculiarly her own and which

(45)
awakened in the mind of intimidated strangers incongruous and improper reminiscences of an elephant, a giraffe, a gazelle; of a gothic tower—of an overgrown angel. Her Thursdays were becoming famous in their world; and their world grew steadily, annexing street after street. It included also Somebody's Gardens, a Crescent—a couple of Squares.

(1913)

46. The primary rhetorical function of the sentence beginning on line 2 is to
    (A) define a term used in the preceding sentence.
    (B) reinforce the idea that the couple were newlyweds.
    (C) prepare the reader for an anecdote later in the passage.
    (D) provide supporting details for the main idea of the previous sentence.
    (E) digress from the main topic of the paragraph.

47. In lines 4–7 ("They moved . . . facts"), the narrator makes use of all the following EXCEPT
    (A) pathos.
    (B) repetition.
    (C) insult.
    (D) comparison.
    (E) irony.

48. From the comment that Alvan Hervey met a literary man "who nevertheless was related to an earl" (lines 16–17), the reader can infer that
    (A) the man pursued his literary endeavors rather casually.
    (B) men of noble blood rarely involve themselves in literary matters.
    (C) the man was a second-rate writer.
    (D) the man was wealthy but went slumming in a low-paying profession.
    (E) the man's social status was more impressive than his literary ability.

49. The humor in the passage derives mainly from

    I. the uniqueness of the Herveys' behavior.
    II. the narrator's sarcasm.
    III. the Herveys' pretentiousness.

    (A) I only
    (B) III only
    (C) I and III only
    (D) II and III only
    (E) I, II, and III

50. Which trait of the Herveys is given the most emphasis in the passage?
    (A) Their obsession to build a good reputation
    (B) Their need to be superior to everyone around them
    (C) Their desire to keep up with their friends and acquaintances
    (D) Their inclination to do charitable works
    (E) Their interest in supporting the arts

51. The reason that Mrs. Hervey joined "various rescuing and reforming societies" (lines 14–15) was to
    (A) form bonds with members of the upper class.
    (B) develop her reputation for helping others.
    (C) enlarge her circle of acquaintance in the community.
    (D) do what Alvan expected of her.
    (E) create an identity for herself apart from her husband.

52. Lines 15–24 serve to show all of the following about Alvan Hervey
EXCEPT that he
(A) was ambitious.
(B) determined the value of things by their profitability.
(C) lacked wit and a sense of humor.
(D) enjoyed being associated with literary people.
(E) craved the approval of others.

53. The narrator describes Alvan Hervey's editor primarily in terms of his
(A) intellectual gifts.
(B) many talents.
(C) professional skill.
(D) manner of speaking.
(E) physical appearance.

54. In line 45, the strangers are "intimidated" in the sense that they
(A) didn't fit into the crowd.
(B) felt themselves being bullied by Mrs. Hervey.
(C) were overwhelmed by Mrs. Hervey's manner and appearance.
(D) could not control their vivid imaginations.
(E) were frightened in Mrs. Hervey's presence.

55. In lines 48–49, the narrator's use of "Somebody's Gardens, a Crescent—a
couple of Squares" rather than the names of specific places implies that
(A) the Herveys continue to expand their world for no other reason than
to expand their world.
(B) the community has grown beyond recognition since the Herveys settled there.
(C) the Herveys have made themselves known in more places than they
can remember.
(D) the Herveys have become less discriminating in their choice of
friends and acquaintances.
(E) the reputation of Mr. and Mrs. Hervey has spread further than they
are aware.

SECTION II
Three essay questions
Total time—2 hours
Suggested time for each essay—40 minutes
Percent of total grade on the exam: 55 percent

Instructions: This section of the exam consists of three questions that require responses in essay form. You may write the essays in any order you wish and return to work on a completed essay if time permits. Although it is suggested that you spend roughly 40 minutes on each essay, you may apportion your time as you see fit.

Each essay will be evaluated according to its clarity, effectiveness in dealing with the topics, and the overall quality of your writing. If you have the time, go over each essay, checking its punctuation, spelling, and diction. Unless plenty of time remains, try to avoid major revisions. In the end, the quality of each essay counts more than its quantity.

For Question 3, please choose a novel or play of at least the same literary merit as the works you have been assigned in your AP English course.

Essays should be written in pen, preferably with black or dark blue ink. Use lined paper and write as legibly as you can. Do not skip lines. Cross out any errors you make. Feel free to make notes and plan your essay on a piece of scrap paper. Please number your essays and begin each one on a new sheet of paper. Good luck.

Essay Question 1
(Suggested time—40 minutes. This question counts as one-third of your score for Section II of the exam.)

Read the following poem carefully, paying particular attention to the personalities of the two neighbors. Then write a well-organized essay in which you explain how the speaker conveys not only the differences between himself and his neighbor but the implications of those differences. You may wish to include analysis of such poetic elements as diction, tone, figurative language, and imagery, among others.

MENDING WALL

Something there is that doesn't love a wall,
That sends the frozen-ground-swell under it,
And spills the upper boulders in the sun,
Line And makes gaps even two can pass abreast.
(5) The work of hunters is another thing:
I have come after them and made repair
Where they have left not one stone on a stone,
But they would have the rabbit out of hiding,
To please the yelping dogs. The gaps I mean,
(10) No one has seen them made or heard them made,
But at spring mending-time we find them there.
I let my neighbor know beyond the hill;
And on a day we meet to walk the line
And set the wall between us once again.
(15) We keep the wall between us as we go.
To each the boulders that have fallen to each.
And some are loaves and some so nearly balls
We have to use a spell to make them balance:
'Stay where you are until our backs are turned!'
(20) We wear our fingers rough with handling them.
Oh, just another kind of out-door game,
One on a side. It comes to little more:
There where it is we do not need the wall:
He is all pine and I am apple orchard.
(25) My apple trees will never get across
And eat the cones under his pines, I tell him.
He only says, 'Good fences make good neighbors'.
Spring is the mischief in me, and I wonder
If I could put a notion in his head:
(30) 'Why do they make good neighbors? Isn't it
Where there are cows?
But here there are no cows.
Before I built a wall I'd ask to know
What I was walling in or walling out,
(35) And to whom I was like to give offense.
Something there is that doesn't love a wall,
That wants it down.' I could say 'Elves' to him,
But it's not elves exactly, and I'd rather
He said it for himself. I see him there
(40) Bringing a stone grasped firmly by the top
In each hand, like an old-stone savage armed.
He moves in darkness as it seems to me
Not of woods only and the shade of trees.
He will not go behind his father's saying,
(45) And he likes having thought of it so well
He says again, "Good fences make good neighbors."

—Robert Frost, 1915

Essay Question 2

(Suggested time—40 minutes. This question counts as one-third of your score for Section II of the exam.)

The passage below is an excerpt from a short story, "Egotism; or The Bosom Serpent" (1843) by Nathaniel Hawthorne. Roderick Elliston, the story's main character, suffers from a rare and puzzling condition, the nature of which is described in the passage. Read the excerpt carefully. Then, in a well-organized essay, analyze the techniques the author uses to explain Elliston's ailment and the reaction it evokes. Consider diction, choice of details, structure, and any other relevant literary element.

Shortly after Elliston's separation from his wife—now nearly four years ago—his associates had observed a singular gloom spreading over his daily life, like those chill, gray mists that sometimes steal away the sunshine from a summer's
Line
(5)
morning. The symptoms caused them endless perplexity. They knew not whether ill health were robbing his spirits of elasticity, or whether a canker of the mind was gradually eating, as such cankers do, from his moral system into the physical frame, which is but the shadow of the former. They looked for the root of this trouble in his shattered schemes of domestic bliss,—willfully shattered by himself,—but could not be satisfied of its existence there. Some thought that
(10)
their once brilliant friend was in an incipient stage of insanity, of which his passionate impulses had perhaps been the forerunners; others prognosticated a general blight and gradual decline. From Roderick's own lips they could learn nothing. More than once, it is true, he had been heard to say, clutching his hands convulsively upon his breast,—"It gnaws me! It gnaws me!"—but, by different auditors, a
(15)
great diversity of explanation was assigned to this ominous expression. What could it be that gnawed the breast of Roderick Elliston? Was it sorrow? Was it merely the tooth of physical disease? Or, in his reckless course, often verging upon profligacy, if not plunging into its depths, had he been guilty of some deed which made his bosom a prey to the deadlier fangs of remorse? There was plausible
(20)
ground for each of these conjectures; but it must not be concealed that more than one elderly gentleman, the victim of good cheer and slothful habits, magisterially pronounced the secret of the whole matter to be Dyspepsia![1]
Meanwhile, Roderick seemed aware how generally he had become the subject of curiosity and conjecture, and, with a morbid repugnance to such notice,
(25)
or to any notice whatsoever, estranged himself from all companionship. Not merely the eye of man was a horror to him; not merely the light of a friend's countenance; but even the blessed sunshine, likewise, which in its universal beneficence typifies the radiance of the Creator's face, expressing his love for all the creatures of his hand. The dusky twilight was now too transparent for
(30)
Roderick Elliston; the blackest midnight was his chosen hour to steal abroad; and if ever he were seen, it was when the watchman's lantern gleamed upon his figure, gliding along the street, with his hands clutched upon his bosom, still muttering, "It gnaws me! It gnaws me!" What could it be that gnaws him?

---

[1]indigestion

Essay Question 3

(Suggested time—40 minutes. This question counts as one-third of your score for Section II of the exam.)

Often in literature a character's life is changed as a result of another person's death. Choose a novel or play of literary merit in which a character undergoes a change following the death of someone else. In a well-organized essay, explain how the death affects the character's life and how the change contributes to the meaning of the work as a whole. Do not merely summarize the plot.

Choose a title from the following list or another play or novel of comparable literary merit.

All My Sons
All the King's Men
All the Pretty Horses
Antigone
Beloved
The Bridge of San Luis Rey
Crime and Punishment
Cry, the Beloved Country
David Copperfield
A Death in the Family
The Grapes of Wrath
Great Expectations
Hamlet
Huckleberry Finn
Light in August
Look Homeward, Angel
Macbeth
Native Son

END OF PRACTICE TEST B

Answer Key for Practice Test B—Section I

1. D	12. C	23. E	34. B	45. B
2. B	13. E	24. A	35. A	46. D
3. E	14. E	25. C	36. C	47. A
4. C	15. A	26. D	37. A	48. B
5. D	16. B	27. D	38. D	49. D
6. E	17. C	28. A	39. B	50. A
7. B	18. C	29. C	40. E	51. E
8. E	19. A	30. D	41. E	52. C
9. C	20. D	31. A	42. D	53. E
10. A	21. B	32. E	43. A	54. C
11. C	22. A	33. A	44. D	55. A

Summary of Answers in Section I Multiple-Choice

Number of correct answers _____

Number of incorrect answers _____

Number of questions not answered _____

Use this information when you calculate your score on this exam. See page 328.

Answer Explanations

SECTION I

1. **D** Autumn is described with such images as the withered sedge, the absence of birdsong, the completion of the harvest—in other words, through its sights and sounds.

2. **B** The poem consists of two sections. In the first part the narrator sets the scene and asks the knight what ails him. The second, and major, part of the poem contains the knight's response, which begins on line 13.

3. **E** Autumn is a season of change. The joys of summer dry up and fade away just as the knight's happiness has dissolved upon waking from his dream and finding himself jilted. Devastated by his loss, he pines for his lost love while loitering sad and lonely around the countryside. He is also in shock. "Fever dew" is the sweat of illness The fading of his cheeks and the pallor on his forehead imply that he is dying, although he himself may not know it, for he is still in thrall to the lady.

4. **C** Melancholy images prevail in the knight's description of his encounter with the lady. That the knight despairs is obvious in the first two lines of the poem. The woman mysteriously entrances the knight, just as she

had enthralled other men (kings, princes, and warriors). While the woman's behavior may be appalling, to call it horrifying is an over-statement.

5. D The dreary setting of the poem goes hand in hand with the knight's "haggard and so woebegone" condition and with the melancholy mood of the poem. The other choices name poetic features of the poem but have less importance than (D).

6. E The lily suggests the whiteness of the knight's forehead, while the "fad-ing rose" implies his increasingly pale cheeks. Both metaphors rein-force the image of the knight "palely loitering," introduced in line 2 and reiterated in line 46.

7. B At this point in the story, the knight is explaining why he was attracted to the lady. One reason is that her irresistible gaze said, "I love you," a sentiment she puts into words in line 28.

8. E Lines 23–24 explain why the knight "nothing else saw all day long." Ordinarily a "faery's song" would not obstruct one's vision, but in this case it blinded the knight with love.

9. C Line 34 marks a turning point in the knight's story. Before exclaiming "Ah woe betide!" he simply tells what happened during his brief affair with the lady. With the dream comes anguish heightened by this uncontrollable outburst of emotion.

10. A Although all the choices allude to events in the knight's story, "this" refers directly to the shock of finding himself "here/ /On the cold hill's side" (lines 43–44) after having been lulled to sleep in the lady's "elfin grot" (line 29).

11. C The poem is basically a story of a lovestruck man saddened by a woman who pretends to love him but then leaves him in the lurch.

12. C The conversation is essentially an argument in which each participant bluntly expresses his views and attacks his opponent with personal insults.

13. E Twice during the conversation Tanner agrees that he is impudent. In lines 37–38, he advises Ramsden to cultivate a little impudence him-self in order to "become quite a remarkable man." Tanner's cockiness and insolence are revealed by almost everything he says. His vicious comment in line 29 is particularly hurtful. Only Choice (E), Tanner's appearance, is not related to his impudence.

14. E The statement seems self-contradictory but Tanner nevertheless believes it to be true. The validity of Tanner's paradox is supported by much of the dialogue that both precedes and follows it.

15. A Tanner harps on the word "ashamed"in arguing that people are con-formists and that their fear of shame lies behind almost everything they do.

16. B Tanner uses his speech to indict people for their conventionality. By alluding to his fairy godmother, he manages to soften the polemical tone of his remarks.

17. C Ramsden refuses to let Tanner treat him as a member of Britain's middle and working classes presumably because he regards himself superior to them. His disdainful comment is one that Tanner, as a compatriot in the upper reaches of British society, would fully appreciate.

18. C Ramsden contradicts Tanner's implication that he is a conformist. In fact, Ramsden regards himself as a progressive thinker.

19. A By calling himself "advanced," Ramsden claims to keeps abreast of advanced ideas and thinking. "Hauling down the flag," therefore, refers to taking a step backward, or returning to the past—something he denies ever having done.

20. D To Tanner, Ramsden seems utterly conventional, so ordinary, in fact, that he can predict what Ramsden will say.

21. B Three-fourths of the passage, beginning with line 15, is devoted to a description of the narrator's avocation, his likes and dislikes, and the office over which he presides.

22. A The narrator says in lines 9–13 that he knows virtually nothing about Bartleby except what he has observed. Evidently, Bartleby kept to himself while in the narrator's employ. Nothing in the passage suggests the existence of affection or friction between the two men.

23. E Appositive modifiers repeat or specify in different words the expression they modify, in this case "set of men" (line 3).

24. A The narrator provokes curiosity about Bartleby by describing him as "the strangest [scrivener] I ever saw" (line 8). The reference in line 14 to a "vague report" is also meant to hook the reader's interest. With respect to II, if you considering the narrator's experience with Bartleby, it is hardly surprising that he lacks material for a biography. Regarding III, nothing in the passage suggests that the narrator is a famous author.

25. C In the given sentence the narrator amplifes the idea in the previous sentence that the complete life story of Bartleby cannot be written.

26. D The phrase means the same as "primary" sources, that is, the words and revelations of Bartleby himself. The narrator says in line 7 that he plans to write "a few passages" about Bartleby because no information exists for a full-length biography.

27. D Several phrases indicate that the narrator favors the "easiest way of life" (line 20). He admits to being "unambitious," and he prefers "cool tranquillity of a snug retreat" (lines 23–24) rather than laboring in public.

28. A Examples of alliteration include "profession proverbially energetic" (lines 20–21) and "pronouncing my first grand point to be prudence" (line 27). Litotes appear in lines 28–29 ("I was not unemployed") and in line 31 ("I was not insensible"). The comment that John Jacob Astor's name "rings like unto bullion" contains a simile, and the word "snug" is repeated in line 24. Only Choice (A), apostrophe—addressing a person or thing not present—is missing.

29. C As one who values tranquillity and peace, the narrator has never allowed frenetic lawyers to influence him.

30. D The choices containing negative connotations should be eliminated because the passage for the most part is written in a friendly, matter-of-fact tone. Although the narrator casts aspersions on hyperactive lawyers and laments the abolition of the office of Master in Chancery, those are incidental to his main purpose—to tell the story of an unusual scrivener.

31. A The dash between "a" and "premature" implies that the narrator paused to think of a suitable word. He claims to have been indignant about the abrogation of the Master in Chancery and is about to say something rash about it (lines 38–40) when he apparently changes his mind and utters "premature," instead of a more expressive word.

32. E To illustrate the meaning of "safe," the narrator cites the opinions of John Jacob Astor, who, in spite of a shortage of "poetic enthusiasm," praised the narrator's "prudence" and "method." In other words, Astor singled out what he believed were the narrator's best qualities: caution and skill in the practice of law.

33. A Claiming that he does not cite Astor out of vanity (line 28), the narrator instead loves to say Astor's name because to him it "rings like unto bullion" (lines 30–31). That is, it sounds like money.

34. B In lines 43–44, the narrator briefly describes a few facts about his office. In the following lines, he interprets the facts, engaging in whimsy, particularly with respect to the views from his windows.

35. A Both windows face unsightly blank walls. With his tongue lodged firmly in his cheek, and using such phrases as "deficient in what landscape painters call 'life'," and "lurking beauties," the narrator describes the views as though they were works of art.

36. C Throughout the poem, the speaker laments bitterly about falling in love and being rejected. The poem's title also suggests the emotional state of the speaker.

37. A The speaker says in line 4 that love can devour ten people in less than an hour. To think otherwise is as crazy as believing that a person can survive the plague for a year or that a quantity of gunpowder can burn for a year instead of exploding instantly.

38. D The phrase "love's hands" gives love a human characterisitic.

39. B Although the poem contains some imagery related to Choices (A), (C), and (D), most images relate to war and devastation: for example, "flash of powder," "chain'd shot," "ranks do die," and "broken glass"—all suggesting the brutality of love.

40. E The speaker asserts that love draws us to it, while other "griefs," come to us, perhaps even seek us out.

41. E The lines in question characterize love as an uncontrollable force that can swallow us whole, as a ruthless destroyer of men, and as a large fish (a "pike") that feeds on our hearts. No suggestion is made that love is hateful.

42. D In lines 19 and 20, the speaker asserts, "I brought a heart into the room,/But from the room I carried none with me." In line 21, he begins to reconsider that account of what had happened, figuring that, had he left his heart behind, his beloved would have taken pity on him. In addition, the speaker concludes that an absent heart could not have shattered like glass within his breast.

43. A The pattern of rhymes, in particular the concluding couplet in each stanza, endows the poem with a cohesiveness it might not otherwise have.

44. D The speaker realizes to his chagrin that with a tattered heart he'll never love again.

45. B The poem begins with some general remarks about the nature of love. Subsequently, the speaker relates his own experience as a lover. Therefore, what starts as theoretical and abstract gradually becomes highly personal and specific.

46. D Because the sentence in question enumerates the people entering the Herveys' circle of acquaintance, it supports the first sentence in the passage.

47. A An example of repetition is "commonest formulas of commonest thought" (lines 6–7). The overall tone is ironic and meant to degrade the "perfectly delightful"—but also commonplace and money-grubbing—"men and women" in the couple's social circle. The narrator also makes a comparison between what these people feared and what they feared even more (lines 5–6). Only pathos, that element in literature that provokes the reader's pity or sorrow, is absent.

48. B The word "nevertheless" suggests that the man was somehow out of the ordinary. Indeed, being a writer, a poet, or a critic would be unusual for an earl or even an earl's relative.

49. D Using sarcasm, the narrator portrays the Herveys searching for happiness "where noble sentiments are cultivated in sufficient profusion to conceal . . . pitiless materialism of thoughts and aspirations" (lines 10–11). That is, they put on airs, mouthed the proper words, and partook of culture not because they wanted to but because it made a good impression on others. In other words, they were phonies, just like everyone else in their circle of acquaintance.

50. A All the choices more or less describe the Herveys, but almost everything they do is intended to enhance and spread their good name.

51. E According to line 13, she volunteered her services in order "to give her individuality fair play."

52. C Nothing in the passage provides evidence that Alvan Hervey, although he may well have been duller than dishwater, lacked wit and sense of humor. The society paper he backed with his money was devoid of wit, but he seems to have had nothing to do with its contents.

53. E The description (lines 25–38) focuses mainly on the man's appearance, particularly on his facial features.

54. C Mrs. Hervey's "tall, ponderous grace" (line 44) so impressed some guests that they could not help being reminded of other tall creatures and objects such as a giraffe and a gothic tower (line 46).

55. A The main point of the passage relates to the expansion of the Herveys' social circle. Over time, they have become so caught up in the process—even to the extent of befriending a man they consider "rather an ass"—that they continue to do it just for the sake of doing it.

SECTION II

Although answers to essay questions will vary greatly, the following descriptions suggest an approach to each question and contain ideas that could be used in a response. Perhaps your essay contains many of the same ideas. If not, don't be alarmed. Your ideas may be at least as valid than those presented below.

Note: Don't mistake these descriptions for complete essays; essays written for the exam should be full-length, well organized, and fully developed. For an overview of how essays are graded, turn to "How AP Essays Are Scored," on page 35.

Essay Question 1

"In lines 1–10 the speaker explains the impetus for the poem: Each winter "something" unseen and unheard knocks down sections of the stone wall that marks the boundary between his and his neighbor's property. Frost heaves and hunters are probably responsible, but the truth remains uncertain, implying that the speaker may probe into deeper questions, perhaps age-old philosophical questions that can never be fully answered. Based on the narrative section of the poem, the speaker has in mind such matters as the barriers between people, the lack of trust that separates one man from another, and the eternal conflict that pits the forces of change against desires to preserve the status quo.

Although the speaker is the one who summons his neighbor to "walk the line/And set the wall between" them once again, he questions the necessity for this annual ritual. He considers it a "game" instead of a serious undertaking and thinks of several sensible and humorous (to him) reasons to abandon it, such as "He is all pine and I am apple orchard./My apple trees will never get across/And eat the cones under his pines" (lines 24–26). The neighbor, however, thinks otherwise, and twice quotes an epigram, "Good fences make good neighbors," passed down to him from his father. To the speaker, this recitation evokes an image of a superstitious savage (lines 41–44), an ignorant man who "moves in darkness" (read *ignorance*), and refuses to "go behind," or relinquish, his father's saying.

The plain language of the poem and frequent references to nature and the land (stones, hills, boulders, pine trees, apple orchard, cows) befit the poem's setting. The lack of rhyme and the colloquial speech of the two neighbors underscore the poem's folksy informality. Yet, the reflections of the speaker, who admits he's full of "mischief" (line 28) raise profound issues. For example, why is the wall rebuilt each year despite the speaker's objections? Are the two farmers in a rut? Is it because they can't communicate? Are barriers between people essential to society? Does the permanence of the barrier symbolize the state of the world? Would it be fair to say, perhaps, that "Mending Wall" is a metaphor for life?

Essay Question 2

The excerpt consists of two paragraphs, each written from a different point of view. The first describes Elliston's symptoms as observed by his "associates." The second deals with Elliston's reaction to his own ailment. Although the focus of the two paragraphs differs, the horrific tone of each unites them. In addition, both show Elliston the victim of a woeful ailment, exacerbated by the mystery of its cause and ignorance of its antidote.

A sense of darkness and ominous decay pervades the entire passage, reflecting Elliston's physical and emotional condition. Images such as "chill, gray mists that sometimes steal away the sunshine" (line 3) and "their once brilliant friend" express changes that have forced Elliston into seclusion. He is so blighted that he can no longer face "the blessed sunshine" (line 27), nor even the "dusky twilight" (line 29). Only "blackest midnight" (line 30) draws him out, but even then he clutches himself and continues to mutter chillingly, "It gnaws me! It gnaws me!"

To add still darker dimensions to the portrait of this unfortunate man, the author alludes to the possibility that he has "canker" (cancer) or that he appears to be going insane. What's worse, however, are hints in each paragraph that Elliston's physical decline may reflect a moral and spiritual decline as well. In lines 27–28, for example, the speaker suggests that by rejecting "blessed sunshine" Elliston is also turning his back on "the radiance of the Creator's face," which is likened to an expression of "love for all creatures of his hand," a first-rate irony considering Elliston's condition. Is the author implying that Elliston is not a creature of God's hand? Or is the poor fellow possessed by some sort of demon.

Because the origins of Elliston's malady remain an "endless perplexity" (line 4), the author crowds the passage with questions asked by people who have seen or heard Elliston in agony and can't figure out what's wrong. Only a group of elderly gentlemen, called by the author victims of "good cheer and slothful habits" (line 21) a label suggesting that they may be slightly out to lunch, dismiss Elliston's problem as indigestion. Their diagnosis adds a surprisingly perverse touch to an account of human suffering at its worst.

Essay Question 3

An essay on any one of the three titles discussed below would be appropriate:

In *Antigone* by Jean Anouilh (based on the play by Sophocles), the title character has her life turned upside down by the death of her brothers. What grieves her most is not losing her brothers, however, but that her uncle, King Creon, declares one of the dead young men, Polynices, a traitor, and decrees that his body may not be properly buried. Antigone defies Creon's word and throws dirt onto the corpse. Her actions, which lead ultimately to her own death, raise issues of resistance to corrupt authority, loyalty to one's family, and standing up for one's principles regardless of the consequences. Antigone may seem like a martyr to her cause but in fighting her uncle, she contributes to social mayhem and the death or destruction of others.

The Bridge of San Luis Rey by Thornton Wilder interweaves the stories of five people who die when an ancient bridge collapses and sends them plunging into a gulf. Brother Juniper, a Franciscan monk, witnesses the catastrophe and spends the remainder of his life gathering evidence to ascertain why God chose these five for premature death. Much of the novel then narrates their life stories up to the fateful moment they cross the bridge. At the end Brother Juniper is condemned as a heretic and burned at the stake for his effort to show that theology can be explained as though it were an "exact science." In a sense, the novel is about meaning—how we seek and perceive meaning, and particularly how some of us assume that we are wise enough to assign meaning to providential occurrences in our daily lives.

In *Native Son* by Richard Wright, Bigger Thomas, a young black in Depression-era Chicago, finds himself stuck without hope in a life of misery and poverty. But a social agency gives him a chance by offering him a chauffeur's job with the Daltons, a wealthy white family. One night, after he accidentally suffocates the daughter Mary Dalton and burns her body, Bigger fabricates a kidnap plot intended to extort money from the family. A manhunt follows. Bigger is caught, tried, and sentenced to die. At death's door Bigger finally searches for an identity. Just as he has been blind to his own potential, white America had been blindly unaware of his and other black people's suffering. In his final moments, Bigger reflects on his miserable life and even though he is afraid of the electric chair, finds relief in his imminent death.

Self-Scoring Guide for Practice Test B

Scoring Section 2   ESSAYS

After referring to "How Essays Are Scored," on page 35 of this book, use this guide to help you evaluate each essay. Do your best to evaluate your performance in each category by using the criteria spelled out below. Because it is hard to achieve objectivity when assessing your own writing, you may improve the validity of your score by having a trusted and well-informed friend or experienced teacher read and rate your essay.

On the following Rating Chart, enter a number (from 1 to 6) that you think represents your level of performance in each category (A–F).

Category A: OVERALL PURPOSE/MAIN IDEA
- 6 extremely well-defined and insightful
- 5 clearly defined and generally insightful
- 4 mostly clear
- 3 somewhat clear but occasionally confusing
- 2 generally unclear and confusing
- 1 virtually incomprehensible

Category B: HANDLING OF THE PROMPT
- 6 self-evident or extremely clear throughout
- 5 mostly clear
- 4 somewhat clear
- 3 somewhat unclear
- 2 generally unclear or ambiguous
- 1 confusing or nonexistent

Category C: ORGANIZATION AND DEVELOPMENT
- 6 insightfully organized; fully developed with excellent supporting evidence
- 5 reasonably well organized; developed with appropriate supporting material
- 4 appropriately organized; developed with some relevant material
- 3 inadequately organized; weak development
- 2 poorly organized; little or no development
- 1 no discernible organization; no relevant development

Category D: SENTENCE STRUCTURE
- 6 varied and engaging
- 5 sufficiently varied to create interest
- 4 some variety
- 3 little variety; minor sentence errors
- 2 frequent sentence errors that interfere with meaning
- 1 serious sentence errors that obscure meaning

Category E: USE OF LANGUAGE
- 6 precise and effective word choice
- 5 competent word choice
- 4 conventional word choice; mostly correct
- 3 some errors in diction or idiom
- 2 frequent errors in diction or idiom
- 1 meaning obscured by word choice

Category F: GRAMMAR AND USAGE
- 6 error-free or virtually error-free
- 5 occasional minor errors
- 4 basically correct but with several minor errors
- 3 meaning somewhat obscured by errors
- 2 meaning frequently obscured by errors
- 1 meaning blocked by several major errors

RATING CHART

Rate your essay:	Essay 1	Essay 2	Essay 3
Overall Purpose/Main Idea	____	____	____
Handling of the Prompt	____	____	____
Organization and Development	____	____	____
Sentence Structure	____	____	____
Use of Language	____	____	____
Grammar and Usage	____	____	____
Composite Scores (Sum of each column)	____	____	____

By using the following chart, in which composite scores are converted to the 9-point AP rating scale, you may determine the final score for each essay:

Composite Score	AP Essay Score
33–36	9
29–32	8
25–28	7
21–24	6
18–20	5
15–17	4
10–14	3
7–9	2
6 or below	1

AP Essay Scores   Essay 1 ____   Essay 2 ____   Essay 3 ____

Calculating Your AP Score on Practice Test B

The scores you have earned on the multiple-choice and essay sections of the exam may now be converted to the AP 5-point scale by doing the following calculations:

I. Determine your score for Section I (Multiple-Choice)

    Step A: Number of correct answers _____

    Step B: Number of wrong answers _____ (Note: Do not count unanswered questions.)

    Step C: Multiply the number of wrong answers by .250 and enter the figure here _____

    Step D: Subtract the figure in Step C from the figure in Step A _____

    Step E: Multiply the figure in Step D by 1.2500 to find your Multiple-Choice Score _____ (if less than zero, enter zero)

II. Determine your score for Section II (Essays)[1]

    Step A: Enter your score for Essay 1 (out of 9) _____

    Step B: Enter your score for Essay 2 (out of 9) _____

    Step C: Enter your score for Essay 3 (out of 9) _____

    Step D: Add the figures in Steps A, B, and C _____

    Step E: Multiply the figure in Step D by 3.0556 _____ (Do not round). This is your Essay Score.

III. Determine Your Total Score

    Add the scores for I and II to find your composite score _____ .

To convert your composite score to the AP 5-point scale, use the chart below. The range of scores only approximates what you would earn on the actual test because the exact figures may vary from test to test. Be aware, therefore, that your score on this test, as well as on other tests in this book, may differ slightly from your score on an actual AP exam.

Composite Score	AP Grade
108–150	5
93–107	4
72–92	3
43–71	2
0–42	1

---

[1]After the AP exam, essays are judged in relation to other essays written on the same topic at the same time. Therefore, the score you assign yourself for an essay may not be the same as the score you would earn on an actual exam.

Answer Sheet for Practice Test C

Section I

1. Ⓐ Ⓑ Ⓒ Ⓓ Ⓔ	21. Ⓐ Ⓑ Ⓒ Ⓓ Ⓔ	41. Ⓐ Ⓑ Ⓒ Ⓓ Ⓔ
2. Ⓐ Ⓑ Ⓒ Ⓓ Ⓔ	22. Ⓐ Ⓑ Ⓒ Ⓓ Ⓔ	42. Ⓐ Ⓑ Ⓒ Ⓓ Ⓔ
3. Ⓐ Ⓑ Ⓒ Ⓓ Ⓔ	23. Ⓐ Ⓑ Ⓒ Ⓓ Ⓔ	43. Ⓐ Ⓑ Ⓒ Ⓓ Ⓔ
4. Ⓐ Ⓑ Ⓒ Ⓓ Ⓔ	24. Ⓐ Ⓑ Ⓒ Ⓓ Ⓔ	44. Ⓐ Ⓑ Ⓒ Ⓓ Ⓔ
5. Ⓐ Ⓑ Ⓒ Ⓓ Ⓔ	25. Ⓐ Ⓑ Ⓒ Ⓓ Ⓔ	45. Ⓐ Ⓑ Ⓒ Ⓓ Ⓔ
6. Ⓐ Ⓑ Ⓒ Ⓓ Ⓔ	26. Ⓐ Ⓑ Ⓒ Ⓓ Ⓔ	46. Ⓐ Ⓑ Ⓒ Ⓓ Ⓔ
7. Ⓐ Ⓑ Ⓒ Ⓓ Ⓔ	27. Ⓐ Ⓑ Ⓒ Ⓓ Ⓔ	47. Ⓐ Ⓑ Ⓒ Ⓓ Ⓔ
8. Ⓐ Ⓑ Ⓒ Ⓓ Ⓔ	28. Ⓐ Ⓑ Ⓒ Ⓓ Ⓔ	48. Ⓐ Ⓑ Ⓒ Ⓓ Ⓔ
9. Ⓐ Ⓑ Ⓒ Ⓓ Ⓔ	29. Ⓐ Ⓑ Ⓒ Ⓓ Ⓔ	49. Ⓐ Ⓑ Ⓒ Ⓓ Ⓔ
10. Ⓐ Ⓑ Ⓒ Ⓓ Ⓔ	30. Ⓐ Ⓑ Ⓒ Ⓓ Ⓔ	50. Ⓐ Ⓑ Ⓒ Ⓓ Ⓔ
11. Ⓐ Ⓑ Ⓒ Ⓓ Ⓔ	31. Ⓐ Ⓑ Ⓒ Ⓓ Ⓔ	51. Ⓐ Ⓑ Ⓒ Ⓓ Ⓔ
12. Ⓐ Ⓑ Ⓒ Ⓓ Ⓔ	32. Ⓐ Ⓑ Ⓒ Ⓓ Ⓔ	52. Ⓐ Ⓑ Ⓒ Ⓓ Ⓔ
13. Ⓐ Ⓑ Ⓒ Ⓓ Ⓔ	33. Ⓐ Ⓑ Ⓒ Ⓓ Ⓔ	53. Ⓐ Ⓑ Ⓒ Ⓓ Ⓔ
14. Ⓐ Ⓑ Ⓒ Ⓓ Ⓔ	34. Ⓐ Ⓑ Ⓒ Ⓓ Ⓔ	54. Ⓐ Ⓑ Ⓒ Ⓓ Ⓔ
15. Ⓐ Ⓑ Ⓒ Ⓓ Ⓔ	35. Ⓐ Ⓑ Ⓒ Ⓓ Ⓔ	55. Ⓐ Ⓑ Ⓒ Ⓓ Ⓔ
16. Ⓐ Ⓑ Ⓒ Ⓓ Ⓔ	36. Ⓐ Ⓑ Ⓒ Ⓓ Ⓔ	
17. Ⓐ Ⓑ Ⓒ Ⓓ Ⓔ	37. Ⓐ Ⓑ Ⓒ Ⓓ Ⓔ	
18. Ⓐ Ⓑ Ⓒ Ⓓ Ⓔ	38. Ⓐ Ⓑ Ⓒ Ⓓ Ⓔ	
19. Ⓐ Ⓑ Ⓒ Ⓓ Ⓔ	39. Ⓐ Ⓑ Ⓒ Ⓓ Ⓔ	
20. Ⓐ Ⓑ Ⓒ Ⓓ Ⓔ	40. Ⓐ Ⓑ Ⓒ Ⓓ Ⓔ	

C English Literature and Composition

SECTION I
Multiple-choice questions
Time—1 hour
Percent of total grade on the exam: 45 percent

Instructions: This section of the exam consists of 55 questions on the content, form, and style of several literary selections, both prose and poetry. Please record your answers on the answer sheet provided.

<u>Questions 1–10</u>. Read the following poem carefully before you decide on your answers to the questions.

BERRY PICKING

Silently my wife walks on the still wet furze[1]
Now darkgreen the leaves are full of metaphors
Now lit up is each tiny lamp of blueberry.
The white nails of rain have dropped and the sun is free.

Line
(5)
And whether she bends or straightens to each bush
To find the children's laughter among the leaves
Her quiet hands seem to make the quiet summer hush—
Berries or children, patient she is with these.

(10)
I only vex and perplex her; madness, rage
Are endearing perhaps put down upon the page;
Even silence daylong and sullen can then
Enamor as restraint or classic discipline.

So I envy the berries she puts in her mouth,
The red and succulent juice that stains her lips;
(15)
I shall never taste that good to her, nor will they
Displease her with a thousand barbarous jests.

How they lie easily for her hand to take,
Part of the unoffending world that is hers;
Here beyond complexity she stands and stares
(20)
And leans her marvelous head as if for answers.

No more the easy soul my childish craft deceives
Nor the simpler one for whom yes is always yes;
No, now her voice comes to me from a far way off
Though her lips are redder than the raspberries.

—Irving Layton, 1958

----
[1]a low-lying evergreen shrub

1. Which of the following best describes the mood of the speaker?
    (A) Sadness
    (B) Envy
    (C) Infatuation
    (D) Frustration
    (E) Confusion

2. In line 1, the image "the still wet furze" exemplifies which of the following poetic techniques?
    (A) Caesura
    (B) Consonance
    (C) Onomatopoeia
    (D) Ambiguity of meaning
    (E) Allusion

3. The woman in the poem is characterized primarily by her
    (A) antisocial behavior.
    (B) patience.
    (C) serenity.
    (D) indifference to her husband.
    (E) hearty appetite.

4. Between line 8 and line 9, the speaker shifts from
    (A) present events to recalled events.
    (B) concrete language to abstract language.
    (C) specificity to generalization.
    (D) cause to effect.
    (E) respect to disapproval.

5. In line 12, the verb "Enamor" is best interpreted as
    (A) charm.
    (B) inflame with love.
    (C) captivate.
    (D) be interpreted.
    (E) trick.

6. The notion that the "leaves are full of metaphors" (line 2) is supported by all of the following EXCEPT
    (A) "tiny lamp of blueberry" (line 3).
    (B) "white nails of rain" (line 4).
    (C) "sun is free" (line 4).
    (D) "she bends or straightens" (line 5).
    (E) "children's laughter among the leaves" (line 6).

7. Throughout the poem, the choice of details and images suggests that
    (A) the events taking place are imaginary.
    (B) the husband and wife have recently had an argument.
    (C) the woman is totally absorbed in what she is doing.
    (D) the man considers himself a second-rate poet.
    (E) the man longs to have as much patience as his wife.

8. The woman in the poem is portrayed primarily through her
   (A) actions.
   (B) facial expressions.
   (C) words.
   (D) physical traits.
   (E) body language.

9. In the course of the poem the speaker discloses that he
   (A) no longer loves his wife.
   (B) has often spoken cruelly to his wife.
   (C) rarely consults his wife while making decisions.
   (D) fears growing estranged from his wife.
   (E) feels guilty about having deceived his wife.

10. Which of the following most significantly contributes to the unity of the poem?
    (A) The poem's last line
    (B) The arrangement of rhymes
    (C) Figures of speech
    (D) Repetition of certain sounds
    (E) The warmth and delicacy of the speaker's feelings

Questions 11–25. Read the following passage carefully before you decide on your answers to the questions.

The wound in my uncle *Toby's* groin, which he received at the siege of *Namur*, rendering him unfit for the service, it was thought expedient he should return to *England*, in order, if possible, to be set to rights.

Line
(5)
He was four years totally confined,—part of it to his bed, and all of it to his room; and in the course of his cure, which was all that time in hand, suffer'd unspeakable miseries,—owing to a succession of exfoliations from the *os pubis*,[1] and the outward edge of that part of the *coxendix* called the *os ilium*,[2]—both which bones were dismally crush'd, as much by the irregularity of the stone, which I told you was broke off the parapet,—as by its size,—(though it was pretty large) which inclined the surgeon all along to think, that the great injury which it had done my uncle *Toby's* groin, was more owing to the gravity of the stone itself, than to the projectile force of it,—which he would often tell him was a great happiness.

(10)

My father at that time was just beginning business in *London* and had taken a house;—and as the truest friendship and cordiality subsisted between the two brothers,—and that my father thought my uncle *Toby* could no where be so well nursed and taken care of as in own house,—he assign'd him the very best apartment in it.—And what was a much more sincere mark of his affection still, he would never suffer a friend or an acquaintance to step into the house on any occasion, but he would take him by the hand, and lead him up stairs to see his brother *Toby*, and chat an hour by his bed side.

(15)

(20)

The history of a soldier's wound beguiles the pain of it;—my uncle's visitors, at least, thought so, and in their daily calls upon him, from the courtesy arising out of that belief, they would frequently turn the discourse to that subject,—and from that subject the discourse would generally roll on to the siege itself.

(25)

These conversations were infinitely kind; and my uncle *Toby* received great relief from them, and would have received much more, but that they brought him into some

---

[1]the hipbone
[2]bone in the upper part of the pelvis

unforeseen perplexities, which, for three months together, retarded his cure greatly; and if he had not hit upon an expedient to extricate himself out of them, I verily believe they would have laid him in his grave.

(30) What these perplexities of my uncle *Toby* were,—'tis impossible for you to guess;—if you could,—I should blush; not as a relation,—not as a man,—nor even as a woman,—but I should blush as an author; inasmuch as I set no small store by myself upon this very account, that my reader has never yet been able to guess at any thing. And in this, Sir, I am of so nice a singular humour, that if I thought you was able to
(35) form the least judgment or probable conjecture to yourself, of what was to come in the next page,—I would tear it out of my book.

(1760)

11. The phrase "rendering him unfit for service" (line 2) is reinforced by all of the following EXCEPT
     (A) "should return to *England*" (line 2).
     (B) "four years totally confined" (line 4).
     (C) "suffer'd unspeakable miseries" (lines 5–6).
     (D) "succession of exfoliations" (line 6).
     (E) "bones were dismally crush'd" (lines 7–8).

12. In context, the word "expedient" (line 2) is best interpreted to mean
     (A) opportune.
     (B) in haste.
     (C) practical.
     (D) advisible.
     (E) efficient.

13. The phrase "if possible" in line 3 casts into doubt that Toby
     (A) can be transported back to England.
     (B) has the wherewithal to make it back to England on his own.
     (C) will recover from his wound.
     (D) will ever be well enough to return to the service.
     (E) has the strength to endure a lengthy convalescence.

14. The narrator uses the Latin names of Toby's bones (lines 6–7) primarily to
     (A) suggest that physicians treated Toby as a specimen not a patient.
     (B) show respect for the reader's erudition.
     (C) endow the passage with the ring of truth.
     (D) reveal the level of anatomical information available at the time.
     (E) impress readers with his knowledge of Latin.

15. Prior to this passage, the author evidently wrote
     (A) a biography of his father.
     (B) a history of England's military operations in foreign lands.
     (C) an exposé of medical practices in London.
     (D) a portrait of his family.
     (E) an account of Toby's experience at the siege of *Namur.*

16. The shift in the narrator's rhetorical stance with the clause "which he would often tell him was a great happiness" (line 12) can best be described as one from
    (A) intellectual to emotional.
    (B) laudatory to critical.
    (C) garrulous to terse.
    (D) objective to sarcastic.
    (E) detached to argumentative.

17. The best interpretation of the word "subsisted" in line 14 is
    (A) persisted.
    (B) continued.
    (C) held.
    (D) fed.
    (E) obtained.

18. The narrator's attitude toward his father may best be described as
    (A) awestruck.
    (B) affectionate.
    (C) dutiful.
    (D) reverential.
    (E) respectful.

19. Which of the following statements about Toby's condition does the narrator imply?
    (A) Toby's wounds healed more rapidly than expected.
    (B) Frequent conversations about the siege of *Namur* slowed Toby's recovery.
    (C) Toby would have recovered sooner had his surgeon administered the proper treatment.
    (D) The dimensions of the rock that hit Toby had little to do with the seriousness of the wound.
    (E) Toby's brother aided considerably in Toby's recovery.

20. The sentence beginning in line 17 does which of the following?
    (A) It lends support to the sentence that preceded it.
    (B) It implies the narrator's real feelings about Toby.
    (C) It addresses details that had been lacking in earlier paragraphs.
    (D) It casts doubt on the accuracy of the previous sentence.
    (E) It adds important details to the portrait of Toby.

21. The sentence "The history of a soldier's wound beguiles the pain of it" (line 21) does which of the following?
    (A) It shifts the focus of the passage from a specific case to generalities.
    (B) It explains why Toby's visitors brought up a particular topic of conversation.
    (C) It introduces a problem that interferes with Toby's recovery.
    (D) It articulates a widely accepted theory of medical professionals.
    (E) It raises a controversial issue.

22. The phrase "if you could" (line 31) suggests that the narrator places great value on
    (A) keeping readers well informed.
    (B) keeping his readers in suspense.
    (C) shocking readers with gruesome details.
    (D) taking readers into his confidence.
    (E) flattering his readers.

23. The last paragraphs (lines 25–36) suggest that this passage is likely to precede an account of
    (A) how Toby overcame unexpected barriers to his recuperation.
    (B) Toby's return to military service.
    (C) Toby's near-death experiences.
    (D) conversations that took place at Toby's bedside.
    (E) the outcome of the siege of *Namur*.

24. The last paragraph of the passage differs from those that preceded it in all of the following ways EXCEPT
    (A) it addresses the reader directly.
    (B) it turns away from the past in order to discuss Toby's future.
    (C) it focuses on the narrator instead of on Toby.
    (D) it shifts from third person to first person.
    (E) it reveals a new aspect of the narrator's personality.

25. Which of the following pairs of adjectives best describes the tone of the passage?
    (A) Disdainful/scornful
    (B) Haughty/pompous
    (C) Courteous/deferential
    (D) Solemn/measured
    (E) Satirical/critical

Questions 26–40. Read the following poem carefully before you decide on your answers to the questions.

GASCOIGNE'S GOODNIGHT

When thou has spent the lingering day in pleasure and delight,
Or after toil and weary way, dost seek to rest at night,
Unto thy pains or pleasures past, add this one labor yet:
Line Ere sleep close up thine eye too fast, do not thy God forget,
(5) But search within thy secret thoughts, what deeds did thee befall;
And if thou find amiss in aught,[1] to God for mercy call.
Yea, though thou find nothing amiss which thou canst call to mind,
Yet evermore remember this: there is the more behind;
And think how well so ever it be that thou hast spent the day,
(10) It came of God, and not of thee, so to direct thy way.
Thus, if thou try thy daily deeds and pleasure in this pain,
Thy life shall cleanse thy corn from weeds, and thine shall be the gain;
But if thy sinful, sluggish eye will venture for to wink,

---

[1]anything, to any degree

Before thy wading will may try how far thy soul may sink,

(15)   Beware and wake; for else, thy bed, which soft and smooth is made,
May heap more harm upon thy head than blows of en'my's blade.
Thus if this pain procure thine ease, in bed as thou dost lie,
Perhaps it shall not God displease to sing thus, soberly:
"I see that sleep is lent me here to ease my weary bones,

(20)   As death at last shall eke[2] appear, to ease my grievous groans.
My daily sports, my paunch full fed, have caused my drowsy eye,
As careless life, in quiet led, might cause my soul to die.
The stretching arms, the yawning breath, which I to bedward use,
Are patterns of the pangs of death, when life will me refuse.

(25)   And of my bed each sundry part in shadows doth resemble
The sundry shapes of death, whose dart shall make my flesh to
   tremble.
My bed itself is like the grave, my sheets the winding sheet,
My clothes the mold which I must have to cover me most meet;[3]

(30)   The hungry fleas, which frisk so fresh, to worms I can compare,
Which greedily shall gnaw my flesh and leave the bones full bare.
The waking cock, that early crows to wear the night away
Puts in my mind the trump that blows before the Latter Day.
And as I rise up lustily when sluggish sleep is past,

(35)   So hope I to rise joyfully to Judgment at the last.
Thus will I wake, thus will I sleep, thus will I hope to rise,
Thus will I neither wail nor weep, but sing in godly wise;
My bones shall in this bed remain, my soul in God shall trust,
By whom I hope to rise again from death and earthly dust."

—George Gascoigne (1539–1578)

26.   In context, "there is the more behind" (line 8) is best interpreted to mean
   (A)   it's impossible for one to remember everything that happens in a day.
   (B)   a day has more meaning to it than you think.
   (C)   another day will be coming tomorrow.
   (D)   don't end a day without reflecting on it.
   (E)   no day passes during which one can do everything properly.

27.   The mood of the poem can best be described as
   (A)   inspirational.
   (B)   suspenseful.
   (C)   pious.
   (D)   skeptical.
   (E)   haunting.

28.   In the metaphor in line 12, "weeds" is used to stand for
   (A)   wasted lives.
   (B)   wickedness.
   (C)   undesirable labor.
   (D)   God's wrath.
   (E)   weariness.

---

[2]also
[3]properly, exactly

29. Which of the following stylistic devices most significantly contributes to the unity of lines 1–19?
    (A) The use of epigrams
    (B) An extended metaphor
    (C) The use of archaic pronouns such as "thou" and "thee"
    (D) Repetition of sentences in the subjunctive mood
    (E) A series of declarative statements

30. The pronoun "it" in line 18 refers to
    (A) "ease" in line 17.
    (B) the recitation of lines 19–39.
    (C) the "song" quoted from line 19 to line 39.
    (D) the bed alluded to in lines 15 and 17.
    (E) the pain mentioned in line 17.

31. Lines 19–24 contain all of the following poetic devices EXCEPT
    (A) personification.
    (B) analogy.
    (C) alliteration.
    (D) internal rhyme.
    (E) synecdoche.

32. The main purpose of the comment "My daily sports, my paunch full fed, have caused my drowsy eye,/As careless life, in quiet led, might cause my soul to die" (lines 21–22) is to
    (A) caution the reader against a life devoid of spiritual things.
    (B) mock anyone who lives only for the present.
    (C) cite reasons why some men ignore God.
    (D) suggest that bodily functions cause fatigue.
    (E) assert that lack of self-control may lead to dire consequences.

33. Which of the following best characterizes the poem's language?

    I. It uses numerous images of farm life.
    II. It is religious in nature.
    III. It is abundant with images of death.

    (A) I only
    (B) II only
    (C) I and II only
    (D) II and III only
    (E) I, II and III

34. Lines 23–29 most resemble which of the following rhetorical devices?
    (A) An elegy
    (B) A metonymy
    (C) A paradoxical understatement
    (D) A mixed metaphor
    (E) An analogy

35. Which of the following is a major concern of the speaker in the poem?
    (A) Fear of dying
    (B) Preparing for sleep
    (C) An unexamined life
    (D) Leading a life without joy
    (E) Excessive hedonism

36. In line 34, "lustily" is best interpreted to mean
    (A) full of desire.
    (B) eagerly.
    (C) loudly.
    (D) without modesty.
    (E) with good intentions.

37. The poem is best described as a
    (A) case study of a sinner.
    (B) lesson in moral behavior.
    (C) type of sermon.
    (D) didactic fable.
    (E) prayer to God.

38. Based on the content of the poem, with which of the following statements is the speaker most likely to agree?

    I. People are so caught up in the daily affairs of life that they neglect God.
    II. Through nature God has provided humanity with a source of freshness and inspiration.
    III. To assure that their souls will ultimately rise to heaven, people must acknowledge and respect God.

    (A) II only
    (B) I and II only
    (C) I and III only
    (D) II and III only
    (E) I, II, and III

39. The "sundry shapes of death" (line 26) include all of the following EXCEPT
    (A) "shadows" (line 25).
    (B) "the winding sheet" (line 28).
    (C) "the mold" (line 29).
    (D) "worms" (line 30).
    (E) "the trump" (line 33).

40. Throughout the poem, the speaker's attitude toward death is best characterized as
    (A) an escape from the burdens of life.
    (B) something for which one should prepare.
    (C) something to look forward to.
    (D) acceptance of the inevitable.
    (E) detached indifference.

<u>Questions 41–55.</u> Read the following passage carefully before you decide on your answers to the questions.

He never asked her whether she had seen Morris again, because he was sure that if this had been the case she would tell him. She had, in fact, not seen him; she had only written him a long letter. The letter, at least, was long for her; and, it may be added, that it was long for Morris; it consisted of five pages, in a remarkably neat and handsome hand. Catherine's handwriting was beautiful, and she was even a little proud of it; she was extremely fond of copying, and possessed volumes of extracts which testified to this accomplishment; volumes which she had exhibited one day to her lover, when the bliss of feeling that she was important in his eyes was exceptionally keen. She told Morris, in writing, that her father had expressed the wish that she should not see him again, and that she begged he would not come to the house until she should have 'made up her mind.' Morris replied with a passionate epistle, in which he asked to what, in Heaven's name, she wished to make up her mind. Had not her mind been made up two weeks before, and could it be possible that she entertained the idea of throwing him off? Did she mean to break down at the very beginning of their ordeal, after all the promises of fidelity she had both given and extracted? And he gave an account of his own interview with her father—an account not identical at all points with that offered in these pages. 'He was terribly violent,' Morris wrote, 'but you know my self-control. I have need of it all when I remember that I have it in my power to break in upon your cruel captivity.' Catherine sent him, in answer to his, a note of three lines. 'I am in great trouble; do not doubt my affection, but let me wait a little and think.' The idea of a struggle with her father, of setting up her will against his own, was heavy on her soul, and it kept her quiet, as a great physical weight keeps us motionless. It never entered into her mind to throw her lover off; but from the first she tried to assure herself that there would be a peaceful way out of their difficulty. The assurance was vague, for it contained no element of positive conviction that her father would change his mind. She only had an idea that if she should be very good, the situation would in some mysterious manner improve. To be good she must be patient, outwardly submissive, abstain from judging her father too harshly, and from committing any act of open defiance. He was perhaps right, after all, to think as he did; by which Catherine meant not in the least that his judgement of Morris's motives in seeking to marry her was perhaps a just one, but that it was probably natural and proper that conscientious parents should be suspicious and even unjust. There were probably people in the world as bad as her father supposed Morris to be, and if there were the slightest chance of Morris being one of these sinister persons, the Doctor was right in taking it into account. Of course he could not know what she knew—how the purest love and truth were seated in the young man's eyes; but Heaven, in its time, might appoint a way of bringing him to such knowledge. Catherine expected a good deal of Heaven, and referred to the skies the initiative, as the French say, in dealing with her dilemma. She could not imagine herself imparting any kind of knowledge to her father; there was something superior even in his injustice, and absolute in his mistakes. But she could at least be good, and if she were only good enough, Heaven would invent some way of reconciling all things—the dignity of her father's errors and the sweetness of her own confidence, the strict performance of her filial duties, and the enjoyment of Morris Townsend's affection.

(1880)

41. The comment that Catherine's letter to Morris "was long for her" (line 3) is most likely intended to
- (A) illustrate one aspect of Catherine's character.
- (B) suggest that Catherine is semiliterate.
- (C) turn the reader against Catherine.
- (D) imply that Catherine usually has more important things to do.
- (E) show that Catherine's love for Morris had cooled.

42. The "accomplishment" mentioned in line 7 refers to
- (A) Catherine's beautiful handwriting.
- (B) an extraordinary letter from Morris to Catherine.
- (C) the five-page letter Catherine wrote to Morris.
- (D) Catherine's fondness for copying.
- (E) Catherine's collection of books containing copied excerpts.

43. In lines 8–9, "when the bliss of feeling that she was important in his eyes was exceptionally keen" implies that
- (A) Catherine fears that she has lost Morris's love.
- (B) Morris is determined to end his affair with Catherine.
- (C) Catherine's attitude toward Morris has undergone a change.
- (D) Catherine and Morris have yet to declare their love for each other.
- (E) Morris has betrayed Catherine.

44. The phrase "in Heaven's name" (line 12) is meant to show
- (A) that Morris is incredulous that Catherine has betrayed him.
- (B) that Morris doubts Catherine's commitment to him.
- (C) how desperately Morris loves Catherine.
- (D) Morris's religious bent.
- (E) Morris's perplexity over Catherine's words.

45. The description of Morris's exchange of letters with Catherine (lines 9–21) suggests that this passage most probably comes after

   I. an account of the the couple's declaration of love for each other.
  II. a narrative of a meeting that occurred between Morris and Catherine's father.
 III. a scene in which Catherine's father instructs his daughter to break up with Morris.

- (A) II only
- (B) III only
- (C) I and II only
- (D) II and III only
- (E) I, II, and III

46. Morris's tone at the beginning of his letter to Catherine (lines 11–17) shifts in the last segment of the letter (lines 17–19, starting with the words "'He was terribly violent . . . '") from
    (A) bewildered to aggressive.
    (B) contrite to pretentious.
    (C) confident to apprehensive.
    (D) hostile to conciliatory.
    (E) forlorn to optimistic.

47. Grammatically, the word "note" (line 20) serves as
    (A) the direct object of the verb "sent" (line 19).
    (B) the subject of the sentence in which the word appears (lines 19–20).
    (C) the indirect object of the verb "sent" (line 19).
    (D) the object of the preposition "in" (line 19).
    (E) an appositive for "answer" (line 19).

48. By comparing the "idea of a struggle with her father" (line 21) with "a great physical weight keeps us motionless" (lines 22–23) the narrator invites the thought that
    (A) Catherine is really looking for an excuse to break off with Morris.
    (B) Catherine is unaccustomed to talking back to her father.
    (C) Catherine is not likely to solve her problem without assistance.
    (D) Catherine and Morris are destined sooner or later to go their separate ways.
    (E) Catherine's father is some sort of petty tyrant.

49. For Catherine, the dominant hindrances to solving the problem with her father include all of the following EXCEPT
    (A) his presumption of his own infallibility.
    (B) proving to him that Morris is a truthful and loving person.
    (C) his desire to be a conscientious parent.
    (D) his propensity for violence.
    (E) her unwillingness to defy or oppose him.

50. Catherine's intuition tells her that her father will change his mind about Morris if she does all of the following EXCEPT
    (A) refrain from exhibiting her true feelings about what her father has done.
    (B) adhere to her father's wishes.
    (C) seek help from a reputable third party to intervene in her behalf.
    (D) try to be a model daughter.
    (E) give her father a chance to reconsider by letting an ample amount of time go by.

51. The structure of the sentence beginning in line 29 and ending on line 32 achieves which of the following?
    (A) It implies that Catherine is accustomed to being treated unjustly by her father.
    (B) It indicates that Catherine, while differing from her father, is aware that he has the right to be unjust.
    (C) It contradicts Catherine's assertion in the previous sentence that she must not judge her father too harshly.
    (D) It suggests that her father's opinion of Morris may be more accurate than her own.
    (E) It emphasizes the callousness of Catherine's father.

52. In context, the phrase "referred to the skies" in line 38 is best interpreted to mean
    (A) left in the hands of God.
    (B) relied on the movement of the stars.
    (C) remained optimistic.
    (D) believed that God controlled her father's behavior.
    (E) waited for Fate to act.

53. Catherine's primary dilemma consists mainly of a conflict between
    (A) satisfying herself and keeping Morris happy.
    (B) protesting her father's decision and displaying her usual tranquillity.
    (C) convincing her father to change his mind and letting fate take its course.
    (D) being a dutiful daughter and basking in a loving relationship with Morris.
    (E) adhering to her pledge to Morris and wrestling with her conscience.

54. Catherine's feelings for her father might best be described as a combination of
    (A) disdain and cynicism.
    (B) respect and fear.
    (C) deference and resentment.
    (D) faithfulness and naïveté.
    (E) appreciation and admiration.

55. The passage is chiefly concerned with a
    (A) misunderstanding and its adjudication.
    (B) romance and its dissolution.
    (C) conflict and its aftereffects.
    (D) plan and its undoing.
    (E) rite of passage and suffering it induces.

SECTION II.
Three essay questions
Total time—2 hours
Suggested time for each essay—40 minutes
Percent of total grade on the exam: 55 percent

Instructions: This section of the exam consists of three questions that require responses in essay form. You may write the essays in any order you wish and return to work on a completed essay if time permits. Although it is suggested that you spend roughly 40 minutes on each essay, you may apportion your time as you see fit.

Each essay will be evaluated according to its clarity, effectiveness in dealing with the topics, and the overall quality of your writing. If you have the time, go over each essay, checking its punctuation, spelling, and diction. Unless plenty of time remains, try to avoid major revisions. In the end, the quality of each essay counts more than its quantity.

For Question 3, please choose a novel or play of at least the same literary merit as the works you have been assigned in your AP English course.

Essays should be written in pen, preferably with black or dark blue ink. Use lined paper and write as legibly as you can. Do not skip lines. Cross out any errors you make. Feel free to make notes and plan your essay on a piece of scrap paper. Please number your essays and begin each one on a new sheet of paper. Good luck.

Essay Question 1
(Suggested time—40 minutes. This question counts as one-third of your score for Section II of the exam.)

The following poem was inspired by "The Man with the Hoe," a painting by Millet. Read the poem carefully and then write an essay in which you characterize the speaker's views of the figure in the painting. Then, analyze how the speaker conveys those views. Consider the poem's structure, figurative language, diction, imagery, or any other relevant poetic devices.

THE MAN WITH THE HOE

(Written after seeing Millet's world-famous painting of a brutalized toiler)

God made man in His own image, in the image of God made He him.

—Genesis

Bowed by the weight of centuries he leans
Upon his hoe and gazes on the ground,
The emptiness of ages in his face,
Line And on his back the burden of the world.
(5) Who made him dead to rapture and despair,
A thing that grieves not and that never hopes,
Stolid and stunned, a brother to the ox?
Who loosened and let down this brutal jaw?
Whose was the hand that slanted back this brow?
(10) Whose breath blew out the light within this brain?

Is this the Think the Lord God made and gave
To have dominion over sea and land;
To trace the stars and search the heavens for power;
To feel the passion of Eternity?
(15) Is this the dream He dreamed who shaped the suns
And marked their ways upon the ancient deep?
Down all the caverns of Hell to their last gulf
There is no shape more terrible than this—
More tongued with censure of the world's blind greed—
(20) More filled with signs and portents for the soul—
More packed with danger to the universe.

What gulfs between him and seraphim!
Slave of the wheel of labor, what to him
Are Plato and the swing of Pleiades?
(25) What the long reaches of the peaks of song,
The rift of dawn, the reddening of the rose?
Thru this dread shape the suffering ages look;
Time's tragedy is in that aching stoop;
Thru this dread shape humanity betrayed,
(30) Plundered, profaned and disinherited,
Cries protest to the Judges of the World,
A protest that is also prophesy.

O masters, lords and rulers in all lands,
Is this the handiwork you give to God,
(35) This monstrous thing distorted and soul-quenched?
How will you ever straighten up this shape;
Touch it again with immortality;
Give back the upward looking and the light;
Rebuild in it the music and the dream;
(40) Make right the immemorial infamies,
Perfidious wrongs, immedicable woes?

O masters, lords and rulers in all lands,
How will the future reckon with this Man?
How answer his brute question in that hour
(45)   When whirlwinds of rebellion shake all shores?
How will it be with kingdoms and with kings—
With those who shaped him to the thing he is—
When this dumb Terror shall rise to judge the world,
After the silence of the centuries?

—Edwin Markham, 1899

Essay Question 2

(Suggested time—40 minutes. This question counts as one-third of your score for Section II of the exam.)

After reading the following excerpt from the British novel, *Vanity Fair* (1848) by William Makepeace Thackery, please write an essay that analyzes how the character of the woman is revealed and how the characterization serves the author's purpose. You may focus on tone, point of view, imagery, diction, choice of detail, or any other literary elements you deem important.

Sometimes—once or twice a week—that lady visited the upper regions in which the child lived. She came like a vivified figure out of the *Magazin des Modes*—blandly smiling in the most beautiful new clothes and little gloves and boots. Wonderful
Line scarves, laces, and jewels glittered about her. She had always a new bonnet on: and
(5)   flowers bloomed perpetually in it: or else magnificent curling ostrich feathers, soft and snowy as camellias. She nodded twice or thrice patronisingly to the little boy, who looked up from his dinner or from the pictures of soldiers he was painting. When she left the room, an odour of rose, or some other magical fragrance, lingered about the nursery. She was an unearthly being in his eyes, superior to his father—to all the
(10)   world: to be worshipped and admired at a distance. To drive with that lady in the carriage was an awful rite: he sat up in the back seat, and did not dare to speak: he gazed with all his eyes at the beautifully dressed princess opposite him. Gentlemen on splendid prancing horses came up, and smiled and talked with her. How her eyes beamed upon them! Her hand used to quiver and wave gracefully as they passed. When he
(15)   went out with her he had his new red dress on. His old brown holland[1] was good enough when he stayed at home. Sometimes when she was away, and Dolly his maid was making the bed, he came into his mother's room. It was the abode of a fairy to him—a mystic chamber of splendor and delights. There in the wardrobe hung those wonderful robes—pink and blue, and many-tinted. There was the jewel-case, silver-
(20)   clasped: and the wondrous bronze hand on the dressing-table, glistening all over a hundred rings. There was the cheval-glass, that miracle of art, in which he could just see his own wondering head, and the reflection of Dolly (queerly distorted, and as if up in the ceiling), plumping and patting the pillows of the bed. Oh, thou poor lonely little benighted boy! Mother is the name of God in the lips and hearts of little children;
(25)   and here was one who was worshipping a stone!

---

[1] a linen or cotton shirt

Essay Question 3

(Suggested time—40 minutes. This question counts as one-third of your score for Section II of the exam.)

In many works of literature a character conquers great obstacles to achieve a worthy goal. Sometimes the obstacle is a personal impediment, at other times it consists of the attitudes and beliefs of others.

Pick a play or novel in which an important character must overcome a personal or social obstacle in order to achieve a worthwhile goal. Then write a well-organized essay that explains the goal and how the character reaches it. Also explain the ways in which the character's struggle contributes to the meaning of the work as a whole. Do not merely summarize the plot.

Choose a title from the following list or another play or novel of comparable literary merit.

Crime and Punishment
The Crucible
Cyrano de Bergerac
An Enemy of the People
Ethan Frome
The Glass Menagerie
The Grapes of Wrath
Great Expectations
The Great Gatsby
Gulliver's Travels
Heart of Darkness
King Lear
Madame Bovary
Native Son
The Picture of Dorian Gray
A Portrait of the Artist as a Young Man
The Red and the Black
The Scarlet Letter
The Stranger
Tess of the d'Urbervilles
Their Eyes Are Watching God
Washington Square

END OF PRACTICE TEST C

Answer Key for Practice Test C—Section I

1. A	12. D	23. A	34. E	45. E
2. D	13. C	24. B	35. B	46. A
3. C	14. C	25. D	36. B	47. A
4. A	15. E	26. B	37. C	48. B
5. D	16. D	27. C	38. C	49. D
6. D	17. C	28. B	39. A	50. C
7. C	18. E	29. D	40. B	51. B
8. A	19. E	30. B	41. A	52. A
9. B	20. A	31. E	42. D	53. D
10. A	21. B	32. A	43. C	54. B
11. A	22. B	33. D	44. E	55. C

Summary of Answers in Section I Multiple-Choice

Number of correct answers _____

Number of incorrect answers _____

Number of questions not answered _____

Use this information when you calculate your score on this exam. See page 359.

Answer Explanations

SECTION I

1. **A** As the speaker observes his wife, he admits that she seems more content picking berries than she is with him. The observation saddens him.

2. **D** The word "still" is somewhat ambiguous. It often means *quiet*, an adjective that certainly fits the tranquil setting of the poem. But the phrase "still wet" also describes foliage that has remained wet after the rain.

3. **C** Starting with the word "Silently" in line 1, the poet piles detail upon detail to portray his wife as a quiet, reserved person. Line 7 ("Her quiet hands seem to make the quiet summer hush") is perhaps the most telling description of her serenity.

4. **A** The first two stanzas are devoted to describing the site and the woman's behavior while picking berries. In the third stanza the poet begins to think about how his wife usually responds to him.

5. **D** Ordinarily *enamor* relates to love, but in this context it suggests misinterpretation. At the end of the day, the poet's long and sullen silence can be mistaken for "restraint or classic discipline."

6. D All of the choices except "she bends or straightens" are figures of speech.

7. C Through much of the poem the speaker scrutinizes the woman, noting that berry picking not only gives her peace of mind but commands her undivided attention.

8. A The speaker concentrates on what the woman does while berry picking. Among other things, he shows her walking, bending, straightening up, and eating the berries.

9. B The speaker admits in line 16 that he has displeased his wife "with a thousand barbarous jests."

10. A The last line succinctly expresses the speaker's feelings, echoing sentiments expressed earlier in the poem. Briefly, he realizes that his wife derives more pleasure and satisfaction from the red and succulent berries than she does from him.

11. A All the choices except (A) cite a reason that Toby can no longer serve. Choice (A), on the other hand, names a consequence, not a cause, of his inability to serve.

12. D The dictionary lists several definitions for "expedient," including *proper, advantageous, opportune, suitable,* and *politic.* In the context of this passage, the best definition is *advisible* because Toby's wound needed expert attention as soon as possible.

13. C In context the phrase refers to "be set to rights." In other words, Toby's wound was so serious that his recovery was questionable.

14. C Using Latin nomenclature creates the impression that the passage was well researched and is scientifically accurate.

15. E Support for this answer is found in lines 8–9, where the narrator mentions that he had previously said that the stone that wounded Toby "broke off the parapet."

16. D Until line 12 the speaker provides an objective account of Toby's wound. His comment that the doctor calls the injury "a great happiness," however, is tinged with sarcasm.

17. C The word is used to indicate that the brothers were held together by a firm and friendly bond.

18. E The passage is full of details that imply the narrator's respect for his father. In particular, see lines 13–20.

19. E Toby's brother went out of his way to help. Toby received particular relief from the conversations with people his brother ushered to his bedside.

20. A The sentence supports the previous one in which the narrator describes how his father took pains to care for his wounded brother.

21. B The paragraph following the given sentence says that visitors thought they would be doing Toby a good turn by inviting him to talk about his wound.

22. B The phrase appears in a brief discussion of the author's desire to keep readers in the dark about what comes next. He would blush if readers could guess.

23. A In this section of the passage the speaker alludes to "unforeseen perplexities" that he intends to explain next.

24. B The speaker virtually ignores Toby's past and future in the final paragraph.

25. D Uncle Toby's story is told in a basically sober and straightforward manner.

26. B Lines 9–10 explain the meaning of the clause: however you spent the day, don't forget that God gave it to you and directed you through it.

27. C The speaker in the poem, as though delivering a sermon, promotes piety and urges the reader never to overlook God's mercy.

28. B The couplet in which the word appears makes the point that assessing each day's experiences will enable you to distinguish between the good things you did ("corn") and the wicked things ("weeds"), and will ultimately work to your advantage ("thine shall be the gain").

29. D At least four of the half-dozen sentences between lines 1–18 use "if" to express a hypothetical condition. In other words, "*if* such-and-such occurred, then the following would happen." The repeated use of "if" sentences corresponds with the speaker's purpose—to show readers the rewards that await them *if* they change their behavior.

30. B Because the entire quotation reads "Perhaps it shall not God displease to sing thus, soberly:" the pronoun "it" refers to the act of singing or reciting the words of the "song" that follows.

31. E In line 20 death is personified. Also in line 20 you'll find an example of alliteration ("grievous groans"). Lines 23–24 contain an analogy. The lines also contain internal rhymes, as in "fed" and "led" (lines 21–22). Only a synecdoche is missing, making (E) the correct answer.

32. A The lines describe the sort of life that causes a "soul to die," meaning a life fit more for a beast perhaps than for a person intent on saving his soul for the hereafter.

33. D Aside from referring to corn and to the crowing of a cock, the poem contains no images related to life on a farm. Rather, the language if full of religious words and phrases, among others, "to God for mercy call," "It came of God," and "rise joyfully to Judgment." In addition, allusions to death pervade the second half of the poem.

34. E In the given lines, the speaker makes an analogy. Using a series of similes, he compares dying and going to sleep.

35. B The speaker in the poem is preoccupied with the rituals associated with going to sleep. He repeatedly makes the point that you shouldn't drop off at the end of a day without thanking God for the gifts He has bestowed upon you.

36. B   The word is used to describe the manner in which a devout worshipper might rise from his bed after a good night's sleep. Expecting God to take his soul into Heaven, he awakens eagerly, as though he is answering God's call to Judgment.

37. C   The prayer (lines 19–39) illustrates what one might say to please God. But the overall purpose of the poem is to persuade readers to let God into their lives. In that sense, the speaker is much like a preacher delivering an inspirational sermon to his flock.

38. C   Statement I is discussed in the first half of the poem, especially in lines 1–10. The latter half of the poem—particularly lines 34–39—deals with the idea expressed in Statement III. Statement II has no relevancy to the poem.

39. A   The "winding sheet" refers to the cloth in which corpses are wrapped. The "mold" and "worms" allude to the decay and gradual decomposition of an interred body. The "trump" is the trumpet blown to announce Judgment Day. Only the word "shadows" fails to count as one of the "sundry shapes" of death.

40. B   According to the poem, because death may come at any time, you must prepare by always trusting God and striving to be in His good graces. With faith in God, you need not fear your demise. On the Day of Judgment your soul will be raised "from death and earthly dust."

41. A   The comment reveals a dimension of Catherine's personality, namely, that she shuns writing lengthy letters, especially at a time like this, when her relationship with Morris appears to be in jeopardy. Her father's insistence that she and Morris never see each other again could also have kept her from writing a longer letter.

42. D   The passage states that Catherine owned volumes of extracts "which testified to this accomplishment," referring to the previous clause, "she was extremely fond of copying" (line 6).

43. C   Only when Catherine had been confident that Morris loved and treasured her unconditionally had she dared to show him volumes of extracts she had copied. The narrator mentions this fact to suggest that in her present state of mind Catherine could no longer do such a thing.

44. E   To Morris it is inconceivable that Catherine would consider siding with her father against him. Therefore, he either feigns bewilderment or is truly puzzled by her assertion that she needs time to think about whether to see him again.

45. E   Morris's letter refers to the time two weeks earlier when he and Catherine had promised fidelity to each other (lines 12–15). The narrator also mentions that an account of Morris's meeting with Catherine's father had been offered earlier "in these pages" (lines 16–17). Catherine's letter alludes to a conversation during which her father had exhorted her not to see Morris again (lines 9–11). Directly or indirectly, therefore, the letters suggest that events I, II, and III appeared earlier in the text.

46. A At first Morris puzzles over suddenly being excluded from Catherine's house and Catherine's apparent change of heart. Later, his words become threatening as he reminds her of the power he has "to break in upon" her "cruel captivity." In other words, he claims to have the wherewithal to stir up some sort of trouble—but the passage fails to explain what the trouble might be.

47. A A direct object receives the action of a verb or shows the consequence of the action. In this case, Catherine "sent" (verb) a "note" (the object receiving the action).

48. B The reason that a potential struggle with her father weighs on Catherine's soul (lines 21–22) is that she is unused to disobeying or challenging his authority. Even her affection for Morris cannot break a longstanding pattern of giving in to her father.

49. D Although Morris reports that Catherine's father was "terribly violent," during their conversation, Catherine disregards the allegation. She is very aware, however, that her father was not one to acknowledge his own mistakes (lines 40–41), that she would be unable to alter her father's opinion of Morris (lines 25–26), and that a consientious parent should be expected to be suspicious of a daughter's beaus (lines 31–32). In addition, the thought of struggling with her father weighed Catherine down (lines 21–23).

50. C Lines 26–29 contain a list of things that Catherine thinks she ought to do. Each of the choices shows up on her list except (C), calling on a third party to intervene.

51. B The sentence consists of three clauses. The first one consists of Catherine's acknowledgment of her father's right to think as he does. The last, or third, clause explains why, and the clause between them describes Catherine's feelings about the matter.

52. A Several allusions to Heaven toward the end of the passage suggest Catherine's inability to change her father's way of thinking about Morris. Therefore, she has no choice but to rely on Heaven, or God, to help solve her dilemma.

53. D Catherine's dilemma, described in lines 42–44, alludes to the conflict between "the strict performance of her filial duties, and the enjoyment of Morris Townsend's affection."

54. B Although Catherine thinks that her father has misjudged Morris, she respects his role as one that is "natural and proper" for a conscientious parent. At the same time she is afraid of setting herself up against him and unwilling to engage him in a struggle that she will certainly lose.

55. C The passage is devoted first to providing background information about a dispute that has arisen between Catherine and her father. It then shows the effect of the conflict on Catherine and to some extent on Morris.

SECTION II

Although answers to essay questions will vary greatly, the following descriptions suggest an approach to each question and contain ideas that could be used in a response. Perhaps your essay contains many of the same ideas. If not, don't be alarmed. Your ideas may be at least as valid as those presented below.

Note: Don't mistake these descriptions for complete essays; essays written for the exam should be full-length, well organized, and fully developed. For an overview of how essays are graded, turn to "How AP Essays Are Scored," on page 35.

Essay Question 1

The figure in the painting horrifies and distresses the speaker. As depicted, he is physically strong ("brother to the ox") but stooped from carrying the "burden of the world" on his back. His head, with its "slanted back" brow, resembles that of a Neanderthal. A victim of death in life ("dead to rapture and despair") the man is a less-than-human creature.

In the second stanza, the speaker rails against the existence of such a brute and asks whether God could have had such a being in mind when He made a man in His own image. The question alludes to the quotation from *Genesis* that precedes the first stanza of the poem.

Next, the speaker decries the huge chasm separating this subhuman beast and the angels (line 22). The man, in effect is "humanity betrayed,/Plundered, profaned and disinherited" (lines 29–30).

In the fourth stanza, the speaker addresses those responsible for such an atrocity, namely the "masters, lords, and rulers in all lands," and demands to know what they intend to do to set things right, to restore the man's humanity.

And in the last stanza, the speaker warns the masters, lords, and rulers that they'd better do something because, when "this Man" (now capitalized to suggest that he represents the downtrodden masses of the world) rises in rebellion, they will have to answer for their actions.

The speaker's response to the painting, then, begins viscerally but evolves into a social/political polemic delivered at a fever pitch with passionate, highly charged diction, including such evocative images as "The emptiness of ages on his face" (line 3), "Down all the caverns of Hell to their last gulf/There is no shape more terrible than this—" (lines 17–18), and "whirlwinds of rebellion shake the world" (line 45). In short, to express his wrath, the speaker relies on hyperbolic, often alliterative bombast: "on his back the burden of the world" (line 4), "Plato and the swing of Pleiades" (line 24), "The rift of dawn, the reddening of the rose" (line 26).

Further, the poem is written in blank verse, a form that fits the content, for a finely crafted rhyme scheme would ill befit the speaker's effusive torrent of fiery words. The poem's emotionalism is heightened still further by a rush of rhetorical questions meant to represent the speaker's moral outrage: "Who loosened and let down this brutal jaw? /. . .Whose breath blew out the light within this brain?" (lines 8 and 10). The speaker answers his own questions. He indicts the demons who remain anonymous but are vaguely categorized as the "masters, lords and rulers in all lands."

The author of "The Man with the Hoe," has tried to be profound and grandiose in thought, language, and idea. Whether he succeeds or whether the poem is little more than windy, melodramatic rant is arguable. Regardless, it's difficult to remain unimpressed by the speaker's empathy for the wretched masses of the world.

Essay Question 2

The woman in the passage seems like a nineteenth century version of a glamor queen. Details about her appearance, her clothes, and the impact she leaves on her admirers dominate her portrait. The imagery is rich in sensuality—for example, her glittering jewels (line 4), her "magnificent curling ostrich feathers, soft and snowy as camellias" (lines 5–6), and the "odour of rose, or some other magical fragrance" (line 8) that she leaves behind after exiting a room.

The voice of the narrator, prevailing in the early part of the passage, gives way to the point of view of the little boy in line 9. From then on, we observe the woman through the innocent eyes of her son, until line 23 when the narrator returns to pass judgment on his subject. To the boy, the woman is like a fairy goddess, an unearthly being deserving of worship and admiration. The narrator, whose opinion differs, however, declares that she patronizes the little boy (line 6). Both the narrator and her son at one point refer to the woman as "that lady," a scornful turn of phrase that suggests her vanity and self-indulgence. Indeed, her aloofness is illustrated by calling her a "beautifully dressed princess" (line 12) who waves gracefully from her carriage. As much as the little boy admires his mother, the two remain distant from each other. For him riding in a carriage with her is "an awful rite" (line 11) for she ignores him and pays attention only to passing gentlemen on horseback.

The last several lines of the passage reinforce how distant the woman is from her son. The boy enters his mother's "mystic chamber of splendor and delights" (line 18) and is virtually overcome with the wardrobe and the room's furnishings. But all this occurs only in her absence.

Concluding the passage, the narrator undercuts everything favorable about the woman by calling her a "stone"—a terrible indictment. At the same time he creates sympathy for her son, referring to him as a "little benighted boy!"

Essay Question 3

All of the listed titles contain material with which to answer the question.

Tom Wingfield in *The Glass Menagerie* by Tennessee Williams, exemplifies a young man leading a life of frustrated dreams. He has the mind and heart of a poet and would like to go out and see the world instead of coping every day with an overbearing mother, a semi-invalid sister, and a job that bores him to tears. One tragic night his patience runs out. He abandons his family and leaves town for good. But he fails to escape completely. As he wanders the earth searching for some elusive paradise, the memory of his sister haunts him. The ending of the play leaves you with the thought that happiness, like so much else in Tom's life, is an illusion.

Another character, Pip, the hero of *Great Expectations* by Charles Dickens, would also serve as the subject of an essay on overcoming obstacles. Pip, who has an abiding dream to be a gentleman, is hindered in his pursuit of success by his low-class background and rustic manners. Throughout the novel Pip struggles to create his own identity. As he matures he realizes the corrupting power of wealth. He also learns to distrust other people and becomes convinced that life will disappoint him. Yet, he maintains a basic goodness. After years of frustration, he achieves the stature he has sought and wins the hand and heart of Estella, a woman he has long but unsuccessfully pursued.

Tom Joad, the protagonist of John Steinbeck's *The Grapes of Wrath*, also represents a man struggling to achieve a goal. Throughout the novel he seeks contentment and security in a world that scorns not only him but his family and countless other refugees from the Dust Bowl of Oklahoma who crisscross the valleys of California in search of work. Tom gets into trouble by killing a deputy sheriff. Suddenly a fugitive, he leaves his family and sets out on his own. What had once been a search for individual happiness broadens into a mini-crusade in behalf of the masses of poor, exploited workers. Tom, in fact, embodies what is perhaps the book's main message—that by working together, people will overcome adversity.

Self-Scoring Guide for Practice Test C

Scoring Section 2   ESSAYS

After referring to "How Essays Are Scored," on page 35 of this book, use this guide to help you evaluate each essay. Do your best to evaluate your performance in each category by using the criteria spelled out below. Because it is hard to achieve objectivity when assessing your own writing, you may improve the validity of your score by having a trusted and well-informed friend or experienced teacher read and rate your essay.

On the following Rating Chart, enter a number (from 1 to 6) that you think represents your level of performance in each category (A–F).

Category A: OVERALL PURPOSE/MAIN IDEA
    6   extremely well-defined and insightful
    5   clearly defined and generally insightful
    4   mostly clear
    3   somewhat clear but occasionally confusing
    2   generally unclear and confusing
    1   virtually incomprehensible

Category B: HANDLING OF THE PROMPT
    6   self-evident or extremely clear throughout
    5   mostly clear
    4   somewhat clear
    3   somewhat unclear
    2   generally unclear or ambiguous
    1   confusing or nonexistent

Category C: ORGANIZATION AND DEVELOPMENT
    6   insightfully organized; fully developed with excellent supporting evidence
    5   reasonably well organized; developed with appropriate supporting material
    4   appropriately organized; developed with some relevant material
    3   inadequately organized; weak development
    2   poorly organized; little or no development
    1   no discernible organization; no relevant development

Category D: SENTENCE STRUCTURE
    6   varied and engaging
    5   sufficiently varied to create interest
    4   some variety
    3   little variety; minor sentence errors
    2   frequent sentence errors that interfere with meaning
    1   serious sentence errors that obscure meaning

Category E: USE OF LANGUAGE
    6   precise and effective word choice
    5   competent word choice
    4   conventional word choice; mostly correct
    3   some errors in diction or idiom
    2   frequent errors in diction or idiom
    1   meaning obscured by word choice

Category F: GRAMMAR AND USAGE
    6   error-free or virtually error-free
    5   occasional minor errors
    4   basically correct but with several minor errors
    3   meaning somewhat obscured by errors
    2   meaning frequently obscured by errors
    1   meaning blocked by several major errors

RATING CHART

Rate your essay:	Essay 1	Essay 2	Essay 3
Overall Purpose/Main Idea	____	____	____
Handling of the Prompt	____	____	____
Organization and Development	____	____	____
Sentence Structure	____	____	____
Use of Language	____	____	____
Grammar and Usage	____	____	____
Composite Scores (Sum of each column)	____	____	____

By using the following chart, in which composite scores are converted to the 9-point AP rating scale, you may determine the final score for each essay:

Composite Score	AP Essay Score
33–36	9
29–32	8
25–28	7
21–24	6
18–20	5
15–17	4
10–14	3
7–9	2
6 or below	1

AP Essay Scores   Essay 1 _____   Essay 2 _____   Essay 3 _____

Calculating Your AP Score on Practice Test C

The scores you have earned on the multiple-choice and essay sections of the exam may now be converted to the AP 5-point scale by doing the following calculations:

I.   Determine your score for Section I (Multiple-Choice)

Step A: Number of correct answers _____

Step B: Number of wrong answers _____ (Note: Do not count unanswered questions.)

Step C: Multiply the number of wrong answers by .250 and enter the figure here _____

Step D: Subtract the figure in Step C from the figure in Step A _____

Step E: Multiply the figure in Step D by 1.2500 to find your Multiple-Choice Score _____ (if less than zero, enter zero)

II. Determine your score for Section II (Essays)[1]

Step A: Enter your score for Essay 1 (out of 9) _____

Step B: Enter your score for Essay 2 (out of 9) _____

Step C: Enter your score for Essay 3 (out of 9) _____

Step D: Add the figures in Steps A, B, and C _____

Step E: Multiply the figure in Step D by 3.0556 _____ (Do not round). This is your Essay Score.

III. Determine Your Total Score

Add the scores for I and II to find your composite score _____ .

To convert your composite score to the AP 5-point scale, use the chart below. The range of scores only approximates what you would earn on the actual test because the exact figures may vary from test to test. Be aware, therefore, that your score on this test, as well as on other tests in this book, may differ slightly from your score on an actual AP exam.

Composite Score	AP Grade
108–150	5
93–107	4
72–92	3
43–71	2
0–42	1

[1]After the AP exam, essays are judged in relation to other essays written on the same topic at the same time. Therefore, the score you assign yourself for an essay may not be the same as the score you would earn on an actual exam.

Answer Sheet for Practice Test D

Section I

1. Ⓐ Ⓑ Ⓒ Ⓓ Ⓔ	21. Ⓐ Ⓑ Ⓒ Ⓓ Ⓔ	41. Ⓐ Ⓑ Ⓒ Ⓓ Ⓔ
2. Ⓐ Ⓑ Ⓒ Ⓓ Ⓔ	22. Ⓐ Ⓑ Ⓒ Ⓓ Ⓔ	42. Ⓐ Ⓑ Ⓒ Ⓓ Ⓔ
3. Ⓐ Ⓑ Ⓒ Ⓓ Ⓔ	23. Ⓐ Ⓑ Ⓒ Ⓓ Ⓔ	43. Ⓐ Ⓑ Ⓒ Ⓓ Ⓔ
4. Ⓐ Ⓑ Ⓒ Ⓓ Ⓔ	24. Ⓐ Ⓑ Ⓒ Ⓓ Ⓔ	44. Ⓐ Ⓑ Ⓒ Ⓓ Ⓔ
5. Ⓐ Ⓑ Ⓒ Ⓓ Ⓔ	25. Ⓐ Ⓑ Ⓒ Ⓓ Ⓔ	45. Ⓐ Ⓑ Ⓒ Ⓓ Ⓔ
6. Ⓐ Ⓑ Ⓒ Ⓓ Ⓔ	26. Ⓐ Ⓑ Ⓒ Ⓓ Ⓔ	46. Ⓐ Ⓑ Ⓒ Ⓓ Ⓔ
7. Ⓐ Ⓑ Ⓒ Ⓓ Ⓔ	27. Ⓐ Ⓑ Ⓒ Ⓓ Ⓔ	47. Ⓐ Ⓑ Ⓒ Ⓓ Ⓔ
8. Ⓐ Ⓑ Ⓒ Ⓓ Ⓔ	28. Ⓐ Ⓑ Ⓒ Ⓓ Ⓔ	48. Ⓐ Ⓑ Ⓒ Ⓓ Ⓔ
9. Ⓐ Ⓑ Ⓒ Ⓓ Ⓔ	29. Ⓐ Ⓑ Ⓒ Ⓓ Ⓔ	49. Ⓐ Ⓑ Ⓒ Ⓓ Ⓔ
10. Ⓐ Ⓑ Ⓒ Ⓓ Ⓔ	30. Ⓐ Ⓑ Ⓒ Ⓓ Ⓔ	50. Ⓐ Ⓑ Ⓒ Ⓓ Ⓔ
11. Ⓐ Ⓑ Ⓒ Ⓓ Ⓔ	31. Ⓐ Ⓑ Ⓒ Ⓓ Ⓔ	51. Ⓐ Ⓑ Ⓒ Ⓓ Ⓔ
12. Ⓐ Ⓑ Ⓒ Ⓓ Ⓔ	32. Ⓐ Ⓑ Ⓒ Ⓓ Ⓔ	52. Ⓐ Ⓑ Ⓒ Ⓓ Ⓔ
13. Ⓐ Ⓑ Ⓒ Ⓓ Ⓔ	33. Ⓐ Ⓑ Ⓒ Ⓓ Ⓔ	53. Ⓐ Ⓑ Ⓒ Ⓓ Ⓔ
14. Ⓐ Ⓑ Ⓒ Ⓓ Ⓔ	34. Ⓐ Ⓑ Ⓒ Ⓓ Ⓔ	54. Ⓐ Ⓑ Ⓒ Ⓓ Ⓔ
15. Ⓐ Ⓑ Ⓒ Ⓓ Ⓔ	35. Ⓐ Ⓑ Ⓒ Ⓓ Ⓔ	55. Ⓐ Ⓑ Ⓒ Ⓓ Ⓔ
16. Ⓐ Ⓑ Ⓒ Ⓓ Ⓔ	36. Ⓐ Ⓑ Ⓒ Ⓓ Ⓔ	
17. Ⓐ Ⓑ Ⓒ Ⓓ Ⓔ	37. Ⓐ Ⓑ Ⓒ Ⓓ Ⓔ	
18. Ⓐ Ⓑ Ⓒ Ⓓ Ⓔ	38. Ⓐ Ⓑ Ⓒ Ⓓ Ⓔ	
19. Ⓐ Ⓑ Ⓒ Ⓓ Ⓔ	39. Ⓐ Ⓑ Ⓒ Ⓓ Ⓔ	
20. Ⓐ Ⓑ Ⓒ Ⓓ Ⓔ	40. Ⓐ Ⓑ Ⓒ Ⓓ Ⓔ	

D English Literature and Composition

SECTION I
Multiple-choice questions
Time—1 hour
Percent of total grade on the exam: 45 percent

Instructions: This section of the exam consists of 55 questions on the content, form, and style of several literary selections, both prose and poetry. Please record your answers on the answer sheet provided.

<u>Questions 1–15</u>. Read the following passage carefully before you decide on your answers to the questions.

When we went down-stairs, we were presented to Mr. Skimpole, who was standing before the fire, telling Richard how fond he used to be, in his school-time, of football. He was a little bright creature, with a rather large head; but a delicate face, and
Line a sweet voice, and there was a perfect charm in him. All he said was so free from
(5) effort and spontaneous, and was said with such a captivating gaiety, that it was fascinating to hear him talk. Being of a more slender figure than Mr. Jarndyce, and having a richer complexion, with browner hair, he looked younger. Indeed, he had more the appearance, in all respects, of a damaged young man, than a well-preserved elderly one. There was an easy negligence in his manner, and even in his dress (his
(10) hair carelessly disposed, and his neckerchief loose and flowing, as I have seen artists paint their own portraits), which I could not separate from the idea of a romantic youth who had undergone some unique process of depreciation. It struck me as being not at all like the manner or appearance of a man who had advanced in life, by the usual road of years, cares, and experiences.
(15) I gathered from the conversation, that Mr. Skimpole had been educated for the medical profession, and had once lived in his professional capacity, in the household of a German prince. He told us, however, that as he had always been a mere child in points of weights and measures, and had never known anything about them (except that they disgusted him), he had never been able to prescribe with the requisite
(20) accuracy of detail. In fact, he said, he had no head for detail. And he told us, with great humour, that when he was wanted to bleed the prince, or physic any of his people, he was generally found lying on his back, in bed, reading the newspapers, or making fancy sketches in pencil, and couldn't come. The prince, at last objecting to this, 'in which,' said Mr. Skimpole, in the frankest manner, 'he was perfectly right,' the
(25) engagement terminated, and Mr. Skimpole having (as he added with delightful gaiety) 'nothing to live upon but love, fell in love, and married, and surrounded himself with rosy cheeks.' His good friend Jarndyce and some other of his good friends then helped him, in quicker or slower succession, to several openings in life; but to no purpose, for he must confess to two of the oldest infirmities in the world: one was, that he had no
(30) idea of time; the other, that he had no idea of money. In consequence of which he never kept an appointment, never could transact any business, and never knew the value of anything! Well! So he had got on in life, and here he was! He was very fond of reading the papers, very fond of making fancy sketches with a pencil, very fond of nature, very fond of art. All he asked of society was, to let him live. *That* wasn't

(35)   much. His wants were few. Give him the papers, conversation, music, mutton, coffee, landscape, fruit in the season, a few sheets of Bristol-board, and a little claret, and he asked no more. He was a mere child in the world, but he didn't cry for the moon. He said to the world, 'Go your several ways in peace! Wear red coats, blue coats, lawn sleeves, put pens behind your ears, wear aprons; go after glory, holiness, commerce,

(40)   trade, any object you prefer; only—let Harold Skimpole live!'

All this, and a great deal more, he told us, not only with the utmost brilliancy and enjoyment, but with a certain vivacious candour—speaking of himself as if he were not at all his own affair, as if Skimpole were a third person, as if he knew that Skimpole had his singularities, but still had his claims too, which were the general

(45)   business of the community and must not be slighted. He was quite enchanting. If I felt at all confused at that early time, in endeavoring to reconcile anything he said with anything I had thought about the duties and accountabilities of life (which I am far from sure of), I was confused by not exactly understanding why he was free of them. That he *was* free of them, I scarcely doubted; he was so very clear about it himself.

(1852)

1. The narrator is quickly caught up in Skimpole's story mainly because of
   (A) the respect he has for Skimpole.
   (B) Skimpole's youthful appearance.
   (C) their mutual interest in football.
   (D) their similar background and education.
   (E) Skimpole's manner of speaking.

2. The narrator is puzzled by one aspect of Skimpole's story primarily because
   (A) the narrator considers Skimpole a kindred spirit.
   (B) the narrator lacks experience in the world.
   (C) the narrator, like Skimpole, has no head for detail.
   (D) Skimpole jumps from subject to subject.
   (E) the narrator is too young to understand Skimpole.

3. In line 8, "damaged" is best interpreted to mean
   (A) unconventional.
   (B) secretly wounded.
   (C) emotionally upset.
   (D) worn out.
   (E) troubled.

4. The antecedent of the relative pronoun "which" in line 11 is
   (A) negligence (line 9).
   (B) manner (line 9).
   (C) dress (line 9).
   (D) hair (line 10).
   (E) neckerchief (line 10).

5. Which of the following pairs of adjectives best describe the narrator's tone?
   (A) Solemn and proud
   (B) Derisive and flippant
   (C) Affable and affectionate
   (D) Laudatory and worshipful
   (E) Envious and uncertain

6. Which of the following best describes the purpose(s) of the excerpt?

   I. To introduce Skimpole through the eyes of the narrator
   II. To reveal some of the narrator's values and biases
   III. To compare Skimpole and the narrator

   (A) I only
   (B) I and II only
   (C) I and III only
   (D) II and III only
   (E) I, II, and III

7. The chief effect of the diction and imagery in lines 3–14 is to
   (A) affirm the congeniality of the gathering taking place downstairs.
   (B) suggest that Skimpole is a pretentious braggart.
   (C) establish a mood of foreboding about Skimpole's future.
   (D) create an impression of an unconventional man.
   (E) provoke the suspicion that Skimpole is concealing something about his past.

8. The shift that occurs between the first and second paragraphs of the passage can best be described as one from
   (A) stating generalities to focusing on details.
   (B) expressing opinions to doling out impressions.
   (C) presenting hypotheses to drawing conclusions.
   (D) observing the present to recalling the past.
   (E) reporting facts to explaining implications.

9. The phrase "rosy cheeks" (line 27) is an example of
   (A) synechdoche.
   (B) personification.
   (C) metaphor.
   (D) metonymy.
   (E) onomatopoeia.

10. In line 28, "in quicker or slower succession" is best interpreted to mean that
    (A) help was rendered according to a prearranged plan.
    (B) some of Skimpole's friends lacked the enthusiasm to lend a hand.
    (C) Skimpole asked for help from his friends as he needed it.
    (D) Jarndyce and others knew that helping Skimpole would be fruitless.
    (E) Skimpole received help as job opportunities became available.

11. The narrator's interjection, "Well! So he had got on in life, and here he was" (line 32), functions in all of the following ways EXCEPT

(A) it conveys the idea that Skimpole had no regrets about his weaknesses.

(B) it editorializes about Skimpole's ineptitude.

(C) it paraphrases something Skimpole said.

(D) it suggests that Skimpole's infirmities had no long-lasting effect on him.

(E) it serves as a transition between sections of Skimpole's story.

12. The structure of the sentence beginning in line 38 ("Wear red . . .") does which of the following?

(A) It demonstrates the intensity of Skimpole's frustrations.

(B) It reflects the failure of society to accept a character like Skimpole.

(C) It supports the earlier assertion that "he didn't cry for the moon" (line 37).

(D) It suggests that Skimpole may be deranged.

(E) It illustrates Skimpole's broadmindedness.

13. The last paragraph (lines 41–49) suggests that this passage most probably precedes an account of

(A) the narrator's increased understanding of what Skimpole was all about.

(B) how Skimpole acquired his skill as a *bon vivant*.

(C) Skimpole's continued efforts to make something of himself.

(D) the narrator's efforts to befriend Skimpole.

(E) the narrator's decision to make Skimpole his role model and to follow in his footsteps.

14. The dominant impression that Skimpole leaves on the narrator is that of

(A) a failure.

(B) a playboy.

(C) a rogue.

(D) a nonconformist.

(E) a freeloader.

15. The passage as a whole draws a contrast between

(A) inclusion and exlusion.

(B) knowledge and ignorance.

(C) conformity and individuality.

(D) illusion and reality.

(E) youth and age.

Questions 16–25. Read the following poem carefully before you decide on your answers.

A LITANY

Ring out your bells, let mourning shows be spread:
For Love is dead.
    All Love is dead, infected
With plague of deep disdain;
    Worth, as nought worth, rejected,
And Faith fair scorn doth gain.
    From so ungrateful fancy,[1]
    From such female franzy,[2]
      From them that use men thus,
      Good Lord, deliver us!

Weep, neighbors, weep! do you not hear it said
That Love is dead?
    His death-bed, peacock's folly;
His winding-sheet is shame;
    His will, false-seeming holy;
His sole executor, blame.
    From so ungrateful fancy,
    From such a female franzy,
      From them that use men thus,
      Good Lord, deliver us!

Let dirge[3] be sung and trentrals[4] rightly read,
For Love is dead.
    Sir Wrong his tomb ordaineth[5]
My mistress Marble-heart,
    Which epitaph containeth,
"Her eyes were once his dart."
    From so ungrateful fancy
    From such a female franzy,
      From them that use men thus,
      Good Lord, deliver us!

Alas, I lie, rage hath this error bred;
Love is not dead.
    Love is not dead, but sleepeth
In her unmatchéd mind,
    Where she his counsel keepeth,
Till due desert she find.
    Therefore from so vile fancy,
    To call such wit a franzy,
      Who Love can temper thus,
      Good Lord, deliver us!

(Sir Philip Sidney, c. 1580)

Line (5), (10), (15), (20), (25), (30), (35), (40)

---

[1]love
[2]frenzy
[3]song for the dead
[4]thirty Roman Catholic masses for the dead
[5]solemnly declares

16. Which of the following events most likely preceded the writing of the poem?
   (A) The speaker's lover passed away.
   (B) A mass was held at the church.
   (C) The speaker was cast aside by his lover.
   (D) The speaker had a dispute with his neighbors.
   (E) The speaker attended a graveside funeral service.

17. The emotional effect of the first stanza (lines 1–10) is achieved mainly by
   (A) use of hyperbole.
   (B) use of alliteration.
   (C) use of a concluding couplet.
   (D) a long first line followed by a terse second line.
   (E) a metaphor comparing love with the plague.

18. One effect of lines 5–6 is to emphasize the speakers's sense of
   (A) pity.
   (B) modesty.
   (C) regret.
   (D) loyalty.
   (E) powerlessness.

19. What does the speaker convey in lines 11–12?
   (A) A desire for company
   (B) Resentment and impatience
   (C) Wrath and guilt
   (D) A need to be pitied and comforted
   (E) The sanctity of the moment

20. The last four lines of stanzas 1, 2, and 3 can best be paraphrased as
   (A) "Lord, let other women be more grateful for my affection."
   (B) "Lord, save me from ungrateful, irrational women."
   (C) "Lord, spare men the emotional turmoil brought on by women."
   (D) "Lord, why must women be so heartless?"
   (E) "Lord, I am suffering; please don't let me fall in love again."

21. The most unconventional and idiosyncratic aspect of the poem is its
   (A) rhymes.
   (B) meter and rhythm.
   (C) spelling.
   (D) syntax.
   (E) figurative language.

22. Lines 37–40 imply all of the following about the speaker EXCEPT that he
   (A) regrets reacting so hysterically.
   (B) is never likely to fall in love again.
   (C) recognizes that his love for the lady was flawed.
   (D) mistook uncontrollable passion for love.
   (E) hopes never to make the same mistake again.

23. Which images are most extensively used in the poem?
  (A) Those pertinent to disorder and chaos
  (B) Those relevant to male-female relationships
  (C) Those alluding to death and dying
  (D) Those relating to religious rituals
  (E) Those concerning love and romance

24. Which of the following marks a turning point in the speaker's tone?
  (A) "And Faith fair scorn doth gain" (line 6)
  (B) "Weep, neighbors, weep!" (line 11)
  (C) "His sole executor, blame" (line 16)
  (D) "'Her eyes were once his dart'" (line 26)
  (E) "Love is not dead" (line 32)

25. The poem is best described as
  (A) a lyric on the death of love.
  (B) a polemic on women's fickleness.
  (C) an allegory about a man's self-discovery.
  (D) a ballad about love's hardships.
  (E) an ironic ode to a heartless woman.

Questions 26–35. Read the following passage carefully before you decide on your answers to the questions.

STREPSIADES: O dear! O dear!
O Lord! O Zeus! these nights, how long they are.
Will they ne'er pass? will the day never come?
Line Surely I heard the cock crow, hours ago.
(5) Yet my servants still snore. These are new customs.
O 'ware of war for many various reasons;
One fears in war even to flog one's servants.
And here's this hopeful son of mine wrapped up
Snoring and sweating under five thick blankets.
(10) Come, we'll wrap up and snore in opposition.
                    (*Tries to sleep.*)
But I can't sleep a wink, devoured and bitten
By ticks, and bugbears,[1] duns,[2] and race-horses,
All through this son of mine. *He* curls his hair,
(15) And sports his thoroughbreds, and drives his tandem;[3]
Even in dreams he rides: while I—I'm ruined,
Now that the Moon has reached her twentieths,[4]
And paying time comes on. Boy! light a lamp,
And fetch my ledger: now I'll reckon up
(20) Who are my creditors, and what I owe them.
Come, let me see then. *Fifty pounds to Pasias!*
Why fifty pounds to Pasias? what were they for?
O, for the hack[5] from Corinth. O dear! O dear!
I wish my eye had been hacked out before—

[1]source of irritation
[2]a brownish-gray horse; also a mayfly; also a creditor
[3]two-seated carriage drawn by horses
[4]the twentieth of the month, when bills were due
[5]taxi ride

(25)   PHEIDIPPIDES (*in his sleep*). You are cheating, Philon; keep to your own side.

STREPSIADES: Ah! there it is! that's what has ruined me!
Even in his very sleep he thinks of horses.
. . . Well then, you sleep: only be sure of this,
These debts will fall on your own head at last.
(30)   Alas! alas! For ever cursed be that same matchmaker,
Who stirred me up to marry your poor mother.
Mine in the country was the pleasantest life,
Untidy, easy-going, unrestrained,
Brimming with olives, sheepfolds, honey-bees.
(35)   Ah! then I married—I a rustic—her
A fine town-lady, niece of Magacles.
A regular, proud, luxurious, Coesyra.
This wife I married, and we came together,
I rank with the wine-lees, fig boards, greasy woolpacks;
(40)   She all with scents, and saffron, and tongue-kissings,
Feasting, expense, and lordly modes of loving.
. . . Well, when at last to me and my good woman
This hopeful son was born, our son and heir,
Why then we took to wrangle on the name.
(45)   She was for giving him some knightly name,
"Callippides," "Xanthippus," or "Charippus:"
I wished "Pheidonides," his grandsire's name.
We compromised it in Pheidippides.
This boy she took, and used to spoil him, saying
(50)   *Oh! when you are driving to the Acropolis, clad*
Like Magacles, in your purple; whilst I said
Oh! when the goats you are driving from the fells,
Clad like your father, in your sheepskin coat.
Well, he cared nought for my advice, but soon
(55)   A galloping consumption caught my fortunes.
Now cogitating all night long, I've found
One way, one marvellous transcendent way,
Which if he'll follow, we may yet be saved.
So,—but, however, I must rouse him first.

(423 B.C.)

26.   The phrase "new customs" (line 5) refers to the
   (A)   seemingly endless nights.
   (B)   speaker's insomnia.
   (C)   crowing of the cock.
   (D)   servants' snoring.
   (E)   servants' indifference.

27.   Strepsiades' distress and discontent come from all of the following
sources EXCEPT
   (A)   an unsuitable marriage.
   (B)   a profligate son.
   (C)   declining health.
   (D)   burdensome debts.
   (E)   a fretful nature.

28. In line 14, "through" is best understood to mean
- (A) as a consequence.
- (B) throughout.
- (C) because of.
- (D) by means of.
- (E) depending on.

29. In line 24, Strepsiades' unfinished thought would most likely pertain to
- (A) his marriage.
- (B) Pasias.
- (C) the trip to Corinth.
- (D) the birth of Pheidippides.
- (E) horses.

30. From the context, the reader can infer that Strepsiades is a former
- (A) gardener.
- (B) woodcutter.
- (C) farmer.
- (D) ploughman.
- (E) goatherd.

31. One effect of lines 28–29 is to suggest Strepsiades' feelings of
- (A) hostility.
- (B) impatience.
- (C) inflexibility.
- (D) jealousy.
- (E) humility.

32. Most of the passage can best be described as a
- (A) villanelle.
- (B) soliloquy.
- (C) peroration.
- (D) dramatic monologue.
- (E) stream of consciousness.

33. Humor in the passage is derived mainly from
- (A) Strepsiades' use of puns.
- (B) the banality of the subjects discussed.
- (C) the speaker's reliance on clichés.
- (D) the background of Strepsiades' wife.
- (E) Strepsiades' sarcasm.

34. Lines 40–41 are used to convey which of the following about Pheidippides mother?
- (A) Her preoccupation with social status
- (B) Her physical charms
- (C) Her reason for marrying Strepsiades
- (D) Her overweening pride
- (E) Her fancy upbringing

35. The content of lines 50–54 does which of the following?

    (A) Explains why Pheidippides is disobedient.

    (B) Illustrates a basic difference between husband and wife.

    (C) Compares the clothing of the rich and the poor.

    (D) Suggests that Strepsiades blames his wife for Pheidippides' faults.

    (E) Shows that Pheidippides is closer to his mother than to his father.

<u>Questions 36–45</u>. Read the following poem carefully before you decide on your answers to the questions.

CHANNEL FIRING

That night your great guns, unawares,
Shook all our coffins as we lay,
And broke the chancel[1] window-squares,
We thought it was the Judgment-day

(Line)
(5)   And sat upright. While drearisome
Arose the howl of wakened hounds:
The mouse let fall the altar-crumb,
The worms drew back into the mounds,

The glebe cow[2] drooled. Till God called, "No;
(10) It's gunnery practice out at sea
Just as before you went below;
The world is as it used to be:

"All nations striving strong to make
Red war yet redder. Mad as hatters
(15) They do no more for Christés sake
Than you who are helpless in such matters.

"That this is not the judgment-hour
For some of them's a blessed thing,
For if it were they'd have to scour
(20) Hell's floor for so much threatening . . .

"Ha, ha. It will be warmer when
I blow the trumpet (if indeed
I ever do; for you are men,
And rest eternal sorely need)."

(25) So down we lay again. "I wonder,
Will the world ever saner be,"
Said one, "than when He sent us under
In our indifferent century!"

And many a skeleton shook his head.
(30) "Instead of preaching forty year,"
My neighbor Parson Thirdly said,
"I wish I had stuck to pipes and beer."

———
[1]area in a church holding the altar and the choir
[2]cow put out to pasture on church land

Again the guns disturbed the hour,
Roaring their readiness to avenge,
(35)   As far inland as the Stourton Tower,[3]
And Camelot[4], and starlit Stonehenge:[5]

(1914)

36. The dramatic situation of the poem can best be described as
    (A) ecclesiastical.
    (B) ethereal.
    (C) naturalistic.
    (D) fantastic.
    (E) suspenseful.

37. In line 14, "Red" metaphorically describes the
    (A) bloodiness of war.
    (B) government's political persuasion.
    (C) passion with which wars are fought.
    (D) debt incurred by warring nations.
    (E) dangers inherent in war.

38. God's laugh ("Ha, ha") in line 21 is meant to illustrate that

    I. God has a sense of humor.
    II. God thinks that some men are fools.
    III. God is not above poking fun at Himself.

    (A) I only
    (B) III only
    (C) I and II only
    (D) II and III only
    (E) I, II, and III

39. In line 27 "sent us under" is best interpreted as
    (A) gave us coffins.
    (B) returned to bed.
    (C) put us to sleep.
    (D) took our lives.
    (E) took care of us.

40. In its context, the word "indifferent" (line 28) can best be interpreted as
    (A) absurd.
    (B) reckless.
    (C) distracted.
    (D) oblivious.
    (E) bewildered.

---

[3]tower built to honor Alfred the Great's victory over the Danes
[4]King Arthur's castle
[5]prehistoric megalithic circle on Salisbury Plain

41. From line 32 to line 33 the tone of the poem shifts from
    (A) whimsical to ominous.
    (B) honest to mendacious.
    (C) serious to ironic.
    (D) facetious to forthright.
    (E) detached to compassionate.

42. The allusions in lines 35 and 36 serve all of the following purposes
    EXCEPT
    (A) to provide the poem with a more poignant ending.
    (B) to suggest that men of the past are hardly different from men of today.
    (C) to propose that readers do all they can to put an end to war.
    (D) to convey a sense of fatalism about men's bellicose nature.
    (E) to ground a basically whimsical poem in reality.

43. The reference to "Christés sake" (line 15) is echoed in
    (A) the broken windows in the chancel (line 3).
    (B) the trumpet blown on Judgment Day (line 22).
    (C) God's comments in lines 21–24.
    (D) Parson Thirdly's words (lines 30 and 32).
    (E) allusions to Camelot and Stonehenge (line 36).

44. The poem's main theme might best be described as
    (A) the universality of death.
    (B) the inevitability of war.
    (C) the influence of the past.
    (D) the power of God.
    (E) man's inhumanity to man.

45. Which of the following literary devices most significantly contributes to
    the poem's unity?
    (A) References to animals
    (B) The use of onomatopeia
    (C) Repetition of key words
    (D) The use of meter
    (E) The use of epigrammatic language

Questions 46–55. Read the following passage carefully before you decide on
your answers to the questions.

As they were sitting together, the prince commanded Imlac to relate his history, and
to tell by what accident he was forced, or by what motive induced, to close his life in
the happy valley. As he was going to begin his narrative, Rasselas was called to a
Line concert, and obliged to restrain his curiosity till the evening.
(5) The close of the day in the regions of the torrid zone, the only season of diversion
and entertainment, and it was therefore midnight before the music ceased, and the
princesses retired. Rasselas then called for his companion and required him to begin
the story of his life.

(10) "Sir," said Imlac, "my history will not be long; the life that is devoted to knowledge passes silently away, and is very little diversified by events. To talk in public, to think in solitude, to read and to hear, to inquire and answer inquiries, is the business of a scholar. He wanders about the world without pomp or terror and is neither known nor valued but by men like himself.

(15) "I was born in the kingdom of Goiama, at no great distance from the fountain of the Nile. My father was a wealthy merchant who traded between the inland countries of Africa and the ports of the Red Sea. He was honest, frugal, and diligent, but of mean sentiments and narrow comprehension: he desired only to be rich, and to conceal his riches, lest he should be spoiled by the governors of the province."

(20) "Surely," said the prince, "my father must be negligent of his charge, if any man in his dominions dares take that which belongs to another. Does he not know that kings are accountable for injustice permitted as well as done? If I were emperor, not the meanest of my subjects should be oppressed with impunity. My blood boils when I am told that a merchant durst[1] not enjoy his honest gains for fear of losing them by the rapacity of power. Name the governor who robbed the people, that I may declare his

(25) crimes to the emperor."

"Sir," said Imlac, "your ardor is the natural effect of virtue animated by youth: the time will come when you shall acquit your father, and perhaps hear with less impatience of the governor. Oppression is, in the Abyssinian dominions, neither frequent nor tolerated; but no form of government has been yet discovered by which

(30) cruelty can be wholly prevented. Subordination supposes power on one part and subjection on the other; and if power be in the hands of men, it will sometimes be abused. The vigilance of the supreme magistrate may do much, but much will still remain undone. He can never know all the crimes that are committed and can seldom punish all that he knows."

(35) "This," said the prince, "I do not understand, but I had rather hear thee than dispute. Continue the narration."

"My father" proceeded Imlac, "originally intended that I should have no other education than such as might qualify me for commerce; and discovering in me great strength of memory and quickness of apprehension, often declared his hope that I

(40) should be some time the richest man in Abyssinia."

"Why," said the prince, "did thy father desire the increase of his wealth when it was already greater than he durst discover or enjoy? I am unwilling to doubt thy veracity, yet inconsistencies cannot both be true."

"Inconsistencies," answered Imlac, "cannot be right, but, imputed to man, they may

(45) both be true. Yet diversity is not inconsistency. My father might expect a time of greater security. However, some desire is necessary to keep life in motion, and he, whose real wants are supplied, must admit those of fancy."

"This," said the prince, "I can in some measure conceive. I repent that I interrupted thee."

(50) "With this hope," proceeded Imlac, "he sent me to school; but when I had once found the delight of knowledge and felt the pleasure of intelligence and the pride of invention, I began silently to despise riches and determined to disappoint the purpose of my father, whose grossness of conception raised my pity. I was twenty years old before his tenderness would expose me to the fatigue of travel, in which time I had

(55) been instructed, by successive masters, in all the literature of my native country. As every hour taught me something new, I lived in a continual course of gratifications; but, as I advanced towards manhood, I lost much of the reverence with which I had been used to look on my instructors; because, when the lesson was ended, I did not find them wiser or better than common men."

(1759)

---

[1]past tense of the verb *to dare*

46. Grammatically, the word "season" (line 5) functions as
    (A) the predicate nominative of the sentence.
    (B) the modifier of "only" (line 5).
    (C) an appositive for "close" (line 5).
    (D) the indirect object of "was" (line 6).
    (E) the object of the preposition "in" (line 5).

47. Which of the following aspects of a scholar's existence (listed in lines 10–13) is most clearly illustrated in the passage?
    (A) It "passes silently away."
    (B) It is "very little diversified by events."
    (C) It consists of reading and hearing.
    (D) It involves thinking in solitude and answering inquiries.
    (E) It requires wandering about the world.

48. In context, the phrase "lest he should be spoiled" (line 18) is best paraphrased as
    (A) unless he wanted to be flattered.
    (B) so that he would not be catered to.
    (C) because he did not want to be influenced.
    (D) to keep himself from being exploited.
    (E) to avoid associating with.

49. The structure of the sentence beginning in line 20 ("Does he . . .?") does all of the following EXCEPT
    (A) make a statement in the form of a question.
    (B) ask a rhetorical question.
    (C) reiterate an assertion made in the previous sentence.
    (D) reflect the prince's confidence in his father.
    (E) cast into doubt the effectiveness of the emperor's rule.

50. The shift in Imlac's rhetorical stance in the paragraph beginning in line 26 can best be described as one from
    (A) informational to instructional.
    (B) tentative to assertive.
    (C) factual to theoretical.
    (D) literal to figurative.
    (E) straightforward to suggestive.

51. Imlac's tone in the passage can best be described as
    (A) satirical.
    (B) supercilious.
    (C) sanctimonious.
    (D) respectful.
    (E) anxious.

52. The passage indicates that Imlac believes which of the following to be true of the prince?
(A) He will be a better ruler than his father.
(B) He will one day become a scholar.
(C) He is young and idealistic.
(D) He is impetuous and unpredictable.
(E) He is petulant and moody.

53. Which of the following best describes Imlac's opinion of his father?
(A) He was an insensitive boor.
(B) He was a self-centered despot.
(C) He was a petty tyrant.
(D) He was a pathetic malcontent.
(E) He was an ignorant money-grubber.

54. Lines 44–47 serve as evidence that Imlac is capable of
(A) holding strong opinions on matters of semantics.
(B) speaking with a forked tongue.
(C) making sense of a paradox.
(D) equivocating without realizing it.
(E) subtly criticizing others.

55. The content of lines 55–59 suggests that what will immediately follow the passage is most likely

I. an admonition to the prince to be skeptical of what others tell him.
II. a warning to the prince to reject what his teachers have told him.
III. an account of Imlac's disillusionment with what he had been taught.

(A) I only
(B) III only
(C) I and II only
(D) II and III only
(E) I, II, and III

SECTION II
Three essay questions
Total time—2 hours
Suggested time for each essay—40 minutes
Percent of total grade on the exam: 55 percent

Instructions: This section of the exam consists of three questions that require responses in essay form. You may write the essays in any order you wish and return to work on a completed essay if time permits. Although it is suggested that you spend roughly 40 minutes on each essay, you may apportion your time as you see fit.

Each essay will be evaluated according to its clarity, effectiveness in dealing with the topics, and the overall quality of your writing. If you have the time, go over each essay, checking its punctuation, spelling, and diction. Unless plenty of time remains, try to avoid major revisions. In the end, the quality of each essay counts more than its quantity.

For Question 3, please choose a novel or play of at least the same literary merit as the works you have been assigned in your AP English course.

Essays should be written in pen, preferably with black or dark blue ink. Use lined paper and write as legibly as you can. Do not skip lines. Cross out any errors you make. Feel free to make notes and plan your essay on a piece of scrap paper. Please number your essays and begin each one on a new sheet of paper. Good luck.

Essay Question 1
(Suggested time—40 minutes. This question counts as one-third of your score for Section II of the exam.)

Read the following sonnet carefully. Then, in a well-organized essay, analyze the techniques the poet uses to develop the dramatic situation in the poem. Comment on the title, tone, figurative language, rhythm, or any other appropriate poetic elements.

SINCE THERE'S NO HELP

Since there's no help, come let us kiss and part.
Nay, I have done, you get no more of me;
And I am glad, yea, glad with all my heart,
Line That thus so cleanly I myself can free.
(5) Shake hands for ever, cancel all our vows
And when we meet at any time again,
Be it not seen in either of our brows
That we one jot of former love retain.
Now at the last gasp of Love's latest breath,
(10) When, his pulse failing, Passion speechless lies,
When Faith is kneeling by his bed of death,
And Innocence is closing up his eyes,
  Now, if thou wouldst, when all have given him over,
  From death to life though mightst him yet recover.

Michael Drayton

Essay Question 2

(Suggested time—40 minutes. This question counts as one-third of your score for Section II of the exam.)

In the following excerpt from Sarah Orne Jewett's story "A White Heron" the narrator describes a little girl's discovery of a heron's nesting place. Read the passage carefully. Then, in a well-organized essay, analyze the techniques the author uses to show the significance of the discovery to the child.

There was a huge tree asleep yet in the paling moonlight, and small and hopeful Sylvia began with utmost bravery to mount to the top of it, with tingling, eager blood coursing the channels of her whole frame, with her bare feet and fingers, that pinched
Line and held like bird's claws to the monstrous ladder reaching up, up almost to the sky
(5) itself. First she must mount the white oak tree that grew alongside, where she was almost lost among the dark branches and the green leaves heavy and wet with dew; a bird fluttered off its nest, and a red squirrel ran to and fro and scolded pettishly at the harmless housebreaker. Sylvia felt her way easily. She had often climbed there, and knew that higher still one of the oak's upper branches chafed against the pine trunk,
(10) just where its lower boughs were set close together. There, when she made the dangerous pass from one tree to the other, the great enterprise would really begin.

She crept out along the swaying oak limb at last, and took the daring step across into the old pine-tree. The way was harder than she thought; she must reach far and hold fast, the sharp dry twigs caught and held her and scratched her like angry talons,
(15) the pitch[1] made her thin little fingers clumsy and stiff as she went round and round the tree's great stem, higher and higher upward. The sparrows and robins in the woods below were beginning to wake and twitter to the dawn, yet she seemed much lighter there aloft in the pine-tree, and the child knew that she must hurry if her project were to be of any use.
(20) The tree seemed to lengthen itself out as she went up, and to reach farther and farther upwards. It was like a great main-mast to the voyaging earth; it must truly have been amazed that morning through all its ponderous frame as it felt this determined spark of human spirit creeping and climbing from higher branch to branch. Who knows how steadily the least twigs held themselves to advantage in this light, weak
(25) creature on her way! The old pine must have loved his new dependent. More than all the hawks, and bats, and moths, and even the sweet-voiced thrushes, was the brave, beating heart of the solitary gray-eyed child. And the tree stood still and held away the

---

[1]pine resin

winds that June morning while the dawn grew bright in the east.

(30) Sylvia's face was like a pale star, if one had seen it from the ground, when the last thorny bough was past, and she stood trembling and tired but wholly triumphant, high in the tree-top. Yes, there was the sea with the dawning sun making a golden dazzle over it, and toward that glorious east flew two hawks with slow-moving pinions.[2] How low they looked in the air from that height when before one had only seen them far up, and dark against the blue sky. Their gray feathers were as soft as moths; they

(35) seemed only a little way from the tree, and Sylvia felt as if she too could go flying away among the clouds. Westward, the woodlands and farms reached miles and miles into the distance; here and there were church steeples, and white villages; truly it was a vast and awesome world.

The birds sang louder and louder. At last the sun came up bewilderingly bright.

(40) Sylvia could see the white sails of ships out at sea, and the clouds that were purple and rose-colored and yellow at first began to fade away. Where was the white heron's nest in the sea of green branches, and was this wonderful sight and pageant of the world the only reward for having climbed to such a giddy height? Now look down again, Sylvia, where the green marsh is set among the shining birches and dark

(45) hemlocks; there where you saw the white heron once you will see him again; look, look! a white spot of him like a single floating feather comes up from the dead hemlock and grows larger, and rises, and comes close at last, and goes by the landmark pine with steady sweep of wing and outstretched slender neck and crested head. And wait! wait! do not move a foot or a finger, little girl, do not send an arrow of light and

(50) consciousness from your two eager eyes, for the heron has perched on a pine bough not far beyond yours, and cries back to his mate on the nest, and plumes his feathers for the new day!

The child gives a long sigh a minute later when a company of shouting catbirds come also to the tree, and vexed by their fluttering and lawlessness the solemn heron

(55) goes away. She knows his secret now, the wild, light, slender bird that floats and wavers, and goes back like an arrow presently to his home in the green world beneath. Then Sylvia, well satisfied, makes her perilous way down again, not daring to look far below the branch she stands on, ready to cry sometimes because her fingers ache and her lamed feet slip. Wondering over and over again what the stranger would say to her,

(60) and what he would think when she told him how to find his way straight to the heron's nest.

Essay Question 3

(Suggested time—40 minutes. This question counts as one-third of your score for Section II of the exam.)

From a novel or play, identify a character (not necessarily the protagonist) who, regardless of the consequences, takes a significant risk of some kind. Then, in a well-organized essay, describe the risk and its motivation. Also explain how the character's action illuminates the meaning of the work as a whole. Choose any of the titles in the following list, or choose one of comparable literary worth. Avoid writing only a plot summary.

Catch-22
The Catcher in the Rye
Crime and Punishment
Don Quixote
An Enemy of the People
Ethan Frome
For Whom the Bell Tolls

---

[2] wings

Going After Cacciato
The Great Gatsby
Hamlet
Henry V
The Invisible Man
Lord Jim
Main Street
Moby Dick
The Odyssey
One Flew Over the Cuckoo's Nest
The Red Badge of Courage
The Sea Gull
A Streetcar Named Desire
A Tale of Two Cities
Their Eyes Were Watching God
War and Peace

END OF PRACTICE TEST D

Answer Key for Practice Test D—Section I

1. E	12. A	23. C	34. E	45. E
2. B	13. A	24. E	35. B	46. C
3. D	14. D	25. A	36. D	47. D
4. A	15. C	26. D	37. A	48. D
5. C	16. C	27. C	38. A	49. D
6. E	17. A	28. C	39. D	50. A
7. D	18. E	29. A	40. D	51. D
8. D	19. B	30. C	41. A	52. C
9. A	20. C	31. A	42. C	53. E
10. B	21. D	32. B	43. D	54. C
11. B	22. B	33. A	44. B	55. B

Summary of Answers in Section I Multiple-Choice

Number of correct answers _____

Number of incorrect answers _____

Number of questions not answered _____

Use this information when you calculate your score on this exam. See page 390.

Answer Explanations

SECTION I

1. E In lines 5–6, the narrator says that Skimpole's words are spoken "with such a captivating gaiety, that it was fascinating to hear him talk."

2. B In line 47, the narrator shows his naïveté by admitting to confusion about why Skimpole was free of the usual "duties and accountabilities of life."

3. D The speaker's impression is that Skimpole looks like a broken-down young man rather than a well-preserved elderly one (lines 7–9).

4. A *Which* refers to the grammatical subject of the sentence's main clause.

5. C The use of such words as "captivating" (line 5) and "enchanting" (line 45) suggests that the narrator is quite taken with Skimpole. Rather than being put off by Skimpole's arrant past, the narrator is impressed with his individuality, although he can't quite fathom it.

6. E To one degree or another, the excerpt accomplishes all three purposes. Almost every sentence adds more details to this portrait of Skimpole. In telling about Skimpole, the narrator reveals his feelings toward his subject, particularly in the first and third paragraphs. At the same time the narrator alludes to differences between himself and Skimpole, especially in lines 45–49 where the narrator's hang-up about "the duties and accountabilities of life" contrast starkly with Skimpole's indifference toward them.

7. D The lines in question are dominated by words and phrases that portray Skimpole as an unusual and free-spirited figure, among them "little bright creature," "loose and flowing," and "romantic."

8. D The first paragraph contains the narrator's observations of Skimpole. The second paragraph consists mainly of an account of Skimpole's life and career.

9. A A synechdoche is a figure of speech in which a part stands for the whole. In this case the phrase "rosy cheeks" could represent a wife, possibly a few children, and perhaps some robust friends.

10. B The phrase implies that some of Skimpole's friends helped him right away, while others, skeptical that their help would make any difference, waited to see what happened to him.

11. B In this section of the passage the narrator, rather than passing judgment on Skimpole, simply recounts in his own words the story Skimpole has told. The statement in line 32 succinctly summarizes Skimpole's experiences and suggests that in spite of his infirmities he suffered no permanent setbacks. It also serves as a break in the narration between an account of Skimpole's weaknesses and a list of his pleasures.

12. A The climax of the sentence—"let Harold Skimpole live!"—is like a plea to the world to get off his back. Its message—"live and let live"—comes straight from Skimpole's guts and vehemently expresses frustration.

13. A In the last paragraph the narrator offers a brief summing up of his introduction to Skimpole. The phrase "at that early time" (line 46) suggests that the story of Skimpole has just begun and that the narrator's confusion alluded to in lines 45–49 will eventually be cleared up.

14. D The passage emphasizes that Skimpole is an unusual fellow. Among other things, his appearance differs considerably from a man "who had advanced in life, by the usual road of years, cares, and experiences." In other words, Skimpole appears to have taken a less-traveled road through life.

15. C The passage portrays Skimpole as a nonconformist. The more expected of him, the more he rebelled. A case in point is his stint as a physician in the home of a German prince. Lacking the know-how to cope with two essentials—time and money—Skimpole could not successfully meet the customary demands of life. In consequence, he created a life and a style of his own.

16. C The speaker's anguish responds to rejection by the woman he loves. That's why he cries out "Love is dead."

17. A The speaker exaggerates the intensity of his dismay by stating that "*All Love is dead*," when the truth is that only he has lost his love. In effect, he views his private misfortune as a public disaster.

18. E In the face of his lady's disdain, the speaker feels impotent. His "worth" was considered worthless (line 5), and his faithfulness to her earned only her scorn (line 6). Is it any wonder that he feels impotent?

19. B Expecting his neighbors to have heard the news that love is dead, the speaker is vexed by their indifference and insists that it's about time that they mourn with him.

20. C The refrain is a short prayer asking God to "deliver"—that is, to remove from his life both "ungrateful fancy" (unrequited or unappreciated love) and "female franzy," an ambiguous phrase that refers to women who behave as though they've lost their minds and to the irrational habit of men to be in love with women.

21. D The poem contains some enigmatic sentence structure. For example, customary word order is reversed in line 35: "Where she his counsel keepeth." The poem also contains elliptical constructions, as in lines 23–26, that may be paraphrased as follows: "Sir Wrong solemnly declares that my mistress's Marble-heart is love's tomb, on which the epitaph says 'His mistress's eyes once sent him love darts.'"

22. B The speaker has not permanently discarded love, but he'll steer clear of the kind of insane passion that ruled him during his recent experience.

23. C Images and words related to death and dying pervade the poem, including "death-bed," "winding-sheet, and "tomb." Religious references such as "dirge" and "tentrals" relate to services for the dead.

24. E Through the third stanza, the speaker is beside himself with woe over losing his love. Then he suddenly comes to his senses. Love had not fled, after all. It had merely been put on hold.

25. A The poem exemplifies a lyric poem—a highly personal expression of emotion by a single speaker.

26. D According to Strepsiades, his servants have recently acquired the habit of snoring, a development that he interprets as their lack of concern for his well-being.

27. C Strepsiades' monologue illustrates that he is uptight, especially about his wife, his son, and his debts. He has nothing to say about the state of his health.

28. C Strepsiades blames Pheidippides for his insomnia.

29. A Pheidippides' utterance briefly distracts Strepsiades from discussing his wife, whom he talks about momentarily, beginning in line 30.

30. C Lines 32–34 provide evidence that Strepsiades was "a rustic" who once grew olives, raised sheep, and kept bees.

31. A In effect, Strepsiades is telling his son 'One day, you'll pay for your errant ways," a vindictive but human reaction to a son who has grieved his father thoughtlessly.

32. B Unlike a dramatic monologue, in which a speaker engages in a one-sided conversation with a silent listener, this passage finds Strepsiades talking to himself except for a few lines addressed to his sleeping son and a demand for a lamp made to a servant. Although some of Strepsiades' language is poetic, his words are not presented in the stanzaic structure of a villanelle. A peroration is a formal piece of oratory, which this passage is definitely not. Nor is it an example of stream of consciousness writing, for it is far too coherent and structured.

33. A Among several puns are "bitten" (line 12), which in the context means chomped on by insects and also financially damaged. In line 13, "duns" has a double meaning: a mayfly and a brownish horse. In line 43, "hopeful" refers both to the parents and to the son. In line 55, "galloping" alludes to the swift consumption of Strepsiades' fortune and also to the horses that contributed to the loss of his fortune.

34. E Strepsiades' description of his wife supports the idea that she was a "fine town-lady" (line 36) accustomed to a life of luxury.

35. B The quotations reveal each parents' approach to child rearing. Strepsiades favors discipline, his wife coddling.

36. D A poem in which skeletons are awakened by the sound of guns and God speaks as though he's just a neighbor is pure fantasy.

37. A While "red" has many connotations—from the political left (communism) to love's passion—in this case "red" alludes to blood.

38. A In lines 17–20, God has humorously explained why some souls will not welcome "the judgment-hour." (Basically, they haven't finished atoning for their sins.) The chuckle He emits in line 21 suggests a slightly sardonic sense of humor.

39. D The speaker, a skeleton, is referring to the time when he or she died.

40. D People paid no attention to the madness that the skeleton is describing.

41. A Until the final stanza, the poem, while dealing with a serious subject, namely mankind's inability to live in peace, is pure fantasy. The last four lines, however, make the threat of war's destruction immediate and chilling.

42. C The place names conjure up poetic or historic associations. Readers are meant to cringe at the prospect of bombing Stonehenge and the other places. (Yet, two of the sites—Stourton Tower and Camelot—stand as memorials to human conflict not much different from that described earlier in the poem.) Mentioning specific places also turns an abstraction into reality. While the poem may open readers' eyes to the implications of war, it stops short of urging readers to actively oppose war.

43. D Parson Thirdly picks up God's observation that men disregard Christ's teachings. He himself regrets having devoted his life to preaching instead of to pipes and beer.

44. B God's words in lines 11–16 and the reactions of the dead reflect the fatalistic view that making war is an aspect of man's nature.

45. E Both God and the skeletons express themselves in everyday speech, as, for example, "Mad as hatters" (line 14) and "'I wish I had stuck to pipes and beer'" (line 32).

46. C An appositive is a noun that explains or defines another noun or pronoun. In this case, "season" figuratively defines the "close of the day."

47. D Through much of the passage Imlac responds to the prince's questions and concerns. His attitude toward his own instructors suggests that he spends much of his time in thought (lines 57–59).

48. D Imlac is saying that, had the authorities in the province known of his father's wealth, they would somehow have taken it away from him.

49. D Rasselas is just beginning to realize that his father may be less well-informed about his duties and obligation than an emperor ought to be.

50. A Until line 26, Imlac tells the prince the story of his life. Then, much like a teacher or an advisor, he begins to explain, interpret, and analyze.

51. D Imlac seems intent on telling the prince his life story, responding to the prince's questions, and trying to help the prince understand issues of government and human nature. Although Imlac knows more about everything than the prince, he still treats the young man with the utmost respect.

52. C After the prince offers to report the "governor who robbed the people" (lines 24–25), Imlac responds, "your ardor is the natural effect of virtue animated by youth" (line 26). In other words, Imlac is struck by the prince's good but rather naïve intention to right a wrong.

53. E In lines 17–18 Imlac says his father, a man of "narrow comprehension," devoted his life to making and hoarding money. Although he claims to pity his father, Imlac emphasizes the "grossness" (line 53) of his father's obsession.

54. C   The prince perceives a paradox in Imlac's account of his father's behavior (lines 41–42). In response, Imlac explains the logic in what appears to be a contradiction.

55. B   Considering the conversational pattern of the passage, Imlac is likely to tell the prince about his loss of reverence for his instructors. There is a chance that he might follow up with advice to the prince about accepting at face value what he is told, but one can't be sure.

SECTION II

Although answers to essay questions will vary greatly, the following descriptions suggest an approach to each question and contain ideas that could be used in a response. Perhaps your essay contains many of the same ideas. If not, don't be alarmed. Your ideas may be at least as valid than those presented below.

Note: Don't mistake these descriptions for complete essays; essays written for the exam should be full-length, well organized, and fully developed. For an overview of how essays are graded, turn to "How AP Essays Are Scored," on page 35.

Essay Question 1

Because the poem is a sonnet written during the Elizabethan era, its structure is familiar: fourteen lines, three quatrains, a concluding couplet, and a prescribed rhyme scheme. But unless you can tie the structure to the dramatic situation that the question asks you to write about, try to avoid a stock structural analysis. Instead, you might focus on the speaker's changing attitude. In the first quatrain he (or perhaps, she) firmly asserts the end of the love affair. As the title says, "there's no help"; love has vanished. The second quatrain refers to a future time when the couple may meet again. (Evidently, the breakup was not as hopeless as it seemed at first.) In next four lines the speaker engages in a flight of poetic fancy, writing what amounts to an allegorical scene in which figures representing Love, Passion, Faith, and Innocence are about to pass on. (Notice that the speaker has wandered from his insistence that he's through with his love.)

In the final couplet the speaker shifts the responsibility to his beloved, telling her, in effect, it's up to you to save our affair. His earlier conviction has dissolved. Not only his sentiment but his language has changed. At first, short and crisp words convey his certainty. In the first four lines, every word but one is made up of a single syllable. As he vacillates, his words grow longer, the tempo slows, and the words roll off the tongue less smoothly, as though he is grasping for a way to postpone the final resolution.

Essay Question 2

Climbing a very tall tree in search of a heron's nest in its upper branches is a significant adventure for a small child. The author uses images and figures of speech that emphasize the enormity and the peril of the undertaking. Early in the passage, a simile compares Sylvia's "bare feet and fingers" to "bird's claws." Later Sylvia is characterized as a "light, weak creature" (lines 24–25). Paradoxically, the delicate little girl conquers a tree that the narrator has described metaphorically as a "monstrous ladder" that reaches (hyperbolically) "up, up almost to the sky." Twigs scratch Sylvia with "angry talons" and pitch causes her little fingers to grow "clumsy and stiff" (line 15). To further emphasize the magnitude of Sylvia's quest, the author compares the tree to "a great main-mast to the voyaging earth" (line 21), and as Sylvia ascends heavenward, her face becomes "like a pale star" (line 29). Below her she sees flying hawks. No longer earthbound, she feels the urge to fly "away among the clouds." In effect, she has had a transcendent experience, the drama of which is heightened by a switch (lines 43 ff.) in the point of view. Instead of continuing to tell Sylvia's story, the narrator, like a coach or mentor, addresses her directly: "And wait! wait! do not move a foot or a finger," says the narrator just as Sylvia locates the heron's nest.

Essay Question 3

Each of the works discussed below contains material appropriate to answering the question.

McMurphy in Ken Kesey's novel, *One Flew Over the Cuckoo's Nest*, is an inmate in a mental hospital. He embodies the individualist willing to do battle against institutional rigidity and oppression represented by Nurse Ratched and administered by a fear-inducing system that mercilessly controls the destiny of the poorest, sickest, and least resilient members of society. Risking punishment, McMurphy fights for freedom and respect. He brings laughter into the life of his wardmates and incites them to join him in breaking the rules. As a consequence, he is given electroshock therapy and a lobotomy that turns him into a human vegetable. The parallel between McMurphy and Christ is self-evident; both sacrificed themselves for others.

Early in *Lord Jim* by Joseph Conrad, the title character deserts a ship that he believes is about to sink, an act that in retrospect he considers scandalous and cowardly. As one who had long fantasized about being a hero, he cannot escape the aftereffects of his conduct. One could argue that Jim's actions were justified. He hadn't a doubt that the ship was doomed and that his presence on board was superfluous. Besides, his escape was driven not by rationality but by impulse. Yet, Jim can't forgive himself. Disgrace lingers in his memory. By novel's end Jim has demonstrated that he's unafraid of death. He has walked fearlessly into perilous situations and undertaken death-defying risks. To prove his courage once and for all, he confronts an adversary whom he knows will kill him. While Jim's bravado serves no purpose other than to bolster his ego, his story raises issues of morality. Jim himself is difficult to judge. He may have done something inexcusable, but his subsequent behavior mitigates the odiousness of his act. Jim's experience raises such moral questions as whether there are circumstances under which supposedly fixed standards of morality may be violated. And if standards shift, how can they serve as guides for human conduct?

Ibsen's play *An Enemy of the People* focuses on Stockmann, a physician in a small Norwegian town, who discovers that the municipal baths are badly contaminated and insists that the condition be corrected. The burgomaster refuses, citing the high cost of repairs and a loss of revenue stemming from closing the baths for two years. Ignoring the health threat to the town's inhabitants, the burgomaster tries to keep Stockmann from informing the public. In fact, he condemns the doctor, officially declaring him "an enemy of the people." Stockmann fights back, putting his reputation on the line, but the townspeople blindly follow their self-serving leaders. Defeated, Stockmann considers leaving town, but changes his mind and founds a school meant to teach young people to think freely and resist corruption. The play advocates the value of truth. Untruth, hypocrisy, fraud: these are crimes against the public and against society; in the end, they are the real "enemy of the people."

Self-Scoring Guide for Practice Test D

Scoring Section 2   ESSAYS

After referring to "How Essays Are Scored," on page 35 of this book, use this guide to help you evaluate each essay. Do your best to evaluate your performance in each category by using the criteria spelled out below. Because it is hard to achieve objectivity when assessing your own writing, you may improve the validity of your score by having a trusted and well-informed friend or experienced teacher read and rate your essay.

On the following Rating Chart, enter a number (from 1 to 6) that you think represents your level of performance in each category (A–F).

Category A: OVERALL PURPOSE/MAIN IDEA
6   extremely well-defined and insightful
5   clearly defined and generally insightful
4   mostly clear
3   somewhat clear but occasionally confusing
2   generally unclear and confusing
1   virtually incomprehensible

Category B: HANDLING OF THE PROMPT
6   self-evident or extremely clear throughout
5   mostly clear
4   somewhat clear
3   somewhat unclear
2   generally unclear or ambiguous
1   confusing or nonexistent

Category C: ORGANIZATION AND DEVELOPMENT
6   insightfully organized; fully developed with excellent supporting evidence
5   reasonably well organized; developed with appropriate supporting material
4   appropriately organized; developed with some relevant material
3   inadequately organized; weak development
2   poorly organized; little or no development
1   no discernible organization; no relevant development

Category D: SENTENCE STRUCTURE
6   varied and engaging
5   sufficiently varied to create interest
4   some variety
3   little variety; minor sentence errors
2   frequent sentence errors that interfere with meaning
1   serious sentence errors that obscure meaning

Category E: USE OF LANGUAGE
6   precise and effective word choice
5   competent word choice
4   conventional word choice; mostly correct
3   some errors in diction or idiom
2   frequent errors in diction or idiom
1   meaning obscured by word choice

Category F: GRAMMAR AND USAGE
6   error-free or virtually error-free
5   occasional minor errors
4   basically correct but with several minor errors
3   meaning somewhat obscured by errors
2   meaning frequently obscured by errors
1   meaning blocked by several major errors

```
┌─────────────────────────────────────────────────────────────────────┐
│                          RATING CHART                                 │
│                                                                       │
│   Rate your essay:          Essay 1      Essay 2      Essay 3         │
│                                                                       │
│   Overall Purpose/Main Idea  _____      _____       _____         │
│                                                                       │
│   Handling of the Prompt     _____      _____       _____         │
│                                                                       │
│   Organization and                                                    │
│     Development              _____      _____       _____         │
│                                                                       │
│   Sentence Structure         _____      _____       _____         │
│                                                                       │
│   Use of Language            _____      _____       _____         │
│                                                                       │
│   Grammar and Usage          _____      _____       _____         │
│                                                                       │
│   Composite Scores                                                    │
│     (Sum of each column)     _____      _____       _____         │
└─────────────────────────────────────────────────────────────────────┘
```

By using the following chart, in which composite scores are converted to the 9-point AP rating scale, you may determine the final score for each essay:

Composite Score	AP Essay Score
33–36	9
29–32	8
25–28	7
21–24	6
18–20	5
15–17	4
10–14	3
7–9	2
6 or below	1

AP Essay Scores   Essay 1 _____   Essay 2 _____   Essay 3 _____

Calculating Your AP Score on Practice Test D

The scores you have earned on the multiple-choice and essay sections of the exam may now be converted to the AP 5-point scale by doing the following calculations:

I. Determine your score for Section I (Multiple-Choice)

   Step A: Number of correct answers _____

   Step B: Number of wrong answers _____ (Note: Do not count unanswered questions.)

   Step C: Multiply the number of wrong answers by .250 and enter the figure here _____

   Step D: Subtract the figure in Step C from the figure in Step A _____

   Step E: Multiply the figure in Step D by 1.2500 to find your Multiple-Choice Score _____ (if less than zero, enter zero)

II. Determine your score for Section II (Essays)[1]

   Step A: Enter your score for Essay 1 (out of 9) _____

   Step B: Enter your score for Essay 2 (out of 9) _____

   Step C: Enter your score for Essay 3 (out of 9) _____

   Step D: Add the figures in Steps A, B, and C _____

   Step E: Multiply the figure in Step D by 3.0556 _____ (Do not round). This is your Essay Score.

III. Determine Your Total Score

   Add the scores for I and II to find your composite score _____ .

To convert your composite score to the AP 5-point scale, use the chart below. The range of scores only approximates what you would earn on the actual test because the exact figures may vary from test to test. Be aware, therefore, that your score on this test, as well as on other tests in this book, may differ slightly from your score on an actual AP exam.

Composite Score	AP Grade
108–150	5
93–107	4
72–92	3
43–71	2
0–42	1

[1]After the AP exam, essays are judged in relation to other essays written on the same topic at the same time. Therefore, the score you assign yourself for an essay may not be the same as the score you would earn on an actual exam.

Glossary of Literary and Rhetorical Terms

Literary and Rhetorical Terms   The following list is made up of words and phrases used by scholars, critics, writers, poets—in fact, all literate people—to exchange ideas and information about language. Knowing these terms won't necessarily transform a mediocre reader into a genius, but familiarity with the terminology will certainly help any aspiring scholar to appreciate the rich possibilities of both written and spoken language.

abstract   An abbreviated synopsis of a longer work of scholarship or research.

adage   A saying or proverb containing a truth based on experience and often couched in metaphorical language.

allegory   A story in which a second meaning is to be read beneath the surface.

alliteration   The repetition of one or more initial consonants in a group of words or lines in a poem.

allusion   A reference to a person, place, or event meant to create an effect or enhance the meaning of an idea.

ambiguity   A vagueness of meaning; a conscious lack of clarity meant to evoke multiple meanings and interpretation

anachronism   A person, scene, event, or other element in literature that fails to correspond with the time or era in which the work is set.

analogy   A comparison that points out similarities between two dissimilar things.

annotation   A brief explanation, summary, or evaluation of a text or work of literature.

antagonist   A character or force in a work of literature that, by opposing the protagonist produces tension or conflict.

antithesis   A rhetorical opposition or contrast of ideas by means of a grammatical arrangement of words, clauses, or sentences, as in the following:

> "They promised freedom but provided slavery."

> "Ask not what your country can do for you, but what you can do for your country."

aphorism   A short, pithy statement of a generally accepted truth or sentiment.

Apollonian   In contrast to Dionysian, it refers to the most noble, godlike qualities of human nature and behavior.

apostrophe   A locution that addresses a person or personified thing not present. An example: "Oh, you cruel streets of Manhattan, how I detest you!"

archetype   An abstract or ideal conception of a type; a perfectly typical example; an original model or form.

assonance   The repetition of two or more vowel sounds in a group of words or lines of a poem.

ballad   A simple narrative verse that tells a story that is sung or recited.

bard   A poet; in olden times, a performer who told heroic stories to musical accompaniment.

bathos   The use of insincere or overdone sentimentality.

belle-lettres   French term for the world of books, criticism, and literature in general.

bibliography   A list of works cited or otherwise relevant to a subject or other work.

Bildungsroman   A German word referring to a novel structured as a series of events that take place as the hero travels in quest of a goal

bombast   Inflated, pretentious language used for trivial subjects.

burlesque   A work of literature meant to ridicule a subject; a grotesque imitation.

cacophony   Grating, inharmonious sounds.

caesura   A pause somewhere in the middle of a verse, often marked by punctuation.

canon   The works considered most important in a national literature or period; works widely read and studied.

caricature A grotesque likeness of striking qualities in persons and things.

carpe diem Literally, "seize the day"; enjoy life while you can, a common theme in literature.

catharsis A cleansing of the spirit brought about by the pity and terror of a dramatic tragedy.

classic A highly regarded work of literature or other art form that has withstood the test of time.

classical, classicism Deriving from the orderly qualities of ancient Greek and Roman culture; implies formality, objectivity, simplicity, and restraint.

climax The high point, or turning point, of a story or play.

conceit A witty or ingenious thought; a diverting or highly fanciful idea, often stated in figurative language.

connotation The suggested or implied meaning of a word or phrase. Contrast with *denotation*.

consonance The repetition of two or more consonant sounds in a group of words or a line of poetry.

couplet A pair of rhyming lines in a poem. Two rhyming lines in iambic pentameter is sometimes called a *heroic couplet*.

denotation The dictionary definition of a word. Contrast with *connotation*.

dénouement The resolution that occurs at the end of a play or work of fiction.

deus ex machina In literature, the use of an artificial device or gimmick to solve a problem.

diction The choice of words in oral and written discourse.

Dionysian As distinguished from *Apollonian*, the word refers to sensual, pleasure-seeking impulses.

dramatic irony A circumstance in which the audience or reader knows more about a situation than a character.

elegy A poem or prose selection that laments or meditates on the passing or death of something or someone of value.

ellipsis Three periods (. . .) indicating the omission of words in a thought or quotation.

elliptical construction A sentence containing a deliberate omission of words. In the sentence "May was hot and June the same," the verb *was* is omitted from the second clause.

empathy A feeling of association or identification with an object or person.

end-stopped A term that describes a line of poetry that ends with a natural pause often indicated by a mark of punctuation.

enjambment In poetry, the use of successive lines with no punctuation or pause between them.

epic A narrative poem that tells of the adventures and exploits of a hero.

epigram A concise but ingenious, witty, and thoughtful statement.

euphony Pleasing, harmonious sounds.

epithet An adjective or phrase that expresses a striking quality of a person or thing; *sun-bright topaz*, *sun-lit lake*, and *sun-bright lake* are examples.

eponymous A term for the title character of a work of literature.

euphemism A mild or less negative usage for a harsh or blunt term; *pass away* is a euphemism for *die*.

exegesis A detailed analysis or interpretation of a work of literature.

exposé A piece of writing that reveals weaknesses, faults, frailties, or other shortcomings.

exposition The background and events that lead to the presentation of the main idea or purpose of a work of literature.

explication The interpretation or analysis of a text.

extended metaphor A series of comparisons between two unlike objects.

fable A short tale often with nonhuman characters from which a useful lesson may be drawn.

falling action The action in a play or story that occurs after the climax and that leads to the conclusion and often to the resolution of the conflict.

fantasy A story containing unreal, imaginary features.

farce A comedy that contains an extravagant and nonsensical disregard of seriousness, although it may have a serious, scornful purpose.

figure of speech, figurative language In contrast to literal language, figurative language implies meanings. Figures of speech include metaphors, similes, and personification, among many others.

first-person narrative A narrative told by a character involved in the story, using first-person pronouns such as *I* and *we*.

flashback A return to an earlier time in a story or play in order to clarify present actions or circumstances.

foot A unit of stressed and unstressed syllables used to determine the meter of a poetic line.

foreshadowing Providing hints of things to come in a story or play.

frame A structure that provides premise or setting for a narrative. A group of pilgrims exchanging stories while on the road is the frame for Chaucer's *Canterbury Tales*.

free verse A kind of poetry without rhymed lines, rhythm, or fixed metrical feet.

genre A term used to describe literary forms, such as novel, play, and essay.

Gothic novel A novel in which supernatural horrors and an atmosphere of unknown terrors pervades the action.

harangue A forceful sermon, lecture, or tirade.

hubris The excessive pride that often leads tragic heroes to their death.

humanism A belief that emphasizes faith and optimism in human potential and creativity.

hyperbole Overstatement; gross exaggeration for rhetorical effect.

idyll A lyric poem or passage that describes a kind of ideal life or place.

image a word or phrase representing that which can be seen, touched, tasted, smelled, or felt.

in medias res A Latin term for a narrative that starts not at the beginning of events but at some other critical point.

indirect quotation A rendering of a quotation in which actual words are not stated but only approximated or paraphrased.

invective A direct verbal assault; a denunciation.

irony A mode of expression in which the intended meaning is the opposite of what is stated, often implying ridicule or light sarcasm; a state of affairs or events that is the reverse of what might have been expected.

kenning A device employed in Anglo-Saxon poetry in which the name of a thing is replaced by one of its functions or qualities, as in "ring-giver" for king and "whale-road" for ocean.

lampoon A mocking, satirical assault on a person or situation.

light verse A variety of poetry meant to entertain or amuse, but sometimes with a satirical thrust.

litotes A form of understatement in which the negative of the contrary is used to achieve emphasis or intensity. Example: *He is not a bad dancer.*

loose sentence A sentence that follows the customary word order of English sentences, i.e., subject-verb-object. The main idea of the sentence is presented first and is then followed by one or more subordinate clauses. See also *periodic sentence*.

lyric poetry Personal, reflective poetry that reveals the speaker's thoughts and feelings about the subject.

maxim A saying or proverb expressing common wisdom or truth. See also *adage* and *aphorism*.

melodrama A literary form in which events are exaggerated in order to create an extreme emotional response.

metaphor A figure of speech that compares unlike objects.

metaphysical poetry The work of poets, particularly those of the seventeenth century, that uses elaborate conceits, is highly intellectual, and expresses the complexities of love and life.

meter The pattern of stressed and unstressed syllables found in poetry. See Chapter 4 for a full discussion of meter.

metonymy A figure of speech that uses the name of one thing to represent something else with which it is associated. Example: *"The White House says . . ."*

Middle English The language spoken in England roughly between 1150 and 1500 A.D.

mock epic A parody of traditional epic form.

mode The general form, pattern, and manner of expression of a work of literature.

montage A quick succession of images or impressions used to express an idea.

mood The emotional tone in a work of literature.

moral A brief and often simplistic lesson that a reader may infer from a work of literature.

motif A phrase, idea, or event that through repetition serves to unify or convey a theme in a work of literature.

muse One of the ancient Greek goddesses presiding over the arts. The imaginary source of inspiration for an artist or writer.

myth An imaginary story that has become an accepted part of the cultural or religious tradition of a group or society.

narrative A form of verse or prose that tells a story.

naturalism A term often used as a synonym for *realism*; also a view of experience that is generally characterized as bleak and pessimistic.

non sequitur A statement or idea that fails to follow logically from the one before.

novel of manners A novel focusing on and describing social customs and habits of a particular social group.

ode A lyric poem usually marked by serious, respectful, and exalted feelings toward the subject.

Old English The Anglo-Saxon language spoken in what is now England from approximately 450 to 1150 A.D.

omniscient narrator A narrator with unlimited awareness, understanding, and insight of characters, setting, background, and all other elements of the story.

onomatopoeia The use of words whose sounds suggest their meaning. Example: *bubbling, murmuring brooks.*

ottava rima An eight-line rhyming stanza of a poem.

oxymoron A term consisting of contradictory elements juxtaposed to create a paradoxical effect. Examples: *loud silence, jumbo shrimp.*

parable A story consisting of events from which a moral or spiritual truth may be derived.

paradox A statement that seems self-contradictory but is nevertheless true.

parody An imitation of a work meant to ridicule its style and subject.

paraphrase A version of a text put into simpler, everyday, words.

pastoral A work of literature dealing with rural life.

pathetic fallacy Faulty reasoning that inappropriately ascribes human feelings to nature or nonhuman objects.

pathos That element in literature that stimulates pity or sorrow.

pentameter A verse with five poetic feet per line.

periodic sentence A sentence that departs from the usual word order of English sentences by expressing its main thought only at the end. In other words, the particulars in the sentence are presented before the idea they support. See also *loose sentence*.

persona The role or facade that a character assumes or depicts to a reader, a viewer, or the world at large.

personification A figure of speech in which objects and animals are given human characteristics.

plot The interrelationship among the events in a story; the *plot line* is the pattern of events, including exposition, rising action, climax, falling action, and resolution.

picaresque novel An episodic novel about a roguelike wanderer who lives off his wits.

point of view The relation in which a narrator or speaker stands to the story or subject matter of a poem. A story told in the first person has an *internal* point of view; an observer uses an *external* point of view.

prosody The grammar of meter and rhythm in poetry.

protagonist The main character in a work of literature.

pseudonym A false name or alias used by writers.

pulp fiction Novels written for mass consumption, often emphasizing exciting and titillating plots.

pun A humorous play on words, using similar-sounding or identical words to suggest different meanings.

quatrain A four-line poem or a four-line unit of a longer poem.

realism The depiction of people, things, and events as they really are without idealization or exaggeration for effect. See also *naturalism*.

rhetoric The language of a work and its style; words, often highly emotional, used to convince or sway an audience.

rhetorical stance Language that conveys a speaker's attitude or opinion with regard to a particular subject.

rhyme The repetition of similar sounds at regular intervals, used mostly in poetry.

rhyme scheme The pattern of rhymes within a given poem.

rhythm The pattern of stressed and unstressed syllables that make up a line of poetry. See also *meter*.

roman à clef French for a novel in which historical events and actual people appear under the guise of fiction.

romance   An extended narrative about improbable events and extraordinary people in exotic places.

sarcasm   A sharp, caustic expression or remark; a bitter jibe or taunt; different from *irony*, which is more subtle.

satire   A literary style used to poke fun at, attack or ridicule an idea, vice, or foible, often for the purpose of inducing change.

scan   The act of determining the meter of a poetic line. The pattern is called *scansion*. If a verse doesn't "scan," its meter is irregular.

sentiment   A synonym for *view* or *feeling*; also a refined and tender emotion in literature.

sentimental   A term that describes characters' excessive emotional response to experience; also nauseatingly nostalgic and mawkish.

setting   The total environment for the action in a novel or play. It includes time, place, historical milieu, and social, political, and even spiritual circumstances.

simile   A figurative comparison using the words *like* or *as*.

sonnet   A form of verse usually consisting of three four-line units called quatrains and a concluding couplet. See Chapter 4 for a discussion of sonnets.

stanza   A group of two or more lines in poetry combined according to subject matter, rhyme, or some other plan.

stream of consciousness   A style of writing in which the author tries to reproduce the random flow of thoughts in the human mind.

style   The manner in which an author uses and arranges words, shapes ideas, forms sentences, and creates a structure to convey ideas.

subplot   A subordinate or minor collection of events in a novel or play, usually connected to the main plot.

subtext   The implied meaning that underlies the main meaning of a work of literature.

symbolism   The use of one object to evoke ideas and associations not literally part of the original object.

synecdoche   A figure of speech in which a part signifies the whole (*fifty masts* for *fifty ships*) or the whole signifies the part (*days* for *life*, as in "*He lived his days under African skies.*") When the name of a material stands for the thing itself, as in *pigskin* for *football*, that, too, is synecdoche.

syntax   The organization of language into meaningful structure; every sentence has a particular syntax, or pattern of words.

theme   The main idea or meaning, often an abstract idea upon which a work of literature is built.

title character   A character whose name appears in the title of the novel or play; also known as the *eponymous* character.

tone   The author's attitude toward the subject being written about. The tone is the characteristic emotion that pervades a work or part of a work—the spirit or quality that is the work's emotional essence.

tragedy   A form of literature in which the hero is destroyed by some character flaw and a set of forces that cause the hero considerable anguish.

trope   The generic name for a figure of speech such as image, symbol, simile, and metaphor.

verbal irony   A discrepancy between the true meaning of a situation and the literal meaning of the written or spoken words.

verse   A synonym for poetry. Also a group of lines in a song or poem; also a single line of poetry.

verisimilitude   Similar to the truth; the quality of realism in a work that persuades readers that they are getting a vision of life as it is.

versification   The structural form of a verse as revealed by scansion.

villanelle   A French verse form calculated to appear simple and spontaneous but consisting of nineteen lines and a prescribed pattern of rhymes.

voice   The real or assumed personality used by a writer or speaker. In grammar, active voice and passive voice refer to the use of verbs. A verb is in the active voice when it expresses an action performed by its subject. A verb is in the passive voice when it expresses an action performed upon its subject or when the subject is the result of the action.

ACTIVE: The crew raked the leaves.

PASSIVE: The leaves were raked by the crew. Stylistically, the active voice makes more economical and vigorous writing.

wit The quickness of intellect and the power and talent for saying brilliant things that surprise and delight by their unexpectedness; the power to comment subtly and pointedly on the foibles of the passing scene.

Index

NOTES

NOTES